THE GENERIC

THE GENERIC BOOK

Edited by

Gregory N. Carlson

and

Francis Jeffry Pelletier

THE UNIVERSITY OF CHICAGO PRESS

Chicago and London

Gregory N. Carlson is professor of linguistics at the University of Rochester. Francis Jeffry Pelletier is professor of philosophy and computing science at the University of Alberta.

THE UNIVERSITY OF CHICAGO PRESS, CHICAGO 60637
THE UNIVERSITY OF CHICAGO PRESS, LTD., LONDON

Printed in the United States of America

04 03 02 01 00 99 98 97 96 95 5 4 3 2 1

ISBN (cloth): 0-226-09291-7
ISBN (paper): 0-226-09292-5

Library of Congress Cataloging-in-Publication Data

The Generic book / edited by Gregory N. Carlson and Francis Jeffry Pelletier.
p. cm.
Includes bibliographical references and indexes.
ISBN 0-226-09291-7. — ISBN 0-226-09292-5 (pbk.)
1. Genericalness (Linguistics). 2. Semantics. 3. Grammar, Comparative and general—Syntax. I. Carlson, Greg N., 1948– . II. Pelletier, Francis Jeffry, 1944– .
P299.G44G46 1995
415—dc20 94-32400
CIP

∞ The paper used in this publication meets the minimum requirements of the American National Standard for Information Sciences—Permanence of Paper for Printed Library Materials, ANSI Z39.48-1984.

CONTENTS

Preface and Acknowledgments vii

List of Contributors ix

1 Genericity: An Introduction 1
Manfred Krifka, Francis Jeffry Pelletier, Gregory N. Carlson, Alice ter Meulen, Gennaro Chierchia, and Godehard Link

2 Stage-Level and Individual-Level Predicates 125
Angelika Kratzer

3 Individual-Level Predicates as Inherent Generics 176
Gennaro Chierchia

4 Truth Conditions of Generic Sentences: Two Contrasting Views 224
Gregory N. Carlson

5 Focus and the Interpretation of Generic Sentences 238
Manfred Krifka

6 Indefinites, Adverbs of Quantification, and Focus Semantics 265
Mats Rooth

7 What Some Generic Sentences Mean 300
Nicholas Asher and Michael Morreau

8 Semantic Constraints on Type-Shifting Anaphora 339
Alice ter Meulen

9 GENERIC INFORMATION AND DEPENDENT GENERICS 358
Godehard Link

10 THE SEMANTICS OF THE COMMON NOUN *KIND* 383
Karina Wilkinson

11 COMMON NOUNS: A CONTRASTIVE ANALYSIS OF CHINESE AND ENGLISH 398
Manfred Krifka

12 THE MARKING OF THE EPISODIC/GENERIC DISTINCTION IN TENSE-ASPECT SYSTEMS 412
Östen Dahl

BIBLIOGRAPHY OF RECENT WORK ON GENERICITY 427

NAME INDEX 451

LANGUAGE INDEX 455

SUBJECT INDEX 457

PREFACE AND ACKNOWLEDGMENTS

In 1987 the National Science Foundation supported a workshop and conference at the 1987 LSA Summer Institute at Stanford University on ''Generics, Habituals, Mass Nouns, and Plurals'' through a grant to Francis Jeffry Pelletier, administered at Stanford University by Ivan Sag (Grant BNS 87-09887). The point of the grant was to allow six researchers with heterogeneous backgrounds and interests to meet during the summer of 1987 at Stanford University to exchange ideas about generics and to try to form some sort of consensus about the leading issues and directions for future research in this area. Each of the six (''The Generic Group'') had previously and independently worked on the philosophic, linguistic, and logical problems raised by the phenomena mentioned in the title of the grant. A subsidiary goal was to develop a terminology to be recommended for use by other researchers, in order to improve the currently chaotic situation. The members of the Generic Group were:

Gregory N. Carlson (then Dept. of Linguistics, University of Iowa; now Dept. of Linguistics, University of Rochester)

Gennaro Chierchia (then Dept. of Literature and Linguistics, Cornell University; now Dept. of Philosophy, University of Milan)

Manfred Krifka (then Seminar für natürlich-sprachliche Systeme, Universität Tübingen; now Dept. of Linguistics, University of Texas at Austin)

Godehard Link (Institut für Philosophie, Logik und Wissenschaftstheorie, Universität München)

Francis Jeffry Pelletier (Depts. of Philosophy and Computing Science, University of Alberta)

Alice ter Meulen (then Dept. of Linguistics, University of Washington; now Cognitive Science Group, Indiana University)

This workshop met not only privately for the six weeks of the Institute, but also twice each week as a class open to the general Institute membership. Scholars who had been active in this field or in related areas attended the meetings and aided us in formulating our views, and often took some of our results and worked them out further. The grant also funded a one-day conference, held at the Summer Institute, at which the members of the Generic Group (plus some others) presented preliminary results of the collaboration.

In August 1988 there was the conference "Genericity in Natural Language," organized by Manfred Krifka at the Universität Tübingen and attended by the members of the Group (plus numerous other researchers from Europe), at which further work was presented, and further discussions took place. In December 1988, Carlson, Pelletier, and ter Meulen presented this joint work in a symposium at the LSA Annual Meeting, at which the commentators were James Higginbotham, Angelika Kratzer, and John Lawler.

This volume represents an attempt to present readers with the main thrust of research on generics from the perspective of the original Generic Group, but includes work from other scholars. We find it somewhat surprising that there was as much agreement as we in fact found among ourselves, and this volume, especially the comprehensive introductory chapter, makes an effort to express those general points of agreement. But the main purpose of this volume is to introduce researchers to the rich variety of questions about generics that have been and can be posed coherently, and to lay out a field that remains wide open to further research, from any number of perspectives, with any number of specific goals.

The contributions to this volume are drawn from a variety of sources, including works that were presented at the 1988 conference and thus have been in informal circulation for some time, as well as some more recent papers. Some of the earlier papers in fact have become "underground classics" and have been widely cited in the published literature. In the case of papers of this "classic nature," we thought it best to encourage the authors *not* to update their presentation, since this could result in a radically different paper. For instance, it seems wrong to have an author discuss a recently published work which was itself a discussion of the "underground classic." However, this decision implies that some papers in this volume will have references that seem a few years behind the times. We trust that the preservation of the "classics" will justify this. Our hope is that the volume, taken as a whole, will display an appealing and wide range of issues, as well as perhaps some promising solutions to the difficult issues one is confronted with in undertaking work in this area.

Gregory N. Carlson and Francis Jeffry Pelletier

CONTRIBUTORS

Nicholas Asher
Department of Philosophy and Cognitive Science Institute
University of Texas
Austin, TX 78712, U.S.A.

Gregory N. Carlson
Department of Linguistics
University of Rochester
Rochester, NY 14627, U.S.A.

Gennaro Chierchia
Dipartimento di Filosofia
Università degli Studi di Milano
Via Festa del Perdono 7
20122 Milano, Italy

Östen Dahl
Stockholms Universitet
Institut för Lingvistik
S-10691 Stockholm, Sweden

Angelika Kratzer
Linguistics Department
University of Massachusetts
Amherst, MA 01003, U.S.A.

Manfred Krifka
Department of Linguistics
University of Texas
Austin, TX 78712, U.S.A.

Godehard Link
Institut für Philosophie, Logik und Wissenschaftstheorie
Universität München
Ludwigstr. 31/I
80539 München, Germany

Michael Morreau
Department of Philosophy
University of Maryland
College Park, MD 20742, U.S.A.

Francis Jeffry Pelletier
Department of Philosophy and Department of Computing Science
University of Alberta
Edmonton, AB, Canada T6G 2E5

Mats Rooth
Universität Stuttgart
IMS
Azenbergstr. 12
70147 Stuttgart, Germany

Alice ter Meulen
Cognitive Science Group
Indiana University
Bloomington, IN 47405, U.S.A.

Karina Wilkinson
Department of Modern Languages and Linguistics
Cornell University
106 Harvard Place
Ithaca, NY 14853, U.S.A.

1 GENERICITY: AN INTRODUCTION

Manfred Krifka, Francis Jeffry Pelletier,
Gregory N. Carlson, Alice ter Meulen,
Godehard Link, and Gennaro Chierchia

1.0. Introduction and Acknowledgments

The purpose of this introduction is to present an overview of topics and issues within the area of generics, and where possible draw conclusions about the current state of the area as agreed upon among the authors. This has proven a formidable task, given the large number of semantic issues that the study of generics directly interacts with, and the number of open questions that remain. This chapter is based on drafts written by Manfred Krifka in consultation with the other authors, starting from a paper written earlier by Krifka, partially in collaboration with Claudia Gerstner-Link. Krifka's final draft was subsequently reworked, in some places extensively, by Francis Jeffry Pelletier and then Gregory Carlson. In attempting to create a synthesis of our views, we found that many of the ideas expressed were not unanimously agreed upon, and the sum total of ideas expressed in this introduction is probably not endorsed by a single one of us.

While all authors listed bear some measure of responsibility for the claims and views expressed, special credit should go to Manfred Krifka for the enormous amount of research and writing that made this introduction possible, and special responsibility (or blame) for the shape of the overall outcome to the volume editors, Gregory Carlson and Francis Jeffry Pelletier. We also want to thank many colleagues who shared with us their ideas on genericity, and those who took the time to discuss earlier versions of this Introduction: Emmon Bach, Henry Churchyard, Ileana Comorovski, Hana Filip, Claudia Gerstner-Link, Randy Goebel, Jim Higginbotham, Janet Hitzeman, David Israel, Ezat Karimi, Boomee Kim, Angelika Kratzer, John Lawler, Bernie Linsky, Jim McCawley, Sally McConell-Ginet, Michael Morreau, Barbara Partee, Ivan Sag, Len Schubert, Andrew Schwartz, Scott Soames, Bob Stalnaker, Rich Thomason, Frank Veltman, Karina Wilkinson, Katsuhiko Yabushita, and Sandro Zucchi. Manfred Krifka wants to thank especially Claudia Gerstner-Link, with whom he developed some central ideas that are presented in this introductory chapter. We also wish to thank the two anonymous University of Chicago Press referees for their many productive comments.

Our joint work was sponsored partly by the National Science Foundation (Grant BNS87-09887 and Grant BNS-8919827), by the Volkswagenstiftung, by the Seminar für natürlich-sprachliche Systeme (Universität Tübingen), by the Canadian Natural Science and Engineering Research Council (OPG 5525), and by the Deutsche Forschungsgemeinschaft (Sonderforschungsbereich 340). The individual contributions record any further debts in our individual research efforts.

1.1. WHAT IS GENERICITY?

1.1.1. The Two Basic Varieties of Genericity

In the history both of philosophy of language and of linguistics, there have been two quite distinct phenomena that have been referred to or classified as 'genericity'. The first is *reference to a kind*—a genus—as exemplified in (1). The underlined noun phrases (NPs) in (1) do not denote or designate some particular potato or group of potatoes, but rather the kind Potato (*Solanum tuberosum*) itself. In this usage a generic NP is an NP that does not refer to an "ordinary" individual or object, but instead refers to a kind.

(1) a. The potato was first cultivated in South America.
b. Potatoes were introduced into Ireland by the end of the 17th century.
c. The Irish economy became dependent upon the potato.

We will call NPs like *potatoes* or *the potato* in these sentences *kind-referring NPs,* or sometimes *generic NPs,* as opposed to *object-referring NPs,* and call the predications in sentences involving such NPs *kind predications,* in opposition to *object predications.*[1]

The second phenomenon commonly associated with genericity are propositions which do not express specific episodes or isolated facts, but instead report a kind of *general property,* that is, report a regularity which summarizes groups of particular episodes or facts. Examples can be found in the natural readings of the sentences in (2). Here (2a) does not report a particular episode but a habit—some kind of generalization over events; and (2b) does not state something about a specific potato but about potatoes in general—a generalization based on properties of individual potatoes. This second notion of genericity is

1. 'Object' is a semantic notion here describing the ontological status of what is being referred to and does not have anything to do with 'object' as a syntactic notion. However, regarding this latter sense of 'object', note that generic NPs can occur as objects of verbs, of prepositions, etc.—as in (1c). For the most part our discussion will revolve around kind-referring NPs in subject position. But we intend our results to apply directly to other syntactic positions as well.

clearly a feature of the whole sentence (or clause), rather than of any one NP in it; it is the whole generic sentence that expresses regularities which transcend particular facts.

(2) a. John smokes a cigar after dinner.
b. A potato contains vitamin C, amino acids, protein and thiamine.

We will call sentences like these *characterizing sentences,* or sometimes simply *generic sentences,* as they express generalizations. They are opposed to *particular sentences,* which express statements about particular events, properties of particular objects, and the like.[2] We will classify the respective predications as *characterizing predications* (as in (2)) and *particular predications* (as in (1)), respectively. Other common terms for characterizing sentences found in the literature are '(g)nomic', 'dispositional', 'general', or 'habitual'. Much of our knowledge of the world, and many of our beliefs about the world, are couched in terms of characterizing sentences. Such sentences, we take it, are either true or false—they are *not* "indeterminate" or "figurative" or "metaphorical" or "sloppy talk". After all, we certainly would want to count the classic *Snow is white* as literally having a truth value!

Both phenomena—kind-referring NPs and characterizing sentences—can occur combined in a single sentence, as the following examples show:

(3) a. Potatoes are served whole or mashed as a cooked vegetable.
b. The potato is highly digestible.

Certainly the subjects of these sentences can be analyzed as kind-referring NPs, and the sentences themselves express regularities which hold for the specimens of this kind. The two phenomena co-occur in the same sentence quite often.

Few studies concentrate explicitly on only one type of genericity. Nonetheless, Langford (1949), Sellars (1963), Bacon (1973a,b, 1974), Platteau (1980), Heyer (1987), Gerstner-Link (1988), Kleiber (1990), and Ojeda (1991) may be cited as concerning themselves mainly with reference to kinds, whereas Chafe (1970), Lawler (1973a), Dahl (1975), Nunberg and Pan (1975), Burton-Roberts (1976, 1977), Biggs (1978), Farkas and Sugioka (1983), Geurts (1985), Strigin (1985), Declerck (1986), and Schubert and Pelletier (1987, 1989) are concerned primarily with characterizing sentences. Smith (1975) and

2. They are also opposed to explicitly quantified general sentences such as (i):
(i) Each potato in this room was grown in Alberta.
But the exact opposition involved here is a topic for later in this chapter; see section 1.1.3.

Carlson (1977a,b, 1982) essentially treat both aspects, trying to analyze one in terms of the other. The two types were contrasted by Gerstner and Krifka (1983);[3] Wilkinson (1988), Wilmet (1988), and Declerck (1991) make similar distinctions.

It is quite obvious that reference to kinds and characterizing sentences have something in common: with kinds we abstract away from particular objects, whereas with characterizing sentences we abstract away from particular events and facts. Furthermore, it seems natural that one way to express a general law about the specimens of a kind is to state it for the kind itself. Nonetheless, it is important to keep these two types of generic phenomena apart, since it turns out that there are linguistic differences between them. So even if in the end we decide (for example) that the best semantic analysis will analyze one in terms of the other, we will still wish to maintain them as separate linguistic phenomena. Also, it will be important to distinguish generic sentences, be they characterizing sentences or sentences containing kind-referring NPs, from nongeneric ones. In section 1.1.3 we will present some linguistic tests to do so.

We want to mention right at the outset that although characterizing sentences sometimes have the flavor of universally quantified sentences, these two categories must be kept apart. One reason is that characterizing sentences, in general, allow for exceptions, whereas universally quantified sentences make a claim for every object of a certain sort. For example, if from time to time, John does not smoke after dinner, sentence (2a) can still be true. And if an occasional potato lacks vitamin C, (2b) can still be true. In both situations, the corresponding universally quantified sentences would be false:

(4) a. Always after dinner/After each dinner, John smokes a cigar.
    b. Every potato contains vitamin C, amino acids, protein and thiamine.

Characterizing sentences allow for exceptions (and as the attentive reader will have recognized, this is a characterizing sentence as well: there might be—and in fact are—characterizing sentences that hold without exceptions). The issue of how to handle possible exceptions in a precise semantic framework is an

3. These authors used the terms 'D-generic' and 'I-generic' for kind-referring NPs and characterizing sentences respectively. The idea was that reference to kinds is often manifested by definite NPs, whereas characterizing sentences often have an indefinite (or bare plural) NP in them. But not only are these not universal properties of the two types; the terms also incorrectly suggest that both types are somehow on a par in that they are manifested by NPs. (It is the terminology that is confused, not the authors.) Also, earlier, "underground" versions of this introductory chapter used 'characteristic sentence' where we now prefer 'characterizing sentence', both for purposes of euphony and for some ineffable and subtle distinction in "feeling" between the two.

extremely interesting one, not only for linguistics but also in logic, cognitive science, and artificial intelligence. We will discuss problems related to this issue in section 1.2.4 of this introductory chapter, and in some of the later chapters in this volume, most notably those by Carlson and by Asher and Morreau (chapters 4 and 7).

1.1.2. Subtypes of the Basic Varieties of Genericity

If we look at the linguistic realization of kind-referring NPs and characterizing sentences, we find that they seldom are encoded in an unambiguous way. Not only are there many linguistically distinct ways to state a particular generic sentence, but also it often happens that a given sentence can have both a particular and a characterizing reading.

Let us first consider kind-referring NPs. In English, many definite singular count nouns, bare plural count nouns, and bare mass nouns can be considered as kind-referring.[4]

(5) a. The lion is a predatory cat.
b. Lions are predatory cats.
c. Gold is a precious metal.

Furthermore, count nouns, and mass nouns like *metal* in a "secondary" count noun reading, can denote subspecies in a taxonomic hierarchy. In this *taxonomic* reading, they clearly have to be analyzed as kind-denoting, even when they appear as indefinite singular NPs.

(6) a. The World Wildlife Organization decided to protect a (certain) large cat, namely the Siberian tiger.
b. One metal, namely copper, went strongly up on the market yesterday.

Of course, the NPs we have considered so far *need* not be analyzed as referring to kinds. Definite singular NPs, bare plural NPs, bare singular NPs, and indefinite singular NPs all can, intuitively, refer to objects as well, as in the following examples:

(7) a. The lion / Lions escaped yesterday from the Hellabrunn zoo.
b. Gold was stolen in yesterday's bank robbery.
c. A cat was sitting on the mat when John arrived at home.

4. We say "can be considered" here because we do not wish to prejudge the final semantic analysis to be given. Certainly at first blush, and on a pretheoretic level, the cited sentences *do* use the underlined NPs to refer to kinds.

One linguistic problem is to identify the clues which help us distinguish between a generic and a nongeneric reading of such NPs—if there is such a distinction, a matter taken up in section 1.4.6 below.

Are there any NPs which can *only* be interpreted as kind-referring? An example is the English NP (not the common noun) *man:*

(8) Man has lived in Africa for more than 2 million years.

There are other unequivocal cases, like *this kind of tiger* and *each species of fish.* But beyond such idiosyncratic examples as *man* and these systematic NPs with special lexical content, no NPs appear to demand unequivocal reference to kinds, at least not at first sight. In section 1.4 we will extend similar consideration to gerunds, infinitive constructions, and deverbal nominalizations as additional possible cases of kind-referring expressions.

Let us now turn to characterizing sentences. Like kind-referring NPs, they often are not clearly marked. Sentences with verbal predicates[5] in the simple present tense, the past tense or the future can (in English) have either a characterizing or a particular interpretation (this even holds for *smokes* with the so-called 'reportive present'):

(9) John smokes/smoked/will smoke a pipe.

Sometimes characterizing sentences are said to express 'timeless truths' (e.g., Lyons 1977, 194). We think that this claim is false, as it is perfectly possible to claim that a characterizing property held in the past or will hold in the future, without any implication for the present. However, there *is* a correlation with aspectual distinctions: progressive and perfect sentences show at least a strong tendency toward a particular, noncharacterizing interpretation:[6]

(10) John is smoking/has smoked a pipe.

5. Once again we use the phrase "verbal predicate" as a pre-analytic, theory-neutral term to pick out what one naively would call the verb phrase. It may be that the correct semantic theory will analyze this verbal predicate in terms of some other predicate which (for example) holds of temporal stages of the verbal subject, and so the verbal predicate may not be the "real" predicate. But here, when we use such terms as "verbal predicate," we wish to focus on the pretheoretical structure of the sentence.

6. Schubert and Pelletier (1987) cite various apparent counterexamples to this "tendency":

(i) Oil is becoming scarce.

(ii) The wolves are becoming bigger as we travel northwards.

It seems that to maintain our claim we need to make caveats about group readings, and about kind-referring NPs; or perhaps say that (i) and (ii) *are* particular statements—about the kind.

There are various constructions which enforce a characterizing reading. First, there are adverbs like *usually, typically, always, often, sometimes, rarely, never,* etc., that lead to lawlike characterizing sentences:

(11a) John usually/always/often/rarely/never smokes a pipe.

This effect can override the previously-noted tendency for progressives to have noncharacterizing interpretations:

(11b) John is usually/always/often smoking a pipe.

Second, in the (English) past tense there is an auxiliary construction that marks a characterizing reading; similar constructions are found in many other languages:

(12) John used to smoke a pipe.

Third, agentive nouns typically have a characterizing meaning, and sentences which have agentive nouns as predicates consequently are characterizing:

(13) John is a pipe smoker.

Similarly, the derivation of deverbal adjectives using *-able* yields characterizing predicates and sentences:

(14) This book is readable.

Furthermore, verbal predicates in the middle voice typically have a characterizing interpretation:

(15) This shirt washes easily.

Finally, there are some rather idiosyncratic ways to describe characterizing generalizations, by using special lexical items:

(16) a. John has an inclination to smoke a pipe.
b. Mary has the habit of carrying an umbrella with her even when the sun is shining.
c. Sue has the disposition / is disposed to get the flu in winter.
d. Bill frequents that pub over there.
e. Milk tends to sour during thunderstorms.
f. Your typical Australian drinks too much beer.

In some languages there are specialized morphological forms for verbs in characterizing sentences. An example is the verbal prefix *hu-* in Swahili (see Dahl 1985, 1988a, and chapter 12, this volume, for further examples):

(17) Wanawake hu-fanya kazi ya kuchokoa pwesa.
women HABIT-do work of catching squid
'The women (generally) do the work of catching squid.'

But normally, these markers are only a sufficient, and not a necessary, condition for the characterizing reading. For example, the same meaning could be expressed in Swahili by using a present tense:

(18) Wanawake wa-na-fanya kazi ya kuchokoa pwesa.
'The women catch squid' *or* 'The women are catching squid.'

In concluding these observations about characterizing sentences, we want to emphasize that characterizing sentences put no limitations on what kinds of NPs may occur in them. For example, we can find proper names, definite singular NPs, indefinite singular NPs, quantified NPs, bare plural NPs, and bare singular NPs in characterizing sentences.

(19) a. John / My brother drinks whiskey.
b. A professor drinks whiskey.
c. Every professor drinks whiskey.
d. Professors drink whiskey.
e. Milk is healthy.

Sometimes the subject NP apparently refers to a kind, as in (19e); sometimes it apparently refers to an individual, as in (19a), and the sentence attributes a characterizing property to this individual; sometimes it is quantified but its values apparently are ordinary individuals, as in (19c), and the sentence attributes a characterizing property to each instance of the quantified NP; and sometimes it is just unclear what the subject NP denotes, as in (19b) and (19d).

Because of the wide variability of NPs in characterizing sentences, it seems implausible that this type of genericity can be traced back to any particular type of NP. Instead, this type of genericity should be analyzed as being a *sui generis* type of sentence.

1.1.3. Genericity vs. Nongenericity: Some Diagnostic Tests

As neither generic (kind-referring) NPs nor generic (characterizing) sentences are typically marked in a clear and unambiguous way, it seems appropriate to list some fairly simple diagnostic tests and typical properties to distinguish them from nongeneric NPs and nongeneric sentences. In this section, we will give five tests of this kind. This series of tests is by no means exhaustive, and of course any test must be applied judiciously, being indicative and not criterial.

The first test. This test distinguishes characterizing sentences from particular sentences as follows: Combine the sentence in question with an adverb like *usually* or *typically*. If the resulting sentence exhibits at most a slight change of meaning, then the original sentence is characterizing. With particular sentences, the change in meaning obtained by applying these adverbs is quite drastic.[7] To be somewhat more precise, if the original sentence is characterizing, then adverbs like *usually* explicitly convey the information that there may be exceptions to the rule which the sentence expresses, and that there actually are instantiations of the rule. If the original sentence is particular, these adverbs change the meaning from a report of a specific event or a particular fact to a general rule. Some examples:

(20) a. A lion has a bushy tail.[8]
b. A lion usually has a bushy tail.

(21) a. A lion stood in front of my tent.
b. A lion usually stood in front of my tent.

In (20), the insertion of *usually* brings about only a minor change in meaning: there is a sense in which (20b) might be called somewhat weaker than (20a), since it points explicitly to the fact that there might be exceptions to the rule. In the case of (21), however, the change is from the report of a specific event to a claim about a regularity of events, which is a much more thorough change of meaning.

Consider another example, though:

(22) a. Mary handled the mail from Antarctica.
b. Mary usually handled the mail from Antarctica.

In this case, (22a) has two readings; it can either mean that Mary was in charge of the mail of Antarctica in general (even if there never was some real mail from Antarctica), or that she handled some particular batch of mail of Antarctica. If we have the former reading in mind, the adverb *usually* in (22b)

7. Naturally enough this test is only applicable if the sentence does not already have a *usually* or *typically* in it. And again, naturally enough, the notion of ''slight change of meaning;'' vs. ''drastic change of meaning'' is pretty fuzzy. But the examples are clear, we hope.

8. Throughout, we follow a well-known dictionary which describes lions' tails as bushy—regardless of whether in fact they are or are not bushy.

generates just slight changes in meaning (it implies that there might have been exceptions to the rule, and consequently also that there was indeed some mail from Antarctica). But if we have the second reading of (22a) in mind, we see that the addition of *usually* in (22b) generates quite a drastic meaning change, despite our contention that even on this latter reading (22a) is still a (dispositional) characterizing sentence.

The second test. This test determines which types of NPs can be used as kind-referring terms. There are some predicates with argument places that can be filled only with kind-referring NPs. Examples are the subject argument of *die out* or *be extinct* and the object argument of *invent* or *exterminate*. The reason is, of course, that only kinds (not objects) can die out or be invented. With some other predicates, such as *be a mammal, be domesticated,* and *be protected by law*, the kind-referring interpretation of the subject is not the only one; indeed, a proper name referring to a particular animal can also be used as subject with these. Yet when a general term is used as subject NP, the kind-referring interpretation of the NP has at least priority over the object-referring interpretation. We call predicates which favor a kind-referring interpretation of an argument *kind predicates;* and we observe, for example, that definite singular NPs such as in (23a), bare blural NPs such as in (23b), and bare singular NPs such as in (23c) pass this test, whereas indefinite NPs such as in (23d) fail, except in the taxonomic reading in (23e) (see also Smith 1975):

(23) a. The lion will become extinct soon.
b. Lions will become extinct soon.
c. Bronze is a metal / was invented as early as 3000 B.C.
d.* A lion will become extinct soon. (nontaxonomic reading)
e. A (certain) lion (namely the Berber lion) will become extinct soon. (taxonomic reading)

This result is quite important, as definite NPs like *the lion,* bare plural NPs like *lions,* and indefinite singular NPs like *a lion* have often been considered the three main types of 'generic noun phrases' (e.g., in the English grammar of Quirk et al. 1985, 265; Dahl 1975; Lyons 1977; Carlson 1977b). But obviously, given the unacceptability of (23d), indefinite singular NPs have to be treated differently, a point that will be substantiated with other tests below. Therefore, we will not consider indefinite NPs as kind-referring (except in their taxonomic reading). Bare plural NPs, on the other hand, can denote a kind, although sometimes they are analyzed as the plural counterpart of indefinite NPs (see Burton-Roberts 1976 and van Langendonck 1980a,b for discussion; see also Kratzer, this volume).

The third test. This test helps to distinguish object-referring NPs from kind-referring NPs. It is based on the fact that it is not possible to form kind-referring NPs with just any nominal constituent. This was pointed out by Vendler (1967), Nunberg and Pan (1975), Carlson (1977b), and Dahl (1985) for singular NPs with definite article in English. Basically, the noun or complex nominal constituent must be semantically connected with a "well-established kind" to which the noun phrase then can refer.[9] A contrast like the following (from Carlson 1977b, who attributes it to Barbara Partee) is quite striking; it can be traced back to the fact that there exists a well-established kind for Coke bottles, but there is no well-established kind for green bottles:

(24) a. The Coke bottle has a narrow neck.
b. ??The green bottle has a narrow neck.

The test can be used to show that certain NPs which can be kind-referring according to our second test, namely bare plurals and bare singular NPs, might have an object-referring reading as well, even in characterizing sentences. The following examples show that bare plural NPs like *green bottles* and bare singular NPs like *gold which is hammered flat* (which do not refer to well-established kinds) pattern with indefinite singular NPs like *a green bottle,* rather than with definite NPs like *the green bottle.*

(25) a. A green bottle (usually) has a narrow neck.
b. Green bottles (usually) have narrow necks.
c. Gold which is hammered flat (usually) is opaque.

Simple bare nouns, like *bottles* or *gold,* may possibly be object-referring, even in characterizing sentences. This becomes apparent when we consider noncharacterizing sentences like *Bottles were standing all over the kitchen,* or *Gold was found all over the place.* In principle, therefore, bare nouns may well have two interpretations: they can be kind-referring, as shown in the previous test, and they may also be object-referring, as shown by the facts cited here (see sections 1.3 and 1.4 for further discussion of this double role

9. We will not attempt to offer any sort of analysis of the notion 'well-established kind'. The distinction is real enough and is quite striking in its effect on example sentences, but we have no well-formed thoughts as to what the contrast owes its origins.

and its controversial aspects). The issue raised by this third test is whether it tests for reference to a kind or whether it tests only for reference to a "well-established" kind, whatever that may turn out to be in the end.

The fourth test. This test helps to distinguish characterizing sentences from particular sentences. Characterizing sentences express regularities and do not report particular events. A roughly corresponding linguistic distinction is the one between stative and nonstative (or dynamic) sentences. Accordingly, characterizing sentences are typically stative, and, most often, particular sentences are nonstative. If the language under consideration has a linguistic form which excludes stative predicates, as the progressive in English does (e.g., **John is weighing 175 pounds*), this form will typically exclude characterizing interpretations as well. Thus it is very difficult to transform a characterizing sentence into the progressive without its losing its generic character. For example, the sentences in (26) clearly have a characterizing reading, which the sentences in (27) lack.

(26) a. The Italian drinks wine with his dinner.
b. An Italian drinks wine with his dinner.
c. Italians drink wine with their dinner.
d. Luigi drinks wine with his dinner.

(27) a. The Italian is drinking wine with his dinner.
b. An Italian is drinking wine with his dinner.
c. Italians are drinking wine with their dinner.
d. Luigi is drinking wine with his dinner.

These facts confirm our observation that there are noncharacterizing sentences with kind-referring NPs, since kind-referring NPs can easily occur with nonstative predicates. Furthermore, they show that indefinite nontaxonomic NPs cannot be kind-referring: when combined with a nonstative predicate, they get either a non-kind-referring interpretation or a taxonomic interpretation. Here are some examples in which *reach Australia in 1770* is used as a clearly nonstative predicate:

(28) a. The rat was (just) reaching Australia in 1770. (kind-referring reading OK)
b. Rats were (just) reaching Australia in 1770. (kind-referring reading OK)
c. Rice was being introduced into East Africa several centuries ago. (kind-referring reading OK)
d. A rat was reaching Australia in 1770. (only non-kind-referring or, perhaps, taxonomic reading)

The fifth test. This last test helps us distinguish characterizing from particular sentences. As noted already by Goodman (1955) and later by Lawler (1973), Dahl (1975), Burton-Roberts (1977), and subsequent researchers, characterizing sentences do not express accidental properties; rather, they state properties that are in some way "essential". To put it in Dahl's (1975) terminology, they are not only "descriptive" generalizations but "normative" ones. With this observation, we can further confirm our claim that indefinite singular NPs in their nontaxonomic reading cannot be kind-referring since they are tied to characterizing sentences. For example, note the following contrast between sentences expressing an accidental property and sentences expressing an essential or at least "central" property (the examples are Lawler's):[10]

(29) a′. The madrigal is popular.
a″. The madrigal is polyphonic.
b′. Madrigals are popular.
b″. Madrigals are polyphonic.
c′. ??A madrigal is popular.
c″. A madrigal is polyphonic.

We assume that being popular is an accidental property of madrigals, whereas being polyphonic is essential to them. Consequently, (29c′), which can only be read as a characterizing sentence, is bad, whereas (29c″) is good. Of course, different properties are essential (in the present sense) to different types of objects. Being popular may not be essential to madrigals but it is to football heroes. Thus, as Nunberg and Pan (1975) say, *A football hero is popular* is acceptable. It's acceptable because the property of being popular is essential or central to football heroes.

Previous observations made in the literature (Lawler 1973, Heyer 1987, Laca 1990) suggest another test for distinguishing between kind-referring and object-referring NPs. In upward-entailing contexts (roughly, non-negative contexts), indefinite object-referring NPs show the usual monotonicity effects: they can be replaced by "less informative" NPs without making the sentence false, as (30a). This is not possible with generic NPs, as shown in (30b).

(30) a. Berber lions escaped from the zoo $\Rightarrow$ Lions escaped from the zoo
b. Berber lions are extinct $\not\Rightarrow$ Lions are extinct

10. Once again (as with "well-established kind") we are not in a position to provide an analysis of what an "essential" vs. an "accidental" property consists in, as it is used by this test. Again, the distinction is real and manifests itself in striking results, but the underlying reason is not clear.

However, this test only works when the kind-referring NP is not also in a characterizing sentence. This is so because characterizing sentences have (what we will soon call) a "restrictor" position; and in this position neither kind- nor object-referring NPs show monotonicity phenomena. For instance:

(30) c. Berber lions are well adapted to cold weather $\not\Rightarrow$ Lions are well adapted to cold weather
d. A Berber lion is well adapted to cold weather $\not\Rightarrow$ A lion is well adapted to cold weather

In (30c), replacing *Berber lions* by *lions* does not block truth preservation just because the subject NPs are kind-referring, but rather because of the specific properties of characterizing sentences. (30d) shows that we obtain the same effect with singular indefinite NPs that are not kind-referring.

1.1.4. A Cross-Classification of Generic Phenomena

In this section, we will develop some more terminology for the classification of generic phenomena. The aim of this classification is a modest one: we wish to put these phenomena into some systematic framework to serve as a reference system for later use. Since some of the phenomena are independent of each other, we expect cross-classification.[11]

We have already introduced a nominal distinction (i.e., a distinction within the NP system), namely the distinction between *kind-referring* and *object-referring* NPs, and a clausal (sentence-level) distinction, namely the distinction between *characterizing sentences* and *particular sentences.* Both the nominal and the clausal distinction can be further refined.

We start with the nominal distinction. We have seen that indefinite singular NPs cannot be simply considered as kind-referring or 'generic' in and of themselves (in contrast to some earlier analyses). The reason is that they get an apparent 'generic' interpretation only when occurring in a characterizing sentence (if we exclude the taxonomic interpretation). The locus of genericity is not in the indefinite singular NP, but rather in the sentence itself; and therefore this type of genericity is outside the nominal system. But there *is* a distinction within singular NPs that is of interest in the present context: the distinction between NPs referring to a particular entity (e.g., definite NPs and indefinite NPs like *a lion* in *A lion stood in front of my tent*) and NPs which do not refer

11. As we shall see, the dimensions are not entirely orthogonal to (or dependent of) one another. We will find certain "gaps" in the classification, which shows some degree of interaction among the dimensions.

to a particular entity (e.g., *A lion* in *A lion has a bushy tail*). Let us call NPs which refer to a particular individual *specific* and NPs which do not refer to a specific individual *nonspecific*. Although this might be reminiscent of the formal distinction discussed by, e.g., Baker (1973) and Fodor and Sag (1982), and further explored by Enç (1991), we view it as a pretheoretic notion at this point.[12]

We want to emphasize that the specific/nonspecific distinction is independent of the kind reference/object reference distinction. It is well known that with ordinary object-level predications we can use an indefinite NP to be either specific or nonspecific; similarly with predications to kinds. For when we are "talking about" kinds, we can do so either specifically (*the lion* or *a cat (namely the lion)*) or nonspecifically. In the latter case we use an indefinite NP, of course, but we consider it as designating some element in this kind taxonomy—as for example in *A different cat is displayed in the zoo each month.*

Then the initial four-way cross-classification with the nominal system can be exemplified as follows:

(31) a. *A lion* (as in *A lion has a bushy tail*) is nonspecific and non-kind-referring.
b. *Simba / a lion, namely Simba* (as in *Simba stood in front of my tent*) is specific and non-kind-referring.
c. *A cat* (in the taxonomic reading, as in *A cat shows mutations when domesticated*) is kind-referring but nonspecific.
d. *The lion / A cat, namely the lion* (taxonomic reading) is kind-referring and specific.

The third of our four dimensions concerns the type of sentence itself, rather than the NP used. Thus we obtain the following cross-classification of characterizing and particular sentences with different NP types as subjects:

(32) a. *A lion has a mane.* (characterizing; nonspecific non-kind reference)
c. *Simba ate lunch.* (particular; specific non-kind reference)
d. *Simba roars when he smells food.* (characterizing; specific non-kind reference)
f. *A predatory cat (usually) is protected by law.* (characterizing; nonspecific kind reference)

12. The actual specific/nonspecific distinction (if there is just one such distinction) is extremely difficult to elucidate in its details. It is for this reason that we wish to remain on a pretheoretic level. Even so, we had better point out that we take, e.g., *a lion* in *A lion must be standing in the bush over there* to be specific rather than nonspecific, even if there is no particular lion that the speaker believes to be in the bush.

g. *The lion vanished from Asia.* (particular; specific kind reference)
h. *The lion roars when it smells food.* (characterizing; specific kind reference)

We observe two gaps, both with particular sentences containing nonspecific NPs. Nonspecific NPs (in the sense in which we intend the term here) only occur with characterizing sentences. In addition, if an NP that may be nonspecific occurs with a characterizing predicate, this NP tends to be interpreted as nonspecific. We should conclude from this that nonspecific NPs are tied to characterizing sentences, or put differently, that particular predications do not allow nonspecific NPs as subjects, whether they make nonspecific reference to objects or to kinds. This affinity between characterizing sentences and nonspecificity has often been observed, for example by Dahl (1975), who remarked that the following sentences only have one interpretation each, instead of two:

(33) a. A dog is barking.
b. A dog barks.

Here (33a) is a particular sentence about a particular (specific) dog, and (33b) is a characterizing sentence which is not about a particular (specific) dog but, intuitively speaking, about dogs in general. Thus, although *a dog* may be either specific or nonspecific in and of itself, (33a) cannot be interpreted as a particular sentence about the kind *Canis familiaris* (or the class of dogs) stating that they happen to bark at the moment, and (33b) cannot be interpreted as a characterizing sentence about a particular dog, stating, say, that Rover barks. We will come back to this important correlation in section 1.2 and again in section 1.4.

Our final dimension concerns clausal distinctions. First, we have the well-known distinction between *stative* sentences and *dynamic* sentences (cf. Vendler 1967; Kenny 1963; Mourelatos 1978, who speaks of states and occurrences; Tichy 1980; Chierchia 1982a; and many others). Stative sentences express a *property* of the subject referent; dynamic sentences report an *event* in which the subject referent is involved. Examples are *Simba has a mane* and *Simba roared,* respectively. Of course, there are further subdistinctions among dynamic sentences, such as that between activities and accomplishments, but they will not concern us now. While it appears that all characterizing (generic) sentences are stative, there appear to be particular sentences which are stative as well: *Simba is in the cage* is one such example. Though stative, these are also episodic, because they do not express long-lasting properties and because they pattern with other episodics (cf., the *ser/estar* distinction in Spanish and existential entailments of bare plural subjects; see Kratzer, this volume, for many more examples of particular states found in the 'stage-level' adjectives, and Carlson 1977b for further discussion). The most important point to note here is that characterizing sentences are always stative: they express a property, and never report a specific event (cf. section 1.2.2).[13] So the stative/episodic distinction only applies to particular sentences and is neutralized for characterizing sentences.

A second clausal distinction, this time for characterizing sentences, is the one between "habitual" sentences and (for lack of a better term) "lexical" characterizing sentences. The verbal predicate of a habitual sentence is morphologically related to an episodic predicate that is commonly used to form episodic sentences, whereas lexical characterizing sentences lack such an episodic counterpart. For example, *John smokes* and *Italians smoke* are habitual characterizing sentences since they contain the episodic verb *smoke,* which also occurs in *John is smoking*. Habitual sentences intuitively generalize over patterns of events as a component of their meaning (e.g., in this case the generalizations is over instances of John or Italians actually engaging in smoking). On the other hand, lexical characterizing verbs do not have such morphologically related episodic predicate, and consequently there is no semantic generalization over events; rather, the generalization would appear to be over characterizing properties of individuals. This class includes many of the verbs that form stative sentences (*know, cost, weigh, love, fear,* the inalienable possession sense of *have,* etc.). For example, *Italians know French* is a characterizing sentence, generalizing about properties of individual Italians but there is no morphologically related episodic sentence and thus no generalization over events. Copular sentences such as *Lions are mammals* or *John is intelligent* likewise lack such episodic counterparts. There is no episodic predicate which is morphologically related to *know French* (this would be an episodic verb which denotes events and which provides evidence that someone knows French), so the sentence *Italians know French* is a lexical characterizing sentence. It will be a task of section 1.2.3 to develop a hypothesis about this distinction (see also Chierchia, this volume).

So among the particular sentences there is a distinction between stative and

13. It does not follow from this that characterizing sentences cannot be in the progressive form—indeed, we gave examples of this earlier. Rather, when the progressive is used in a characterizing sentence, then that progressive is in fact reporting a stative property. As we said before, this is atypical but not unheard of.

dynamic sentences, and among the characterizing sentences there is a distinction between habitual and lexical characterizing sentences; one question left open here is whether these two distinctions are related. We can now derive a more comprehensive classification of sentence types, which can be illustrated with the following list of examples:

(34) A. HABITUAL SENTENCES
Simba (usually) roars when he smells food. (specific non-kind-referring)
A lion (usually) roars when it smells food. (nonspecific non-kind-referring)
A predatory cat (e.g., the leopard) (usually) is exterminated when it is dangerous to people. (nonspecific kind-referring)
The lion (usually) roars when it smells food. (specific kind-referring)

B. LEXICAL CHARACTERIZING SENTENCES
A lion (usually) weighs more than 200 lbs. (nonspecific non-kind-referring)
The lion weighs more than most animals. (specific kind-referring)
A predatory cat (e.g., the lion) (usually) knows its young. (nonspecific kind-referring)
Simba has a mane. (specific non-kind-referring)

C. EPISODIC DYNAMIC SENTENCES
Simba roared. (non-kind-referring)
The lion disappeared from Asia. (kind-referring)

D. EPISODIC STATIVES
Simba is in this cage. (non-kind-referring)
The lion is in the cage next to the tiger. (kind-referring)

As noted earlier, there are no nonspecific episodic predications, either of (''regular'') objects or of kinds, but the rest of the paradigm is filled in. One puzzle in this is that lexical characterizing sentences with non-kind subjects do not seem to have a basis for generalization, unlike those that have kind-referring subjects. Possible counterexamples to this claim are sentences like (35):

(35) John (usually) has pink hair.

But one could argue that here the basically stative predicate *have pink hair* is ''coerced'' into an episodic meaning, and that only then can the quantificational adverb *usually* be applied in order to produce a habitual. See section 1.2.3 below, and also Chierchia (this volume).

In the next section, we will start by looking at the range of meanings exhibited by characterizing sentences and their linguistic expression.

1.2. CHARACTERIZING VS. PARTICULAR SENTENCES

1.2.1. Basic Properties

We have argued that the type of genericity found in characterizing sentences is tied to sentences rather than to NPs. Two main arguments were used to support this thesis.

The first argument was that characterizing sentences may contain virtually any NP, including indefinite and definite NPs of any type, and proper names (even of "ordinary" objects, which are clearly not kinds). The variety of NPs acceptable in characterizing sentences makes it implausible that this type of genericity is conditioned by the meaning of an NP.

The second argument was that in those few cases where a characterizing sentence is marked formally, the operator is clearly more tightly related to the finite verb (that is, the head of the sentence) than to some argument of that finite verb. In these cases, the marker of characterizing is either some auxiliary (as in the English *used-to* construction, or the corresponding German *pflegt-zu* construction), an adverb (such as English *usually*), or an affix of the main verb (as in Swahili and many other languages). There are no clear cases where the marker is part of the NP. (A possible counterexample to this claim are NPs with the adjective *typical,* as in *A typical lion has a mane.* Note, however, that this adjective occurs freely not only in characterizing sentences but with nongeneric NPs as well. For example, it occurs in episodic sentences such as *A typical house was built next to ours,* where it does not unequivocally indicate a characterizing property.)[14] The syntactic position of the markers of characterizing sentences, then, shows clearly that this type of genericity is independent of verbal predicates.

Recalling the results of section 1.1, we can summarize our findings concerning characterizing genericity as follows:

1. In characterizing sentences the property described by the verbal predicate is an "essential" property of some entity mentioned in the sentence.
2. The subject (or other NP) of a characterizing sentence may be any type of NP.
3. Characterizing predicates may be *habitual* (i.e., derived from episodic predicates) or *lexical.*

One requirement on a semantic theory of characterizing sentences is that it specify the semantic relationship between instances or objects of a kind and a characterizing sentence about that kind. For example, how is the truth of *A*

14. See also the discussion of 'average property interpretations' in section 1.3.4.

lion has a bushy tail related to particular lions? Or, how is the truth of *John smokes a cigar after dinner* related to actual smoking events? As mentioned earlier, characterizing sentences differ from universally quantified sentences in that they allow for exceptions. This is the real puzzle of characterizing sentences; we do not claim to have solved it, but in the following sections we will present some linguistic facts which a solution must address, and some linguistic clues which may facilitate a solution.

1.2.2. Theories with a Monadic Generic Operator

In the first semantic theories of characterizing sentences, genericity was traced to a verb phrase operator taking as its argument an ordinary verbal predicate and yielding a characterizing predicate. We will, for present purposes, call this a "monadic" analysis, in contrast to the "dyadic" analyses to be presented below. For example, Lawler (1972), Dahl (1975), and Carlson (1977a,b) postulate generalization operators which change a particular predicate to a characterizing one. If **Gn** is such operator, we have formalizations such as the following:[15]

(36)	a.	John is smoking.	**smoke(John)**
	b.	John smokes.	**Gn(smoke)(John)**
(37)	a.	Italians are smoking.	∃x[**italians**(x) & **smoke**(x)][16]
	b.	Italians smoke.	**Gn(smoke)(Italians)**

In (36) and (37), **smoke** is a particular predicate (true of individuals at a time, or—depending on the semantic theory adopted—true of temporal stages of individuals), and **Gn(smoke)** is the derived characterizing predicate. In (37) it is assumed that **italians** is a predicate applying to Italians and that **Italians** refers to the kind, Italians (*Homo sapiens italicus*). Of course, we should have a theory of how the predicate **italians** and the kind **Italians** are related. There are several ways such a theory can be constructed (see section 1.3.2). The most interesting and influential theory was developed by Carlson (1977a,b, 1982).[17] According to Carlson's theory, we must distinguish between three types of basic entities: ordinary *objects* and *kinds* (which jointly form the category of *individuals*) and *stages* (which are temporal slices of an individual—that is, individuals-at-a-certain-time-interval). Carlson postulates a "real-

15. Here and below, tense is not captured in the formalism. We use boldface for semantic representations, except for variables, logical connectives, and operators.

16. Plurality is discussed below. We believe that sentences such as (37a) are true if but one individual satisfies the predicate; however, the use of the plural form conversationally implies that the use of the singular would be less accurate.

17. See section 1.4.6 for a more detailed discussion of Carlson's theory.

ization'' relation **R** which holds between stages and their associated individuals. For example **R(s,Simba)** expresses that **s** is a stage of the object **Simba,** and **R(s,Lion)** expresses that **s** is a stage of the kind **Lion.** Arguably, we should assume that if **R(s,Simba),** and Simba is a lion, then also **R(s,Lion)**: every Simba-stage will be a lion-stage.[18] In addition, Carlson also uses **R** for the relation between objects and the kinds they belong to, giving us **R(Simba,Lion)**.

Carlson introduced two kinds of verbal predicates: *individual-level* and *stage-level* predicates. Individual-level predicates are predicated of individuals (kinds or objects); they are stative predicates such ask *know French* and *have red hair* (for objects) or *be extinct* (for kinds). Stage-level predicates are non-stative (or episodic) predicates such as *is speaking French* or *are smoking.* They also appear as predicates of individuals; Carlson described such uses as an existential quantification over stages plus the predicate on stages. For example, a sentence such as *John is smoking* can be paraphrased as: There is a stage of John which is engaged in smoking. A sentence such as *John knows French,* on the other hand, cannot be reduced in this way to a proposition concerning a stage of John.

With this understanding of the ''types'' of the basic predicates (that is, of the ontological level of their arguments), we see that the representations in (36a) and (37a) were not quite correct—since the predicate *smoke* only applies directly to stages, we must redefine what it is for John to be smoking as some stages of John smoking. By contrast, stative predicates like *know French* already apply directly to objects, so we have the following:

(38)	a.	John knows French.	**know.French(John)**
	b.	John is smoking	$\exists y^s$ [**R**(y^s,**John**) & **smoke**(y^s)]
	c.	Italians are smoking.	$\exists y^s$ [**R**(y^s,**Italians**) **smoke**(y^s)]

If we wished, we could introduce a special operator **Ep** on episodic sentences which maps basic stage-level predicates onto their derived individual-level forms. **Ep** would be defined as $\lambda P \lambda x \exists y^s$[**R**(x,y) & P(y)], where y is a variable over stages and x is a variable over individuals. (38b,c) would then be presented as follows:

(38) b.′ **Ep(smoke)(John)**

(38) c.′ **Ep(smoke)(Italians)**

18. At least if Lion is a ''natural kind'' of the sort such that any object which manifests it does so throughout its existence. So if Simba ever manifests Lion then Simba does so throughout his existence—and hence any *stage* of Simba does so also. But artifactual kinds such as table do not so obviously obey this restriction.

After replacement of **Ep** by its definition, these expressions become (38b,c). (38b) (and 38b′)) states that a stage of the object **John** is engaged in smoking; (38c) (and (38c′)) states that a stage of the kind **Italians** is engaged in smoking. In the latter case, we must assume that the stages y, which consist of the stages of several Italians, also stand in the **R**-relation to the kind **Italians,** and that the predicate **smoke** handles this in an adequate way by distributing the property **smoke** to stages of single Italians (see Hinrichs 1985 for such refinements).

Among individual-level predicates, we can make a further distinction between *object-level* and *kind-level* predicates; and we can view the **Gn**-operator as a function which raises the predicate level by mapping stage-level predicates to object-level predicates and object-level predicates to kind-level predicates. For example:

(39) a. John smokes. **Gn(smoke)(John)**
b. Italians smoke. **Gn(smoke)(Italians)**
c. Italians know French. **Gn(know.French)(Italians)**

The correct formulation of **Gn** is a central and difficult problem (as shown by Carlson 1977b) which we will not attempt to solve here. In any case, the truth of **Gn**(α)(β), where α is a verbal predicate and β a term denoting an individual, must be spelled out in terms of the realizations of β and the predicate α. For example, we could require the following:

TENTATIVE GN-RULE: Whenever **Gn**(α)(β) holds, there are several times t and realizations **y** of β, **R**(y,β), such that α(y) holds at t.

In (39a), for example, this would mean that there are several times t and stages y^s such that [**R**(y^s,**John**) & **smoke**(y)] holds at t. In the case of (39b), this means that there are times t and stages y^s such that [**R**(y,**Italians**) & **smoke**(y)] holds at t. Sentence (39c) is analyzed as: There are several times t and objects y^o such that [**R**(y,**Italians**) & **know.French**(y)] holds. This formalism allows us to give a second rendering of *Italians smoke* as **Gn(Gn(smoke))(Italians),** which will be true according to our tentative **Gn**-rule if there are several times t and objects y^o such that [**R**(y^o,**Italians**) & **Gn(smoke)**(y^o)], which in turn is true if there are several times t′ and stages x^s such that **R**(x^s,y^o) & **smoke**(x^s). In the first analysis of (39b), the generalization holds because of certain stages of Italians who are engaged in smoking. In this second analysis, the generalization holds because of individual Italians who are smokers.

We conclude this section with some remarks on the individual-level/stage-level distinction (see also Kratzer, this volume). Carlson (1977b), making use of observations by Milsark (1974), noted that stage-level predicates allow for *there*-constructions.

(40) a. There are students smoking in the classroom.
b.* There are students knowing French.

Stump (1985) observed that absolute constructions as in the following examples can be paraphrased by conditional clauses only if they are based on stage-level predicates:

(41) a. Smoking a cigarette, John can enjoy the trip.
= If he smokes a cigarette, John can enjoy the trip.
b. Knowing French, John can enjoy the trip.
≠ If he knows French, John can enjoy the trip.

The stage/individual distinction seems to cut across many established category distinctions. For example, verbal predicates may be either individual-level or stage-level, as we have seen. Predicative adjectives are also found in both categories: *available* is a case of a stage-level predicate, and *intelligent* a case of an individual-level predicate.

(42) a. There are firefighters available.
b. *There are firefighters intelligent.

Locative prepositional phrases in predicative positions can occur in both classes as well; witness the two readings of *Books are on the shelf.* Predicative nominals were considered to be individual-level by Carlson; however, Weir (1986) remarked that they also may be stage-level, as shown by a sentence like *Rain clouds were a welcome sight* in its "particular" reading.

We will return to Carlson's theory and its motivations and consequences in section 1.4. In the next subsection, we will present an alternative, "dyadic" description of the nature of generic sentences which makes use of the insights of discourse-based semantics (Heim 1982, Kamp 1981) and, at least in certain respects, improves on the monadic predicate-operator analysis.

1.2.3. Theories with a Dyadic Generic Operator, Plurality Phenomena, and Specificity

Carlson (1989) points out that a treatment of characterizing sentences based on a monadic predicate operator such as **Gn** leads to several difficulties. There are many sentences with more than one characterizing reading, such as:[19]

19. The example is from Milsark 1974, the second due to Barbara Partee (reported in Carlson 1989), and the third from Schubert & Pelletier 1987.

(43) a. Typhoons arise in this part of the Pacific.
1. Typhoons in general have a common origin in this part of the Pacific.
2. There arise typhoons in this part of the Pacific.
b. A computer computes the daily weather forecast.
1. Computers in general have the task of computing the daily weather forecast.
2. The daily weather forecast is computed by a computer.
c. A cat runs across my lawn every day.
1. Cats in general run across my lawn every day.
2. Every day, a cat runs across my lawn.

In these examples, the 2-readings are the natural interpretations, whereas the 1-readings are less favored and seem pragmatically odd. The examples in (44) below also contrast in terms of which reading is the most salient, exhibiting an ambiguity with the modal *must* that is strongly reminiscent of the ambiguities above:[20]

(44) a. Dogs must be carried. (Sign in front of an escalator)
1. A dog must be carried in order to use the escalator.
2. Any dogs on the escalator are to be carried.
b. Shirts must be worn. (Sign at a restaurant entrance)
1. If you want to enter this restaurant, you must wear a shirt.
2. The only thing you can do with a shirt is to wear it.

The monadic analysis of the **Gn**-operator yields only the nonpreferred, 1-readings of the examples in (43).[21] (43a) would be analyzed as **Gn(arise.in.that.part.of.the.Pacific)(Typhoons)**, for example, which means, according to our tentative **Gn**-rule, that there are times t and stages y^s such that [**R**(y^s, **Typhoons**) & **arise.in.that.part.of.the.Pacific**(y^s)]. This is paraphrased as 'It is in some way typical for typhoons that they arise in that part of the Pacific', which is the 1-reading rather than the desired 2-reading.

The fact that some sentences have these multiple readings suggests that the monadic operator analysis of characterizing sentences is on the wrong track. Carlson (1989) proposes to replace it with what he calls a "relational" analysis, which is based on the assumption that characterizing sentences use a specific relation to relate two semantic constituents to each other, and that the different readings can be obtained by varying which of these constituents is related to the other in that way. For example, the two readings of sentence (43a) can be interpreted in the following informal manner:

20. These examples are from Halliday 1970.
21. And, with work, it could probably generate the preferred meanings of (44).

(45) 1. For typhoons it holds: They arise in this part of the Pacific.
2. For this part of the Pacific it holds: There arise typhoons.

Here the two constituents are separated by a colon. Such cases, in which there are two distinct generic readings of one sentence, can now be said to be due to different partitions of the sentence into these two constituents. These observations lead us to conclude that the generic operator should be not monadic but rather dyadic, relating these two constituents.

Similar dyadic operators have been proposed earlier for characterizing sentences which contain a conditional or a *when*-clause, as in *John smokes when he comes home.* (See Lewis 1975, Kamp 1981, Kratzer 1981, Heim 1982, Farkas & Sugioka 1983, Rooth 1985, ter Meulen 1986a, Schubert & Pelletier 1987, 1989, and Declerck 1988). Heim (1982) was the first to propose a theory of characterizing sentences with indefinite generic NPs using a dyadic operator.

A dyadic operator may be seen as a quantificational adverb—an adverbial operator that relates one set of conditions (containing one or more variables) to another set (which may share some variables with the first set). Consider the following example, due to Lewis (1975):

(46) When m and n are positive integers, the power m^n can be computed by successive multiplication.
$\forall$(m,n are positive integers; m^n can be computed by successive multiplication)

Here, '$\forall$' is a quantifier expressed in English by *always* which relates two open propositions. They will be called the *restrictor* and the *matrix,* respectively. In Lewis's theory, '$\forall$' is a so-called unselective quantifier, as it binds any free variables in its scope (here, *m* and *n*). This same tripartite analysis is a general form applying to a variety of constructions (Partee 1991).

This representation has the advantage of capturing our observations that the genericity of characterizing sentences takes sentential scope, and that it should be treated as similar to adverbs such as *always, often, seldom,* and the like. Adverbs such as *usually, typically,* and *in general* are closest in meaning to the generic operator, which often is not realized phonologically.[22]

But if we want to represent characterizing sentences in general, we cannot simply assume that the adverbial quantifier binds every free variable. For example, the 2-reading of (43a) makes no claim about typhoons in general, so the variable for *typhoons* should be bound existentially within the matrix (rather than universally with a wide-scope quantifier). We therefore assume

22. See Farkas & Sugioka 1983 and Schubert & Pelletier 1989.

that the quantifier indicates which variables it binds and which variables are to be found existentially within the matrix. (See Heim 1982 for the formulation of a syntactic construction algorithm which accomplishes this, and Schubert & Pelletier 1989 sect. 7 for a series of examples to illustrate the different possibilities of binding.) So, if **Q** is a dyadic adverbial quantifier, the general form of adverbial quantification will be given as follows:

(47) **Q**[x_1,..,x_i;y_1,...,y_j] (**Restrictor** [x_1,...,x_i]; **Matrix** [{x_1},...,{x_i}, y_1,...,y_j])

Here, x_1,...,x_i are the variables to be bound by **Q,** and y_1,...,y_j are the variables to be bound existentially with scope just in the matrix. The notation $\Phi[\ldots x_m \ldots]$ is a formula where x_m occurs free, and $\Phi[\ldots\{x_m\}\ldots]$ is a formula where x_m possibly occurs free. So (47) is equivalent to (47′):

(47′) **Q**[x_1,...,x_i;] (**Restrictor** [x_1,...,x_i]; $\exists y_1$,...,y_j **Matrix** [{x_1},...,{x_i}, y_1,...,y_j])

Although the preceding material is just notation, as yet without any semantic interpretation and without any direct tie to the syntax, it nonetheless gives us a convenient way of representing the various readings of our characterizing sentences. Let **GEN** be the generic quantifier underlying characterizing sentences that lack an overt quantificational adverb. Then example (43a) is represented as follows:

(43) a.′ Typhoons arise in this part of the Pacific.
1. **GEN**[x;y](x **are typhoons;** y **is this part of the Pacific** & x **arise in** y)
2. **GEN**[x;y](x **is this part of the Pacific;** y **are typhoons** & y **arise** in x)
= **GEN**[x;](x **is this part of the Pacific;** ∃y[y **are typhoons** & y **arise in** x])

In this formalization, the different readings of sentences such as those in (43) can be captured by assuming a single dyadic generic operator. This partition of the semantic material into two parts is related to linguistic phenomena. For example, the "universal" vs. "existential" interpretation of bare plurals in German (Diesing 1988, 1992) and in Dutch (de Mey 1982, where the following examples are taken from) depends on their syntactic position.

(48) a. In Duitsland worden hoge posten nod steeds door Nazi's bekleed.
'In Germany, high posts are still being filled by Nazis.'
Gen[x;y,s](x **are high posts** & x **in Germany;** x **are filled by** y **in** s & y **are Nazis**)

b. In Duitsland worden er nog steeds hoge posten door Nazi's bekleed.
'In Germany, there are still high posts filled by Nazis.'
Gen[s;x,y](s **in Germany;** x **are high posts** & x **are filled by** y **in** s & y **are Nazis**)

In (48a) the bare plural *hoge posten* has scope over the adverbial *nog steeds* 'still'; in (48b) we have an *er*-construction (similar to a *there*-construction in English), and *nog steeds* has scope over *hoge posten.* We conclude therefore that the first sentence is a generalization over high posts in Germany, whereas the second is a generalization over situations in Germany (see section 1.2.4 for generalizations over situations). Diesing (1988, 1992) discusses additional syntactic reflexes of the semantic partition, for example the position of modal particles in German and topic marking in Japanese.

The partition of the semantic material into two parts is also related to stress placement, sentence intonation, and word order. These phenomena are discussed by Krifka (this volume) and Rooth (this volume). For example, the two readings of (43a) differ in the placement of the main sentence pitch agent. If we mark the main sentence accent by capitalization and the pertinent pauses by a vertical line, we find the following accentuations go with the 1- and 2-interpretations:

(49) a. 1. Typhoons | arise in THIS part of the Pacific.
2. TYPHOONS arise in this part of the Pacific.

If we assume (following much recent work) that sentence accent marks the focused part of an utterance,[23] it then becomes clear that the focused part of an utterance with an operator such as **GEN** is always in the matrix and not in the restrictor.

An analysis of such sentences as (43a) raises another issue that intersects with the study of genericity—the role of plurality, especially in bare plural NPs. Chomsky (1975), for example, has raised basic issues concerning generics based on plurality (see below), and de Mey (1982) has developed a concept of "dependent plurals" that interacts with the treatment of generics. A sentence like (43a) requires an interpretation for plural noun phrases and for predicating things of plural noun phrases. Let us assume, for the sake of convenience here, that plural nouns, in general, represent *sum individuals*—that is, individuals which consist of other individuals. Link (1983) and others have developed formal models which structure individual domains so that a

23. The exact placement of the accent is a matter of syntactic and morphological rules which is of no concern for us now.

sum operation on individuals '$\oplus$', and a concomitant 'part-of' relation '$\leq$', can be defined ($x \leq y$ iff $x \oplus y = x$). For example, if x is a typhoon and y is a typhoon, then x and y together. i.e., the sum individual (written $x \oplus y$) will be in the extension of the property 'typhoons' (along with other typhoons), with each typhoon as a part. This structure has an influence on predication as well, since we will have to distinguish between different modes of predication—such as distributive and cumulative predication—once we allow sum individuals into the domain. This shows up clearly in sentences such as the following:

(50) a. The losers got a lemon.
b. The losers got lemons.

Assume that *the losers* applies to a sum individual $j \oplus m$ which consists of two elementary, or atomic, individuals, j and m. Let us use the relation '$\leq_a$' for 'be an atomic part of'; for example, j is an atomic part of $j \oplus m$, so it is true that $j \leq_a j \oplus m$. We can now express the two interpretations of (50a): The cumulative interpretation, as shown below in (50a′.1), says that there is a lemon such that $j \oplus m$ got it. In the distributive interpretation, the predicate *got a lemon* must be distributed over the atomic individuals. Following Link (1983), we define a distributivity operator **DST** which does this:

$$\mathbf{DST}(\delta)(\alpha) \leftrightarrow \forall z[z \leq_a \alpha \rightarrow \delta(z)]$$

The distributive reading is shown in (50a′.2):

(50) a.′ 1. $\exists x[x\ \mathbf{is\ a\ lemon}\ \&\ j \oplus m\ \mathbf{got}\ x]$
2. $\mathbf{DST}(\delta y \exists x[x\ \mathbf{is\ a\ lemon}\ \&\ y\ \mathbf{got}\ x])(j \oplus m)$
$= \exists x[x\ \mathbf{is\ a\ lemon}\ \&\ j\ \mathbf{got}\ x]\ \&\ \exists x[x\ \mathbf{is\ a\ lemon}\ \&\ m\ \mathbf{got}\ x]$

Example (50b) also has both a cumulative and distributive interpretation, but we are only interested here in the cumulative interpretation, in which the two losers j and m each got one lemon. We can describe this interpretation as in (50b′):

(50) b.′ $\exists x[x\ \mathbf{are\ lemons}\ \&\ j \oplus m\ \mathbf{got}\ x]$

We can describe (50b) in this manner by the rule of summativity (see Krifka 1989, 1992b), which states that, in the example at hand, if 'u got y' and 'v got z' are true, then '$u \oplus v$ got $y \oplus z$' is also true. We furthermore need to assume that the semantics for count nouns allows us to conclude from 'y is a lemon' and 'z is a lemon' that '$y \oplus z$ are lemons'. It then follows from 'j got y', 'y is a lemon', 'm got z', and 'z is a lemon' that $\exists$x[x are lemons & j$\oplus$m got x].

To return to the interaction of generics and the treatment of plurals, consider the examples in (51). Chomsky (1975) proposed to explain the plural *horns* in (51a) as a syntactic phenomenon:

(51) a. Unicorns have horns.
GEN[x;y](x **are unicorns;** y **are horns** & x **has** y)
b. Unicorns have a horn.
GEN[x;](x **are unicorns; DST**($\lambda x \exists y$[y **is a horn** & x **has** y])(x))
= **GEN**[x;](x **are unicorns;** $\forall z[z \leq_a x \rightarrow \exists y$[y **is a horn** & z **has** y]])

An alternative, and quite possibly better, explanation for the data would be semantic in nature. The most natural interpretation of (51a) is a cumulative interpretation of the matrix: If x *are* unicorns, then for every atomic part z of x (i.e., for every unicorn), there is a horn y which z has, and therefore there are horns w such that the unicorns x have w. (Note that the sentence would also be true if the atomic entities had more than one of the objects in question, as in the natural interpretation of *Cows have horns*.)[24] To get the most natural interpretation of (51b), namely, that each unicorn has one horn, we must assume that the matrix contains the distributivity operator, and that the existential quantifier is in the scope of that operator. The issue that is being alluded to here is one of *dependency*—a unicorn has a horn, and therefore unicorns have horns; but no individual unicorn has the kind, Horn. The intricacies involved with the important notion of dependency are investigated by Link (this volume).

This focus on singular and plural indefinites emphasizes their propensity for being bound by other operators, resulting in a nonspecific reading. However, we wish to remind the reader that indefinite NPs can also be interpreted as referring to specific entities. This behavior of indefinites is explained in the theories of Kamp (1981) and Heim (1982) on the assumption that indefinite NPs (including many instances of bare plurals) are, in general, predicates which introduce variables that are bound by other operators. They can be bound either by some local operator (as in the cases discussed so far), or by the quantifier *every* (as in (52a) below), or, especially, by existential closure (where an existential operator ranges over the whole text). If they are bound by existential closure, they refer to a specific entity, as in example (52b),

24. The same property is expressed by the predicate whether one or more horns are intended. *Cows have horns and unicorns do too* is true, and so is *Both cows and unicorns have horns*.

where ∃ is a text-level unselective existential operator that binds the free variable x.

(52) a. Every man who has a cat likes to pet it.
∀[x,y;](x **is a man** & y **is a cat** & x **has** y; x **likes to pet** y)
b. A cat came in. It meowed.
∃ [x **is a cat** & x **came in** & x **meowed**]

The availability of these two ways of interpreting indefinite NPs—allowing indefinite NPs to be interpreted either in the context of a local operator (e.g., a quantificational adverb or a generic operator) or outside of it (by existential closure)—can perhaps be used to explain why a sentence like *A dog is barking* has only a specific interpretation of *a dog*. This suggests that we might reinterpret the specific reading of indefinite NPs as follows: An NP is interpreted specifically if its variable is bound by existential closure; it is nonspecific if its variable is bound by a local operator. The other gap mentioned earlier, where *A dog barks* has only the nonspecific interpretation of *a dog,* remains something of a mystery, though. Although we know that *A dog barks* is a characterizing sentence, and therefore by our theory must have a local quantifier that binds the variable of the NP *a dog,* making it nonspecific, still, at this stage we cannot explain why this variable *must* be bound by that operator and cannot simply be left for later binding by existential closure. We will discuss this problem further in section 1.4.6.

1.2.4. Generalizations over Situations and over Objects

In sentences like *A dog barks* or *Lions have manes,* the generic quantifier **GEN,** under the dyadic analysis described here, quantifies over individuals (dogs, lions, etc.). But there are characterizing sentences in which the generic quantifier quantifies not over individuals, but over what might be called situations or occasions or cases, a notion introduced by Lawler (1972) and further refined by Schubert and Pelletier (1989).[25] Consider, for example, (53a):

(53) a. Mary smokes when she comes home.
b. **GEN**[s,x;](x = **Mary** & x **comes home** in s; x **smokes** in s)

This says that, in general, if there is a situation of Mary coming home, she will smoke in that situation. Letting s be a variable for situations, we represent this interpretation as in (53b). (One might note that reference to situations here

25. Other authors who make similar assumptions for the treatment of genericity and quantificational adverbs are Lawler (1973a), Spears (1974), Newton (1979), Stump (1981, 1985), Conrad (1982), Partee (1984), Kleiber (1985), Krifka (1987), and Schubert and Pelletier (1987).

plays a role similar to reference to stages in Carlson's original theory.) Where does the situation argument s come from? Kratzer (chapter 2, this volume) argues that episodic verbs have, in addition to their usual syntactic arguments, an argument for the location where the event described by the verb occurs. This argument can be bound by quantificational adverbs.

Although it is natural to assume generalizations over situations in conditional characterizing sentences such as (53), simple sentences such as (54) are more difficult, since it is unclear what should count as the restrictor in these cases:

(54) Mary smokes.

One way to handle these examples is to assume that even in these cases there *is* a restrictor, but that this restrictor must be derived pragmatically. Spears (1974), Newton (1979), Conrad (1982), Kleiber (1985), Krifka (1987), and Schubert and Pelletier (1989) have all made suggestions along these lines. In the example at hand, the restrictor could be situations which contain Mary and which are somehow "normal" situations with respect to smoking. With this idea in mind, we would get the following semantic interpretation:

(54′) **GEN**[s,x;](x = **Mary** & s **is a normal situation with respect to smoking** & s **contains** x; x **smokes** in s)

However, this interpretation forces us to make reference to "normalcy conditions," in addition to relying on unspecified pragmatic factors, both in the interpretation of the operator **GEN** and in the interpretation of the antecedent. That is, our analysis says: 'In a normal smoking situation, Mary normally smokes'. We thereby have two separate places that appeal to "normalcy." As an alternative, we could consider interpreting **GEN** in such a way that, in and of itself, it takes into account only those situations that are relevant for the generalization at hand, which in our case are only those situations that are normal for Mary's smoking. This interpretation is further investigated in section 1.2.5.

We now turn to an issue raised at the end of section 1.1, namely the source of the peculiarity for an example like (55a), as opposed to (55b–e):

(55) a. ??Minette is infertile when she is tricolored.
b. A cat is infertile when it is tricolored.
c. The cat is infertile when it is tricolored.
d. Minette is hungry when she meows.
e. A cat is hungry when it meows.

That is, why do characterizing sentences with a specific subject, as in (55a), need a habitual predicate—in contrast with other characterizing sentences, which have a nonspecific subject? Intuitively, the source of the difficulty comes from the implication on the part of (55a) that a given cat, Minette, must undergo a fundamental change in her fur color from time to time, being tri-colored sometimes, but not at others. Let us try to be a bit more precise.

The first question is: What is a habitual sentence? In section 1.1.4 above, we defined habitual sentences as characterizing sentences whose predicates are derived from an episodic verbal predicate. This can now be refined by saying that habitual sentences express generalizations over situations that are specified by the corresponding episodic verbal predicate. That is, habitual sentences can be defined as follows:

(56) A sentence is *habitual* if and only if its semantic representation is of the form
GEN[...s...;...](**Restrictor**[...s...]; **Matrix**[...s...])
where s is a situation variable.

Let us take a closer look at the notion of generalization over entities of a certain type, e.g., over objects or over situations. Roughly, a generalization expresses that if an entity satisfies certain conditions (or has certain properties) A, then it also satisfies certain conditions (or has certain other properties) B to a certain degree; the degree is specified by the quantifier. For example, (53) expresses the fact that if s is a situation of Mary coming home, then usually, s is also a situation of Mary smoking. In our formal representation it is therefore essential that a variable of the type generalized over occurs free in the restrictor and in the matrix, and is bound by the quantificational operator. Furthermore, the variable must not be *explicitly* tied to *exactly* one entity by the restrictor, as such a case would not result in a "generalization."[26] Our formal account is shown in (57):

(57) An expression **Q**[...x...;...](**Restrictor**[...x...]; **Matrix**[...{x}...]) is a *generalization over x* iff it allows for models in which there is more than one value for x for which ∃[**Restrictor**[...x...]] is true (where ∃ binds all free variables except x).

Characterizing sentences must have at least one variable to generalize over. That is, there must be at least one variable which is not explicitly tied to some particular object. If this were not the case, they would merely state that a certain particular object (as described by the restrictor) has a certain property

26. The notion of *explicitness* in this condition is important. As Quine (1960) remarked long ago, *is a natural satellite of the Earth* is a general term despite its being true of exactly one entity. Here we only wish to rule out *explicit* claims of being true of exactly one entity (claims like *x is identical to Mary*), not claims that are "accidentally" true of exactly one entity (like *x is a natural satellite of the Earth*).

(as described by the matrix), and they could no longer express a "generic" fact. Note that (57) does allow for the possibility that x has only one value with respect to certain models; this is because an indefinite NP might happen to be applicable to only one entity in a certain model (see footnote 26).

With these preliminaries out of the way, we are finally able to discuss the cause of the gap noted in (55a). Consider the semantic representations of the non-kind-referring sentences in (58):

(58) a. ??Minette is infertile when she is tricolored.
   i) (??)**GEN** [x;] (x = **Minette** & x **is tricolored;** x **is infertile**)
   ii) **GEN** [x, s;] (x = **Minette** & x **is tricolored** in s; x **is infertile** in s)
b. A cat is infertile when it is tricolored.
   GEN[x;](x **is a cat** & x **is tricolored;** x **is infertile**)
c. A cat is hungry when it meows.
   GEN[x,s;](x **is a cat** & x **meows** in s; x **is hungry** in s)
d. Minette is hungry when she meows.
   GEN[x,s;](x = **Minette** & x **meows** in s; x **is hungry** in s)

The representations of (58b–d) are generalizations in our sense, because there are variables bound by the **GEN**-operator that are not explicitly tied to one particular object in the restrictor. In (58b), x can have any cat as a value. In (58d), x is bound to one entity, namely Minette, but s still can vary over all situations in which Minette is meowing. In (58c), we have generalizations over x as well as over s. Conversely, in (58a.i), the most plausible representation of (58a), the only variable is tied to a specific individual, Minette. The representation is therefore not a generalization in our sense, and (58a) is therefore not a proper characterizing sentence. A similar point is made by Kratzer (chapter 2, this volume), who argues that a stative predicate does not supply a situation variable. De Swart (1991) showed that even if we have a situation variable, we get an unacceptable sentence if the variable is tied to a particular event and there is no other variable to quantify over, as in *(??)Usually, when Minette dies, Mary is unhappy*. There is, however, a possible interpretation of (58a), namely one in which the basic predicates *be tricolored* and *be infertile* are given an episodic reading, that is, are represented with a situation variable as in (58a.ii). Although these predicates are not normally interpreted as episodic—as having an open situation variable—they can be coerced into that interpretation in certain syntactic contexts.[27] Here that means that Minette

27. Schubert and Pelletier (1989) note that such coercion often happens in *when*-clauses. For example, *People are overweight* has a non-episodic meaning, although in the context of a *when* clause it becomes episodic—*When people are overweight, they often exercise*.

changes back and forth between being tricolored and not, and between being fertile and not. This coercion is of the same type as, for example, the coercion of a count noun into a mass noun in, say, *ten kilograms of book* or *too much car,* as discussed in Pelletier & Schubert 1989. Coercions such as these typically lead to an expression which is grammatically unusual but can be saved by some special interpretation.[28]

If we analyze *when*-clauses as restrictors of quantificational structures which may bind any open variable, we get a simple explanation for the intuitive distinction between the so-called temporal and atemporal *when*-clauses. The *when*-clauses in examples (58c,d) are temporal because they quantify over a situation variable; the *when*-clause in (58b) is atemporal because it does not quantify over a situation variable. In the meaningful reading of (58a), viz., (58a.ii), the *when*-clause is temporal because of the situation variable—but it is difficult to make predicates such as *be tricolored* be understood temporally, as this reading requires.

A kind of *when*-clause construction that we have not yet considered is illustrated by (59):

(59) When the party was over, John did the dishes.

What is the relationship between the *when*-clauses we have considered so far (restrictive *when*-clauses and the *when*-clause shown in (59)? To give the correct account of (59), we will assume that such sentences do not contain an adverbial quantifier which could bind the free variables in the *when*-clause. Instead, the *when*-clause specifies a situation in which the main clause holds, and the free variables left in the sentence must then be interpreted by existential closure (i.e., by the "unselective" existential closure quantifier, ∃):

(59′) ∃s(**the party is over in** s & **John does the dishes in** s)

An interesting question is to which extent the restrictor must be specified overtly. In some cases, this may be left pretty much to the context, as in *Mary smokes* (see Roberts 1989). Another example of context dependence is (60):

(60) [Don't worry if I'm not here at 8. You know—] planes arrive late.
GEN[s;x](s **is a situation;** x **are planes in** s & x **arrive late in** s)

28. Moens and Steedman (1988) define and discuss coercion of a sentence or verb phrase from one aspectual class to another. Such coercions are common and generally perfectly acceptable, but those which are unusual can often be saved by some special interpretation, as stated in the text. Pelletier (1991) argues that the mass/count examples are so common and acceptable that they should not be called coercions at all.

The most probable reading of *Planes arrive late* is not that it is typically true for planes that they arrive late. Instead, it says that for a specific type of situation, there are planes which arrive late. Note that the type of situation (e.g., situations at an airport) is not specified overtly here. Our preference is that this is how the semantics given for the **GEN**-operator should handle cases like this one—with underspecified restrictors.

Are there any further semantic conditions for the restrictor? Declerck (1988) discusses contrasts such as (61a,b) to show that the restrictive clause must be "unbounded," which is to say (in this case) that the restrictive indefinite NP must not be numerically specified:

(61) a. Cats are beautiful when they have white fur.
b. ?Twelve cats are beautiful when they have white fur.

Our theory gives the following interpretations for (61) (note that the subject NP forms part of the restrictor; that is, the *they* of the *when*-clause has been interpreted as referring to the subject NP):[29]

(61) a.′ **GEN**[x;](x **is a cat** & x **has white fur;** x **is beautiful**)
b.′ **GEN**[x;](x **are twelve cats** & x **have white fur;** x **are beautiful**)

In (61b′), we assume that x ranges over sum individuals which consist of parts (in this case, of twelve individual cats). Contrary to Declerck's analysis, we find this interpretation to be semantically correct, and only pragmatically deviant. The problem, we claim, is that the predicates *have white fur* and *are beautiful* must be interpreted as distributive. A condition such as *x have white fur* is true just in case every atomic part y of x is such that *y has white fur* is true (as our analysis of distributivity and plurality puts it, following Link 1983). But then it would be mysterious why the speaker has chosen the predicate *twelve cats* in the restrictor when he could have made the point with *ninety-nine cats* as easily, or simply with *a cat.* Note that examples with number-specified NPs in the restrictor become acceptable with nondistributive predicates. In these cases, the number specification is essential:

(62) a. Two canaries can be kept in the same cage if it is large enough.
b. Two magnets either attract or repel each other.
c. Two's company; three's a crowd.

Declerck (1988) developed the notion of "unboundedness" as a general property of restrictive *when*-clauses and generic sentences. This concept was in-

29. See Schubert & Pelletier 1989 for a discussion of the difficulties encountered in carrying out this sort of interpretation in a uniform and compositional manner.

tended to refer not only to numerical restrictions, but also to the temporal anchoring of sentences. We cannot follow him closely in this latter point either, since generic sentences may in fact be temporally located by adverbs, as in the sentence *In 1989, Mary played tennis.* Declerck (1986, 1988) also used "unboundedness" to explain the fact that restrictive *when*-clauses do not refer to a specific situation or group of objects; and he argued that this, rather than the presence of a generic operator, is the essence of restrictive *when*-clauses. We agree with his observation concerning the "unspecified" nature of *when*-clauses, but we claim that it is the presence of a generic operator (or of explicit quantificational adverbs) which *causes* the *when*-clause to be "unspecific."

In concluding this subsection, we want to point out that we did not postulate stages in developing the semantics of habituals (see section 1.2.1 and cf. Carlson 1977b, 1982). In a sense, reference to situations here plays a role very similar to reference to stages in Carlson's original theory. While there are theories that employ both concepts, e.g., Hinrichs 1985, most theories make use of just one such construct.

1.2.5. Habitual and Lexical Stative Predicates; The Treatment of Object NPs.

The theory of characterizing sentences developed above sheds some light on why habitual predicates are stative, and also on the relationship between episodic and stative predicates in general. Episodic sentences are those whose main predicate has a situation argument bound by existential closure; they report on a specific event or occasion. Sentences that lack such a situation argument are generally stative, the other aspectual classes being confined to the category of episodics. There are two cases of stativity: either the verbal predicate is inherently independent of situations, as is the case with lexical statives such as *be infertile* and *know French,* or else the situation variable is bound by some operator other than existential closure, such as *usually.* In either case, the statements do not report on specific situations; and it seems natural to see this independence from specific situations as the core of stativity (though the existence of episodic statives such as progressives and such predicates as *be available* may demand a reformulation of the roots of stativity). It then follows that habitual sentences, which generalize over situations, are stative.[30]

30. See Newton 1979 for a similar explanation as to why the predicates in habitual sentences have imperfective aspect in Modern Greek.

Rather than taking lexical items as unitary, atomic items, one might take a "lexical decomposition" attitude and analyze certain lexical statives as involving generalizations over situations. For example, consider the minimal pair *speak French* and *know French.* The first item, *speak French,* has an episodic reading which refers to situations and a characterizing reading which expresses a generalization over situations (*John is speaking French* and *John speaks French,* respectively). The former type of situations—where John is speaking French—can be considered evidence for the truth of the characterizing reading. Although the second item, *know French,* lacks the episodic meaning, there nonetheless are situations which count as evidence for knowing French and (in some abstract sense) *could* have been described by *knowing French,* were English just slightly different. (We are thinking of such activities as speaking French, or listening to French and reacting in an appropriate way.) But it so happens that there is no corresponding episodic predicate in the lexicon that characterizes all the situations which count as direct evidence of the "knowing French" behavior.[31] So, one difference between verbs which are lexically stative and verbs which have a stative (habitual)/non-stative (episodic) alternation is merely that the former have no episodic counterpart in the language. Ryle (1949, chap. 5) observed such lexical gaps with certain dispositional predicates, and explained them by saying that because there are so many different ways to show a given behavior (so many different ways to show "knowing French behavior," for instance), there can be no single episodic verb to denote them all. The situation can be pictured like this:

(63)

	Habituals	Lexical Statives
Characterizing Predicates	*speak French*	*know French*
Episodic Predicates	*be speaking French*	—

The similarity between the habitual *speak French* and the lexical stative *know French* will perhaps become clearer in the following analyses. The difference is that the semantic relation **speak French in** (a situation) is denoted by a predicate in the language, namely the episodic *speak French,* whereas there is no lexical item denoting the semantic relation **show knowledge of French**

31. Of course, we can coerce *knows French* into a habitual—perhaps that state of mind brought about by those special French-language-learning pills John eats after dinner sometimes. But this is to assimilate the case to that of *speaks French.*

in (a situation)—despite the fact that the states of affairs which are relevant to the two can quite easily be semantically described:

(64) a. speak French: λx**GEN**[x,s;](x **in** s; x **speaks French in** s)
b. know French: λx**GEN**[x,s;](x **in** s; x **shows knowledge of French in** s)

We will refer to stative predicates which express a generalization over situations as *dispositional;* this term applies to both habituals and lexical statives. However, habituals and dispositional lexical statives do differ in one respect: whereas the language provides a morphologically related form to denote the type of situation involved in a habitual, such a form is lacking with respect to dispositional lexical statives.

Another case of a dispositional lexical stative predicate is *like John.* If this is attributed to a person, we'd expect that this person typically shows ''liking John behavior,'' for which English, again, lacks an episodic predicate. Dispositional lexical statives need not be based on verbs; examples based on copular sentences are *be intelligent* and *be a friend of John.* The dispositional nonverbal predicates most naturally occur with the 'active *be*' of English (Partee 1977), to form sentences like *John is being intelligent* or *Mary is being a hero.*

Not all lexical stative predicates are dispositional, however. Take as an example *be married.* In order to count as being married, one need not show any particular regular behavior. It suffices that one event, a wedding, has occurred, and that other specified events, such as a divorce or a death, have not yet occurred. This is an essential difference between nondispositionals such as *be married* and dispositionals such as *be in love.* Other nondispositional statives are *own* (related to an event of buying), *be thirty years old* (related to an event of birth), and *be a student* (related to an event of registration). Some statives are not related to an event at all, such as *be male.* (Even if the correct applicability of such a predicate depends upon certain situations (in this case, the conception event), it is implausible to assume that the details of this play any role in the semantics of natural language!)

The general property of all or at least most stative predicates, be they dispositional or not, is that they lack reference to a specific situation. A stative predicate either expresses a generalization over situations (as with habituals and dispositional lexical statives) or is tied only indirectly to situations (as with nondispositional statives, and perhaps with episodic statives as well). We should remark here that the stative/episodic distinction may not be very strict for a given lexical item; recall the coercion phenomena discussed in connection with example (58b). Also, Campbell (1989) pointed out that there are verbs that show a systematic variation between an episodic and a stative interpretation, such as *upset, amuse, satisfy, show*. With an agentive subject, he claimed, they are basically episodic, as in *John is upsetting me,* and can be habitual, as in *John upsets me;* but with a causative subject, they are, he claimed, lexically stative and not easily interpreted as episodic, as in *John's behavior upsets me*. (See Chierchia, this volume, for further remarks on this general topic.)

Let us now consider the origin of the **GEN**-operator in dispositional predicates. There are two possibilities: either the **GEN**-operator is introduced at some point in the syntactic derivation or we have a **GEN**-operator provided in the lexicon. It seems to us that we should assume the first option for habitual predicates and the second option for lexical dispositional predicates. Consider examples such as the following:

(65) a. John speaks French after dinner.
b. ??John knows French after dinner.

In (65a), the prepositional phrase *after dinner* clearly can restrict the **GEN**-quantifier; hence its structure must be transparent for the syntax, which would be a natural consequence if we assume that *after dinner* is introduced in the syntactic derivation. In (65b), however, *after dinner* cannot restrict the proposed generic quantifier, yielding something like (65b′):

(65) b.′ ??**GEN**[s;](s **is after-dinner** and **john in** s; **john shows knowing-French behavior in** s)

Hence, if we assume a quantificational analysis of *knowing French* at all, we must guarantee that it is syntactically opaque.

Let us have a look at the number feature of NPs in habitual sentences, a topic that follows up on the discussion of number marking in nonhabitual characterizing sentences in section 1.2.3. Consider the following examples:

(66) a. Mary smokes cigarettes / *a cigarette.
b. John sells vacuum cleaners / *a vacuum cleaner.

The situations which justify these habitual sentences are situations in which Mary smokes a cigarette or John sells a vacuum cleaner. Under the syntactic derivation analysis, the **GEN**-operator would be applied to the representation of an episodic predicate such as *smoke a cigarette*. But this will result in *Mary smokes a cigarette,* and we would be at a loss to explain why the object NPs in (66) are plural. So why do we have plural NPs?

One explanation of this phenomenon was put forward by Declerck (1988,

1991) and Laca (1990), namely that the absence of a number restriction is a precondition for the generic, "unbounded" interpretation in the first place. We have seen that this explanation does not work with subject NPs (see the discussion of example (62)); it does not work with object NPs either, as shown by the following examples, which clearly are characterizing sentences:

(67) a. Mary smokes (a cigarette)/(cigarettes) after dinner.
b. Mary smokes a pipe.

The two versions of (67a) have different truth conditions, claiming (respectively) that in after-dinner situations, Mary typically smokes one cigarette, or an unspecified number of cigarettes. One way to capture the difference between (66) and (67a) would be to assume that we have a quantification over simple situations with explicit restrictions in (67a), but over "sum situations" with implicit restrictions in (66). That is, we would propose the following:

(68) a. **GEN**[s;](Mary **in** s; ∃x(**cigarettes**(x) & Mary **smokes** x **in** s))
b. **GEN**[s;](Mary **in** s & **after-dinner**(s); ∃x**cigarette**(x) & Mary **smokes** x **in** s))

In (68a) the situation s is unrestricted as to its "size"—in particular, it may be a sum situation, $s = s_1 \oplus s_2 \oplus \ldots \oplus s_n$, where all the situations s_i contain Mary, and Mary smokes different cigarettes $x_1, x_2, \ldots, x_n$ in each situation. But then the object x that is smoked in the sum situation is a sum individual $x_1 \oplus x_2 \oplus \ldots \oplus x_n$, which is in the extension of the plural predicate **cigarettes**. In this way, the assumption that implicit restrictors leave open the "size" of the situations that are quantified over predicts that we will use plural predicates. However, this would hold only if we can also assume that each simple situation is related to a different object, as here with different cigarettes for different smoking situations. If, on the other hand, every simple situation could be related to one and the same simple object, we would expect a singular NP. This explains, for example, why we have the singular *a pipe* in (67b).

In (68b), the situation s is explicitly restricted to after-dinner situations. If we assume that this explicit restriction implies a restriction to simple situations, then we should expect the singular predicate *cigarette* when it is being expressed that Mary smokes one cigarette in after-dinner situations. And we should expect the plural predicate *cigarettes* when the number is being left unspecified.

There is another use of plural objects, as in *Mary hates cigars*. In cases like these, the object NP has to be interpreted as kind-referring. We will discuss such interpretations in section 1.3.2.

To close this subsection on the semantics of dispositional predicates, it is interesting to look at a problem concerning the semantics of the genericity operator. We have provisionally assumed that it is much like some sort of universal quantifier; this will be discussed in greater detail in section 1.2.6. However, Lawler (1973a) and Dahl (1975) have pointed out that there might be two different generic interpretations, one "universal" and the other "existential." In its universal generic reading (a habitual reading), sentence (69) means that beer is the (favorite) alcoholic beverage John drinks. In its existential reading (a dispositional reading), it says that John does not object to drinking beer.

(69) John drinks beer.

Lawler employed two different generic operators to represent these two readings. But although we believe that these two readings exist, and that the precise interpretation of the generic operator is dependent on the context of utterance, we nonetheless think that a proposal to have two different, unrealized generic operators would considerably weaken any predictions of a theory of characterizing sentences. Furthermore, Lawler's "two-hidden-operators" proposal is problematic in another direction. According to Lawler's theory, the overt presence of a quantificational adverb requires that there is no unrealized operator. Thus in the sentences in (70), there can be no hidden operators. Yet these sentences have more than one reading, even though they contain an overt quantificational adverb. Therefore, it cannot be simply two phonologically unrealized operators with different meanings which give these sentences their two different meanings.

(70) a. John always drinks beer.
 b. John usually drinks beer.
 c. John sometimes drinks beer.
 d. John seldom drinks beer.

Example (70a) has (at least) two interpretations: it can mean either (i) that whenever John drinks something, it is beer, or (ii) that he drinks beer on every occasion on which it is available. The other examples behave similarly. These two interpretations are similar to the two interpretations of the original example, (69), which did not have any overt operator; indeed, especially (70b) can be considered a near-synonym of (69) in both its interpretations. Thus, whatever is causing the ambiguity in (69) also occurs in (70)—but then it cannot be hidden operators. Furthermore, note that (69) has yet another reading over and above the "existential" and "universal" readings. It can also mean that

John has the habit of drinking beer, not excluding the possibility that he has the habit of drinking other beverages as well. After all, one can habitually drink beer *and* habitually drink wine.

In our relational analysis, which we prefer, we can stay with one meaning of the generic operator, the universal one, and account for the different readings of the examples above by postulating different partitions of the underlying semantic material. Since two of the readings are indicated by different accent placements, it is plausible to suppose that in these cases we are dealing with distinct syntactic objects. The three readings of (69) are given in (71) below.

(71) a. John drinks BEER.
GEN[x,y,s;](x = **John** & x **drinks** y **in** s; y **is beer**)
b. John DRINKS beer.
GEN[x,y,s;](x = **John** & y **is beer** & y **in** s & x **in** s; x **drinks** y **in** s)
c. John drinks BEER.
GEN[x,s;y](x = **John** & x **in** s; y **is beer** & x **drinks** y **in** s)

The "universal" interpretation in (71a) can be rendered as: In appropriate situations in which John drinks something, this is normally beer. The "existential" interpretation in (71b) says that in appropriate situations where there is some beer available, John normally drinks it. The "habitual" interpretation in (71c) says that in appropriate situations which contain John, he will drink beer. In the latter interpretation, the accent is on *beer* by the usual rules of focus projection because the entire predicate, *drink beer,* is in focus and hence is interpreted as part of the matrix. Arnauld (1662) was already aware of the fact that the restrictor can contain semantic material from different parts of the sentence. He claimed that in *All men are just through the grace of Jesus Christ,* the term *just* is understood as belonging to the subject, and hence that the sentence does not say that all men are just, but that all men who are just are so through the grace of Jesus Christ. (For further reflections on these phenomena, see Krifka, this volume, and Rooth, this volume, on the topic of focus.)

The influence of focus on the interpretation of generic sentences has been discussed by Newton (1979); Rooth (1985) developed a theory to treat the focus sensitivity of explicit adverbial quantifiers (like *always*). Schubert & Pelletier (1987) discussed the ways stress might influence the selection of what they called "cases"—essentially, the restrictor of our current framework. Laca (1990) examined cases with verb focus, such as (71b), and also cases with predicative constructions, such as *John eats salmon raw,* which naturally are interpreted with the predicate (here, *raw*) in the matrix and the object NP (here, *salmon*) in the restrictor (see also Léard 1984). The data discussed by Laca also suggest that sentences whose verbs show a particularly close verb-object relation (such as *smokes cigarettes* and *worships idols*) typically have both the verbal predicate and the object NP in the matrix.

Furthermore, Laca's (1990) discussion of Spanish data suggests that NPs in the restrictor tend to be marked with a definite article:

(72) a. Los guamba-mamba comen salmón.
'The Guamba-mamba eat salmon.'
b. Los-guamba-mamba comen el salmón crudo,
'The Guamba-mamba eat salmon raw.'

(73) a. Los arquitectos construyen casas.
'Architects build houses.'
b. Los arquitectos construyen las casas y los decoradores de interiores las arruinan.
'Architects BUILD houses, and interior decorators RUIN them.'

This analysis implies that the definite article in Spanish may be used with semantically indefinite NPs; it would indicate the position of the NP in the partition of the sentence, namely that it occurs in the restrictor. As the restrictor can be related to the thematic part of a sentence, the definite article should be analyzed as a theme marker. (See section 1.3.7 for similar cases in French, and Newton 1979 for similar observations in Modern Greek.)

1.2.6. The Semantics of the Generic Operator

In section 1.2.3 above we began with a monadic interpretation of the generic operator in characterizing sentences and supplanted it with an analysis where this operator is dyadic. Here, we will examine ways in which the semantics of such operator might be specified, casting it in terms of the dyadic analysis.

A first approximation to the semantics of the **GEN**-operator might be to analyze it as a universal quantifier. For example, consider (74):

(74) A cat has a tail.
GEN[x;y](x **is a cat;** y **is a tail** & **has** y)

This sentence is given the semantics of *Every cat has a tail:*

$\forall$x[x **is a cat** $\rightarrow$ $\exists$y[y **is a tail** & **has** y]]

However, it has often been observed that the analysis is both too strong and too weak (vide Ziff 1972, Lawler 1972, 1973a,b, Putnam 1975, Dahl 1975,

Lyons 1977, Carlson 1977b, Schubert & Pelletier 1987). We have already mentioned that an analysis of **GEN** as a universally quantified sentence might be too strong, since a characterizing sentence often allows for exceptions while a universal quantifier does not. For example, (74) can be true even if there are some cats which have lost their tail or were born without one. The type of quantification that we find in such sentences has already been identified by Arnauld (1662, part 2 chap. 13), who noted that we cannot conclude from *Cretans are liars* that every particular Cretan is a liar. Arnauld called such sentences ''morally universal'' and distinguished them from ''metaphysically universal'' sentences, which hold without exception. This suggests that we require a weaker quantifier, such as *most* for characterizing sentences. However, Carlson (1977b) has shown that this move is futile, in part because we can find generic sentences which are considered to be true but which nevertheless cannot be satisfactorily described by any ordinary quantifier. For example, the following sentences are certainly true characterizing sentences although less than half of all birds lay eggs (only the healthy and fertilized female ones), not more than five percent of the *Anopheles* mosquitos carry malaria, and the chance of a turtle having a long life is extremely small, as most turtles are eaten by predators early in life.

(75) a. A bird lays eggs.
b. An *Anopheles* mosquito carries malaria.
c. A turtle lives a long life.

On the other hand, the analysis is too weak, since true characterizing sentences cannot capture a mere accidental generalization. For example, it might be true that every child ever born in Rainbow Lake, Alberta, was right-handed. Still, the generic sentences *Children born in Rainbow Lake are right-handed* and *A child born in Rainbow Lake is right-handed* are not true—unless there is something special about Rainbow Lake that causes right-handedness (e.g., perhaps the water in Rainbow Lake is nomically connected with right-handedness). Or imagine a zoo where the two last surviving lions in the world are kept, and by some accident both of these poor creatures lose one leg. Then the sentences *Every lion has three legs* and *The lions have three legs (each)* would be true, but the characterizing sentence. *A lion has three legs* would nonetheless still be false. Characterizing sentences express ''principled'' generalizations over the entities of a class, and do not capture mere ''accidental'' facts about them. (See also section 1.1, examples (29) and (30), about madrigals and football heros.)

Another difference from nominal quantifiers such as *every* or *each* is that the generic operator, in common with other adverbial quantifiers, cannot be contextually restricted (Dahl 1975, Croft 1986). For example, a sentence such as (76a) below need not mean that every professor in the world wears a tie, but may mean that each of the professors in a contextually restricted set, say, the set of all professors at UCLA, wears a tie. This contextual restriction can be either explicit (by stating the restriction, as in (76b)) or implicit. However, with adverbial quantifiers as in (77), implicit contextual restriction is not possible. For example, although in the right circumstances (76a) might be used with an implicit restriction so as to mean what (76b) does, one cannot use (77a) to mean (77b). A generic sentence states a lawlike regularity, and such regularity does not admit of contextual restrictions.

(76) a. Every/Each professor wears a tie.
b. At UCLA, every/each professor wears a tie.

(77) a. A professor (always/usually/often/seldom) wears a tie.
b. At UCLA, a professor (always/usually/often/seldom/∅) wears a tie.

Several methods have been proposed to capture the semantics of the generic operator in characterizing sentences. In the rest of this section, we will sketch and discuss six of these—without coming to any hard and fast, final conclusion. First, the **GEN**-operator might be spelled out as a 'relevant quantification'. Second, the notion of prototypical entities might be employed. Third, **GEN** can be seen as a statement of a stereotype. Fourth, **GEN** might be analyzed as a modal operator, to be interpreted in a possible-worlds semantics. Fifth, **GEN** might be analyzed as combining with a sentence to express a constraint in the theory of Situation Semantics. And sixth, **GEN** might be analyzed in such a way as to indicate a nonmonotonic inference rule. We will look at these approaches in turn.

1. Relevant quantification. In a pragmatic account of genericity, the generic operator might be spelled out as a quantification over *relevant entities,* as suggested by Declerck (1991). Declerck adopted a principle which says that when a statement is made of a "set," the hearer will use his or her world knowledge to restrict the statement to just those members of the "set" to which it can be applied in a suitable way. For example, consider (78):

(78) Whales give birth to live young.

$\forall x[\mathbf{whale}(x)\ \&\ \mathbf{R}(x) \rightarrow x\ \mathbf{gives\ birth\ to\ live\ young}]$

This statement will be a predication over female, nonsterile whales, as only they could possibly give birth to live young in the first place. In the formulation above, this would be expressed by specifying the restriction variable **R** in a suitable way. One obvious problem with this approach is that the principle, as it stands, can easily justify all kinds of generic sentences—it is easy to find restrictions which would make *any* quantification come out true. For example, the analysis could make (79) be a true generic, since we could take **R** to be the predicate **sick** and hence to restrict the quantification to sick whales.

(79) Whales are sick.

So this approach calls for a theory of suitable restrictions, and it is unclear how or whether this can be developed.

2. *Prototypes.* The prototype approach assumes that from among the entities which are categorized as being an instance of a certain concept, we can choose those entities which are the "best" representations of that concept (Hempel & Oppenheim 1936). The fundamental idea behind this approach is that those entities which are the most typical representatives of a concept are called 'prototypes', a concept popularized in cognitive psychology especially by Rosch (1978). Platteau (1980), Nunberg and Pan (1975), and Heyer (1985, 1987, 1990) propose treatments for characterizing sentences which make use of this notion of prototypes. In these treatments, a characterizing sentence is seen as a universal quantification over the prototypical elements of a concept. For example, a sentence such as *A cat has a tail* can be paraphrased as *Every prototypical cat has a tail.* If we represent *cat* as the predicate **cat** and adopt an operator **TYP** which restricts the extension of a predicate to the entities that are "prototypical" for that predicate, then the "prototype analysis" of generics generates the following:[32]

(80) A cat has a tail.
$\forall x[\mathbf{TYP(cat)}(x) \rightarrow \exists y[y\ \mathbf{is\ a\ tail}\ \&\ x\ \mathbf{has}\ y]]$

When developing a unified treatment for all characterizing sentences, however, we must assume a very general prototypicality operator, because the contents of a restrictor can vary widely; and we must also allow such a **TYP**-operator to be applied to predicates of different adicities. Note that this operator cannot be defined in terms of sets or other extensional entities, but must be specified as an operator whose arguments are intensional expressions. For if **GEN** were

32. This analysis is similar to Heyer's (1985, 1987, 1990) treatment, but Heyer is concerned only with kind-referring NPs in characterizing sentences, and interprets kinds as having a set of "typical specimens," which is a subset of the set of all specimens of that kind.

defined in terms of extensional entities, then, for example, in a world in which all birds except penguins became extinct, the notions of typical bird and typical penguin would coincide. But leaving these considerations of intensionality aside, **GEN** can be defined, using **TYP,** by a universal quantifier operating on a **TYP**-modified restrictor as follows:

(81) **GEN**$[x_1,\ldots,x_i;y_1,\ldots,y_j]$(**Restrictor; Matrix**) is true if and only if
$\forall x_1,\ldots,x_i[$**TYP**$(\lambda x_1\ldots x_i$**Restrictor**$[x_1,\ldots,x_i])(x_1,\ldots,x_i) \rightarrow$
$\exists y_1\ldots y_j$**Matrix**$[\{x_1\},\ldots,\{x_i\},y1,\ldots,y_j]]$

One problem with this approach is that it replaces one puzzle (that of determining the semantics of characterizing sentences) with another (that of determining the semantics of the **TYP**-operator). In addition, the approach does not give a fine-grained enough representation, as shown by the following true characterizing sentences:

(82) a. A duck has colorful feathers.
$\forall x[$**TYP(duck)**$(x) \rightarrow$ x **has colorful feathers**]
b. A duck lays whitish eggs.
$\forall x[$**TYP(duck)**$(x) \rightarrow$ x **lays whitish eggs**]

The problem with the representations of these sentences is that only male ducks have colorful feathers, and only female ones lay whitish eggs. As the sets of male and female ducks are disjoint, the predicate **TYP(duck)** does not apply to any object at all. And this would have the untoward logical consequence that *any* characterizing sentence of the form '*A duck Fs*' would be true (because the antecedent of the universal quantifier would always be false). Another example comes from the concept 'human being': One expects, and indeed hopes, that each one of us is atypical in at least one respect, which once again brings us to the conclusion that the class of prototypical elements is empty, and hence that we cannot make characterizing statements about them. (Or rather, that every such sentence is true.) Clearly, the notion of prototypicality must be relativized to the property being expressed in order to save this approach.

There are ways within the prototype approach to avoid this problem. They all involve denying the fundamental idea that the prototypes of a predicate include *all* the typical exemplars of a predicate; instead they "construct" a special exemplar (or group of special exemplars) for each concept. For example, we might assume a special class of objects that may have conflicting properties, as in the theory of arbitrary objects proposed by Fine (1985), in which, for example, arbitrary numbers are allowed to be even and odd at the same time. Another method involves the use of the notion of partial, or underspecified, objects, as developed in Landman (1986b). In this approach, a prototypical object can lack specific properties in one information state, but can acquire these properties in more detailed information states. We will not pursue these possible remedies for the prototype approach, but it seems clear that some such alterations are required before any prototype theory can be pressed into the semantic service of characterizing sentences. We will not comment upon whether the adoption of such things as arbitrary objects, or partial objects, takes away from the initial plausibility of prototypes.

3. Stereotypes. A related approach is to analyze characterizing sentences as expressing stereotypes. Consider the following contrast:

(83) a. A lion has a mane.
 b. A lion is male.

Why are we ready to accept (83a) but not (83b)?[33] Note that arbitrary lions are more likely to be male than to have a mane, since only male lions but not all male lions (e.g., not male cubs) have a mane. Nonetheless, (83a) is definitely true and (83b) is definitely false. Why? One possible answer, proposed by Geurts (1985) and Declerck (1986), is to say that (83a) but not (83b) expresses a stereotype about lions in our culture: it is part of our linguistic knowledge about the kind *Leo leo* that it has a mane. The concept of a stereotype was developed by Putnam (1970, 1975) in philosophy and Rosch (e.g., 1978) in psychology (as a distinct part of her theory of prototypes—the two parts of Rosch's work are separable, and here we are concerned only with the stereotype portion). Putnam broke down the meaning of a lexical expression into several components, including its extension and some stereotypical properties. These properties are considered to be the "core facts" (about the extension of the entities) which everyone speaking the language in question must know. Their truth-functional status is undetermined, however. As Putnam says, "The fact that a feature . . . is included in the stereotype associated with a word X does not mean that it is an analytical truth that all X's have that feature, nor that most X's have that feature, nor that all normal X's have that feature, nor that some X's have that feature" (1975, 250).

If **GEN** expresses stereotypical knowledge, then all we need to do in order to understand **GEN** is to investigate the formation of stereotypes, but there is little hope that we will find principles of general logical interest. For example,

33. Cf. also Carlson (1977b), who observed that *Chickens lay eggs* is considered true, but *Chickens are hens* is considered false.

one reason why having a mane is part of the stereotype of a lion is that the lion is the only cat that has a mane, making this a distinguishing property for lions. Our task would be to search out other stereotype formations in which distinguishing properties play a role. (For our views on distinguishing properties see section 1.3.4.) But again, we think it unlikely for there to be anything of general logical interest in stereotype formation. Another potential difficulty for a stereotype analysis arises if one thinks that cultural norms are the source of stereotyping properties. For instance, suppose it is the norm in some culture to assume that snakes are slimy. Even in that culture, the sentence *Snakes are slimy* is a false sentence—although believed to be true by most members of the culture—since snakes, those real-world objects, are in fact not slimy. That is, generics are construed as making claims about the world, rather than what is considered a cultural norm.

Besides, even if **GEN** does occasionally express stereotypes, that in itself is not an adequate description of **GEN,** for stereotypes are tied to single words or well-known and "fixed" concepts, whereas the restrictor of **GEN** can be made up by novel concepts as well. A sentence such as *Mary smokes when she comes home* requires a generalization over situations in which Mary comes home. This sentence can be understood and believed to be true even though the hearer probably does not have a stereotype about situations in which Mary comes home. Furthermore, even if there were such a stereotype, it surely would not be part of our linguistic knowledge (as it is with Putnam's examples of stereotypes of lemons and the like). Instead it would merely be chance knowledge we happened to have encountered or generated. If the stereotype theory were correct, **GEN** would not have a uniform interpretation after all, or, equivalently, there would have to be numerous different generic operators. In either case there would be no general theory of the semantics of **GEN**.

4. *Modal interpretations.* The modal approach (Dahl 1975, Nunberg & Pan 1975, Heim 1982, Delgrande 1987, 1988), which uses a possible-worlds semantics in the analysis of generic sentences, seems more promising. For one thing, it has often been remarked (e.g., by Lawler 1973a, Burton-Roberts 1977, Thrane 1980) that characterizing generic sentences resemble conditional sentences. For example, a characterizing sentence such as *A lion has a bushy tail* can be rephrased as *If something is a lion, it has a bushy tail.* (In section 1.2.4 we discussed restrictive *when*-clauses, which are similar to conditional clauses in some respects.) So the extensive literature on the modal treatment of conditionals and counterfactuals is relevant here as well (see Lewis 1973, Kratzer 1981, van Benthem 1984, Delgrande 1987, and the articles in Traugott

et al. 1986). Heim (1982) explicitly treats both conditionals and characterizing sentences as containing modal quantification. Furthermore, the philosophical literature on dispositional predicates is related to the modal approach. Dispositional predicates, like *be soluble in water,* are generally reduced to lawlike sentences (*If x is put into water, it will dissolve*), and lawlike sentences are in turn analyzed as modalized sentences. In chapter 7 of the present volume, Asher and Morreau consider the modal approach from the point of view of knowledge representation in Artificial Intelligence.

We will first give a sketch of the possible-worlds semantics of modal operators and conditionals, based on Stalnaker 1968, Lewis 1973, and especially Kratzer 1981. According to Kratzer, we must distinguish three parameters of modal operators in natural language. One parameter, the *modal relation,* distinguishes operators such as *must* from *may* and *can,* and *necessarily* from *possibly,* or, in a more formal turn of phrase, $\Box$ from $\Diamond$. Let us call the former class of operators 'necessity' and the latter class 'possibility'.

A second parameter is called the *modal base* (or *conversational background*). Consider the following sentence:

(84) John must have a car.

This sentence can be interpreted in terms of several different modal bases, yielding different interpretations:

a. Epistemic modality: Given the evidence we have (e.g., that John was in Tübingen at 5:00 and in Stuttgart at 5:30), it is necessary that John has a car.

b. Deontic modality: In order to fulfill some requirement (e.g., to be a salesperson), it is necessary that John has a car.

c. Instrumental modality: In order to achieve some goal (e.g., commuting between Tübingen and Stuttgart), it is necessary that John has a car.

The modal base is often left unspecified and must be provided by the context of the utterance, but it may be specified by expressions such as *in view of what we know,* or *according to the company's directives for salespeople,* or *given that there are no other reasonable means of transportation.* Formally, the modal base should specify the set of possible worlds quantified over by the modal operator. This set of possible worlds may vary from possible world to possible world. (E.g., the rules of salespeople may be different in different worlds.) We therefore must assume that the modal base is a function which maps a possible world (the one considered the actual world) onto a set of possible worlds. In this reconstruction, the modal base is simply the accessibility relation for possible worlds in modal logic.

These two parameters must be supplemented by a third. For example, although sentence (84), in the epistemic interpretation, asserts that John could not have used a helicopter or resorted to witchcraft in order to reach his destination, its analysis as an epistemic modality does not contradict the existence of such possible worlds. The idea is that these worlds are not "similar enough" to the real world to be taken into account. In order to formalize this intuition, we need a third parameter, the *ordering source,* to give us an ordering among possible worlds. For example, the epistemic interpretation of (84) will say, based on such ordering, that worlds in which John uses a helicopter and in which he resorts to witchcraft (and in which witchcraft works!) are more abnormal than worlds in which he uses a car. The ordering is dependent upon the actual world and can be specified by expressions of the types mentioned above. For example, *according to the law* will specify an ordering relation which reflects that, the more violations of the law a world contains, the more abnormal it is. (From the description of this ordering relation, it should be clear that it is taken to be reflexive.)

Given these parameters, we can define a necessity modal operator **must** (Kratzer's "human necessity") as follows:

must Φ is true in world w with respect to a modal base B_w and an ordering source $\leq_w$ ('be at least as normal as') under the following condition:
For all worlds w′ in B_w there is a world w″ in B_w such that w″ $\leq_w$ w′, and for every other world w‴ $\leq_w$″, Φ is true in w‴.

This definition states that **must** Φ is true in w if Φ is true in those worlds of the modal base (with respect to w) which are closest to the ideal (or most normal) worlds with respect to w. (Note that since $\leq_w$ is not required to be a total order, there will typically be many "most normal" worlds). The corresponding possibility operator **may** can be defined as follows:

may Φ is true in w with respect to B_w and $\leq_w$ iff it is not the case that **must not-**Φ is true in w with respect to B_w $\leq_w$.

Conditional sentences can be treated in this framework by assuming that they contain a modal operator. This operator can be overt as in (85a,b) or covert as in (85c):

(85) a. If John is in Stuttgart now, he must/may/could have a car.
b. Maybe/Possibly, if John is in Stuttgart now, he has a car.
c. If John is in Stuttgart now, he has a car.

The method assumes that the conditional clause restricts the modal base B_w to those worlds which are compatible with the conditional clause's semantic content. For example, the modal base of (85a) is restricted to the set of possible worlds which are in B_w and for which *John is in Stuttgart now* is true. The matrix sentence then is evaluated with respect to this modified modal basis. In (85c), the covert operator is clearly a necessity operator, as (85c) does not merely express the possibility that John has a car, given that he is in Stuttgart now, but definitely something stronger.

Now let us return to characterizing sentences. A characterizing sentence such as *A lion has a bushy tail* expresses the same concept as the conditional sentence *If something is a lion, it has a bushy tail.* We can try, therefore, to extend the modal semantics for conditionals to the realm of characterizing sentences that do not have an explicit adverb of quantification. Note that in order to capture the quasi-universal force of characterizing sentences, we will want to employ a necessity operator in our representation. More specifically, we will give the following interpretation to the GEN-operator (with a slight blurring of object- and metalanguages):

(86) **GEN**[$x_1,\ldots,x_i;y_1,\ldots,y_j$](**Restrictor; Matrix**) is true in w relative to a modal base B_w and an ordering source $\leq_w$iff:
For every $x_1,\ldots,x_i$ and every $w' \in B_w$ such that **Restrictor**[$x_1,\ldots,x_i$] is true in w', there is a world w'' in B_w such that $w'' \leq_w w'$, and for every world $w''' \leq_w w''$, $\exists y_1,\ldots,y_j$**Matrix**[$\{x_i\},\ldots,\{x_j\},y_1,\ldots,y_j$]] is true in w'''.

This is similar to the definition for **must** given above except that it takes into account the binding of variables, as in the similar definition from Heim (1982, 179). Consider the example below (again with a slight blurring of object- and metalanguage in the interpretation):

(87) A lion has a bushy tail.
GEN[x;y](x **is a lion;** y **is a bushy tail** & x **has** y) is true in w relative to B_w and $\leq_w$ iff:
For every x and every $w' \in B_w$ such that 'x is a lion' is true in w', there is a world w'' in B_w such that $w'' \leq_w w'$, and for every world $w''' \leq_w w''$, $\exists$y[y **is a bushy tail** & x **has** y] is true in w'''.

This representation states that everything which is a lion in the worlds of the modal base is such that, in every world which is most normal according to the ordering source, it will have a bushy tail. Note that this does not presuppose the existence of lions in the real world (B_w might not include w). It also does not require that every lion has a bushy tail, not even of those lions in B_w worlds. It merely states that a world which contains a lion without a bushy tail is less normal than a world in which that lion has a bushy tail.

An obvious question at this point is whether the covert operator in conditionals is the same as the covert operator in characterizing sentences. Both clearly express some sort of necessity, but Heim (1982, 194) argues that they are not the same. In her view, a conditional sentence must be interpreted with respect to a "realistic" modal base and ordering source, which includes the actual world and hence entails universal quantification with respect to the actual world. A characterizing sentence, however, allows for exceptions; and hence its covert operator can be interpreted with respect to modal bases which are not "realistic." So, on this view, we cannot always replace the covert quantifier by an overt quantifier such as *must,* since it might evoke a different modal basis and ordering sources. Consider the following examples:

(88) a. If someone owns a dog, he pays tax on it.
b. If someone owns a dog, he must pay tax on it.

According to Heim, (88a) can only be true if everyone in the real world who owns a dog pays tax on it. Sentence (88b), on the other hand, is a lawlike statement that can be true even if many dog owners do not pay tax on their dogs. Unlike (88a), it evokes a deontic modal base and ordering source which does not include the actual world.

However, if we look at a wider range of examples, we actually find that conditionals need not be interpreted with respect to a "realistic" base. For example, the following conditional clearly has a deontic interpretation (it can be used to control the behavior of rude tourists in British manor homes).

(89) If a gentleman is in the company of a lady, he doesn't peel bananas.

So we can entertain the simpler hypothesis that the covert operator in conditional sentences and the covert operator in characterizing sentences are the same.

There are many different ways to vary the modal bases and the ordering sources. Let us see how our approach fares with a few different examples:

(90) Two and two equals four.

This sentence expresses a mathematical necessity. Here we assume that the most normal worlds are those in which our mathematical laws hold (arguably the set of all possible worlds). Consequently, in this domain we should not encounter any exceptions. This is indeed the case; for example, the characterizing sentence *Prime numbers are odd* is definitely false, even if there is only one exception (the number 2) and an infinite number of confirming cases.

(91) A spinster is an old, never-married woman.

This is a definitional sentence that expresses a linguistic necessity. The ordering source is given by the language, so that the most normal worlds are those in which English is interpreted as it is in the real world. If we take, as usual, the meanings of terms in the language as fixed, then the set of most normal worlds for such a sentence is the set of all possible worlds, and hence sentences of this type also will not have exceptions. Burton-Roberts (1977) attempts to reduce characterizing sentences in general to such definitional sentences, where the "relevant area of evaluation" is allowed to vary.

Another sort of interpretation seems required for examples like (92):

(92) This machine crushes oranges.

We interpret this sentence with respect to a modal base and ordering source, where the machine performs the action for which it was designed. As observed by Laca (1990), this is quite typical for characterizing sentences about artifacts. In particular, we do not need any corroborating past instances to judge whether (92) is true; (92) can be true even if the machine never has and never will have crushed a single orange.

Another type of problems is illustrated by (93) and (94), due to Ewald Lang.

(93) This boat floats.
(94) a. ?This boat can float.
b. This tank can float.

In (93) we express that this boat works properly insofar as it stays above water. As noted before, we can justify such a generic sentence by evaluating it with respect to all the worlds where the machine performs the action it was designed for. (94) sounds a bit strange by comparison. This can be explained by assuming that the modal *can* expresses a weaker generalization than (93): it says that the boat floats in some worlds but not necessarily in all. When we take the same set of worlds as before, then we can infer that the boat actually does not work properly. (94b) is normal again, because we can assume that not all the worlds in which this tank works properly are worlds in which it has to float, and hence the weaker modality is warranted. Now consider (95):

(95) Mary smokes cigarettes.

In contrast to (92), we would hesitate to say that (95) is true if Mary didn't smoke now and then. This can be explained as follows: the modal base and ordering source are related to worlds in which Mary shows her typical behavior. Now, with living beings, the usual evidence we have for typical behavior is their behavior in the past. Hence, the usual and expected evidence for (95) are events of Mary smoking cigarettes.

Some further examples are provided by (96)–(99):

(96) John sells vacuum cleaners.

In this case, we might have circumstantial evidence other than actual performances of the act expressed by the verbal predicate. For example, we might know that John signed a contract with a company.

(97) Bob jumps 8.90 meters.

This sentence will be considered true if Bob accomplished the feat described once. We can explain this by employing a modal base and ordering source where Bob performs as well as he can, and where no adverse conditions interfere. It might be difficult to produce these conditions, and so it might be that Bob typically jumps a shorter distance. But there must be at least some evidence that he can jump the specified distance, and this is given by the fact that he managed to do so once. Examples such as (83a), repeated here as (98), are also amenable to a modal analysis:

(98) A lion has a mane.

According to our earlier discussion, this sentence expresses a stereotype. We can incorporate this as a special case into our analysis by assuming a "stereotypical" ordering base (Kratzer 1981, Heim 1982). For such an ordering base, the closer the worlds are to the ideal, the more stereotypical properties hold in them. Again, stereotypically interpreted characterizing sentences will have exceptions in the real world. One last, rather different example:

(99) Six apples cost one dollar.

In contrast with the examples above, this sentence must be evaluated with respect to a very restricted modal base and ordering source, namely one which is restricted to the current world (and time and place). In this "collapsed" modality, the sentence does not allow for exceptions.

Since characterizing sentences as a group have a wide variety of interpretations, it is sometimes suggested (e.g., Lawler 1973a, Heyer 1987, Kleiber 1988a) that they do not form a uniform class. Thus the sort of theory we have been suggesting would simply be going beyond the evidence. But we disagree. It is indeed true that different characterizing sentences which are superficially similar in appearance may be paraphrased in quite different ways. For example, (91) can be paraphrased by *A spinster is necessarily unmarried*, and (92) by *A boy should not cry*. However, we would prefer to have this difference in paraphrase follow from the different modal bases and ordering sources we assume, and to stand by our simpler assumption that there is only one covert genericity operator.

As stated earlier, the modal base and ordering source are often not specified overtly. As with other context-dependent sentences, we must assume that hearers construct a modal base and ordering source for the interpretation of a sentence, in order to *accommodate* it, in the terminology of Lewis (1983). For example, if the speaker uses a definite description such as *the girl* and hearers have no specific individual available as a referent of that description, they will construct a context in which this definite description makes sense. Similarly, they may accommodate suitable modal bases and ordering sources. Accommodation may also be a way to handle the problem of simple habituals which lack an overt restrictor, such as *Mary smokes*. In these sorts of cases, we might assume that the restrictor is generated by accommodation, and that hearers accommodate modal bases in which a smoker can be expected to show smoking behavior.

Although the modal approach is promising, it sometimes forces us to accept unusual modal bases and orderings. Consider the following example:

(100) A turtle is long-lived.
GEN[x;](x **is a turtle;** x **is long-lived**)

According to the definition of **GEN** given in (86), this is true if and only if every turtle in the modal base is long-lived in all the most normal worlds with respect to the ordering source. This sentence evokes a kind of ''realistic'' modality in which the laws of biology hold. However, the worlds in which no turtle ever dies a premature death are biologically highly abnormal. Normalcy conditions may contradict one another, as do in this case the conditions for single organisms and for whole ecological systems. Consider another example (again with a simplified formal representation):

(101) A pheasant lays speckled eggs.
GEN[x;](x **is a pheasant;** x **lays speckled eggs**)

Again, we assume that (101) is interpreted with respect to biological normality and is true if and only if every pheasant in the worlds of the modal base lays speckled eggs in every most normal world. To get this universal quantification, we must restrict our attention to worlds in which there are only pheasants, since only they may lay speckled eggs. We know, however, that only *fertilized* female pheasants may lay speckled eggs, and according to the laws of biology, there must then be some male pheasants around as well. Those won't lay eggs, though. The precise mechanism for achieving the appropriate restrictions necessary for such interpretations remains controversial.

5. *Situations.* It would be convenient to use, as conversational background, domains smaller than complete possible worlds or sets of such worlds. A useful domain might be one in which we look only at single turtles or only at fertilized female pheasants. Our fifth approach does exactly this by considering *situations* instead of possible worlds, modeling characterizing sentences as *constraints on situations*. Constraints of the appropriate sort have already been used in Situation Semantics to model conditional sentences (e.g., Barwise 1986). Since characterizing sentences are basically conditionals, a constraint technique would seem to be applicable to them as well; constraints have in fact been used for this purpose by ter Meulen (1986a) and Gerstner-Link (1988).

Constraints are relations between types of situations (cf. Barwise & Perry 1983). A constraint such as $\Sigma \Rightarrow \Sigma'$, where Σ and Σ' are situation types, says that Σ *involves* Σ', or that whenever Σ is realized, Σ' is realized as well; that is, whenever there is a situation σ of type Σ there is also a situation σ' of type Σ'. The situation types may contain parameters which can be *anchored* to specific entities, locations or types. (In such an approach, parameters are similar to variables, and anchors similar to variable assignments). An important rule is that whenever f is an anchor for Σ (i.e., $\Sigma(f)$ differs from Σ insofar as some parameters of Σ are anchored) and we have a constraint $\Sigma \Rightarrow \Sigma'$, we also have a constraint $\Sigma(f) \Rightarrow \Sigma'(f)$. This rule captures the dependencies between parameters, and can be used to express these dependencies in sentences with adverbial quantifiers if we analyze the variables as parameters. It is important to note that it may be the case that a constraint holds only with respect to some background B. Such a conditional constraint is given as $(\Sigma \Rightarrow \Sigma') \mid B$, read as '$\Sigma$ involves Σ', given that B', where B is a situation type as well. It is plausible to express the conditional constraint $(\Sigma \Rightarrow \Sigma') \mid B$ as an unconditional constraint, by putting the background in the antecedent—that is, as $(\Sigma \cup B) \Rightarrow \Sigma'$—following Barwise & Perry (1983). However, Barwise (1986) explicitly refrains from doing so and treats conditional constraints as three-place relations. Gerstner-Link (1988) proposes the notation '$\Sigma \Rightarrow_c \Sigma$', where C stands for some conditions similar to the modal dimensions discussed above.

The formalism we have developed can easily be integrated into Situation Semantics, by interpreting variables as parameters and formulas as situation types. If we ignore the fact that, in Situation Semantics, the notion of truth must be relativized to a specific situation referred to by a declarative sentence, we have the following:

> **GEN**[$x_1,\ldots,x_i;y_1,\ldots,y_i,\ldots,y_j$](**Restrictor; Matrix**) is true relative to a background B in which $x_1,\ldots, x_i$, and possibly others, occur as parameters (i.e., relative to B[$\ldots,\{x_1\},\ldots\{x_i\},\ldots$]) iff:
> There is an anchor *f* for the parameters in B such that for every situation σ which is of type B(*f*) it holds that if **Restrictor**(*f*) is true, then *f* can be extended to *f′* such that **Matrix**(*f′*) is true.

The background B can be more specific than possible worlds could possibly be. For example, in sentence (101), *A pheasant lays speckled eggs,* B can be restricted to situations containing female animals, because the sentence tells us something about the mode of giving birth and therefore only female animals should count. But our considering here only situations that contain no male pheasants does not in any way commit us to denying that there are also mating situations in which there are both male and female pheasants. More formally:

(101′) A pheasant lays speckled eggs.
GEN[x,s;y](x **is a pheasant in** s; x **lays** y & y **are speckled eggs in** s) is true with respect to the background 's is a situation of giving birth' iff:
For every situation σ which is a situation of giving birth it holds that for any x which is a pheasant in σ, there is a y which are speckled eggs, and x lays y in σ.

As with the modal approach, the pertinent background is often left unspecified; and again we must assume some rule of accommodation.

6. *Nonmonotonic inferences.* The sixth approach for handling the semantics of characterizing sentences is actually a set of related approaches currently under development in the literature on nonmonotonic reasoning both in logic and in artificial intelligence. Although this literature does not contain an explicit discussion of generic sentences, the crucial examples that guide its development are always characterizing sentences, and so, if these theories are successful, we should expect from them an adequate semantics of characterizing sentences. The term 'nonmonotonic' indicates that these frameworks provide a formal mechanism for retracting a previous conclusion when given new evidence. Formally speaking, an inference is nonmonotonic if the set of premises Γ generates conclusion φ, but the premises (Γ∪ψ) do not generate conclusion φ. For example, learning that the supermarket is open and knowing that it carries wine and that I have enough money to buy wine, I can conclude that

I can buy wine. However, I might (later) learn in addition that city laws prohibit the selling of alcoholic beverages between midnight and 6:00 in the morning, and as it is after midnight now, I must retract my earlier conclusion. Linguistic treatments of characterizing sentences in terms of nonmonotonic theories are sketched in Strigin 1985, Carlson 1987, Kleiber 1988b, Morreau 1988, 1992b, and, in more detail, Asher and Morreau (this volume), and Veltman 1995.

The question of how to treat exceptions is at the core of the enterprise. A typical problem is that we may infer from the fact that Bruce is a bird the fact that he can fly, although there are many types of birds which are exceptions to this rule, such as kiwis, penguins, ostriches, emus, dead birds, and birds with clipped wings. We might try to include all these exceptions in our rule by saying that, if Bruce is a bird that is not a kiwi, not a penguin, not an ostrich, not an emu, is not dead, doesn't have clipped wings, etc., then he can fly. But it may not be possible to give a complete list of exceptional properties; and in any particular case, we may not know whether the entity in question has an exceptional property. Still, we typically reason that if Bruce is a bird, then he can fly, and retract this conclusion at a later time if we learn that Bruce is, in fact, an emu.

We consider here three varieties of nonmonotonic reasoning and examine the extent to which they can be used to handle generic sentences. Consider the following example, which illustrates the three approaches:

(102) A bird is feathered.
- a. If *x is a bird* is true, and if *x is feathered* can be consistently assumed, then conclude that *x is feathered* is true.
- b. If x is a bird and it is not known that x is not feathered, then conclude that x is feathered.
- c. If x is a bird, and x is not abnormal for a bird with respect to being feathered, then conclude that x is feathered.

The reasoning in (102a) is an example of a *default rule* in default logic (Reiter 1980). This is an inference rule that allows us to reach a conclusion C (here, *x is feathered*) from a sentence A (here, *x is a bird*), given that another sentence B (the so-called justification; here, *x is feathered*) is consistent with the facts assumed so far, that is, we cannot infer its negation from these or other facts.

The reasoning in (102b) is an example of *autoepistemic reasoning* (McDermott & Doyle 1980, Moore 1984). The various approaches which fall into this category differ with respect to the epistemic modality they invoke, as well as in certain technical details. In general, this type of approach can be characterized as reasoning in the absence of positive knowledge; it is similar to default logic in this respect. Unlike default logic, however, modalized nonmonotonic reasoning allows the default rule to be made explicit in the object language by employing the modal operator **it is not known that**.

The reasoning in (102c) represents McCarthy's theory of *circumscription,* or *minimal entailment* (McCarthy 1980, 1986). The central idea is to cover all exceptions by one predicate which indicates that these cases are abnormal, and to restrict the domain of that predicate merely to those entities which *must* be abnormal given the positive knowledge we have. This minimization of the predicate domain is called 'circumscription'. Clearly, the abnormality must be relativized to a certain property. For example, the emu Bruce is abnormal for a bird because he cannot fly, but not abnormal in the sense of having no feathers. To emphasize the fact that the abnormality predicate in Circumscription must be relativized in this manner, we assume here that this predicate is dependent upon the semantic constituents of the sentence. Note that (102c) can be used in two directions: Either we learn about a bird x which is not feathered and then conclude that x is abnormal for a bird with respect to being feathered, or, if we already know or can derive that x is abnormal for a bird with respect to being feathered (because it's molting, for example), then we refrain from deriving that x is feathered.

We won't go into the technical details of the various formats of nonmonotonic reasoning at this point, such as the treatment of conflicting rules (see Asher and Morreau, this volume, for some remarks, and Reiter 1987 for a general discussion of nonmonotonic formalisms). However, we *do* wish to point out that the default logic approach in (102a) differs from the two other approaches in that it uses a formula of the metalanguage rather than of the representation language to state how characterizing sentences are to be understood. Default rules are rules, and therefore are sound or unsound—in contrast with sentences, which are either true or false. If we analyzed characterizing sentences using default rules, these sentences would not have truth values, and their meanings could not be specified by an ordinary semantic interpretation function. If we were to accept this, we would need to find a way to handle cases with nested **GEN**-operators such as the following:

(103) A cat is healthy if it chases an object when that object is moved in front of its eyes.
GEN[x;](x **is a cat** &
GEN[y,s;](y **is an object** & y **is moved in front of** x's **eyes in** s; x **chases** y **in** s); x **is healthy**)

Default logic can't work here because in such an approach the embedded **GEN**-formula would have to be spelled out as a default rule—which is a statement in the metalanguage and cannot be conjoined with a sentence such as *x is a cat* in the object language as required for the treatment of the other **GEN**-phrase. Another manifestation of the problems associated with treating characterizing statements as metalinguistic default rules is that as such they are neither true nor false—they are not *in* the language, and therefore do not "talk about the world"; instead they "talk about" which inferences to draw. But as we claimed very early in this chapter, it is with characterizing statements that most of our knowledge about the world is represented. What shall we make of a theory that refuses to tell us the conditions under which *Snow is white* is true? Indeed, one that refuses even to admit that it *is* true?

The main reason that nonmonotonic logics appear to be useful for representing the meaning of characterizing statements is that they explicitly allow for exceptions to general rules, and thus can accommodate the fact that characterizing sentences typically allow for exceptions. Furthermore, there is a correspondence between the "modal" quality of these generic sentences and the way generalizations are captured in nonmonotonic logics: Generic sentences are "modal" in that they make claims about an open (or open-ended) class of entities. For example, the sentence *A lion has a mane* does not make a claim about the closed class of all existing lions, but rather about every ("realistically") possible lion. This excludes the possibility of simply listing the properties of the entities in question, or of formulating universal sentences and enumerating their exceptions. Default reasoning seems to be just what is called for in such a circumstance.

The nonmonotonic reasoning approach fares well in certain cases that are problematic for the modal approach. For example, the sentence *A turtle lives a long life* does not require us to construct biologically inconsistent possible worlds; it simply says that when x is a turtle and we have no information to the contrary, we can assume that x lives a long life. Despite the apparent success of the approach along this dimension, however, the original problem might reappear in the guise of the "lottery paradox" (Kyburg 1988): Given a box with a suitably large number of lottery tickets, only one of which is a winner, a rule such as "If x is a ticket, and we have no information to the contrary, then x is not a winner" is sound; however, we cannot apply that rule to *every* ticket, because we know that one of them is indeed a winner. Similarly, we know that we cannot apply the rule "If x is a turtle, x lives long'' to every turtle; if we were to do it, the notion of biological inconsistency would make its appearance again.

Nonmonotonic reasoning can handle the problems with simple generic sentences such as (54), repeated here with a new interpretation that makes no reference to the situations which are normal with respect to smoking:

(54) a. Mary smokes.
b. **GEN**[x,s;](x = **Mary** & s **contains** x; x **smokes** in s)

At first glance, this representation appears to be too strong, since even a heavy smoker doesn't necessarily smoke in every situation. However, there seems to be a way to use the nonmonotonic reasoning paradigm in such a way that (54b) could be seen to be a reasonable representation—at least if one has considerable explicit knowledge concerning smoking. Consider (54c):

(54) c. If s is a situation which contains Mary, and if s is not an abnormal situation for Mary with respect to smoking, then Mary is smoking in s.

For example, in a given situation s, there may be many properties of s from which we can derive the conclusion that s is an unlikely situation for Mary to be smoking in. Which situations we would consider abnormal situations for Mary to be smoking in depends upon our theories concerning smoking and Mary. For example, we could assume that s is abnormal in this respect if Mary is sleeping or eating in s, or if Mary is a guest and her hosts object to smoking, or if s immediately follows a situation s′ in which Mary has smoked a cigarette. There are, of course, many other reasons why we might conclude that s is abnormal for Mary's smoking. A perhaps more striking case is provided by our earlier sentence (97), repeated here:

(97) a. Bob jumps 8.90 meters.
b. If s is a situation which contains Bob, and if s is not an abnormal situation for Bob with respect to jumping, then Bob jumps 8.90 meters in s.

Again, there could be many reasons why Bob did not jump 8.90 meters on a specific occasion: he might have been asleep or watching an opera performance, or perhaps he was not really trying, or he had a hangover, or there was some head wind. . . . Sports fans are never at a loss for arguments as to why a specific situation was abnormal for an athlete's performing his best in some particular situation s.

Our final remark on nonmonotonic reasoning is that there is nothing in current theories which corresponds to the different modal bases and ordering sources of the modal approach presented earlier. We have argued that the interpretation of characterizing sentences clearly shows a dependency on these parameters. To give an adequate semantics to characterizing sentences in a nonmonotonic reasoning framework requires a reconstruction of those parameters in this framework.

It is time to conclude our inconclusive discussion of the semantics of characterizing sentences. We have great empathy for the reader who is dissatisfied with all of the approaches outlined here. The semantics of characterizing sentences (more specifically, the semantics of the **GEN**-operator) is one of the deepest problems not only for linguistic semantics but also for disciplines such as cognitive psychology, analytic philosophy, and Artificial Intelligence. We wish we could answer all the questions raised in this section, but we console ourselves with the belief that this is a large and interesting area, connecting with deep issues of broader import, that calls for much more research.

1.3. KIND-REFERRING AND OBJECT-REFERRING NPs

1.3.1. Basic Properties

In this section we turn our attention toward the other type of genericity we identified in section 1.1, that is, toward kind-referring NPs. Our basic observations in section 1.1 about these NPs can be recapitulated as follows:

i) Nominal predicates that are tied to an established kind can safely be regarded as yielding a kind-referring NP (*the Coke bottle* vs. **the green bottle*).
ii) The verbal predicate in a sentence with a kind-referring NP need not be stative (*The panda is dying out*).
iii) There are verbal predicates (kind predicates like *be extinct, invent*) which require a kind-referring NP in some argument place.
iv) Observations (i–iii) can be most easily explained if we assume that the phenomenon under consideration is tied to the NPs in question, and not to the sentences as a whole.
v) Although observation (iii) might suggest that we deal with a phenomenon that is verb oriented, we can most easily handle these cases simply as selectional restrictions of specific verbs.

To illustrate point (v): we would say that a verb like *invent* selects for kinds in its direct object position. In this way, a nominal distinction is reflected in a concomitant verbal distinction, but would nevertheless remain a nominal distinction. This is rather like our practice of saying that although *kill* requires an animate object (in non-metaphorical uses), the feature [$\pm$ animate] is still a nominal feature. Thus (103) has the kind-selecting verb *invented* select the kind-denoting NP *the computer* as a direct object.

(103) Charles Babbage invented the computer.

We will assume throughout that what we call kind-referring NPs actually *do* refer to kinds, which are modeled as special types of individuals. This is, of course, not the only theory that can be found in the literature (see Kleiber 1990 for a recent survey and discussion). First, kind-referring NPs might be claimed not to refer at all, but to be quantificational in force (Bacon 1973a, 1974). This may work with examples like *The lion is ferocious* (which will be rendered as, perhaps, 'All lions are ferocious'), but it is unclear how sentences with kind predicates like *The lion is extinct* would be handled. A possibility is that kind-referring NPs are ambiguous between a quantifying and a nonquantifying use—an assumption that can be found already in Frege 1892 with examples like *Das Pferd ist ein Vierbeiner* 'The horse is a four-legged (animal)' and *Der Türke belagert Wien* 'The Turk is occupying Vienna'. However, this ambiguity obviously depends on the verbal predicate and certainly does not strike one as a particularly elegant solution. (See Carlson 1982 and Heyer 1987 for discussion.)

Second, kind-referring NPs might be analyzed as denoting the intension of their nominal predicate, and hence kinds would be intensions (see, inter alia, Mayer 1980 and Martin 1986). This approach accounts for some properties of kind-referring NPs quite nicely—for example, that we can distinguish between *the tyrannosaurus* and *the brontosaurus,* even though their extensions in the current world are the same, namely the empty set. However, in other respects this analysis raises questions. In a sentence like *The rat reached Australia in 1770,* we need to ensure that the truth of the sentence depends upon the arrival of concrete, non-intensional rats. This in turn suggests that we should instead think of kinds as relatively ''concrete'' entities. A third position that points in this direction, namely that kind-referring NPs denote the sum of the entities to which the nominal predicate applies (Kleiber 1990, Ojeda 1991), will be discussed in section 1.3.4 below.

We will start with nontaxonomic NPs and then consider taxonomic NPs and the associated taxonomic hierarchies. Finally, we will examine the range of possible meanings of sentences that contain kind-referring NPs and discuss some items that seem closely related to kinds.

1.3.2. Nontaxonomic Kind-Referring NPs

We begin by looking at the possible linguistic forms of (nontaxonomic) kind-referring NPs in English and some other languages. In English, kind-referring NPs are typically definite singular NPs like *the Panda,* bare plurals like *pandas,* bare mass terms like *gold,* or proper names like *Ailuropoda melanoleuca:*

(104) a. The panda will become extinct soon.
b. Pandas will soon become extinct.
c. Gold has the atomic number 79.
d. *Ailuropoda melanoleuca* will become extinct soon.

Why do we find these forms and not others? Our hypothesis is that kinds are (a certain type of) individual entities, and kind-referring NPs consequently should be NPs which refer to these entities. It follows from this hypothesis that the subclass of kind-referring terms we are considering in this section might be semantically analyzed as proper names (Langford 1949, Carlson 1977b, Heyer 1985). That is, when these terms (which, after all, can be used in various other ways) are in fact being used to "talk about" kinds (in the manner indicated in (104)), then in that usage they may well be functioning like proper names.

There are a number of arguments for this analysis. To begin with, there is a conceptual relationship between this notion of a kind-referring NP and the notion of a proper name: both are definite, referring expressions. Secondly, the class of kind-referring NPs actually does contain some ordinary proper names, like *Ailuropoda melanoleuca.* Maybe even the more common *man* (as an NP, not as a noun) must be analyzed as a proper name, as well as poetic names like *Bruin* or German *Meister Petz* for bears:

(105) a. *Homo sapiens* lived in Australia for at least 40,000 years.
b. Man lived in Australia for at least 40,000 years.
c. Bruin likes to take a nap after eating.
d. Meister Petz macht gern ein Schläfchen nach dem Fressen.
'Bruin likes to take a nap after eating'.

Another context in which kind-referring NPs behave like proper names is provided by the so-called *so-called* construction (this was observed by Carlson 1977b for bare plural NPs).

(106) a. The Incredible Hulk was so called because of his shape.
b. The liger is / Ligers are so called because it is / they are the offspring of a lion and a tiger.
c. *This fat man is so called because he is corpulent.

Now, why do the other kind-referring NPs (the ones which are not proper names by the usual syntactic tests) take precisely the forms they have? This can be explained by the assumption that normally, a common noun like *panda* has to perform at least two functions: first, it refers to a kind, and second, it has as its extension the set of entities which belong to this kind. To be more specific, let **R** be the *realization relation* which relates kinds to their specimens. It is similar to Carlson's realization relation (cf. Carlson 1977a,b; also, section 1.2.2 above), with the exception that we do not consider stages here. Thus a formula **R**(x,k) states that the object x belongs to the kind k. For example, it holds that **R(Xinxin, Ailuropoda melanoleuca)**, that is, Xinxin is a panda. **R** arguably should be an irreflexive relation,[34] as no entity can be a specimen of itself. The hypothesis being put forward can then be recast by saying that a common noun like *panda* has two functions: first, it is related to a kind, in this case *Ailuropoda melanoleuca,* and second, it is related to a set (or property), in this case λx[**R**(x,**Ailuropoda melanoleuca**)]—or the set of all pandas. If δ is a common noun, let us designate its kind-referring use by δ_k and its predicate use by δ_p.

According to its kind-referring function (K-function), a common noun should behave like a proper name, that is, as an NP. According to its predicative function (P-function), it should behave like a nominal predicate, that is, as an N. This ambivalence between a referring interpretation and a predicate interpretation was first investigated with mass nouns, as mass nouns in English actually occur in both functions. According to Quine (1960), a mass noun like *water* is a singular term when in subject position, as in *Water is a fluid,* and a general term when occurring after the copula, as in *This puddle is water.* Ter Meulen (1980, 1981) distinguished more generally between 'nominal' mass terms and 'predicative' mass terms. The tension between these two uses can be resolved in different ways (Parsons 1970, Pelletier 1974, Bealer 1975, Bunt 1985, Pelletier & Schubert 1989). We may either take the kind-referring use as semantically primitive and derive the predicate use from it, as δ_p equals $\lambda x[\mathbf{R}(x,\delta_k)]$; that is, δ_p equals the set of objects which realize the kind δ_k. Or we may take the predicate use as primitive and define the kind-referring use in terms of it, as δ_k equals $\iota x \forall y[\delta_p(y) \leftrightarrow \mathbf{R}(y,x)]$; that is, δ_k equals that kind of which every object in the extension of δ_p is a realization. (We leave it open as to whether every predicate has a corresponding kind individual). And of course there is also the option of taking each term to be ambiguous; on that

34. Otherwise we might run into some (Platonic-style) Third Man Argument, or maybe a Russell-style contradiction.

view, both uses are primitive and should be related (when necessary) by meaning postulates. (See Bunt 1985 for this option, and see Carlson 1977b for the correspondence between kind-referring and predicative nouns generally).

It seems that common nouns in many languages are primarily predicates, that is, of category N, and that the kind-referring use, which requires the category NP, has to be marked somehow. But there are certainly counterexamples, and even distinctions within a language, between different types of nouns (count nouns vs. mass nouns, for instance).[35] Let us have a look at a sampling of a few different languages in this respect (cf. also Gerstner-Link 1988).

English. The basic syntactic difference between simple NPs (e.g., names) and common nouns is that NPs can be used directly as arguments of verbs, whereas an N normally needs a determiner to do so. But note that there are cases where a proper name has a definite article, like *The Sudan.* This should not be surprising: proper names are semantically definite and so the definite article is not out of place. Common nouns, on the other hand, come in three classes: mass nouns like *rice* can stand as an NP without determiner; the same holds for plural nouns like *pandas,* whereas singular count nouns like *panda* require a determiner. Now, if a common noun has to be used like a proper name, as in the case of the kind-referring interpretation, it must somehow be transformed into a member of the NP category. The three options at hand are these: (i) If the common noun is a mass noun, it can be used directly as an NP without any change. If it is a count noun, this option is usually not available in English (*man* is an exception, see below). The two minimal changes are (ii) to put it into the plural form, or (iii) to add a definite article as a determiner. Option (ii) certainly does not distort the meaning of the count noun—indeed, some people have even argued that the plural form is the semantically unmarked form anyway (see Krifka 1989). Neither does option (iii) distort the meaning: for as we have observed, the definite article is compatible with the meaning of proper names. (Mufwene 1986 reports on a tendency of English-based creoles not to mark generic nouns as plural.)

Chinese. In this language, any noun is syntactically also an NP—witness the NP *xíongmao* '(the panda(s)' in sentences like (107). Therefore we need no

35. Note, however, that Pelletier and Schubert (1989) argue that in English the predicative use is primary, even in the case of mass nouns.

determiner at all for kind-referring NPs. This is shown by examples like the following (the glosses ASP and CL stand for 'aspect' and 'classifier'):

(107) a. wǒ kànjiàn xíongmao le.
I see bear-cat ASP
'I saw (the/some) panda(s).'
b. Xíongmao jué zhōng le.
bear-cat vanish CL ASP
'The panda is extinct.'

French. In French there is a syntactic requirement that, with the exception of very few syntactic constructions, every noun needs a determiner in order to be an NP. Therefore we cannot have bare nouns as kind-referring NPs in the manner encountered in Chinese. Instead, kind-referring NPs have to be constructed with a definite article.

(108) a. *Pandas sont éteint.
Le panda est éteint.
Les pandas sont éteint.
'The panda is extinct.'
b. *Or prend de la valeur.
L'or prend de la valeur.
'Gold is going up in value.'

We conclude that if a language is forced to construct a kind-referring noun with a determiner, it will use the definite article. This corresponds best to the fact that these NPs are definite.

German. In this language, proper names are constructed more often with the definite article than happens in English. For example, personal names frequently occur with definite articles, as in *Der Karl ist gekommen* 'Charles has arrived'. It fits in perfectly with the proper name analysis of kind-referring NPs that we find the definite article more often with them as well. For example, mass nouns and, to a somewhat lesser extent, plural count nouns in this interpretation can employ the definite article:

(109) a. (Das) Gold steigt im Preis.
'(The) Gold is getting more expensive.'
b. (Die) Pandabären sind vom Aussterben bedroht.
'(The) Pandas are facing extinction.'

In general then, the syntax of kind-referring NPs tends to be similar to the syntax of kind-referring NPs tends to be similar to the syntax of proper names. This makes best sense if kind-referring NPs *are* proper names of kinds.

German dialects. In some German dialects (see Scheutz 1988 for Bavarian), as well as in Frisian (see Ebert 1971a), there are two sorts of definite articles. There is a long form used for anaphoric reference and a short form used to refer to entities that are part of the shared background knowledge of speaker and hearer. This short form is used with proper names as in (110a), with NPs referring to unique entities as in (110b), and with kind-referring NPs as in (110c), but is not used to refer to an entity which is introduced in the text, as in (110d). The following examples are Bavarian.

(110) a. Da/*Dea Kare is kema.
'Karl has arrived.'
b. Da/*Dea Kini is gschtoabm.
'The King has died.'
c. Da/*Dea Schnaps is daia.
'Schnaps is expensive.'
d. I hab a Bia un an Schnaps bschdait. Dea/*Da Schnaps war daia.
'I have ordered a beer and a schnaps. The schnaps was expensive.'

Indonesian. A similar situation is reported for Indonesian by Porterfield and Srivastav (1988) (who also discuss the situation in Hindi). In this language, definite NPs are normally overtly marked (by the determiner *-itu* or the suffix *-nya*). But NPs which refer to unique entities, like the president of the country, occur as bare nouns, and this holds also of kind-referring NPs.

The fact that languages which mark definite NPs whose referent is furnished by the background knowledge also mark kind-referring NPs in this way supports our hypothesis, put forward in section 1.1.3 with examples like the *Coke bottle/*the green bottle,* that kind-referring NPs refer to well-established entities in the background knowledge of speaker and hearer. If kind-referring NPs denote kinds which are not 'construed' in the text but are well-established in the background knowledge of speaker and hearer, we should conclude that they are lexical entries, even if they are syntactically complex. In case they are syntactically complex, they have to be counted as idiomatic expressions; that is, their meaning cannot be derived systematically from the meaning of their parts. As an example, consider (111a,b) below.

(111) a. The German shepherd is a faithful dog.
b. *The German fly is a lazy insect.

The clear difference in acceptability is related to the fact that *German shepherd* is an idiomatic expression specified as such in the lexicon, whereas *German fly* is not. (People who do not find (111b) so bad presumably accommodate their lexicon and conceptual universe such that it contains a hitherto unknown kind, *Musca germanica*). Kind-referring NPs share this property with proper names. Even when proper names are syntactically complex (like *John Smith*) or descriptive (like *William the Conqueror* and *Sitting Bull*), their meaning (the object to which they refer) cannot be systematically derived from the meanings of their parts.

A similar example was discussed by ter Meulen (1980), who contrasted *heavy water,* which refers to a kind (deuterium oxide), with *muddy water,* which does not. There are some borderline cases, that is, complex kind-referring NPs whose composition is still transparent; one example is *Coke bottle.* And of course, nouns of any complexity can occur in generic (characterizing) sentences, like *Lions without teeth are vegetarian;* but then they clearly do not refer to a well-established kind, but instead can be analyzed as predicates occurring in characterizing sentences in accord with our remarks in section 1.2. Just when a language will promote an NP to kind-referring status is quite difficult to specify. And it is even more difficult to contemplate the ontology this picture presupposes. (Are kinds created and destroyed by our use of language?) On the other hand, the analysis of Carlson (1977b) treats all bare plurals, regardless of complexity, as denoting kinds, and holding on to that sort of analysis requires that bare plurals and definite generics in English be differentiated in other ways. Some predicates that are apparently kind-selecting can take complex bare plurals, as in *Lions without mates at mating time are quite common.* For this and other reasons, we give a different treatment of such predicates in section 1.4.1.

Up to now, we have only considered kind-referring NPs in subject position. It is interesting to look at them when they occur in other syntactic environments, for example in object position. In section 1.2.5 we analyzed cases like *John loves dogs* by claiming that *dogs* does not refer to a kind, but is a predicate instead. However, there are fairly clear cases of kind-referring NPs in object position (Smith 1975); in the following examples they are in the direct object position.

(112) a. The Americans invented chewing gum.
b. The Italians improved German food quite a lot.
c. Shockley invented the transistor / ?transistors.

d. The Sumerians invented the pottery wheel / ?pottery wheels.
e. The French settlers in Mauritius exterminated the dodo / ?dodos.

Examples (112a,b) show that kind-referring mass mouns can occur in object position. Examples (112c–e) show that kind-referring count nouns with a definite article can occur in object position as well, whereas bare plural NPs in this position are not normally accepted by speakers (indicated by the question marks). One should note, however, that this may have something to do with the nature of the direct object position itself rather than the semantics of the predicate, since the bare plural form is much more acceptable as the subject of the passivized versions of (112) (e.g., *Dodos were exterminated by the French settlers in Mauritius* is much more acceptable than (112e) with the bare plural). To be sure, a bare plural NP in direct object position *can* be interpreted as an indefinite NP denoting elements of a class of kinds—that is, here, as subkinds of the transistor, of the pottery wheel, or of the dodo. These interpretations are cases of taxonomic readings, which we will examine in the next sections. And those who accept the plurals in (112) but who insist they are not taxonomic seem to agree that they are interpreting *invented* as *constructed,* and *exterminated* as *killed* (i.e., they are not really using kind-selecting verbs but rather object-selecting verbs). It seems, then, that the bare plurals in this position may not designate kinds for such people but rather specimens of the kind.

In (112a–e), the direct objects must be kind-referring terms. But recall that there are also sentences (such as *John loves dogs* and *Mary smokes cigarettes*) in which we claim that the direct object is to be analyzed as a predicate rather than as a kind-denoting term. In part, the difference between the two is that, for instance, while one smokes *a* cigarette, one does not invent *a* transistor.[36] But there are many verbs which are "intermediate" along such intuitive dimension:

(112) f. John hates coffee / cigarettes / the lion.
g. Dutchmen despise Belgians.
h. Rust erodes iron.

How shall we analyze these sentences? Are they kind-denoting or predicative in their object positions? Our claim is that they are kind-denoting, and are not cases of a predicate within the scope of a generic operator.[37] For one thing,

36. Except, of course, in the taxonomic sense.
37. See Kanouse 1972, Lawler 1973b, Declerck 1987, and Laca 1990.

sentences (112f–h) can be put into the passive without changing their truth conditions, unlike *Mary smokes cigarettes:*

a. John hates coffee ⇔ Coffee is hated by John
b. Dutchmen despise Belgians ⇔ Belgians are despised by Dutchmen
c. Rust erodes iron ⇔ Iron is eroded by rust
d. Mary smokes cigarettes ⇎ Cigarettes are smoked by Mary

Also, the object NPs in (112f–h) cannot be replaced by subordinate kinds *salva implicatione,* unlike the case of *Mary smokes cigarettes.*

a. John hates Columbian coffee ⇏ John hates coffee
b. Mary smokes French cigarettes ⇒ Mary smokes cigarettes

Furthermore, as Laca (1990) mentions, the NPs we would intuitively consider to be kind-referring occur with the definite article in Spanish, yielding contrasts like the following:

a. Juan detesta el café.
b. Juan fuma cigarros.

In sum, there is enough evidence to conclude that the object NPs in examples like (112f–h) refer to kinds, much in the same way as the object NPs in (112a–e) and in contrast to the object NPs in examples like *Mary smokes cigarettes*. Obviously, the truth conditions of a sentence like *John likes coffee* should ultimately be related to quantities of the kind Coffee, and this relationship will be different from the relationship between Shockley and the kind Transistor in (112c). In both cases, though, we will claim that this relationship is ''intensional'' (as we argued above when considering sentences like *Mary handles the mail from Antarctica* and *Kim helps her friends in emergencies,* which can be true even if there never has been mail from Antarctica or any opportunity for Kim to help friends).

There is, though, an interesting difference between the sentences in (112a–e) and those in (112f–h): plural objects are considerably better in the latter. A possible explanation of this effect might go like this: the usual interpretation of a bare plural NP is an indefinite NP, and the definite interpretation is only possible in suitable syntactic environments. There are at least two environments that are suitable:

1. The subject of so-called categorical sentences. These are sentences whose subject is in the topic position; they are contrasted with so-called the-

tic sentences (Kuroda 1972, Sasse 1987). (113 is an example of this contrast:[38]

(113) a. Pandas | are facing EXTINCTION. [the kind *Ailuropoda melanoleuca*]
b. PANDAS were roaming the camp. [some specimens of *Ailuropoda melanoleuca*]

2. The object position of stative verbs. These verbs favor the definite interpretation of bare plurals.

So why is the kind-referring interpretation of a bare plural NP tied in this way to its syntactic position in the sentence? One idea would be that the default interpretation of a bare plural NP is the indefinite one, and that the definite, kind-referring interpretation of a bare plural may be coerced by additional means. These means include, in English, sentence-initial position as in (113a) (which must be a sentence about the kind *Ailuropoda melanoleuca* because of (i) the selectional restrictions of the verbal predicate *face extinction* and (ii) the progressive form, which excludes a characterizing interpretation over subspecies of *Ailuropoda melanoleuca*). (In addition to being sentence initial, the bare plural NP must occur in a sentence with a certain accentual structure.) A further way to coerce the interpretation can be to have the bare plural NP in the object position of stative verbs. These two positions—the subject position of categorical sentences and the object position of stative verbs—are not particularly well-suited to introduce new discourse referents (the usual task of indefinite NPs) and so they may be free to be interpreted differently.

The obvious generalization that follows from this reasoning, then, is that bare plurals can be easily interpreted as definite (and hence kind-referring) only when they are in topic position; if they are in the subject position of a thetic sentence like (113b) or in a nonsubject position, they tend to be interpreted as indefinite (see also Gerstner-Link 1988, for German). In (112c–e) the verbs require kind-referring objects, and bare plural NPs are coerced to the definite interpretation. The assumption that the topic position enables a definite interpretation of bare plural NPs is a natural one, given the fact that topics are definite (or at least specific), whereas indefinite bare plurals are nonspecific. Thus the accentual topic marking in (113a) forces the bare plural NP *panda* into its definite (kind-referring) reading. In object position, on the other hand, there is no accentual marking for definiteness, and so we tend

38. As before, a vertical line marks a pause, and capitalization marks the main sentence accent.

toward the normal indefinite interpretation of bare NPs. Interestingly, the same subject–object asymmetry in the interpretation of some types of bare NPs holds for other languages as well, e.g., for bare plural NPs in German and for bare singular NPs in Hindi and Indonesian (cf. Porterfield & Srivastav 1988).

However, this whole discussion about whether and when an instance of a bare plural NP is interpreted as referring to a kind or as designating objects of that kind is at the moment lacking clear guiding criteria; and this theory, like the one assuming that all instances of bare plural NPs denote kinds, stands in need of considerable refinement.

1.3.3. Taxonomic Kind-Referring NPs

We now turn to what we have called taxonomic NPs. Consider a noun like *whale*. Up to now, we have identified two uses of such a noun, one as a predicate applying to the specimens of the kind *Cetacea*, the other as a name of the kind *Cetacea* itself. There is a third use, namely as a predicate applying to the *subkind* of the kind *Cetacea*, that is, the blue whale, the sperm whale, the dolphin, etc. Thus taxonomic NPs were identified by Galmiche (1985) as forms "pour référer à une sous-espèce," and by Declerck (1987a, 1991) as NPs in the "subkind interpretation." (See also Burton-Roberts 1981 and Wilmet 1988.)

In which forms do taxonomic NPs occur? The underlined expressions in the following examples give some indication for the range of possible forms.

(114) a. The dolphin is a whale.
b. The dolphin and the porpoise are whales.
c. One whale, namely the blue whale, is nearly extinct.
d. Two whales, namely the blue whale and the fin whale, were put under protection.
e. This whale, namely the blue whale, is nearly extinct.
f. The whale which was most recently put under protection is the blue whale.
g. Every whale (from the pygmy whale to the blue whale) is protected by law.

These examples show that taxonomic NPs need not be indefinite. Instead, taxonomic NPs show the whole gamut of syntactic behavior that we observe with every count noun: we find singular indefinites like *a whale,* bare plurals like *whales,* NPs with numerals like *one whale, two whales,* NPs with demonstratives like *this whale,* NPs with definite article like *the whale which was most recently put under protection,* and quantified NPs like *every whale*. The count-noun-like character of taxonomic NPs also shows up in the fact that if we put a mass noun in a count noun context, it typically gets the taxonomic reading, as in the following example (cf. Pelletier & Schubert 1989):

(115) *Two red wines* are produced in Württemberg: Lemberger and Trollinger.

There are count nouns, like *species, halogen, metal,* and *alloy,* which seem to have only a taxonomic reading:

(116) a. Chlorine is a halogen.
b. There was chlorine/?halogen in the water.

And furthermore, the taxonomic reading does not make much sense if the noun is associated with a kind which has no species, as is the case for *dodo:*

(117) ?A dodo is extinct.

But taxonomic NPs do not only occur in the form of simple count nouns. For example, we find constructions based on nouns like *type* or *kind* which resemble numerative constructions like *five glasses of wine* but which denote subkinds (for further remarks see Wilkinson, this volume):

(118) This kind of whale lives mainly in Arctic and Antarctic waters.

In a classifier language like Chinese, which has to use classifier construction to render the equivalent of count noun constructions, we find different classifiers in the object-related case than we find in the taxonomic case.

(119) a. yi zhī xíong
one CL bear
'an individual bear'
b. yi zhōng xíong
one CL bear
'a kind of bear, a bear species'

In German, there is a productive morphological process to derive taxonomic count nouns, which consists in suffixing *-art* or *-sorte.* In the following example, which represents the equivalent of (115), *-sorte* is added to the mass noun *Rotwein* 'red wine', making it a count noun referring to subkinds of red wine. (Alternatively, the noun itself could be used taxonomically, as in *zwei Rotweine* 'two red wines'.)

(120) Zwei Rotweinsorten werden in Württemberg angebaut: Lemberger und Trollinger.

Let us now look at the nature of the subkind relation. It is obvious that it should be analyzed in terms of *taxonomic hierarchies*. As an example, consider the following (parts of) taxonomic hierarchies:

(121) a.

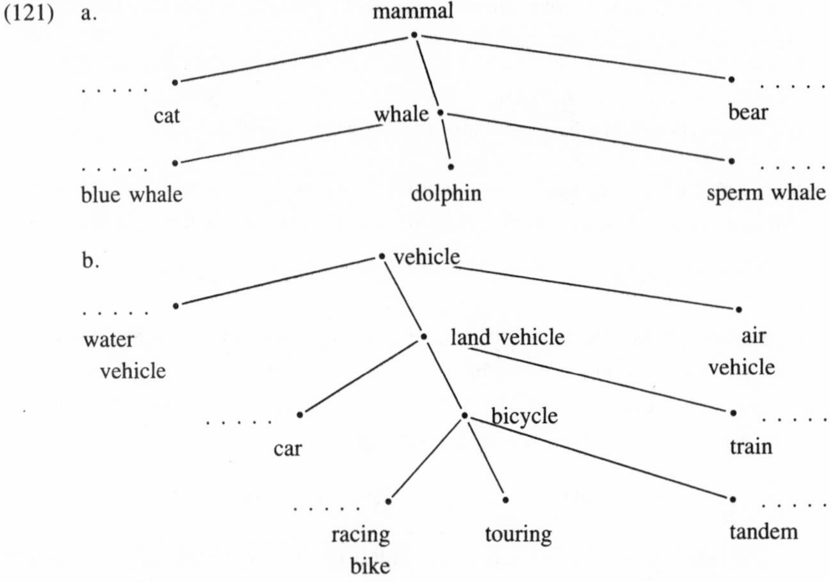

See Kay 1971, Berlin, Breedlove & Raven 1973, Cruse 1986, and Pelletier & Schubert 1989 for a discussion of such hierarchies in language and of their mathematical structure. Basically, they can be considered as partial orderings or lattice structures. There typically is a distinguished level of "everyday words" (Berlin et al. call them "generic," though more commonly they are referred to as "basic-level" terms). These words are frequent and noncomposite; in our example, the *cat/whale/bear* level and the *car/bicycle/train* level are basic in this sense. The words at this distinguished level are most readily used to describe an object. For example, to refer to some bicycle, a speaker is less likely to use *vehicle* or *15-speed racing bike* than to just use *bicycle* (or *bike*).

Taxonomic hierarchies also play a role in the determination of the comparison class in a characterizing sentence with positive adjectives (Bierwisch 1987). For example, the sentences *A pony is small* and *A Saint Bernard is big* are probably considered true, although Saint Bernard dogs typically are smaller than ponies. The reason is that the positive adjectives *small, big* implicitly refer to some standard given by the comparison class, and that the comparison class of *pony* and that of *Saint Bernard* are different and hence may yield different standards. The comparison class in these cases is given by the taxonomic hierarchy; it is horses for *pony* and dogs for *Saint Bernard*.

Let us call the taxonomic subkind relation **T**, with **T**(x,y) meaning that x is a subkind of y.[39] This is reminiscent of our previously mentioned realization relation **R**(x,y): x is an instance of y. There is the following relation between the two:

(122) [**T**(x,y) & **R**(z,x)] ⇒ **R**(z,y)

That is, if x is a subspecies of y and the object z belongs to x, then z also belongs to y. For example, every sperm whale is a whale. We might be tempted to conflate the subkind relation **T** and the realization relation **R**, that is, to make no distinction between kinds and individual objects. This is frequently done in the AI literature on semantic nets (see, for example, the articles in Findler 1979—a standard reference), which have only one relation, ISA, to cover both **T** and **R**. However, not only are there logical reasons to distinguish kinds and objects (as philosophers have been claiming for decades); there are also linguistic reasons to make the distinction. For example, an object could never be in the extension of a nominal predicate which is clearly marked as taxonomic, say, German *eine Walart* 'a kind of whale'. This even holds in the case where a kind happens to be realized by only one object. That is, even in extreme cases like this one, there is a type distinction between kinds and objects. This requires that **T** and **R** must be different, because as they have different domains, namely, **T** relates kinds to kinds while **R** relates objects to kinds.

The notion of a taxonomic hierarchy can be exploited to cover the well-known *type–token ambiguity* as well. For example, *this book* can either refer to a specific copy or to a title:

(123) a. This book got wet in the rain. (= copy)
b. This book sells well. (= title)

The first reading can be treated as an individual-related one, and the second as a taxonomic one. In this case, a book type (a title) can be analyzed as a subkind of the kind book.

39. **T** is asymmetric, as no kind can be a *sub*kind of itself, and it is transitive—if a kind x is a subspecies of a kind y and y is a subspecies of a kind z, then x should count as subkind of kind z as well. The relation **T** is also "intensional" in that (for example) there can be two distinct species both of which are empty. It furthermore ought to be noted that a species might have only one subkind, and yet the species and subkind are nonetheless distinct.

1.3.4. The Meanings of Sentences with Kind-Referring NPs

In this section, we will present the range of meanings we find with sentences containing a kind-referring NP and give a rough-and-ready analysis in order to elucidate each phenomenon further. The following list gives some typical examples, as well as a preliminary descriptive classification of the phenomena:

(124) a. The dodo is extinct.
(kind predicate interpretation)

b. Linguists have more than 8,000 books in print.
The German customer bought 11,000 BMWs last year.
(collective property interpretation)

c. The American family contains 2.3 children.
German teenagers watch six hours of TV daily.
(average property interpretation)

d. The potato contains vitamin C.
(characterizing property interpretation)

e. Dutchmen are good sailors.
The Dutchman is a good sailor.
(distinguishing property interpretation)

f. Be quiet—the lion is roaming about!
In Alaska, we filmed the grizzly.
(representative object interpretation)

g. Man set foot on the Moon in 1969.
(avant-garde interpretation)

h. The wolves are getting bigger as we travel north.
(internal comparison interpretation)

We will discuss these interpretations in turn and given some more examples for each of them.

A. *Kind predicates* can only be applied to kinds in the first place, and so it is quite clear that (124a) uses the kind-referring NP to name a kind directly and then to predicate something of it. These kind predicates have been described by several authors, e.g., Smith (1975), Heyer (1985, 1987), and Wilkinson (1988). Of our eight examples in (124), this is the only one that clearly and straightforwardly "says something" about the kind without talking about the instances of the kind.

But note that even kind predicates are related to properties of *instances* of the kind, if we engage in an analysis of the lexical meaning of such predicates (which does not affect the ability of these predicates to select for kinds). For example, in order to show that the dodo is extinct, one has to show that there have been realizations of this kind in the past, that there are no present realizations of this kind now, and, perhaps, that there will be no more in the future. This reduction of kind predicates to predicates about objects can be handled by meaning postulates for kind predicates. To give a fairly simple case, we can derive from 'x is *a* liquid' and **R**(y,x) that 'y is liquid' holds, at least under normal temperature conditions. (See Pelletier & Schubert 1989 for similar simple examples.) Often, though, the reduction of kind predicates is quite complex; consider for example 'x is extinct'. Here, something like the following must hold: x must be a (biological) kind, there did exist objects y such that **R**(y,x) in the past, but there exists no object now such that **R**(y,x) in the present. When we take into account that there are kinds which may survive over long periods in form of spores or even as frozen sperm, we must claim in addition that the genetic propagation of the kind is irreversibly disrupted. As an even more complicated example for the reduction of kind properties to object properties, consider the following (from Schubert & Pelletier 1987):

(125) The lemur evolved from the tree shrew.

We might call kind predicates like *be extinct, invent,* or *evolve from,* which cannot be reduced to morphologically related predicates of objects, *lexical kind predicates;* and we might contrast them with *derived kind predicates* (the cases in (124b–h)), since these other predicates all have parallel, morphologically related predicates which hold directly of objects. This distinction is reminiscent of the one between lexical dispositional predicates like *love* and habitual predicates like *smoke* (see section 1.2.5), as only habituals are related to situation-dependent predicates.[40]

B. If the predicate applies collectively to all existing objects belonging to a kind, the property can be projected from the objects to the kind. We call this the *collective property interpretation.* This interpretation might seem to be "at the opposite end of the scale" from the kind predicate interpretation, for here it seems clear that the property in question is something that holds of the actual

40. A special property of sentences containing kind-referring NPs in this interpretation concerns the past tense. Consider (i):

(i) The dodo was a bird.

This sentence suggests that the dodo is extinct. In general, when a necessary property is asserted of a kind in the past tense, we infer that the kind does not exist anymore. Contrary to Anderson (1973), we assume that this is a mere pragmatic effect—note that (ii) is true as well, in spite of the dodo's being extinct.

(ii) The dodo is a bird.

instances (as a group), and not of the abstract object, the kind. One might even argue, using this sort of example, that a kind should be analyzed as the sum of its realizations (cf. Sharvy 1980, Kleiber 1990, Ojeda 1991 for this 'mereological' reconstruction). The reason is that collective interpretations can often be rendered formally in mereological models. For example, the collective interpretation of *The girls ate seven apples* can be given as: The collection of the girls ate seven apples. Similarly, in (124b) we could argue that the property of having eight thousand books in print is applied to the collection of all linguists.

But one should carefully distinguish between these entities (mereological sum vs. kinds), since not every predicate which holds for the collection of the specimens of a kind holds for the kind itself, nor vice versa. For example, it may be true that the collection of all existing rabbits has a weight of more than one million tons, but generic sentences like (126) are quite strange.[41]

(126) The rabbit has a weight of more than one million tons.
Rabbits have a weight of more than one million tons.

It remains to be investigated under which conditions the collective property interpretation is available (see Condoravdi 1992).

C. It is interesting to contrast collective property interpretations with *average property interpretations*. Certainly there are no syntactic differences, as can be seen from the example sentences in (124b,c). Rather, our choice of interpretation is conditioned upon facts such as these: that it would be extremely implausible for the average German customer to have bought eleven thousand BMWs last year, and we know (from our own case?) that the average linguist could not have published eight thousand books last year (thus the sentences in (124b) must receive collective property interpretations); that no actual family can contain 2.3 children, and that it would be extremely unlikely for the total daily German-teenager-TV-watching-time to be only six hours (thus the sentences in (124c) must receive average property interpretations). The average property interpretation is sometimes marked in the NP by nominal adjectives such as *typical, average, ordinary, normal, usual,* etc. (*The average American family* . . . , *Your typical German teenager* . . .). The lack of syntactic distinction between these two types of interpretation means that there can be instances of properties for which we cannot tell which interpretation is meant. Consider sentences such as these:

41. This same argument is applied against mereological interpretations of mass terms in Pelletier & Schubert 1989.

The American family used less water this year than last year.
The small businessperson in Edmonton paid nearly $30 million in taxes but only made $43,000 in profits last year.

The former sentence is ambiguous between the collective and average property interpretations. It could be true that the average American family used less water this year than last while the collective American family used more (due to more families); conversely, it could be true that the average family used more but the collective family used less. As to the latter sentence, which is admittedly somewhat strange (but might be used to further the political interests of Edmonton businesspeople), our world together tells us that the first conjunct of the VP must be interpreted as a collective property, since certainly the average businessperson, even in wealthy Edmonton, does not pay $30 million in taxes; but our world knowledge also tells us that the second of the VP conjunctions is to be given an average property interpretation.

D. In (124d), we find our "kind-referring NP" genericity and our "characterizing" genericity combined. (The subject NP is kind-referring, and the sentence is of the characterizing type). Heyer (1985, 1987) calls these sentences "personal generic," since the kind-referring NP can be replaced by an indefinite NP without much change in meaning. Ideally the analysis of this case should be logically derived from a combination of the semantics of kind reference and of characterizing predication. We will discuss this issue in section 1.3.6 below. Here, we just label the case as the *characterizing property interpretation,* to indicate that the property expressed by the verbal predicate must be characterizing for the objects of the kind.

E. Another case in which we can project a property from an object to its kind is shown in (124e) (an example from Arnauld 1662). Some more examples of this type are the following (due to Schubert & Pelletier 1987):

(127) a. Italians are good skiers.
b. Frenchmen eat horsemeat.

At first sight, these might seem to be just some more cases of the characterizing property interpretation, that is, characterizing sentences. If they were, we would try to analyze them as we do a characterizing sentence with an indefinite subject NP (see section 1.2 above):

(128) Dutchmen are good sailors.
GEN[x;](x **are Dutchmen;** x **are good sailors**)

But the generic quantification in (128) is not warranted; for although *Dutchmen are good sailors* is true, we certainly would not conclude that any randomly picked Dutchman will turn out to be a good sailor. There are several possibilities which might save this general style of analysis. One is to assume that (128) is evaluated with respect to a stereotypical modality; then it would only claim that being a good sailor belongs to the stereotypes of a Dutchman. Or we could tamper with the restrictor or with the interpretation of **GEN**, changing it in such a way that it yields truth conditions which seem to be correct (cf. Geurts 1985). For example, it seems that the main sentence stress in (128) can be on *good*. Given the correlation between sentence accent and the partitioning between restrictor and matrix (see section 1.2.2), we can claim that **good** is part of the matrix, whereas **sailor** is part of the restrictor. We then get a more plausible semantic representation that amounts to 'Dutch sailors are good sailors', an analysis which was already suggested by Arnauld (1662).

(129) Dutchmen are GOOD sailors.
GEN[x;](x **are Dutchmen** & x **are sailors;** x **are good (as sailors)**)

However, we also get this reading with an accent on *sailors* (where we can assume that *good sailors* is in focus), and so just assuming different partitionings will not give us a general solution.

It should be noted that these examples require kind-denoting subjects, for they are not adequately paraphrased by indefinite singulars (e.g., *A Dutchman is a good sailor* and *A Frenchman eats horsement* are in fact *not* true.) Consider the following examples:

(130) a. The potato contains vitamin C.
b. Potatoes contain vitamin C.
c. A potato contains vitamin C.

(131) a. The Dutchman is a good sailor.
b. Dutchman are good sailors.
c. A Dutchman is a good sailor.

Whereas the examples in (130) have the same truth conditions (at least at the level of detail with which we are concerned here), examples (131a,b) differ from (131c) in that (131c) makes a stronger claim than (131a,b). With (131c) we can more or less expect that a random Dutchman we pick out will turn out to be a good sailor—must as with all the examples of (130), we can expect a random potato to contain vitamin C. The somewhat weaker claim of (131a,b) can be paraphrased as: The Dutch are known to have good sailors. Or: The Dutch distinguish themselves from other comparable nations by having good sailors. It is this somewhat weaker interpretation which we call the *distinguishing property interpretation,* as it seems to express a property that distinguishes the subject referent from other entities that might belong to the same category. (See also Wilmet 1988.)[42]

F. If the object in the situation described is only relevant as a representative of the whole kind, then a property can be projected from the object to the kind. We call this the *representative object interpretation.* Languages, and maybe registers within a language, seem to differ in their readiness to employ this interpretation. For example, whereas German speakers agree that example (132a) has a representative object interpretation, English speakers have difficulties in getting this reading with the English equivalent, (132b).

(132) a. Der Fuchs ist wieder in den Hühnerstall eingebrochen.
 b. The fox broke into the chicken house again.

But elsewhere English allows for this kind of interpretation, witness (124f). Also, certain dialects of English can get the representative object interpretation with *Mister;* compare (132c):

 c. Mister Fox broke into the chicken house again.

G. If some object belonging to a kind has a property which is exceptional for objects of that kind, the kind can be assigned the same property. The property is felt to be relevant not only to the object, but also to the kind itself. Let us call this the *avant-garde interpretation,* since the exceptional object can be considered the 'avant-garde' of the kind (Gerstner & Krifka 1987; see also Carlson 1977b, Heyer 1985, 1987, and Corblin 1987, who describes these cases as expressing "un record à porter au crédit de l'espèce"). Note that not just any old exceptional property will give rise to this interpretation, but that the property really must be considered relevant and important for the kind. Note also that such properties are episodic. This can be seen in the following squish of examples:

(133) a. Man learned to solve cubic equations in the 16th century.
 b. ?Man broadjumped further than 8.90 meters in 1968.
 c. *Man ate 128 pretzels in one hour in 1976.

42. There have been attempts to reduce all sentences with kind-referring NPs to this type, e.g., Platteau 1980 and Galmiche 1983. But such a "reduction" comes with a price: it means that we cannot take such sentences as *The lion has four legs* to be felicitous, because the property of having four legs certainly is not distinctive for lions with respect to other cats, or mammals, or even vertebrates.

These sentences differ in acceptability because achievements in sports like broad jumping are not considered as particularly relevant for man, and the pastime of pretzel eating even less so. This is in contrast with the solving of mathematical equations or landing upon celestial bodies.

Another aspect of the avant-garde interpretation is that we have to pick out the "right" kind in the kind hierarchy to which to attribute the property (see Kleiber 1990). For example, we might express the first landing on the Moon also as follows:

(124) g.′ The American set foot on the Moon in 1969.
g.″ The primate set foot on the Moon in 1969.

But (124g′) seems to be a predication on a kind that is too "low" in the hierarchy, whereas (124g″) seems to be too "high." It seems that predications of this type preferably are about "basic-level" kinds (cf. section 1.3.3); predications on lower-level subkinds are possible if a contrast with other subkinds on the same level is implied. For example, (124g′) is good in case, say, the Chinese had set foot on the Moon before 1969.

H. Examples like (124h) (cf. Carlson 1977b, Schubert & Pelletier 1987) involve a comparison of the specimens of a kind along a certain dimension of their occurrence. Note that they cannot be treated as characterizing sentences, as they do not involve properties of individual specimens—thus, (124h) cannot be rephrased as *A wolf is getting bigger as we travel north*. We have to analyze such *internal comparison interpretations* as yet another class, perhaps comparable to sentences about normal objects like *The road is getting rougher as we travel north*.

Let us now reconsider the examples in (124) as a whole. It is surely quite astonishing to get such an array of different interpretations. The readings range from attributing properties strictly to an (abstract?) kind, to attributing properties to all members of the kind acting in concert, to attributing properties to the "average" of a group (and not necessarily to any instances), to attributing characteristic properties which hold of "randomly chosen" individuals, to attributing distinguishing properties, to attributing exceptional properties to the kind because of an avant-garde member of the species, to attributing a comparative property to a kind that relates specimens along a dimension. Furthermore, it is remarkable that these different readings do not hinge on the presence of specific linguistic elements. The situation is clearly different from our prototypical characterizing sentences, where we can claim to have only one interpretation scheme, and where the covert operator can be made explicit by adverbs such as *typically, in general,* or *usually*. So how should we treat the range of meanings we find? This is a fertile topic for future research. We will comment a bit further on this problem in the following section.

1.3.5. Kind-Oriented and Object-Oriented Modes of Talk

In this section, we will look at the notion of a kind and its relation to objects more thoroughly. We start with an unusual, but not at all far-fetched, example. Imagine a cage in a zoo with three lions in it, and a father pointing at them and telling his children:

(134) Look kids, this is the lion.

It seems obvious that *the lion* should be analyzed as a kind-referring NP here. In the case at hand, we deal with what we have called the representative object interpretation of the NP. Note, for example, that (134) can be continued with a generic sentence:

It lives in Africa.

Here *it* should clearly be analyzed as coreferent with *the lion* in (134) and therefore as referring to the kind *Leo leo*. But how could this be? The father is pointing at three actual animals, which surely do not make up the whole kind *Leo leo*. And even if it were the case that the lion was a more endangered species than it actually is and these three lions in the cage were the last surviving lions, it still seems clear that the father is not pointing at the kind *Leo leo,* since kinds are not defined solely by their existing specimens. So, how *can* this be?

One way to explain it might be to assume an ontology where it is possible that a kind is in some way ''identical'' with the objects, or with collections of objects, that belong to it.[43] With such an ontology the father could point to three lions and say that ''this is the lion'' (as the three are, in this new sense of the term, ''identical'' with the kind *Leo leo*), and later say that this same kind lives in Africa. Of course, such a move needs a somewhat unusual notion of identity—so unusual that we probably ought not call it ''identity', so let's call this relation **IS** (plural: **ARE**) instead. An important difference between

43. An alternative way of looking at this puzzle is to view reference to collections as providing a ''deferred reference'' to the kind. The following discussion is couched in terms of ''identity'' rather than ''deferred reference'', but it seems to us that the points made could equally well be phrased in terms of the latter, *mutatis mutandis*. See Nunberg (1993) for further discussion on deferred reference.

identity and **IS** is that the latter relation must be relativized to the sort of entities we identify. Otherwise, we could prove that, for example, any two lions **ARE** the same, because they **ARE** the kind *Leo leo* and normal identity is a transitive and commutative relation.

It is actually easy to define the **IS**-relation we need in terms of normal identity and the realization relation **R** (see section 1.3.2 above).

(135) $\mathbf{IS}(x,y) \Leftrightarrow_{df} (x=y \vee \mathbf{R}(x,y))$

That is, if x and y are either both objects or both kinds, then **IS**(x,y) holds if and only if they are identical. And if x is an object and y a kind, then **IS**(x,y) holds if and only if x is a realization of y. Note that **IS** is still reflexive and transitive, but not symmetric; thus it fails to be an equivalence relation.[44] Our initial example (134) can now be rendered as follows. Let **a** be the object which is the collection of the three lions in the cage. Then we have:

(134′) a. This [**a**] is the lion [**Leo leo**]: **IS**(**a, Leo leo**).
b. It [**Leo leo**] lives in Africa: **lives in**(**Leo leo, Africa**).

As natural as this approach appears to be, there is a problem with it. For, if the approach is correct, then it should *always* be possible to talk about kinds instead of their realizations; after all, the objects **ARE** the kinds. For example, the sentences in (136) should be equally appropriate to describe a situation in which a gorilla walks across a street into a pub.

(136) a. A gorilla walked across a street into a pub.
b. The gorilla [generic interpretation] walked across the street [generic interpretation] into the pub [generic interpretation].

To develop a stable terminology, we will say that (136a) belongs to the *object-oriented mode* of speaking, whereas (136b) belongs to the *kind-oriented mode* of speaking. Roughly, in the kind-oriented mode, NPs that are ambiguous between a kind reading and an object reading are generally intended to be interpreted at the kind level. Although the kind-oriented mode of speaking in (136b) sounds rather odd at first sight, we have already pointed to examples in which it is perfectly natural to talk in this mode, namely (134) and the

44. Compare the discussion in Grice & Code 1979 (and in Code 1985, 1986), who also use **IS** for this sort of relation, and use what they call **HAS** for a somewhat different one. They are explicating Aristotle, but it seems nonetheless that their **IS**-relation is quite similar to ours, in that it relates items within a given hierarchy. The **HAS**-relation relates items from different hierarchies, as in *Callicles is pale,* which is analyzed as **HAS(callicles,paleness).** On the semantics of the unusual notion of identity in Artisotle, see Pelletier 1979.

examples of the avant-garde interpretation and the representative object interpretation given in (124f,g).

Considering the nature of the data, it seems futile to look for hard grammatical criteria that determine when we can use the kind-oriented mode. Instead, the criteria we expect to find will have a more pragmatic flavor. For example, when we do not care about the object-level identity of the objects, as in the sentence *We filmed the grizzly in Alaska,* we can (and often will) choose to talk in the kind-oriented mode. If we *do* care about object-level identity, then we have to switch to the more fine-grained object-oriented mode.

The "default" mode surely is the object-oriented mode.[45] The reason probably is that this mode is more informative and versatile. It is more informative as it provides the hearer with "quantitative information." It is more versatile as it allows for anaphoric reference to the same object, and not only to the same kind. For example, in (136a) it is said that one gorilla, one street, and one pub are involved in the reported event, and it is possible to refer back to the same objects later, say, in *He found that it was closed.* In (136b), on the other hand, it is unclear how many individual men, hats, streets, and pubs are involved, and it would be impossible to refer explicitly to the same objects in later discourse. To sum up: there are pragmatic reasons why we normally choose the object-oriented mode, and there are also pragmatic reasons why we sometimes deviate from this default and choose the kind-oriented mode.

Some facts suggest that there is variation between languages and speech communities in their readiness to choose the kind-oriented mode. An important test case is the use of noun incorporation. In many languages, a syntactic object can occur in two forms; either as a separate phrase or incorporated into the verbal predicate. According to Mithun's survey of noun incorporation (Mithun 1984), kind-referring nouns, nouns which do not introduce a discourse referent, and nouns which do not refer to salient entities in a discourse are normally incorporated (in those languages that make use of incorporation). Furthermore, the incorporated nouns must be syntactically simple; typically, they consist only of a noun stem. One might argue from this that incorporated nouns refer to kinds, and that noun incorporation is a syntactic device to stay in the kind-oriented mode.

Mithun observes that anaphoric reference to incorporated nouns is at least strongly disfavored. Unfortunately, she does not discuss anaphoric reference to kinds; but we might consider some data from German, a language in which

45. At least in the cultures and languages we are familiar with. Perhaps science fiction stories can make us believe that there are other possibilities; and we regularly hear of tales from "pop" anthropology describing cultures and languages that do not view object-oriented talk as primary.

noun incorporation is not infrequent. Here we find that with the incorporated nouns, anaphoric reference to objects *is* blocked indeed, whereas anaphoric reference to kinds is still possible.

(137) a. Hans fuhr Mercedes$_i$. *Er$_i$ war grau. / Das$_i$ ist ein zuverlässiger Wagen.
'Hans drove Mercedes$_i$. *It$_i$ was gray. / That$_i$ is a reliable car.'
b. Hans fuhr einen Mercedes$_i$. Er$_i$ war grau.
'Hans drove a Mercedes$_i$. It$_i$ was gray.'

The noun *Mercedes* in (137a) is incorporated, even though this is not reflected in the orthography. (For example, it is a bare word stem which cannot be expanded to a phrase—e.g., **Hans fuhr schnellen Mercedes;* this is a clear sign of incorporation (Baker 1988).) If indeed noun incorporation indicates the kind-oriented mode, then languages which noun-incorporate heavily are languages which employ this kind-oriented mode more extensively than (for example) English does.

1.3.6. Kind Reference in Characterizing Sentences

In this section, we will look at sentences which exhibit both types of genericity at the same time, that is, both kind reference and characterizing predication. One set of examples consists of sentences with kind-referring NPs in the characterizing property interpretation, such as (124c). In them, both types of genericity—kind-referring NPs and characterizing predication—occur simultaneously. With the introduction of the **IS**-relation, we are in a position to tackle this problem. The general solution will be to assume that there is a variable which **IS** the kind the NP refers to. This is not simply an ad hoc rule invoked only for this purpose, because the same analysis is in effect with ordinary proper names. Consider the following examples:

(138) a. Simba roars when he smells food.
GEN[x,s;]**IS**(x,**Simba**) & x **smells food in** s; x **roars in** s)
= **GEN**[x,s;](x = **Simba** & x **smells food in** s; x **roars in** s)
b. The lion roars when it smells food.
GEN[x,s;](**IS**(x,**Leo leo**) & x **smells food in** s; x **roars in** s)
i) = **GEN**[x,s;](**R**(x,**Leo leo** & x **smells food in** s; x **roars in** s)
or: ii) = **GEN**[x,s;](x = **Leo leo** & x **smells food in** s; x **roars in** s)

Since *Simba* refers to an object, in (138a), the **IS**-relation reduces to ordinary identity. On the other hand, *the lion* in (138b) refers to the kind *Leo leo,* so the relation **IS** can be either the realization relation R or the identity relation, depending on whether x refers to an object or to a kind.

In the second interpretation of (138b), (138b,ii), where x refers to a kind, the predications 'x smells food in s' and 'x roars in s' of course have to be understood in the kind-oriented mode of speaking. And this in turn allows for situations s in which the lions that are smelling the food are different from the lions that roar. That this is indeed a possible meaning of the generic sentence (138b) can be verified by considering the scenario in which lions live in packs, the more sensitive females smell the food, but only the oldest male has the right to roar. Sentence (138b) might be uttered to describe this scenario. (But due to our tendency to avoid the kind-oriented mode, this interpretation is chosen only very rarely.)

Under our analysis, sentence (138b) in its interpretation (138b.i) is quite similar in meaning to (139):

(139) A lion roars when it smells food.
GEN[x,s;](x **is a lion** & x **smells food in** s; x **roars in** s)

The only difference between the representations concerns what the values of x can be. In (139) x has to be a single lion. But under the reasonable assumption that groups, or sum individuals, can stand in the **R**-relationship to kinds as well as ordinary individuals can,[46] the x in (138b.i) could also be a group of lions.[47] This leads us to conclude that our set of objects *does* contain sum individuals, and that the predicate use of the bare plural NP *lions* applies to sum individuals of lions—including single lions as a limiting case. We would then predict that *the lion* (in its kind-referring interpretation) patterns more closely with *lions* (in its kind-referring interpretation) than with *a lion*. This is indeed borne out: *the lion* and *lions* allow for collective predicates like *gather near acacia trees*, whereas *a lion* does not allow for those predicates (Gerstner 1979).

(140) a. *A lion gathers near acacia trees when it is tired.
GEN[x,s;y](x **is a lion** & x **is tired in** s; y **are acacia trees** & x **gathers near** y **in** s)

46. The assumption is reasonable, at least given example (134), where *the lion* refers to a group of three lions.

47. The similarity between (138b.i) and (139) is already predicted in fact by our earlier description of the relation between predicative and kind uses. Accepting the plausibility of defining δ_p as $\lambda x[\mathbf{R}(x,\delta_\kappa)]$ (that is, as the set of objects which realize the kind δ_k), and also the plausibility of defining the kind-referring use in terms of the predicative use (so that δ_κ equals $\iota x \forall y[\delta_p(y) \leftrightarrow \mathbf{R}(y,x)]$—that kind of which every object in the extension of δ_p is a realization), amounts to predicting the noted similarity between these sentences.

b. Lions gather near acacia trees when they are tired.
GEN [x,s;y](x **are lions** & x **is tired in** s; y **are acacia trees** & x **gathers near** y **in** s)

c. The lion gathers near acacia trees when it is tired.
GEN[x,s;y](**R**(x **Leo leo**) & x **is tired in** s; y **are acacia trees** & x **gathers near** y **in** s)

The fact is that whenever the predicate *gather* can be felicitously applied to an x, that x must be a group of individuals. The reason that (140a) is ruled out is that x cannot refer to a group of individuals in such a scenario. Examples (140b,c) are good, in contrast, because the value of x *can* be a group of individuals in these cases. As we said, this is our reason for assuming that bare plural NPs can apply to groups and that the realization relation **R** can have groups in its domain. (In passing, note that (140b) also has a second interpretation, similar to the one in (140c), as *lions* may refer to the kind *Leo leo* as well.)

It may seem problematic to allow that not only single entities, but also sum individuals may stand in the **R**-relation to kinds, given examples like the ones in (141) below (from Hinrichs 1985). It might seem as though (141a) ought to be true if we allow sum individuals—whereas it is intuitively false, and it might seem as though (141b) would be false for a sum individual—although it is intuitively true.

(141) a. The lion has bushy tails.
GEN[x;y](**R**(x, **Leo leo**); y **are bushy tails** & x **has** y)

b. The lion has a bushy tail.
GEN[x;](**R**(x,**Leo leo**); **DST**(λz∃y[y **is a bushy tail** & z **has** y)])(x))

However, we can explain why the intuitive truth values result, even if we allow sum individuals to be specimens of kinds. The answer has to do with verbal predicates being distributive. Recall from section 1.2.3 that the **DST**-operator distributes the basic predicate to atomic entities. When x refers to an atomic entity, the **DST** operator will simply apply the verbal predicate to that entity. So (141b) gets the intuitively correct interpretation. (141a), on the other hand, is bad because x might refer to an atomic entity, and in that case there is no corresponding y to which the predicate *are bushy tails* applies—there is only a y of which *is a bushy tail* holds.

This explanation is at odds with a theory developed by Kleiber (1990) to explain certain differences between definite singular and definite plural generic NPs in French. His observations carry over to English:

a. The bobcats avoid each other.
The armadillos are numerous in Texas.
b. *The bobcat avoids each other.
*The armadillo is numerous in Texas.

According to Kleiber, the explanation for these differences is that singular definite NPs are mass-noun-like; it is for this reason that they shun reciprocals and predicates like *be numerous*. But if that's so, then we should not expect there to be distributive readings either, because distributing terms also don't combine with mass nouns (consider the oddness of *The cattle has a bushy tail*). So, we need some other explanation of these phenomena. Our conclusion is that the (b)-examples violate a ''formal'' constraint each rather than a semantic or conceptual one: reciprocals require plural antecedents, and the predicate *be numerous* requires a plural subject. Indeed, we find that these constraints *can* be violated without any conceptual difficulty, as in the following attested German example:

> Der Deutsche ist ja selbst ein Ausländer, jedenfalls, behandelt er sich gegenseitig so.
> 'The German himself is a foreigner, at least he treats one another like that.'

Coming at the problem from the opposite direction, we find that singular collective NPs that semantically *should* allow for reciprocals and predicates like *be numerous* in fact resist them, as seen in **The family hates each other* and **The family is numerous,* adding evidence to the assumption of a purely ''formal'' morphological restriction rather than any semantic or conceptual restriction.

In section 1.2.4 we noted that although there do not exist sentences like (142a) below, examples like (142b) may be found. The **IS**-relation helps us explain this. Consider the following contrast (for simplicity, we treat *have a mane* as a one-place predicate):

(142) a. *Simba has a mane when it is male.
GEN[x;](x **Is Simba** & x **is male;** x **has a mane**)
= **GEN**[x;y](x = **Simba** & x **is male;** x **has a mane**)
b. The lion has a mane when it is male.
GEN[x;y](x **IS Leo leo** & x **is male;** x **has a mane**)
= **GEN**[x;y](x **R Leo leo** & x **is male;** x **has a mane**)

We argued in section 1.2.4 that the reason why a sentence of the type in (142a) is bad is that it fails to be a proper generalization, since the variable x is ''tied to just one individual'' and there is no other variable over which we are generalizing. The situation is different in (142b), where x is not "tied to just one individual" but ranges over all realizations of the kind **Leo leo,** that is, over all lions. This is our explanation of why object-referring specific NPs and kind-referring specific NPs behave differently in characterizing sentences of this sort.

Another case of "mixed" genericity can be constructed with indefinite nouns in their taxonomic interpretation. Since taxonomic nouns are predicates true of kinds, we should be able to construct characterizing sentences with them, that is, sentences which are both characterizing and kind-referring at the same time. This is indeed possible, as already shown with the examples in (31) (section 1.1.4). Consider the following:

(143) A bird flies. (cf: 'One bird flies'.)

This sentence has at least two readings: It may claim that any individual bird typically flies, which would be a 'nonspecific' reading; or it may claim (though not everyone gets this reading easily) that an individual bird species typically flies—that is, the species will have specimens that fly—which would be a 'specific' reading. The first interpretation is a generalization over individual birds, and the second one is a generalization over bird species. These two interpretations follow from the possible interpretations of the count noun *bird,* which can apply either to individual birds or to bird species. Our method generates the following two representations:

(143′) a. **GEN**[x,s;](x **is a bird** & **in** s; x **flies in** s)
b. **GEN**[x;](x **is a bird species;** x **flies**)

In the first case, *flies* has to be interpreted as an episodic predicate, as it is related to a situation s. In the second case, *flies* must be interpreted as a predicate with a kind-referring subject, x, in the characterizing property interpretation (an instantiation would be, for example, *The robin flies*). As we have seen, sentences in the characterizing property interpretation can be spelled out with the help of the **IS**-relation. Therefore we can transform (143′b) into the following equivalent representations:

(143′) b. i) **GEN**[x;](x **is a bird species; GEN** [y,s;](**IS**(y,x) & y **in** s; y **flies in** s))
ii) **GEN**[x;](x **is a bird species; GEN**[y,s;](**R**(y,x) & y **in** s; y **flies in** s))

(At least they are equivalent formulas if we disregard the arcane possibility that x = y). Here we have another case of a nested **GEN**-operator. The formula says that for the usual bird species x, it will usually fly, that is, for the typical specimen y of x in a normal situation s, y will usually fly in s.

1.3.7. Notions, Concepts, and Other Pseudo-Kinds

In this subsection we discuss several cases that look like kind-referring NPs at first sight, but, as we will ultimately conclude, refer to something else after all. Let us start with examples of the following type, which were discussed (for French) by Corblin (1987) and Kleiber (1990):

(144) In medieval times, the child didn't exist.

This constitutes a problem, as an NP like *the child* does not occur as a kind-referring term in many other contexts. For example, a sentence like *The child is demanding* does not sound very good (in the kind-referring interpretation), even though it would be considered true if *the child* were to refer to a kind. We follow here the explanation of Kleiber (1990), who proposed that *the child* in (144) does not refer to a kind at all, but to something we will call a *notion,* and that can (144) can be paraphrased as 'In medieval times, people didn't have the notion of 'child'.' One test that distinguishes notion-referring NPs from regular kind-referring NPs is that they can be replaced by constructions like *the notion of . . .* , or *the concept of . . .* , which is not possible for kind-referring NPs. It seems that only singular definite NPs can refer to notions; in (144) we cannot replace *the child* by *children,* or *the children,* without distorting its meaning.

Reference to notions is certainly interesting in its own right, especially the problem of separating it from reference to words themselves. But it is not a case of kind-reference, and we will not be concerned with it any further here.

Consider now the difference between singular definite NPs and plural definite NPs. At first sight, it seems that plural definite NPs can act as kind-referring NPs as well, since examples like (145) seem to have a natural reading:

(145) The dinosaurs are extinct.

However, plural definite NPs differ in several respects from singular definite NPs (see Kleiber 1990 for an extensive survey on French). Most importantly, they are not restricted to well-established kinds.

(146) a. The lions that have toothaches are particularly dangerous.
b. ?The lion that has toothaches is particularly dangerous.

In chapter 11 of this volume, Krifka develops a theory that assumes, in addition to kinds the designation of nominalizations of "well-established" predicates), also what we might call *concepts* (which are the designation of nominalizations of arbitrary predicates).

Another case of NPs that at first look to be kind-referring, but in fact are not, can be seen in examples like the following:

(147) a. The nose is in the center of the face.
b. The meat is more expensive than the vegetables.

According to Kleiber (1981, 1990), the subjects in these examples are not kind-referring, but instead are "dependent" definite NPs. The examples express generalizations over certain entities or situation types: faces in (147a) and meals, perhaps, in (147b)—where for each such entity or situation there is a unique object that can be denoted by *the nose* or *the meat*. (See also Link, this volume, for a discussion of cases of "dependency.")

Furthermore, we have seen that in Spanish, the definite article may be used as an indication that the NP occurs in the restrictor of the generic operator (see the end of section 1.2.5, where we discussed Laca's (1990) treatment of sentences such as *Los arquitectos construyen las casas* 'Architects build houses'). Again, this is not a case of a kind-referring use of definite NPs; the NP itself should be analyzed as semantically indefinite, the definite article being only something like a "theme marker." There seem to be similar cases in other Romance languages, such as Romanian (as Ileana Comorovski informs us) and French; consider the following example of Kleiber's (1990):

(148) Le chien qui aboie ne mord pas.

Here *le chien qui aboie* should not be understood as designating a kind; after all, this NP contains an episodic predicate, which we already know not to designate a kind. We capture the meaning of (148) better if we translate it as a characterizing sentence with an indefinite subject (or with a bare plural subject with the same meaning):

(148′) a. A dog that barks doesn't bite.
b. Barking dogs don't bite.

These both are to be represented as characterizing sentences, with the definite article of (148) serving only to indicate that the predicate *dog* is in the restrictor of the characterizing sentence:

(148″) **GEN**[x,s;] (x **is a dog** & x **barks in** s: ¬x **bites in** s)

1.4. FURTHER ISSUES

In sections 1.2 and 1.3, we discussed the essential properties of characterizing sentences and kind-referring NPs. In this final section we will take up some subjects that we had set aside in order to simplify the discussion of those central topics. We will not offer any detailed discussion of the various analytic options available with the issues raised below, nor do we have any fixed position about them that we wish to advocate. Rather, these issues are merely laid out and their resolution is left to the readers and to future research.

1.4.1. Quantificational Predicates

Some readers may be wondering why we have not mentioned such verbal predicates as *be widespread, be common, be abundant, be rare,* and *be scarce*. In the literature, these predicates are normally treated as kind-selecting predicates, on a par with *be extinct* or *be invented* (see, e.g., Carlson 1977b). These predicates are different from kind predicates, however, in that some of them can be combined with indefinite noun phrases without forcing a taxonomic reading. This is borne out in the following examples:

(149) a. The rhino will become extinct soon.
b. Rhinos will become extinct soon.
c. *A rhino will become extinct soon. (only taxonomic reading O.K.)

(150) a. The rhino is common.
b. Rhinos are common.
c. A rhino is common. (nontaxonomic reading)

Example (150c) is not acceptable for all speakers; the parallel (152b) below is more universally accepted. Furthermore, verbal predicates such as *be common* can easily be combined with subjects which do not refer to well-established kinds, unlike the classic kind-selecting predicates (as before, we assume here that rhinos with blue eyes do not constitute some special type of rhino, but rather that this is a truly accidental, hit-or-miss property of rhinos):

(151) a. *Rhinos with blue eyes will become extinct soon.
b. *A rhino with blue eyes will become extinct soon.

(152) a. Rhinos with blue eyes are common.
b. A rhino with blue eyes is cómmon.
c. *A rhino with blue eyes is widespread.

These examples indicate that predicates of the class of *be common* (in contrast to *be widespread,* as indicated in (152c)) should not be treated as ordinary kind predicates, because they lack the selectional restriction that says they may only apply to kinds. On the other hand, sentences with predicates such as *be common* can't be analyzed as characterizing sentences either. For one thing, sentences such as *Rhinos are common* or *The rhino is common* express generalizations for the kind Rhino rather than for individual rhinos or groups of rhinos. Furthermore, insertion of adverbial quantifiers, such as *always* and *usually,* leads to a drastic change in meaning, as in the following sentences, which can only be understood on a taxonomic reading of the subject NP:

a. Rhinos are always/usually common.
b. A rhino is always/usually common.

Also, predicates such as *be common* cannot be applied to ordinary individuals at all, as in **Simba is common,* contrary to predicates of characterizing sentences.

How, then, should we analyze such predicates as *be common?* Consider the sentence *A rhino (with blue eyes) is common.* It does not express a property of a specific rhino, nor does it express a generalization over individual rhinos. Instead its meaning is 'The chance of encountering a (blue-eyed) rhino is high', that is, it is a statement about the distribution of rhinos. It seems most natural then to analyze such predicates as extensional second-order predicates, that is, as predicates which can be applied to such first-order predicates (NPs) as *a rhino.*

Such an analysis of predicates like *be common* would be similar to the analysis of quantified noun phrases (such as *every rhino*) found in generalized quantifier theory (see Barwise & Cooper 1981, Westerståhl 1989). In this theory, quantifiers such as *every* are analyzed as two-place relations between sets, and quantified noun phrases are analyzed as second-order predicates which are applied to verbal predicates. A sentence such as *Every rhino yawned* is true if and only if the set of rhinos is a subset of the set of yawning entities. In generalized quantifier theory, a quantifier is dependent upon a universe of quantification, M. The interpretation of most natural language quantifiers does not depend on the size of M (see the "extension" postulate in Westerståhl 1989, sec. 3.2). There are some natural-language quantifiers, however, which do seem to depend on M. One example proposed in the literature is the context-dependent interpretation of *many* and *few* (Westerståhl 1985, 1989). A sentence like *Many A's are B* is true in case the number of A's which are B exceeds some fraction of the cardinality of the universe. For example, in a universe of 10 entities, 5 may count as many, but not in a universe of 1,000 entities. Clearly, this fraction cannot be given a fixed value because *many* (and *few*) are vague.

Returning now to predicates such as *be common:* it seems natural to analyze these predicates in a manner similar to that applied to quantified NPs such as *many rhinos* or *few rhinos,* where the interpretation depends on the size of the universe or on the frequency of occurrence in the universe of the elements described by the subject predicate. For this reason we shall call such predicates *quantificational.* However, they differ from quantificational NPs, especially syntactically. Syntactically, these verbal predicates cannot be decomposed into a quantifier and another predicate (unlike, say, *many rhinos,* which can be decomposed into *many* and *rhinos*). Furthermore, they are applied to a nominal predicate (unlike quantificational NPs, which are applied to a verbal predicate).[48] Semantically, however, quantificational predicates such as *be common* depend on the universe of quantification in a manner similar to that of the interpretations of *many* and *few* as indicated above.[49]

Up to now, we have taken for granted a universe M which is accessible to the interpretation of quantificational predicates. The choice of universe is often left open, that is, it must be inferred from the context. But it can also be linguistically specified, most typically by a locational or temporal phrase as in (154). This is true for quantified sentences in general, as shown in (155):

(154) a. Rhinos are rare in the Serengeti.
b. Two hundred years ago, rhinos were common.
c. Water is rare in the Kalahari.

(155) a. Many rhinos were killed in the Serengeti.
b. Two hundred years ago, few rhinos were killed.
c. This summer, little water was used.

The analysis of quantificational predicates must be refined in other respects as well. For example, in *be common,* as well was in the similar *be widespread,* there is a meaning component implying that one can come across the entities in question at many places all over the universe; a sentence such as *Rhinos are common in Africa* seems to be false in case there are many rhinos in Africa, but all of them gathered at a single place, say, in the Ngorongoro crater. Therefore, a proper formulation of quantificational predicates such as *be common* or *be widespread* would need some topological component. (Moltmann 1991 discusses these types of quantifiers, which she calls "metrical quantifiers," also suggesting the need for a topological component).

48. They may not be the only quantifiers of this type; for example, one could analyze the existential predicates *there is* and *there are* similarly as quantificational predicates which must be applied to a nominal predicate.

49. Note that this makes them nonconservative in the sense of Barwise and Cooper (1981): we need information about the whole universe to evaluate a sentence like *A rhino is common.*

An interesting case of interaction of quantificational predicates with kind reference can be seen with the following examples, due to Barbara Partee:

(156) a. Endangered species are common.
b. Endangered species are rare.

In one reading, the most natural one, (156a) says that there are many endangered species, or that the frequency of endangered species in the universe is greater than some limit. Such sentences presuppose a Platonic universe with kinds as entities. On this reading (156a) is perfectly consistent with (156b), on the reading of the latter that it is typical for an endangered species to be rare (that is, to have few specimens). Of course, the truth conditions of this reading of (156b) must be checked with respect to the universe of objects, not of kinds.

In concluding this section, we should point out that the category of quantificational predicates is larger than the few examples mentioned here might suggest. In fact, there are operators which can transform an ordinary verbal predicate into a quantificational predicate, for example *on average* (which was mentioned, e.g., by Smith 1975) or *up to* with individual-level predicates:

(157) a. The rhino weighs four tons on average.
b. Rhinos weigh four tons on average.
c. A rhino weighs four tons on average.
d. Rhinos weigh up to six tons.

We shall not explicitly formulate a semantic rule for the modifiers *on average* or *up to* here. But it should be obvious that such a rule will need the extension of the subject to determine an average value for whatever the relevant dimension for the verbal predicate may be. Therefore we must assume, again, that a complex verbal predicate, such as *weighs four tons on average,* is a second-order predicate.

1.4.2. *Any*-NPs in Characterizing Sentences

We haven't yet considered NPs with the determiner *any,* such as in (158):

(158) Any tiger is dangerous.

The relation of *any* and the so-called indefinite generic article has been discussed by Vendler (1967), Perlmutter (1970), Smith (1975), Nunberg and Pan (1975), and Burton-Roberts (1976), among others. In fact, Perlmutter (1970) derives the ''generic'' indefinite article *a* from the determiner *any.*

Two different analyses of *any* have been proposed in the "classical" literature: *any* has been analyzed as a wide-scope universal quantifier (by, e.g., Hintikka 1980) and as an indefinite determiner with certain co-occurrence restrictions (by, e.g., Ladusaw 1979). From our data we can derive an argument for the second analysis. As mentioned in section 1.2.5, nominal quantifiers can be contextually restricted, whereas this is not possible for characterizing sentences and sentences with adverbial quantifiers in general. Generic sentences with *any*-NPs clearly pattern with characterizing sentences in that they do not allow for contextual restrictions, as shown by the following examples:

(159) There were lions and tigers in the circus ring.
  a. Every lion / all lions / each lion / the lions / most lions / many lions / no lion had a mane.
  b. A lion had a mane.
  c. Lions had a mane.
  d. Any lion had a mane.

The quantificational universe of the NPs in (159a) is restricted to the lions introduced in the initial sentence. This is not possible in (159b) and (159c) if these sentences are read as characterizing sentences.[50] (Sentence (159b) can be read as a particular sentence as well, in which case *a lion* is naturally interpreted with respect to the restricted universe. The point we are making is that (159b,c) cannot be understood as characterizing sentences and simultaneously be interpreted with respect to the restricted universe.) Sentence (159d) patterns like (159b,c) in that it is not restricted to the lions which were introduced in the initial statement. Therefore, according to this argument, *any lion* should not be analyzed as a quantified NP, but as an indefinite NP similar to *a lion*.

In contrast to *a lion,* the NP *any lion* is (at least in certain instances) a *negative polarity item.* According to Ladusaw (1979), negative polarity items occur within the scope of *downward-entailing operators*. An operator is defined as downward-entailing if an expression in its scope can be replaced *salva veritate* (i.e., without affecting the truth of the sentence) with a semantically stronger expression, that is, an expression with a more restricted extension. The paradigm case of a downward-entailing context is the scope of negation:

(160) John didn't see a tiger.
  ⇒ John didn't see a female tiger.

50. To readers having difficulty interpreting (159b,c) as characterizing, we point out that we have all along given examples of characterizing sentences in the past tense (see section 1.2), and have remarked that the past tense *had* can generally be replaced by *used to have* (section 1.1.2). The characterizing reading of (159c) is the same as that of *Lions used to have a mane.*

If the first sentence of (160) is true, then the second sentence, where *tiger* has been replaced by the more restrictive expression *female tiger,* is also true. It is in these contexts that negative polarity items are acceptable, for example in *John didn't see any tigers.*

If negative polarity items only occur in downward-entailing contexts, then we should be able to show that the restrictor of the **GEN**-operator is a downward-entailing context, since negative polarity items such as *any*-NPs may be found there. As we remarked in section 1.2.2, characterizing sentences can be analyzed as a special type of conditional sentences where the restrictor corresponds to the protasis (i.e., the antecedent):

(161) a. A tiger has orange fur, marked with black stripes.
b. If something is a tiger, it has orange fur, marked with black stripes.
GEN[x;](x **is a tiger;** x **has orange fur, marked with black stripes**)

Since the protasis of a conditional sentence is known to be a context which licenses negative polarity items (Ladusaw 1979)—as in *If you spot any tigers then report to the Ministry of Tourism*—we should not be surprised to find negative polarity items such as *any tiger* in the restrictor of characterizing sentences.

If being in a negative-polarity-licensing position (such as the restrictor of the **GEN**-operator) is what really allows for *any*-NPs, then we should not find them in positions which have sometimes been considered generic, namely the subjects of quantificational predicates (see section 1.4.1 above). And indeed, as noted by Smith (1975), we cannot replace an indefinite NP with an NP with the determiner *any* in these cases:

(162) a. A rhino (with three legs) is common.
b. *Any rhino (with three legs) is common.

(163) a. A rhino weighs four tons on average.
b. *Any rhino weighs four tons on average.

However, a serious theoretical problem with the downward-entailingness of the main clause of conditional sentences and the restrictor of characterizing sentences in that these contexts actually fail to be strictly downward-entailing, as demonstrated in (164):

(164) A tiger has orange fur, marked with black stripes.
a. ⇏ A female tiger has orange fur, marked with black stripes.
b. ⇏ An albino tiger has orange fur, marked with black stripes.

(Nor, for that matter, are they upward-entailing, as the reader can easily verify.) One story line we could phrase is this: The reason we cannot draw the conclusion in (164b) is that the strengthening from *tiger* to *albino tiger* introduces the more specific rule that albino animals are white, interacting with and preempting the generic rule concerning the color of tigers. Interestingly, if (165), which makes use of NPs with *any,* is true, then so are (165a,b), as well as (164a,b):

(165) Any tiger has orange fur, marked with black stripes.
  a. ⇒ Any female tiger has orange fur, marked with black stripes.
  b. ⇒ Any albino tiger has orange fur, marked with black stripes.

Heim (1984) develops a theory in which it is not *general* downward-entailingness which licenses a negative polarity item in a position, but rather downward-entailingness with respect to the position of a negative polarity item and with respect to a set of alternatives determined by the negative polarity item in question (see also Rooth 1985 and Krifka 1993). Clearly this phenomenon is also related to the nonmonotonic reasoning considerations we pursued in section 1.2.6 in trying to account for the semantics of the **GEN**-operator. We shall not pursue this topic further here, and refer the reader to the works cited in this paragraph as well as to Asher & Morreau (chapter 7, this volume).

Burton-Roberts (1976) notes some differences in acceptability between indefinite NPs and *any*-NPs in generic sentences. One of her examples is *A beaver / *Any beaver is an amphibious rodent.* The reason why the *any*-sentence sounds odd seems to be that the predicate expresses a necessary, even definitional property which holds of every beaver. But then the ''strengthening'' of *a beaver* to *any beaver* does not make much sense because the default rule held without exception in the first place. This explanation can perhaps be made more precise by assuming that a sentence with an *any*-NP is more ''complex'' than the corresponding sentence with an indefinite NP, and that, as a pragmatic maxim, the simpler expression is used if the more complex one does not differ from it in meaning. (See the more recent analysis by Kadmon and Landman (1993), which makes critical use of the notion of strengthening for the analysis of *any*.)

Nunberg and Pan (1975) try to capture the difference between *a*-NPs and *any*-NPs by assuming that the extension of the *a*-NP is restricted to individuals which are typical representatives, whereas the *any*-NP is to be understood more widely, including all the atypical cases as well. A problem with adopting this analysis is that it cannot explain why sentences such as **This is any lion* (pointing to a specific lion which is possibly not very typical for its species) are bad. (See also Kadmon & Landman 1993.)

In discussions of the treatment of English *any,* a controversial point is whether the *any* in generic sentences like *Any tiger eats meat* is "the same word" that appears in negative polarity contexts such as *I didn't see any cars on that street.* While it is commonly assumed that the most desirable analysis would unify the treatment of these two instances (the line of thought tentatively pursued above), the notion of a unitary analysis has not gone unchallenged in the literature (Carlson 1982 presents some empirical reasons to distinguish between the two); it is, furthermore, commonplace to talk descriptively about a "free-choice *any*" in opposition to a "negative polarity *any.*" When classified this way, the free-choice *any* has a distribution that is almost entirely limited to generic, as opposed to episodic, sentences, a matter emphasized by Enç (1991), while the polarity *any* may appear equally well in either.

1.4.3 Gerundives, Infinitives, and Nominalizations

In the preceding sections, we have only considered sentences with nominal arguments. However, the notion of genericity can also be applied to (sentences containing) different kinds of verb-based arguments, as already observed by Carlson (1977b). Conrad (1982) offers a survey of the relevant phenomena, and Chierchia (1982a, 1984) and Weir (1986) give a treatment in a formal semantic theory; see also Portner 1992.

There is quite a range of syntactically and morphologically different types of verb-based arguments in English (and in other languages). In English, we observe gerundives such as *driving a car* or *John's chewing tobacco,* infinitives such as *to chew tobacco* or *for John to drive a car,* and nominalizations like *the winning of the chess match.* Also, there are derived nominals such as *the resistance,* which we will not examine here.

First, we note that all these deverbal expressions may be kind-referring. This is brought out by the following examples, which combine them with a predicate that selects for kinds (the predicate nominal *a bad habit*). Here the subjects of the sentences refer to a type of event, namely, events of chewing tobacco.

(166) a. Chewing tobacco is a bad habit.
b. To chew tobacco is a bad habit.
c. The chewing of tobacco is a bad habit.

Second, we observe that they may be subjects of characterizing sentences:

(167) a. Chewing tobacco (usually) calms John down / upsets John.
b. To chew tobacco (usually) calms John down / upsets John.
c. The chewing of tobacco (usually) calms John down / upsets John.

The first versions of (167a–c) most normally assert that whenever John chews tobacco, this (usually) calms him down. We assume that the subject argument place is controlled by an NP in the main clause (here, *John*). The second versions of (167a–c) most normally assert (although the (b)-sentence might be questioned) that whenever someone chews tobacco, this (usually) upsets John. These cases are instances of so-called "arbitrary control," similar to the kind-referring cases of (166).

Finally, we have cases where gerundives and nominalizations are used to refer to a specific situation. This seems impossible for infinitives.

(168) a. Chewing tobacco calmed John down / upset John.
b. *To chew tobacco calmed John down / upset John.
c. The chewing of tobacco calmed John down / upset John.

The first version of (168a) says that a particular situation in which John chewed tobacco calmed him down. The status of (168b) is not quite clear. According to the survey of Conrad (1982), infinitives cannot refer to particular situations; however, he cites examples like *To hear her expressing it made me feel that I could hide nothing from her,* which seem to us to be commonplace.

Disregarding the issue of control (a large issue to disregard, to be sure!), these facts can be described by assuming that gerundives and infinitives behave similar to bare NPs. They have two readings. First, they have an indefinite reading in which they apply to events or situations and refer either specifically to some event (as in 168a)), or in which they are subjected to a quantificational operator like **GEN** (as in (167a,b)). Second, there is a definite reading in which they refer to a kind (which has as realizations the events of the indefinite reading); this is the case with (166a,b) and also, in a second analysis, with (167a,b). Nominalizations can be analyzed as definite NPs. In (166c) and (167c), they refer to a kind, and in (168c), they refer definitely to some event. Thus, verb-based arguments do not constitute something new; they are simply special cases of the phenomena we have analyzed above.

There is a problem with the analysis of verb-based arguments as kind-referring NPs: unlike the kind-referring NPs we have considered so far, which were related to well-established kinds, these verb-based arguments can be formed quite productively. For example, we can construe such kinds as *the trespassing of this area*. Therefore, we would probably conclude that the verb-based NPs refer to ''concepts'' (see section 1.3.8 for this wider notion). This holds even for NPs like *chewing tobacco,* which might arguably be related to a well-established kind, since the meaning of these NPs clearly is built up compositionally and hence should not be a lexical entry, like well-established kind-referring NPs.

Of course, there are important differences between gerundives, infinitives, and deverbal nominalizations—differences having to do with aspectual distinctions (gerundives and nominalizations are telic and infinitives are atelic), specify (infinitives tend to be nonspecific), or the syntactic categorization (nominalizations are NPs, whereas infinitives and gerundives are clearly verbal categories).

Up to now we have taken the verb-derived subject in its simplest analysis, namely as a predicate over events. However, this subject might itself be a generic predicate, at least in the gerundive case (see Weir 1986). One example is (169):

(169) John's chewing tobacco impresses Mary.

In addition to one generic reading saying that whenever John chews tobacco this impresses Mary, there is a second one saying that John's habitually chewing tobacco impresses Mary. Gerundives of characterizing predicates behave similar to gerundives of other stative predicates. They generally can be paraphrased by the expression *the fact that . . . ;* this implies that they refer to propositions or facts. We also note that they cannot be paraphrased by a *when*-clause if they do not contain some argument that has an open variable.

(170) a. The fact that John chews tobacco impresses Mary. (paraphrase of (169))
b. When John chews tobacco, this impresses Mary. (only the noncharacterizing reading of the *when*-clause)

(171) a. John's knowing French impresses Mary.
b. The fact that John knows French impresses Mary.
c. *When John knows French, this impresses Mary.

If we render the sentence *John chews tobacco* as

GEN[s;y,e](**John in** s; **chew**(**John**,y,e) **in** s & **tobacco**(y))

and we take ^p to refer to the proposition expressed by p, then we can give the following analysis for (169):

(169′) **impress(^GEN[s;y,e](John in** s; **chew(John,**y,e) **in** s & **tobacco**(y)), **Mary**)

This says that Mary is impressed by the proposition that John habitually chews tobacco. Of course, a more detailed semantic analysis would also express that it is presupposed that John chews tobacco. (See also Zucchi 1990.)

1.4.4. Generic Anaphora

We will briefly discuss generic anaphora.[51] Consider the following examples:

(172) a. John killed a $spider_i$ because $they_i$ are ugly.
b. John didn't keep a $spider_i$ because $they_i$ are ugly.

The natural reading of the second clause of (172a,b) is that generally, spiders are ugly. *They* should be analyzed as referring to a kind (see Carlson 1977b and Webber 1978, who assume that *they* refers to a "generic class"). For example, *they* in this configuration allows for the interpretations typical for kind-referring NPs, such as the representative object reading in *John killed the spider because they once frightened his girlfriend.* Generic anaphora of this sort can be explained if one assumes that an NP composed of a common noun always introduces the kind that is associated with the common noun into the discourse. (See, e.g., Webber 1978, Frey & Kamp 1986, and Root 1986. See also ter Meulen, this volume, for another discussion of similar sentences.)

In the examples we have so far considered, the generic pronoun is plural. But it can also be singular, as in (173a). If the antecedent is plural, as in (173b), the pronoun must be plural as well. In the case of a mass noun antecedent, given in (173c), the pronoun has to be singular.

(173) a. John found a $dodo_i$, although it_i was believed to be extinct.
b. John found some $dodos_i$ although $they_i$ were / $*it_i$ is believed to be extinct.
c. John drank some $milk_i$ even though he's allergic to it_i/$*them_i$.

These facts can be explained via certain interacting principles. The first principle is that a plural NP can refer to a kind if the kind is denoted by a count noun, as in (173b) (cf. the use of bare plurals as kind-referring terms), but not if it is denoted by a mass noun, as in (173c). This allows for *they* to refer to a kind like *Raphus Cucullatus,* since this kind is denoted by the count noun *dodo,* but it excludes that *they* could refer to a kind like *Lac* since this is denoted by the mass noun *milk.* The second principle concerns agreement; it

51. See ter Meulen (this volume) for a more comprehensive and slightly different treatment.

says that if the antecedent is plural—that is, has a marked agreement feature—then the pronoun must bear the same feature. This excludes the use of *it* in (173b) to refer to *dodos*. The third principle says that in cases where a singular pronoun would be ambiguous as to reference to an individual entity or to the kind, a plural pronoun will be chosen to refer to the kind. But if it is clear for other reasons that the pronoun refers to the kind, for example because it is an argument of a kind predicate as in (173a), then singular pronouns are also allowed. The third principle, then, serves to disambiguate between different readings.

Another phenomenon which is related to generic anaphora is indefinite pronouns such as *one* and *some,* or German *ein-* and *welch-*, as in the following examples:[52]

(174) a. John saw a spider$_i$, and Mary saw one$_i$, too.
b. John bought milk$_i$, and Mary bought some$_i$, too.

(175) a. Otto sah eine Spinne$_i$, and Anna sah auch eine$_i$.
b. Otto kaufte Milch$_i$, und Anna kaufte auch welche$_i$.

Indefinite pronouns can be analyzed as *referring* to a kind which is introduced in the preceding context, and as *introducing* a realization of this kind.[53] Thus, although they are indefinite expressions, they share some referential properties with definite expressions.

Finnish offers an interesting case of indefinite pronouns; in that language it is possible to distinguish between reference to a group and reference to a kind, by using pronouns in the elative or partitive case, respectively (I. Alho, pers.comm.):

(176)	Markku tuntee kymmemem lingvistiä,	(a)	heistä	kuusi
	Mark knows ten linguists		them.ELATIVE	six.ACC
	ja Fred tuntee	(b)	heitä	kuusi
	and Fred knows		them.PARTITIVE	six.ACC

'Mark knows ten linguists, and Fred knows { (a) six of those ten. / (b) six of them, i.e., six linguists. }

Let us now turn to indefinite generic NPs. First, there are cases in which indefinite generic NPs can be antecedents of anaphora (note that the opening sentence of (177) is a characterizing sentence):

(177) A lion$_i$ is a ferocious beast. It$_i$ has huge claws.

52. See also van Langendonck 1980a for French and Dutch examples.
53. See Webber 1978 for a similar account.

There are two ways this example can be interpreted. First, if we assume that the indefinite NP *a lion* is the antecedent of *it,* then we must explain how it is possible that an indefinite NP in a quantificational structure (which is what we assume it to be in the first sentence of (177)) can be related to a pronoun outside of the scope of this quantification. One answer might be to claim that, actually, the pronoun is not outside the scope at all, but that the second sentence has to be interpreted with respect to the restrictor introduced by the first one. That is, in interpreting the second sentence, one must be able to "look into" the first one. There are different ways this can be done. One option was investigated as *modal subordination* by Roberts (1987); another was investigated as *context change semantics* by Schubert and Pelletier (1989). But we also can take another route and claim instead that the indefinite NP *a lion,* even in these characterizing sentences, introduces a kind just as the indefinite NPs discussed above did—and it is this kind which the pronoun picks up.

Another interesting piece of behavior of generic indefinites was identified by Postal (1970) and Wasow (1972). Contrary to other indefinite NPs and to quantificational NPs, generic indefinites allow for backwards anaphora:

(178) If he_i can't afford to rent an entire house, then a new faculty $member_i$ should rent a simple room to save money.

Heim (1982, 226) suggests a special rule that says that indefinites have widest scope with respect to the generic operator. Essentially then, (178) would not be analyzed as containing two generic sentences, one embedded in the other as in (179a), but rather only one, as in (179b).

(179) a. **GEN**($\neg\Diamond$ x **affords to rent entire house; GEN** (x **is a new faculty member;** x **should rent a simple room to save money**)
b. **GEN**($\neg\Diamond$ x **affords to rent entire house** & x **is a new faculty member;** x **should rent a simple room to save money**)

One way or another we have to construct the restrictor using the *if*-clause and the generic indefinite NP. The details of this are quite unclear.

1.4.5. Natural and Nominal Kinds, and the Establishment of Kinds

We have analyzed kinds as a special sort of individual and kind-referring NPs as names of kinds. The semantics of proper names and of natural kind terms forms an important topic of discussion in modern works in philosophy of language, including Donnellan 1966, 1972, Putnam 1970, 1975, and Kripke 1972, among others. In this section we want to recapitulate this discussion and ask whether the basic conceptual distinctions developed in it are relevant to a linguistic treatment of kind reference. For reasons of space, the summary of the philosophical discussion will be quite sketchy; for a more detailed overview, the reader is referred to the introduction of Schwartz 1977 and to Salmon 1989.

According to the semantic framework accepted as standard since the time of Frege, there is a distnction between the *sense* (or *intension*) and the *denotation* (or *extension*) of an expression. The sense can be seen as something like a "conceptual description" which serves to pick out the denotation; for example, the sense of the phrase *the author of "Der Mann ohne Eigenschaften"* is some conceptual description which picks out the man Robert Musil (in the actual world). According to this standard, Fregean ("descriptional") view, every designating expression has both an intension and an extension; hence proper names like *Robert Musil* have them too. This leads to problems, however. To begin with, it is not obvious what should count as a valid conceptual description for a proper name. We could choose some arbitrary identifying properties—for example, we could give *Robert Musil* the sense *the author of "Der Mann ohne Eigenschaften,"* or maybe the sense *the winner of the Kleist award in 1923,* or some conjunction or cluster of such properties. But then we could never be sure whether people are talking about the same individual, since the identifying properties a speaker connects with a name may differ between speakers, and the standard view takes it that a necessary condition for "talking about the same entity" is to use the same intension or sense. And even if speakers agree on some prominent properties, there remain problems. For example, if we take *the author of "Der Mann ohne Eigenschaften"* as the defining property of the name *Robert Musil,* then the sentence *Robert Musil is the author of "Der Mann ohne Eigenschaften"* becomes a necessary truth, which is obviously not the case—Robert Musil could have decided not to write that novel. A related problem in such theories is that the denotation of a name is world-dependent. For example, if we take the sense of *Robert Musil* to be *the winner of the Kleist award in 1923*, then *Robert Musil* would pick out Franz Kafka in those possible worlds where the Kleist award was conferred on Franz Kafka in 1923.

For reasons such as these, Kripke (1972) and others proposed a *nondescriptional* theory of meaning for proper names, with the central tenet that proper names refer directly to entities, without a mediating descriptive concept. For example, the name *Robert Musil* directly refers to the person Robert Musil. Consequently, speakers have to rely on something other than conceptual descriptions in order to be sure they are talking about the same individual when using a proper name. The basic assumption, in the most common variants of this new view, is that when using a proper name, $speaker_1$ refers to the same individual as $speaker_2$ who first acquainted him_1 with that individual under that name. And this transmittal process might be traced back until we get to speakers with firsthand experience. For example, a speaker may associate the name *Robert Musil* with the person who is referred to by the term *Robert Musil* in some history of German literature; and the author of that history might associate the name with the person called *Robert Musil* by Adolf Frisé (Musil's editor), who in turn may have firsthand knowledge of Musil, having met the author in his Swiss exile. This is called the *causal theory of reference,* because reference is fixed by causal links of acquaintance, and the first or fundamental use of a certain name to refer to a person or object called a "baptism". Note that the causal theory of reference essentially embodies an equivalence relation, since it assumes that a speaker using a proper name refers to the same individual as another speaker using that proper name.

Names of kinds often behave similarly to proper names, a point which was brought forward by Kripke and especially by Putnam. A famous example concerns the kind name *gold.* We cannot reduce the meaning of *gold* to a list of necessary conceptual descriptions. For example, if we were to assume that *a yellow metal* is one of gold's necessary descriptions, it could turn out that this coloration is an optical illusion or caused by ever-present impurities. But even in such a case, we would still be referring to the same substance as *gold* refers to.[54] One might be tempted to think that some "better" conceptual description would work. Perhaps a better candidate would be *the chemical element with atomic number 79.* But note that *gold* was used to refer to gold before science found this property, which we today consider to be essential. Also, the sentence *Gold is the element with atomic number 79* would be an analytical truth, although its truth was, in fact, a scientific discovery. Furthermore, using this meaning of *gold* we would never know whether we were talking about the same stuff as people in the last century, for whom other properties were essential.

The gist of the nondescriptional theory for kind terms is that we use kind terms to refer to the things that are "the same as" some things considered to be *paradigms* of the kind, and not to whatever happens to satisfy a certain description. Therefore we have two essential components for the semantics of natural kind terms: some sort of equivalence relation (embodied in "the same as") and some sort of indexical relation (embodied in the reference to paradigm cases).

54. Actually, pure gold is *not* yellow.

The problems now are (i) to determine the nature of the equivalence relation, and (ii) to determine the nature of the paradigms. The nature of the paradigms might seem to be the easier question to answer: any exemplar should do—any quantum of gold, any lion. But of course, this is not quite right: the exemplars have to be *prototypical* and may not be "abnormal" or "exceptional." As for the equivalence relation, we can distinguish among, and make use of, several criteria. For chemical elements like gold, the current view is that the essential criteria is the number of protons in the atomic nucleus. For biological species such as *Leo tigris,* the tiger, we came to agree upon criteria such as capability of inbreeding (which reflects similarities on the DNA level). For languages, we came to agree upon criteria such as mutual comprehensibility. For diseases, we often use common causes, like infection with the same virus. For chairs, we can have functional criteria such as the intended use of the object. For more culturally determined items such as music, we would have to take into consideration a criterion like function in society. (There might be a tribe that claps hands at certain social occasions, and although this doesn't count as music in familiar western and eastern societies, it might nonetheless perform the same social function in this tribe's society as music does in ours, and for that reason we might wish to refer to it by the kind term *music*.)

We can combine the nondescriptional view with our earlier formalization by claiming that for any object x and any kind y, the fact that x is a realization of y can be traced back to the existence of a paradigm x′ of y and an equivalence relation between x and x′. If we have a predicate $\mathbf{PARADIGM}_y$ which applies to paradigm cases of a kind, and a relation '$\approx_y$' which is the relevant equivalence relation for the kind y, we can define the realization relation **R** for kinds as follows:

(180) $y \in \text{KIND} \rightarrow [\mathbf{R}(x,y) \leftrightarrow \exists x'[\mathbf{PARADIGM}_y(x') \;\&\; x \approx_y x']]$

There might be variations and historical changes in both conjuncts on the righthand side of the definition of **R,** that is, both in the relevant equivalence relation and in the relevant-paradigm cases. A good example is the somewhat recent conceptual separation of the kind *fish* into the kinds *whales* and *fish* (proper). Here, the older equivalence relation (which had to do with shape and place of living) got replaced by another one (genetic similarity), and the new paradigm cases were chosen such that they belong to the class *fish* (proper). Putnam (1975) argues that we can employ different equivalence criteria in different contexts; for example, a plastic lemon can be called *lemon* in certain contexts, although it surely fails to be species-equivalent to paradigm cases of lemons: In general, the type of equivalence relation we choose is likely to be determined by the classification of kinds; for example, we use the atomic number for *gold* because gold is an element, and we use genetic similarity for *fish* because fish are animals.

There are two concepts of natural kind terms, a narrow one and a broad one, which differ in the nature of their equivalence relations. Kripke (1972) considers mainly equivalence relations associated with the physical internal structure of things, and therefore uses examples such as *gold, heat, hot,* etc. Putnam (1975) employs a wider usage of 'natural kind term', including terms denoting artifacts such as *pencil* whose equivalence relation is likely to include functional criteria.[55] As far as natural language goes, there seems to be no difference between strict natural kind terms such as *gold* or *tiger* and more general ones such as *music* or *pencil.* For example, both allow for definite generic NPs:

(181) a. Gold was one of the first metals to attract man's attention.
b. Music was developed in a very early stage of human history.
c. The tiger is thought to have originated in northern Eurasia.
d. The pencil was first described in 1565 by the Swiss scholar Conrad Gesner.

(To be sure, there are some distinctions between very specific kinds; for example, *be extinct* is applicable only to biological kinds, and *be invented* only to artifact kinds, except of course for metaphorical uses.)

Is there a linguistic distinction between natural kind terms (in the broad sense) and the so-called *nominal kind terms,* which must be analyzed as descriptions? Standard examples cited for nominal kinds are nouns such as *bachelor* (which can be described as "an unmarried male of marriageable age"), *pediatrician* ("doctor specializing in the care and medical treatment of children"), or *weed* (which the *Encyclopedia Britannica* ingeniously defines as "any plant growing where it is not wanted"). However, it seems that we can get definite generic NPs with these nouns, suggesting that they are not pure nominal kind terms:

(182) a. The bachelor had a major influence on the *Sturm und Drang* movement of the late 1700s.
b. Although the pediatrician has specialized in childhood maladies, he remains a generalist who looks after the whole patient.
c. The weed was an important factor in last year's economic disaster.

55. One might object to calling artifacts natural kinds, but Putnam (and others) argue for a strong similarity between them.

This might be taken as an argument that natural kind terms do not correspond to formal linguistic categories, even if we allow for a very wide interpretation of "natural kind" (cf. Abbott 1989). To counter this sort of objection, Putnam (1975) has argued that many terms which seem to be descriptional, or which were introduced as descriptional, can easily acquire the status of natural kind terms in which reference is not fixed by description anymore but by satisfying an equivalence relation to paradigm cases. This could easily be the case with examples such as *bachelor, pediatrician, weed,* or *outhouse.* (Nowadays this last is a natural kind term true of small buildings without running water whose sole function is to contain a pit used for eliminating body wastes; the original meaning of *outhouse* was "(small) building which is outside the main living area," which described many farm buildings other than the privy. So the designation of this term is no longer fixed by description, but rather by being the same as certain paradigms.)

Since these are not clear cases of nominal kind terms, perhaps should look at syntactically complex nouns such as *loud music, sweetened lemon,* or *melancholy bachelor* as possibly clearer cases. It would seem that unless they are idioms, their denotation is at least partly fixed descriptionally. For example, *sweetened lemon* denotes things which are lemons and which are sweetened. So even if *sweetened* and *lemon* are natural kind terms, their combination must count as a description.[56] We have seen that we can use definite generic NPs only with "well-established" kinds such as *the lemon,* not with newly constructed concepts—*the sweetened lemon* does not make a pleasant generic NP. Thus at least we can say that clear cases of nominal kinds cannot be referred to by definite generic NPs. This seems to be the only general statement we can make about linguistic correlations to the nominal/natural kind distinction.

We should add here, however, that the notion "well-established" should not be taken too literally. We can accommodate kinds relatively easily even when we hear of them for the first time, or have not thought about the corresponding concepts as kinds. For example:

(183) a. The wolpertinger roams the mountains and forests of the Bavarian Alps.
b. The green bottle saved the lives of hundreds of children.

Most readers probably have not heard of, let alone seen, the kind *Chimaera bavarica;* nonetheless (183a) can be easily understood by tacitly adding such a kind to one's knowledge base. This is quite similar to cases where the speaker

56. Some caveat is needed here about NPs containing nonintersective adjectives, like *toy gun,* but we shall not concern ourselves with the details.

uses a proper name that is new to the hearer. By accommodation, we may even accept strange kinds such as the one mentioned in (183b). As a context for that sentence, imagine a story about the invention of some sort of green glass that turned out to protect a certain pediatric medicine from decomposing, or maybe a situation where all and only poisons are put into green bottles and children are taught this at a very young age. Such cases are especially interesting, since the contexts which license them can reveal the principles behind the establishment of kinds. In the case at hand, the assumption is that green bottles are not just bottles which happen to be green, but that they have a certain additional property which cannot simply be derived from the meanings of the constituent expressions (cf. the discussion surrounding *the German fly* vs. *the German shepherd* in section 1.3.2). In (183b) this might be the property of green glass to preserve the medicine, or to warn children. It seems reasonable to assume that this example illustrates a necessary condition for kinds in general: their specimens must show similar behavior in one or more sufficiently important and relevant respects. (See Gerstner-Link 1988 for additional data concerning the construction of kind-referring NPs in different domains.)

In concluding this section, we want to mention that the readiness of language users to assume the existence of kinds corresponding to some definite NP may change over time. If we take the construction with the definite article as indicative of speakers "assuming the existence of a kind," then there was a definite shift in German this century away from assuming kind entities corresponding to peoples. For example, whereas a sentence like (184a) would have been normal in the first half of this century, it now sounds rather old-fashioned and conservative, both linguistically and ideologically, and would be replaced by (184b):

(184) a. Der Italiener singt gerne. 'The Italian likes to sing.'
b. Italiener singen gerne. 'Italians like to sing.'

A similar change occurred in English. With the current vogue for nostalgia posters, one can easily see just how common the archaic usage was. André Fuhrmann has shown one of us (FJP) a British WWI poster using the sentence (185a); the standard WWII poster would put it as (185b):

(185) a. The Hun is a sly and cunning beast! Do not divulge secrets to strangers!
b. Germans are sly and cunning! Do not tell strangers secrets!

And a reading of the classic English authors and playwrights will yield corroboration and documentation of this shift.

1.4.6. Generic vs. Episodic Interpretations of Bare NPs: The Early Theory of Carlson

The analysis of genericity we have argued for in this introductory chapter appears to differ in several respects from the first elaborate formal theory of the semantics of generic sentences, which was developed by Carlson (1977a,b, 1979, 1982).[57] In this section, we will compare that theory to the framework developed here and discuss the interpretation of bare NPs, for which Carlson's theory provides an ingenious treatment. Further discussion can be found in Carlson's contribution to this volume (chapter 4). We will see that, although there are indeed a number of important differences between the two theories, many of the apparent conflicts are merely a matter of emphasis, and on some issues either theory could adopt either approach.

Carlson's theory is mainly concerned with bare plural NPs in English, although he also examines bare mass nouns and kind-referring NPs containing the definite article. His basic idea is to unify the two interpretations of bare plural NPs, the *generic* (kind-referring) and the *existential* (indefinite), by claiming that the existential interpretation is kind-referring as well. For example, the subject NPs in the both of the following sentences are analyzed as referring to the kind *Canis:*

(186) a. Dogs are good pets.
b. Dogs are sitting on my lawn.

Carlson gives a battery of convincing arguments for this unified analysis of bare plurals:

1. *Lack of ambiguity.* If bare plural NPs were ambiguous between a generic and an existential interpretation, we should expect sentences in which a bare plural occurs to be ambiguous as well. However, we do not find such ambiguities. Sentence (186a) only means that, in general, realizations of the kind *Canis* are good pets, whereas (186b) only means that some realizations of that kind are sitting on my lawn.

2. *Scope phenomena.* If bare NPs in the 'existential' interpretation are indefinite NPs, then they should behave similarly to other indefinites. In particular, they should have a specific (or wide-scope) and a nonspecific (or narrow-scope) interpretation when they interact with other scope-ambiguous operators. How-

57. See also Chierchia 1982b for another version of this theory; and compare our remarks in section 1.2.2 above.

ever, Carlson argues with several types of examples that bare plural NPs in the 'existential' interpretation are always nonspecific (have narrow scope). This distinction between bare plurals and other indefinite NPs is borne out in examples such as the following:

(187) a. Minnie wishes to talk to a young psychiatrist.
   i) Minnie wishes that there is a young psychiatrist and she talks to him.
   ii) There is a young psychiatrist and Minnie wishes to talk to him.
b. Minnie wishes to talk to young psychiatrists.
   i) Minnie wishes that there are young psychiatrists and she talks to them.

Example (187a) has two readings: *a young psychiatrist* may take narrow scope or wide scope. (187b), however, has only the narrow-scope reading. Therefore a treatment of this phenomenon along the lines of indefinite NPs would be implausible.

3. *Anaphora phenomena.* Carlson observes that it is possible to have anaphoric links between 'generic' and 'existential' bare NPs, as in these examples:

(188) a. My mother hates raccoons$_i$ [generic] because they$_i$ [existential] stole her sweet corn last summer.
b. Raccoons$_i$ [existential] have stolen my mother's sweet corn every year, so she really hates them$_i$ [generic] a lot.

Another case in point, observed by Mats Rooth (1985), concerns the anaphoric connection between bare plural subjects and reflexive pronouns (see Rooth, Chapter 6, and ter Meulen, Chapter 8 in this volume):

(189) a. At the post-WW III peace meeting, Martians$_i$ presented themselves$_i$ as almost extinct.
b. *At the post-WW III peace meeting, some Martians$_i$ presented themselves$_i$ as almost extinct.

According to Rooth, (189a) is acceptable for most people with the reading that *themselves* refers to a kind even if *Martians* has an existential interpretation, whereas he claims that this reading is unavailable for (189b). If we assume that the reflexive is coreferential with the subject and must refer to a kind because of the kind-level predicate *be extinct,* then we have an argument for Carlson's analysis: *Martians* in (189a) refers to the kind *Homo(?) martis* even in the 'existential' interpretation, whereas the NP *some Martians* in (189b) can't refer to the kind (since it is an indefinite NP), and hence the sentence is bad.

4. *Multiple interpretations with conjoined predicates.* This argument was brought forward by Schubert and Pelletier (1987) in support of Carlson's theory. In sentences such as those in (190) below, the bare NP is the subject of a conjoined verbal predicate. (They bring up similar arguments with relative clauses a la (190c) and with other constructions.) One of the conjuncts requires a 'generic' interpretation and the other an 'existential' one. If there is an ambiguity to be traced to bare NPs, we would predict that such sentences are unacceptable because the 'generic' interpretation does not satisfy the second conjunct and the 'existential' interpretation does not satisfy the first conjunct. But these sentences are good, which leads us to prefer Carlson's uniform analysis.

(190) a. Snow is white and is falling right now through Alberta.
b. Dogs are mammals and are barking right now in front of my window.
c. Sulfuric acid, which is a transparent liquid, can be found in the lower cabinet.

Carlson's theory captures these observations with the assumption that 'generic' and 'existential' bare plural NPs are interpreted uniformly as names of kinds, and that the different interpretations are generated solely by the verbal predicates (see section 1.2.2 above). This assumption explains the lack of ambiguity. It also explains why bare plurals have narrow scope: because the existential quantifier is part of the word meaning of the verb, it cannot interact with other operators in the sentence and consequently must take narrow scope. Carlson's theory also accounts for the anaphora phenomenon: in cases such as (188a,b), both *raccoons* and *they* refer to the same entity, the kind *Procyon;* it is the verbal predicates which introduce or do not introduce an existential quantifier over realizations. In particular, this explains the fact that an 'existential' bare plural subject can show coreference with a kind-referring reflexive pronoun, as in (189). Finally, the different interpretations of conjuncts, as in (190), are no longer a problem since the predicate of each conjunct applies to the kind denoted by the subject; the only difference is that one is "internal" to the verbal predicate, and this difference will generate the 'existential' vs. 'generic' interpretations.

However, Carlson's theory also faces some problems, which have led van Langendonck (1980b), de Mey (1982), Weir (1986), Gerstner and Krifka (1987), and Wilkinson (1988) to abandon it in favor of the assumption that bare NPs are ambiguous between an indefinite and a definite, kind-referring interpretation. We shall mention some of these problems and how they are handled by these new theories. And then we shall contrast these theories with the initial one of Carlson (1977b), leaving it somewhat open as to how much of the original theory can be maintained in a new theory.

One problem is presented by the distributional differences between bare NPs like *horses* and NPs with a definite article that denote a kind, like *the horse*. Carlson's theory, in which they denote the same entity, the kind *Caballus,* must explain, then, why bare NPs easily yield an episodic reading as in (191a), whereas kind-referring NPs with a definite article either do not, as seen in (191b), or else do only in the avant-garde or representative object readings, as in (191c) (see also section 1.3.4):

(191) a. Horses stampeded through the gate.
b. The horse stampeded through the gate. (not same meaning as (a))
c. The horse came to America with Columbus.

The theory also has to explain why bare NPs are possible in *there*-constructions whereas definite NPs are not (Weir 1986):

(192) a. There are horses stampeding through the gate.
b. *There is the horse stampeding through the gate.

One way to account for this is to assume that the bare NP *horses* is an indefinite NP, and not a kind-denoting name.

A second problem is that even in characterizing sentences, bare NPs and kind-referring definite NPs may behave differently. For example, (193a) is a characterizing sentence which might say: Whenever a farm has pigs, they are kept in the pen behind the farmhouse. (193b) does not have this reading.

(193) a. Pigs are kept in the pen behind the farmhouse.
b. The pig is kept in the pen behind the farmhouse. (not same meaning as (a))

Again, one way to account for this is to assume that *pigs* is an indefinite NP and not a kind-denoting game.

Another problem becomes more obvious when we look at other languages, since some languages seem to distinguish syntactically between a 'generic' and an 'existential' interpretation of bare NPs. One example is Finnish. In this language, a bare NP in subject position is in the nominative case when interpreted as 'generic', and in the partitive case when interpreted as 'existential' (note that the verb is singular with partitive subjects):

(194) a. Koirat haukkuvat.
dogs.NOM bark.PL
'Dogs bark.'
b. Koiria haukku.
dogs.PART bark SG
'Dogs are barking.'

(195) a. Maito on makeaa.
'Milk (NOM) is sweet.'
b. Maitoa kaatui pöydälle.
'Milk (PART) was spilled over the table.'

French uses a definite article in the first type of case, and an indefinite (or partitive) article in the second:

(196) a. Le lait est doux.
b. Du lait était renversé sur la table.

(Both in Finnish and in French, partitive subjects also have a tendency to be postposed.) In Japanese, in the 'generic' case the subject is marked by the topic postposition *wa,* and in the 'existential' case it is marked by the nominative postposition *ga:*

(197) a. Inu wa hasiru.
dog TOP run
'Dogs run.'
b. Inu ga hasitte iru.
dog NOM run PROGR
'Dogs are/A dog is running.'

Even in English, there are some differences between the two interpretations. Bare NPs in the 'existential' interpretation appear to pattern with indefinite NPs; for example, they bear the same sentence accent as the corresponding sentence with an indefinite NP, and both bare NPs and indefinite NPs have a tendency to move to a postverbal position with the *there*-construction. Bare NPs in the 'generic' interpretation lack these properties (see also Laca 1990).[58]

(198) a. A DOG is sitting on my lawn.
DOGS are sitting on my lawn.
b. There is a DOG sitting on my lawn.
There are DOGS sitting on my lawn.
c. DOGS are good pets. (only good with a contrastive interpretation)
d. *There are DOGS good pets.

58. Recall that main sentence stress is indicated by capitalization.

Carlson explains these differences with the nature of the verbal predicates; he points out, for example, that it is a property of stage-level predicates to allow the *there*-construction (see also Milsark 1974). However, it is not a natural consequence of his theory that indefinite NPs like *a dog* and bare NPs in the 'existential' interpretation should act similarly.

Another set of problems concerns the narrow scope phenomena. Although there is a clear tendency for bare NPs in the 'existential' interpretation to be interpreted with narrow scope, this is not always the case, as pointed out for German by Kratzer (1980); the same point can be made for English (Schubert and Pelletier (1987) discuss a variety of similar examples):

(199) a. Hans wollte Tollkirschen an den Obstsalat tun, weil er sie mit richtigen Kirschen verwechselte.
b. John intentionally put belladonnas into the fruit salad because he took them for cherries.

On a plausible reading (though a reading not everyone seems to get), John didn't want belladonnas in the fruit salad, nor did he believe that the kind *Atropa belladona* is the kind *Cerasus*. This, however, is implied by the only reading (199a,b) have in Carlson's theory. The more plausible reading says that John wanted to put some objects x into the fruit salad which were, in fact, belladonnas; and the reason for this was that he (mis)took x for cherries. To get this reading, *belladonnas* must have wide scope with respect to *intentionally,* as it refers to specific belladonnas; and the pronoun *they* must refer to x. These two requirements cannot be reconciled if the object x is introduced by a verb-internal existential quantifier. But there seems to be no problem at all if we analyze *belladonnas* on a normal indefinite NP, which can have wide scope over embedding operators, and whose referent can be picked up by pronouns in later discourse. An account in Carlson's theory would at least have to involve additional assumptions.

Even in cases which lack scope ambiguities, anaphoric reference to the objects in question is possible:

(200) John saw apples_i on the plate, and Mary saw them_i, too.

In the most natural reading, *apples* and *them* refer to the same objects. According to Carlson, they refer to the same kind, and it is only the predicate *saw* which introduces objects. But since the existential quantifier has necessarily narrow scope (because it is introduced internally in the lexical semantics of the verb), *them* isn't within the scope of this existential quantifier, and it is therefore not obvious how to express that *apples* and *them* should refer to the same apples. Whatever solution to this problem can be found within Carlson's framework also needs to work for sentences where the anaphoric relation is not to the objects but rather to the kind (under the guise of "different manifestations of the same kind"). Consider (201):

(201) John ate apples$_i$ and Mary ate them$_i$, too.

Surely there is a reading of this sentence where John and Mary ate the same apples, and another in which John and Mary ate different apples. How can we arrange it so that both readings are available?

Note that there is no problem with the anaphoric relationship in cases such as (188b) if we assume (as suggested above) that indefinite NPs introduce not only an object, but also a kind into discourse. In (188b), the indefinite *raccoons* in the antecedent position would introduce some specific raccoon(s) as well as the kind *Procyon*. It is this kind which is picked up by the pronoun *they*. We find the same phenomenon with other types of indefinite NPs, for example in *A raccoon has stolen my mother's sweet corn last year, so she really hates them.*

The kind reflexive phenomena (cf. (189)) seem to be a good argument for Carlson's original theory. Certainly they are more convincing than cases with an existential antecedent and a generic pronoun (like (188b)), since we must assume that the reflexive enforces coreference between the relevant argument places. And if *Martians* in (189) were an indefinite NP, the antecedent argument would be an x such that **R**(x,**Homo martis**); this cannot be identical with the kind **Homo martis** as required by the reflexive pronoun and the predicate *be extinct*. Unlike Carlson, we need to say that speakers who find (189a) acceptable have a kind-referring interpretation of *Martians,* even if in fact only some members of this kind were actually involved. The theory developed here allows for this, calling it an example of the representative object interpretation of sentences with kind-referring NPs (cf. section 1.3.4).

The case of conjoined predicates constitutes another argument for the early Carlson theory. The theory under development here is forced to deny sentences such as (190a,b) full semantic acceptability. Intuitions of the authors of this chapter differ on their acceptability. But even if they are not fully acceptable, Carlson's theory might explain this by saying that the coordination of a proper kind-level predicate such as *be white* and a predicate like *be falling right now throughout Alberta* (which reduces kinds to specific realizations) is stylistically awkward because the predicates express very different types of properties. The theory developed here might be able to cope with these sentences as well, by claiming that the bare plural indeed refers to a kind, and that the verbal predicates such as *be falling right now throughout Alberta* are interpreted in the kind-oriented mode (see section 1.3.5). The alleged marginal status of these examples would be explained, then, by the fact that the kind-oriented mode is quite rare in English.

One further clear strength of Carlson's theory is its ability to explain the lack of ambiguity in sentences with bare NP subjects. He is clearly correct in assuming that it is the nature of the verbal predicate which determines the interpretation of bare NPs as 'generic' or 'existential'.

The theory of bare plural NPs presented in Carlson (1977b) assumes that *all* such NPs denote kinds. When the sentence as a whole is about "ordinary" individuals or about stages of such individuals, then it is the role of other elements in the sentence to convert the basic NP meaning (of denoting a kind) into a sentence which mentions, or otherwise brings into play, these other types of things. Thus, in Carlson's early theory, *dogs* designates the kind Dog; *dogs with three legs* designates the kind Dog with Three Legs; and *Dogs Barking in the Kitchen* designates the kind Dog Barking in the Kitchen. It is a separate question whether *sentences* such as (202) below are "about" the kind Dog or "about" individual dogs.

(202) a. Dogs make good pets.
b. Dogs with three legs are rare.
c. Dogs barking in the kitchen irritate me.

(And indeed, except impressionistically, it is quite difficult to know what it means for a sentence to be "about" something. After all, the various levels of semantic representations of even such sentences as *Dogs are barking outside right now* "mention" both a kind and individuals in Carlson's theory. This seems merely a matter of which representation we are investigating.) Some predicates, such as *be extinct,* are kind-selecting, and therefore sentences employing them will (at the intuitive level) be "about" kinds and not "about" ordinary entities. Other predicates, such as *be barking,* are "stage selecting," and therefore sentences employing them will (at the intuitive level) be "about" stages (or ordinary individuals, in certain other theories). So much is pretty well agreed by all theories. Sentence (203a) below is "about" kinds while sentence (203e) is "about" individuals (ordinary ones or stages, depending on the theory). However, the status of other sentences in (203) is not so clear. Carlson (1977b) tended to favor interpreting all of them as being "about" kinds.[59] The theory presently being developed suggests that, on the contrary,

59. He noted that this was not forced upon us by his theory, but that it was the most "natural" interpretation of these sentences.

these three sentences are "about" individual dogs; however, we wish to point out that this is not required by the theory—merely suggested. Various of the authors of this chapter characterize these intermediate cases differently.

(203)	a.	Dogs are extinct.	(kind predicate)
	b.	Dogs are common.	(quantificational predicate)
	c.	Dogs make good pets.	(NP in restrictor)
	d.	DOGS bark when the bell rings.	(NP in matrix)
	e.	DOGS are barking.	(NP not in scope of **GEN**-operator)

The centerpiece for both analyses (Carlson 1977b and the present one), at least with respect to bare plural NPs, is the analysis of sentences such as (203c). The two theories make similar claims in two important respects: First, they both trace back two seemingly distinct uses of bare NPs to a uniform interpretation—kind names in Carlson 1977b and indefinites in the present theory. Second, both theories burden the rest of the sentence (that is, the verbal predicate) with the task of distinguishing between the two uses of bare NPs—in Carlson 1977b by distinguishing between individual-level and stage-level predicates, and here by distinguishing between sentences which have the bare NP in the restrictor of a **GEN**-operator and sentences in which the bare NP occurs outside of the scope of a **GEN**-operator.

1.5. CONCLUDING REMARKS AND OUTLOOK

Let us repeat here the main points of this introduction to the syntax and semantics of genericity.

Perhaps the most important result is that genericity is not a uniform concept. We must distinguish between kind reference on the one hand and characterizing predication on the other. Each of these has been called 'genericity' in the past, and there are certain intuitive similarities between them. Furthermore, they may interact with one another. However, we think that it will be crucial for future research to keep these notions separated.

In the case of characterizing predication, we argued for the assumption of a dyadic operator that relates a restrictor to a matrix and binds at least one variable. We then used this arrangement to explain different generic readings by assuming different partitions of the semantic material into the restrictor and the matrix, a matter that requires far more detailed investigation than given here (see Diesing 1992 for a recent investigation). We treated habitual sentences as quantifications over situations, in contrast to generalizations over individuals. And we discussed possible ways to spell out the semantics of the genericity operator.

In the case of kind-referring NPs, we showed that the nontaxonomic variety behaves like proper names, whereas the taxonomic variety arises as a special interpretation of common nouns. We had a look at the range of meanings that sentences with kind-referring NPs can exhibit, and we suggested investigation of two "modes of speaking": the standard object-oriented mode and the kind-oriented mode, which, although simpler, occurs only in special circumstances. We examined kind-referring NPs in characterizing sentences, and we looked at NPs that refer to entities similar to kinds ("notions" and "concepts").

Finally, we discussed some additional subjects. We argued for a distinction between quantificational predicates (such as *be common*) and proper kind-predicates (such as *be extinct*). And we showed that *any*-NPs can be seen as behaving like indefinite NPs in characterizing sentences. We also looked at gerundives, infinitives, and nominalizations, arguing that they are semantically similar to NPs. Generic anaphora was explained as a second layer in the anaphorical process, on top of the well-known "object anaphora." We summarized the philosophical discussion of natural kinds and made some observations concerning the establishment of kinds. Finally, an analysis of bare plurals in English that is connected with the present theory was compared with their treatment in Carlson 1977b.

Several other, relevant subjects were not treated in this chapter. An example is the interaction of genericity and negation; note that we have only looked at affirmative sentences. One interesting phenomenon is the scope of negation. A sentence like *Mary doesn't smoke a cigarette after dinner* can mean that it is not the case that Mary habitually smokes a cigarette after dinner, that is, negation may have wide scope. It is not so clear whether it can have narrow scope as well, that is, whether the sentence can mean that Mary habitually does not smoke (≟ objects to smoking) a cigarette after dinner. Other cases can have either scope. For example, *Cows do not eat nettles* can mean either that cows do not have the habit of eating nettles, or that they have the habit of not eating nettles (that is, in situations that contain nettles, they do not eat them).

Furthermore, in the discussion of characterizing sentences, we concentrated on the covert **GEN**-operator. We did not investigate in any detail the relationship between this operator and others that are overtly expressed, such as *always, typically, usually, mostly, sometimes,* etc. Sometimes the differences are rather subtle, sometimes quite evident.

Also, we did not mention the lively research going on under the title of "arbitrary interpretations," which often have been seen as related to genericity. Arbitrary interpretations occur within a range of different constructions, for example with the suppressed and uncontrolled subject argument of infinitival constructions as in (204a), with unspecified arguments as in Italian

(204b), with overt arbitrary pronouns such as French *on* or German *man* as in (204c), and with reflexive constructions as in Italian (204d).

(204) a. It is not clear how [to solve this problem].
b. L'ambizione spesso spinge e [a comettere errori].
'Ambition often pushes one [to make mistakes].'
c. Man zeigt nicht mit dem Finger auf Leute.
'One doesn't point with the finger at people.'
d. In Italia si beve molto vino.
'In Italy, people drink a lot of wine.'

Recent research on a number of languages, such as Italian (Jaeggli 1986, Rizzi 1986, Cinque 1988, Chierchia 1990), Greek (Condoravdi 1989a), French (Authier 1989), Polish (Kanski 1992), Persian (Karimi 1989), and Korean (Kim 1991), points toward the view that arbitrary interpretations are essentially like a general indefinite referring to persons; if the sentences have a generic flavor, then this is due to additional generic operators in them. Interestingly, it seems that in many cases this indefinite cannot be the only predicate in the restrictor. For example, Karimi points out the following contrast in Persian:

(205) a. *Mamolan ghost-e khook ne-mikhorand.
usually meat-GEN pig not-eat.3PL
'Usually, people don't eat pork.'
b. Dar een shahr, mamolan ghost-e khook ne-mikhorand.
In this city, usually meat-GEN pig not-eat.3PL
'In this city, people usually don't eat pork.'

Another area which we have neglected is semantic models for nominalization phenomena. The problem here is that a predicate, like *lions* or *chewing tobacco,* can be treated as a referring expression (as in *Lions are extinct* or *Chewing tobacco is a bad habit*). And sometimes it even seems that a predicate is applicable to itself, as in *Fun is fun.* The challenge is to provide model structures that allow for this. Perhaps one way is to carefully relax the type theory that underlies traditional model-theoretic semantics—of course without allowing the antinomies for the prevention of which type theory was invented to arise again. Several theories have been developed to do just this; see Chierchia 1982a, Turner 1983, Bealer & Mönnich 1989, and articles in Chierchia, Partee & Turner 1989.

2 STAGE-LEVEL AND INDIVIDUAL-LEVEL PREDICATES

Angelika Kratzer

That I am sitting on this chair is a very transitory property of mine.[1] That I have brown hair is not. The first property is a *stage-level property* in the terminology of Carlson (1977b). The second property is an *individual-level property*. Stage-level properties are expressed by *stage-level predicates*. And individual-level properties correspond to *individual-level predicates*. A number of grammatical phenomena have been shown to be sensitive to the distinction between stage-level and individual-level predicates. *There*-insertion sentences (Milsark 1974), bare plurals (Carlson 1977b), and absolute constructions (Stump 1985) are relevant examples. Here are some illustrations:

THERE-INSERTION

(1) a. There are firemen available.
    b. *There are firemen altruistic.

BARE PLURALS

(2) a. Firemen are available.
    b. Firemen are altruistic.

ABSOLUTE CONSTRUCTIONS (Stump 1985, 41–43)

(3) a. Standing on a chair, John can touch the ceiling.
    b. Having unusually long arms, John can touch the ceiling.

Altruistic and *having unusually long arms* are typical individual-level predicates. *Available* and *standing on a chair* are typical stage-level predicates. The contrast between (1a) and (1b) is a contrast in grammaticality. The contrasts between (2a) and (2b) and between (3a) and (3b) are contrasts in interpretation. (2a) can mean that there are available firemen, but (2b) cannot mean that there are altruistic ones. (3a) can mean 'If John stands on a chair, he can touch the ceiling', but (3b) cannot mean 'If John has unusually long arms, he can touch the ceiling'.

If a distinction between stage-level and individual-level predicates is operative in natural language, it cannot be a distinction that is made in the lexicon

1. This paper was completed and submitted in December 1988, and appears here unchanged. Naturally my thinking about these topics has changed, largely due to the responses the paper has received during the six years it has circulated informally.

of a language once and for all. If I dyed my hair every other day, my property of having brown hair would be stage-level. Usually we think of having brown hair as an individual-level property, though, since we don't think of persons dying their hair capriciously. Hence we classify predicates like *having brown hair* as individual-level predicates. We now know that there may be some problems with such classifications. This being said, we will make use of the convenient classifications just the same. As long as we are careful, no harm is likely to result from this simplification.

In this chapter, I am going to argue that stage-level predicates and individual-level predicates differ in argument structure. That is, the argument structure of *having brown hair* changes when you start using it as a stage-level predicate. I will propose that stage-level predicates are *Davidsonian* in that they have an extra argument position for *events* or *spatiotemporal locations* (Davidson 1967). Individual-level predicates lack this position.

This view is different from the proposal defended in Carlson 1977b and subsequent work. Carlson assumes that stage-level properties and individual-level properties are ¬ properties of different types of entities. Stage-level properties are properties of stages, and individual-level properties are properties of individuals. An individual can be a kind like the kind of pots or the kind of pans, but it can also be an object like this pot or that pan. A stage is a spatiotemporal part of an individual: this pot here and now, or that pan there and then.

The view advanced here also differs from some neo-Davidsonian approaches that have it that *all* kinds of predicates have an eventuality argument in the sense of Bach 1981. Predicates may then differ as to the kind of eventuality involved. We may have events, processes, or states, for example. (This approach is taken in Higginbotham 1985, among others.)

The proposal that stage-level predicates are Davidsonian will not come as a surprise at a time when Davidsonian approaches to the semantics of verbs are becoming ever more popular (see in particular Parsons 1980, 1985; Higginbotham 1985, 1988). What I want to show here is that this proposal has a number of truly unexpected consequences. We will see that it can shed light on phenomena as diverse as extraction facts in German and the proportion problem for donkey sentences.

2.1. Locatives as Evidence for an Extra Argument Position

This section presents a first set of data supporting a Davidsonian treatment of the distinction between stage-level and individual-level predicates. The following sentences illustrate some uses of spatial and temporal expressions in German.

STAGE-LEVEL PREDICATES

(4) . . . weil fast alle Flüchtlinge in dieser Stadt umgekommen sind.
since almost all refugees in this city perished are
a. '. . . since almost all of the refugees in this city perished.'
b. '. . . since almost all the refugees perished in this city.'

(5) . . . weil ihn fast alle Flöhe in diesem Bett gebissen haben.
since him almost all fleas in this bed bitten have
a. '. . . since almost all of the fleas in this bed bit him.'
b. '. . . since almost all the fleas bit him in this bed.'

(6) . . . weil fast alle Antragsteller in diesem Wartesaal saßen.
since almost all petitioners in this waiting room sat
a. '. . . since almost all of the petitioners in this waiting room were sitting.'
b. '. . . since almost all the petitioners were sitting in this waiting room.'

(7) . . . weil uns heute fast alle Kandidaten beeindruckt haben.
since us today almost all candidates impressed have
a. '. . . since almost all of today's candidates impressed us.'
b. '. . . since almost all the candidates impressed us today.'

INDIVIDUAL-LEVEL PREDICATES

(8) . . . weil fast alle Schwäne in Australien schwarz sind.
since almost all swans in Australia black are
a. '. . . since almost all swans in Australia are black.'

(9) . . . weil fast alle Lebewesen auf diesem Planet von der Amöbe abstammen.
since almost all living beings on this planet from the amoeba descend
a. '. . . since almost all living beings on this planet descend from the amoeba.'

(10) . . . weil fast alle Schüler in dieser Schule Französisch können.
since almost all students in this school French know.
a. '. . . since almost all of the students in this school know French.'

(11) . . . weil heute fast alle Kandidaten "Hans" hiessen.
since today almost all candidates "Hans" were named
a. '. . . since almost all of today's candidates were named "Hans".'

In the above examples, the sentences with stage-level predicates have two readings (sometimes corresponding to a difference in intonation), while the sentences with individual-level predicates have only one. The readings differ as to the role played by spatial and temporal expressions like *in this city* or *today*. In the (a)-readings, the spatial or temporal expression modifies the restricting predicate of the quantifier *fast alle* ('almost all'). In the (b)-readings, the spatial or temporal expression modifies the main predicate of the sentence. On a Davidsonian account, temporal and spatial expressions accompanying verbs relate to the verb they modify via the Davidsonian argument. The verb introduces an *event variable,* and the modifiers of the verb impose further restrictions on this variable. If stage-level predicates do, but individual-level predicates don't, have a Davidsonian argument, we can explain why temporal and spatial expressions can modify stage-level predicates but not individual-level predicates. Here are some examples illustrating how spatial and temporal expressions modify verbs on a Davidsonian approach:

(12) Manon is dancing on the lawn.
[**dancing**(**Manon,** l) & **on-the-lawn**(l)]

(13) Manon is dancing this morning.
[**dancing**(**Manon,** l) & **this-morning**(l)]

(14) Manon is a dancer.
dancer(**Manon**)

Is dancing is a stage-level predicate. Consequently, it has a Davidsonian argument that appears in the form of a variable. The locatives *on the lawn* and *this morning* relate to the verb *is dancing* by taking another occurrence of the same variable as their argument. *Is a dancer* is a fairly typical individual-level predicate. It normally lacks a Davidsonian argument, hence cannot be modified by locatives. If it can, it has turned into a stage-level predicate. At this point, I don't want to commit myself to a particular view with respect to the precise nature of the Davidsonian argument. It may not be an event argument. It may simply be an argument for spatiotemporal location. This is the minimal assumption necessary to explain the data presented above. It is also the minimum assumption needed for the data to be discussed in the remainder of this chapter. In what follows, then, I will try out the minimal assumption, being curious about how far it can be carried. The proposal to consider the Davidsonian argument as an argument for spatiotemporal location was first made by E. J. Lemmon in his comments on Davidson's paper "The Logical Form of Action Sentences" (Lemmon 1967). Lemmon meant to identify events with their spatiotemporal locations, though, a view I don't want to embrace here.

Let us assume, then, that in the logical representations given above 'l' is a variable ranging over spatiotemporal locations. A spatiotemporal location is a space-time chunk like the space occupied by this room today. The logical representations for (12) and (13) contain free occurrences of l. These free occurrences of l may become bound by quantifiers when the sentences appear as parts of more complex constructions, or else they may be supplied with a value by the context of use. (12) says that Manon is dancing at l, and the spatial extension of l consists of the surface of the lawn. The context of use may now specify the temporal extension of l. (13) says that Manon is dancing at l, and the temporal extension of l is this morning. This time, the context of use may specify the spatial extension of l. (14) simply says that Manon is a dancer.

Having looked at some aspects of the technical implementation of a Davidsonian treatment of the stage-level/individual-level distinction, let us now turn to another argument in favor of our position.

2.2. *When*-Clauses: A Second Argument for the Extra Argument Position

This section will present a second argument for the presence of an extra argument position in stage-level predicates. This time, the argument has to do with variable binding, and it makes use of certain features of 'Discourse Representation Theory' (Kamp 1981, Heim 1982). Consider the following sentences:

(15) a. *When Mary knows French, she knows it well.
b. When a Moroccan knows French, she knows it well.
c. When Mary knows a foreign language, she knows it well.
d. When Mary speaks French, she speaks it well.
e. *When Mary speaks French, she knows it well.
f. *When Mary knows French, she speaks it well.

Following Kratzer (1978, 1986), I am assuming that, quite generally, the antecedents of conditionals have no other function apart from restricting the domain of some operator. This extends Lewis's treatment of *if*-clauses in connection with adverbs of quantification to all types of conditionals (Lewis 1975). For an *if*-clause, the operator to be restricted can be a determiner quantifier, an adverb of quantification, or any kind of modal operator. *When*-clauses are more selective in that they don't seem to be able to restrict epistemic modals. Hence the following contrast:

(16) a. *When the library has this book, it must be on the second floor.
b. If the library has this book, it must be on the second floor.

If *if*-clauses and *when*-clauses are both devices for restricting the domain of operators, we have to stipulate non-overt operators whenever a conditional sentence introduced by *if* or *when* lacks an overt one. An adverb of quantification like *always* or an epistemic necessity operator seem to be the available options (Kratzer 1986). If *when*-clauses cannot restrict epistemic modals, the non-overt operator in sentences (15a–f) must be *always*. Following Lewis 1975 and some further developments in Kamp 1981 and Heim 1982, the analysis of (15a–f) will now be as follows.

(15′) a. ***Always [knows(**Mary, French**)] [knows-well(**Mary, French**)]**
b. **Always**$_x$**[Moroccan(**x**) & knows(**x, **French)] [knows-well(**x, **French)]**
c. **Always**$_x$**[foreign-language(**x**) & knows(Mary,** x**)] [knows-well(Mary,** x**)]**
d. **Always**$_l$**[speaks(Mary, French,** l**)] [speaks-well(Mary, French,** l**)]**
e. ***Always**$_l$**[speaks(Mary, French,** l**)] [knows-well(Mary, French)]**
f. ***Always[knows(Mary, French)]** $\exists_l$**[speak-well(Mary, French,** l**)]**

(15′a–f) are all tripartite quantifier structures consisting of the quantifier *always,* a restrictive clause, and a 'nuclear scope' (Heim 1982). The adverb of quantification is indexed with all those variables that occur free in its restrictive clause. As a consequence, it binds all free occurrences of these variables in its entire scope. The nuclear scope of a tripartite quantifier construction is closed by an existential operator binding all occurrences of variables in its scope which are not bound otherwise. Indefinite noun phrases like *a Moroccan* or *a foreign language* are not analyzed as existential quantifiers. They are treated as predicates introducing a variable into the logical representation. This variable may then be bound by the quantifier *always.* For details of this analysis, see Lewis 1975 and Heim 1982. See also Kamp 1981 for an analogous approach. Note, however, that contrary to assumptions in Discourse Representation Theory, I didn't let proper names and referential pronouns introduce variables into logical representations.

Alternatively, we might assume that proper names and referential pronouns do introduce variables, but these variables are "anchored" to the context of use, hence not available for binding. In what follows, I will not be able to do justice to directly referential expressions. Since they are not our main concern here, I will occasionally be satisfied with ad hoc solutions.

We are now in the position to explain why sentences (15a, e, f) are ungrammatical. Assuming that stage-level predicates do but individual-level predicates don't introduce a variable that can be bound by *always,* we predict that (15a, e,

f) should be excluded, given the following natural prohibition against vacuous quantification (see Chomsky 1982 for a similar proposal):

Prohibition against Vacuous Quantification
For every quantifier Q, there must be a variable x such that Q binds an occurrence of x in both its restrictive clause and its nuclear scope.

In (15a), the main predicate in the antecedent and in the consequent is individual-level. Hence there is no Davidsonian argument introducing a variable. No other expression in (15a) introduces variables. The sentence, then, is excluded by the prohibition against vacuous quantification. Similar considerations apply to (15e) and (15f), which lack a bindable variable in the consequent and in the antecedent respectively. (15b) and (15c) are good since variables are introduced by indefinites in the antecedent and reappear again in the consequent. The interesting case is (15d). (15d) is exactly like (15a), except that it contains the stage-level predicate *speak* where (15a) contains the individual-level predicate *know*. If stage-level predicates introduce a free variable but individual-level predicates don't, (15a) will but (15d) will not violate the prohibition against vacuous quantification. Assuming that the prohibition against vacuous quantification is well motivated and that there is ample support for a Lewis/Kamp/Heim analysis of sentences like (15a–f), we now have another argument in favor of the view that stage-level predicates are Davidsonian but individual-level predicates are not.

There is one loose end that I should attend to before closing this section. Why is (15b) good? Or, why is it that (15a, e, f) all become grammatical as soon as we replace *when* with *if*? Recall that *if*-clauses differ from *when*-clauses in being able to restrict epistemic modals. In fact, (15a, e, f) all turn into epistemic conditionals after the replacement. (17a, b, c) correspond to (15a, e, f) respectively.

(17) a. If Mary knows French, she knows it well.
b. If Mary speaks French, she knows it well.
c. If Mary knows French, she speaks it well.

If (17a–c) are epistemic conditionals, the *if*-clause restricts an epistemic modal. While some modals can act as quantifiers and bind variables, as argued in Heim 1982, it seems that epistemic modals cannot. Consider the following example:

(18) A car must be in the garage.

When *must* is interpreted deontically, the indefinite noun phrase in (18) can have an existential or a universal (generic) interpretation. On Heim's account, the universal reading of *a car* is due to the modal *must,* which can function as a universal quantifier just like *always.* On this reading, (18) would be represented as follows:

(18′) $\mathbf{Must}_{x,l}$[**car**(x) & **be**(x, l)] [**in-the-garage**(l)]

(18′) means (roughly) that whenever there is a car in an accessible world w, then its location is within the garage in w. If *a car* is understood existentially, the logical representation would be (18″):

(18″) **Must** $\exists_{x,l}$[**car**(x) & **be**(x, l) & **in-the-garage**(l)]

(18″) means that in all accessible worlds there is a car in the garage. (18″) is only well formed if the modal *must* is not *necessarily* a quantifier. Otherwise, it would be ruled out by the prohibition against vacuous quantification. We have to conclude, then, that deontic modals are only optionally quantificational. When *must* is interpreted epistemically, *a car* in (18) can only be interpreted existentially. This suggests that epistemic modals are never quantifiers and can therefore never bind variables. But if epistemic modals are not quantifiers, (17a–c) don't violate the prohibition against vacuous quantification.

2.3. A Syntactic Argument for the Extra Argument Position in Stage-Level Predicates

2.3.1. Extraction Facts from German

Recent work by a variety of scholars suggests that configurational sentence structures with VPs seem to be plausible for many languages, including Japanese (Saito 1985), German (Webelhuth 1985, 1989), Breton, Niuean, Chamorro, Jacaltec, Papago, and Warlpiri (Woolford 1988). Most of this work also converges on the conclusion that VPs may contain D-structure subjects even if their heads are not unaccusative verbs (Koopman & Sportiche 1985, Kuroda 1989, Kitagawa 1986, Tateishi 1988, Diesing 1990). These subjects are claimed to appear in the specifier-of-VP (Spec VP) position. They may stay there in S-structure provided that they can get case in this position. The Spec VP position is the highest position within the VP. It is distinct from the customary object position, which is the position adjacent to V. Neglecting any variation concerning the position of heads, the structure of simple sentences is usually assumed to be as shown in (19):

(19)

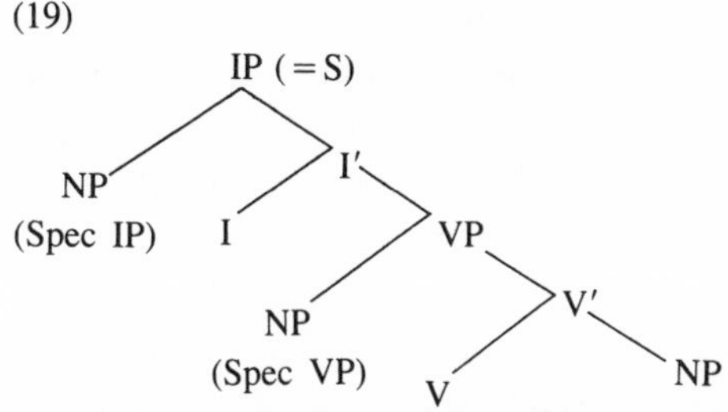

In Diesing 1988, 1990, Molly Diesing argues that certain extraction facts from German can be explained if we assume that at the relevant level of representation, subjects of stage-level predicates are within VP, while subjects of individual-level predicates are in the specifier-of-IP (Spec IP) position. While Diesing is very careful in not making unwarranted claims as to the level of representation involved, I will adopt the common assumption that the level for generalizations about the realization of arguments is D-structure (rather than Logical Form, for example). The exploration of alternatives might be worthwhile, but will be left for another occasion. Here are two examples illustrating some facts relevant for what we might call "Diesing's Conjecture."

(20) a. . . . weil uns viele Lehrer geholfen haben.
since us many teachers helped have
'. . . since many teachers helped us.'

b. Lehrer haben uns viele geholfen.
teachers have us many helped
'As for teachers, many of them helped us.'

(21) a. . . . weil das viele Lehrer wissen.
since this many teachers know
'. . . since many teachers know this.'

b. *Lehrer wissen das viele.
teachers know this many
'As for teachers, many of them know this.'

The above examples illustrate the so-called "quantifier split" construction in German. The (a)-sentences give examples of subordinate clauses with unsplit quantifier phrases. In the corresponding (b)-sentences, verb-second has taken place, allowing the quantifier phrase to split, with a portion preceding the finite verb. (20) involves a stage-level predicate, (21) has an individual-level predicate. Quantifier split is possible with subjects of stage-level predicates, but impossible with subjects of individual-level predicates.

Diesing (1988) proposes a CED (Condition on Extraction Domains; Huang

1982) explanation for those facts, and I will follow her in this respect. Let us assume that the quantifier split construction is the result of moving a common noun phrase out of its NP, as argued by van Riemsdijk (1987). Suppose now that subjects of individual-level predicates are base-generated in Spec IP. They will then have several options at S-structure. They may stay in their original position, or else may scramble, that is, adjoin to IP. In either case, they are ungoverned. Hence movement from subjects of individual-level predicates will *always* lead to a CED violation. (Subjects can also move to Spec CP, of course. This option is not relevant here, since there is never movement out of Spec CP.) As for subjects of stage-level predicates, suppose that they are base-generated within VP. They, too, will then have several options at S-structure. They may stay in their original position. In this case, they are in a governed position and movement from these subjects will not lead to a CED violation. If they move on to Specific IP or scramble, they will occupy an ungoverned position. Movement from such subjects, then, will again violate the CED. Little is known about the factors that make a subject move in German. At this point, all we can say is that assuming that subjects of stage-level predicates are base-generated within VP and that they can stay there at S-structure, we expect to find cases where movement from those subjects is possible. (20b) is such a case. We also expect that sometimes, movement from subjects of stage-level predicates might not be possible. This expectation is borne out, as illustrated by the following pair of sentences:

(22) a. . . . weil viele Nachbarn einem alten Ehepaar geholfen haben.
since many neighbors an old couple helped have
'. . . since many neighbors helped an old couple.'

b. *Nachbarn haben viele einem alten Ehepaar geholfen.
neighbors have many an old couple helped
'As for neighbors, many of them helped an old couple.'

A similar CED explanation might be given for the following data illustrating extraction possibilities for relative clauses. (23) involves a stage-level predicate, (24) an individual-level predicate. Subjects of stage-level predicates permit the extraposition of a relative clause, but subjects of individual-level predicates don't.

(23) . . . weil zwei Kinder hier waren, mit denen niemand spielen wollte.
since two children here were, with whom nobody play wanted
'. . . since two children were here with whom nobody wanted to play.'

(24) *. . . weil zwei Bücher teuer waren, die niemand lesen wollte.

since two books expensive were that nobody read wanted
'. . . since two books were expensive that nobody wanted to read.'

In the next section, I am going to show that our assumptions concerning the argument structure of the two types of predicates, plus some plausible additional premises, will allow us to derive a result that is *almost* Diesing's Conjecture (as modified above). In particular, we will be able to derive that subjects of stage-level predicates are always base-generated within the maximal projection of their predicates, and that subjects of individual-level predicates are base-generated outside of the maximal projection of their predicates unless the predicates are unaccusatives (in the sense of Perlmutter 1978). We will also see that this slight deviation from Diesing's original proposal has the right consequences.

2.3.2. Deriving (Almost) Diesing's Conjecture

The reasoning in this section will closely follow the structure of an argument given in Williams 1981. Williams argues that in nominalizations like *Caesar's destruction of the city,* the agent argument *Caesar* may be realized within the maximal projection of *destruction,* since nominalizations like *destruction* have an event argument. Consequently, the event argument, and not the agent argument, is the external argument here.

Following Williams, let us assume that the argument structure of lexical items consists of a list of thematic role labels like 'agent', 'experiencer', 'theme', 'goal'. Let us assume furthermore that we also have a Davidsonian thematic role, in our case a role for spatiotemporal location. At most one of the thematic role labels of a predicate may be underlined. The underlined label corresponds to the external argument of the predicate. All other arguments are internal. There may be some generalizations as to which argument of a lexical item will wind up as its external argument. Here are some candidates: If a predicate has a Davidsonian argument, it will always be its external argument. If a predicate has no Davidsonian argument, but has an agent argument, the agent argument will be its external argument. The arguments of a predicate are linked to their syntactic positions in D-structure according to the following principle:

Argument Linking (Williams 1981)
In D-structure, all arguments except the external argument are realized within the maximal projection of their predicate.

There may be further principles guiding the realization of internal arguments. Maybe internal agent arguments have to occupy the specifier position while internal theme arguments have to occupy the object position, for example. This may lead to a more hierarchical view of argument structure, as proposed in Grimshaw 1987, 1990, among others. There will also be principles regulating case assignment and agreement. All of these issues are addressed in the literature mentioned above, so I will not go into details here.

Let us now look at some examples illustrating possible argument structures for different types of predicates.

(25) Stage-Level Predicates That Are Not Unaccusatives

hit	**⟨location, agent, theme⟩**
dance	**⟨location, agent⟩**

(26) Stage-Level Predicates That Are Unaccusatives

die	**⟨location, theme⟩**
fall	**⟨location, theme⟩**

(27) Individual-Level Predicates That Are Not Unaccusatives

know	**⟨experiencer, theme⟩**
altruistic	**⟨theme⟩**

(28) Individual-Level Predicates That Are Unaccusatives

belong	**⟨theme, goal⟩**
be known to	**⟨theme, experiencer⟩**

The above examples are at best suggestive. We have seen that the stage-level/individual-level distinction is context dependent and vague. And the distinction between predicates that are unaccusatives and those that are not is likewise unstable. What is important here is (i) that there are prototypical examples, (ii) that we know which factors contribute to context dependency and vagueness, (iii) that whatever kind of vagueness and context dependency we may find will be transmitted to all the grammatical phenomena in which the two distinctions play a role.

Let us now look at the predictions made by these lexical representations in conjunction with Williams's linking rule. All stage-level predicates have an external argument for spatiotemporal location. In languages like English or German, this argument seems to be implicit, that is, it has no realization at D- or S-structure. As a consequence, spatial and temporal expressions are adjuncts. They don't fill argument positions. All but the event argument of stage-level predicates are internal, hence they have to be realized within the maximal projection of the predicate in D-structure. Subjects of stage-level verbs, then, are always base-generated inside of their VP, subjects of stage-level adjectives are always base-generated within their AP, and so on. This gives us one part of Diesing's Conjecture.

Let us now turn to individual-level predicates. Those predicates don't have a Davidsonian argument. Hence some other argument may be external. If there is such an argument, it has to be base-generated externally, and the usual option is the Spec IP position. If the predicate is unaccusative, its subject will be base-generated within its maximal projection. Individual-level predicates, then, may come in two kinds. One kind has external subjects in D-structure and the other kind has internal ones. This gives us a slightly different version of the second part of Diesing's Conjecture. The following data support this revision.

INDIVIDUAL-LEVEL PREDICATES THAT ARE NOT UNACCUSATIVES

(29) a. . . . weil das fast alle Bürger in dieser Stadt wissen.
since this almost all citizens in this town know
'. . . since almost all of the citizens in this town known this.'

b. *When Mary knows this, she knows a lot.

c. *Bürger wissen das viele.
citizens know this many
*'As for citizens, many of them know this.'

(30) a. . . . weil fast alle Bürger in dieser Stadt altruistisch sind.
since almost all citizens in this city altruistic are
'. . . since almost all of the citizens in this city are altruistic.'

b. *When Ann is altruistic, she will give us a hand.

c. *Sanitäter sind viele altruistisch.
paramedics are many altruistic
'As for paramedics, many of them are altruistic.'

INDIVIDUAL-LEVEL PREDICATES THAT ARE UNACCUSATIVES

(31) a. . . . weil mir fast alle Esel in dieser Stadt gehören.
since to me almost all donkeys in this town belong
'. . . since almost all of the donkeys in this town belong to me.'

b. *When this donkey belongs to Pedro, it is lucky.

c. Esel gehören ihm viele.
donkeys belong to him many
'As for donkeys, there are many that belong to him.'

(32) a. . . . weil mir fast alle Buchläden hier bekannt sind.
since to me almost all bookshops here known are
'. . . since almost all of the bookshops here are known to me.'

b. *When this fact is known to her, she keeps it secret.

c. Häßliche Gegenbeispiele sind mir mehr als genug bekannt.
nasty counterexamples are to me more than enough known
'As for nasty counterexamples, there are more than enough that are known to me.'

The (a)- and (b)-sentences above establish that we are indeed dealing with individual-level predicates. The main predicate of the sentence has no Davidsonian argument that a locative could relate to. And there is no extra variable that a non-overt quantifier could bind. The (c)-sentences are bad for *know* and *altruistic,* showing that the subjects of these predicates are sitting in an ungoverned position. But the (c)-sentences are good for the unaccusatives *belong to* and *be known to,* suggesting that their subjects can appear in a governed position.

We have seen in this section that the presence of a Davidsonian argument can be held responsible for the fact that subjects of stage-level predicates are always internal arguments and are base-generated within the maximal projection of their predicates. In a language like German, they can receive case in their D-structure position and can stay there. As a consequence, extraction from those subjects is permitted. Subjects of individual-level predicates may or may not be external arguments. Hence they may or may not allow extraction. Assuming, then, that individual-level predicates and stage-level predicates differ in argument structure as proposed here, we can derive certain facts about the syntactic behavior of their subjects, given independently motivated assumptions about the link between argument structure and D-structure representations.

2.4. The Different Readings of Bare Plurals

The work of Gregory Carlson has shown convincingly that the distinction between stage-level and individual-level predicates plays a crucial role in the interpretation of bare plurals. Carlson's particular approach to bare plurals faces some serious problems, however, most of which are already raised in his dissertation (Carlson 1977b). Various attempts to deal with those problems led to various alternatives. In what follows, I will briefly sketch Carlson's analysis as well as the most promising alternative proposal, developed independently by Karina Wilkinson (1986) and Claudia Gerstner and Manfred Krifka (1987). I will then discuss some apparent difficulties with Wilkinson's and Gerstner and Krifka's approach, and we will see how Diesing's syntactic treatment of the stage-level/individual-level distinction might help us to overcome those difficulties.

2.4.1. Carlson's Analysis

On Carlson's analysis, bare plurals are always interpreted as names of a kind. The logical counterparts of English stage-level predicates are predicates of stages. A stage is a temporal "slice" of an individual. Since kinds are not the sort of entity to which a stage-level property can apply, the relationship between the denotation of a bare plural NP and a stage-level property has to be mediated by a 'realization relation.' The counterparts of English individual-level predicates are predicates of individuals. Individuals may be kinds or objects, as mentioned above. An individual-level property, then, may apply to the denotation of a bare plural NP directly; no mediation is necessary. To illustrate the details of Carlson's analysis, let us examine the translations for the English adjectives *available* and *altruistic*.

(33) available
$\lambda y_i \exists x_s[\mathbf{R}(y_i, x_s) \ \& \ \mathbf{available}(x_s)]$
altruistic
$\lambda y_i[\mathbf{altruistic}(y_i)]$

The translations make use of two sorts of variables. Stage variables are subscripted by 's', individual variables are subscripted by 'i'. The translations for sentences like (34) and (35) will be (34′) and (35′) respectively.

(34) Firemen are available.
(35) Firemen are altruistic.
(34′) $\exists x_s[\mathbf{R}(\mathbf{firemen}, x_s) \ \& \ \mathbf{available}(x_s)]$
(35′) $\mathbf{altruistic}(\mathbf{firemen})$

(34) illustrates the existential reading of bare plurals. (35) represents the generic reading. (34′) says roughly that there is a stage x such that x realizes the kind of firemen and x is available. (35′) says that the kind of firemen is altruistic. On this proposal, the logical counterparts of *altruistic* and *available* are both predicates with one argument. These arguments are of different sorts, though.

2.4.2. A Lewis/Kamp/Heim Analysis

There are a number of problems with Carlson's proposal. Here is an example (Milsark 1974; see also Carlson 1977b, 1989):

(36) Typhoons arise in this part of the Pacific.

(36) has two readings. It may mean that it is a typical property of typhoons that they arise in this part of the Pacific. Or else that it is a typical property of this part of the Pacific that there are typhoons that arise there. Carlson's analysis only predicts the first of those readings. The difficulty with the second reading is that the verb *arise* is understood generically, but the bare plural noun phrase *typhoons* can still get an existential reading. On Carlson's proposal, the

existential reading of a bare plural can only be provided by a stage-level predicate. But if *arise* in (36) were translated as a stage-level predicate, the resulting translation would mean that typhoons are arising in this part of the Pacific. Difficulties of this sort motivated Wilkinson (1986) and Gerstner and Krifka (1987) to propose that at least certain kinds of bare plurals should be analyzed along the lines of Lewis, Heim, and Kamp (see also Farkas & Sugioka 1983 for an earlier articulation of a similar view, and Schubert & Pelletier 1987 for an overview and some further developments). The two readings of (36) can now be represented as (36′a) and (36′b).

(36′) a. $\mathbf{G}_x$[**typhoon**(x)]$\exists_l$[**this-part-of-the-Pacific**(l) & **arise-in**(x, l)]
b. $\mathbf{G}_l$[**this-part-of-the-Pacific**(l)]$\exists_x$[**typhoon**(x) & **arise-in**(x, l)]

These representations are quantifier structures of the sort discussed above. *G* is some kind of adverb of quantification, a generic operator like *typically,* whose exact nature is not at issue here (overt quantifiers like *always* or *usually* may be substituted without changing the point of the example). Like other indefinites, bare plurals are treated as predicates introducing variables into the logical representation. The generic reading of *typhoons* arises when *typhoons* appears in the restrictive clause of the quantifier construction. In this position, the variable introduced by *typhoons* can be bound by the non-overt generic operator. The existential reading of *typhoons* arises when *typhoons* appears in the nuclear scope. Recall that the nuclear scope of a logical representation is always existentially closed (Kamp 1981, Heim 1982). If the variable that comes with *typhoons* is introduced in the nuclear scope, it will be caught by existential closure. This is the source of the existential reading.

2.4.3. Too Many Readings? Diesing's Proposal

Wilkinson (1986) is well aware that while her approach to bare plurals is successful in predicting certain plausible readings of bare plural sentences that Carlson's analysis excludes, it also runs the risk of admitting some very implausible ones. This point is taken up in Diesing 1988. Diesing's main concern is to predict the correct range of available readings for bare plurals. She proposes an analysis of sentences with bare plurals that crucially exploits the fact that subjects of stage-level predicates and subjects of individual-level predicates may be in different positions at the relevant level of representation. I have argued above that this syntactic difference is in fact a consequence of a difference in argument structure. If Diesing's analysis of bare plural sentences is plausible, it can be understood as yet another piece of evidence for our main hypothesis. Consider again sentence (34), repeated here as (37):

(37) Firemen are available.

Diesing argues that a Lewis/Kamp/Heim approach (as advocated by Wilkinson and by Gerstner and Krifka) correctly admits at least three possible readings for a sentence like (37).

(37′) a. $\exists_{x,l}$[**fireman**(x) & **available**(x, l)]
b. $\mathbf{G}_{x,l}$[**fireman**(x) & **be**(x, l)] [**available**(x, l)]
c. $\mathbf{G}_{l}$[**here**(l)]$\exists_{x}$[**fireman**(x) & **available**(x, l)]

(37′a) says that there are firemen available. (37′b) says that it is a characteristic property of a fireman that he is available. And (37′c) means that there are typically firemen available around here. While a Lewis/Kamp/Heim approach to bare plurals fares better than Carlson's analysis in allowing at least three possible readings for (37), it must make special provisions to block the impossible (b)-reading for sentence (35) above, repeated here as (38):

(38) Firemen are altruistic.

(38′) a. $\mathbf{G}_{x}$[**fireman**(x)] [**altruistic**(x)]
b. $\exists_{x}$[**fireman**(x) & **altruistic**(x)]

(38′a) says that a fireman is typically altruistic. (38′b) means that there are altruistic firemen. (38′a) but not (38′b) is a possible interpretation for (38). Diesing proposes a syntactic solution to this problem. Her proposal says roughly that when sentences like the ones we have been discussing so far are mapped into logical representations, material in the VP goes into the nuclear scope, while material outside of the VP goes into the restrictive clause. For a language like English, we can implement Diesing's proposal as follows.

While all subjects appear in Spec IP position at S-structure, subjects of stage-level predicates and subjects of unaccusative individual-level predicates don't originate there. They have been moved from their D-structure position within VP, leaving a trace. This distinguishes them from subjects of individual-level predicates that are not unaccusatives. Those subjects are base-generated in Spec IP, hence don't bind a trace within VP. Let us say that a subject in Spec IP that binds a trace within VP appears "simultaneously" within and outside of the VP. When surface structures are mapped into quantifier structures, those subjects may then be mapped into the restrictive clause or else into the nuclear scope. That the effects of NP movement can be optionally "undone" in this way is supported by examples like (39), as observed by May (1977).

(39) [A unicorn]$_1$ seems [t_1 to be in the yard].

(39) has two readings. The noun phrase *a unicorn* may have narrower or wider scope than *seems*. The narrow scope reading arises through undoing the effects of NP movement at Logical Form. Subjects of individual-level predicates that are not unaccusatives, then, are always mapped into the restrictive clause. All other subjects have an option. They may be mapped into the restrictive clause or into the nuclear scope. We have seen that within a Lewis/Kamp/Heim approach, bare plurals have no quantificational force of their own. They only introduce a predicate and a variable into the logical representation. If they appear in the nuclear scope, the variable they introduce will be bound by existential closure, hence the existential reading. If they appear in the restrictive clause, the variable will be bound by a suitable overt quantifier or by the non-overt generic operator. This is the source of the generic reading. *Available* is a stage-level predicate. Diesing's proposal correctly predicts that a bare plural subject of *available* may have an existential or a generic reading. *Altruistic* is an individual-level predicate that is not unaccusative (as shown by the German extraction facts). Diesing's proposal implies that a bare plural subject of *altruistic* cannot get an existential reading through existential closure of the nuclear scope.

If this proposal is to exclude the reading (38′b) for sentence (38), we must be sure that existential closure operations are indeed limited to nuclear scopes. This is not Heim's or Kamp's view, however. For them, there is a second existential closure operation (or some analogue) affecting texts. Problems with Kamp and Heim's existential closure operation for texts have been pointed out by Kadmon (1987), using examples like (40) (inspired by Evans 1977).

(40) John owns sheep. Harry vaccinates them.

If existential closure of texts applied to (40) as shown in (40′) below, (40) would be incorrectly predicted to mean that John owns sheep that Harry vaccinates (as before, we are neglecting all specific aspects of plurality).

(40′) $\exists_x$[**sheep**(x) & **own**(**John**, x) & **vaccinates**(**Harry**, x)]

To avoid this consequence, Evans proposes to treat pronouns like *them* in (40) as *E-type* pronouns (Evans 1977, 1980; cf. also Cooper 1979, Partee 1978, Kadmon 1987, Heim 1987a). E-type pronouns are pronouns that are anaphorically related to quantifier phrases that don't c-command them. They are interpreted as definite descriptions (''the sheep that John owns''). But if we treat pronouns like *them* above as E-type pronouns, we can dispense with the existential closure operation for texts altogether. This means that the only available existential closure operation is existential closure of the nuclear scope. And it also means that a bare plural noun phrase that is base-generated outside of the nuclear scope can never get an existential reading. This is why (38′b) is not a possible reading for (38).

Diesing's proposal also implies that subjects of unaccusative individual-level predicates might get existential readings. This prediction is borne out. Consider the following examples involving the predicates *belong to* and *be known to,* which patterned as unaccusatives with respect to the German extraction data.

(41) PONDS belong to this lot.

(42) She thinks that COUNTEREXAMPLES are known to us.

Emphasizing the subjects (as indicated by capitalization) favors an existential reading here. Note, however, that emphasizing the subject in (38) will still not give us an existential reading. This suggests that whatever the precise role of intonation is, it can merely help us to choose among the options provided by grammar.

It seems, then, that Diesing's Slogan, "Material in the VP is mapped into the nuclear scope, material outside of the VP is mapped into the restrictive clause," may indeed be used as a first step toward explaining why sentences like (37) and (38) have the readings they have.

Up to now, our discussion has raised two major issues. The first issue had to do with syntactic differences between stage-level and individual-level predicates. I argued that the two types of predicates differ in argument structure, and that this property may result in a syntactic difference concerning the position of subjects in D-structure. The second issue addressed the connection between S-structure VPs and the nuclear scope of quantifier constructions at Logical Form. I argued that it is nuclear scopes, and only nuclear scopes, that can be existentially closed. As a consequence, all existential NPs that have no quantificational force of their own have to appear in the nuclear scope at the level of Logical Form. We found that those NPs are already restricted to certain positions in S-structure, and this observation led to the hypothesis that there is a tight connection between S-structure VPs and the nuclear scope of quantifier representations ('Diesing's Slogan'). The two issues are closely related, of course, with VP-external versus VP-internal subjects providing the link. In the remainder of this chapter, I am going to pursue both of these issues further. We will look at a diverse body of data jointly supporting the conclusions we have reached so far.

2.5. NEGATIVE QUANTIFIERS IN GERMAN

In German, plural negative quantifier phrases show unexpected scope interactions with modals (Bech 1955/1957; Lerner & Sternefeld 1984).[2] Consider the following example:

(43) . . . weil keine Beispiele bekannt sein müssen.
since no examples known be must
'. . . since it is not necessary that examples be known.'

If *keine Beispiele* were a normal quantifier phrase, we would expect that it is raised at logical form (let us neglect the question of precisely how quantifier raising interacts with the other proposals developed here). And if the modal is raised as well, we should find the following readings for (43), neglecting plurality as usual.

(43′) a. $\mathbf{no}_x[\mathbf{example}(x)]\ [\Box\ \mathbf{known}(x)]$
b. $\Box\ \mathbf{no}_x[\mathbf{example}(x)]\ [\mathbf{known}(x)]$

(43′a) would give the quantifier phrase wide scope over the modal. (43′b) would represent the narrow scope reading. However, sentence (43) has neither of these readings. The only reading it has is represented by (43′c).

(43′) c. $\mathbf{not}\ \Box\ \exists_x[\mathbf{example}(x)\ \&\ \mathbf{known}(x)]$

This suggests that *keine Beispiele* is not a normal quantifier phrase. It seems to be a particular realization of the string *nicht Beispiele,* consisting of the negation adverb *nicht* ('not') and the bare plural *Beispiele* ('examples'). The bare plural NP has to receive existential force through existential closure. *Keine Beispiele,* then, involves two operators: negation and the existential closure operator. A third operator may intervene. This is what happens in (43) (for some reason, the modal cannot have scope over the negation). If there is no other operator, *nicht* and the existential closure operator jointly give us the effect of 'no'. That the true source of *keine N* is *nicht* plus a bare plural noun is further supported by the following data:

(44) a. *Wir haben nicht Kürbisse gekauft.
we have not pumpkins bought
'We didn't buy any pumpkins.'

b. Wir haben keine Kürbisse gekauft.
we have no pumpkins bought
'We bought no pumpkins.'

2. I think it was Irene Heim who first made me aware of the special properties of plural negative quantifiers in German.

c. Kürbisse haben wir nicht gekauft.
pumpkins have we not bought
'As for pumpkins, we didn't buy any.'

(44a) shows that the negation adverb *nicht* cannot appear adjacent to a plural indefinite noun phrase. One way of accounting for this fact is to assume that *nicht* and the zero determiner have to "merge" so as to yield *keine,* as shown in (44b). (Bech's term for this phenomenon is 'Kohäsion'.) In (44c), the indefinite noun phrase has been moved away from its D-structure position. It is not adjacent to *nicht* anymore. The unmerged form can appear here, suggesting that it is indeed the unmerged forms that are inserted at D-structure. The merging of *nicht* with a zero determiner, then, may be a rather superficial phenomenon, perhaps taking place at the level of phonetic form.

There is another argument showing that plural negative quantifier phrases in German originate from *nicht* plus a bare plural NP. Suppose that just like its English counterpart *not, nicht* is base-generated somewhere between the subject and the VP, that is, in the usual position for sentence adverbs. (An assumption like this seems justified in the light of Webelhuth's 'Identical Projection Function Model'; Webelhuth 1989.) If *nicht* is to merge with the zero determiner of an adjacent bare plural NP to its right, this NP has to be within the VP. We now expect that plural negative quantifier phrases in German must be VP-internal, and this is exactly what we find. Consider the following data:

OBJECTS

(45) . . . weil wir keine Birnbäume haben.
since we no pear trees have
'. . . since we have no pear trees.'

(46) . . . weil wir keinen Bären begegnet sind.
since we no (dat.) bears (dat.) come upon are
'. . . since we didn't come upon any bears.'

SUBJECTS OF STAGE-LEVEL PREDICATES

(47) . . . weil uns keine Freunde helfen.
since us no friends help
'. . . since no friends are helping us.'

(48) . . . weil hier keine Fliederbäume wachsen.
since here no lilacs grow
'. . . since no lilacs are growing here.'

SUBJECTS OF UNACCUSATIVE INDIVIDUAL-LEVEL PREDICATES

(49) . . . weil ihr keine Fahrräder gehören.
since to her no bicycles belong
'. . . since she owns no bicycles.'

(50) . . . weil keine Beispiele bekannt sind.
since no examples known are
'. . . since no examples are known.'

SUBJECTS OF INDIVIDUAL-LEVEL PREDICATES THAT ARE NOT UNACCUSATIVES

(51) * . . . weil keine Ärzte altruistisch sind.
since no physicians altruistic are
'. . . since no physicians are altruistic.'

(52) * . . . weil das keine Kandidaten wissen.
since this no candidates know
'. . . since no candidates know this.'

These data show again the by now familiar behavior of subjects. Subjects of stage-level predicates and subjects of unaccusative individual-level predicates can be VP-internal, but subjects of individual-level predicates that are not unaccusative cannot.

Before I close this section, I should add a few remarks on singular negative quantifier phrases. In German, singular and plural negative quantifier phrases have quite different properties. (This doesn't concern phrases like *kein Gold* 'no gold', where the noun is a mass noun. Mass nouns pattern with bare plurals in all important respects. See Carlson 1977b, chap. 7.) Consider the following examples illustrating the scope possibilities of a singular negative quantifier phrase with respect to a modal:

(53) . . . weil kein Beispiel bekannt sein muß.
since no example known be must
a. '. . . since there is no example that must be known.'
b. '. . . since it is not necessary that an example be known.'

(53′) a. $\mathbf{no}_x[\mathbf{example}(x)]\ [\Box\ \mathbf{known}(x)]$
b. $\mathbf{not}\ \Box\ \exists_x[\mathbf{example}(x)\ \&\ \mathbf{known}(x)]$

Unlike (43) above, sentence (53) has two readings. The first reading is expected if *kein Beispiel* is a "true" quantifier phrase that is raised at Logical Form. For reasons that don't have to concern us here, this quantifier phrase can only have wider scope than the modal *muß*. The second reading of (53) is the reading that we encountered with plural negative quantifiers. It requires *kein Beispiel* to be analyzed as consisting of the negation adverb *nicht* and the indefinite noun phrase *ein Beispiel*. This reading is given in (53′b). Since *ein Beispiel* has no quantificational force of its own, (53′b) involves the existential closure operator. The phrase *kein Beispiel,* then, may be a genuine quantifier phrase or else a string resulting from "negation merging." That singular indefinites, too, are subject to negation merging is further supported by the following examples:

(54) a. *Wir haben nicht einen Kürbis gekauft.
we have not a pumpkin bought
'We didn't buy a pumpkin.'
b. Wir haben keinen Kürbis gekauft.
we have no pumpkin bought
'We bought no pumpkin.'
c. Einen Kürbis haben wir nicht gekauft.
a pumpkin have we not bought
'As for a pumpkin, we didn't buy one.'

If singular negative quantifier phrases can optionally be "true" quantifiers, they should be able to appear as subjects of individual-level predicates that are not unaccusatives. They can indeed, as shown by the following examples:

(55) . . . weil kein Arzt altruistisch ist.
since no physician altruistic is
'. . . since no physician is altruistic.'

(56) . . . weil das kein Kandidat weiß.
since this no candidate knows
'. . . since no candidate knows this.'

Unlike sentences (51) and (52), sentences (55) and (56) are fully grammatical.

We have shown in this section that German plural negative quantifier phrases provide another piece of evidence that stage-level predicates and certain individual-level predicates (those that are not unaccusatives) differ with respect to the base position of their subjects. We have also seen that existential closure plays a crucial role in the interpretation of those quantifier phrases. This lends further support to the assumption that there is a process of existential closure tied to VPs.

The properties of plural negative quantifier phrases in German are reminiscent of the genitive-of-negation construction in Russian (Babby 1980, Pesetsky 1982). Further research will have to show whether the genitive-of-negation phenomenon is amenable to an analysis where an existential closure operation linked to VPs (rather than quantifier raising and the ECP as proposed by Pesetsky) carries the main burden of explanation.

2.6. OBJECTS AND EXISTENTIAL CLOSURE

We have seen that on Diesing's analysis, bare plurals (and other indefinites without quantificational force) can be interpreted existentially only if they end up in the nuclear scope at Logical Form. This is where the variable they introduce can be bound by existential closure. We have also seen that Diesing assumes that quite generally, VPs are mapped into nuclear scopes. In a language like English, objects always appear within VP (we may neglect topicalization here). We expect, then, that whenever a variable is introduced by an indefinite object in English, it will be bound by existential closure (Heim's Novelty Condition (Heim 1982) prevents it from being bound by any other quantifier). As a consequence, all indefinite objects should be interpreted existentially. In what follows, I am going to show that these predictions hold for some objects, but not for others. I will then argue that the main features of Diesing's analysis can still be maintained, provided we allow objects to be scrambled at Logical Form.

2.6.1. Well-Behaved Indefinite Objects

Let us start this section with another set of *when*-conditionals. The conditionals below all contain an individual-level predicate in the *when*-clause. This ensures that they can only satisfy the prohibition against vacuous quantification if a variable is introduced by an indefinite noun phrase. All conditionals considered are arranged in pairs. The (a)-sentences contain indefinite subjects, the (b)-sentences indefinite objects. The (a) sentences are grammatical, the (b)-sentences are not.

(57) a. When a proof contains this line of argumentation, it is seriously flawed.
  b. *When this proof contains a mistake, Mary will point it out to us.

(58) a. When a proposal requires his formal approval, it is doomed to failure.
  b. *When this proposal requires a formal approval, we will try to obtain it soon.

(59) a. When a lot is close to Lawrence Swamp, it is subject to many restrictions.
  b. *When this lot is close to a swamp, construction must be kept 200 feet away from it.

(60) a. When a farmer has a donkey, he beats it.
  b. *When Pedro has a donkey, he beats it.

The (b)-conditionals above are all ungrammatical, provided that the main predicates in their antecedents are interpreted as true individual-level predicates. I emphasized above that most individual-level predicates can also be used as stage-level predicates. Take sentence (57b), for example. Imagine that you and Mary are going through a long proof together. On this scenario, you might find (57b) relatively acceptable. But then you are talking about a proof containing mistakes here right now or there a little bit later. You are using *contains a mistake* as a stage-level-predicate. Similarly, if (60b) is interpreted as stage-level, the sentence is fine (e.g., if (60b) relates to donkeys that Pedro occasionally borrows from his neighbors; cf. the most natural reading of *When John has a spare dollar, he buys a lottery ticket with it*).

Why are the (b)-sentences bad on the primary reading? The discussion of bare plurals in section 2.4 suggests an answer to this question. Recall Diesing's Slogan, "Material in the VP is mapped into the nuclear scope, material outside of the VP is mapped into the restrictive clause." This procedure (properly formalized) splits a sentence into two parts when it is mapped into a logical representation. In the examples discussed in earlier sections, the two parts always ended up as the restrictive clause and the nuclear scope of a tripartite quantifier structure. This doesn't have to be the only possibility, however. Consider the following sentence.

(61) Pedro has a donkey.

If Diesing's proposal is a general procedure for dividing sentences into two parts, (61) will be divided into a restrictive clause and a nuclear scope as well. Since there is no quantifier, the result is a bipartite structure, rather than a tripartite one. Let us assume that in cases like this, restrictive clause and nuclear scope are conjoined by '&'. The logical representation of (61), then, might be something like (61′).

(61′) [**be-now**(**Pedro**$_3$)] & $\exists_x$[**donkey**(x) & **have**(**he**$_3$, x)]

In (61′), *Pedro* (with a suitable predicate; see section 2.7 below) appears in the restrictive clause, since it is realized outside of VP at S-structure. The VP itself is mapped into the nuclear scope. (Recall that there are open issues concerning the treatment of proper names and referential pronouns throughout this chapter. In (61′), indices are used to indicate coreference between directly referential expressions.) If sentences like (61) are part of other sentences, the corresponding Logical Forms might become rather complex. We may now have embedded restrictive clauses and nuclear scopes. Take sentence (60b) from above. The antecedent of (60b) is (61). At the level of Logical Form, (61′) is the restrictive clause of the whole sentence. But this restrictive clause contains another restrictive clause and a nuclear scope as parts. The consequent of (60b) is mapped into the nuclear scope of the whole sentence. This nuclear scope is complex again, since the consequent of (60b) is split up according to Diesing's Slogan as well. The result is something like (60′b).

(60′) b. ***Always**[**be-now**(**Pedro**$_3$) & $\exists_x$[**donkey**(x) & **have**(**he**$_3$, x)]]
$\exists_l$[**location**(l) & [**beat**(**he**$_3$, ιx[**donkey**(x) & **have**(**he**$_3$, x)],l)]]

With existential closure binding the variable introduced by *a donkey,* the pronoun *it* cannot be a bound variable. It is then interpreted as an E-type pronoun (cf. section 2.4.3. above). E-type pronouns in turn are interpreted as definite descriptions. That is, the E-type pronoun *it* above is analyzed as 'the donkey Pedro has'. If definite descriptions are given a Russellian analysis, [*beat*(*he*$_3$, ιx[*donkey*(x) & *have*(*he*$_3$, x)],l)] can be taken as an abbreviation for ∃y[∀x[*donkey*(x) & *have*(*he*$_3$, x)] ≡ [x = y]] & *beat*(*he*$_3$, y, l)]]. (60′b) is not well formed, since the quantifier *always* doesn't bind a variable.

Given representations of this kind, we expect the following. Subjects always have the option of becoming part of a restrictive clause. Objects, however, as long as they stay in their VP, have to go into a nuclear scope. If nuclear scopes are existentially closed, variables introduced by indefinite objects will be bound by the existential closure operator. In all of the above sentences, then, variables introduced by indefinite objects are bound by existential closure, while variables introduced by indefinite subjects are not. These variables can now be bound by the implicit adverb of quantification that is restricted by the *when*-clause. The resulting representation is well formed if no vacuous quantification occurs. Vacuous quantification occurs in the (b)-examples, but not in the (a)-examples.

We have already discussed a (b)-example. A representative (a)-example is (60a), which has the following logical representation:

(60′) a. **Always**$_x$[**farmer**(x) & ∃$_y$[**donkey**(y) & **have**(x, y)]]
∃$_l$[**location**(l) & [**beat**(x, ιy[**donkey**(y) & **have**(x, y)],l)]]

(60′a) is well formed since the quantifier *always* binds an occurrence of x in its restrictive clause and in its nuclear scope. As before, the pronoun *it* is interpreted as an E-type pronoun. Simply interpreting *it* as an E-type pronoun doesn't give us the desired interpretation for (60a), however. (60a) doesn't imply that whenever a farmer has a donkey, he has only one. Heim proposes to treat this case as a case of presupposition accommodation (Heim 1983a, 1987a; see also Lewis 1975). Quite generally, presuppositions of the nuclear scope can be accommodated into the restrictive clause (nice examples are Schubert and Pelletier's *Cats always land on their feet,* or *Robin Hood never misses;* Schubert & Pelletier 1987). After accommodating the uniqueness presupposition introduced by the E-type pronoun in (60a), we have the following:

(60″) a. **Always**$_x$[**farmer**(x) & ∃!$_y$[**donkey**(y) & **have**(x, y)]]
∃$_l$[**location**(l) & [**beat**(x, ιy[**donkey**(y) & **have**(x, y)],l)]]

The status of (60″a) is still controversial. Are we really considering only those farmers who have exactly one donkey? I will return to this point below.

2.6.2. "Ill-Behaved" Objects

The indefinite objects discussed in the previous section behaved as we expected them to. There was evidence that they were indeed caught by existential closure. Not all kinds of objects are as "well-behaved," however. Here are some examples of "ill-behaved" ones:

(62) a. When Sue likes a movie, she recommends it to everyone.
b. When Ann appreciates a paper, she tries to really understand it.
c. When Mary knows a foreign language, she knows it well.
d. When Robin isn't responsible for a mistake, he won't correct it.
e. When this assignment is too hard for a student, you may offer to help him.
f. When these dresses don't fit a customer, we will alter them for her.

All predicates in the antecedents of these conditionals are individual-level predicates. This is shown by the ungrammaticality of the following examples:

(63) a. *When Sue likes "Wings of Desire," she recommends it to everyone.
b. *When Ann appreciates this paper, she tries to really understand it.
c. *When Mary knows French, she knows it well.
d. *When Robin isn't responsible for this mistake, he won't correct it.
e. *When this assignment is too hard for Chris, you may offer to help him.
f. *When these dresses don't fit your daughter, we will alter them for her.

If all predicates in the antecedents of the conditionals (62a–f) are individual-level predicates, the prohibition against vacuous quantification can only be satisfied if their indefinite objects can move into the embedded restrictive clause (of the main restrictive clause) when Logical Forms are constructed.

We have to assume, then, that in English, objects can sometimes leave their VPs at the level of Logical Form. Transformations that move objects out of their VPs have been studied for a number of languages. These are the scrambling transformations which play a crucial role in configurational analyses of so-called "nonconfigurational" languages like Japanese (Saito 1985) or German (Webelhuth 1985, 1989; von Stechow & Sternefeld 1988). Scrambling is a transformation that adjoins a constituent to IP (and maybe to other maximal projections). It is an instance of Move α, hence has all the usual properties of transformations. As a consequence, scrambling may move a constituent out of VPs, but it could never move a constituent into VPs, for example. If it is scrambling that saves sentences (62a–f), scrambling must be possible for some indefinite objects, but not for others. If scrambling were always possible, no indefinite object would have to be caught by existential closure. Scrambling, then, must discriminate between "well-behaved" and "ill-behaved" indefinite objects. If this is so, we expect that S-structure scrambling in German and Japanese should be sensitive to this distinction. The following examples with scrambled indefinite objects confirm this expectation for German. In sentences (64a–d) indefinite objects of the sort we identified as "well-behaved" before have been scrambled to the left of the negation *nicht*. The result is ungrammatical. In (65a–f) "ill-behaved" indefinite objects have been scrambled. The result, again, is ungrammatical. Note that in all of those cases, the indefinite object could appear to the right of *nicht*. It would then have to undergo negation merging, though.

INDEFINITE OBJECTS THAT CANNOT BE SCRAMBLED

(64) a. *. . . falls ein Beweis einen Fehler nicht enthält.
if a proof a mistake not contains
b. *. . . falls ein Projekt eine Genehmigung nicht erfordert.
if a proposal an approval not requires
c. *. . . falls ein Grundstück an einen Sumpf nicht grenzt.
if a lot on a swamp not borders
d. *. . . falls ein Bauer einen Esel nicht hat.
if a farmer a donkey not has

INDEFINITE OBJECTS THAT CAN BE SCRAMBLED

(65) a. . . . falls ein Kritiker einen Film nicht mag.
if a critic a movie not likes
b. . . . falls ein Leser einen Artikel nicht schätzt.
if a reader a paper not appreciates
c. . . . falls ein Dolmetscher eine Fremdsprache nicht beherrscht.
if an interpreter a foreign language not knows
d. . . . falls ein Kollege für einen Fehler nicht verantwortlich ist.
if a colleague for a mistake not responsible is
e. . . . falls ein Übungsblatt einem Schüler nicht schwerfällt.
if an assignment to a student not hard is
f. . . . falls ein Kleid einer Kundin nicht paßt.
if a dress to a customer not fits

In the above sentences, an indefinite object precedes the negation *nicht*. If the negation *nicht* is placed somewhere between Spec IP and the VP (an assumption we made earlier), the object (as well as the subject) must have been scrambled. Scrambling of "ill-behaved" indefinite objects is permitted, but scrambling of "well-behaved" indefinite objects is not.

We don't know yet what makes it possible for an indefinite object to scramble. And I will make no attempt at an explanation. There are probably several factors involved. Apart from the type of verb, the type of noun phrase seems to play a role. For our present purposes, it is sufficient that we found a relevant correlation. Whenever an indefinite object can scramble at S-structure in German, it can scramble at Logical Form in English (and vice versa). The "ill-behaved" indefinite objects, then, present no real challenge to Diesing's way of explaining why bare plurals have the readings they have: VPs are always mapped into nuclear scopes—but there may be some scrambling first.

We are now in the position to make some predictions about possible readings of indefinite objects in English. Indefinite objects in English should always have an existential reading. In the presence of a suitable operator a generic reading might also be available. We expect that a generic reading will be available in precisely those cases where S-structure scrambling is possible in German. The following examples confirm this expectation:

INDEFINITE OBJECTS THAT CANNOT BE SCRAMBLED

(66) a. . . . weil Anton meistens einen Anzug trägt.
since Anton usually a suit wears
b. *. . . weil Anton einen Anzug meistens trägt.
since Anton a suit usually wears
c. . . . since Anton usually wears a suit.

(67) a. . . . weil Paula meistens Tulpen pflanzt.
since Paula usually tulips plants
b. *. . . weil Paula Tulpen meistens pflanzt.
since Paula tulips usually plants
c. . . . since Paula usually plants tulips.

(68) a. . . . weil diese Zeitung meistens einen schlechten Artikel enthält.
since this paper usually a bad article contains
b. *. . . weil diese Zeitung einen schlechten Artikel meistens enthalt.
since this paper a bad article usually contains
c. . . . since this paper usually contains a bad article.

INDEFINITE OBJECTS THAT CAN BE SCRAMBLED

(69) a. . . . weil sie immer Briefe aus Europa beantwortet.
since she always letters from Europe answers
'. . . since she is always engaged in answering letters from Europe'.
b. . . . weil sie Briefe aus Europa immer beantwortet.
since she letters from Europe always answers
'. . . since she never leaves a letter from Europe unanswered'.
c. . . . since always answers letters from Europe.

(70) a. . . . weil wir immer ein gutes Projekt fördern.
since we always a good project sponsor
'. . . since there is always a good project that we sponsor'.

b. . . . weil wir ein gutes Projekt immer fördern.
since we a good project always sponsor
'. . . since we sponsor any good project'.

c. . . . since we always sponsor a good project.

(71) a. . . . weil ein Pianist immer eine Sonate auswendig kann.
since a pianist always a sonata by heart knows
'. . . since a pianist always has a sonata that he knows by heart'.

b. . . . weil ein Pianist eine Sonate immer auswendig kann.
since a pianist a sonata always by heart knows
'. . . since a pianist knows any sonata (he plays) by heart'.

c. . . . since a pianist always knows a sonata by heart.

The (a)-sentences above are German sentences with an indefinite object following a sentential adverb like *meistens* or *immer*. These objects are not scrambled and can only have an existential interpretation. The (b)-sentences are like the (a)-sentences, except that the indefinite object has been scrambled out of its VP and precedes the adverb (the subject must have been scrambled as well, but this is not relevant here). The result is grammatical for some indefinite objects, but not for others. If the (b)-sentences are grammatical, the indefinite object can only have a generic interpretation. The (c)-sentences give the closest English equivalent to the German (a)- and (b)-sentences. The objects of all (c)-sentences have an existential reading. The objects of (60c), (70c), and (71c) also have a generic reading. What is important is that the English (c)-sentences have a generic reading in precisely those cases where the corresponding German (b)-sentences are grammatical. And this shows again that the English indefinite objects can be scrambled at Logical Form in precisely the cases where the German indefinite objects can be scrambled at S-structure. Indefinite objects that cannot scramble must stay in their VPs. They are then mapped into nuclear scopes and are caught by existential closure.

2.7. Where Does the Davidsonian Argument Go?

In the preceding sections, we investigated how S-structure subjects and objects are mapped into logical representations. This section will present some thoughts about the Logical Form representation of Davidsonian arguments.

We assumed above that Davidsonian arguments are implicit arguments in languages like English or German. Diesing's slogan, then, does not affect them. At S-structure, Davidsonian arguments don't appear within VP. Nor do they appear outside of VP. In fact, they don't appear anywhere. They will be present at the level of Logical Form, though. For them to be present there, they need a predicate that takes them as an argument. Stage-level predicates of all kinds are one possibility. Wherever a stage-level predicate appears at Logical Form, a variable ranging over spatiotemporal locations will be present. Locatives are another possibility. In his comments on Davidson's paper, Lemmon (1967) proposes to treat tense predicates like 'is before now', 'is now', 'is after now' as expressing properties of spatiotemporal locations ("space-time zones"). Tense predicates, then, are yet another tool for introducing a Davidsonian argument into a logical representation. Tense is realized by the inflectional element I(NFL) at S-structure. Hence tense predicates are realized outside of VP, and have to appear in the restrictive clause at Logical Form. Let us look at an example.

(72) Firemen were available.

A possible logical form of (72) is (72′) (this is a slight revision of my earlier analysis of a similar example, (37) in section 2.4).

(72′) [**before-now**(l)] & $\exists_x$[**fireman**(x) & **available**(x, l)]

The expression *before-now* is the tense predicate of (72′). It introduces an occurrence of the variable l into the restrictive clause. Being introduced in the restrictive clause, the variable l cannot be bound by existential closure. If there is no other quantifier to bind it, the context of use has to supply a value. This consequence is welcome. In an influential paper, Partee (1973) argues that sentences like (72) do not mean that there was some time in the past when firemen were available. We are talking about a particular occasion here, and this is just what our proposal implies. Note that something has to prevent the second occurrence of the variable l in (72′) from being caught by existential closure. It seems reasonable to stipulate that whenever one occurrence of a variable is supplied with a value by the context of use, all other occurrences of the same variable are supplied with the same value. They are then all anchored to the context and cannot be caught by existential closure. Further investigations into the nature of indexicality will have to clarify these issues.

Tense is not just a property of sentences where the main predicate is stage-level. Consider the following example:

(73) Henry was French.

(73) has two possible interpretations. On the first interpretation, we are treating *be French* as a stage-level predicate. Imagine that Henry used to be French, but is now an American citizen. The past tense is an effective tool for turning individual-level predicates into stage-level predicates. In this case, the tense predicate is a predicate for a Davidsonian argument, as expected. On the

second interpretation, *be French* stays an individual-level predicate. The tense predicate now applies to the unique argument of *be French.* (73′) gives a suitable logical form.

(73′) [**before-now(Henry$_3$)**] & [**French(he$_3$)**]

In (73′), the property of being before now is not predicated of a spatiotemporal location, but of the individual denoted by the subject. (73′) says that the individual Henry is located in the past and has the property of being French. We may conjecture that the tense predicate always relates to the external argument of the main predicate. This gives us an interesting prediction. Take my aunt Theresa, for example. She is an almost perfect clone of my grandmother. Yet unlike my poor grandmother, Aunt Theresa is still alive. In this situation, (74b) and (74c) are true. (74a) and (74d), however, are either false or are cases of presupposition failure. (There is a close connection between restrictive clauses and presuppositions, a topic that we cannot go into here.)

(74) a. Aunt Theresa resembled my grandmother.
b. My grandmother resembled Aunt Theresa.
c. Aunt Theresa resembles my grandmother.
d. My grandmother resembles Aunt Theresa.

These facts are easily explained if the tense predicate of the above sentences applies to the external argument of the main predicate. Note also that the data displayed under (74) seem to argue against those neo-Davidsonian approaches that assume the presence of state arguments for verbs like *resemble*. The tense predicate in the sentences above would then apply to this state argument, and the asymmetry observed in (74) would be unaccounted for. (74a) and (74b) would both be claimed to mean that there was a contextually specified state in the past that consisted in my aunt and my grandmother's resembling each other.

Other relationships between the tense predicate and the external argument of the main predicate are possible. Here is an example:

(75) All applicants were French.

The most likely reading of (75) is (75′).

(75′) **All**$_x$[**applicant**(x, l) & **before-now**(l)] [**French**(x)]

In (75′), the tense predicate relates to the Davidsonian argument of the predicate *applicant;* (75′) says that everybody who applied at a particular occasion in the past has the individual-level property of being French.

If the tense predicate always relates to the external argument of the main predicate of the sentence, it follows that a variable ranging over spatiotemporal locations must appear in the restrictive clause of every tensed sentence whose main predicate is stage-level. This fact is important for our discussion of *when*-clauses throughout this chapter. Take example (15d) from section 2.2, repeated here as (76):

(76) When Mary speaks French, she speaks it well.

A possible logical representation of (76) is (76′).

(76′) **Always**$_l$[**location**(l) & [**speak**(**Mary**$_3$, **French**$_2$, l)]]
[**location**(l) & [**speak-well**(**she**$_3$, **it**$_2$, l)]]

(76′) is well formed, since the quantifier *always* binds the variable l in both its restrictive clause and its nuclear scope. The tense of (76) is what we may call "generic tense." One way of thinking about generic tense is that it introduces predicates of the most general kind. In (76′) the tense predicate expresses nothing but the sortal property 'is a spatiotemporal location'. If there weren't a tense predicate in (76), the variable l would only appear in the nuclear scope. It would then be bound by existential closure, and the whole structure would be ruled out as a violation of the prohibition against vacuous quantification.

The preceding sections gave a rough idea of some basic principles guiding the mapping from S-structures to Logical Forms. The remainder of this chapter will use the insights gained so far for a fresh look at some of the hardest problems surrounding the analysis of the so-called "donkey sentences."

2.8. UNIQUENESS AND PROPORTIONS

2.8.1. A Dilemma

The "proportion problem" for the Lewis/Kamp/Heim approach to adverbs of quantification and indefinites was first noted by Irene Heim[3] and has since been discussed by a number of scholars (Partee 1984, Bäuerle & Egli 1985, Heim 1987a, Kadmon 1987, Berman 1987, and others). The problem is illustrated by the following sentence.

(77) When a house has a fireplace, it (the house) is usually old.

The classical Lewis/Kamp/Heim analysis of sentence (77) is given in (77′).

3. Irene Heim discussed the proportion problem in an earlier draft of her dissertation (Heim 1982). She also proposed a technical solution, but then became dissatisfied with it and discarded the whole section in the final version.

(77′) $\textbf{Usually}_{x,y}$[**house**(x) & **fireplace**(y) & **have**(x, y)] [**old**(x)]

(77′) is true if and only if most pairs of individuals that satisfy the restrictive clause of (77′) also satisfy its nuclear scope. Imagine now a situation with 50 houses. Of these houses, 20 are old, 30 are new. Each of the old houses has five fireplaces. The new houses have only one. This means that there are 130 house/fireplace pairs that satisfy the restrictive clause of (77′). Out of those 130 pairs, 100 satisfy the nuclear scope. The classical Lewis/Kamp/Heim analysis, then, predicts that sentence (77) should be true in the situation given. But it is not.

The antecedent of (77) was constructed in such a way that the main predicate is a relatively clear case of an individual-level predicate, and the object is hard to scramble. On our analysis, then, the logical form of (77) should be (77″) rather than (77′).

(77″) $\textbf{Usually}_{x}$[**house**(x) & $\exists_y$[**fireplace**(y) & **have**(x, y)]] [**old**(x)]

In (77″), the restrictive clause of the quantifier *usually* is split into two parts conjoined by '&' as proposed above. The subject appears in the first conjunct (an embedded restrictive clause), since it was base-generated outside of VP. The object must appear in the second conjunct, since it cannot be scrambled. The second conjunct is an embedded nuclear scope, hence is existentially closed. (77″) is true if and only if most individuals that satisfy the restrictive clause of the whole sentence also satisfy its nuclear scope. On our scenario, there are 50 individuals that satisfy the restrictive clause. But out of those, only 20 satisfy the nuclear scope. Sentence (77), then, is correctly predicted to be false in such a situation.

Now consider the next example, which is a version of Heim's famous "sage plant example" (Heim 1982).

(78) When a house has a barn, it often has a second one right next to it (the first barn).

As before, the main predicate of the antecedent of (78) is individual-level, and the object cannot be scrambled. The logical form of (78) should then be (78′).

(78′) $\textbf{Often}_{x}$[**house**(x) & $\exists!_y$[**barn**(y) & **have**(x, y)]]
$\exists_z$[**barn**(z) & **have**(x, z) & z≠ιy[**barn**(y) & **have**(x, y)] &
next-to(z, ιy[**barn**(y) & **have**(x, y)])]

(78′) says that often, if there is a house with exactly one barn, the house has a second barn right next to the first one. But this is absurd. And it is not what

(78) means. We are not assuming that we are only talking about houses with exactly one barn. Yet our approach seems to commit us to some such assumption. Let us briefly review why. *A barn* is an object that cannot be scrambled, hence is caught by existential closure. The phrase *a second one* is best analyzed as 'a barn different from it'. The implicit pronoun 'it' here (as well as the explicit occurrence of *it* in *next to it*) is anaphorically related to *a barn* in the antecedent of the conditional. Since *it* cannot be bound by the same quantifier, it has to be analyzed as an E-type pronoun. Recall that following Evans and Cooper, E-type pronouns are treated as definite descriptions. As such, they carry uniqueness presuppositions. In our case, the uniqueness presupposition is incorporated into the restrictive clause of *often* through presupposition accommodation.

Sentence (78) throws us into a real dilemma. It is sentences like this one that motivated Heim (1982) to pursue what we have been calling "the classical Lewis/Kamp/Heim analysis":

(78″) $\textbf{Often}_{x,y}[\textbf{house}(x)\ \&\ \textbf{barn}(y)\ \&\ \textbf{have}(x, y)]$
$\exists_z[\textbf{barn}(z)\ \&\ \textbf{have}(x, z)\ \&\ z \neq y\ \&\ \textbf{next-to}(z, y)]$

But giving (78) the analysis (78″) will immediately bring back the proportion problem. Here it is. Suppose we have a total of 30 houses. Ten of those houses have five barns each, nicely placed next to each other. The remaining 20 houses have only one barn. Analysis (78″) predicts sentence (78) to be true in such a situation. But it is false.

It seems, then, that there is no way out. We seem to be either stuck with the proportion problem or else committed to absurd uniqueness assumptions.

Let us not give up that fast. The approach taken in this chapter tells us that we should opt for representations like (78′) under any circumstances. These representations are independently motivated and avoid the proportion problem. And there might be a way of getting rid of unwelcome uniqueness assumptions.

We have been following Evans and Cooper in treating E-type pronouns as definite descriptions. Evans and Cooper both adopted Russell's treatment of definite descriptions. And so did we—out of habit. I think that we should continue to treat E-type pronouns as definite descriptions. But we should adopt Heim's theory of definite descriptions (Heim 1982). The consequences of such a move are far-reaching and cannot be properly explored here. Yet we might pursue the proposal up to a point where we can see its promise. On Heim's approach, definite and indefinite noun phrases are treated very much alike. They both introduce a predicate and a variable into logical representations. All by themselves, they are neither quantificational nor referring. But the variable introduced has to be a new variable for indefinite NPs and an old variable for definite NPs. There is also a difference in presuppositions. Definite NPs presuppose their descriptive content, but indefinite NPs don't. Let us look at two simple examples:

(79) a. Harry vaccinated a sheep. He owns it.
b. Harry vaccinated a sheep. He owns the sheep he vaccinated.

(80) a. Mary always wears a dress. Usually, it has polka dots.
b. Mary always wears a dress. Usually, the dress she wears has polka dots.

The (a)-texts both contain an E-type pronoun *it*. In the (b)-texts, the E-type pronoun is replaced by a suitable definite description as proposed by Evans and Cooper (let's assume we know how to get a suitable description). Using Heim's analysis of definite descriptions, we arrive at the following logical representations for (79) and (80):

(79′) a. **past**(l) & $\exists_y$[**sheep**(y) & **vaccinate**(**Harry**$_3$, y, l)]
b. [**sheep**(y) & **vaccinate**(**Harry**$_3$, y, l) & **past**(l) & **own**(**he**, y)]

(80′) a. **Always**$_l$[**location**(l) & **at**(**Mary**$_3$, **l**)] $\exists_y$[**dress**(y) & **wear**(**she**$_3$, y, l)]
b. **Usually**$_{y,l}$[**dress**(y) & **wear**(**she**$_3$, y, l)] [**have polka dots**(y)]

The second part of (79′) consists of a restrictive clause and a nuclear scope conjoined by '&'. As a result of presupposition accommodation, the restrictive clause contains the descriptive content of the definite description 'the sheep Harry vaccinated'. The variable y occurs free in the restrictive clause and in the nuclear scope. It has to receive a value by the context of use. A suitable value is not difficult to find. The first part of (79′) conversationally implicates that Harry vaccinated exactly one sheep at the time under consideration (see Kadmon 1987 for a very detailed discussion of this point). The unique sheep Harry vaccinated, then, will be the value for y.

If a free variable receives a referent from the context of use, the referent has to be familiar in that context. Definiteness in English indicates familiarity. Indefiniteness indicates lack of familiarity. It follows that variables introduced by definite noun phrases can, but variables introduced by indefinite noun phrases cannot, receive a value from the context of use. (This is important. *Firemen are altruistic* cannot mean that some contextually specified firemen are altruistic.)

The second part of (80′) is a tripartite quantifier construction. As before, the restrictive clause contains the descriptive content of the definite description. This time, the adverbial quantifier *usually* binds all variables that occur free in the sentence, and no recourse to contextually supplied values is necessary. A scalar implicature and world knowledge suggest that Mary wears exactly one dress on each occasion.

Combining Evans's and Cooper's analysis of E-type pronouns with Heim's theory of definite descriptions, then, seems to yield the appropriate analysis for sentences like (79) or (80).[4]

Let us now return to example (78). After some simplifications (eliminating stacked nuclear scopes, for example), its final Logical Form will be (78‴).

(78‴) $\mathbf{Often}_x[\mathbf{house}(x)\ \&\ \exists_y[\mathbf{barn}(y)\ \&\ \mathbf{have}(x, y)]]$
$\exists_{z,y}[\mathbf{barn}(z)\ \&\ \mathbf{have}(x, z)\ \&\ \underline{\mathbf{barn}(y)\ \&\ \mathbf{have}(x, y)}\ \&\ z \neq y\ \&$
$\mathbf{next\text{-}to}(z, y)]$

(78‴) correctly captures the meaning of (78). The important part is *barn*(y) & *have*(x, y) in the nuclear scope. This part constitutes the descriptive content of the definite description replacing the two occurrences of E-type pronouns. Since the variable y is not bound from outside the nuclear scope, it is caught by existential closure. The logical representation (78‴) corresponds to the "indefinite Lazy Reading" of donkey pronouns in the terminology of Schubert and Pelletier (1989). On our approach, such a reading can only arise under very special conditions. The donkey pronoun has to be an E-type pronoun, and the variable it introduces must be caught by existential closure.

Heim's theory of definite descriptions, then, may help us solve uniqueness problems with donkey sentences. We are now free to dedicate the remaining pages to proportions. Our approach makes a number of very concrete predictions here, which should not go unmentioned.

2.8.2. Experiments with Donkey Sentences and Proportions

Experimenting with donkey sentences and proportions is a subtle affair. Fragile phenomena like unaccusativity, the stage-level/individual-level distinction, scrambling possibilities, and the topic-focus organization of the sentence can all influence the outcome. Yet the task is not an impossible one. We know the main factors influencing judgments here and will try to keep them under control.

In this section, we examine a special brand of donkey sentences. They are

4. Analyzing E-type pronouns as Heimian definite descriptions allows us to derive the "Accommodation of a Missing Antecedent" approach to discourse subordination discussed in Roberts 1987, 1989. The missing antecedent is the presupposition of the definite description associated with the E-type pronoun. And the accommodation needed is a special case of the general mechanism of presupposition accommodation.

all conditionals with antecedents restricting an adverb of quantification. And the main predicates of the antecedents are always transitive individual-level predicates with indefinite subjects and objects. Following Kadmon (1987), let us distinguish three possible interpretations for such sentences. The three interpretations correspond to the following three types of Logical Forms.

(81) SYMMETRIC INTERPRETATION
Usually$_{x,y}$[**subject**(x) & **object**(y) ...] [.......]
Quantification is over pairs <a,b> such that a satisfies the subject predicate and b satisfies the object predicate.

(82) ASYMMETRIC INTERPRETATION
Usually$_{x,y}$[**subject**(x) ... & $\exists_y$ **object**(y) ...] [.......]
Quantification is over individuals a such that a satisfies the subject predicate and there is an individual b satisfying the object predicate.

(83) OBJECT ASYMMETRIC INTERPRETATION
Usually$_y$[**object**(y) ... & $\exists_x$[**subject**(x) ...]] [.......]
Quantification is over individuals b such that b satisfies the object predicate and there is an individual a satisfying the subject predicate.

These Logical Forms are tripartite quantifier structures with the quantifier *usually,* a restrictive clause, and a nuclear scope. We are interested in the position of subjects and objects within the restrictive clause. Our previous discussion has shown that the restrictive clause itself is split into an embedded restrictive clause and a nuclear scope. On the symmetric reading, subject and object are part of the embedded restrictive clause. On the subject asymmetric reading, the subject is part of the embedded restrictive clause and the object is part of the embedded nuclear scope. On the object asymmetric reading, it is the other way around. Note that these three possibilities are the only ones, given just one object. The fourth conceivable possibility, (84) below, is excluded by the prohibition against vacuous quantification (recall that we are only considering individual-level predicates).

(84) IMPOSSIBLE INTERPRETATION
Usually[... $\exists_{x,y}$[**subject**(x) & **object**(y) ...] [.......]

Given our assumptions about how S-structures are mapped into Logical Forms, we are committed to a number of predictions concerning the possible interpretations of English donkey sentences of the sort considered here. If the main predicate in the antecedent is not unaccusative, its subject is base-generated outside of VP and has to be mapped into the embedded restrictive clause at Logical Form (recall again that we are only talking about individual-level predicates here). If the object is not scrambled, we get the subject asymmetric interpretation. If the object is scrambled, we get the symmetric interpretation. If the predicate is unaccusative, its subject appears outside of VP at S-structure. But in that case, the subject binds a trace within VP, hence can optionally appear in the embedded restrictive clause or in the embedded nuclear scope at Logical Form. If it appears in the restrictive clause and the object is not scrambled, we arrive at the subject asymmetric interpretation. If the object is scrambled, we have the symmetric interpretation. If the subject appears in the nuclear scope, the object has to be scrambled, which gives us the object asymmetric interpretation. Here is a summary of all the predictions.

(85) PREDICTIONS
  a. A subject asymmetric interpretation is possible with any individual-level predicate.
  b. A symmetric interpretation is only possible if the object can be scrambled.
  c. An object asymmetric interpretation is only possible if the predicate is unaccusative and the object can be scrambled.

These predictions are predictions about the possibilities permitted by grammar. If we want to test them, we have to be aware that for each interpretation, there are intonational properties favoring that particular interpretation (see Kadmon 1987, Heim 1987a for discussion). That is, if grammar allows several interpretations for a given sentence, intonation may bias us toward one of them. Quite generally, deaccenting is tied to restrictive clauses, and accenting is tied to nuclear scopes. Here is an overview.

(86) FAVORABLE INTONATION CONDITIONS
  a. *Symmetric:* both subject and object deaccented
  b. *Subject asymmetric:* subject deaccented, object emphasized
  c. *Object asymmetric:* object deaccented, subject emphasized

For each interpretation, there are also specific anaphora conditions that favor that particular interpretation (see Bäuerle & Egli 1985, Kadmon 1987, Heim 1987a for the relevant observations). That is, for each interpretation, there is a particular configuration of donkey pronouns that facilitates that interpretation. (A "donkey pronoun" is any pronoun in the consequent of a conditional that is anaphorically related to an indefinite noun phrase in the antecedent.) For our present purposes, it is not important to know why certain donkey pronoun configurations facilitate certain interpretations. Likewise, we don't have to know why certain intonation conditions bias us toward certain readings. At this point, we only have to know that there *are* additional factors influencing interpretations. This will help us to design appropriate proportion experiments. The following table summarizes the crucial facts about donkey pronoun configurations:

(87) MOST-FAVORABLE DONKEY PRONOUN CONFIGURATIONS

a. *Symmetric:* two donkey pronouns, one related to antecedent subject, the other one related to antecedent object
b. *Subject asymmetric:* one donkey pronoun, related to antecedent subject
c. *Object asymmetric:* one donkey pronoun, related to antecedent object

We are now in the position to test a few selected predictions. Out of the three possible interpretations, the object asymmetric interpretation is predicted to be the most constrained. We should only find it with unaccusative predicates. How can we tell whether a predicate doesn't permit a particular interpretation? I think a relatively safe method is to create the most favorable conditions for the reading we are after. If the reading doesn't emerge under optimal conditions, we may conclude that it is not available.

Let us first examine the verb *adore*. *Adore* is individual-level, it is not unaccusative, and its object can be scrambled. All of those properties can be established with the help of the tests discussed earlier in this chapter. We expect, then, that the symmetric and the subject asymmetric interpretation should be possible for a donkey sentence involving this verb in the antecedent, whereas the object asymmetric interpretation should be excluded. Let us check this last prediction. Consider the following sentence:

(88) When a SICILIAN adores a piece of music, it is rarely a Bellini opera.

In (88), the intonation and anaphora conditions are set up as to be most favorable to the object asymmetric reading. Does (88) have this reading? Suppose we have 300 Sicilians. The following list gives an overview of their favorite pieces of music:

(89) BELLINI OPERAS

Norma	80
La Sonnambula	150
I Puritani	50

OTHER PIECES OF MUSIC

Schubert Mass in E-flat Major	1
Archduke Trio	1
Trout Quintet	1
Kreutzer Sonata	1

Mozart Piano Concerto K.414	5
Brahms Sextet op. 18	1
Brahms Horn Trio op. 40	1
Schubert String Quintet C Major	1
String Quartets "Rasumovsky"	1
Stadler Quintet	1
Cantata BWV 106 "Gottes Zeit"	5
Cantata BWV 82 "Ich habe genug"	1
Don Giovanni	0
Le Nozze di Figaro	0
Wozzeck	0

On this scenario, sentence (88) is intuitively false. Yet the object asymmetric interpretation predicts it to be true. All in all, 15 pieces of music are adored by at least one Sicilian. And very few of those pieces are Bellini operas. Since the conditions were optimal for an object asymmetric reading to arise, we may conclude that verbs like *adore* can't give gise to such readings at all. We have to be careful, though. Take the following sentence:

(90) When a SICILIAN adores a piece of music, we usually include it in our "Morning Pro Musica" program

It seems that the policy expressed in (90) has to lead to the inclusion of a certain percentage of non-Bellini music in the program. As long as there is one Sicilian adoring a piece of music, the piece counts. But then (90) seems to have an object asymmetric reading. Note, however, that there is a crucial difference between (88) and (90). The main predicate in the consequent of (88) is individual-level, while the main predicate in the consequent of (90) is stage-level. This seems to have an effect on how to interpret the main predicate in the antecedent. (90) suggests that we have a pile of letters from listeners, on the basis of which we make our decisions. Whenever a Sicilian expresses her adoration for a piece of music, the piece is given consideration. But this means that the verb *adore* is being pushed toward being a stage-level predicate.

Let us now examine an unaccusative case. Take the verb *belong to*. The tests proposed earlier establish that it is individual-level, unaccusative, and that its object can be scrambled. The following sentence expresses a generalization from real estate catalogs:

(91) When a LAKE belongs to a lot, it (the lot) is usually in Minnesota.

As before, intonation and anaphora conditions are chosen so as to bias us toward an object asymmetric interpretation. This time, we predict that the interpretation will emerge. And it does. Suppose we have a total of 30 lots being offered. Out of those 30 lots, ten are in Minnesota and they have five lakes each. The remaining 20 lots are all in the Adirondacks, and they have just one lake. In this situation, (91) is intuitively false, and the object asymmetric interpretation is the only interpretation that predicts this. A verb like *belong to,* then, can give rise to the object asymmetric interpretation as expected. It should be able to give rise to the other two kinds of interpretations as well, if only we create the right conditions. Take the following example:

(92) (When a linguist merely attends the CONFERENCES of a professional organization, she often doesn't care about its other activities. But) when a linguist BELONGS to a professional organization, she usually identifies with its political stand.

In (92), the text in parentheses is meant to evoke a context for the conditional we are interested in. The intonation and anaphora conditions bias us toward a symmetric interpretation. Imagine now the following scenario.

We have 20 linguists. They are all members of the Linguistic Society of America, of GLOW, and of the Deutsche Gesellschaft für Sprachwissenschaft. They don't care about the politics of any of those organizations, however. Each of the linguists is a member of a fourth professional organization, and this is the organization she really identifies with. Here is a list of the linguists (represented by numbers) and their primary professional organization.

(93)
1 Acoustical Society of America
2 American Anthropological Society
3 American Association of Applied Linguistics
4 American Dialect Society
5 American Sociological Association
6 Association Venezolana de Linguistica
7 Association for Computational Linguistics
8 Association for Symbolic Logic
9 Australian Linguistic Society
10 Berkeley Linguistics Society
11 Canadian Linguistic Association
12 Chicago Linguistic Society
13 Indiana University Linguistics Club
14 International Society of Phonetic Sciences
16 Linguistic Society of India
17 Linguistic Society of the Philippines

18 Linguistic Association of Great Britain
19 Modern Language Association of America
20 Societas Caucasologica Europea

I think that sentence (92) is intuitively false, given our scenario. The only interpretation that predicts it to be false is the symmetric interpretation. We have 80 linguist-organization pairs such that the linguist is a member of the organization. But we only have 20 linguist-organization pairs such that the linguist identifies with the politics of the organization. The subject asymmetric interpretation predicts the sentence to be true, since each linguist is a member of an organization she identifies with. The object asymmetric interpretation predicts the sentence to be true as well, since for most organizations, there is a member who cares about its politics.

We have seen that a verb like *belong to* can have an object asymmetric and a symmetric interpretation. The next example shows that, as expected, it can also have a subject asymmetric interpretation. As before, intonation and anaphora conditions are chosen to fit.

(94) When a linguist belongs to a professional ORGANIZATION, she is usually not affiliated with a university.

Imagine that we have 40 linguists. Of these, 20 are the linguists from the previous example, so we know about their involvement in professional organizations. None of them is affiliated with a university. The remaining 20 linguists are members of the Linguistic Society of America and belong to no other professional organization. They are all affiliated with some university. In this situation, (94) is intuitively false, and the subject asymmetric interpretation is the only interpretation that predicts it to be false.

An unaccusative verb like *belong to,* then, can indeed give rise to three interpretations, whereas the readings for a verb like *adore* are more constrained. While we didn't check all possible predictions, of course, the results obtained so far are encouraging and lend further support to our conception of the link between S-structure and Logical Form representations.

2.8.3. Stage-Level Predicates and Proportions

In this section, we will continue our investigation of donkey sentences and proportions. This time, we will only consider conditionals with stage-level predicates in the antecedent. As before, I will be quite selective with respect to the issues discussed, and open up many questions for further research. The following example is inspired by an example from Bäuerle & Egli 1985. A similar example plays a crucial role in Berman 1987.

(95) When a birder spots an owl, it is usually night.

Since we are interested in proportions, we are interested in the antecedent of (95), repeated as (96).

(96) . . . a birder spots an owl. . . .

Four possible logical forms for (96) are permitted by the approach we have been arguing for in this chapter:

(96′) a. **location**(l) & $\exists_{x,y}$[**birder**(x) & **owl**(y) & **spot**(x, y, l)]
b. **location**(l) & **birder**(x) & $\exists_{y}$[**owl**(y) & **spot**(x, y, l)]
c. **location**(l) & **birder**(x) & **owl**(y) & [**spot**(x, y, l)]
d. **location**(l) & **owl**(y) & $\exists_{x}$[**birder**(x) & **spot**(x, y, l)]

In all four logical representations, a variable for spatiotemporal location is present in the restrictive clause. It has to be there, since it is introduced by the tense predicate, and the tense predicate is base-generated outside of VP. Both the subject and the object of (96) can optionally appear in the restrictive clause. The subject can appear in the restrictive clause since it appears outside of VP at S-structure. It can also appear in the nuclear scope, since it binds a trace within VP. The object can appear in the nuclear scope since it appears within VP at S-structure. And it can also appear in the restrictive clause, since it is the sort of object that can scramble. The free variables in (96′a–d) may become bound by a quantifier, if the sentences are embedded into more complex structures. In fact, the variables introduced by the subject or object *have* to be bound. Being introduced by indefinite NPs, these variables cannot receive values from the context of use.

Let us now examine the possible Logical Forms for (95).

(95′) a. **Usually**$_{l}$[**location**(l) & $\exists_{x,y}$[**birder**(x) & **owl**(y) & **spot**(x, y, l)] [**night**(l)]
b. **Usually**$_{l,x}$[**location**(l) & **birder**(x) & $\exists_{x}$[**owl**(y) & **spot**(x, y, l)]] [**night**(l)]
c. **Usually**$_{l,x,z}$[**location**(l) & **birder**(x) & [**owl**(y) & **spot**(x, y, l)] [**night(l)**]
d. **Usually**$_{l,y}$[**location**(l) & **owl**(y) & $\exists_{x}$[**birder**(x) & **spot**(x, y, l)]] [**night(l)**]

All four representations (95′a–d) involve quantification over spatiotemporal locations. While quantification over spatiotemporal locations is a topic that I cannot seriously pursue here, I should at least add a few remarks as to its main properties. Spatiotemporal locations are related to each other by part-whole relationships, and this means that we must be careful with quantification. Quite generally, any sort of quantification seems to require that the domain of quantification is set up in such a way that its elements are truly distinct. Take the objects in this room. There are two tables, two chairs, and a bed. There are at least five objects, then. Each of those pieces of furniture has four legs. Can we conclude that there are at least 25 objects in this room? No way. This is not how counting works.

Let us now return to the conditionals in (95′a–d). How do we manage to quantify over spatiotemporal locations here? Well, we have to make sure that the main restrictive clauses of those conditionals specify appropriate domains. One way of achieving this is through the interpretation mechanism for sentences with a free Davidsonian variable. We expect differences for different aktionsarten here, an issue I cannot develop in this paper. As an illustration take (97), which contains the achievement verb *spot*.

(97) **spot**(**Megan, Bubo,** l)

We are looking for an interpretation of (97) that guarantees that the set of spatiotemporal locations satisfying (97) constitutes an appropriate domain of quantification. A requirement of this kind is needed in view of sentences like *When Megan spots Bubo, it is usually night,* or *Megan spotted Bubo twice.* We know that a domain of quantification is never appropriate if there are part-whole relationships holding among its members. There are two part-whole relationships to watch out for in our case. The first one is spatial in nature. Whenever Megan spots Bubo on Mulholland Drive, she also spots Bubo in Los Angeles. The second one is temporal. If Megan spotted Bubo yesterday, she also spotted Bubo this year. If the set of entities satisfying (97) has to consist of distinct members, then we should say that (97) is satisfied by any spatiotemporal location l such that l is a *minimal* location where a spotting of Bubo by Megan takes place.

A representation like (95′a) will now be true if and only if most minimal spatiotemporal locations l such that a spotting of an owl by a birder takes places in l are locations where it is night. These are the correct truth conditions for (95′a) (see Berman 1987 for a similar proposal within a situation-based semantics).

We are now in the position to return to our main topic, donkey sentences and proportions. I have argued that the grammar allows four possible representations for (95). What I want to show next is that these four representations all seem to mean the same, given some plausible assumptions. Compare (95′a) and (95′c), for example, which are repeated here:

(95′) a. **Usually**$_l$[**location**(l) & $\exists_{x,y}$[**birder**(x) & **owl**(y) & **spot**(x, y, l)]] [**night**(l)]

c. **Usually**$_{l,x,y}$[**location**(l) & [**birder**(x) & **owl**(y) & **spot**(x, y, l)] [**night**(l)]

In (95′c), quantification is over triples. The set of triples satisfying the main restrictive clause of (95′c) has very special properties, however. Whenever two triples ⟨l,a,b⟩ and ⟨l,c,d⟩ are in the set, then a = c and b = d. Why is this? The main restrictive clause of (95′c) is satisfied by any triple ⟨l,a,b⟩ such that a is a birder and b is an owl and l is a minimal spatiotemporal location where a spots b. If l is to be a minimal spatiotemporal location where a spots b, then a and b have to be at l, but there couldn't be other birders or owls at l. If there were, the location wouldn't be minimal any more. It is now easy to establish that there is a one-to-one correspondence between the locations satisfying the main restrictive clause of (95′a) and triples satisfying the main restrictive clause of (95′c). Whenever a location l satisfies the main restrictive clause of (95′a), there is a unique pair ⟨a,b⟩ such that ⟨l,a,b⟩ satisifies the restrictive clause of (95′c). And whenever a triple ⟨l,a,b⟩ satisfies the main restrictive clause of (95′c), l satisfies the main restrictive clause of (95′a). It can now be shown that a location satisfies the main restrictive clause and the main nuclear scope of (95′a) if and only if the corresponding triple satisfies the main restrictive clause and the main nuclear scope of (95′c). But this means that (95′a) is true if and only if (95′c) is. Similar arguments can be made to show that all four representations (95′a–d) are assigned the same meaning. The interpretation of those sentences should always amount to something that looks like the symmetric interpretation we discussed for individual-level predicates. It isn't, of course. We only get a similar effect by quantifying over locations.

The discussion in Bäuerle & Egli 1985 suggests that this last expectation might not be quite right. Suppose we have 100 bird-watchers. They go bird-watching on Mulholland Drive. One half of the birders goes in groups of ten. The other 50 birders go on individual outings. Each party takes off on a different day and spots exactly one owl. The five groups of ten spot their owl during the day. The 50 individual bird-watchers spot their owl at night. On this scenario, (95) is intuitively true. Yet it seems that our analysis predicts it to be false. There are 50 minimal spatiotemporal locations l such that a birder spots an owl at l and l is a day time location. And there are no more minimal spatiotemporal locations l such that a birder spots an owl at l and l is a night location.

Using examples of this kind, Berman (1987) argues convincingly that there is a certain amount of leeway as to what a minimal location ('situation' in his framework) is. In our case, he would reason that if a birder is part of a group, the minimal location in which she spots an owl might sometimes be taken to be identical with the minimal location in which the whole group spots the owl. This is what it means to spot an owl together. Likewise, should a birder spot several owls at the same time, we would sometimes want to treat those owls as a group. The minimal spatiotemporal location where the birder spots one owl would then be identical with the minimal spatiotemporal location where he spots the whole group.

With stage-level predicates in the antecedent, then, we may get group effects in donkey sentences. These group effects might be mistaken for "true" asymmetric readings. And "true" asymmetric readings might be misanalyzed as group effects. Within a Davidsonian framework, the latter proposal would require that individual-level predicates have a Davidsonian argument (an eventuality argument), too. While this approach is attractive, the evidence accumulated in this chapter argues against such a move.

But for the sake of the argument, suppose that, contrary to what I have argued earlier, individual-level predicates do have a Davidsonian argument after all. Would it then be plausible to analyze all asymmetric readings as group effects? I think not. A major difficulty for such a proposal would be to account for the distribution of asymmetric readings with individual-level predicates. We would have to explain, for example, why an object-asymmetric reading is possible with some verbs, but not with others. Why should the privilege of being treated as a group be granted to the lakes that belong to the same lot, but not to the Sicilians who like the same piece of music? If this line of reasoning is on the right track, then there are two sources for what looks like asymmetric readings in donkey sentences: a syntactic source with individual-level predicates, and a conceptual source with stage-level predicates. This means that Kadmon's account of asymmetric readings seems to be correct for individual-level predicates. And the proposal of Berman (1987) is likely to turn out to be the adequate account for stage-level predicates.

2.8.4. Comparisons and Concluding Remarks

Several recent discussions of donkey sentences have considered the possibility of going back to a position where all indefinites are uniformly treated as existential quantifiers (Heim 1987a, Groenendijk & Stokhof 1987, Chierchia 1988, Schubert & Pelletier 1989). All of those proposals were intended to overcome some apparent shortcomings of the original Lewis/Kamp/

Heim proposal. Major concerns include the proportion problem and a commitment to implausible readings for sentences like the following (adapted from Schubert & Pelletier's sentence):

(98) If I find a quarter in my pocket, I'll put it in the parking meter.

Schubert and Pelletier argue that on its most plausible reading, sentence (98) doesn't mean that all quarters that I find in my pocket will have to go into the parking meter. This intuition seems right, contrary to what the classical Lewis/Kamp/Heim approach seems to predict.

In this last section, I will briefly address the major issues raised by these new proposals. And I will conclude that the slight amendments to the classical Lewis/Kamp/Heim approach that I have been arguing for in this chapter are to be preferred.

If all indefinite noun phrases in the antecedents of donkey sentences are treated as existential quantifiers, all donkey pronouns are E-type pronouns, since they are not c-commanded by their antecedents. We considered two possible analyses of E-type pronouns. The standard analysis takes them to be Russellian definite descriptions. Our own analysis treats them as Heimian definite descriptions. This means that they are like indefinite descriptions if they are caught by existential closure. Heim 1987a critically examines the first proposal for donkey pronouns. The analysis of Chierchia 1988 can be seen as a version of the second proposal. Both Heim and Chierchia rely on a neo-Davidsonian framework where all predicates have an eventuality argument. Here is a sketch of the essence of the two types of analyses for a simple donkey sentence (let us call these analyses ''E-type only'' analyses).

(99) When a donkey is stubborn, it is usually from Andorra.

E-TYPE PRONOUNS AS DEFINITE DESCRIPTIONS

For most minimal eventualities e such that there is a stubborn donkey in e, there is an eventuality e′ such that the unique donkey that is stubborn in e is from Andorra in e′.

E-TYPE PRONOUNS AS INDEFINITE DESCRIPTIONS

For most minimal eventualities e such that there is a stubborn donkey in e, there is an eventuality e′ such that a donkey that is stubborn in e is from Andorra in e′.

Assuming that quantification in (99) is over *minimal* eventualities where a donkey is stubborn (as it has to be, given the arguments above), the two analyses yield the same truth conditions for (99). Every minimal eventuality where a donkey is stubborn is an eventuality where exactly one donkey is stubborn. There are other sentences, however, where the two types of analyses make different predictions. The following type of example is an individual-level version of a parallel stage-level example ascribed to Hans Kamp ("When a bishop meets another man, he blesses him"; Mats Rooth, pers. comm.).

(100) When a man resembles another man, he tries to avoid him.

E-TYPE PRONOUNS AS DEFINITE DESCRIPTIONS
For every minimal eventuality e such that a man resembles another man in e, there is an eventuality e′ such that in e′, the unique man who resembles another man in e tries to avoid the unique man who resembles another man in e.

E-TYPE PRONOUNS AS INDEFINITE DESCRIPTIONS
For every minimal eventuality e such that a man resembles another man in e, there is an eventuality e′ such that in e′, a man who resembles another man in e tries to avoid a man who resembles another man in e.

Neither 'E-type only' analysis gets the truth conditions for (100) right. Given that 'resemble' is a symmetric relation, the first analysis makes (100) true in all worlds in which no man resembles another man and false in all other worlds. There simply cannot be a unique man who resembles another man. The second analysis doesn't capture the fact that (100) says that whenever two men resemble each other they *both* try to avoid *the other*. It only requires that one of the two men tries to avoid the other.

Examples like (100) provide one of the strongest arguments in favor of a Lewis/Kamp/Heim analysis. Since our proposal preserves the essential features of this analysis, it is able to treat those examples correctly. Depending on whether the object *another man* in the antecedent of (100) is scrambled or not, our approach admits the following two logical representations:

(100′) $\mathbf{Always}_x[\mathbf{man}(x)\ \&\ \exists_y[\mathbf{man}(y)\ \&\ x \neq y\ \&\ \mathbf{resemble}(x, y)]]$
$\exists_y[\mathbf{man}(y)\ \&\ x \neq y\ \&\ \mathbf{resemble}(x, y)\ \&\ [\mathbf{try\text{-}to\text{-}avoid}(x, y)]]$

(100″) $\mathbf{Always}_{x,y}[\mathbf{man}(x)\ \&\ \mathbf{man}(y)\ \&\ x \neq y\ \&\ [\mathbf{resemble}(x, y)]]$
$[\mathbf{try\text{-}to\text{-}avoid}(x, y)]$

Both representations predict that whenever two men resemble each other they both try to avoid the other.

Example (100) shows that 'E-type only' analyses of donkey sentences face serious empirical problems that our version of the Lewis/Kamp/Heim analysis avoids. Let us now turn to some of the problems with the classical Lewis/Kamp/Heim approach that 'E-type only' analyses are designed to overcome.

We have already discussed the proportion problem. One important point to keep in mind is that the task here is not just to overcome a problem. An adequate analysis has to be able to actually predict the subtle proportion facts we've encountered above. An approach that treats all indefinite noun phrases uniformly as existential quantifiers and all donkey pronouns uniformly as E-type pronouns is unlikely to achieve this. To illustrate this, let us finally examine sentence (98), which is repeated here.

(98) If I find a quarter in my pocket, I'll put it in the parking meter.

Recall that Schubert and Pelletier observe that on the prominent reading of (98), not all quarters that I find in my pocket have to go into the parking meter, contrary to what the classical Lewis/Kamp/Heim analysis seems to require. The reading of (98) that Schubert and Pelletier are interested in is the reading where *if* cannot be replaced by *when*. I have argued above that in this case, the *if*-clause restricts an epistemic modal. We have also seen that epistemic modals cannot bind variables. Our approach now permits the following Logical Form for (98):

(98′) **Must[location**(l) & $\exists_x$[**quarter**(x) & **in-my-pocket**(x, l)]
$\exists_{l',x}$[**after-now**(l′) & **quarter**(x) & **in-my-pocket**(x, l)
& [**put**(I, x, **parking meter,** l′)]]

In (98′) the variable l is left free, since *must* cannot bind it. It will have to receive a value from the context of use, hence has a definite interpretation. The indefinite noun phrase *a quarter* has to be mapped into the embedded nuclear scope of the main restrictive clause, where the variable it introduces can be caught by existential closure. If it were mapped into the embedded restrictive clause of the main restrictive clause, the variable could not be bound. Nor could it receive a value from the context of use (due to the indefiniteness of *a quarter*). The donkey pronoun *it* must be interpreted as an E-type pronoun ('the quarter in my pocket'). It is analyzed as a Heimian definite description. The result is precisely the reading Schubert and Pelletier want to get for (98). If I find a quarter in my pocket, I will put a quarter from among the quarters I find in my pocket into the parking meter.

It seems, then, that the slight amendments to the classical Lewis/Kamp/Heim approach that I have been advocating here not only overcome the problems of the original proposal, but also avoid the empirical shortcomings of the 'E-type only' theories that were intended to be its successors.

ACKNOWLEDGMENTS

Research for this chapter was supported in part by NSF grant BNS 87-19999. Previous versions of the paper were read at the Seminar für natürlichsprachliche Systeme in Tübingen, at CSLI in Stanford, at the MIT Center for Cognitive Science, at Cornell University, and in David Pesetsky's seminar at MIT. I'd like to thank the organizers of these talks for the opportunity to present my thoughts, and I am grateful for the comments and suggestions I received from the various audiences. I'd also like to thank my colleagues Emmon Bach and Barbara Partee for very helpful conversations in connection with our NSF grant. During the past years, I have been working with Karina Wilkinson, Nirit Kadmon, Steve Berman, and Molly Diesing on related topics, and their insights and proposals had a considerable and visible influence on the present work. Lisa Selkirk, Irene Heim, and Arnim von Stechow all gave me detailed and much appreciated comments on various drafts. Very special thanks go to David Pesetsky for his sustained interest and invaluable feedback during all stages of the research that led to the final 1988 version of this chapter.

3 INDIVIDUAL-LEVEL PREDICATES AS INHERENT GENERICS

Gennaro Chierchia

3.1. INTRODUCTION

Carlson (1977b) noted that predicates can be classified as belonging to two natural classes, which he dubbed *individual-level* vs. *stage-level* (*i-level* and *s-level* henceforth), and proposed an account for this distinction. Among other things, Carlson showed that this distinction has important implications for our understanding of genericity. Recently Diesing (1992) and Kratzer (1988; cf. chapter 2, this volume) have developed an interesting alternative to Carlson's approach, based on the idea that while s-level predicates have an extra Davidsonian argument for space-time locations, i-level predicates lack such an argument. They have argued that the bulk of the properties of i-level predicates can be derived from this difference. In this chapter, I would like to explore an approach that, while preserving the spirit (and even some of the specific insights) of the aforementioned approaches, might arguably take us a little further in our understanding of the relevant contrast. In line with, for example, Parsons (1990) among many others, I will argue that all predicates have a Davidsonian argument ranging over occasions/eventualities, but that in i-level predicates this argument has to be bound by a generic operator. In this sense, i-level predicates are claimed to be inherently generic.[1]

This chapter is organized as follows. In the remainder of this introduction, I will review the bulk of the properties that make i-level predicates into a natural class. In section 2, I will sketch some background assumptions. In section 3, I will discuss genericity. In section 4, I will articulate my proposal; in section 5, I will discuss its consequences, and finally, in section 6, I will compare it with other approaches.

I-level predicates express properties of individuals that are permanent or tendentially stable. S-level predicates, per contrast, attribute to individuals transient, episodic properties. As Carlson argues, there are three basic types of i-level predicates, namely:

1. For a recent view different from both Diesing's and the one presented here, cf. Bowers 1993.

(1) a. Stative verbs, like *know, love, hate,* etc. (vs. *hit, run,* etc.)
b. All (predicative) NPs, like *be a man, be mammals,* etc.
c. Adjectives like *intelligent, tall, blue,* etc. (vs. *drunk, available,* etc.)

In what follows I give a list of six key properties that have been identified in the literature as criterial for the characterization of i-level predicates.

1. Stable stativity. The first property is simple and self-evident. I-level predicates are all aspectually stative. They all have the characteristics typical of statives (like being ungrammatical in the progressive, having the subinterval property, and so forth; cf. Dowty 1979). The only statives that are s-level are adjectives which express "transient" or "episodic" qualities (like being drunk or being sick) and pure locatives (like being on the roof). Deciding whether a state is "transient" or "stable" is sometimes difficult, for the notions involved are vague. Nonetheless, we seem to be able to settle the issue in most cases. For example, normally, if one is intelligent or tall, one clearly tends to retain these properties. Of course, accidents capable of altering such tendentially permanent states can occur. But this does not affect their being tendentially stable. Per contrast, a single state of, say, drunkenness lasts relative little. If it doesn't pass, you are not just drunk—you are an alcoholic. This difference manifests itself in the behavior of temporal adverbials. Consider (2):

(2) a. John was drunk yesterday / last month / a year ago.
b. ??John was tall yesterday / last month / a year ago.

While (2a) is wholly normal, the interpretation of (2b) calls for special scenarios (e.g., an accident capable of affecting John's height).

There is also another factor that needs to be taken into consideration. Sometimes one and the same state can be viewed as either stable or transient. For example, in saying "John is sick," we may mean that he is chronically sick, or that he just has an occasional ailment. So *sick* can perhaps be classified as belonging to both classes. Moreover, a verb that is normally classified as stable can in certain cases be reclassified as transient. Again, this will generally involve setting up a special context of some kind. Consider (3), for example:

(3) a. John was intelligent on Tuesday, but a vegetable on Wednesday.
b. A friend of mine likes DRT on Mondays and Thursdays and hates it on Tuesdays and Fridays.

Be intelligent, be a vegetable, like all express stable states; that is, they are i-level. However, in (3) they are being used as s-level predicates. For example, in (3a) we either must interpret the VP as "behave intelligently" or else we must imagine that John has a double personality which involves switching his mental capacities on and off in an abnormal manner. If we all were like him, *intelligent* would be s-level. It is intuitively clear that a shift from i-level to s-level (akin to the well-known shifts from one aspectual class to another or, for nouns, from mass to count) is taking place in these examples.

Modulo these caveats, the first feature that makes i-level predicates into a natural class is the fact that they express stable states, which manifests itself linguistically in the oddity of sentences with temporal modifiers such as (2b).

2. *Locatives.* Not only are there restrictions on the cooccurence of temporal modifiers with i-level predicates. There also are even tighter restrictions on their cooccurrence with locative modifiers. In fact, as Carlson (1982) noticed, modification of an i-level predicate by a locative is quite generally impossible. This can be seen by the following kind of contrast:

(4) a. ??John is a linguist in his car.
b. ??John is intelligent in France.
c. ??John knows Latin in his office.

(5) a. John is always sick in France.
b. John works in his office.

Intuitively, it is as if i-level predicates were, so to speak, unlocated. If one is intelligent, one is intelligent nowhere in particular. S-level predicates, on the other hand, are located in space.[2]

3. *Perception sentences.* A third property of i-level predicates is that they do not occur felicitously within the 'small clause' complements of perception verbs:

(6) a. *I saw John a linguist.
b. *I saw John tall.
c. *I heard John like Mary.

(7) a. I saw John drunk.
b. I heard Mary beat John.

2. Locatives become more acceptable if the sentence contains an indefinite or bare plural;
(i) In Italy, five-year-olds know how to play soccer.
I believe that in these cases the locative is understood as modifying the noun. For instance (i) is interpreted as (ii):
(ii) [Five-year-olds in Italy] know how to play soccer.

It is unclear why this should be so. Notice that one cannot get away with saying that certain states cannot be seen or otherwise perceived. Height, for example, is prominently perceivable. One can certainly see that John is tall (or that he is not). Yet one cannot describe this perception using (6b). Moreover, the ungrammaticality of (6a–c) cannot just be due to a ban against having states in the complement of perception reports, for *drunk* in (7a) is a state. Perceptual reports seem to exclude just i-level predicates, and it is not obvious why.

4. There-*sentences.* Another seemingly unrelated grammatical structure that appears to single out i-level predicates is the existential construction with *there*. In particular, the coda position of *there*-sentences does allow adjectives, as in (8a), but as it turns out, only s-level ones.

(8) a. There are two men drunk/sick/available, ...
b. ??There are two men intelligent/white/altruistic, ...

Again, this cannot be construed as a ban against stativity, for adjectives are all aspectually stative. Moreover, there is nothing patently wrong with the meaning of the sentences in (8b). It is quite clear what they should mean, if they were grammatical. They ought to mean something like:

(9) There are two intelligent/white/altruistic men around.

Yet we cannot express what (9) does by means of (8b).

5. Bare plurals. I-level predicates also interact in an interesting way with bare plurals. A prominent property of i-level predicates is that they select the universal reading of bare plurals, in contrast with s-level predicates:

(10) a. Humans are mammals.
b. Firemen are altruistic.
c. Dogs hate cats.

(11) a. Firemen are available.
b. Dogs are barking in the courtyard.

This observation played a central role in the theory of Carlson (1977b). The bare plural subjects in (10) must all be interpreted universally (or generically). The bare plurals in (11), on the other hand, are naturally interpreted existentially. They may also arguably have a universal reading. But the relevant point is that for the bare plurals in (10) an existential interpretation is just impossible.

The NPs we focused on in (10) and (11) are all subjects. For objects, we have a broader range of options. Consider the following examples:

(12) a. Lions have manes.
b. Dogs hate cats.

The object in (12a) is interpreted existentially. Sentence (12a) says roughly that for every lion there is a mane that it has. The object in (12b) is instead interpreted universally. Sentence (12b) says that for every dog and every cat the former hates the latter.

A further interesting fact, noted by Kratzer (chapter 2, this volume), is that subjects of i-level unaccusatives (or passives) *can* be interpreted existentially. For example:

(13) a. Ponds belong to this property.
b. Counterexamples to this claim are known to me.

Quite clearly, (13a)'s most natural interpretation is that there are ponds that belong to this property. Similarly for (13b).

These observations on the interaction of i-level predicates with bare plurals can be schematically summarized as follows:

(14) a. The bare plural subject of non-unaccusative i-level predicates must be interpreted universally.
b. The bare plural subjects of i-level unaccusatives and passives, as well as other bare plural arguments of i-level predicates, can be interpreted existentially.

The distribution of universal readings of bare plurals seems to form a quite regular pattern, sensitive to the nature of the grammatical relations involved.

6. *Adverbs of quantification.* The following set of facts has also been noticed by Kratzer. It concerns the interaction of i-level predicates with adverbs of quantification. Consider the following contrast:

(15) a. ??When John knows Latin, he always knows it well.
b. ??When John is intelligent, he is always pleasant.

(16) a. When John speaks Latin, he always speaks it well.
b. When John is drunk, he is always obnoxious.

The sentences in (15), which involve i-level predicates, sound strange, in contrast with the fully parallel s-level sentences in (16), which are quite natural. Kratzer notices further that if we replace one of the NPs in the *when*-clause of (15a) or (15b) with an indefinite or a bare plural, the sentence becomes grammatical:

(17) a. When a Moroccan knows French, she knows it well.
b. When a student is intelligent, it is a pleasure to work with him or her.

A closely related pattern can be observed in the absence of a *when*-clause:

(18) a. John always speaks French.
b. ??John always knows French.
c. A Moroccan always knows French.
d. Moroccans always know French.

Thus here, too, we find a pretty regular behavior. The generalization seems to be that sentences involving an adverb of quantification and an i-level predicate must for some reason have an indefinite or a bare plural as argument.

This cursory overview should suffice to illustrate that i-level predicates display a fairly systematic and interesting clustering of properties that calls for an explanation. A number of diverse grammatical constructions seem to single them out. The question is why. In order to formulate my hypothesis, I will first need to spell out a number of background assumptions.

3.2. BACKGROUND

In what follows I adopt a particular combination of syntactic and semantic assumptions, the one I feel is best suited to supplement my main hypothesis. These assumptions are widely shared and arguably independently needed. They do not, however, represent the only way in which the thesis I am exploring can be cast.

3.2.1. The Syntax-Semantics Map

I will adopt a run-of-the-mill version of the Principles and Parameters framework. In this framework, S(urface)-structures are mapped into L(ogical) F(orms) by Move α. One of the effects of this operation is the adjunction of NPs to S, which fixes their scope (Quantifier Raising). LF is the syntactic level that feeds into semantic interpretation, which takes the form of a recursive mapping of LF-structures into Intensional Logic. Each lexical entry is associated with a restricted range of logical types that determine its semantic makeup. For example, NPs come in (at least) two types: the type *e* of basic individuals and the type *gq* ($= \langle\langle e,t\rangle,t\rangle$) of generalized quantifiers.[3] Verbs also come in different basic types, depending on how many arguments they take and whether they are extensional or intensional. I will adopt Montague's theory of intensional verbs. I also assume that all verbs take an extra argument ranging over situations, in the spirit of Davidson (1967) and Parsons (1990), among many others. I will use e_s for the type of situations. (19) gives a list of some common categories:

3. I am ignoring predicative NPs for the moment. See below (sec. 3.4.3) for some discussion.

(19)

Category	Type	Example	Name
S	t	John runs	sentence
V	$\langle e_s, \langle e,t\rangle\rangle$	walk, run	intransitive extensional verbs
V	$\langle e_s, \langle\langle s,gq\rangle, t\rangle$	be missing	intransitive intensional verbs
V	$\langle e_s, \langle e, \langle e,t\rangle\rangle\rangle$	hit, love	transitive extensional verbs
V	$\langle e_s, \langle\langle s,gq\rangle, \langle e,t\rangle\rangle\rangle$	seek, need	transitive intensional verbs
V	$\langle e_s, \langle\langle s,t\rangle, \langle e,t\rangle\rangle\rangle$	know, believe	proposition taking verbs
NP	e	John, he	e-level NPs
NP	gq	a man, every man	gq-level NPs

The situation argument is automatically filled by an appropriate variable, which is then bound by tense operators and modified by adverbs. The core rule of semantic interpretation is functional application. In a configuration of the form $[_{XP}$ A B$]$ one constituent is going to be a function and the other the argument to which the function is applied. Which of the constituents is interpreted as function depends on the types of A and B. For example:

(20) $[_{V'}$ kiss John$]$ ⇒ tr(kiss)(tr(john)) = [**kiss**(**s**)](**j**)
where tr(α) is the translation of α in IL

In (20) the type of the verb (after the situation argument has been saturated) is going to be $\langle e,\langle e,t\rangle\rangle$ and the type of the NP is going to be e, so the interpretation of V′ will be derived by applying the verb meaning to the noun meaning.

When the types of functions and arguments do not match, one can resort to a limited set of type-shifting principles. These include, for example, intensional abstraction and type promotion:

(21) a. *Intensional Abstraction*
$^\wedge\alpha \rightarrow \langle s,a\rangle$
$\alpha \mapsto {}^\wedge\alpha$

b. *Type Promotion*
Lift: a $\rightarrow \langle\langle a,b\rangle,b\rangle$
$\alpha \mapsto \lambda\beta\beta(\alpha)$

Here are some examples of where these type-shifting principles would be used:

(22) a. $[_{V'}$ believe that John is smart$]$ ⇒ tr(believe (^tr(that John is smart))
= **believe**(**s**)(^**smart**(**j**))

b. $[_{V'}$ seek Bill$]$ ⇒ tr(seek)(^lift(tr(Bill))) = **seek**(^λPP(**b**))

In (22a) 'believe' is looking for a proposition, but the complement denotes, under the present assumptions, a truth value. This mismatch is fixed by using intensional abstraction. Similarly, in (22b) 'seek' is looking for a $\langle s,gq \rangle$, while '**b**' is of type *e;* however, by applying 'Lift' and intensional abstraction to it we obtain an object of the right kind. Quantifier raising (QR) is interpreted as Montague's 'quantifying in', as illustrated in (23):[4]

(23) a. $[NP_i\ S] \Rightarrow tr(NP)(\lambda x_i tr(S))$
b. $[\text{every cat}_i[\text{John likes } t_i]] \Rightarrow \lambda P \forall x[\mathbf{man}(x) \rightarrow P(x)](\lambda x_i\ \mathbf{like}(\mathbf{j}, x_i))$
$= \forall x[\mathbf{man}(x) \rightarrow \mathbf{like}(\mathbf{j}, x)]$

Following many current proposals, I assume that QR can adjoin NPs to other categories besides S, such as, in particular, VP and NP. The semantics for such structures is a pointwise extension of the basic quantifying-in rule. I refer to, for example, Rooth 1985 for details.

I do not assume that QR is, in general, obligatory (although there may be constructions that force it). Quantified NPs can be interpreted in situ when the types allow for it. So for example, a sentence like (24a) can have either the LF in (24b) or the one in (24c). The corresponding interpretations are indicated:

(24) a. Every man walks.
b. $[_S \text{ every man}[_{VP} \text{ walks}]] \Rightarrow \lambda P \forall x[\mathbf{man}(x) \rightarrow P(x)](\mathbf{walk})$
c. $[_S \text{ every man}_i[t_i \text{ walks}]] \Rightarrow \lambda P \forall x[\mathbf{man}(x) \rightarrow P(x)](\lambda x_i\ \mathbf{walk}(x_i))$

Quantified NPs can also be interpreted in situ within the VP by means of a type-shifting operation such as Partee and Rooth's (1983) 'argument raising'. This operation turns an *e*-taking function into a *gq*-taking one. In (25a) I give a simplified definition (for the case of two-place relations) which I exemplify in (25b). See Partee & Rooth 1983 for extensions and motivation.

(25) a. $[_Q\ R] = \lambda \mathcal{P} \lambda y[\mathcal{P}(\lambda x[\mathbf{R}(x)(y)])]$ where $\mathcal{P}$ is of type *gq*
b. $[_Q \text{ love}](\text{a man}) = \lambda y \exists x[\mathbf{man}(x) \wedge \mathbf{love}(x)(y)]$

To assume that QR is obligatory would be inconsistent with Montague's theory of intensional verbs.

Another construction that will be relevant to some of our concerns is NP-raising. I assume that its interpretation involves λ-conversion in the manner illustrated in the following example:[5]

(26) a. A unicorn seems to be approaching.
b. $[_S \text{ a unicorn}_i[_{VP} \text{ seems}[t_i \text{ be approaching}]]]$
i. $\Rightarrow \lambda \mathcal{P}\ \mathbf{seem}(\mathcal{P}(\mathbf{approach}))(\mathbf{a\text{-}unicorn})$
$= \mathbf{seem}((\mathbf{a\text{-}unicorn}(\mathbf{approach})))$
ii. $\Rightarrow \text{a unicorn } (\lambda x_i\ \mathbf{seem}(\mathbf{approach}(x_i)))$

4. As usual, **like**(x,y) is taken as an abbreviation for **like**(y)(x).

5. In fact, I think that raising is best construed as a case of function composition (cf. Jacobson 1990 and Williams 1987).

c. a unicorn_i $[_S\ t_i\ [_{VP}$ seems $[t_i$ be approaching]]]
⇒ **a unicorn** $(\lambda x_i[$**seem**(**approach**$(x_i))])$

Since NPs come in two types, it is plausible to maintain that NP traces do too. If an NP trace is assigned the type *gq,* then the raised NP will be "λ-ed in" back into its original position and interpreted as if it was in its D-structure site, as (26b.i) illustrates. If we assume instead that a particular instance of NP movement leaves an *e*-level variable behind, then the raised NP ends up having scope over *seem;* cf. (26b.ii). Although not strictly speaking necessary, one can assume that the traces left behind by QR are always *e*-level (for if QR were to leave behind *gq*-level traces, it would have no semantic effect). Under this assumption, (26c), where the subject has undergone QR, unambiguously represents the wide scope reading of (26a) (type coherence forces the type of the two occurrences of t_i to match). In interpreting traces of NP movement at the *gq*-level we achieve the effects of the downgrading movement transformation proposed by May (1977) to deal with the narrow scope reading of *a unicorn* in (26a), but the operation is recast now as a purely interpretive phenomenon, without an actual LF movement. Downward movement has always been problematic for movement theory, which makes its elimination arguably desirable.

Following much recent work, I take the basic structure of the clause to be as follows:

(27)

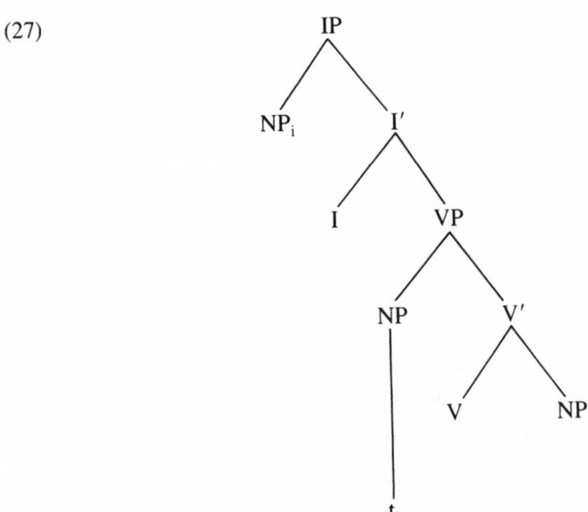

As the reader can see, I adopt the view that S is the maximal projection of I, as well as the 'Internal Subject Hypothesis', that is, the hypothesis that subjects are base-generated in Spec VP.[6] I am going to ignore the inner articulation of I into further functional heads, except when relevant. The interpretation of VPs is also going to play an important role in what follows. Since it is a somewhat unclear and controversial issue, it is worth discussing with some care; to this the following subsection is devoted.

3.2.2. Internal Subjects

In the spirit of Kitagawa (1989), I will regard VPs as predicates and traces in Spec VP as a sort of predication operator, represented here by the λ-abstractor. The general schema, in two parts, is as follows:

(28) $[_{VP}\ t_i\ V']\Rightarrow$
  a. $\lambda v_i\, tr(V')$, if V′ is of type *t*
  b. $\lambda v_i\, tr(V')(v_i)$, otherwise

Case (28a) is meant to deal with derived subjects (like, e.g., the subjects of unaccusatives), while (28b) deals with underived ones. Consider first an example of the latter:

(29) a. kiss John
  b. Tree

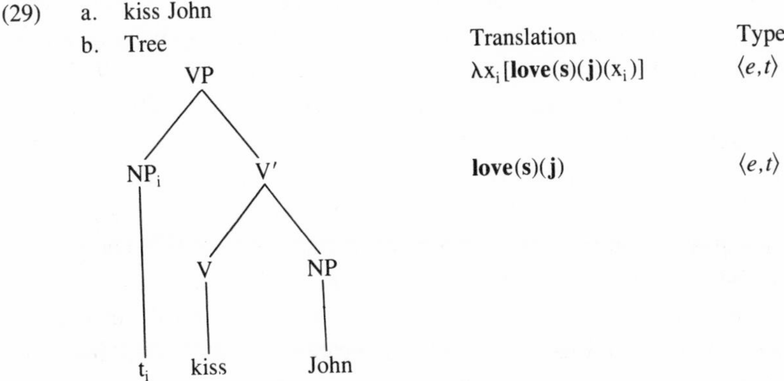

Here basically nothing happens. The type and meaning of the V′ is not changed (with the possible exception of the binding of embedded pronouns carrying the index i within the V′). The property thus obtained is then predicated of

6. Cf., e.g., Kuroda 1988 or Koopman & Sportiche 1988, among many others. See Bowers 1991 for an alternative that would also fit well with the present approach.

the external subject (i.e., Spec IP). Consider now what happens in the case of, say, an unaccusative:

(30) a. John arrived.

b. Tree

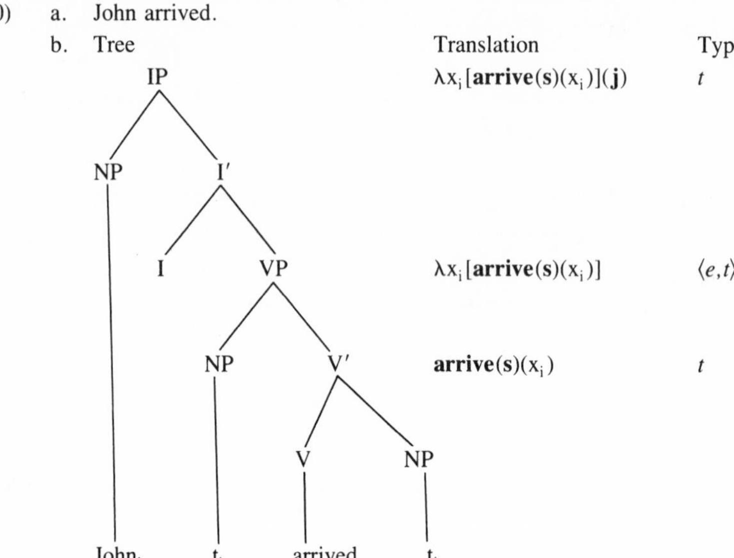

Here the subject position is nonthematic. This means that the lexical verb combines first with a variable in object position, resulting in something of type t (i.e., we are dealing with a propositional structure already at the V′-level). The trace in Spec VP, being in a nonthematic position, presumably makes no contribution to the VP meaning. At the VP-level, then, we have to "reopen" the structure, forming a property that can be predicated of the lexical subject in Spec IP. The semantics of raising and passive is essentially the same.

This semantics can be viewed as a plausible way of compositionally interpreting the process of "externalization" of the subject (or, in the case of unaccusatives/passives, the object) as embodied in the Internal Subject Hypothesis. Let us call traces in Spec VP 'predication phrases', while reserving 'NP traces' for other kinds of traces left behind by NP movement. Under this view, the role of predication phrases vs. NP traces is quite distinct. NP traces relate to their antecedent by binding. Predication phrases, on the other hand, relate to their antecedent by predication; that is, they form a complex predicate which is then predicated of the external subject.[7]

7. In languages where the subject can remain in Spec VP at S-structure, such as German or Japanese (cf., e.g., Diesing 1992, Kuroda 1988), the default rule of functional application will apply of course.

This interpretation of VPs has as a consequence that it is not possible, in general, to "reconstruct" an NP in Spec VP (contrary to what, e.g., Kratzer and Diesing maintain). This is so because reconstruction means putting back an NP meaning into its original site via λ-conversion; cf. (26). But the schema in (28b) assumes that, in general, predication traces will not be NP-level (at least for active transitive and unergative verbs, if they are extensional), for the type of the variable being introduced in (28), namely v_i, will depend on the type of V′. The absence of reconstruction into predication traces, besides being technically simpler, is also empirically justified by the following considerations, involving VP deletion. Assume that predication phrases could freely be interpreted at the higher NP type in examples like the following:

(31) a. some $student_i$ [t_i loves every professor]
b. [t_i loves every professor] ⇒ $\lambda\mathcal{P}[\mathcal{P}$ **loves every professor**]

Now a quantified NP in object position can be assigned VP scope. So the structure of (31b) can actually be this:

(32) [$_{VP}$ every $professor_j$ [t_i loves t_j]]
⇒ $\lambda\mathcal{P}[\forall x[\mathbf{professor}(x) \rightarrow \mathcal{P}(\lambda y\, \mathbf{love}(y,x))]]$

If (32) is predicated of *some student,* the latter ends up having narrow scope relative to *every professor*. There is nothing wrong with that, since (31a) can have this interpretation. The problem comes from the fact that if (32) is an admissible interpretation for the VP in (31a), what is to stop it from being used in VP anaphora cases? Nothing, it would seem. But then the following ought to be possible:

(33) Some student loves every professor and some secretary does too.

Here it should be possible to interpret *every professor* as having wide scope over both *some student* and *some secretary*. But as has long been noticed (Williams 1977, Sag 1976), this reading is impossible. Its impossibility follows straightforwardly from our interpretation of VP shells, which bans predication phrases from having the higher *gq* type.

It is also well known that there are "exceptions" to this generalization. Hirschbühler (1982) discusses cases of the following sort:

(34) A Canadian flag was hanging in front of every window and an American flag was too.

Here it seems possible for the VP-internal quantified NP *every window* to have scope over the subject in both clauses. I believe that this is so because the verb in (34) is unaccusative (as can be seen from the way in which its Italian counterpart *pendere* behaves; Italian is a language that marks unaccusativity overtly). Accordingly the structure of the VP is as follows:

(35) [t_i was hanging t_i in front of every window]

Here we have a genuine NP trace in object position, which according to our hypothesis *can* be interpreted at the *gq*-level. The schematic interpretation of the VP will be as follows:

(36) $\lambda\mathcal{P}$[**in-front-of-every-window**($\mathcal{P}$(**hang**))]

This interpretation makes the reading observed in (34) possible.

So our semantics for VPs predicts that across-the-board wide scope for VP-internal NPs is only possible with unaccusatives or passives, but not with plain active or unergative verbs. As far as I can tell, this prediction is borne out. I am not aware of any other solution to this problem (none, that is, that can account for the facts with fewer stipulations).

This concludes our overview of the basic background assumptions adopted for the purposes of subsequent discussion.

3.3. The Generic Operator

My goal in this section is to give an idea of the line I will be taking on generics and to suggest how my proposals fit with (and, when appropriate, differ from) current research on the topic. As much work has highlighted, there are several key properties that the generic operator shares with *adverbs of quantification (Q-adverbs),* a circumstance that has led many to conclude that such operator itself is just a Q-adverb with a special, modal character. I believe this insight to be basically correct. Accordingly, my strategy will be the following. First, I will review the main properties that Q-adverbs and the generic operator share and lay out my assumptions concerning how Q-adverbs in general work. Having done that, I will indicate the way in which I think the generic operator fits into this picture.

3.3.1. Some Properties of Adverbs of Quantification

The interpretation of a Q-adverb requires establishing a relation between a restriction (or, restrictor) and a scope.[8] The clause has to be ''split'' into two parts, and the task is to determine what options are available. In trying to do so, the following properties of Q-adverbs should be borne in mind.

PROPERTY A: Q-adverbs can bind eventualities.

8. See, e.g., Carlson 1989 or Gerstner & Krifka 1987.

This property is exemplified by sentences of the following kind:

(37) a. Fred always smokes.
b. ∀s [C(**f**,s)] [**smoke**(**f**, s)]
c. ∃s ∀s′ [**Overlap**(s,s′) ∧ C(**f**,s′)] ∃s″[**Overlap**(s′,s″) ∧ **smoke**(**j**,s″)]

external situation (s) — internal situation (s′) — scope situation (s″)

A sentence like (37a) is typically understood as quantifying over a set of contextually specified occasions involving Fred (e.g., after meals, during every break, etc.). For example, suppose that Fred has the habit of spending his frequent breaks in my office, where he knows he can smoke. Bill, witnessing one of these scenes, utters (37a). Relative to a context of this kind, the truth conditions that (37a) ends up having can be roughly paraphrased as follows: "Every situation in which Fred is in Gennaro's office is a situation in which Fred smokes." This is what (37b) would express in such a context. *Always* is translated as '∀'; the material in the left pair of brackets forms the restriction of '∀' and the material in the right pair its scope. The formula in (37c) is a more explicit rendering of (37a). Formula (37c) says that there is a situation s in the actual world such that every situation s′ that temporally overlaps with it in which Fred is in Gennaro's office overlaps with a situation s″ of Fred's smoking. I will call s the *external* situation, s′ the *internal* one (or the *restriction* situation), and s″ the *scope* situation. Normally, I will be representing truth conditions of sentences like (37a) using simpler formulas like the one in (37b), which I take to be abbreviations for formulas like (37c). I will, however, switch to (37c) when appropriate.[9]

A second general property of Q-adverbs is the following:

PROPERTY B: Q-adverbs can bind variables provided by indefinites.

For example, consider (38):

(38) a. An Italian is usually short.
b. **Most** x [**Italian**(x)] [**short**(x)]

Sentence (38a) is naturally understood as saying that most Italians are short, which is what (38b) expresses. The variable that the Q-adverb binds is provided by the indefinite *an Italian*. Within Discourse Representation Theory, it is assumed that indefinites are generally interpreted as free variables, which,

9. The nature of the context variable is affected by focus. For discussion, see, e.g., Rooth 1985, Kadmon 1990, Krifka 1992b, among many others. A theory that would fit well with the general line I am taking is Rooth's. I do not believe, however, that the restriction of Q-adverbs is wholly determined by focus as, e.g., Krifka 1992b claims. But this is not something I can get into within the limits of the present discussion.

where appropriate, get existential force by rules of existential closure. Within Dynamic Intensional Logic, indefinites are treated as existentially quantified terms and their variable-like behavior is captured by a rule of "existential disclosure" (the term is due to Paul Dekker), which reopens existential terms within the restriction of Q-adverbs.[10] Our main thesis is compatible with both approaches. Accordingly, I will remain neutral on this issue here. However, for the sake of explicitness, I will assume that indefinites are treated as generalized quantifiers, and I will posit a type-shifting function '$!_y$' that turns them into open formulas. This type-shifting operation is a simple modification of Montague's meaning for BE, namely:

(39) $!_y\text{NP} = \lambda\mathcal{P}\, \mathcal{P}(\lambda x[y=x])$, if $\mathcal{P}$ is indefinite, else undefined.[11]
Example: $!_y$ a man′ $= !_y\, \lambda P\, \exists x[\mathbf{man}(x) \wedge P(x)] = \exists x[\mathbf{man}(x) \wedge y=x)] = \mathbf{man}(y)$

This operation will be used in setting up the restriction in cases like (39). Let me give an illustration of what I have in mind.

(40) [an Italian$_i$ usually [t$_i$ is short]]
$\Rightarrow \mathbf{Most}_{y_i}[!_{y_i}\, \lambda P\, \exists x[\mathbf{man}(x) \wedge P(x)]][\mathbf{short}(y_i)]$
$= \mathbf{Most}_{y_i}[\mathbf{Italian}(y_i)]\, [\mathbf{short}(y_i)]$

We will arrive at a more precise formulation of the splitting algorithm shortly, after we have identified the other major properties that must be taken into account.

It is apparent that there are certain definites that can provide variables for Q-adverbs to bind:

PROPERTY C: Q-adverbs can bind variables provided by kind-denoting definites.[12]

For example:

(41) a. This dog is usually easy to train. (pointing at a dog in a pet shop)
b. $\mathbf{Most}\ x[x \leq \mathbf{d}]\ [\mathbf{easy\text{-}to\text{-}train}(x)]$
c. $x \leq y$ = x is an instance of y

The definite *this dog* in (41a) can be understood as referring to a kind of dog salient in the context. The Q-adverb is used to quantify over instances of such a kind. The term **d** in (41b) is taken to refer to the contextually specified kind

10. See, e.g., Groenendijk & Stokhof 1990, Dekker 1990, or Chierchia 1992.

11. The notion 'indefinite' can be defined explicitly along the lines of, e.g., Barwise & Cooper 1981.

12. I believe that Property C is actually more general. All definites that have instances, in an intuitive sense, can provide variables for Q-adverbs to bind. A case in point is represented by free relatives, which are arguably definites and can provide a restriction for Q-adverbs. See Jacobson 1990 and Berman 1990 for relevant discussion.

that the definite *this dog* picks out. The formula '$x \leq \mathbf{d}$' is interpreted as saying that x is an instance of **d**. There are various ways in which one can imagine that '$x \leq \mathbf{d}$' is accommodated in the restriction. Within the present set-up this can be done by a straightforward generalization of the type-shifting operation defined in (39), namely:

(42) a. $!y\ NP = \lambda\mathcal{P}\ \mathcal{P}(\lambda x[y \leq x])$ if $\mathcal{P}$ is indefinite or definite, else undefined

Examples:

b. $!y\ \lambda P[P(\mathbf{d})] = y \leq \mathbf{d}$

c. $!y\ \lambda P\ \exists x[\mathbf{man}(x) \wedge P(x)] = \exists x[\mathbf{man}(x) \wedge y \leq x)] = \mathbf{man}(y)$

I assume that every individual is an instance of itself. So when '!' applies to a non-kind-denoting indefinite we will get the same results as before, as (42c) illustrates.

Other NPs (i.e., NPs that aren't either definites or indefinites) do not provide variables that Q-adverbs can bind. So, for example, a sentence like (43) has only the interpretation where the Q-adverb binds situations.

(43) Every man usually smokes.

a. $\forall x[\mathbf{man}(x)]\ [\mathbf{most}\ s[C(x,s][\mathbf{smoke}(x,s)]]$
(= every man smokes on most occasions)

b. $\mathbf{Most}\ s[C(s)][\forall x[\mathbf{man}(x)]\ [\mathbf{smoke}(x,s)]]$
(= on most occasions, every man smokes)

These NPs are usually referred to as 'quantificational' within the DRT literature, a term I will stick with for the purposes of this chapter.[13] Since quantificational NPs do not provide variables that adverbs of quantification can bind, the type-shifting operation '!' will be undefined for them.

Bare plurals, by contrast, are another type of NP that can provide variables for adverbs of quantification. Consider (44):

(44) a. Dogs are usually easy to train.

b. $\mathbf{Most}\ x[x \leq \mathbf{d}]\ [\mathbf{easy\text{-}to\text{-}train}(x)]$

The interpretation of a sentence like (44a) seems to be essentially the same as that of (41a), namely (44b). This is uncontroversial. However, the way this interpretation is to be obtained is the object of discussions. Some, e.g., Gerstner and Krifka (1987), argue that this interpretation comes about because bare plurals, at least on one reading, are indefinites. The bare plural in (44a) would

13. Within the theory I subscribe to, indefinites, being treated in the standard Frege-Russell way as existentially quantified terms, are also 'quantificational'. But in this text I will stick with DRT terminology and reserve the term 'quantificational' for quantificational NPs other than definites and indefinites.

have roughly the same interpretation as *sm dogs* (where "*sm*" is the unstressed *some*). This would make sentences like (44a) similar to sentences with overt indefinites, like (38a). The variable in (44b) would come about by whatever mechanism enables indefinites to act like variables in certain contexts. Carlson (1977b), however, argues against the view that bare plurals are indefinites. He gives a list of many properties (seven, by my count) that differentiate bare plurals from plural indefinites, and argues that bare plurals unambiguously name kinds. While I am inclined to believe that Carlson is more on the right track than his critics on this issue, it is clear that given the way we have set things up we can stay neutral on this as well. The type-shifting operation in (39), which is what we will use to obtain the free variables we need, will work equally well however bare plurals are treated. Again, for explicitness' sake, I will assume that they denote kinds.

Let us turn now to another relevant property of Q-adverbs. So far we have only considered cases involving intransitive VPs. If there are more arguments around, however, it turns out that there is a fair amount of variability as to which arguments provide the variables that a Q-adverb can bind. Below, I give some examples, along with what I perceive their most natural interpretations to be.

(45) a. A cat usually chases a mouse.
b. **Most** x,y,s[**cat**(x) ∧ **mouse**(y) ∧ C(x,y,s)] [**chase**(x,y,s)]

(46) a. A cowboy usually carries a gun.
b. **Most** x[**cowboy**(x)] ∃y[**gun**(y) ∧ **carry**(x,y)]

(47) a. A computer usually routes a modern plane.
b. **Most** y[**modern-plane**(y)] ∃x[**computer**(x) ∧ **route**(x,y)]

In (45) the Q-adverb seems to bind symmetrically all the variables that are around (namely, the one provided by the subject, the one provided by the object, and the situation variable). Sentence (46), on the other hand, seems to be most naturally construed as quantifying over cowboys (i.e., the subject), and sentence (47) as quantifying over modern planes (i.e., the object). In fact, the interpretation of one and the same sentence can vary depending on factors like what the context (i.e., common ground) is and what is focused. These observations can be summarized in the following terms:

PROPERTY D: Q-adverbs can bind more than one variable.
PROPERTY E: Q-adverbs can (by and large) freely select the arguments they bind.

These are the main properties of Q-adverbs that are going to be relevant for the following discussion. Before turning to generics, I will sketch how I think these properties are to be accounted for.

3.3.2 The Splitting Algorithm

Our main task is to establish how the partition of the clause into restriction and scope is to be accomplished. My proposal on this score is a modification of Diesing's. Diesing proposes that the scope of a Q-adverb is set quite rigidly: it is the VP. This raises an issue concerning subjects. As is clear from the above considerations, subjects can be part of the scope (cf., e.g., (47a)). However, in languages like English, subjects must always appear outside of the VP (for case-theoretic reasons, it is generally maintained). So how can they be incorporated in the scope, if the scope is rigidly set to be the VP? Diesing suggests that there is always the option of reconstructing subjects back into their D-structure position, viz. Spec VP. However, this alternative is not open to us, as we have argued that for independent reasons subjects cannot in general be interpreted as if they were in Spec VP. So we have to look for a different way to partition the clause. I would like to propose that adverbs of quantification can freely choose any semantically compatible maximal projection as their scope. Q-adverbs are propositional operators; so any category that denotes a proposition (or a propositional function) will, in principle, constitute an admissible scope for a Q-adverb.[14] This subsumes the scope proposed by Diesing as a special case. We can implement this idea very simply by assuming that wherever Q-adverbs are at S-structure, they remain free to select their scope via LF adjunction. This operation (an instance of Move α) provides us with a scoping mechanism fully analogous to QR. The restriction is then drawn from the material which is external to the scope and locally c-commands the Q-adverb.[15] The net result will be LF configurations of the following type:

(48) $\underbrace{[_{XP}\ NP_1, \ldots, NP_n}_{\text{restriction}}\ ADV\ \underbrace{XP_s}_{\text{scope}}]$, where XP_s is a clausal constituent

The NPs (and possibly other constituents) in the restriction get there either by overt (S-structure) movement or by covert (LF) movement. I assume that clauses bear the index of the situation variable which is an argument of their main predicate. In this way, the situation variable will always be locally available for the adverb of quantification to bind.

14. Actually, in a generalized quantifier framework, the type of both restriction and scope would be that of an n-place relation. See the appendix to this chapter for details.

15. I adopt May's (1985) definition of 'domination'. According to May, a constituent A is dominated by XP iff it is dominated by every segment of XP. Moreover, following Chomsky's (1993) terminology, if only some segment of a multisegmental category XP dominates (in the traditional sense) a node, then that node is 'contained' within (but not dominated by) XP. Containment is thus weaker than domination. Finally, we say that a constituent is in the 'checking domain' of a head X iff it is contained within XP.

To see these ideas at work in some concrete examples, let us consider what LFs would correspond to the preferred interpretations of the examples in (45)–(47). They would be, respectively, as follows (in general, there will be more than one option available):

(49) a. $[_{IP}$ a cat$_i$ a mouse$_j$ usually $[_{IP}$ t$_i$ $[_{VP}$ t$_i$ chases t$_j$]]]
a′. **Most** x,y,s[**cat**(x) ∧ **mouse**(y) ∧ C(x,y,s)] [**chase**(x,y,s)] (= 45b)
b. $[_{IP}$ a cowboy$_j$ $[_{VP}$ usually [t$_j$ carries a gun$_i$]]]
b′. **Most** x[**cowboy**(x)] ∃y[**gun**(y) ∧ **carry**(x,y)] (= 46b)
c. $[_{IP}$ a modern plane$_i$ usually $[_{IP}$ a computer$_j$ routes t$_i$]]
c′. **Most** y[**modern plane**(y)] ∃x[**computer**(x) ∧ **route**(x,y)] (= 47b)

The primed versions of the formulas in (49) do not constitute a further linguistic level. They merely represent the intended interpretation of the LFs in the unprimed versions of (49).

Using the ideas outlined in section 3.3.1., it is rather straightforward to provide explicit truth conditions for LFs of the form in (49). Informally, the type of each NP that locally[16] c-commands the Q-adverb gets suitably shifted to that of a proposition with a free variable. These propositions jointly form the interpretation of the restriction. Each free variable thus introduced is then bound by the Q-adverb. The c-command domain of the Q-adverb constitutes its scope. All this can be schematically summarized as follows (see appendix for details):

(50) $[_{XP}\ NP_1, \ldots, NP_n\ ADV\ XP_s] \Rightarrow$
$ADV\ x_1, \ldots, x_n[!x_1NP_1 \wedge \ldots \wedge !x_nNP_n \wedge C(x_1,\ldots, x_n,s)][XP]$

This approach directly accommodates Properties A–E. For one thing, quantification over situations is always an option (Property A). Quantification over indefinites and definites is accomplished by shifting their type to that of a formula containing a variable (Properties B and C). The fact that Q-adverbs can bind more than one variable is captured by allowing more than one NP in the restriction (Property D). Finally, which NPs can end up in the restriction is left open, modulo standard assumptions on movement (Property E). This simple splitting algorithm appears to yield the necessary flexibility as to what is incorporated in the restriction and what in the scope.

It should be noted that this approach uses a relatively modest apparatus. In setting up the relevant LFs, we use no construction-specific rule (merely Move α). In interpreting them, we use the standard procedures for interpreting quanti-

16. "Locally" essentially means that the material in the restriction and the Q-adverb have to m-command each other (or alternatively, using the terminology of footn. 15, that they have to be in the same checking domain).

ficational structures, plus a type shift which "discloses" indefinites (and kind-level definites). In any framework, the interpretation of Q-adverbs is going to require a partitioning of clausal structures into a restriction and a scope. And the basic ideas outlined here should carry over in a fairly direct manner.[17]

3.3.3. The Gen-Operator

Turning now to the generic operator, it is easy to observe that it shares with overt Q-adverbs all of Properties A–E. This can be most simply illustrated by dropping the Q-adverb throughout from the above examples. As a result, we will obtain typical generic sentences whose interpretation is fairly close to that of the corresponding sentence with an *always*-like Q-adverb. This is the basis for concluding that the generic operator **Gen** must essentially be a phonologically null Q-adverb. What is specific to **Gen** relative to other Q-adverbs is the nature of its modal dimension. To spell this out is a very hard task. Rather than trying to do so, which well exceeds what can be done at this point, I will illustrate the general line I would like to take with a couple of simple cases. Consider (51):

(51) a. Fred smokes.
b. $[_{IP}$ Fred [**Gen** $[_{VP}$ t_i smokes]]
c. **Gen** s[C(**f**,s)] [**smoke**(**f**,s)]

I assume that sentence (51a) has roughly the LF in (51b), which is interpreted as in (51c). In this example, no indefinite (or kind-denoting definite) is present; thus, **Gen** can just bind the situation variable. To understand the intended modal force of **Gen,** we must bear in mind that each activity or state comes with a set of "felicity" conditions.[18] For example, in order for Fred to engage in smoking, he must feel like it; that is, he must intend, or perhaps feel compelled, to do it; he also must be in a place where there is enough oxygen, he must not be asleep or disabled, and so on. So in evaluating (51a), we have to look at worlds similar to ours where the felicity conditions for smoking are met. These felicity conditions are what provides a value for the variable C in the restriction. (51a) is true iff in all the worlds maximally similar to ours where the felicity conditions for Fred's smoking are met, he does smoke. The similarity of this analysis with the (Lewis/Stalnaker) semantics of conditionals

17. For example, in a Montague-style categorial grammar, this could be done by a rule of quantifying-in that employs the same type-shifting operation.

18. Searle's (1969) analysis of performatives is relevant in this connection. Searle argues that performatives are subject to a set of 'felicity conditions' and provides some examples of how these can be spelled out. But of course performative verbs are just a special kind of activity verb (viz., activities that crucially involve verbal behavior), and thus Searle's insight extends to activities in general.

is obvious.[19] Being more explicit than this is a titanic task that I cannot possibly undertake here.

Let us consider another typical case, involving an indefinite:

(52) a. A bird flies.
b. $[_{IP}$ a bird$_i$ $[_{VP}$ **Gen** $[t_i$ flies$]]]$
c. **Gen** s[**bird**(x) $\wedge$ C(x,s)] [**fly**(x,s)]

The expression in (52c) says: Take any bird and any situation in any world maximally similar to ours where the felicity conditions for flying (such as, e.g., presence of the right triggers) are satisfied and assume, furthermore, that inhibiting factors (such as birth defects, diseases, etc.) are absent. Any bird will fly in such a situation. In considering the felicity conditions for the relevant activity, an extra dimension is brought in by the common noun. For example, penguins are birds that fail to have the structural characteristics necessary for flying and are thus excluded from consideration. I assume that this is somehow done via the context variable C.[20]

Another feature of generics is that they tend to last. When someone has a habit or a disposition, we expect it to occupy a significant portion of his lifespan. In reality, some habits or dispositions can be very shortlived. I may become a smoker and then stay one for only a day. But this forces us to imagine a somewhat unusual set of circumstances. Laws, routines, habits, and the like are without doubt tendentially stable in time. This fact should somehow be built into the semantics of **Gen.** For example, we might require that whenever a property holds generically of an individual, in all the stereotypical cases (i.e., cases where nothing unexpected takes place) that property holds for a substantial part of the existence of that individual (where what counts as "substantial" must remain somewhat vague). I will assume that some axiom to this effect suitably constrains **Gen,** without trying to be more explicit about it.[21]

One way of implementing these ideas, consistent with the framework we are

19. See, e.g., Lewis 1973, Stalnaker 1968, or Kratzer 1989b.

20. Actually, it seems intuitively that there are two kinds of contextual restrictions. One comes, as it were, from the verb; it determines what conditions have to be met for an individual to undertake an action. The other comes from the noun; it determines what features of the species are relevant for the action. This intuition could be accommodated by employing more than one context variable. However, I will not pursue this here.

21. The notion of 'stereotypical state of affair' is taken from Kratzer 1981. Dowty's (1979) 'inertia worlds' and Landman's (1992) 'continuation branches' are another possible way of thinking about this issue. As a very rough first approximation toward a formalization of what is informally discussed in the text, we might adopt the following definition of **Gen**:

(i) **Gen** s′ [**Overlap**(s,s′) $\wedge$ ϕ] [ψ] $=_{df}$ $\forall$s′ [[**Overlap**(s,s′) $\wedge$ ϕ] $\Rightarrow$ ψ] $\wedge$ $\Box_{st}$ **long**(s)
where '$\Rightarrow$' is a Lewis-style conditional, $\Box_{st}$ is to be read as 'in every stereotypical world,' and **long** is to be treated along the lines of Kamp 1975.

assuming, might be along the following lines. Genericity manifests itself overtly in the aspectual system of a language. In English the simple present (which is aspectually imperfective) has a predominant habitual interpretation. The simple past and the future also have natural generic interpretations. In other languages, genericity is marked by explicit aspectual morphemes. Accordingly, we can assume that all languages have a distinctive habitual morpheme (say, Hab) which can take diverse overt realizations. In the spirit of much recent work on the structure of inflection, this morpheme can be taken to be a functional head in an aspectual projection. The semantically relevant characteristic of this morpheme is that of carrying an agreement feature requiring the presence of the **Gen**-operator in its Spec. On the basis of this hypothesis, the structure of, say, (51a) can be spelled out as follows (irrelevant details aside):

(53)

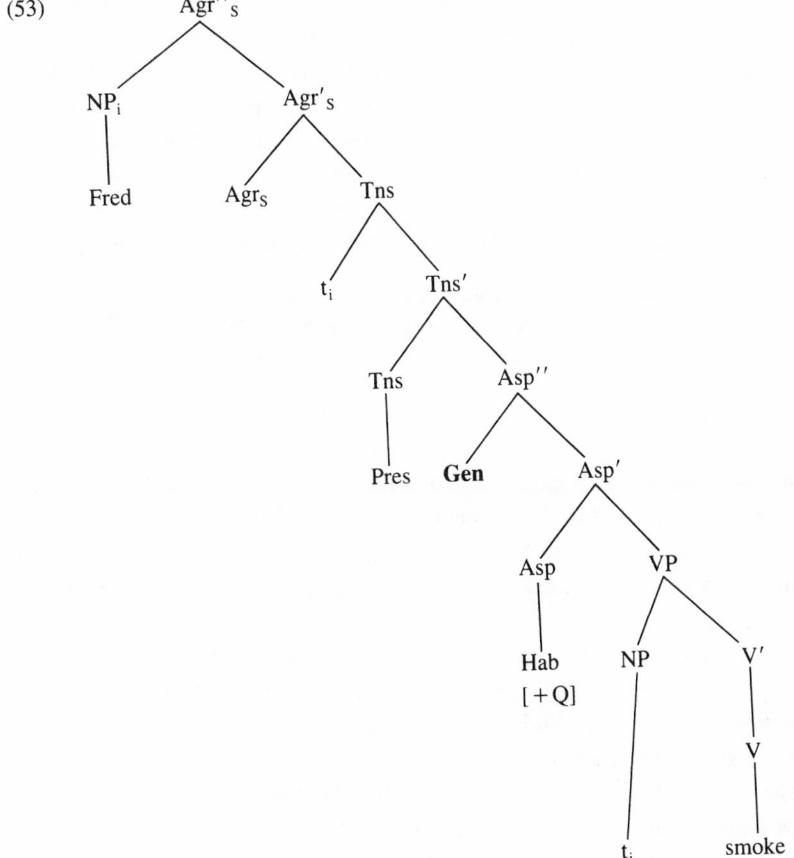

The lexical verb *smoke* undergoes head raising, picking up the habitual aspectual marker, the present tense, and agreement. The habitual aspectual marker, we may assume, has an agreement feature (call it '+Q', for quantificational) requiring a suitable adverb (the null **Gen** or, possibly, some other quantificational adverb) in its Spec. This adverb can then, if necessary, be scoped out at LF. Obviously, this is no more than a rough sketch, and not a particularly original one at that. Many similar proposals can be found in the literature. My goal here is merely to identify the properties of generics that are going to be relevant for the following discussion and to place my proposal within a more general approach to the semantics and syntax of generics.

3.4. INHERENT GENERICITY

As noted at the outset, the main characteristic of i-level predicates is that they ascribe tendentially permanent properties to their arguments. It seems that one can say of an argument with an i-level property P, "Once a P, tendentially always a P." This is, of course, a prominent property of generics. It is therefore very tempting to take this intuition at face value. Perhaps, i-level predicates are simply predicates that *must* cooccur with a **Gen**-like quantificational adverb. In contrast, s-level predicates are free to occur or not occur with **Gen.** In other words, i-level predicates have no natural nongeneric uses.

If i-level predicates are generic, they must have the following form:

(54) a. John knows Latin ⇒ **Gen** s [C(**j**,s)[**know**(**j**,**L**,s)]
 b. John is a smoker ⇒ **Gen** s [C(**j**,s)] [**smoker**(**j**,s)]
 c. John is intelligent ⇒ **Gen** s [C(**j**,s)] [**intelligent**(**j**,s)]

In order to test this claim we should try to give some content to the restriction expressed by the variable C in these formulas. In the informal discussion of **Gen** above, we said that C ought to be filled by the felicity conditions for the relevant activities (and by the absence of inhibiting factors). What could these be in the case of states like knowing, being a smoker, or being intelligent? It is very hard to tell. For example, smoking does require that one feels like it, is not asleep, and so on. But being a smoker does not. If, say, Fred is a smoker, he is also a smoker when he sleeps. The same goes for being intelligent. It is very hard to find felicity conditions for these states other than those very conditions that are constitutive of the state itself. If one is intelligent, one remains such even when acting silly.

The upshot of these considerations is that the restrictions on i-level predicates appear to be rather meager in content, if contentful at all. Perhaps, the only restriction we want to impose on s in (54) is that John be part of it. This means that the content of C in (54) might be set to a maximally general locative relation **in.** Accordingly, (54a–c) wind up saying that whenever John is or might be located, he knows Latin, is a smoker, and is intelligent, respectively.[22]

On the basis of this hypothesis, one might be led to conclude that the meaning of i-level lexical entries is as follows:

(55) a. $\alpha = \lambda x_1, \ldots, \lambda x_n$ **Gen** s [**in**$(x_1,\ldots,x_n,s)$] [$\alpha^+(x_1,\ldots,x_n,s)$]

Examples:

b. know ⇒ $\lambda x_1\ \lambda x_2$ **Gen** s [**in**(x_1,x_2,s)] [**know**(x_1,x_2,s)]

c. smoker ⇒ λx_1 **Gen** s [**in**(x_1,s)] [**smoker**(x_1,s)]

d. intelligent ⇒ λx_1 **Gen** s [in(x_1,s)] [**intelligent**(x_1,s)]

This is a way of giving content to the idea that i-level predicates are inherently generic. They have **Gen** built into their lexical entry. The restriction on the **Gen**-operator is taken to be the property of being at an arbitrary location. In a sense, this amounts to saying that in the case of i-level predicates, the restriction on **Gen** is fairly trivial: being located anywhere. This, right off the bat, seems to capture the fact that one carries i-level predicates along as one changes location and that they are tendentially stable through time.

In order for this approach to be really viable, we must see how it accounts for other properties of i-level predicates. It is this issue that the remainder of this section is devoted to. We will start by further exploring the lexicalist approach outlined above. We will see that while it can be made to work for a number of cases, there are also difficulties with it that will lead us to modify it somewhat.

3.4.1. The Lexicalist Approach

It is prima facie not clear how defining i-level predicates as in (55) would account for their behavior with indefinites and bare plurals. If, for example, the lexical entry for *intelligent* is as in (55d), where only individual variables are used, why should, say, *Dogs are intelligent* select the universal reading?

22. These considerations apply only to generic predications of singular individuals. For example:

(i) Italians know Latin.

When we say (i), we do not mean to say that any Italian, wherever he is, knows Latin. We are presumably talking about Italians of normal intelligence, average upbringing, and so on. These restrictions would be part of C and would be triggered by the common noun. However, those instances of the Italian population that support the truth of (i) do know Latin wherever they may be. To make this explicit, one could assume that the following is a presupposition of i-level predicates:

(ii) $\forall x\ \forall y\ \forall R$ [[**Ind**(x) $\wedge$ **locative**(R) $\wedge$ **Gen** s [$^{\vee}$R(x,s)][**know**$^+$(x,y,s]] $\rightarrow$ R = $^{\wedge}$ **in**]

This sets the value of the context variable C only vis-à-vis locative restrictions, and only with respect to singular individuals.

Perhaps this difficulty stems from the fact that we haven't really used the full-blown version of the **Gen**-operator in the definitions we have considered so far. On the basis of the discussion in section 3.3.3, we are assuming that the general form of the generic operator (cf. (50)) is roughly the following:

(56) $\mathbf{Gen}\ x_{i_1} \ldots x_{i_n}\ s\ [!x_{i_1}NP_{i_1} \wedge \ldots \wedge !x_{i_n}NP_{i_n} \wedge C(x_{i_1},\ldots,x_{i_n},s)]\ [XP_s]$

So this is, presumably, what we want to use. We should restate the definitions of (55) along the following lines:

(57) a. know $= \lambda\mathcal{P}\,\lambda\mathcal{P}'\ \mathbf{Gen}\ x_i\ x_j\ s\ [!_{x_i}\mathcal{P} \wedge !_{x_j}\mathcal{P} \wedge \mathbf{in}(x_i,x_j,s)]\ [\mathbf{know}(x_i,x_j,s)]$
b. smoker $= \lambda\mathcal{P}\ \mathbf{Gen}\ x_i\ s\ [!_{x_i}\mathcal{P} \wedge \mathbf{in}(x_i,s)]\ [\mathbf{smoker}(x_i,s)]$
etc.

This amounts to lifting the type of i-level predicates so that they can take *gq*-type arguments, by using the independently motivated definition of **Gen.** As a consequence, a sentence with bare plurals, for example, such as (58a), ends up being interpreted as in (58b):

(58) a. Italians know pasta recipes.
b. $\mathbf{Gen}\ x_i\ x_j\ s\ [x_i \leq \mathbf{Italians} \wedge x_j \leq \mathbf{pasta\ recipes} \wedge \mathbf{in}(x_i,x_j,s)]$
$[\mathbf{know}(x_i,x_j,s)]$

Similarly for indefinites. For example:

(59) a. An Italian knows Latin.
b. $\mathbf{Gen}\ x_i\ s\ [\mathbf{Italian}(x_i) \wedge \mathbf{in}(x_i,L,s)]\ [\mathbf{know}(x_i,L,s)]$[23]

So the **Gen**-operator induces universal readings of bare plurals and indefinites just as it does in the generic forms of s-level predicates. But while s-level predicates can of course be nongeneric (and in the nongeneric mode, will select existential readings of bare plurals), for i-level predicates there is no choice. The **Gen**-operator has to be there. This is why i-level predicates only allow for universal readings of bare plurals.

These considerations suggest that the lexicalist approach we have sketched might indeed be on the right track. However, there are certain difficulties that stem from the assumption that the argument structures of i-level predicates are actually created in the lexicon. I'll illustrate these difficulties by means of two

23. In sentence (59a), the indefinite could also be quantified in. This would give rise to the 'specific indefinite' reading, namely, 'Some Italian (I have in mind) knows Latin'. Notice that given the definition of **Gen,** the function **know** as defined cannot directly apply to quantificational NPs. However, quantificational NPs *can* be interpreted as arguments of i-level predicates if they are scoped out. In other words, our definition of i-level predicates requires quantificational NPs in their argument structure to undergo QR.

examples. Consider first the following, pointed out by Schubert and Pelletier (1987):

(60) Sheep are black or white.

Black and *white* are i-level predicates. Now, this sentence clearly has a reading which can be paraphrased roughly as 'Every sheep is black or white'. This reading would be naturally represented as follows:

(61) **Gen** x s [x $\leq$ **sheep** $\wedge$ **in**(x,s)] [**black**(x,s) $\vee$ **white**(x,s)]

But how could (61) be obtained on our current approach? We would first need to form the complex predicate *black or white*. Then we would have to generically attribute this predicate of the sheep-kind. The generic operator would then induce the quasi-universal quantification over sheep. However, on the lexicalist hypothesis each i-level predicate comes out of the lexicon with its own **Gen**-operator attached. So there is no way of creating the complex predicate *black or white* without each disjunct carrying along this attached **Gen**-operator. Consequently, the only reading for (60) one should get could be paraphrased roughly as:

(62) Sheep are black or sheep are white.

While this is arguably a possible reading for (60), it clearly isn't the only one.

A similar problem arises in connection with the following kind of sentence, discussed in Carlson 1977b:

(63) Cats like themselves.

A natural reading for this sentence is: Every instance of the cat-kind in the appropriate circumstances bears the 'like'-relation to itself. In our formalism this reading is expressed as follows:

(64) **Gen** x,o [x $\leq$ **cats** $\wedge$ C(x,o)] [**like**(x,x,o)]

To obtain (64), one should first form the reflexive predicate *like oneself* and then predicate it generically of the cat-kind. But it is not clear how to do that, if *like* comes out of the lexicon with its **Gen**-operator already built in.

So the lexicalist approach to i-level predicates seems to face serious difficulties. In view of these difficulties, it appears to be impossible to handle i-level predicates simply by exploiting the **Gen**-operator as part of the word formation component of the grammar.

3.4.2. Local Licensing

If the idea that i-level predicates are somehow inherently generic cannot be straightforwardly implemented in strict lexicalist terms, we must find some other way to force i-level predicates to cooccur with a generic operator. The intuition we want to formalize is that i-level predicates (as delivered by the lexicon) are somehow incomplete. They cannot stand on their own and need to be operated on by **Gen.** In other words, they have a quantificational, ''operator-like'' character. The parallel that comes to mind is with negative polarity items. They too cannot stand by themselves and need to be licensed by negation under certain strict locality conditions.

Here is one way of capitalizing on this parallelism. We have assumed that the habitual morpheme Hab carries a feature [+Q] that induces the presence of **Gen** in its local environment. Suppose that i-level predicates have this morpheme inherently (i.e., in the lexicon). This entails that they will be directly associated with the feature [+Q], which requires the presence of **Gen.** Hence, unless they find the **Gen**-operator in their immediate environment (i.e., in their checking domain), ungrammaticality will result. In other words, by assuming Hab to be, as it were, lexicalized in the verbal head, we derive the fact that i-level predicates are subject to licensing by **Gen.** They are generic polarity items.

According to this hypothesis, the structure of a VP headed by an i-level predicate will be, schematically:[24]

(65)

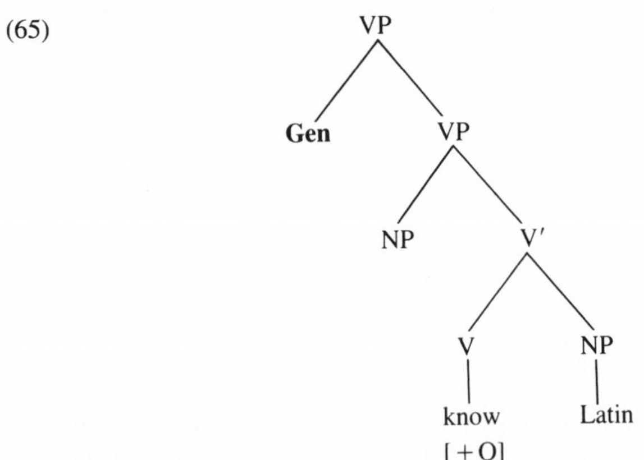

24. Since the Spec position is occupied by the subject, satisfaction of the [+Q] feature cannot take place via Spec-Head agreement. There are two possibilities that come to mind in this connection. Either (as assumed in the text) we maintain that having **Gen** in the checking domain of the head suffices to license [+Q]. Or we can assume that the verb moves into a higher empty functional head in whose Spec **Gen** is located. At present, I have no evidence that helps me choose between these two hypotheses.

We could go further by spelling out the semantics of [+Q] in appropriate ways. We could assume, for example, that what [+Q] does is turn the VP into a function that looks for **Gen.** So if the VP doesn't find a Q-adverb locally, the resulting structure will be uninterpretable. In this way the syntactic requirement of being licensed by a Q-adverb would be rooted in the semantics of i-level verbs.[25]

I will refer to the approach I have just sketched as *local licensing* and contrast it with the strict lexicalist approach. It should be clear that the local-licensing approach doesn't run into the difficulties that the lexicalist view runs into. Let us consider the cases that were problematic for the lexicalist approach. The first one, repeated here, was of the following form:

(66) Sheep are black or white.

For the sake of explicitness, let us adopt Stowell's (1978) analysis of copular sentences as small clauses (sc). According to such an analysis, the copula is a raising verb that takes a small clause as complement. So, for example, two possible syntactic structures for (66) would be these:

(67) a. [sheep_i are [$_{sc}$ t_i **Gen**[$_{AP_{[+Q]}}$ black or white]]]
b. [sheep_i are [$_{sc}$ [$_{sc}$ t_i **Gen**[$_{AP_{[+Q]}}$ black]] or [$_{sc}$ t_i **Gen**[$_{AP_{[+Q]}}$ white]]]]

In (67a) we first form the complex AP *black or white* and then apply **Gen** to it, which will license [+Q] across the board, on both disjuncts. This will result in the interpretation according to which each (typical) individual sheep is either black or white. In (67b) we have a coordination of small clauses (each with its own occurrence of **Gen**) out of which the subject is extracted across the board. This yields the reading according to which every sheep is typically black or every sheep is typically white.

It should be noted that nothing hinges on the details of this particular analysis of copular sentences. The point is that in coordinate structures involving i-level predicates, we will in general have more than one way to satisfy the requirement that [+Q] be licensed by the **Gen**-operator. On the lexical approach, we had no such choice.

25. In a framework that uses Cooper-storage, this would amount to storing the operator **Gen** in the lexical entry of i-level predicates and have it retrieved out of store at the VP level. This is analogous to the way in which reflexives are treated in categorial grammar. Cf., e.g., Bach & Partee 1980.

Essentially the same considerations apply to the other kind of problem for the lexical approach, involving reflexives (cf. (63) above):

(68) a. [cats **Gen**[$_{VP_{[+Q]}}$ like themselves$_i$]]
b. **Gen** x o [x ≤ **cats** ∧ C(x,o)] [λy **like**(y,y,o)(x)]

The interpretation of reflexives requires an operation that identifies two argument slots in a relation. Such an operation, which is represented by the λ-abstractor in (68b), must clearly be allowed to apply at the VP-level. This is shown, for example, by well-known VP anaphora facts. In sentences like *Norman likes himself and Templeton does too,* the missing VP must be interpreted as the property of loving oneself. The right interpretation will arise only if the reflexivization operation is construed as having VP scope. Consequently, nothing can prevent **Gen** from taking scope over the reflexivized VP. Moreover, if reflexivization is syntactically instantiated in the form of an operator binding the reflexive pronoun, the operator will presumably be in an adjunction structure, which would not create a barrier for the **Gen**-operator.

It thus seems that the idea that i-level predicates are inherently generic can be successfully worked out. Inherent genericity cannot simply be equated to lexical genericity. Rather, it is to be thought of in terms of local licensing. I-level predicates must be licensed by a (modalized) quantifier in their local environment. This is what makes them "operator-like."

3.4.3. Nouns

So far I have been assuming that predicate NPs are treated just like other i-level predicates, without paying much attention to their internal structure. Before moving on, it might be appropriate to be more explicit about this internal structure, even though I will certainly not be able to solve all the problems that it poses.

A basic assumption I am making is that every VP, whatever its internal structure and aspectual characteristics, has an extra argument position for eventualities, in the spirit of Davidson's proposal. It is through the Davidsonian argument that temporal and adverbial modification is realized. That is to say, adverbs and tense are construed as properties of eventualities. In a way, having this extra argument slot is part of what makes something a VP, whatever its inner structure. Predicate NPs, I would like to maintain, are no exception to this. Accordingly, I assume that their basic structure is roughly as follows:

(69) a. Mary is a doctor.

b.

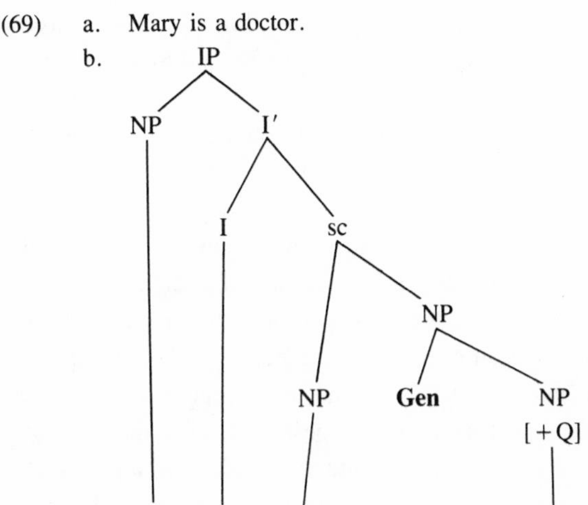

c. **Gen** s [**in**(**m**,s)] [**doctor**(**m**,s)]

The meaning of the lexical item *doctor* in (69) is that of a predicate marked [+Q]. The Davidsonian slot is filled by a variable ranging over states. The determiner *a* in predicative NPs is interpreted as a cardinality predicate, in the sense of, e.g., Milsark (1974). So the type of the whole predicative NP is that of a propositional function. All this is summarized in (70):

(70)

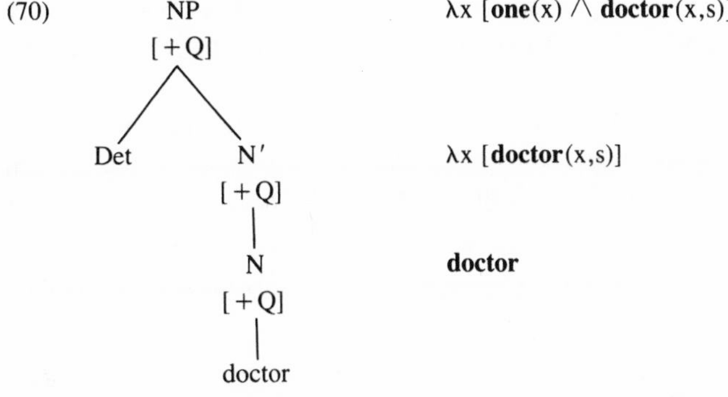

Predicative NPs can, therefore, be operated on by the **Gen**-operator in the manner indicated in (69). I am assuming that determiners that do not have a natural adjectival interpretation are not felicitous within predicative

NPs.[26] The details of this analysis are not so important for my purposes as the claim that the type of a predicate NP is that of a predicate which, like other VPs, has a Davidsonian argument.

The assumptions I am making raise the issue, of course, of the other main role of common nouns, namely that of being restrictors of quantifiers in quantificational NPs like *every man*. Clearly, we do not want to say that nouns in their role as quantifier restrictors have a Davidsonian argument. The purpose of having a Davidsonian argument is that tense and adverbs can operate on it. But nouns, qua quantifier restrictions, do not take adverbs or tense. To the extent that nouns in argument position enter into temporal relations, they do so in a radically different manner than VPs (cf., e.g., Enç 1981). We can account for this by assuming that every noun, besides having the type of a two-place relation α between individuals and situations, also has a predictable variant of the type of (sortal) one-place predicates (which we will denote as α*). The relation between α and α* is roughly as follows.

(71) $\alpha^* = \lambda x\, \mathbf{Gen}\ s\ [\mathbf{in}(x,s)][\alpha(x,s)]$
Example: $\mathbf{doctor}^* = \lambda x\, \mathbf{Gen}\ s\ [\mathbf{in}(x,s)][\mathbf{doctor}(x,s)]$

Viewed as an operation, (71) can be regarded as an "internalization" of the Davidsonian argument. I assume that nouns are freely assigned either type. However, if a noun without Davidsonian argument wound up in predicate position, tense and adverbials would have nothing to operate on and hence the derivation would be ruled out. Conversely, if a noun with the Davidsonian variable were to occur in argument position, the Davidsonian argument would remain unbound and hence, one can argue, the resulting structure would be uninterpretable.

In a sense the analysis I just sketched amounts to saying that the inherent genericity of i-level predicates can be satisfied in two ways: in the lexicon for (nonpredicative) nouns, and locally in the syntax (via the Q-feature) for predicative nouns, verbs, and adjectives.[27] That it couldn't be the other way around follows from general principles concerning the way tense is instantiated and how adverbial modification works.

26. It is well known that definites like *the president* can also occur after the copula, as in *John is the president*. For our present purposes, I assume that these are equational sentences, to be treated on a par with *John is him*. A classical reference on this and related topics is Higgins 1973.

27. I-level adjectives can also, of course, be used as noun modifiers, as in *yellow car*. The simplest way of accounting for this that I can think of is to assume that i-level adjectives, like nouns, exist in two forms, and that these forms are related to each other in just the way nouns are.

3.5. CONSEQUENCES

It is now time to reconsider the properties of i-level predicates listed at the beginning of this chapter. We will argue that they follow naturally if we adopt the hypothesis that i-level predicates are inherent generics (as articulated in the previous section) and other independently plausible assumptions.

1. Stable stativity. Some of the observed properties are immediately obvious now and hardly deserve any comment. Generics express tendentially stable properties, and hence i-level predicates will too. Consequently, a temporal modifier that is somehow incompatible with this presumption of stability (like *yesterday, an hour ago,* etc.) will be odd when it applies to an i-level predicate. Moreover, generics are known to be aspectually stative. Hence i-level predicates will be stative as well. The stativity of generics follows in turn from the fact that their semantics is based on the semantics of conditionals, also generally taken to express states. Notice that the stativity of i-level predicates is expected no matter what aspectual class the (abstract) underlying predicate—*know, intelligent,* etc.—might belong to. These predicates never surface as such. They only occur within the scope of **Gen** (i.e., as conditionals).

2. Locatives. Consider next the oddity of i-level predicates with locative modifiers. Some relevant examples from (4) are repeated in (72).

(72) a. ??John is a linguist in his car.
b. ??John is intelligent in France.
c. ??John knows Latin in his office.

We have argued that the generic quantifier present in the argument structure of i-level predicates ranges over situations that are *arbitrarily* located. The introduction of a locative modifier clearly clashes with the fact that the location of i-level predicates is arbitrary, that is, unrestricted. This is, in a nutshell, the source of the ungrammaticality of sentences like (72).

It is worth pursuing a bit further how this incompatibility of i-level predicates and locative modification actually comes out on our formalization. The full-blown representation of something like *John knows Latin* is as follows:

(73) $\exists s' [\mathbf{Overlap}(s',\mathbf{now}) \wedge \mathbf{Gen}\ s\ [\mathbf{Overlap}(s,s') \wedge \mathbf{in}(\mathbf{j},s)]\ \exists s'' [\mathbf{Overlap}(s,s'') \wedge \mathbf{know}^{+}(\mathbf{j},\mathbf{L},s)]]$

There are three possible targets for a locative modifier in formula (73). Such a modifier could in principle restrict the external situation s′, the internal one s, or the scope situation s″. Modification of the internal situation, however, is ruled out by the fact that the restriction already contains a locative. The contextual variable C is set to **in** and there is no room for further locative modification in the restriction. Modification of the scope situation would yield the following expression:

(74) SCOPE MODIFICATION
$\exists s'$ [**Overlap**(s′,**now**) $\wedge$ **Gen** s [**Overlap**(s,s′) $\wedge$ **in**(**j**,s)] $\exists s''$ [**Overlap**(s,s″) $\wedge$ **know**$^{+}$(**j**,**L**,s″) $\wedge$ **in-j's-office**(s″)]]

But this is clearly logically false. Formula (74) says: *Any* situation s where John is or might be located (including, that is, situations where he is not in his office) is a situation in which he is in his office.

Finally, modification of the external situation would result in something like (75):

(75) EXTERNAL SITUATION MODIFICATION
$\exists s'$ [**Overlap**(s′,**now**) $\wedge$ **in-j's-office**(s′) $\wedge$ **Gen** s [**Overlap**(s,s′) $\wedge$ **in**(**j**,s)] $\exists s''$[**Overlap**(s,s″) $\wedge$ **know**$^{+}$(**j**,**L**,s)]]

But formula (75) is trivially equivalent to the logical form of the unmodified sentence *John knows Latin,* namely (73). To see this, assume that there is a situation **s′** such that

$[\![$[**Overlap**(s′,**now**) $\wedge$ **in-j's-office**(s′) $\wedge$ **Gen** s [**Overlap**(s,s′) $\wedge$ **in**(**j**,s)] $\exists s''$ [**Overlap**(s,s″) $\wedge$ **know**$^{+}$(**j**,**L**,s)]]$]\!]^{g[s'/s']} = 1$.

For this to hold, any situation temporally overlapping with **s′** must satisfy a certain condition. But if this is the case, then an *arbitrary* situation **s*** temporally overlapping with **s′**, no matter what its spatial location, cannot fail to also verify (73) when assigned as a value to the variable s′. In other words, if we can find any situation at all in the actual world that constitutes a verifying assignment for s′ in (73), then any actual situation temporally overlapping with it will. And among such situations, there will also be some whose spatial location is John's office.

Kratzer (1989b) makes exactly this point. She argues that if the truth of a generic statement is supported by one situation in a world, it must be supported by all. Generic statements, as it were, distribute through every part of a world.[28]

28. Kratzer formulates her claim within a situation-based semantics. Our semantics is compatible with hers as well as with more traditional approaches.

So if the locative modifier were taken to modify the external situation, it would add nothing to the meaning of what it modifies—not an efficient way to communicate.

Having exhausted all possible targets for locative modification, we can conclude that our semantics for i-level predicates actually predicts that there is just no way that they can be meaningfully modified by locative adverbials.

3. Perception sentences. The next property of i-level predicates to be considered involves perception sentences. Why are i-level predicates bad as complements of perception verbs? Here are some relevant examples again:

(76) a. I could see that John was tall.
b. I could see John on the roof.
c. *I could see John tall.

The explanation for this unexpected restriction is parallel to the one offered for the impossibility of locative modification. Following Higginbotham (1983), Parsons (1990), and many others, I assume that verbs of perception can either express relations between individuals and propositions, as in (76a), or relations between individuals and eventualities, as in (76b). Naked infinitive complements are, I assume, small clauses of some kind (cf. (77a)) that in the complement of perception verbs are interpreted roughly as in (77b).

(77) a. I could see [$_{sc}$ John on the roof]
b. $\exists$s [**could-see**(**I**,s) $\wedge$ **on-the-roof**(**j**,s)]

Formula (77b) says that there is a state I saw which is a state of John's being on the roof. The contribution of the meaning of the small clause to the meaning of (77b) is that of determining the type of the eventuality which is taken as an argument of the verb. Now why are sentences like (76c) ungrammatical? As mentioned in the introductory section, this cannot have anything to do with the relevant state being perceivable or not. The state of being tall is uncontroversially perceivable. I think that what gets in the way in sentences like (76c) is the **Gen**-operator. Given our hypothesis on the nature of i-level predicates, the LF of (76c) must be as in (78a), which is then interpreted as in (78b):

(78) a. I saw [$_{sc}$ John **Gen**[$_{AP_{[+Q]}}$ tall]]
b. $\exists$s′ [**saw**(**I**,s′) $\wedge$ **Gen** s [**Overlap**(s,s′) $\wedge$ **in**(**j**,s)] [**tall**(**j**,s)]]

The problem is that the situation that can be taken as argument by *see* must be the external one (for the internal one, being bound by **Gen,** is not accessible). But since we are dealing with a generic sentence, if the right conjunct is true of some s′ in the actual world, it will be true of every s′, for the reasons discussed in connection with locatives above. Consequently, (78b) says nothing more than 'John is tall and I saw something (possibly totally unrelated to John's tallness)''. The complement of a perception verb, if it is an inherent generic, will be incapable of specifying or in any way narrowing down the nature of the observed situation, which, I submit, is sufficient cause for ungrammaticality.

4. There-*sentences.* Another peculiarity of i-level predicates we observed is that they are not good in *there*-sentences. To my knowledge, this phenomenon has not received a satisfactory account as of yet. I believe that a plausible one is at hand, if one adopts the perspective developed in the present paper. *There*-sentences state the existence of entities of a certain kind and are known to give rise to a 'definiteness effect': the NPs that can occur in *there*-sentences have to be indefinite (the *weak* NPs of Milsark 1974). There are two main lines on the definiteness effect, namely, Milsark 1974 and Barwise & Cooper 1981). Depending on which line one adopts, the explanation for the ban against i-level predicates takes a slightly different form. In what follows, I briefly go over both approaches.

According to Milsark, weak NPs are constituted by determiners which can be analyzed as cardinality predicates, while strong NPs cannot. The determiners within strong NPs are quantificational. 'There-be' is an existential quantifier and looks for a variable to bind (i.e., for an open sentence). Weak NPs provide just that. Strong NPs, being already quantified, do not. Hence the definiteness effect is essentially a case of vacuous quantification.[29] Now, according to our hypothesis, i-level predicates require a **Gen**-operator in their local environment, which is a (modalized) universal quantifier. This operator will bind the indefinite NP, making the quantifier associated with 'there-be' vacuous. It is exactly as if there was a strong determiner. In fact, that is just what **Gen** is: a phonologically null strong determiner. Schematically, we are dealing with a structure of this form:

(79) a. ??There is $[_{sc}$ a man **Gen** tall]
b. $\exists\ \mathbf{Gen}_{x,s}\ [\mathbf{a\ man}_x\ \mathbf{tall}_s]$

By definition, the subject of the small clause in (79a) is the restrictor of **Gen** and hence gets bound by it. The existential quantifier in (79b), therefore, has

29. The main difficulty with this line of explanation concerns NPs like *no man,* whose determiner cannot be analyzed as a cardinality predicate and yet is acceptable in *there*-sentences.

nothing to bind. Notice that this also explains, right off the bat, why predicative NPs are disallowed in the coda of *there*-sentences, as in (80):

(80) *There is [a woman a doctor]

Predicative NPs are of course all i-level predicates.

As mentioned, the second main line on *there*-sentences stems from Barwise and Cooper (1981).[30] Details aside, the basis of their proposal is that strong NPs are tautologous or contradictory in the context 'NP exists', while weak NPs in that same environment give rise to contingent statements. *There*-sentences are of course interpreted just as 'NP exists', and the deviance of strong NPs in that environment is thus attributed to the uninformativeness of the resulting structure.[31] This second account presupposes that the semantic type of what follows 'there-be' is that of generalized quantifiers. If we adopt (some version of) Stowell's analysis of *there*-sentences, according to which what follows the copula is a small clause, we must, therefore, assume an interpretive procedure of the following kind:

(81) a. There is $[_{sc}$ a man in the garden]
b. $[_{sc}$ a man in the garden] $\Rightarrow \lambda P \exists x\, [\mathbf{man}(x) \wedge \mathbf{in\text{-}the\text{-}garden}(x) \wedge P(x)]$[32]
c. There be sc $\Rightarrow$ **sc**(**exist**)
(where **exist** $= \lambda x[x=x]$; cf. Barwise & Cooper 1981)
d. There is $[_{sc}$ a man in the garden] $\Rightarrow$
$\lambda P \exists x\, [\mathbf{man}(x) \wedge \mathbf{in\text{-}the\text{-}garden}(x) \wedge P(x)]\, (\mathbf{exist})$
$= \exists x\, [\mathbf{man}(x) \wedge \mathbf{in\text{-}the\text{-}garden}(x) \wedge \mathbf{exist}(x)]$
$= \exists x\, [\mathbf{man}(x) \wedge \mathbf{in\text{-}the\text{-}garden}(x)]$

In (81b), the small clause gets an NP meaning (i.e., its type is that of a generalized quantifier). In (81c) the contribution of 'there-be' is taken to be

30. See also Keenan 1987.

31. The weak point in this explanation is that uninformativeness might not be sufficient ground for ungrammaticality. In particular, as Heim (1987b) points out, there are pairs of equivalent sentences that pattern differently in *there*-sentences, like *There is no perfect relationship* vs. **No perfect relationship is such that there is it.*

32. There are a variety of ways in which this interpretation may be obtained. For example, in order to treat relative clauses, one arguably needs an interpretation for NPs of the following kind:

(i) a man $\Rightarrow \lambda P \exists x[\mathbf{man}(x) \wedge R(x) \wedge P(x)]$
(ii) a man + that I met $\Rightarrow \lambda R \lambda P \exists x[\mathbf{man}(x) \wedge R(x) \wedge P(x)](\lambda x \mathbf{met}(\mathbf{I},x))$
$= \lambda P \exists x[\mathbf{man}(x) \wedge \mathbf{met}(\mathbf{I},x) \wedge P(x)]$

'R' is a variable that is going to be filled by a relative clause, roughly in the manner indicated in (ii) (if no relative clause comes along, its value is simply going to be some property salient in the context; see Bach & Cooper 1978, Jacobson 1990, and Srivastav 1991 for relevant discussion). We can use the same type of procedure to interpret small clauses when they occur in *there*-sentences.

that of saying, essentially, 'NPs are in the universe of discourse'. And in (81d), it is shown how this reduces to a statement of existence.

Suppose now we have an i-level predicate. The structure of the sentence will be:

(82) There is **Gen** [$_{sc}$ a man tall]

At this point we have two options. Either we first apply **Gen** to the small clause and then go through the steps in (81) or the other way around. Suppose we follow the latter route and first apply to the small clause in (82) the interpretive procedure outlined in (81), where the coda is ''absorbed' within the NP. Then the result will be an NP meaning—and this will be the only thing left for **Gen** to operate on. But **Gen** needs two arguments: an NP (or a set of NPs) and a clause. Thus, in this case, there will be a type mismatch, which will make the sentence uninterpretable.

Suppose, on the other hand, we first apply **Gen** to the small clause, so that the small clause winds up being interpreted roughly as follows:

(83) $\mathbf{Gen}_{xs}$ [$\mathbf{man}$(x) $\wedge$ $\mathbf{in}$(s,x)] [$\mathbf{tall}$(x,s)]

Then the interpretation of 'there-be' structures as outlined in (81) (which requires an NP meaning) will be unable to operate (again because of a type mismatch) and the structure will be uninterpretable.

So on either one of the two main interpretive hypotheses for *there*-sentences (i.e., Milsark's and Barwise and Cooper's) there is a quite natural account of the ungrammaticality of i-level predicates, under the assumption that they are inherent generics. The point is basically this: the semantics for *there*-sentences and the **Gen**-operator compete for the same structure (i.e., they must operate on the same structure) and it is quite plain that they pull in different directions. Their respective semantics cannot be smoothly integrated. And it seems very reasonable to blame this semantic incompatibility for the ungrammaticality of the relevant sentences.

5. Bare plurals. Let us now turn to the distribution of readings of bare plurals with i-level predicates. The first basic fact in this connection, as mentioned in the Introduction, is that i-level predicates select universal readings of bare plural subjects. On the present theory this follows from the locality requirement on the licensing of i-level predicates. Consider the following example:

(84) a. Italians know Latin

b.

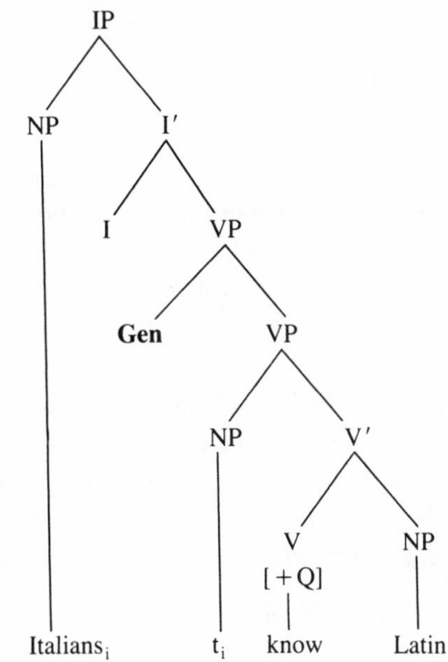

The [+Q] feature on *know* has to be locally licensed on the lexical head by the presence of **Gen** within the head's checking domain. If **Gen** were to select IP scope (as it would be necessary for the subject to be incorporated in the scope), it wouldn't be in the checking domain of the lexical head and hence be too far to license [+Q] on the verb. The guiding principle of our splitting algorithm is that once the scope of **Gen** is fixed, what is external to it is part of the restriction. We assume that in general no "reconstruction" of the material in Spec IP into Spec VP is possible (not even as a purely interpretive phenomenon). Since **Gen** has to be VP-adjoined for it to be able to license [+Q], it follows that the subject of i-level predicates will generally be forced to be part of the restriction (and thus pick up universal force). Singular indefinites work in the same way (modulo the fact that with them, 'specific' readings are always possible).

It is conceivable that **Gen** is generated first in VP-adjoined position, where it licenses the Q-feature on the verb, and then scoped out. This possibility must be ruled out, perhaps by insisting that a trace is too weak to license [+Q].

Note that something of exactly this sort is needed for negative polarity items

(NPIs). To see this, recall the fact often noticed in the literature that negation can have scope over the subject position, as (85) illustrates.

(85) a. Did every student come to the party?
b. No, every student didn't come to the party. ($\Rightarrow \neg\forall$)

While for some, (85b) on the intended reading is less than perfect, most people do get it. Now, in contrast with (85b), it seems that when negation licenses a NPI, it cannot be scoped out. This is attested by two facts. First, in languages like English a NPI cannot be licensed by negation in subject position.

(86) *Anyone didn't come.

This fact would be unexpected if negation could be scoped out to a level where it locally c-commands the subject position, while it follows under the assumption that negation is a proper NPI-licensor only from its base position. Second, and independently of this fact, when negation is an NPI-licensor it cannot take scope over the subject in any case. Contrast (85) with (87):

(87) Every student didn't do anything. ($\Rightarrow \forall\neg\exists$)

Sentence (87) lacks the reading 'Not every student did anything', in sharp contrast with sentence (85b). Again, we assume that whatever mechanism allows negation to have wide scope in (85b) is blocked when it acts as NPI-licensor. I suggest that what happens with i-level predicates is fully parallel. The licensor of a polarity trigger (an NPI or an i-level predicate) can act only under conditions of strict locality.

As far as objects are concerned, whether they are part of the restriction or not will depend, as is generally the case, on whether they are scoped out of the VP or not. In (88) I give two examples with a schematic representation of their LFs:

(88) a. Mice hate cats.
a′. [$_{IP}$ mice$_j$ [$_{VP}$ cats$_i$ **Gen** [$_{VP}$ t$_i$ hate t$_j$]]]
b. Lions have manes.
b′. [$_{IP}$ lions$_i$ [$_{VP}$ t$_i$ have manes]]

In (88a′) the object is scoped out and thus gets universal force, since it is part of the restriction of **Gen**. In (88b′), on the other hand, the object remains in situ and thus is interpreted existentially. As is clear from these examples (and well known from the literature), certain verbs strongly prefer a reading where the object is scoped out, others the one where it stays within the VP. I have nothing to say about this (see Diesing 1992 for interesting considerations).

Things are different with unaccusatives (or, for that matter, passives). NP traces can be interpreted as *gq*-level variables, and the antecedents of NP traces can be interpreted as if they were in the trace position. Which means that the subjects of i-level unaccusatives will be able to escape from the restriction and be interpreted as part of the scope. Below I provide a simple example, taken from Kratzer 1989b (for more details, see the appendix to this chapter).

(89) a. A pond belongs to this property.
b. LF: [a pond$_i$ [$_{VP}$ this property$_j$ **Gen** [$_{VP}$ t$_i$ belong t$_i$ to t$_j$]]]
c. $\lambda\mathcal{P}$ [**Gen** x,s [x = **this-property** $\wedge$ **in**(x,s)] [$\mathcal{P}$ (**belong**$^+$(s)(x))]] (**a-pond**)
= **GEN** x,s [x = **this-property** $\wedge$ **in**(x,s)] [**a-pond**(**belong**$^+$(s)(x))]
= **Gen** x,s [x = **this-property** $\wedge$ **in**(x,s)] [$\exists$y[**pond**(y) $\wedge$ **belong**$^+$(y,x,s)]]

The subject in (89a) is most naturally interpreted existentially. Yet the sentence involves an i-level predicate which carries **Gen** with itself. However, since the predicate is unaccusative, the subject can be λ-ed in back into the position of the object trace. As we know, this option is not available with predication traces, which is why subjects of unergative i-level predicates must be caught in the restriction.

6. *Adverbs of quantification.* Let us now turn to Kratzer's generalizations which concerns contrasts of the following type:

(90) a. ??When John knows Latin, he usually knows it well.
b. When an Italian knows Latin, he usually knows it well.

As it turns out, this kind of behavior is not restricted to i-level predicates (cf. De Hoop and De Swart 1989 and Chierchia 1992:

(91) a. ??When John kills Fido, he kills him cruelly.
b. When John kills a dog, he kills it cruelly.
c. ??When John wins the 1991 Boston marathon, he wins it by a wide margin.
d. When John wins a marathon, he wins it by a wide margin.

The predicates in (91) are all s-level, and yet they pattern just like i-level predicates with respect to this phenomenon. What seems to be playing a role here is the fact that the events described in (91) are not naturally iterable. Not being naturally iterable means that two instances of the same event (with the same protagonists) cannot naturally occur (e.g., two killings of John by Bill cannot naturally occur). In the deviant sentences in (91), the only thing that the Q-adverb can quantify over is the situation variable (since there are no indefinites or kind-level NPs). But we know that in any given world there is going to be at most one situation in which, e.g., John kills Fido. This makes the Q-adverb useless. Thus the ungrammaticality of the sentences in (91) does not stem from a formal ban against vacuous quantification (as Kratzer proposes), for there is in (91a–d) a variable over which to quantify. Instead, it seems plausible to maintain that not only do variables have to be there but also that they must in principle be satisfiable by more than one entity. Let's call this the "*nonvacuity presupposition*." It is the nonvacuity presupposition that appears to be violated in the examples in (91).

The question that arises is, however, why should i-level predicates not be principally naturally iterable? This seems to be a straightforward consequence of their tendential stability. Their duration tendentially occupies a significant portion of an individual's lifespan. To imagine a situation where there can be two distinct knowings of Latin by John, we have to imagine an unusual scenario. So on the present approach, we can relate the deviance of (90a) to the deviance of (91a,c) on principled grounds. The tendential stability of i-level predicates triggers a presupposition that there is going to be at most one state of the relevant sort, which clashes with the nonvacuity presupposition of Q-adverbs.

7. *I-level predicates and counterfactuals*. There is a further interesting property of i-level predicates that follows from this analysis, mentioned in Kratzer 1989b, fn. 7, which we haven't considered in the Introduction. It involves the way they behave in counterfactual reasoning. The example that follows is taken from Kratzer's work. Imagine a situation where five people are in this room, including Otto and Paula. It so happens that Otto and Paula are the only two people in the room that are bored. In such a situation, we would be inclined to regard (92a) as true, but (92b) as false:

(92) a. If Otto and Paula weren't in the room, nobody in the room would be bored.
b. If nobody in the room were bored, Otto and Paula wouldn't be in the room.

Kratzer argues quite forcefully that her analysis of counterfactuals predicts exactly these judgments. In order to sketch why this is so, I will now present some key ingredients of Kratzer's analysis. I will do so in a completely informal way and without any pretense of doing justice to the richness of her analysis.

The basic semantics for *would*-conditionals is as follows:

(93) A *would*-counterfactual is true in a world w if and only if every way of adding propositions which are true in w to the antecedent while preserving consistency reaches a point where the resulting set of propositions logically implies the consequent. (Kratzer 1989b, 626)

For this statement to work, it has to be qualified in a crucial way. In adding a true proposition p to the antecedent of a counterfactual, we must also add the propositions that p 'lumps'. The notion 'lumping' is defined as follows:

(94) p lumps q in w iff:
i. p is true in w
ii. For any situation s which is a part of w, if p is true in s, then q is true in s.

The intuitive idea behind this definition can be put in the following terms. Facts come structured in blocks, or 'lumps'. Reasoning about a certain fact involves considering all that comes with it. This includes not just what the fact in question entails, but the various aspects that are inherent to the situation it characterizes. For example, in the state of affairs just considered, (95a) lumps (95b):

(95) a. Exactly two people in this room are bored.
b. Otto and Paula are in this room.

In the world as we have described it, any situation that supports the truth of (95a) will support the truth of (95b). This is obviously not a matter of entailment. Now consider (92a) in light of definitions (93) and (94). For (92a) to be true, every consistent way of adding true propositions and what they lump to 'Paula and Otto are not in this room' reaches a point where the result entails 'Nobody in this room is bored'. Now, obviously (95b) cannot be added consistently to the antecedent of (92a). And since (95a) lumps (95b), (95a) cannot be added consistently either. But if we leave (95a,b) out and add the rest of the facts to the antecedent, we reach a point where the result entails the consequent. Hence (92a) is true in the state of affairs in question. Consider now (92b). (95a) is incompatible with its antecedent, so it cannot be added to it. But (95b) is compatible with 'Nobody in this room is bored' and can be added to it. Moreover, as Kratzer puts it, ''[(95b)] doesn't lump any dangerous proposition like [(95a)]'' (p. 633). So there is a way of adding facts to the antecedent of (92b) that do not entail the consequent (in fact, they entail its negation). Hence (92b) is not true in the relevant state of affairs.

The counterfactuals under discussion so far involve an s-level predicate, like *be bored*. What is interesting from our point of view is that if we use i-level predicates instead, judgments are reversed. Suppose that Otto and Paula are the only tall people in this room, then consider the following sentences:

(96) a. If Otto and Paula weren't in the room, nobody in the room would be tall.

b. If nobody in the room were tall, Otto and Paula wouldn't be in the room.

We would still be inclined to regard (96a) as true in the relevant state of affairs. But contrary to what happens with (92b), we would also be inclined to regard (96b) as true. In observing this asymmetry, Kratzer remarks that it would be explained if i-level predicates could be taken to express ''nonaccidental generalizations'' (i.e., generics). This is so because nonaccidental generalizations, if true in a world, are true in any situation of that world. Consequently, they will be lumped by any true proposition whatsoever. So the fact that Otto and Paula are tall is lumped by any true proposition, which means that however we add facts to the antecedent of (96b), the result will be something that is incompatible with them being in this room; whence the truth of (96b). This is a reflection of the general fact that in counterfactual reasoning nonaccidental facts always take precedence over accidental ones.

On the approach presented here, i-level predicates are generics. Hence, by adopting Kratzer's approach to counterfactuals and lumping, the contrast between (92) and (96) is predicted. From our perspective, it would be surprising and problematic if i-level predicates didn't pattern as ''nonaccidental generalizations.''

3.6. Some Comparisons

I will indicate now what I think the main differences are between the approaches of Kratzer and Diesing, on the one hand, and the one I have developed here, on the other. I will only focus on what I understand to be the central aspects of their proposals, whose scope goes well beyond what I was able to cover here. Also, I will not comment directly on the differences between their approaches.

The main assumptions of the two theories (Kratzer and Diesing's vs. my own) can be summarized as follows:

(97) THE KRATZER-DIESING HYPOTHESIS

a. S-level predicates have a Davidsonian argument ranging over occasions or eventualities (or perhaps space-time locations). I-level predicates do not.
b. The subject of i-level predicates is base-generated in Spec IP, the one of s-level predicates is generated in Spec VP.
c. VP is the scope of existential closure (for indefinites) and gets mapped into the scope of a Q-adverb.
d. Reconstruction of a raised NP into its base position is always possible (on a language-particular basis).[33]

These assumptions account for most of the empirical generalizations discussed in the preceding section. For example, the fact that i-level predicates cannot be smoothly modified by locatives follows from the fact that they lack a Davidsonian argument that the locative could modify. Moreover, an indefinite (which Kratzer and Diesing interpret as a free variable) in the subject position of a sentence involving i-level predicates will not be able to undergo existential closure. Hence, either it gets quantificational force from somewhere (like a generic operator) or else the sentence will contain a free variable floating around, which can arguably be regarded as the source of the ungrammaticality of the sentences in question (on the existential reading).

(98) THE INHERENT GENERICITY HYPOTHESIS

a. Every verb has a Davidsonian argument. Uniformly, the subject of a verb is generated in Spec VP.
b. I-level predicates must be licensed locally by a **Gen**-operator.
c. The scope of a Q-adverb is free.
d. Interpretive reconstruction is only possible into NP traces (not into predication phrases).

Of these assumptions, those in (98a) are in no way specific to my theory. Assumption (98b) is really the plank of the whole approach. As for (98c), I think it is fair to say that it should constitute the null hypothesis, assuming that scoping is an instance of Move α. Finally, (98d) is, as I have suggested, independently needed.

From the point of view of genericity, one way of looking at these two approaches is as follows. Kratzer and Diesing stipulate that the function-argument structure of i-level predicates is special in certain ways and try to derive their inherent genericity (and their other properties) from these assump-

33. This restriction is necessary on Diesing's approach to handle certain contrasts between English and German; see Diesing 1992.

tions on function-argument structure. My approach stipulates that what is special about the function-argument structure of i-level predicates is just the fact that they need a generic operator. I then try to derive their properties from this assumption. Kratzer and Diesing's hypothesis in effect almost succeeds in deriving the fact that i-level predicates need a **Gen**-operator (which I take as basic), but only when indefinites are involved. According to their hypothesis, something like *John is tall* is not in any obvious way "generic." We have seen reasons for wanting to regard even sentences of this form as generic. In so far as English is concerned, the present theory covers all the facts addressed by Kratzer and Diesing.[34] Moreover, it enables us to derive the predicate restriction on *there*-sentences and the behavior of i-level predicates in counterfactuals. It is not obvious how a theory based solely on (97) would derive these generalizations.

On the syntactic side, the approach I have developed here is consistent with a strong version of the Internal Subject Hypothesis, whereby the subject of every verb is uniformly generated in the same place. Various arguments have been put forth in the literature in favor of this view. For example, one is based on the conjoinability of passive and active VPs illustrated in (99):

(99) a. John loves Mary and is loved by her.
b. John [$_{VP}$ t_i loves Mary] and [$_{VP}$ t_i is loved t_i by her]

If there was no trace within the active VP in (99a), this sentence ought to constitute a violation of the Across-the-Board constraint on extraction. The problem disappears if we assume that there is a trace in Spec VP of *love*. But this appears to be inconsistent with the claim that subjects of i-level predicates originate outside the VP. The same point can be made in connection with the conjunction of i- and s-level predicates:

(100) a. Sue married John thirty years ago and still loves him very much.
b. Sue [[t_i married John thirty years ago] and [PRO still loves him very much]]

The analysis of (100a) according to the Kratzer-Diesing hypothesis would be (100b), which should be ruled out by constraints on Across-the-Board movement. A possible way out might be to assume that the conjunction in (100a) involves a functional category higher than VP, such as, say, TP. Under the assumption that the subjects of i-level predicates are actually generated in Spec TP and then move up, the coordinated structures would both contain a trace.

34. Kratzer and Diesing also discuss many facts from German. I address them in Chierchia (1994), where I argue that they too follow naturally from the inherent genericity hypothesis.

However, this way out is rather implausible in view of facts such as the following:

(101) a. Which of your colleagues married her husband thirty years ago and always loved him like the first day?
b. Sue did ____.

Here the antecedent for the VP anaphor in (101b) is the coordinated structure in (101a). Yet, the tense (and aspectual) features appear on *did* in (101b). Hence it is implausible to maintain that the missing predicate is a coordinated Tense Phrase or Aspect Phrase.

On the semantic side, the present theory is consistent with the view that temporal and adverbial modification is done uniformly through the Davidsonian situation argument. And there may be reasons for viewing this uniformity as a positive feature. For example, we can borrow from Parsons (1990) the following argument. Consider the following set of sentences:

(102) a. John loved Mary with great passion in his youth.
b. John loved Mary with great passion.
c. John loved Mary in his youth.
d. John loved Mary.

These sentences give rise to the following entailment pattern:

(103)

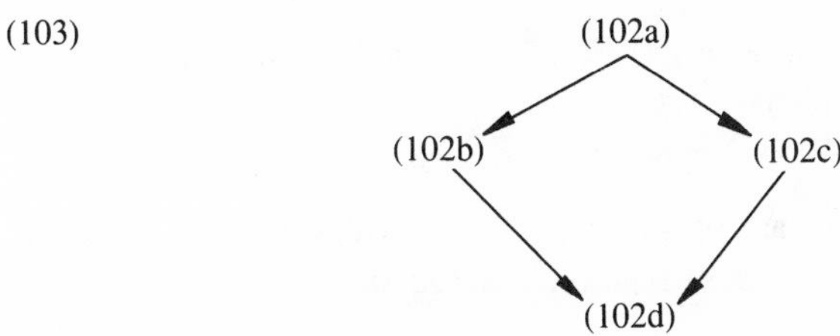

Each sentence in this diagram entails the ones below it but is not entailed by them. As Parsons argues, this fact follows in a rather direct fashion under the assumption that adverbs apply to the eventuality argument of verbs. If i-level predicates lack such an argument, this behavior (which is fully parallel to that of s-level predicates) would appear to be hard to explain.[35]

35. The logical form of (102a) on our approach would have to be:

(i) $\exists$s [**in-John-youth** (s) $\wedge$ **Gen** s′ [**Overlap**(s,s′) $\wedge$ **in**(**j**,s′)] $\exists$ s″[**Overlap**(s′,s″) $\wedge$ **love**(**j**,**m**,s″) $\wedge$ **with-great-passion** (s″)]]

I leave it to the reader to verify that the desired entailment pattern does follow from (i).

3.7. CONCLUSIONS

The idea that i-level predicates are inherent generics can be implemented in a fairly elegant way. Polarity phenomena are rooted in the lexicon but have effects on whole phrases. My main contention is that i-level predicates give rise to a kind of polarity phenomenon (namely, inherent genericity). By assuming that i-level predicates must be licensed by **Gen,** under a strict form of locality we can derive all of their observable properties in an arguably principled manner. This hypothesis also sheds some light on genericity in general and exposes interesting aspects of the syntax/semantics interface.

APPENDIX

Here I will make more explicit the 'splitting algorithm' developed in the text and give some detailed examples. I will begin by considering cases where IP is selected as scope. Then I will turn to cases of VP scope.

(104) $[NP_{i_1},\ldots,NP_{i_n}\ \mathbf{Gen}\ IP_s] \Rightarrow$
$\mathbf{Gen}\ x_{i_1},\ldots,x_{i_n}\ [!x_{i_1}\ NP_{i_1} \wedge \ldots \wedge !x_{i_n}\ NP_{i_n} \wedge C(x_{i_1},\ldots,x_{i_n},s)][IP_2]$

Example:

(105) a. A cat chases a mouse.
b. $[\text{a cat}_i\ \text{a mouse}_j\ \mathbf{Gen}\ [_{IP_s}\ t_i\ \text{chase}\ t_j]$
c. $\mathbf{Gen}\ x_i\ x_j\ [!x_i\ \mathbf{a\text{-}cat}_i \wedge !x_j\ \mathbf{a\text{-}mouse}_j \wedge C(x_i,x_j,s)]\ [\mathbf{chase}(x_i,x_j,s)]$
Reductions of (c):
i) $\mathbf{Gen}\ x_i\ x_j\ [!x_i\ \lambda P\exists x[\mathbf{cat}(x) \wedge P(x)] \wedge !x_j\ \lambda P\exists y[\mathbf{mouse}(y) \wedge P(y)] \wedge C(x_i,x_j,s)]\ [\mathbf{chase}(x_i,x_j,s)]$
ii) $\mathbf{Gen}\ x_i\ x_j\ [\mathbf{cat}(x_i) \wedge \mathbf{mouse}(x_j) \wedge C(x_i,x_j,s)]\ [\mathbf{chase}(x_i,x_j,s)]$

Let us consider now the case of VP scope. This divides into two subcases, depending on whether the VP is of type $\langle e,t\rangle$ or $\langle gq,t\rangle$

(106) Case (a): the VP is of type $\langle e,t\rangle$
$[_{VP}NP_{i_1},\ldots,NP_{i_n}\ \mathbf{Gen}\ VP_s] \Rightarrow$
$\lambda\mathcal{P}\ [\mathbf{Gen}\ x_k,\ x_{i_1},\ldots,x_{i_n},s\ [!x_k\mathcal{P} \wedge !x_{i_1}\ NP_{i_1} \wedge \ldots \wedge !x_{i_n}\ NP_{i_n} \wedge C(x_k,\ x_{i_1},\ldots,x_{i_n},s)][VP_s(x_k)]$
where k is the predication index (i.e., the index of the trace in Spec VP)

Example:

(107) a. A lion has a mane.
b. $[_{IP}\ \text{a lion}_i[\text{VP}\ \mathbf{Gen}\ [_{VP_s}\ \text{has a mane}]]$
c. Interpretation of the components:
i) $[_{VP_2}\ \text{has a mane}] \Rightarrow \lambda x\exists y[\mathbf{mane}(y) \wedge \mathbf{has}(x,y,s)]$

ii) $[_{VP}$ **Gen** $[_{VP_s}$ has a mane$]] \Rightarrow$
$\lambda\mathcal{P}$ **Gen** x_i,s[!$x_i\mathcal{P} \wedge C(x_i,s)$][$\lambda x\ \exists y$[**mane**(y) $\wedge$ **has**(x,y,s)](x_i)]
= $\lambda\mathcal{P}$ **Gen** x_i,s[!$x_i\mathcal{P} \wedge C(x_i,s)$][$\exists y$[**mane**(y) $\wedge$ **has**(x_i,y,s)]]
iii) $[_{IP}$ a lion$_i$ $[_{VP}$ **Gen** $[_{VP_s}$ has a mane$]] \Rightarrow$
$\lambda\mathcal{P}$ **Gen** x_i,s[!$x_i\mathcal{P} \wedge c(x_i,s)$][$\exists y$[**mane**(y) $\wedge$
have(x_i,ys)]]($\lambda P\exists x$[lion(x) $\wedge$ P(x)])

Reduction of (iii):
iv) **Gen** x_i,s[!$x_i\lambda P\exists x$[**lion**(x) $\wedge$ P(x)] $\wedge$ C(x_i,s)][$\exists y$[**mane**(y) $\wedge$
has (x_i,y,s)]]
v) **Gen** x_i,s[**lion**(x_i) $\wedge$ C(x_i,s)][$\exists y$[**mane**(y) $\wedge$ **have**(x_i,y,s)]]

(108) Case (b): the VP is of type $\langle gq,t\rangle$
$[_{VP}$ $NP_{i_1},\ldots,NP_{i_n}$ **Gen** $VP_s] \Rightarrow$
$\lambda\mathcal{P}$ [**Gen** $x_{i_1},\ldots,x_{i_n}$,s [!x_{i_1} $NP_{i_1} \wedge\ldots\wedge$!$x_{i_n}$ $NP_{i_n} \wedge C(x_{i_1},\ldots,x_{i_n},s)$][$VP_s(\mathcal{P})$]

Example:

(109) a. A pond belongs to Morrill Hall.
b. [a pond$_i$ $[_{VP}$ Morrill Hall$_j$ **Gen** $[_{VP_s}$ t_i belongs t_i to t_j]]]
c. Interpretation of the components:
i) $[_{VP_s}$ t_i belongs t_i to $t_j] \Rightarrow \lambda\mathcal{P}$ [$\mathcal{P}$(**belong-to**(x_j,s))]
This interpretation is licensed by the fact that the NP trace t_i can be interpreted at the *gq*-level.
ii) $[_{VP}$ Morrill Hall$_j$ **Gen** $[_{VP_s}$ t_i belongs t_i to $t_j]] \Rightarrow$
$\lambda\mathcal{P}'$ **Gen** x_j,s [!x_j **Morrill-Hall**$_j$ $\wedge$
C(x_j,s)][$\lambda\mathcal{P}$ [$\mathcal{P}$ (**belong-to**(x_j,s))]($\mathcal{P}'$)]
$\lambda\mathcal{P}'$**Gen** x_j,s [!x_j **Morrill-Hall**$_j$ $\wedge$ C(x_j,s)][$\mathcal{P}'$(**belong-to**(x_j,s))]
= $\lambda\mathcal{P}'$**Gen** x_j,s [!x_j λPP(**mh**) $\wedge$ C(x_j,s)][$\mathcal{P}'$(**belong-to**(x_j,s))]
= $\lambda\mathcal{P}'$**Gen** x_j,s [x_j = **mh** $\wedge$ C(x_j,s)][δ'(**belong-to**(x_j,s))]
= $\lambda\mathcal{P}'$**Gen** s [C(**mh**,s)][$\mathcal{P}'$(**belong-to**(**mh**,s))]
iii) [a pond$_i$ $[_{VP}$ Morrill Hall$_j$ **Gen** $[_{VP_s}$ t_i belongs t_i to t_j]]] $\Rightarrow$
$\lambda\mathcal{P}'$**Gen** s [C(**mh**,s)][$\mathcal{P}'$(**belong-to**(**mh**,s))]($\lambda P\exists x$[**pond**(x) $\wedge$ P(x)])
= **Gen** s [C(**mh**,s)][$\lambda P\exists x$[**pond**(x) $\wedge$ P(x)](**belong-to** (**mh**,s))]
= **Gen** s [C(**mh**,s)][$\exists x$[**pond**(x) $\wedge$ **belong-to** (**mh**,s)(x)]]

ACKNOWLEDGMENTS

I wish to thank Andrea Bonomi, Paolo Casalegno, Polly Jacobson, and the participants of the 1992 ''Movement, Partition and Definiteness'' seminar at Cornell for helpful discussion. Special thanks are due to John Bowers and Molly Diesing, my co-teachers at that seminar. It was great fun.

4 TRUTH CONDITIONS OF GENERIC SENTENCES: TWO CONTRASTING VIEWS

Gregory N. Carlson

In this chapter, which is intended to form a very general backdrop for considering the semantics of generic sentences, we are going to examine some basic assumptions about how work on generics is to proceed, and what basic, empirical issues need to be accounted for by any adequate theory of generic meaning. There are two generally opposed perspectives on how generic sentences can be true or false. One view takes induction as its primary model and attempts to understand generics in terms of the inductive process. The other perspective takes rules and regulations (e.g., of games or legally regulated activity) as its primary model, and seeks to understand generics in those terms. Our present purposes are to review the primary features of the two opposed views, to evaluate the strengths and weaknesses of each, and to discuss reasons for choosing one over the other. The discussion will be cast in terms of a simple opposition, though one must eventually allow for mixed or intermediate positions. Work on the semantics of generics, however, tends indeed to take one point of view or the other as its guiding feature, and so considering the opposition in this unqualified form has some merit.

Before proceeding, though, I'd first like to get a couple of matters out of the way. First, I will take it for granted that I know what a generic sentence is—any sentence expressing a generalization—and that the opposing category consists of episodic sentences—sentences which relate specific occurrences. On this view, generics form a single class of sentence types constituting a unified phenomenon. This is a very strong claim, one that ultimately requires careful resolution. If one divides the domain of data in different ways, different analyses will emerge as a result of that initial division. The strategy pursued here is to assume that an all-encompassing semantics is indeed possible (and desirable), and to retreat from this strong position only when convincing reasons are given to do so.

The second matter I wish to dispense with is the question of whether generic sentences have any truth conditions associated with them at all. I will only answer this conditionally for present purposes: if episodic sentences are true or false, then generics are as well. Certainly we *speak* as if such sentences were true or false, as when we say *It is true that cats chase mice* or *It is false that bears migrate from North to South America.* This does not have the feel of a category mistake, unlike what might be said about calling questions true or false (e.g., *??It is true whether John eats light breakfasts*). I am quite willing to grant the possibility that some generics may be epistemically indeterminate. I also grant that generics are quite vague as compared to episodics like *The cat is on the mat* or *Sam drove the bus from Amsterdam to Rotterdam.* But both difficulties also plague episodics, and are therefore by no means special to generics.

These preliminaries out of the way, I wish to begin by contrasting the two basically different views of generic sentences, each of which handles with apparent ease what the other handles only clumsily. The first approach, one I have argued against in the past (e.g., Carlson 1982), is what I will call the *inductive* approach. The driving intuition behind it lies in the conviction that generics essentially express inductive generalizations, where the base of the generalization is some observed set of instances; after "enough" instances have accumulated, the generic form can be truly asserted. Paradigm cases of generics under this view would be sentences like *Dogs bark, The sun rises in the East, Max spends every Friday at his mother's,* and *Jill walks to school.* The most natural adherents of this approach would be empiricists, verificationists, and nominalists of varying stripes.

On the other side of the coin is what I will call the *rules-and-regulations,* or *realist,* approach, which does not hold that generics are truly asserted on the basis of any array of observed (or even unobserved) instances. According to this approach, generic sentences depend for their truth or falsity upon whether or not there is a corresponding structure in the world, structures not being the episodic instances but rather the causal forces behind those instances. The paradigm cases of generics on the realist approach are rules and regulations that we can stipulate, and hence know directly, such as *Bishops move diagonally, The Speaker of the House succeeds the vice president,* or *Tab A fits in slot B* (on a cereal box cut-out toy), or, for that matter, the content of a computer program. People who take properties and propositions as real entities would be most naturally inclined toward this approach, as would many realists, though this dichotomy between realists and inductivists, so grossly put, allows for rather free travel from side to side. We will develop this latter view a bit more before returning to the former.

There are many activities that we understand to be explicitly and highly consciously guided by rules and regulations. If we play a game, for instance, we are first taught some rules (typically by conscious instruction), and from there on the form of our activities depends in large part on the rules that we have learned. I move my knight in chess in that particular way, I am to keep the tennis ball between the white lines, I play trump card on my opponent's ace, and so forth, all because of the rules I know about these various games. In other types of activity, a similar notion of rules informing events applies, as when we fill out our tax forms (e.g., "Add line 6b to the total on line 5, subtract the figure on line 33 Form 1209B from the total on line 5, and enter the result on line 8"), when you learn how to perform a job (answer the telephone saying "Good day, this is XYZ Enterprises, may I help you?," bring the incoming mail to Mrs. Santini, attend department meetings monthly, . . .). Instructions about how to assemble a bicycle fall into this category, how to address persons of distinction appropriately ("Mr. President," "Your Highness," "Herr Professor," . . .), how to go about the legalities of renting an apartment. One could with very little effort come up with hundreds of such examples—where we have been told something (or read it), accept it as authoritative knowledge, and apply that knowledge to a situation at hand so that a certain type of behavior emerges.

To be sure, most of our behavior is not guided by such consciously acquired rules and regulations. Nevertheless, a common practice is to assume that, at least in certain domains, there is a discoverable body of largely unconscious knowledge which constitutes a set of rules and regulations for executing certain behaviors. Take language, for example. I aspirate my stops in syllable-initial position, diphthongize tense vowels, put determiners before nouns, say *cat* instead of *chat* or *Katze* or *felis* in reference to feline animals, etc., because there is a presumed body of rules and regulations which, taken collectively, define (my variety of) English. I "know" these rules, and their application informs my behavior. The study of these rules and regulations constitutes the substance of at least one major brand of current theoretical linguistics. The key point is the presumed direction of explanation: that we engage in certain types of behavior *because* we have a certain body of knowledge. On one view, all forms of "unconscious" knowledge have this basic character. (From this perspective, classical and operant conditioning techniques may be viewed as roundabout ways of informing an organism what the rules are—e.g., "To obtain food, peck a green triangle.")

Taking another step in this same direction, we may think of there being rules and regulations to order events in general, not just those events counting as behavior in organisms. Under this view, something like Newton's laws of motion may be seen as the rules and regulations that govern the movements of bodies in space in the same way that the rules of chess determine what chess piece gets moved where on the board under what circumstances. Obviously there are some glaring differences between the two—there are matters of universality, and the concept of 'cheating' applies in one case but not the other, for instance—but there is also a fundamental commonality which permits us to see them both as examples of the same thing: rules informing a sequence of events so that things occur *this* way rather than *that* because of the rules themselves. The basic consequence of this view is that the world (including minds/brains) is in part constituted of these rules and regulations.

All the rules and regulations I have discussed or alluded to so far are statable as generic sentences, but not as episodic sentences; the latter express the instances informed by the rules (note, e.g., the difference between the generic *Bishops move diagonally* and the episodic *Max moved his king's bishop from K2 to Q1*). The rules-and-regulations view is very popular, in fact, both in terms of theory and in terms of everyday accounts of behavior. (Why does Jack Nicklaus use a golf club to move the golf ball along? Why didn't Alexis move his rook over the opponent's pawn? How come Sam fills out a tax form for the government each year?) However, for a long time, this view did not predominate in the more narrow study of the semantics of generic sentences. Instead, the prevailing perspective tended toward an inductive, or in more linguistic terms, a quantificational view, which appears the most natural perspective to take when first examining the data. In the main, this inductive perspective holds that a generic sentence is true (or false) not by virtue of there being any corresponding constituents of the world so described, but instead by virtue of there being some array of instances (episodes) from which language users can abstract the stated regularities. Hence, on the inductive view, the real-world grounding of the truth of generics lies in the same sort of thing that also grounds the truth of episodics. Leaving the mind out of it for the time being, it is very easy to see one of the good reasons for preferring this view over the rules-and-regulations model: it is ontologically more frugal, trading only in the extensional entities necessary to construct the grounding of episodics, such as times and places and individuals and events. The ontology of the alternative view, however, must include whatever the inductive view includes, and rules and regulations in addition.

Other initially attractive reasons for holding the inductive view emerge when we begin to consider natural language. Generic sentences would appear to be formally based on episodics—a generic like *The sun rises in the East* has a corresponding episodic *The sun rose in the East,* matters of tense aside. As a wider array of languages are examined, this basic observation receives consistent support. No language I am aware of takes generic forms as basic and derives episodics from them (though there are some interesting challenges to this view), yet there are a lot that seem to work the other way around (and there is a very large class, including German, French, and English, in which the two sentence types are treated roughly the same). In other words, if one holds the view that episodic truth conditions are basic, and that generic truth conditions are derived from these, the facts about natural language forms are consistent, based on what little is presently known, though also compatible with the rules-and-regulations approach. (See especially Dahl 1985, and also Dahl, this volume, for a survey; my own (unpublished) survey of grammars has also influenced my thinking.)

Another factor in favor of the inductive view lies in what I will call the problem of weak and descriptive generalizations. Let us frame the problem as follows. The rules-and-regulations model, in its most naive form, would take it that a true generic directly corresponds to a real rule—an actual condition of the world. It is reasonable to think of basic (unquantified) episodic sentences thus: *The cat is on the mat* is true because there is a directly corresponding real-world condition where the cat *is* on the mat, supporting its truth. Now if we apply the same strategy to generics in, for instance, the case of games, the directly corresponding condition would be the presence of a rule. For games, there is a finite, usually small, set of rules governing play. Hence, on this naive view, evaluating the truth or falsity of a generic should be a matter of consulting some finite list of rules and laws that are "in force" for the domain under consideration.

Let us turn to a different domain to illustrate the problem. Let us suppose that much about an animal can be explained in terms of its genetics. So, for example, this crow is black because there is a genetic structure determining its color, and the truth of the sentence *Crows are black* finds its grounding in that genetic structure. So far so good. But now let's consider the grounding for the sentence *Crows are smaller than ravens*. Again, genetics has something to do with size; let's pretend it's the sole determinant for the moment. However, there will (in all likelihood) be no genetic structure that corresponds to crows being smaller than ravens. After all, is there to be another that corresponds to crows being larger than bullfinches, another to being smaller than zebras, and still another to their being smaller than breadboxes? The problem is that if the truth of a generic is modeled on, say, rules of games, one could propose that a generic sentence is true iff one finds the relevant rule in the instructions. Thus, just as *Bishops move diagonally* is true because it is in the rules—let us suppose—*Crows are black* is true because there's a rule for it out there as well (in the genetic structure of crows). So, determining the truth of generics is a matter of consulting a finite list—let us assume for simplicity's sake a list of propositions.

But once one gets beyond this preliminary guiding vision of every true generic having a directly corresponding condition, things break down very badly, since one is confronted with a possibly unlimited number of true generic sentences which do not simply appear to be alternative descriptions of the same thing (crows being bigger than bullfinches is not an alternative description of crows being smaller than storks). So, from the start, the most straightforward view of the truth conditions of generics based on the rules-and-regulations model can be seen to be hopelessly inadequate and in need of immediate modification. The problem is compounded by there being increasingly "weaker" generalizations that seem nevertheless to be true or false, for which anything but an inductive model seems at first sight inappropriate. Consider examples like *Mike sometimes goes to school by way of Elm Street, Mary shows up at psychology conferences every once in a while,* or *Max occasionally smokes cigars.* (Note: these are generic sentences despite the presence of overt quantifiers.) The thought of such sentences sending realists trooping around the world in search of rules and regulations that say, in effect, "Mary, go to a psychology conference every once in a while" or "Max, smoke an occasional cigar" is probably enough to convince most people that it is preferable to pursue the inductivist approach as the saner model.

Also, to be sure, most real-world patterns we describe via generics turn out to be the results of innumerable interacting factors. Consider what sorts of factors interact to determine traffic patterns in a city, or how many coat hangers are used by the population of North America annually. To even think of there being some list of rules and regulations that are real constituents of the world in such cases (e.g., "Traffic increases steadily on Elm Street during the early morning hours") is patently implausible. Thus, one of the strengths of the inductive approach is its very agnosticism about the existence of and the source of real patterns found in the world. On the inductive view, if the generic generalization can be derived via inductive operations from the basic observations, it is true—that is that, whatever the source of the real-world patterns, if indeed there are any real patterns at all. The rules-and-regulations model deems it necessary not only to insist that there are real-world patterns, but also that the source of these patterns be identified in evaluating the truth of generic sentences. This does not, initially, play in favor of the rules-and-regulations approach.

I wish to argue, however, that the appeal of the inductive approach lies in paying more attention to the full portion of the glass than the empty, and I think the full portion is considerably less than half the glass. First, while the realist approach to generics owes an account of the relationship between real-world conditions and the truth or falsity of generic sentences, the inductive approach in turn owes an account of the abstraction process as an operation performed on (take your pick) episodic sentences or the conditions in the world they correspond to. Thus, it bears the full complement of difficulties coming under the heading "the problem of induction." In particular, its most straightforward instantiation as a linguistically motivated theory of truth conditions, in the form of the "quantificational" analysis of generic sentences, meets with failure. So, to take one analysis that has been suggested (by, e.g., Lawler 1973a), the generic sentence *The sun rises in the East* is taken to be some function of the open sentence *The sun rise in the East at x,* where x ranges over times. Inserting a value for x, such as 'this morning', results in a nongeneric sentence meaning about the same thing as *The sun rose in the East this morning*. The generic sentence itself is thus taken to have a logical form in which some operator O (which itself might contain complex descriptive material) binds the variable in the open sentence, resulting in a structure that is essentially '(Ox) [The sun rise in the East at x]'. (My playing fast and loose with tenses in these examples is defensible, by the way, though I omit such a defense here.) Other suggestions put the free variable in place of certain NPs in the sentence, or quantify over "cases," or combine these approaches; there are other things one could do as well and remain within the spirit of this analysis.

Any similarly straightforward attempt to model generics as some sort of quantification over episodics containing free variables is open to all sorts of empirical challenges; once one gives any remotely testable characterization of the quantifier, or quantifiers, supposedly involved, it turns out to be demonstrably incorrect, as can be shown with very little effort. (See Lawler 1973a and Carlson 1980 for discussion; the literature on propensities, such as being flammable or brittle, actually points up the same moral, though in quite a different way).[1]

The inductive approach also appears to insist on some very unrealistic scenarios regarding how we come to judge a generic as true or false. For example,

1. The device of 'default quantification,' as proposed in Krifka 1987, I take to be an example of a nonquantificational analysis, even though it does incorporate elements of classical quantificational analyses in it. The reason, quite simply, is that there are no clear cases of natural language quantifiers (such as 'all,' 'some,' 'no') the semantics of which requires the notion 'default' independent of genericity. In a similar vein, modalized approaches (e.g., Dahl 1975) also count as nonquantificational, since they introduce an intensional element into the analysis otherwise unnecessary in quantification theory.

the fact is that we learn most rules of games we play not by watching someone else play (cf. Wittgenstein 1953, p. 27), but rather by being told what the rules are. When I learned the rules of chess, I did not observe n bishop moves and then have it pop into my head that bishops move diagonally. And none of us, to be sure, learned that bachelors are unmarried by observing bachelors and then noting the strong tendency for them not to be married. Instead, we found these things out in other ways.

One might object that an utterance of a true generic on the part of a given individual does not require that *that individual* must have observed enough instances himself or herself for the sentence to be true. That's fair enough, at least for the time being. Still, if the truth of a generic requires that there have been ''enough'' instances observed—or even just, to water it down further, that there have been enough instances, whether observed or not—this in itself is sufficient to cause difficulties. Suppose in Supermarket A bananas sell for $.49/lb (a generic statement), and they are selling well at that price. Now, the store manager wishes to up the price a bit, to, say, $1.00/lb. The manager does not up the price (i.e., make a new generic sentence true) by seeing to it that n customers come through the registers and just so happen to pay $1.00/lb. No, the manager changes the sign (and maybe does some other things), and upon his doing so the price has been changed—bananas now sell for $1.00/lb—whether anyone buys bananas at that price or not. Or, suppose a toy manufacturer creates a new game, listing the rules on the box cover. Are we to say that the rules are false (or at least, not true) until the game has been played n times? In cases such as these, the inductive approach puts the cart squarely before the horse.

In the limiting case, the most direct challenge to the inductive approach comes from those circumstances which make the rules-and-regulations model most plausible, namely, rules for which there are, have been, and will be no corresponding instances (such as no bananas actually selling for a dollar a pound in the example above), and hence no episodes to perform any inductive operations on in the first place. The following all seem quite possibly to be true even under circumstances where the corresponding episodes do not ever take place.

(1) This machine crushes up oranges and removes the seeds. (said of a new machine to be later destroyed accidentally in shipping)

(2) Tab A fits in slot B. (cut-out toy instruction on a cereal box which is thrown out)

(3) The Speaker of the House succeeds the vice president.

(4) Sally handles the mail from Antarctica. (an unfulfilled office function)

In short, for examples and situations such as these, the inductive approach appears *in principle* incapable of giving a convincing account. In fact, if the inductive approach would rule out anything at all, such examples would surely be paradigm cases of what could not possibly ever occur.

But there is more. Further problems with the inductive approach are more linguistic in character. One is that generic sentences are aspectually stative (as seen by applying the tests outlined in, e.g., Dowty 1979). If the linguistic meaning of a generic is derived from some operation over value substitutions for variables in episodic sentences, then any generic sentence should retain its original aspectual class. So, for example, *John pushed carts to Cleveland* is an event, and hence *John pushes carts to Cleveland* ought to test out as an event as well. But it does not: it is a state. Normally quantification has no such stativizing effect: *Every man pushed a cart to Cleveland* is still eventive; *John pushed a cart to Cleveland on two occasions* is still eventive; and so forth. Thus the device of quantification itself does not introduce any aspectual shift (nor, for that matter, does intensionality).

A second major linguistic difficulty arises from the existence of sentences like *John is intelligent, Zebras are mammals,* and *Cats like to chase mice*. It appears that such sentences should be treated as non-episodic sentences, on a par with generics like *Sam does smart things* or *Zebras are hunted by lions,* (I will call these lexical statives *basic generics*). Yet, examples such as these must be presumed consistent with the inductive approach if one is to maintain it for generics as well. It will be strange indeed if there were a non-inductive set of truth conditions for *Sam is a poor liar* but an inductive set for *Sam lies poorly,* a non-inductive set of truth conditions for *Cats are carnivores* but an inductive set for *Cats eat meat,* and so forth. If there exists some episodic condition in the world to support the assertion that cats are carnivores, then why couldn't that selfsame episodic condition be used to support the assertion that cats eat meat? If it can, then such generics need not be defined inductively, there being a supporting condition in the world, and the inductive analysis collapses. But if not—if examples like *Cats are carnivores* do require an inductive analysis—then a corresponding episodic must be sought for each true 'basic generic'. In many instances, it is reasonably clear what the supporting instances would have to be, but in others, the problem of identifying what counts as a supporting instance becomes insurmountable—and this is just a *preliminary* to the problem of finding out what array of instances must occur to support the assertion (the fundamental problem of generics, so viewed). What are the supporting instances for *Cats are mammals* or *Bob is a bachelor?* (Fodor 1987 embarks on a lengthy discussion of this particular problem, though with a different set of aims in mind.) Yet, to be consistent, the inductive approach is committed to an inductive account of all such sentences, and dealing with basic generics inductively is even more difficult (not less) than dealing with generics derived from episodics inductively. (This problem comes out quite clearly in attempts to deal inductively with belief, for example, as a generic state corresponding to certain episodic behaviors, such as assent.) I think these problems are just too much for this approach to take on, particularly given its difficulties in dealing with generics.

Finally, to reemphasize a point made by Goodman (1955) and more recently by Dahl (1975) (among a host of others), the truth of generics depends on a notion of 'nonaccidental generalization'. The world contains in its extension all manner of possible patterns and convergences, many of which we judge to be purely accidental, but others of which we take to be principled. Only the principled patterns are taken to support true generics. There is no obvious way that any inductive approach operating on real instances to derive inductively driven generalizations can make this distinction, yet it is central to any account of the truth conditions of generics. This is where the rules-and-regulations approach, which insists on there being some real, non-episodic conditions of the world to support the truth of generics, would appear to offer a promising avenue of explanation.

I have now summarized my reservations about the inductive approach, and I judge the weight of the criticisms to militate against it. As a matter of fact, this approach has lost some prominence in more recent research on the nature of rules and regulations. Let me mention two trends in the study of generalizations that I take to be roughly in keeping with a "rules and regulations" approach. One is the large amount of work that has been done on the nature of nonmonotonic reasoning and/or logics. In the introductory chapter to this volume, the strengths and weaknesses of this approach are discussed in extensive detail (see also Asher & Morreau, this volume). A second area that also holds considerable promise is the study of rules and regulations from the point of view of contrafactuals, especially as presented in Lewis 1973, Stalnaker 1987, and Kratzer 1989b. Analyzing generics, however indirectly, in terms of contrafactuals is a promising and interesting approach. The weakness I detect in it is that invariably, some qualitative relation must be defined among the possible worlds (or whatever plays the role of such in the theory). For instance, the theory of Lewis (1973) requires a notion of 'similarity' to order the accessibility of worlds to one another (other theories make use of a notion of 'normalcy'). Now, similarity is a generic notion (*A is similar to B* is a generic sentence), so we end up analyzing generics in terms of other generics. This may well be an improvement, but it runs the risk of circularity (one then needs to define similarity, or else argue for the plausibility of treating it as a primitive). I believe that in the end a certain kind of circularity is required, but if one is intent upon doing mathematical modeling, then what is needed as foundation for expressing the notion of a generalization are mathematically expressed generic truths, and these do not include such notions as similarity and normalcy.

In concluding this chapter, I wish to discuss why the ontologically less modest rules-and-regulations approach, whatever form it may take, can nevertheless provide a better framework for dealing with the problems of generics, and to sketch the major challenges that this approach faces. The ontological-parsimony argument must be conceded to the inductivists from the outset, so more or less lost ground needs to be made up elsewhere, depending on how important one thinks the parsimony argument is. (Note, by the way, that the inductivists still need a mind, which weakens their case considerably; if we are to model the mind as a programmed computer, there is the risk of getting into a regress, since a program is a paradigm case of a bit of generic information). We clearly owe some kind of account of the connection between a set of real generic states and the truth of generic sentences, since on the face of it, the phenomenon of 'weak generalizations' shows that the most naively straightforward application—that of direct correspondence—will not work. Let us assume for now, following the game model, that real rules and regulations are propositions (real constituents of the world), and that any domain will have a finite list of rules associated with it at any given time (i.e., the rules "in force"). Yet these rules must be able to support the truth of more propositions than just themselves—possibly an unlimited number of propositions. In keeping with attempting the simplest things first, let us briefly explore whether the following might work:

> A generic sentence S is true with respect to a set of rules R iff R entails the proposition expressed by S.

One can see how this will allow for an unlimited number of true generic propositions not in R. But can anything so simple be actually made to work? It certainly requires supplementation. I have several concerns. One, of course, is the presumption that rules are propositions. This is plausible at the level of consciously known rules; it remains plausible, though controversial, at the level of subconscious psychological regularities. It may seem more dubious at the level of physical laws. If one wants to claim that physical principle P (which is stated as a proposition) is a real constituent of the world, one must show (a) that this is not simply a descriptive generalization (i.e., one entailed but not on the original list—this requires deep theory, and I doubt that such claims can ever be fully demonstrated to everyone's satisfaction), and (b) that the proposition is the law, and not our linguistic means of expressing the law, which itself may have quite a different character. However one does it, there are many instances where we must concede that we just do not know which descriptions correspond directly to laws and which do not, since in these cases we do not know the governing laws directly (unlike games, etc., which have standard codebooks). But this causes a grave difficulty, for how can we judge whether a generic sentence is true or false when we do not know what the real rules are in the first place? Hence, our semantics must be an "agnostic" system which need not depend on the particular propositional identity of a law in the first place. However, entailment requires reference to this very identity. For example, suppose some group of people believes that oak trees grow from acorns, but ascribes the source of this generalization to some god or other that lives in oak trees, has nineteen wives, and so on. Suppose another group of people also believes that oak trees grow from acorns, but ascribes the grounding for this generalization to some very fancy modern theory of biology. And suppose a third group of people also thinks oak trees grow from acorns, but hasn't been curious enough about things to come up with any sort of explanation, scientific or not. The point is a simple one: *Oak trees grow from acorns* is true in the mouths of all, however far-fetched their account of why it is true, or even if there is no account at all. People can still judge a generic true or false in the presence of misconceptions—or even the absence of any conceptions—of the grounding real-world conditions.

As I have already pointed out, another concern centers on the possibility of rule interaction, that is, cases where some regular, describable behavior is the result of the interplay of a variety of more primitive rules. This has got to be the standard case in the real world. Take, for instance, principles of gravity and of magnetism. If one measures the movement of a body under the influence of both forces, its path will not be predictable from either alone. Yet, something like vector analysis may yield a generalization about the path of a body under the influence of both forces, i.e., a generic proposition, that is neither in the original list nor in any standard sense entailed by the list of propositions.

Another problem results from the possibility of having incommensurate theoretical terms in a proposition. Let us take a linguistic example: Using late-'60s transformational terminology, one could observe that the 'pronominalization transformation' was not sensitive to the Ross Island Constraints. Now these days, transformational grammar no longer countenances any pronominalization transformation, nor are there Ross Island Constraints. Nevertheless, the above statement was accepted as true at the time and, I would argue, is still a true observation about natural language, so long as one accepts it as a description and not as a theoretical claim (Churchland 1984, in questioning the worth of folk psychology, appears to ignore this distinction). Yet the proposition cannot possibly be entailed by the ''real'' grammatical theory, on the assumption that the latter lacks the notions 'passive transformation' and 'Ross Island Constraint'. It chops things up in the wrong way, and in the end the key terms cannot be decomposed into new terms yet still maintain a fit: that would be mere ''notational variation,'' and I certainly do not have that in mind. Yet another phenomenon that requires an account is *rule preemption*—application of one rule precluding application of another as a matter of the relation between the rules themselves. For example, an ace takes a lower card in bridge, but a trump takes any nontrump. In linguistics this appears as the 'Elsewhere Principle' (Kiparsky, 1973), characterizing cases where rules that should interact fail to. These principles of interaction and preemption can be thought of as real relations between the rules themselves (hence the world, and not the semantics, is the locus of the phenomenon), providing perhaps the best litmus concerning which rules are ''real'' and which are not.

We might summarize the above concerns with an example, that of the debate over connectionism vs. nonconnectionism. In a connectionist system, the theoretical vocabulary expresses order functions determining levels of activation between connected nodes (the vocabulary consisting of talk of nodes, connections, activation, and some measure of activation). This is not a very rich vocabulary. The level corresponding to the rules of propositions is a long list of activation functions (''If input to node x is A, compute F(A).'') Yet one can ascribe much richer true descriptions to such a model; these are referred to in the literature as 'emergent properties'. Now, the emergent properties are not simply arbitrarily chosen true descriptions, but rather conform to certain patterns that the network gives rise to. That is, they correspond to something real about the operations of the network in a way that other, purely descriptive generalizations (which carve things up along different lines) may not. However, such propositions are not in the original list of propositions, nor are they in any classical sense entailed by the underlying set. One solution of course is to claim that this just shows that the emergent properties *are* in fact among the list of basic propositions (i.e., the ones that the lower-level propositions were arranged to express). However, this solution, which may or may not be correct, violates our original assumptions—that the rules governing the system really are limited in number and there really are true emergent properties.

So framed, the fundamental difficulty for the rules-and-regulations approach remains how to deal with weak and descriptive generalizations. They point us back in the direction of the episodic phenomena "caused" by the basic laws and rules, whether known or unknown. I am not optimistic that an entailment approach modeled along standard lines will work, for there seems to be a certain preservation of vocabulary implicit in such approach; more importantly, it does not shed any light on how people judge generics to be true or false, and it seems likely that nonlogical notions would be required in the end, particularly that of 'applying a rule'. Note that none of these issues constitute difficulties for the inductive approach; in fact, they constitute its strengths. So, in constructing an alternative semantics for generics based on the rules-and-regulations model, one of the primary tasks must be to deal with those very examples which lend the most prima facie plausibility to the inductive model.

It may well be possible that there is no single successful analysis of the domain of generics *in toto,* and that the domain must be split for the sake of arriving at tractable semantic analyses. If one type of analysis or the other could be demonstrated, though, the study of generics would take on a more certain air.

ACKNOWLEDGMENT

I gratefully acknowledge the support of NSF grant #BNS 89-19827.

5 FOCUS AND THE INTERPRETATION OF GENERIC SENTENCES

Manfred Krifka

5.1. THE FOCUS SENSITIVITY OF GENERIC SENTENCES

In Chapter 1 (section 1.2.3), we have argued for a dyadic operator **GEN** for the semantic representation of generic (or characteristic) sentences, following Carlson (1989). In that framework we could represent the different readings of generic sentences as given in (1) and (2).

(1) Mary smokes after dinner.
 a. **GEN**[x,s;] (x = **Mary** & **after.dinner**(s) & **in**(x,s); **smoke**(x,s))
 b. **GEN**[x,s;] (x = **Mary** & **smoke**(x,s); **after.dinner**(s))

(1a) represents the reading which says that in after-dinner situations which contain Mary, she usually smokes. (1b) represents the reading which says that when Mary smokes, it is usually in after-dinner situations.

(2) Planes disappear in the Bermuda Triangle.
 a. **GEN**[x;] (**planes**(x); ∃s[**in**(s, **the.Bermuda.Triangle**) & **disappear**(x,s)])
 b. **GEN**[s;] (**in**(s, **the.Bermuda.Triangle**); ∃x[**planes**(x) & **disappear**(x,s)])
 c. **GEN**[x,s;] (**planes**(x) & **in**(x,s) & **in**(s, **the.Bermuda.Triangle**); **disappear**(x,s))

(2a) represents the reading which says that it is generally true for planes that they disappear in the Bermuda Triangle, or more precisely, that there exist situations in the Bermuda Triangle in which they disappear. (2b) says that it is generally true for situations in the Bermuda Triangle that there are planes which disappear in these situations. And (2c) says that it is generally true that if planes are in the Bermuda Triangle, they disappear. The different readings, then, are the result of a different partitioning of the semantic material into the restrictor and the matrix of the **GEN**-operator (see Diesing 1992 for this notion of semantic partition).

In chapter 1 we also have shown that intonational features, in particular stress placement, play a role in distinguishing between these different partitions. The readings of (1) and (2) are associated with the following accentual patterns:

(1′) a. Mary SMOKES after dinner.
b. Mary smokes after DINNER.

(2′) a. Planes disappear in the BERMUDA Triangle.
b. PLANES disappear in the Bermuda Triangle.
c. Planes DISAPPEAR in the Bermuda Triangle.

It appears that accented constituents, in general, are part of the matrix. However, we will see that this statement has to be modified.

Sentence accent marks that a constituent is in focus. For example, it serves to differentiate between the readings that show up with focus-sensitive operators like *only:*

(3) a. John only introduced BILL to Sue.
b. John only introduced Bill to SUE.
c. John only introduced BILL to SUE.
d. John only INTRODUCED Bill to Sue.

(3a) can be paraphrased as: The only person that John introduced to Sue was Bill. (3b) has two readings. (i) The only person that John introduced Bill to was Sue, and (ii) The only thing John did was introducing Bill to Sue. (3c) can be rendered as: The only two persons such that John introduced one to the other are Bill and Sue. And (3d) means: The only thing John did to Bill and Sue is that he introduced him to her.

Several theories have been developed to account for the sensitivity of the interpretations of sentences like (3) to the placement of the sentence accent; suffice it to mention Jackendoff (1972), von Stechow (1982, 1989), Jacobs (1983, 1991), and Rooth (1985). In addition, several researchers as early as Lawler (1973a), and more recently Schubert and Pelletier (1987), have noticed that the interpretation of generic sentences is influenced by sentence accent. But up to now, no systematic theory of focus in generic sentences has been offered (with the exception of Rooth, this volume). The present chapter is an attempt to do precisely that. It will relate the influence of focus in generic sentences to the influence of focus in adverbial quantifications in general, as first described in Rooth 1985. In contrast to Rooth (1985) and Rooth (this volume) it works with so-called *structured meanings* as the basic semantic representation format.

The organization of this chapter is as follows: In section 5.2 I introduce *structured meanings*. Section 5.3 presents a framework of dynamic interpretation for the representation of anaphoric bindings that are crucial for generic sentences. In section 5.4, structured meanings and dynamic interpretation will be combined, and I will show that this allows for a treatment of quantificational adverbials. In section 5.5 I will come back to our initial examples and give an explicit analysis of them in the framework developed.

5.2. THE STRUCTURED MEANING REPRESENTATION OF FOCUS

The basic function of focus is to give prominence to meaning-bearing elements in an expression. The highlighted constituents are called *focus,* the complement notion is *background.* Certain operators, like *only,* make use of this partitioning of expressions into focus and background.

We can investigate the focus-background structuring in two respects: We may be interested in the syntactic, morphological and phonological correlates of it, that is, in the marking of focus. Or we may look at how the information inherent in the focus-background structuring is put into use, that is, we may be interested in the semantics and pragmatics of focus. I will be mainly concerned with the latter in this chapter. I will follow the theory of Jacobs (1983, 1991), which has its roots in Jackendoff (1972).

According to Jacobs, focus cannot be interpreted independently (e.g., as the part of an utterance that is "new"), but only in relation to a *focus operator (FO)* that is associated with that focus. Technically, constituents in focus bear a feature [F], and this feature is coindexed with its focus operator (where the index may be suppressed). Let us give a representation of the two readings of (3b).

(3) b′.

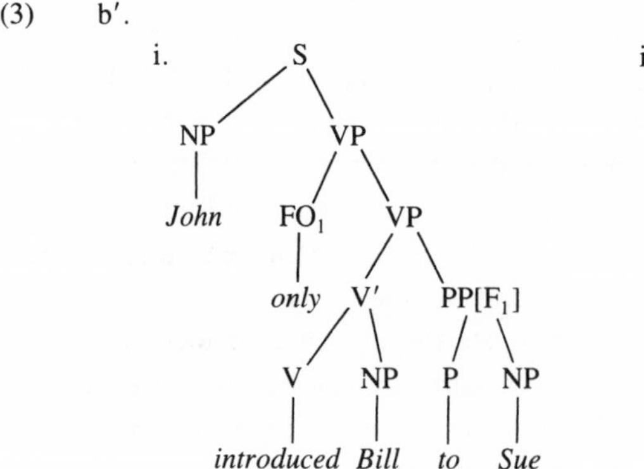

The feature $[F_1]$ is spelled out by sentence accent, following rules that are sensitive to syntactic structure (see, e.g., Selkirk 1984, von Stechow & Uhmann 1986, Jacobs 1991, Féry 1991, Uhmann 1991 for some details of these rules in English and German). In (3′b.i, ii), it happens to be the case that the F-feature is realized in the same way, with the stress on *SUE*.

On the meaning side, focus induces a partition of the semantic representation into a background B and a focus F, which is commonly represented by the pair ⟨B,F⟩, where B can be applied to F, and the application B(F) yields the standard interpretation. Focus operators apply to such focus-background structures. In the example at hand, we would get the following semantic representations for readings (i) and (ii) (to keep things simple, I assume that *only* is a sentence operator instead of a VP operator):

(3) b″. i. **only**(⟨λx.**introduced**(**j**,x,**b**),**s**⟩)
ii. **only**(⟨λP.P(**j**), λx.**introduced**(x,**s**,**b**)⟩)

Let us assume that *only* has the following interpretation:

(4) **only**(⟨B,F⟩) :⇔ B(F) & ∀X[X∈ALT(F) & B(X) → X = F],
where X is a variable of the type of F and ALT(F) is the set of alternatives to F.

Here, **only** is interpreted with respect to a set of alternatives ALT(F) to the interpretation of the focus constituent F. This set of alternatives is typically provided by the context. The meaning of **only**(⟨B,F⟩) can be paraphrased as 'B applies to F, and B applies to no alternative to F'. (A more adequate analysis would analyze the first part as presupposition and the second part as assertion; cf. Horn 1969.) For our examples this will yield the following interpretations:

(3) b.‴ **introduced**(**j**,s,**b**) &
i. ∀x[x∈ALT(**s**) & **introduced**(**j**,x,**b**) → x = **s**]
ii. ∀P[P∈ALT(λx.**introduced**(x,**s**,**b**)) & P(**j**) →
P = λx.**introduced**(x,**s**,**b**)]

The Structured Meaning representation of focus has been elaborated to capture various additional phenomena. Jacobs (1984) shows that we can treat so-called *free focus,* that is, focus that is not associated with an overt focusing operator, as being associated instead with the illocutionary operator of the sentence, for example an assertion operator. In such cases, focus typically has an influence on the felicity conditions of the sentence. For example, (5b.i) is a felicitous answer to (5a.i), but not to (5a.ii), whereas (5b.ii) is a felicitous answer to (5a.ii), but not to (5a.i).

(5) a. i. To whom did John introduce Bill?
ii. What did John do?
b. i. ASSERT_1 [John introduced Bill to $[\text{SUE}]_{F_1}$]
ii. ASSERT_1 [John [introduced Bill to $\text{SUE}]_{F_1}$]

Also, the Structured Meaning framework can capture complex foci such as shown in (6a) (by list representations, where '·' is the list connector) and multiple foci such as shown in (6b) (by recursive focus-background structures).

(6) a. John only_1 introduced BILL_{F_1} to SUE_{F_1}.
only(⟨λx·y.**introduced**(**j**,y,x), **s**·**b**⟩
b. Even_1 JOHN_{F_1} drank only_2 WATER_{F_2}
even(⟨λx.**only**(⟨λP.**drank**(x,P), **water**⟩), **j**⟩)

In cases with multiple focus, it is only the focus associated with the highest operator that is clearly marked by sentence accent (in (6b), this is *JOHN*), whereas other foci are marked less prominently (cf. Jacobs 1991). This point is especially important when we consider the fact that the highest operator is the illocutionary operator of a sentence, which will typically obliterate the accentual marking of other foci. For example, we can obtain the reading (3b′.i) with stress on *John* in a context like the following one:

(7) Speaker A: Jim only introduced Bill to SUE.
Speaker B: No, JOHN only introduced Bill to Sue.
ASSERT_1 $[\text{JOHN}]_{F_1}$ only_2 introduced Bill to $[\text{Sue}]_{F_2}$

In Krifka 1991a I have developed a theory in which focus-background structures are analyzed in a compositional way. In this framework the focus on a constituent with the semantic representation A introduces a focus-background structure with an "empty" background, ⟨λX.X,A⟩, where X is of the type of A. This focus-background structure is projected through semantic compositions. For example, if the original semantic composition rule called for the application of a semantic representation B to A, then the application of B to ⟨λX.X,A⟩ will yield ⟨λX.B(X),A⟩, and if the original rule called for an application of A to B, then the application of ⟨λX.X,A⟩ to B will yield ⟨λX.X(B), A⟩. Finally, focus-sensitive operators are applied to such background-focus structures.

Let me give a simple illustrative example. I will assume here that the semantic representation of noun phrases maps verbal predicates with n arguments to verbal predicates with $n-1$ elements. Let us use the notation '$\vec{v}$' for (possibly empty) vectors of terms, and let us use Q as a variable for predicates with arbitrary arity. Then a name like *John* will be interpreted as a generalized quantifier $\lambda Q\lambda\vec{v}.Q(\vec{v},\mathbf{j})$. For example, the application of this meaning to a transitive verb like **love** will result in $\lambda\vec{v}.\mathbf{love}(\vec{v},\mathbf{j})$, which can be reduced to $\lambda x.\mathbf{love}(x,\mathbf{j})$, for $\vec{v}$ must be a single variable since **love** is two-place. The application of $\lambda Q\lambda\vec{v}.Q(\vec{v},\mathbf{m})$ to that predicate gives us $\lambda\vec{v}[\lambda x.\mathbf{love}(x,\mathbf{j})(\vec{v},\mathbf{m})]$, where $\vec{v}$ turns out to be empty, such that we arrive at $\lambda x.\mathbf{love}(x,\mathbf{j})(\mathbf{m})$, that is, $\mathbf{love(m,j)}$. In the following, I illustrate the syntactic derivation and the corresponding semantic interpretation in tandem. Semantic combination typically is by functional application.

(8) John only met $[\text{MARY}]_F$

Mary, $\lambda Q\lambda\vec{v}.Q(\vec{v},\mathbf{m})$

$[\text{Mary}]_F$, $\langle\lambda T.T,\ \lambda Q\lambda\vec{v}.Q(\vec{v},\mathbf{m})\rangle$

met, **met**

met $[\text{MARY}]_F$, $\langle\lambda T.T,\ \lambda Q\lambda\vec{v}.Q(\vec{v},\mathbf{m})\rangle(\mathbf{met})$, $= \langle\lambda T.T(\mathbf{met}),\ \lambda Q\lambda\vec{v}.Q(\vec{v},\mathbf{m})\rangle$

John, $\lambda Q\lambda\vec{v}.Q(\vec{v},\mathrm{j})$

John met $[\text{MARY}]_F$, $\lambda Q\lambda\vec{v}.Q(\vec{v},\mathbf{j})\ (\langle\lambda T.T(\mathbf{met}),\ \lambda Q\lambda\vec{v}.Q(\vec{v},\mathbf{m})\rangle)$

$= \langle\lambda T[\lambda Q\lambda\vec{v}.Q(\vec{v},\mathbf{j})\ (T(\mathbf{met}))],\ \lambda Q\lambda\vec{v}.Q(\vec{v},\mathbf{m})\rangle$

$= \langle\lambda T\lambda\vec{v}.T(\mathbf{met})\ (\vec{v},\mathbf{j}),\ \lambda Q\lambda\vec{v}.Q(\vec{v},\mathbf{m})\rangle$

only, $\lambda\langle B,F\rangle.\mathbf{only}(\langle B,F\rangle)$

John only met $[\text{MARY}]_F$,

$\mathbf{only}(\langle\lambda T\lambda\vec{v}.T(\mathbf{met})\ (\vec{v},\mathbf{j}),\ \lambda Q\lambda\vec{v}.Q(\vec{v},\mathbf{m})\rangle)$

$= \lambda T[\lambda\vec{v}.T(\mathbf{met})\ (\vec{v},\mathbf{j})]\ (\lambda Q\lambda\vec{v}.Q(\vec{v},\mathbf{m}))\ \&$
$\forall T[T\in ALT(\lambda Q\lambda\vec{v}.Q(\vec{v},\mathbf{m}))\ \&\ \lambda\vec{v}.T(\mathbf{met})\ (\vec{v},\mathbf{j}) \rightarrow T = \lambda Q\lambda\vec{v}.Q(\vec{v},\mathbf{m})]$

$= \mathbf{met(j,m)}\ \&\ \forall T[T\in ALT(\lambda Q\lambda\vec{v}.Q(\vec{v},\mathbf{m}))\ \&\ T(\mathbf{met})(\mathbf{j}) \rightarrow$
$T = \lambda Q\lambda\vec{v}.Q(\vec{v},\mathbf{m})]$

Here I have treated names as quantifiers, and consequently focus alternatives to names as sets of quantifiers. We can assume a plausible restriction for alternatives of quantifiers generated by an individual, such as names, namely, that the alternatives are quantifiers that are generated by an individual as well. Then we can reduce the last representation to one that takes the alternatives of individuals instead, and we arrive at:

$$\mathbf{met(j,m)}\ \&\ \forall x[x\in ALT(\mathbf{m})\ \&\ \mathbf{met}(\mathbf{j},x)) \rightarrow x = \mathbf{m}]$$

Other types of operators that have been identified as focus sensitive include adverbial quantifiers. Rooth (1985) discusses examples like the following:

(9) a. [In St. Petersburg] OFFICERS$_{F_1}$ always$_1$ escorted ballerinas.
b. [In St. Petersburg] officers always$_1$ escorted BALLERINAS$_{F_1}$.

We have the following prominent readings: (9a) means that whenever ballerinas were escorted, it was by officers, whereas (9b) means that whenever officers escorted someone, they were ballerinas.

Rooth (1985) develops an analysis for these readings within the framework of Alternative Semantics. It can be imitated in the Structured Meaning representation. Let us concentrate on a somewhat simpler example of Rooth's to explain how it works:

(10) Mary always$_1$ took JOHN$_{F_1}$ to the movies.

This means: Whenever Mary took someone to the movies, she took John along. I will leave open whether she has to take ONLY John in order to make (10) come out as true; see Krifka 1992b for discussion and a treatment that covers both the exhaustive and the non-exhaustive interpretation. Here I will only treat the weaker, non-exhaustive reading. Also, bear in mind that a sentence like *Mary always took JOHN to the movies* can be interpreted in ways where focus on *John* does not influence quantification, for example, when *JOHN* is the focus of assertion, as in an answer to the question *Whom did MARY always take to the movies?*

Following Rooth (1985) I will concentrate in this section on sentences that contain quantifications over situations. Let us assume that episodic sentences are true of situations. Then the meaning of a sentence like (11a) can be given as the set of situations in which Mary took John to the movies, shown in (11b), which can be applied to a specific situation the speaker has in mind, or alternatively be existentially bound.

(11) a. Mary took John to the movies.
b. {s|**took.to.the.movies(m,j**,s)}

With focus on *John,* and interpreting *John* as a simple term, we get the following representation:

(12) a. Mary took [JOHN]$_F$ to the movies.
b. ⟨λx.{s|**took.to.the.movies(m**,x,s)}, **j**⟩

A focus-sensitive quantifier like *always* can then be spelled out as follows:

(13) **always**(⟨B,F⟩) :⇔ **EVERY**({s|∃X[X∊ALT(F) & s∊B(X)]}) ({s|s∊B(F)}),

Here, **EVERY** is the universal quantifier in generalized quantifier format: **EVERY**(X)(Y) :⇔ X⊆Y. For our example, this will give us the following:

(12′) a. **EVERY**({s|∃x[x∈ALT(**j**) & **took.to.the.movies(m**,x,s)]})
({s|**took.to.the.movies(m,j**,s)})

That is, in every situation in which Mary took some alternative to John to the movies, she took John to the movies. This captures the non-exhaustive reading of our example. The context may provide a set of alternatives, as in the following little text:

(14) Mary liked John and Bill a lot. One day, she would make a day trip to the countryside with John, and on the next day, she would go to a concert with Bill. However, she always took JOHN to the movies.

The last sentence, in the given context, means: Whenever Mary took John or Bill to the movies, she took John to the movies.

If the context does not provide any restriction of alternatives, we can assume that the alternatives are the set of all suitable entities of the type of the expression in focus. For example, the alternatives of **j** will be the set of all individuals (or of all persons, given a sortal restriction to humans). Then the meaning of our example is reduced to the following, which amounts to: Whenever Mary took someone to the movies, she took John to the movies.

(15) EVERY({s|∃x.**took(m**,x,s)}) ({s|**took(m,j**,s)})

A problem with this analysis is that it works only with episodic sentences and cannot capture bindings other than those related to the situation variable. Thus, examples like the following cannot be treated in the framework developed so far:

(16) a. A girl that sees a cat (always) STROKES it.
b. A three-colored cat is always INFERTILE.

In the most straightforward representation for (16a), the variables for the girl and the cat cannot be bound. Using our current way of interpretation we get something like this:

(16) a′. EVERY({s|∃x,y[**girl**(x) & **cat**(y) & **see**(x,y,s)]})({s|**stroke**(x,y,s)})

In (16b), we would like to quantify over cats, but the representation format given so far only allows us to quantify over situations.

Obviously, what we need is something like a quantification over cases, in the sense of Lewis (1975). A combination of focus representations with frameworks like Discourse Representation Theory (Kamp 1981), File Change Semantics (Heim 1982, 1983b), or another dynamic semantic representation (e.g., Rooth 1987, Groenendijk & Stokhof 1991) can offer a suitable setting.

5.3. A FRAMEWORK FOR DYNAMIC INTERPRETATION

The dynamic framework I will employ is related to Rooth 1987, the main differences being that I will work with partial assignment functions (cf. Heim 1983b) and that I will assume indices for possible worlds to capture modal quantifications and, in general, the increase of propositional information (cf. Stalnaker 1978, Heim 1982).

For a countable infinite set of *discourse referents* (or *indices;* henceforth DR) I will use natural numbers 1, 2, 3, etc. Let us call the domain of entities D, and let G be the set of *assignment functions,* that is, the set of partial functions from DR to D; thus $G = \cup\{G'|\exists X[X \subseteq DR \ \& \ G' = D^X]\}$. If g is an assignment function and d is an index in its domain, then I will write 'g_d' instead of 'g(d)'; for example, I will write 'g_3' instead of 'g(3)'. Two assignment functions g, k are said to be *compatible,* $g \approx k$, iff they are identical for their shared domain: $g \approx k$ iff $\forall d[d \in DOM(g) \ \& \ d \in DOM(k) \rightarrow g_d = k_d]$. The *augmentation* of g with k, $g+k$, is defined as $g \cup k$ if $DOM(g) \cap DOM(k) = \emptyset$, and undefined otherwise.

I will use the following notations for *variants* of assignment functions; contrary to usual conventions, they will denote sets of assignment functions. First, g[d] should be the set of assignment functions that is like g, with the added property that they map the index d to some entity in D; that is, $g[d] = \{k|\exists x[x \in D \ \& \ k = g+\{\langle d,x\rangle\}]\}$. Second, g[d/a] is the set of assignment functions that is like g, with the additional property that they map the index d to the entity a; that is, $g[d/a] = \{k|k = g+\{\langle d,a\rangle\}\}$. Note that this will be a singleton set. Be aware that these notations are defined only if $d \notin DOM(g)$. The two notations can be combined; for example, g[1/a,2,3/b] stands for $\{k|\exists x[x \in D \ \& \ k = g+\{\langle 1,a\rangle,\langle 2,x\rangle,\langle 3,b\rangle\}]\}$.

In general, the interpretation of natural language expressions will be with respect to an *input assignment,* an *output assignment,* and a *possible world.* NPs are related to discourse referents. Their syntactic indices are interpreted as semantic indices. Indefinite NPs bear indices that are new with respect to the input assignment, definite NPs bear old indices, and quantificational NPs bear new indices that are "active" only within the scope of quantification. The situation variable of episodic verbs will in addition be related to an index.

The individuals in the domain D are sorted. I assume here a minimal distinction between normal individuals (for which I use variables x,y,...), situations (with variables s,s',...), and worlds (with variables w,w',...). For situations I assume a relation **then**; 's-**then**-s'' means that the situation s is temporally succeeded by the situation s' and that s and s' form a larger, spatiotemporally coherent situation. Worlds determine the meanings of constants, which have a world argument, written as a subscript.

As above, I will use $\vec{v}$ as a meta-variable over vectors of individual terms of length ≥ 0. Tupels are written without commas and brackets when no confusion can arise. For example, instead of '$\langle g,k,w,y,k_2,s \rangle$' I will write '$gkwyk_2s$'. I use Q,Q', etc. as variables for entities of type $\{gkw\vec{v} \mid ... \}$; T,T', etc. as variables for entities of type $\lambda Q.\{gkw\vec{v} \mid ... \}$; and X for variables of any type. For assignments, I will use variables g,h,k,j,f. Semantic combinations are typically produced by functional application.

Let us start by giving some examples of syntactic derivations and corresponding semantic representations. I will not provide the respective syntactic and corresponding semantic rules, but it should be straightforward to infer them from the examples given.

The first example illustrates the treatment of indefinite NPs and episodic verbs. Indices of NPs are introduced by determiners, the functional heads of NPs. For indefinite NPs, the indices of indefinite determiners are new. The situation variable of an episodic verb is bound by an operator that introduces a new index for that situation; this operator may be associated with the syntactic position of INFL as the functional head of a sentence, and hence I will attach the corresponding syntactic index to the finite verb. Temporal and local adverbials specify the situation argument of a predicate. Tense will be kept implicit throughout. I will use capital letters in brackets, like '[A]', as abbreviations.

(17) A_1 plane $started_2$ on August 15, 1991.

plane, $\{ggwx|\mathbf{plane}_w(x)\}$

a_1, $\lambda Q'\lambda Q.\{gkw\vec{v}|\exists h \exists j[ghwh_1 \in Q' \ \& \ j \in h[1] \ \& \ jkwh_1\vec{v} \in Q]\}$

a_1 plane,
$\lambda Q.\{gkw\vec{v}|\exists h[h \in g[1] \ \& \ \mathbf{plane}_w(h_1) \ \& \ hkwh_1\vec{v} \in Q]\}$

start, $\{ggwxs|\mathbf{started}_w(x,s)\}$

a_1 plane start,
$\{gkws|k\epsilon g[1]\ \&\ \mathbf{plane}_w(k_1)\ \&\ \mathbf{started}_w(k_1,s)\}$

on August 15, 1991,
$\lambda Q.\{gkw\overrightarrow{vs}|gkws\overrightarrow{vs}\epsilon Q\ \&\ \mathbf{on(8\text{-}15\text{-}91},s)\}$

a_1 plane start on August 15, 1991,
$\{gkws|k\epsilon g[1]\ \&\ \mathbf{plane}_w(k_1)\ \&\ \mathbf{started}_w(k_1,s)\ \&\ \mathbf{on(8\text{-}15\text{-}91},s)\}$,

INFL_2, $\lambda Q.\{gkw\vec{v}|\exists h[h\epsilon g[2]\ \&\ hkw\vec{v}h_2\epsilon Q]\}$

a_1 plane started_2 on August 15, 1991,
$\{gkw|k\epsilon g[1,2]\ \&\ \mathbf{plane}_w(k_1)\ \&\ \mathbf{started}_w(k_1,k_2)\ \&\ \mathbf{on(8\text{-}15\text{-}91},k_2)\}(=[A])$

This analysis shows that episodic predicates are analyzed as having a situation argument, following Davidson (1967). The situation argument can be modified by temporal or locative adverbials. It is bound by an operator which can be related to the INFL node and hence is called 'INFL' here. In the example above, the INFL-operator has scope over the subject, representing a thetic sentence. It might also be applied to a VP. The INFL-operator also introduces an index attached to the finite verb.

The following example shows the treatment of transitive sentences, of definite NPs, and of temporal coherence. NPs with definite articles and definite pronouns presuppose that their index is already in the domain of the input assignment. The bare plural term *goods* is treated like an indefinite NP and introduces its own index. Temporal coherence is established by a device that allows to relate the situation index of an INFL-operator to some situation index introduced previously. The two situation indices are either identified, as in the case of an atelic predicate, or the situation index of the second predicate is located after the situation index of the first predicate (see Hinrichs 1981, Partee 1984 on temporal anaphora in narrative discourses). Technically this is solved by assuming that the INFL-operator can relate its index to an antecedent situation index. Thus the INFL-operator can have two indices, an anaphoric index and a new index. In the example below representing a categorical sentence, I assume that the INFL-operator is applied before the subject NP:

(18) The_1 plane $\text{carried}_{2,3}$ goods_4.
carry, $\{ggwyxs|\mathbf{carried}_w(y,x,s)\}$

goods_4, $\lambda Q.\{gkw\vec{v}|\exists h[h\epsilon g[4]\ \&\ \mathbf{goods}_w(h_4)\ \&\ hkwh_4\vec{v}\epsilon Q]\}$

carry goods$_4$,
$= \{gkwsx|k\epsilon g[4]$ & $\mathbf{goods}_w(k_4$ & $\mathbf{carried}_w(x,k_4,s)\}$

INFL$_{2,3}$, $\lambda Q.\{gkw\vec{v}|\exists h[h\epsilon g[3]$ & $h_2 = h_3$ & $hkw\vec{v}h_3\epsilon Q]\}$

carried$_{2,3}$ goods$_4$,
$\{gkwx|k\epsilon g[3,4]$ & $\mathbf{goods}_w(k_4)$ & $k_2 = k_3$ & $\mathbf{carried}_w(x,k_4,k_3)\}$

the$_1$ plane, $\lambda Q.\{gkw\vec{v}|\mathbf{plane}_w(g_1)$ & $gkwg_1\vec{v}\epsilon Q\}$

the$_1$ plane carried$_{2,3}$ goods$_4$, $\{gkw|k\epsilon g[3,4]$ & $\mathbf{plane}_w(k_1)$ & $k_2 = k_3$ & $\mathbf{goods}_w(k_4)$ & $\mathbf{carried}_w(k_1,k_4,k_3)\}$ (= [B])

We can combine the first sentence with the second by dynamic conjunction, for which I use the semicolon:

(19) A$_1$ plane started$_2$ on August 15, 1991. [A]

The$_1$ plane carried$_{2,3}$ goods$_4$. [B]

A$_1$ plane started$_2$ on August 15, 1991. The$_1$ plane carried$_{2,3}$ goods$_4$. [A];[B]
$= \{gwk|\exists h[ghw\epsilon[A]$ & $hkw\epsilon[B]]\}$
$= \{gkw|k\epsilon g[1,2,3,4]$ & $\mathbf{plane}_w(k_1)$ & $\mathbf{started}_w(k_1,k_2)$ & $\mathbf{goods}_w(k_4)$ & $\mathbf{on(8\text{-}15\text{-}91},k_2)$ & $k_2 = k_3$ & $\mathbf{carried}_w(k_2,k_4,k_3)\}$

Let us look at another small text in which the second situation follows the first one:

(20) A$_1$ girl saw$_2$ a$_3$ cat,
$\{gkw|k\epsilon g[1,2,3]$ & $\mathbf{child}_w(k_1)$ & $\mathbf{cat}_w(k_3)$ & $\mathbf{saw}_w(k_1,k_3,k_2)\}$

She$_1$ stroked$_{2,4}$ it$_2$, $\{gkw|k\epsilon g[4]$ & k_2-**then**-k_4 & $\mathbf{stroked}_w(k_1,k_3,k_4)\}$

A$_1$ girl saw$_2$ a$_3$ cat. She$_1$ stroked$_{2,4}$ it$_2$, $\{gkw|k\epsilon g[1,2,3,4]$ & $\mathbf{child}_w(k_1)$ & $\mathbf{cat}_w(k_3)$ & $\mathbf{saw}_w(k_1,k_3,k_2)$ & k_2-**then**-k_4 & $\mathbf{stroked}_w(k_1,k_3,k_4)\}$

A stative predicate, like *be infertile,* does not introduce any situation argument. That is, the INFL-operator cannot be applied (or alternatively, we assume that it can be applied vacuously). We get analyses like the following:

(21) is infertile, $\{ggwx|\mathbf{infertile}_w(x)\}$

the$_3$ cat, $\lambda Q.\{gkw\vec{v}|\mathbf{cat}_w(g_3)$ & $gkwg_3\vec{v}\epsilon Q]\}$

the$_3$ cat is infertile, $\{ggw|\mathbf{cat}_w(g_3)$ & $\mathbf{infertile}_w(g_3)\}$

To complete our overview of the dynamic framework, it might be interesting to have a look at the treatment of quantified NPs. Quantified NPs do not introduce any anaphoric possibilities beyond their scope, that is, their input assignment and output assignment are the same: they are "tests" in the terminology of Groenendijk and Stokhof (1991). For example, the meaning of the determiner $most_d$ can be given as follows:

(22) $most_d$:
$\lambda P \lambda Q.\{gg w\vec{v} | \mathbf{MOST}(\{x | \exists h,k[h \in g[d/x] \ \& \ hkwx \in P\})$
$(\{x | \exists h,k,j[h \in g[d/x] \ \& \ hjwx \in P \ \& \ jkwx\vec{v} \in Q]\})\}$

where **MOST** represents the usual generalized quantifier: MOST(X)(Y) $\Leftrightarrow$ card(X$\cap$Y) > ½card(X). In the following example, we use a noun with a relative clause that introduces a situation argument:

(23) a. planes that $started_2$ on August 15, 1991,
$\{gkwx | k \in g[2] \ \& \ \mathbf{plane}_w(x) \ \& \ \mathbf{started}_w(x,k_2) \ \& \ \mathbf{8\text{-}15\text{-}91}(k_2)\}$
b. $carried_{2,3}$ $goods_4$,
$\{gkwx | k \in g[3,4] \ \& \ \mathbf{goods}_w(k_4) \ \& \ k_2 = k_3 \ \& \ \mathbf{carried}_w(x,k_4,k_3)\}$
c. $Most_1$ planes that $started_2$ on August 15, 1991, $carried_{2,3}$ $goods_4$,
$\{ggw|$
$\mathbf{MOST}(\{x | k \in g[1/x,2] \ \& \ \mathbf{plane}_w(k_1) \ \& \ \mathbf{started}_w(k_1,k_2) \ \& \ \mathbf{8\text{-}15\text{-}91}(k_2)\}$
$(\{x | k \in g[1/x,2,3,4] \ \& \ \mathbf{plane}_w(k_1) \ \& \ \mathbf{started}_w(k_1,k_2) \ \&$
$\mathbf{8\text{-}15\text{-}91}(k_2) \ \& \ \mathbf{goods}_w(k_4) \ \& \ k_2 = k_3 \ \& \ \mathbf{carried}_w(x,k_4,k_3)\})\}$

That is, most x that are planes and that started on August 15, 1991, are planes that started on August 15, 1991, and carried goods.

Until now we have constructed the dynamic meaning of expressions. The truth condition for a discourse is given by existential closure over the assignments and the world arguments with respect to the "actual" world: A text A is true with respect to the world w iff there are assignments g,k such that gkw$\in$A. And A is true with respect to an input assignment g and a world w iff there is an assignment k such that gkw$\in$A.

5.4. STRUCTURED MEANINGS AND DYNAMIC INTERPRETATION

In this section, the Structured Meaning representation will be combined with the dynamic framework. Technically this is fairly easy—we have structured meanings ⟨B,F⟩, where B and F are now dynamic meanings. However, dynamic interpretation adds some complexity to the notion of alternatives: since focus meaning (and in fact, every meaning) is dynamic, the meanings in alternative sets will be dynamic as well. The task now is to decide what to do with the dynamic component of alternatives.

First of all, we should make sure that the added complexity is not only forced upon us as a technical consequence, but that we actually need it to describe the linguistic data correctly. Look at the following example:

(24) John only introduced every_1 woman to $[\text{her}_{1,2}\ \text{partner}]_F$

Here, the reference of *her partner,* in the bound reading indicated, essentially depends on the choice of woman, which is captured by the dynamic component. But as the focus meaning itself is necessarily dynamic, the alternatives, which are of the same type, must be dynamic as well.

Furthermore, in constructing alternatives we must refer to the context in which the focus constituent enters the semantic composition. For the following example, imagine a dinner table situation in which every woman has a partner at her left and a partner at her right:

(25) Speaker A: Did John introduce every lady to her partner at left and her partner at right?
Speaker B: John only introduced every_1 woman to $[\text{her}_{1,2}$ partner at $\text{LEFT}]_F$

Here, the set of alternatives will depend on the choice of woman again—for each woman x, it will contain x's partner at left and x's partner at right. I will capture this by relating alternative sets to input assignments; for example, the alternative set of F, given input assignment g, is $\text{ALT}_g(F)$.

Another complication arises because two expressions may refer to the same entity but still have different meanings when their anaphoric possibilities differ. To see this, look again at example (8), *John only met* $[MARY_1]_F$. Assume that $Mary_1$ and *the*$_1$ *woman with a*$_2$ *hat* refer to the same person at the given input assignment; nevertheless, their meaning will differ, as the second NP introduces the index 2 for the hat. Assume also that the context does not restrict the alternatives. Then both $\mathbf{the_1.woman.with.a_2.hat} \in \text{ALT}(\mathbf{MARY_1})$ and $\mathbf{John(the_1.woman.with.a_2.hat(met))}$ hold, but $\mathbf{the_1.woman.with.a_2.hat}$ does not equal $\mathbf{Mary_1}$, in the dynamic interpretation. Hence we should require that every pair of two alternatives in an alternative assignment refer to different entities, given the specified input assignment:

(26) a. For all dynamic meanings X,Y, where $X \neq Y$, and assignments g, if $Y \in \text{ALT}_g(X)$, then X and Y have the same type.
b. If X is of a type $\{gkw\vec{v} \mid \ldots\}$, and $Y \in \text{ALT}_g(X)$, then for all $k, w, \vec{v}, k', \vec{v}'$:
if $gkw\vec{v} \in X$ and $gk'w\vec{v}' \in Y$, then $\vec{v} \neq \vec{v}'$.

c. If X is of a type $\lambda X_1 \ldots X_n.\{gkw\vec{v}| \ldots\}$, and $Y \epsilon ALT_g(X)$,
then for all $k, \vec{v}, k', \vec{v}', X_1, \ldots, X_n$:
if $gkw\vec{v} \epsilon X(X_1) \ldots (X_n)$ and $gk'w\vec{v}' \epsilon Y(X_1) \ldots (X_n)$, then $\vec{v} \neq \vec{v}'$.

This restriction excludes that both **Mary$_1$** and **the$_1$.woman.with.a$_2$.hat** are in $ALT_g(F)$ if these meanings refer to the same object, given input g.

Now we are well equipped to give meaning rules for focus-sensitive quantification. Let us start with the nonmodal adverbial quantifier *most of the time*—a fairly typical representative—which will be rendered by 'MOSTLY'. The meaning rule looks as follows; here, B and F are used as variables of arbitrary types representing background and focus, and I assume that we also have variables of structured types, like $\langle B,F \rangle$.

(27) **MOSTLY**($\langle B,F \rangle$) =
$\{ggw|\mathbf{MOST}(\{h|\exists f[f = g+h \ \& \ gfw \epsilon B(\{ggw\vec{v}|\exists Q \exists j[Q \epsilon ALT_g(F) \ \& \ gjw\vec{v} \epsilon Q]\})]\})$
$(\{h|\exists j[j \approx g+h \ \& \ gjw \epsilon B(F)]\})\}$
if F is of a type $\{gkw\vec{v}| \ldots\}$

MOSTLY expresses a quantification over augmentations h of the input assignment g. In the first argument, h is restricted to the cases in which the input g and the output f (where f=g+h) satisfy the background applied to some alternative of F. The set of alternatives is again taken with respect to that input assignment at which the focus constituent is interpreted. We prevent the alternatives from introducing their own binding possibilities by binding the assignment j existentially—in a sense, we are skipping over the indices introduced within the focus. In the second argument, we require that g+h satisfies the background applied to the focus directly. Actually, we have to introduce an assignment j that is compatible with g+h, as the focus might introduce its own binding possibilities that are not captured by h.

Let us see how things work out by looking at an example in which we implicitly quantify over entities and situations:

(28) Most of the time, a_1 girl that $sees_2$ a_3 cat $[\text{STROKES}_{2,4}]_F$ it_3.
stroke, $\{ggwyxs|\mathbf{stroke}_w(x,y,s)\}$ (= [C])

$[\text{STROKE}]_F$, $\langle \lambda Q.Q, [C] \rangle$

it_3, $\lambda Q.\{ggw\vec{v}|ggwg_3\vec{v} \epsilon Q\}$ (= [D])

$[\text{STROKE}]_F$ it_3, $\langle \lambda Q.[D](Q),[C] \rangle$

$\text{INFL}_{2,4}$, $\lambda Q.\{gkw\vec{v}|\exists h[h \epsilon g[4] \ \& \ h_2\text{-}\mathbf{then}\text{-}h_4 \ \& \ hkw\vec{v}h_2 \epsilon Q]\}$

$[\text{STROKES}_{2,4}]_F$ it_3,
$\langle \lambda Q.\{gkwx|\exists h[h \in g[4]$ & h_2-**then**-h_4 & $hkwxh_4 \in [D](Q)]\},[C]\rangle$

| a_1 girl that sees_2 a_3 cat, $\lambda Q.\{gkw\vec{v}|\exists h[h = g[1,2,3]$ & $\textbf{girl}_w(h_1)$ & $\textbf{cat}_w(h_3)$ & $\textbf{see}_w(h_1,h_3,h_2)$ & $hkwh_1\vec{v} \in Q]\}$ (= [E])

a_1 girl that sees_2 a_3 cat $[\text{STROKES}_{2,4}]_F$ it_3,
$\langle \lambda Q.[E](\{gkwx|\exists h[h \in g[4]$ & h_2-**then**-h_4 & $hkwxh_4 \in [D](Q)]\}),[C]\rangle$

| most of the time, $\lambda\langle B,F\rangle.\text{MOSTLY}(\langle B,F\rangle)$

most of the time, a_1 girl that sees_2 a_3 cat $[\text{STROKES}_{2,4}]_F$ it_3,
MOSTLY$(\langle \lambda Q.[E](\{gkwx|\exists h[h \in g[4]$ & h_2-**then**-h_4 & $hkwxh_4 \in [D](Q)]\}),[C]\rangle)$
= $\{ggw|$**MOST**$(\{h|\exists f[f = g+h$ & $gfw \in [E](\{gkwx|\exists h[h \in g[4]$ & h_2-**then**-h_4 & $hkwxh_4 \in [D]\{ggw\vec{v}|\exists Q\exists j[Q \in \text{ALT}_g([C])$ & $gjw\vec{v} \in Q]\})]\})]\})$
$(\{h|\exists j[j \approx g+h$ & $gjw \in [E](\{gkwx|\exists h[h \in g[4]$ & h_2-**then**-h_4 & $hkwxh_4 \in [D]([C])]\})]\})\}$

The first argument of MOST reduces to:
$\{h|\exists f[f = g+h$ & $f \in g[1,2,3,4]$ & $\textbf{girl}_w(f_1)$ & $\textbf{cat}_w(f_3)$ & $\textbf{see}_w(f_1,f_3,f_2)$ & f_2-**then**-f_4 & $\exists q\exists j[Q \in \text{ALT}_f([C])$ & $fjwf_3f_1f_4 \in Q]]\}$

The second argument of MOST reduces to:
$\{h|\exists j[j \approx g+h$ & $j \in g[1,2,3,4]$ & $\textbf{girl}_w(j_1)$ & $\textbf{cat}_w(j_3)$ & $\textbf{see}_w(j_1,j_3,j_2)$ & j_2-**then**-j_4 & $\textbf{stroke}_w(j_1,j_3,j_4)]\}$

Hence we get an interpretation that accepts input assignments g (without changing them) and worlds w such that
– most augmentations h of g where f = g+h and f_1 is a girl, f_3 is a cat, f_1 sees f_3 in situation f_2, and f_4 is a situation after f_2 such that f_1 does some alternative to stroking f_3 in f_4 (where the alternatives are determined with respect to the input assignment f)
– are such that f_1 is a child, f_3 is a cat, f_1 sees f_3 in f_2, and f_1 strokes f_3 in f_4.

Note that we refer in both cases to the same child, cat, seeing situation, and situation after the seeing situation, by virtue of the relation '≈'. In a paraphrase closer to English: 'For most x,s,y,s′ such that x is a child that sees a cat y in s and s′ follows s, x strokes y in s′'.

Until now, we have investigated cases where a verbal predicate, that is, an expression of a type $\{gkw\vec{v}| \dots \}$, was in focus. How should we extend the rule for MOSTLY to focus constituents of other types? Let us have a look at quantifiers, which are of type $\lambda Q.\{gkw\vec{v}| \dots Q \dots \}$, where Q stands for the verbal predicate to which the term is applied. As in (27), we have to introduce in the restrictor some existentially bound assignment j that allows us to skip over the indices introduced by the item in focus. But in this case we must make sure that we do not skip over the indices introduced by the verbal predicate which Q stands for—that is, we have to exempt those indices that are introduced within Q. A meaning rule for *most of the time* which does that is the following (where the relevant part is $\exists\vec{v}'[gkw\vec{v}'\epsilon Q]$):

(29) **MOSTLY**($\langle B,F\rangle$) =
$\{ggw|MOST(\{h|\exists f[f = g+h \;\&\; gfw\epsilon B(\lambda Q.\{gkw\vec{v}|\exists\vec{v}'[gkw\vec{v}'\epsilon Q] \;\&$
$\exists T\exists j[j\approx f \;\&\; T\epsilon ALT_g(F) \;\&\; gjw\vec{v}\epsilon T(Q)]\})]\})$
$(\{h|\exists j[j\approx g+h \;\&\; gjw\epsilon B(F)]\})\}$
if F is of a type $\lambda Q.\{gkw\vec{v} \mid \ldots\}$

Let us have a look at the treatment of an example. Imagine that little Mary has several dolls and teddy bears which she likes to take to bed with herself. Her parents can observe:

(30) Most of the time, Mary takes [a TEDDY bear]$_F$ to bed.
a_3 teddy bear,
$\lambda Q.\{gkw\vec{v}|\exists h[h\epsilon g[3] \;\&\; \mathbf{teddy}_w(h_3) \;\&\; hkw\vec{v}\epsilon Q]\}$ (= [F])
|
[a_3 TEDDY bear], $\langle\lambda T.T,$ [F]$\rangle$
|
take to bed, $\{ggwyxs|\mathbf{take}_w(x,y,s)\}$ (= [G])
↓
take [a_3 TEDDY bear] to bed, $\langle\lambda T.T([G]),[F]\rangle$
|
$INFL_2$, $\lambda Q.\{gkw\vec{v}|\exists h[h\epsilon g[2] \;\&\; hkw\vec{v}h_2\epsilon Q]\}$
↓
$takes_2$ [a_3 TEDDY bear] to bed,
$\langle\lambda T.\{gkw\vec{v}|\exists h[h\epsilon g[2] \;\&\; hkw\vec{v}h_2\epsilon(T([G]))]\},[F]\rangle$
|
$Mary_1$, $\lambda Q.\{gkw\vec{v}|g_1 = \mathbf{m}_w \;\&\; gkwg_1\vec{v}\epsilon Q]\}$ (= [H])
↓
$Mary_1$ $takes_2$ [a_3 TEDDY bear] to bed,
$\langle\lambda T.[H](\{gkw\vec{v}|\exists h[h\epsilon g[2] \;\&\; hkw\vec{v}h_2\epsilon(T([G]))]\}),[F]\rangle$
|
most of the time, $\lambda\langle B,F\rangle.MOSTLY(\langle B,F\rangle)$
↓
most of the time, $Mary_1$ $takes_2$ [a_3 TEDDY bear] to bed,
$MOSTLY(\langle\lambda T.[H](\{gkw\vec{v}|\exists h[h\epsilon g[2] \;\&\; hkw\vec{v}h_2\epsilon(T([G]))]\}),[F]\rangle)$,

$$= \{ggw|\mathrm{MOST}(\{h|\exists f[f = g+h \;\&\; gfw\in[H](\{gkw\vec{v}|\exists h[h\in g[2] \;\&\; hkw\vec{v}h_2\in$$
$$(\{gkwxs|\exists y'x's'[gkwy'x's'\in[G]] \;\&\; \exists T\exists j[j\approx f \;\&$$
$$T\in \mathrm{ALT}_g([F]) \;\&\; gjwxs\in T([G])]\})]\})]\})$$
$$(\{h|\exists j[j\approx g+h \;\&\; gjw\in[H](\{gkw\vec{v}|\exists h[h\in g[2] \;\&$$
$$hkw\vec{v}h_2\in[F]([G])]\})]\})\}$$

The first argument of MOST reduces to:

$$\{h|\exists f[f = g+h \;\&\; g_1 = m_w \;\&\; f\in g[2] \;\&\; \exists yxs[\mathbf{take}_w(x,y,s)] \;\&$$
$$\exists T\exists j[j\approx f \;\&\; T\in \mathrm{ALT}_g([F]) \;\&\; fjwg_1k_2\in T([G])]]]\}$$

The second argument of MOST reduces to:

$$\{h|\exists j[j\approx g+h \;\&\; g_1 = m_w \;\&\; j\in g[2,3] \;\&\; \mathbf{teddy}_w(j_3) \;\&\; \mathbf{take}_w(j_1,j_3,j_2)]\}$$

This accepts input assignments g (without changing them) and worlds w such that

– most augmentations h of g with DOM(h) = {2} and $f = g+h$ where f_1 is Mary, f_2 is a situation where f_1 takes something to bed, and f_1 takes some alternative to a teddy bear to bed

– are such that they can be extended to j, where j_1 (= f_1) is Mary, j_3 is a teddy bear, and j_1 takes j_3 to bed in situation j_2 (= f_2).

This gives us the right analysis, at least for the non-exhaustive reading. We effectively quantify only over situations in which Mary takes something to bed with her. Krifka (1992b) discusses the meaning rules for the exhaustive readings.

In the final section we will take a closer look at generic sentences and at the role of the alternative sets.

5.5. GENERIC SENTENCES

In chapter 1 we have discussed different ways to render the semantics of the generic quantifier, **GEN.** Here I will adopt a modal treatment—a quantification over possible worlds—inspired by Lewis (1973) and Kratzer (1981).

GEN is dependent on a modal background N (e.g., a deontic or epistemic background) and a possible world, here, the actual world a. We assume a partial order relation '$\leq_{N,a}$' between cases, where '$u \leq_{N,a} v$' means: u is at least as normal (close to the ideal) as v, with respect to N and a. Then we can state the following:

(31) $\mathbf{GEN}_{\mathbf{N,a}}(A)(B)$ iff
$$\forall u[u\in A \rightarrow \exists v[v \leq_{N,a} u \;\&\; \forall v'[v' \leq_{N,a} v \;\&\; v'\in A \rightarrow v'\in B]]]$$

That is, for any case u that satisfies the restrictor A, there is a case v that is at least as close to the ideal as u, such that all cases v′ that are at least as close to v and that satisfy the restrictor A also satisfy the matrix B. That is, for the "most normal" cases v′, it holds that satisfaction of the antecedent entails satisfaction of the consequent.

The adverbial quantifier that incorporates **GEN** will be called '$\mathbf{GENER}_N$', where N refers to some modal background; its definition is similar to that of **MOSTLY** above:

(32) $\mathbf{GENER}_N(\langle B,F\rangle) =$

a. $\{ggw|\mathbf{GEN}_{N,w}(\{h|\exists f[f = g+h \;\&\; gfw\in B(\{ggw\vec{v}|\exists Q\exists j[Q\in ALT_g(F) \;\&$
$gjw\vec{v}\in Q]\})\})$
$(\{h|\exists j[j\approx g+h \;\&\; gjw\in B(F)]\})\}$
if F is of a type $\{gkw\vec{v}|\ \ldots\ \}$.

b. $\{ggw|\mathbf{GEN}_{N,w}(\{h|\exists f[f = g+h \;\&\; gfw\in B(\lambda Q.\{gkw\vec{v}|\exists\vec{v}[gkw\vec{v}\in Q] \;\&$
$\exists T\exists j[j\approx f \;\&\; T\in ALT_g(F) \;\&\; gjw\vec{v}\in T(Q)]\})]\})$
$(\{h|\exists j[j\approx g+h \;\&\; gjw\in B(F)]\})\}$
if F is of a type $\lambda Q.\{gkw\vec{v}|\ \ldots\ \}$

Let us now look at the treatment of our initial examples. I start with the derivations of the two readings of (1), *Mary smokes after dinner.* I assume that a phrase like *after dinner* introduces a dinner situation and links the situation argument of the verb to that situation; more specifically, the situation argument should follow that situation.

(33) $[\text{SMOKE}]_F$, $\langle\lambda Q.Q, \{ggwxs|\mathbf{smoke}_w(x,s)\}\rangle$, $= \langle\lambda Q.Q,[I]\rangle$

after dinner_3,
$\lambda Q.\{gkw\vec{v}s|\exists h[h\in g[3] \;\&\; h_3\text{-}\mathbf{then}\text{-}s \;\&\; \mathbf{dinner}_w(h_3) \;\&\; hkw\vec{v}s\in Q]\}$ (= [K])

$[\text{SMOKE}]_F$ after dinner_3, $\langle\lambda Q.[K](Q),[I]\rangle$

INFL_2, $\lambda Q.\{gkw\vec{v}|\exists h[h\in g[2] \;\&\; hkw\vec{v}h_2\in Q]\}$

$[\text{SMOKES}_2]_F$ after dinner_3, $\langle\lambda Q.\{gkw\vec{v}|\exists h[h\in g[2] \;\&\; hkw\vec{v}h_2\in[K](Q)]\},[I]\rangle$

Mary_1, $\lambda Q.\{gkw\vec{v}|g_1 = \mathbf{m}_w \;\&\; gkwg_1\vec{v}\in Q\}$ (= [L])

Mary_1 $[\text{SMOKES}_2]_F$ after_2 dinner_3,
$\langle\lambda Q.[L](\{gkw\vec{v}|\exists h[h\in g[2] \;\&\; hkw\vec{v}h_2\in[K](Q)]\}),[I]\rangle$

ø, $\lambda\langle B,F\rangle.\mathbf{GENER}_N(\langle B,F\rangle)$

Mary_1 $[\text{SMOKES}_2]_F$ after_2 dinner_3,
$\{ggw|\mathbf{GEN}_{N,w}(\{h|\exists f[f = g+h \;\&\; gfw\in[L](\{gkw\vec{v}|\exists h[h\in g[2] \;\&$
$hkw\vec{v}g_2\in[K](\{ggw\vec{v}|$

$\exists Q \exists j[Q \in ALT_g([I]) \ \&\ gjw\vec{v} \in Q]\})]\})]\})$
$(\{h|\exists j[j \approx g+h \ \&\ gjw \in [L](\{gkw\vec{v}|\exists h[h \in g[2] \ \&$
$hkw\vec{v}g_2 \in [K]([I])]\})]\})\}$

The first argument of $\mathbf{GEN}_{N,w}$ reduces to:

$\{h|\exists f[f = g+h \ \&\ g_1 = \mathbf{m}_w \ \&\ f \in g[2,3] \ \&\ f_3\text{-}\mathbf{then}\text{-}f_2 \ \&\ \mathbf{dinner}_w(f_3) \ \&$
$\exists Q \exists j[Q \in ALT_f([I]) \ \&\ fjwf_1f_2 \in Q]]\}$

The second argument of $\mathbf{GEN}_{N,w}$ reduces to:

$\{h|\exists j[j \approx g+h \ \&\ g_1 = \mathbf{m}_w \ \&\ j \in [2,3] \ \&\ j_3\text{-}\mathbf{then}\text{-}j_2 \ \&\ \mathbf{dinner}_w(j_3) \ \&$
$\mathbf{smoke}_w(j_1, j_2)]\}$

This accepts input assignments g (without changing them) and worlds w such that g_1 is Mary and
– augmentations h of g with $f = g+h$ and $DOM(h) = \{2,3\}$ such that f_3 is a dinner situation followed by a situation f_2 in which f_1 ($= g_1$) does some alternative Q to smoking
– can typically be extended to j such that j_2 ($= f_2$) is a situation following the dinner situation j_3 ($= f_2$), and j_1 ($= f_1$) smokes in j_2.

The other reading of (1) can be derived as follows:

(34) smoke$_2$, $\{ggwxs|\mathbf{smoke}_w(x,s)\}$ (= [I])

after dinner$_3$, [K]

[after DINNER$_3$]$_F$, $\langle \lambda T.T, [K] \rangle$

smoke [after DINNER$_3$]$_F$, $\langle \lambda T.T([I]), [K] \rangle$

INFL$_2$, $\lambda Q.\{gkw\vec{v}|\exists h[h \in g[2] \ \&\ hkw\vec{v}h_2 \in Q]\}$

smokes$_2$ [after DINNER$_3$]$_F$, $\langle \lambda T.\{gkw\vec{v}|\exists h[h \in g[2] \ \&\ hkw\vec{v}h_2 \in T([I])]\}, [K] \rangle$

Mary$_1$, $\lambda Q.\{gkw\vec{v}|\exists h[h \in g[1] \ \&\ hkwh_1\vec{v} \in Q]\}$ (= [L])

Mary$_1$ smokes$_2$ [after DINNER$_3$]$_F$,
$\langle \lambda T.[L](\{gkw\vec{v}|\exists h[h \in g[2] \ \&\ hkw\vec{v}h_2 \in T([I])]\}), [K] \rangle$

ø, $\lambda \langle B,F \rangle.GENER_N(\langle B,F \rangle)$

Mary$_1$ smokes$_2$ [after DINNER$_3$]$_F$,
$\{ggw|\mathbf{GEN}_{N,w}(\{h|\exists f[f = g+h \ \&\ gfw \in \{gkw\vec{v}|\exists h[h \in g[2] \ \&\ hkw\vec{v}h_2 \in \{gkw\vec{v}|$
$\exists \vec{v}[gkw\vec{v} \in [L]] \ \&\ \exists T \exists j[j \approx f \ \&\ T \in ALT_g([I]) \ \&$
$gjw\vec{v} \in T([L])]\}]\}]\})$
$(\{h|\exists j[j \approx g+h \ \&\ gjw \in \{gkw\vec{v}|\exists s[gkw\vec{v}s \in [I]([L])]\}]\})\}$

The first argument of $\mathbf{GEN}_{N,w}$ reduces to:
$\{h|\exists f[f = g+h \& f\epsilon g[2] \& g_1 = \mathbf{m}_w \& \mathbf{smoke}_w(f_1,f_2) \&$
$\exists T\exists j[j\approx f \& T\epsilon ALT_f([I]) \& gjwf_2\epsilon T([L])]\}$
The second argument of $\mathbf{GEN}_{N,w}$ reduces to the same expression as in (33).

This accepts input assignments g (without changing them) and worlds w such that g_1 is Mary and
– an augmentation h of g such that DOM(h) = {2} and f = g+h, where f_1 (= g_1) smokes in f_2, and there is some alternative T to the temporal determination "after dinner" such that f_1 smokes in f_2, and f_2 is related to T
– typically can be extended to an assignment j such that there is a dinner situation j_3, and j_2 (= f_2) follows j_3.

In both cases we get the intuitively correct readings. In the first case, we quantify over after-dinner situations and say that Mary smokes in these situations; in the second case, we quantify over situations in which Mary smokes and say that they are after-dinner situations.

One potential problem with this analysis arises from the fact that we should count only those dinner situations that involve Mary. This is not expressed directly in the representations given. In our informal formalizations in (1a,b), we had to represent the fact that Mary had to be "in" the dinner situation by a relation **in** whose presence was not licensed by any linguistic element.

Where can we locate the implicit requirement that the dinner situations should include Mary? The proper place for that is within the set of alternatives and the relation between situations **then.** In the analysis of the first reading, (33), we require that the alternatives to [I] are with respect to the assignment f, where f contains reference to a dinner situation f_3 followed by a situation f_2 in which the alternatives are located. Now, it is a reasonable requirement that all the alternatives Q to [I] (i.e., smoking, with respect to f) such that f_1 (= Mary) has the property Q in f_2 must be located after f_3. Furthermore, when two situations stand in the relation **then,** we should be allowed to draw the inference that the participants in the situation are the same. In our example, if f_3 is a dinner situation, f_2 is a smoking situation with Mary as the agent, and f_2 is related to f_3 by **then,** we can infer that f_3 contains Mary as a participant as well.

In the second reading, (34), the condition that Mary be part of the dinner situation need only be expressed in the matrix. It follows, under the assumption mentioned above, that the **then**-relation between situations invites the inference that the situations have the same participants.

Generic sentences that lack a situation variable can be treated as well. Let us derive the following example:

(35) A$_1$ three-colored cat [is INFERTILE]$_F$
is infertile, $\{ggwx|\mathbf{infertile}_w(x)\}$ (= [M])
|
[is INFERTILE]$_F$, $\langle\lambda Q.Q,[M]\rangle$
|
a$_1$ three-colored cat, $\lambda Q.\{gkw\vec{v}|\exists h[h = g[1]\ \&\ \mathbf{cat}_w(h_1)\ \&\ \mathbf{3\text{-}colored}_w(h_1)\ \&\ hkwh_1\vec{v}\in Q]\}$ (= [N])
↓
a$_1$ three-colored cat [is INFERTILE]$_F$, $\langle\lambda Q.[N](Q),[M]\rangle$
|
ø, $\lambda\langle B,F\rangle.\mathbf{GENER}_N(\langle B,F\rangle)$
↓
a$_1$ three-colored cat [is INFERTILE]$_F$

$$\{ggw|\mathbf{GEN}_{N,w}(\{h|\exists f[f = g+h\ \&\ gfw\in[N](\{ggw\vec{v}|\exists Q\exists j[Q\in ALT_g([M])\ \&\ gjw\vec{v}\in Q]\})\})$$
$$(\{h|\exists j[j\approx g+h\ \&\ gjw\in[N]([M])]\})\}$$
$$= \{ggw|\mathbf{GEN}_{N,w}(\{h|\exists f[f = g+h\ \&\ f\in g[1]\ \&\ \mathbf{cat}_w(f_1)\ \&\ \mathbf{3\text{-}colored}_w(f_1)\ \&\ \exists Q\exists j[Q\in ALT_f([M])\ \&\ gjwf_1\in Q]]\})$$
$$(\{h|\exists j[j\approx g+h\ \&\ j\in g[1]\ \&\ \mathbf{cat}_w(j_1)\ \&\ \mathbf{3\text{-}colored}_w(j_1)\ \&\ \mathbf{infertile}_w(j_1)]\})\}$$

This accepts those inputs g (without changing them) and worlds w such that in general, augmentations h of g such that h_1 is a three-colored cat that has some alternative property to being infertile are such that h_1 is a three-colored cat that is infertile. Effectively we do quantify over individuals in this case.

In chapter 1 we mentioned that a sentence like *Simba is infertile* cannot be interpreted as a characteristic sentence, because there is no variable to quantify over—the subject does not provide for it, since it is a name, and neither does the predicate, since it is stative. In our reconstruction, these sentences would have degenerate representations, as the augmentations h have an empty domain. This is illustrated by the following derivation, where h has as its domain the empty set:

(36) Simba$_1$ is infertile.

$$\{ggw|GEN_{N,w}(\{h|\exists f[f = g+h\ \&\ f = g\ \&\ g_1 = \mathbf{s}_w\ \&\ \exists Q\exists j[Q\in ALT_f([M])\ \&\ gjwf_1\in Q]]\})$$
$$(\{h|\exists j[j\approx g+h\ \&\ j = g\ \&\ g_1 = \mathbf{s}_w\ \&\ \mathbf{infertile}_w(j_1)]\})\}$$

Finally, let us go over the treatment of the readings of example (2), *Planes disappear in the Bermuda Triangle.* The three readings are related to the following focus assignments:

(37) a. Planes$_1$ [disappear$_2$ in the$_3$ BERMUDA Triangle]$_F$.
b. [PLANES$_1$ disappear$_2$]$_F$ in the$_3$ Bermuda Triangle.
c. Planes$_1$ [DISAPPEAR$_2$]$_F$ in the$_3$ Bermuda Triangle.

We assume the following meanings:

(38) a. Planes$_1$:
$\lambda Q.\{gkw\vec{v}|\exists h[h\epsilon g[1] \;\&\; \mathbf{planes}_w(h_1) \;\&\; hkwh_1\vec{v}\epsilon Q]\}$ (= [P])
b. disappear: $\{ggwxs|\text{disappear}_w(x,s)\}$ (= [D])
c. in the$_3$ Bermuda Triangle:
$\lambda Q.\{gkw\vec{v}s|g_3 = \text{BT}_w \;\&\; \text{in}_w(s,g_3) \;\&\; gkw\vec{v}s\epsilon Q\}$ (= [B])

Now, the first of the three readings can be derived as follows:

(37) a′. disappear in the$_3$ Bermuda Triangle, [B]([D])

INFL$_2$, $\lambda Q.\{gkw\vec{v}|\exists h[h\epsilon g[2] \;\&\; hkw\vec{v}h_2\epsilon Q]\}$

disappear$_2$ in the$_3$ Bermuda Triangle,
$\{gkwx|\exists h[h\epsilon g[2] \;\&\; hkwxh_2\epsilon[B]([D])]\}$ (= [DB])

[disappear$_2$ in the$_3$ BERMUDA Triangle]$_F$, $\langle\lambda Q.Q,[DB]\rangle$

planes$_1$, [P]

planes$_1$ [disappear$_2$ in the$_3$ BERMUDA Triangle]$_F$, $\langle\lambda Q.[P](Q),[DB]\rangle$

ø, $\lambda\langle B,F\rangle.\text{GENER}_N(\langle B,F\rangle)$

planes$_1$ [disappear$_2$ in the$_3$ BERMUDA Triangle]$_F$,
$\{ggw|$
$\text{GEN}_{N,w}(\{h|\exists f[f = g+h \;\&\; gfw\epsilon[P](\{ggw\vec{v}|\exists Q\exists j[Q\epsilon \text{ALT}_g([DB]) \;\&\; gjw\vec{v}\epsilon Q]\})]\})$
$(\{h|\exists j[j\approx g+h \;\&\; gjw\epsilon[P]([DB])]\})\}$

The first argument of GEN$_{N,w}$ reduces to:
$\{h|\exists f[f = g+h \;\&\; f\epsilon g[1] \;\&\; \mathbf{planes}_w(f_1) \;\&\; \exists Q\exists j[Q\epsilon \text{ALT}_f([DB]) \;\&\; fjwf_1\epsilon Q]]\}$

The second argument of GEN$_{N,w}$ reduces to:
$\{h|\exists j[j\approx g+h \;\&\; j\epsilon g[1,2] \;\&\; j_3 = \mathbf{BT}_w \;\&\; \mathbf{in}_w(j_2,j_3) \;\&\; \mathbf{disappear}_w(j_1,j_2)]\}$

This derivation accepts input assignments g and worlds w for which it is the case that

- an augmentation h of g with DOM(h) = {1} and f = g+h such that f_1 are planes and f_1 has some alternative property Q to disappearing in the Bermuda Triangle
- typically can be extended to j such that j_2 is a situation in the Bermuda Triangle in which j_1 (= f_1) disappears.

This represents the intended reading correctly: Disappearing in the Bermuda Triangle is the typical fate of planes.

Next, let us drive the reading corresponding to (37b):

(37) b′. Planes$_1$ disappear, [P]([D]) (= [PD])

[PLANES$_1$ disappear], ⟨λQ.Q,[PD]⟩

in the$_3$ Bermuda Triangle, [B]

[PLANES$_1$ disappear]$_F$ in the$_3$ Bermuda Triangle, ⟨λQ.[B](Q),[PD]⟩

INFL$_2$, $\lambda Q.\{gkw\vec{v}|\exists h[h\epsilon g[2]\ \&\ hkw\vec{v}h_2\epsilon Q]\}$

[PLANES$_1$ disappear]$_F$ in the$_3$ Bermuda Triangle,
$\langle\lambda Q.\{gkw\vec{v}|\exists h[h\epsilon g[2]\ \&\ hkw\vec{v}h_2\epsilon[B](Q)]\},[PD]\rangle$

ø, λ⟨B,F⟩.GENER$_N$(⟨B,F⟩)

[PLANES$_1$ disappear$_2$]$_F$ in the$_3$ Bermuda Triangle,
$\{ggw|GEN_{N,w}(\{h|\exists f[f = g+h\ \&\ \exists h[h\epsilon g[2]\ \&\ hfwh_2\epsilon[B](\{ggws|\exists Q\exists j$
$[Q\epsilon ALT_g([PD])\ \&\ gjws\epsilon Q]\})]]\})$
$(\{h|\exists j[j\approx g+h\ \&\ \exists h[h\epsilon g[2]\ \&\ hjwh_2\epsilon[B]([PD])]]\})\}$

Here the first argument of $GEN_{N,w}$ reduces to:
$\{h|\exists f[f = g+h\ \&\ f\epsilon g[2]\ \&\ f_3 = \mathbf{BT}_w\ \&\ \mathbf{in}_w(f_3,f_2)\ \&\ \exists Q\exists j[Q\epsilon ALT_f([PD])$
$\&\ gjwf_2\epsilon Q]]\}$

The second argument reduces to the same as in (37a′).

This accepts input assignments g and worlds w such that
- an augmentation h of g where DOM(h) = {2}, f = g+h, and f_2 is a situation in the Bermuda Triangle such that some alternative Q to the disappearing of planes happens in f_2
- can typically be extended to j such that j_2 (= f_2) is a situation in which there are planes f_1 that disappear in f_2.

That is: It is characteristic for situations in the Bermuda Triangle that planes disappear there.

Finally, we have arrived at perhaps the most plausible reading, the one corresponding to (37c):

(37) c′. $[\text{DISAPPEAR}]_F$, $\langle \lambda Q.Q,[D]\rangle$

in the_3 Bermuda Triangle, [B]

$[\text{DISAPPEAR}]_F$ in the_3 Bermuda Triangle, $\langle \lambda Q.[B](Q),[D]\rangle$

INFL_2, $\lambda Q.\{gkw\vec{v}|\exists h[h\epsilon g[2]\ \&\ hkw\vec{v}h_2\epsilon Q]\}$

$[\text{DISAPPEAR}]_F$ in the_3 Bermuda Triangle,
$\langle \lambda Q.\{gkw\vec{v}|\exists h[h\epsilon g[2]\ \&\ hkw\vec{v}h_2\epsilon [B](Q)\},[D]\rangle$

planes_1,[P]

planes_1 $[\text{DISAPPEAR}_2]_F$ in the_3 Bermuda Triangle,
$\langle \lambda Q.[P](\{gkw\vec{v}|\exists h[h\epsilon g[2]\ \&\ hkw\vec{v}h_2\epsilon [B](Q)\}),[D]\rangle$

$\lambda\langle T,Q\rangle.\text{GENER}_{N,w}(\langle T,G\rangle)$

planes_1 $[\text{DISAPPEAR}_2]_F$ in the_3 Bermuda Triangle,
$\{ggw|\text{GEN}_{N,w}(\{h|\exists f[f = g+h\ \&\ gfw\epsilon[P](\{gkwx|\exists h[h_2 g[2]\ \&$
$hkwxg_2\epsilon[B](\{ggwxs|\exists Q\exists j[Q\epsilon \text{ALT}_g([D])\ \&\ gjwxs\epsilon Q]\})]\})\})$
$(\{h|\exists j[j\approx g+h\ \&\ gjw\epsilon[P](\{gkw\vec{v}|\exists s[gkw\vec{v}s\epsilon[B]([D])]\})]\})\}$
The first argument of $\text{GEN}_{N,w}$ reduces to:
$\{h|\exists f[f = g+h\ \&\ f\epsilon g[2,3]\ \&\ \mathbf{planes}_w(f_1)\ \&\ f_3 = \mathbf{BT}_w\ \&\ \mathbf{in}_w(f_3,f_2)\ \&$
$\exists Q\exists j[Q\epsilon \text{ALT}_f([D])\ \&\ fjwf_1f_2\epsilon Q]\}$
The second argument reduces to the same as in (37a′).

This accepts input assignments g and worlds w such that
– an augmentation h of g with DOM(h) = {1,2} and f = g+h, where f_1 are planes and f_2 is a situation in the Bermuda Triangle, and where f_1 does some alternative to disappearing in f_2,
– typically is such that f_1, in fact, disappears in f_2.

Again, we have imposed certain conditions on the three interpretations (37a′,b′,c′): In (37a′), we have quantified over planes f_1 that have some property Q that is an alternative to disappearing in the Bermuda Triangle. Q need not be related to the Bermuda Triangle here at all, but may refer to the ways in which a plane can get lost. We say that an f_1 that has this property—that is, an f_1 that gets lost—typically has the property of disappearing in a situation

j_2, where j_2 is in the Bermuda Triangle; consequently, f_1 must be in the Bermuda Triangle too at the moment it disappears.

In (37b′), we quantify over situations in the Bermuda Triangle that have some property which is an alternative to containing disappearing planes. Again, the alternatives might be restricted appropriately, in this case perhaps to the situation type of catastrophic events. Then (37b′) could even be true if most situations in the Bermuda Triangle turned out to be rather unspectacular.

In (37c′), we quantify over planes and situations in the Bermuda Triangle that satisfy some alternative Q to the planes disappearing in the situations. One plausible requirement is that all planes and situations that satisfy Q are such that the planes participate in the situations, and the situations, moreover, are located in the Bermuda Triangle. Consequently, we only quantify over planes that are in the Bermuda Triangle.

These considerations show that it is a promising enterprise to formulate the implicit restrictions we often find in generic sentences in terms of suitable alternatives. I think that the set of alternatives is crucial for the interface between the semantics and the pragmatics of generic sentences.

We should expect that simple generic sentences without explicit restrictor, like *Mary smokes*, can be captured by assuming suitable alternatives as well. For this example, we would get the following semantic representation:

(39) $\text{Mary}_1\ [\text{smokes}_2]_F.$

$$\{ggw|\text{GEN}_{N,w}(\{h|\exists f[f = g+h\ \&\ g_1 = \mathbf{m}_w\ \&\ f\epsilon g[2]\ \&\ \exists Q\exists j[Q\epsilon \text{ALT}_g(\{ggwxs|\mathbf{smoke}_w(x,s)\})\ \&\ fjwf_1f_2\epsilon Q]\})$$
$$(\{h|\exists j[j\approx g+h\ \&\ g_1 = \mathbf{m}_w\ \&\ j\epsilon g[2]\ \&\ \mathbf{smoke}_w(j_1,j_2)]\})$$

Here we quantify over situations f_2 in which Mary (= f_1) does some alternative to smoking, and we say that, in fact, she smokes in these situations. Many situations may not count as alternatives to smoking situations—for example, all situations that exclude smoking to begin with, like being asleep, but also other situations, such as those in which Mary has just finished a cigarette. So it seems that proper restrictions of the alternatives can lead us to a proper interpretation of generic sentences even in these cases.

5.6 OPEN ISSUES

I have developed in this chapter a framework for the meanings of generic sentences that captures the influence of focus. I have shown that a combination of the Structured Meaning representation of focus with a dynamic interpretation allows us to formulate an adequate description.

There are several issues that require further elaboration. On the top of the list is a closer investigation into the notion 'alternatives', since it is here that the semantics and the pragmatics of generic sentences, and quantificational sentences in general, meet. In particular, there are two aspects that require further investigation: First, how does the context or the situation of utterance influence the set of alternatives? Secondly, what are the general principles behind the construction of alternatives? For example, I have suggested that the alternatives to a situation predicate like *Planes disappear* are predicates that describe other catastrophic situations. So it seems that one important principle in constructing sets of alternatives is that we generalize from a relatively specific type of situations, objects, or cases to a more general type, perhaps using a universal ontological hierarchy.

In this chapter, I did not cover generic sentences that contain generic, or kind-referring, NPs, such as *The cat meows.* (See chapter 1 for a discussion of how generic NPs relate to generic sentences, and how generic sentences with generic NPs can be treated. Also, I did not go into the role of the plural in sentences like (2). Chapter 1 contains some discussion of the treatment of plurality and distributivity within a lattice-theoretic semantic representation.

A final point is the question of how predictive focus is in determining the semantic partition that is necessary for the generic operator and for adverbial quantifiers in general. Schubert and Pelletier (1987), in their discussion of "reference ensembles" (i.e., the restrictor of the quantification), give a number of examples where they do not refer to the role of focus, but where focus seems to play a role. For instance, their example *Cats usually land on their feet* can easily be explained in terms of background-focus structure: The main accent probably is on *feet;* hence we have *Cats usually land [on their FEET]$_F$* as a plausible analysis, which would generate the reading 'Usually, when cats land on something (one of their body parts), then they land on their feet'. However, there certainly are other examples where focus doesn't seem to play a role. For example, sentence (30),—*Most of the time, Mary takes [a TEDDY bear]$_F$ to bed*—might also be interpreted with respect to situations in which Mary goes to bed. Here, Schubert and Pelletier's suggestion that presuppositions may furnish the reference ensembles seems to be on the right track. Thus, taking a stuffed animal to bed implies going to bed. It remains to be clarified whether the role of focus-background structure can be subsumed under a general theory of the role of presupposition in quantification.

6 INDEFINITES, ADVERBS OF QUANTIFICATION, AND FOCUS SEMANTICS

Mats Rooth

6.1. INTRODUCTION

A sentence with an indefinite description in subject position may be intuitively equivalent to one where the material from the indefinite subject has been moved to an initial *when*-clause:

(1) a. A green-eyed dog is usually intelligent.
    b. When a dog is green-eyed, it is usually intelligent.

Suppose we adopt the view that adverbs of quantification such as *always* and *usually* are semantically two-place operators, and assume that one way of specifying their arguments is this: an initial *when*- or *if*-clause contributes the restrictor (or first argument) and the corresponding main clause, minus the adverb, contributes the scope (or second argument). Then we can use intuited equivalences with initial *when*-clause examples to make observations about how the arguments are filled in other cases. According to this test, in the variety of generic sentence illustrated in (1), semantic material coming from an indefinite description (in this case, *a green-eyed dog*) fills the restrictor of a quantificational adverb. Such readings of indefinite descriptions are not limited to subject position (see, for instance, Carlson 1989). In (2a), the indefinite description contributing the restriction is in object position.

(2) a. Knowing who to interview usually cracks a case like this.
    b. When a case is like this, knowing who to interview usually cracks it.

Indeed, the position of the indefinite description seems quite unrestricted. In (3a) it is inside a relative clause modifier of the subject. (3b) is a near-*when*-clause paraphrase indicating that the indefinite description is supplying the restrictor (first argument) of the quantification.

(3) a. At least one person an AIDS victim works with is usually misinformed about the disease.
    b. When someone has AIDS, at least one person he or she works with is usually misinformed about the disease.

The fact that the restriction can be supplied by indefinite descriptions in a variety of positions leads to ambiguities in examples with several indefinite descriptions. In (4a), the restriction can be supplied either by the subject *a big female* or by *a group,* as suggested by the *when*-paraphrases (4b,c).

(4) a. A big female is usually the leader of a group.
    b. When a female is big, she is usually the leader of a group.
    c. When a something is a group, the leader of it is usually a big female.

With regard to the readings above, bare plural noun phrases are like singular indefinite descriptions: the restriction of an adverb of quantification can be supplied by a bare plural in various positions.

(5) a. People who commit mass murders usually suffer from an extraordinary lack of impulse control.
    b. If a person commits/has committed a mass murder, he or she usually suffers from an extraordinary lack of impulse control.
    c. The Soviet Union usually responds to Western complaints about its human rights record.
    d. When a Western complaint is about the Soviet human rights record, the Soviet Union usually responds to it.

This chapter elaborates an approach to how semantic material from various parts of a sentence gets to serve as the restrictor of an adverb of quantification with that sentence as its scope. This enterprise takes for granted a particular view about the semantics of sentences with adverbs of quantification, the one developed by David Lewis, Hans Kamp, and Irene Heim, and is concerned with the mechanisms—the systems of semantic values and the recursive rules manipulating them—by which sentences get this semantics. Consequently, certain aspects of indefinites and quantificational adverbs which Lewis, Kamp, and Heim did not focus on, in particular the issue of the semantic analysis of genericity, are not focused on here either. This omission is worth worrying about, since most (though by no means all) of the examples discussed are generic, but is ameliorated by the fact that the derivation of equivalences like those above is only weakly tied to the semantics assumed for the quantificational adverbs. For instance, the same equivalences would result in a semantics which gave them simultaneous modal and quantificational force, as long as their semantic type remained the same.

6.1.1. The Association-with-Focus Theory

In earlier work (Rooth 1985, chap. 3), I suggested a theory of how the restrictor argument of adverbs of quantification is filled based on a semantics for intonational focus. The initial motivation was examples with focus on an individual-denoting NP. The sentences in (6), where focus is notated with the subscript F, have different truth conditions. For instance, if Mary took John to the movies exactly five times and Bill did so exactly ten times, the first generalization might be true, but the second is certainly false.

(6) a. Mary usually took John_F to the movies.
b. Mary_F usually took John to the movies.

In outline, the treatment of (6), using a Montague grammar framework, was the following:

— The adverb *usually* denotes a relation between sets of time intervals, analogous to the nominal quantifier *most,* and combines compositionally with the sentence *Mary took John to the movies.*
— The S with which an adverb of quantification combines denotes a *temporal abstract,* a set of time intervals which fills the second argument (scope) of the adverb.
— The first argument (restrictor) is unspecified as far as the normal recursive semantics goes: formally, the first argument is a free *context variable* C over sets of time intervals.
— In line with the theory of focus-related effects proposed in Rooth 1985, focus contributes to fixing the value of this context variable.

The first two points originate with Stump (1981). A simple and perhaps desirable revision is to replace "time" with "event" throughout, so that an adverb of quantification denotes a relation between sets of events rather than sets of times.[1] Here is how C is determined. Focus is interpreted in a separate component of recursive semantics: in addition to an ordinary semantic value function $[\![.]\!]^o$, there is a focus semantic value $[\![.]\!]^f$. In the appendix to this chapter, I will say exactly what $[\![.]\!]^f$ is taken to be; the important point here is that it can be mapped rather directly to an object just like the ordinary semantic value, except that there is an existentially quantified variable in the position of the focused phrase (or, in the case of multiple foci, existentially quantified variables in the positions of the focused phrases). In the case of (6a), this will be (7), the set of times or events at which Mary takes someone to the movies.

1. It has been pointed out that cardinal adverbs such as *twice* clearly quantify something other than times. It seems that *At the last department party, a libertarian twice insulted an anarcho-syndicalist* can be true even if the insulting which took place on the volleyball court happened to be cotemporal with the insulting which took place in the kitchen. By this logic, even nominal adverbs headed by *times* quantify something other than times (or perhaps in addition to them), as one can see by substituting *two times* into the example.

The association-with-focus theory says that this object, which I will call a *focus closure,* is the value of the context variable C. The end result for (6) is then: Most times (events) at which Mary takes someone to the movies are times (events) at which Mary takes Bill to the movies.[2] This seems to be the right result.

(7) {t | ∃y[AT(t, [$_S$Mary take y to the movies])]}

Rooth (1985) showed that this theory can be applied to ambiguities involving temporal adverbial clauses, such as (8), which can be read either as *Every laundry day is a rainy day* or as *Every rainy day is a laundry day.*

(8) John always does his laundry when it is raining.

This chapter investigates how the theory works out in the examples involving indefinite descriptions introduced above. Section 6.2 presents the issues and problems and sketches a solution, the formal statement of which is given in the Appendix. Section 6.3 works out the consequences of the theory in examples like (4) with multiple indefinite descriptions. Section 6.4 extends the theory to bare plural noun phrases, and section 6.5 evaluates the theory in a general setting.

6.2. Focus Semantics and Kamp/Heim Semantics

The issue of indefinites and anaphora was broached in Rooth 1985 in the form of a partially formalized treatment within a Discourse Representation Theory (DRT) framework (Kamp 1981, Heim 1982, 1983), but not given a clear solution. The root of the unclarity was that the semantics for focus was stated in a version of Montague grammar, while temporal adverbial clauses were analyzed using DRT, following Hinrichs (1981) and Partee (1984). The version of DRT I was working with (essentially Kamp's) deals with indefinite descriptions and anaphora in part by manipulating syntactic objects corresponding to NPs (i.e., discourse markers or referents) at the syntactic level of discourse representation. The focus semantics, on the other hand, is model theoretic: it gives an interpretation of the focus feature F in the model. This difference made it difficult to see what the focus theory of fixing the domains

2. The formula uses the AT-operator familiar from tense logic (see, e.g., Dowty 1979). The syntax of this operator is consistent with the event logic discussed in Kamp 1983.

of quantificational adverbs says about indefinite descriptions and anaphora: essentially, any semantic phenomenon with which focus interacts should be treated model theoretically, if we are committed to a model-theoretic analysis of focus.[3] The thing to do, then, is to develop a unified model theory for focus and the phenomena of concern in Kamp/Heim semantics. Although we are really concerned with meaning in the model, it remains convenient to work with a formal language.[4] Mine mixes phrases of English logical form (LF or compositional structure) with logical operators.[5] Example expressions are the equivalent logical representations in (10) of the donkey sentence in (9).

(9) When a farmer owns a donkey, he always beats it.

(10) a. [always$[_S[_{NP}$ a farmer$]_1$ $[_S[_{NP}$ a donkey$]_2$ $[_S$ e_1 owns e_2]]] $[_S[_{NP}$ he$]_1$ beats $[_{NP}$ it$]_2$]]

b. **always**($[_{NP}$ a farmer$]_1$ $\wedge$ $[_{NP}$ a donkey$]_2$ $\wedge$ $[_S$ e_1 owns e_2], $[_S[_{NP}$ he$]_1$ beats $[_{NP}$ it$]_2$])

c. **always**($\exists x_1$ [**farmer**(x_1)] $\wedge$ $\exists x_2$[**donkey**(x_2)] $\wedge$ **own**(x_1,x_2), **beat**(x_1,x_2))

The logical form in (10c) is the one proposed by Heim. I also follow her type assignments, according to which $[_{NP}$ *a donkey*] has the type of a sentence.[6] It is simplest to say that indefinite descriptions cannot occur in the argument position of an extensional verb, and must in such examples be scoped to give

3. See the remarks on pp. 195–196 of Rooth 1985, which conclude that one should try to combine the focus theory with a version of DRT that, like Heim's file change theory, treats the indices of indefinites semantically. That is the objective concern of the present analysis.

4. Since this language might in principle be the DRT language, what I was saying above was not that it is impossible or inconvenient in the present context to use DRT expressions to name semantic values. Rather, the point is that we have to figure out how focus interacts with indefinite descriptions and anaphora at the level of semantic values (i.e., in the model), rather than at the level of expressions of one kind or another.

5. I use logical forms to simplify exposition, without necessarily committing myself to LF as a syntactic level. It will be obvious how to restate all or most of what I say in a rule-by-rule framework, using either quantifying-in or a storage device for scope. Indeed, a simple transformation turns logical forms into the derivation trees of Montague grammar.

6. This may ultimately be unsatisfactory. See Rooth 1987, Groenendijk & Stokhof 1987, and Chierchia 1988 for some other options. Rooth gives [*a donkey*] a property type, while Groenendijk and Stokhof and Chierchia give it a generalized quantifier type. The first option fits in with the fact that indefinite descriptions can be used predicatively. An argument for the second (or some other system in which any two NPs have, or at least can have, the same semantic type) can be based on NP conjunction: unless $[_{NP}$ *a woman*] and $[_{NP}$ *every man*] can have a like type, how do we execute the standard Boolean method for giving a semantic value to $[_{NP}$ *a woman or every man*]? Partee has argued for a family of systematically related denotations with differing types, which might be the right answer here, although I have not worked out the systematic relations.

an interpretable LF. Since we already need scoping of NPs, this does not involve us in any incremental noncompositionality. (10c) is an expression which looks more like predicate logic in its syntax. Here, **always** is an operator combining with two formulas. (10b) illustrates that English phrases and logical symbols can be mixed. We will assume that the occurrences of x_1 and x_2 as arguments in (10b,c) and the corresponding traces and pronouns in (10a) are bound.[7] This will work out because we are using the DRT semantics for anaphora and quantification. Also, when I say below that two expressions are equivalent, this is supposed to be substantiated by the model theory in the Appendix.

Given (10), it is clear that the classical DRT semantics for adverbs of quantification proposed by Heim and Kamp differs from the standard relational one in that the arguments have a proposition-like type, rather than a property-like type. Though there are alternatives to the former approach (see in particular Chierchia 1988 also this volume), I will assume the original version throughout.

According to the association-with-focus theory, a quantificational adverb has sentence scope. In examples involving indefinite descriptions, this has the consequence that the semantic material coming from the indefinite shows up in the scope of the quantification. To take a specific example, *A dog is usually intelligent* will have a compositional structure where *usually* combines with a sentence:

(11) [usually $[_S[_{NP}$ a dog$]_2$ $[_2$ e_2 is intelligent]]]

The S fills the second argument of the adverb, and the first argument is a free variable. Given that the semantics for the scoping construction is conjunctive, the above is equivalent to (12):

(12) **usually**(C, $[_{NP}$ a dog$]_2 \wedge [_2$ e_2 is intelligent])

The strategy of the theory was to say that the part of the sentence which does not show up in the restriction is focused. In (11), this means there should be a phonologically marked focus on [*intelligent*] or on [*is intelligent*]. In this discussion, I would like to leave aside the question whether this expected focus marking is really phonologically defensible. At a superficial level, however, note that the sentence has greatest prominence on *intelligent,* which is presum-

7. Or, if you do not care for this terminology in this context, that (10a–c) are closed expressions.

ably consistent with focus on *intelligent* or *is intelligent.* In examples like (6) above with a narrow focus on an individual-denoting NP, the first argument of the quantificational adverb was filled by a version of the second argument in which an existentially quantified variable had been substituted for the second argument. What does this amount to in the case of a focused VP? The second argument we are concerned with is this:

(13) $[_{NP}$ a dog$]_2 \wedge [_S\ e_2$ is intelligent$_F]$

A corresponding expression with an existentially quantified variable in the position of the focused phrase might be (14):[8]

(14) $[_{NP}$ a dog$]_2 \wedge \exists P[P(x_2)]$

Here P is a property variable and x_2 is an individual variable semantically indistinguishable from the trace e_2. Now, the second conjunct is a trivial condition on the variable x_2: as long as x_2 has at least one of the properties the existential quantifier ranges over, it will be true. For instance, anything is presumably either intelligent or non-intelligent. Accordingly, (14) is equivalent to (15a), and the association-with-focus theory says that (15b) is the semantics for (11).

(15) a. $[_{NP}$ a dog$]_2$
b. **usually**($[_{NP}$ a dog$]_2$, $[_{NP}$ a dog$]_2 \wedge [_S\ e_1$ is intelligent$]$)

Is this the right result? The target meaning is (16), where material coming from the indefinite supplies the restriction of the quantificational adverb and binds a variable in the scope.

(16) **usually**($[_{NP}$ a dog$]_2$, **intelligent**(x_2))

The question then is: Is (15b) equivalent to (16)? This of course depends on the semantics for the expressions involved. The discussion above makes assumptions about this, but is consistent with a number of different versions of the Kamp/Heim theory. We need to choose a version which will make the equivalence fall out. Not any version will do: Heim's file change theory (Heim

8. The procedure specified in the appendix for filling the second argument will give a result equivalent to quantifying the variable at the maximal level. This will prove to be equivalent to (14).

1982, chap. 3), by means of a semantic device analogous to presupposition, imposes the condition that the index of a noun phrase $[_{NP}$ *a* $N]_k$ be novel. Since the semantics for quantificational adverbs evaluates the scope relative to a context created by the restriction, and since the index 2 occurs with maximal scope in the restrictor of (15b), it is not a novel index in the scope, and the occurrence of $[_{NP}$ *a dog*$]_2$ there gives a violation of the semantic novelty condition amounting to a presupposition failure.

Another version which does not work in one which says that $[_{NP}$ *a* $N]_k$ has existential force; see Rooth 1987. The problem with this is suggested by a version of (15b) written with existential quantifier symbols:

(17) $\mathbf{usually}(\exists x_2[\mathbf{dog}(x_2)], \exists x_2[\mathbf{dog}(x_2)] \wedge \mathbf{intelligent}(x_2))$

Because the variable is requantified in the scope, its occurrence as an argument of **intelligent** in the scope has nothing to do semantically with its occurrence in the restrictor as an argument of **dog.**[9] The result is a rather trivial assertion: Most dogs are such that some dog is intelligent.

What is apparently required is a semantics which makes the occurrence of $[_{NP}$ *a dog*$]_2$ in the scope merely redundant. That this is possible is suggested by one of the versions of DRT in Kamp 1981, which associated with (18a) a representation like (18b).

(18) a. When a dog is blue-eyed, it is always intelligent.
b.

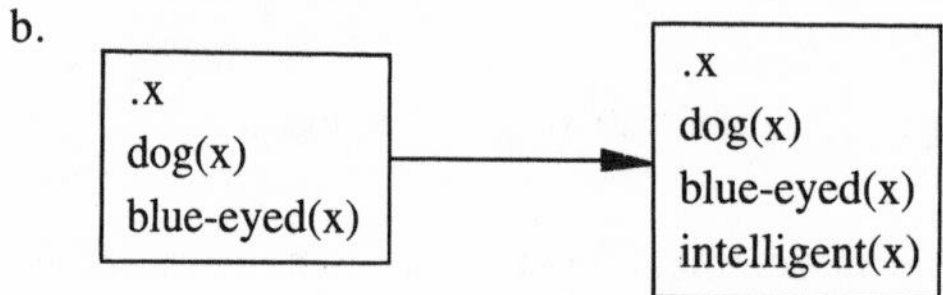

The semantics for the DRT language makes this equivalent to (19):

(19)

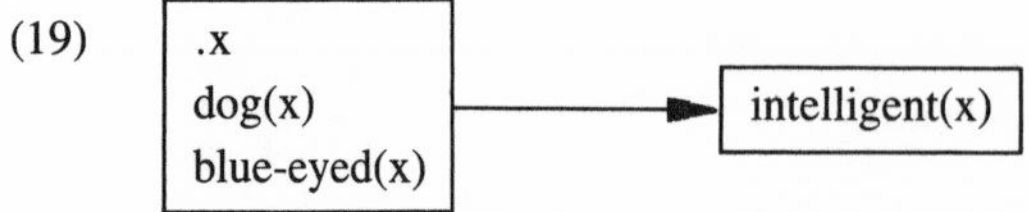

At least at the graphical level, this is the kind of equivalence we require: compare the "box examples" above to (15) and (16). To see how one may achieve this desired equivalence, we have to look at the semantics for discourse representations. The reference markers at the top of the box (e.g., '.x' above) give information about the domain of a partial assignment function: since x occurs in both the left and right boxes, an assignment (or embedding) function

9. This is substantiated by the formalization in the Appendix of the existential force semantics for indefinites.

for either is supposed to have x in its domain.[10] The semantics for quantification says, in addition, that an embedding function for the right box is supposed to be an extension of an embedding function for the left box. Notice that this allows an embedding function for the right box in (18b) to be identical to the corresponding embedding function for the left box.[11] In an expression like $[_{NP}$ *a dog*$]_2$, the index 2 roughly corresponds to a discourse representation reference marker. Consequently, to make our revised focus theory work, we should treat the index on $[_{NP}$ *a* N$]_k$ as a regulator of the domain of assignments—something which imposes the condition that k be in the domain of an assignment—rather than as an index which is presupposed to be novel or as an existentially quantified variable. As formalized in the Appendix, this move makes expressions (15b) and (16) logically equivalent. Returning to the *when*-clause test, we also derive the equivalence of (15b) with (20).

(20) When something is a dog, it is usually intelligent.

The remainder of this section surveys other lines of evidence on the treatment of indefinites in the Kamp/Heim theory. For purposes of reference, here are the three options under consideration.

1. *The semantic novelty condition:* This requirement semantically forces the index of an indefinite to be novel.
2. *The existential force theory:* On this view, the semantics of indefinites is similar to existential quantification. If the index is old, it is requantified, giving a non-anaphoric reading for the repeated index.
3. *The domain regulator theory:* Here the index gives a restriction on the domain of a partial assignment function. As far as the semantics goes, the index may be new or old.

In the argument of Heim (1982), the novelty condition is motivated in part by the desire to eliminate two rules for constructing LFs which were necessary in the alternative presented in her chapter 2: the rule adjoining an existential quantifier to the scope of a two-place quantifier and to the maximal discourse level, and the rule copying the index of an indefinite to the minimal c-commanding quantifier. (21) exemplifies the output of these rules. As we have already seen, the semantic novelty theory requires neither copied indices nor inserted existential quantifiers.

10. Just as in Tarskian semantics for first order logic, an embedding or assignment function in DRT can be thought of as a table of values for variables.

11. In this case, the definitions enforce identity, since an assignment for a right-hand box is only allowed to have new values at most on markers in that box.

(21) a. When a farmer owns a donkey, he always beats it with a stick. One donkey is resentful.

b.

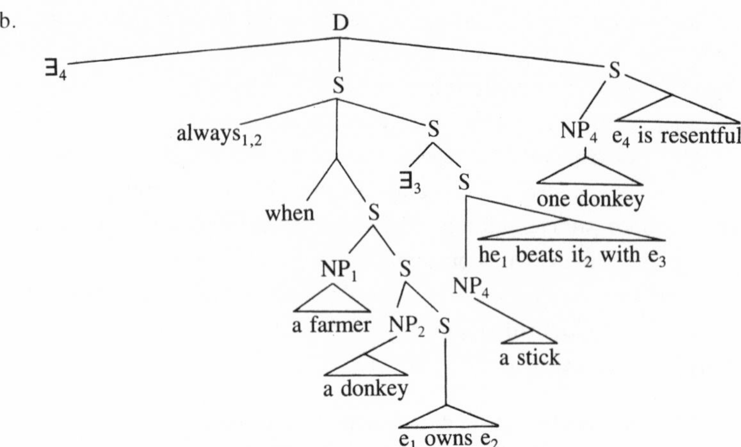

This is a compelling argument of elegance for Heim's chapter 3 theory, since the LF construction rules appear rather arbitrary: Why should the indices be copied to the minimal quantifier rather than to any quantifier? Why do the existential quantifiers show up exactly where they do? Other things being equal, one would prefer to do without them. But eliminating the ∃-insertion and index copying rules is not very closely tied to a presuppositional novelty condition. Each of the other alternatives under discussion can assume an LF without indices on the adverb of quantification or inserted existential quantifiers.

The domain regulator theory does, however, require something the others do not, namely a "syntactic" device ruling out the coindexing of two indefinite descriptions; for example:

(22) $[_{NP}$ A man$]_3$ walked in. $[_{NP}$ A man$]_3$ sat down.

If coindexing is allowed, the domain regulator theory predicts an anaphoric reading equivalent to:

(23) $[_{NP}$ A man$]_3$ walked in. $[_{NP}$ He$]_3$/$[_{NP}$ the man$]_3$ sat down.

This reading seems impossible. Neither of the alternative treatments of indefiniteness requires a syntactic contra-indexing device: Heim's chapter 3 theory filters (23) semantically, and the existential force theory makes the indices semantically independent.

A second consideration is based on disjunctive sentences with split antecedency:

(24) When John sails a yacht or flies a plane, he always wrecks it.

Within a single reading the pronoun can refer either to a yacht or a plane.[12] The most direct treatment of this example seems to be to coindex $[_{NP}$ *a plane*], $[_{NP}$ *a yacht*], and $[_{NP}$ *it*] and rely on the semantics to give the right meaning. It is perhaps surprising that this works out in a theory employing the semantic novelty condition. The reason that a coindexed structure gives no novelty violation is that, in a disjunction, neither conjunct is evaluated in the context of the other. The existential force theory can also give the coindexed logical form the right semantics. But the domain regulator solution, given that it is forced to stipulate that indefinites have different indices, can obviously not take a coindexing approach to (24).

The result of this survey is that what independent evidence there is favors the novelty and existential force semantics for indefiniteness over the domain regulator approach.

This completes the informal exposition of the application of the association-with-focus theory to indefinite descriptions. Given a logical form for a sentence where an adverb of quantification is the top operator, including focus markings, the theory delivers a semantic value in a given model. To argue that the theory works in a particular example, we have to exhibit an LF, including a focus marking (hopefully a phonologically plausible one), and use the semantics to argue that it has the right meaning.

6.3. MULTIPLE INDEFINITE DESCRIPTIONS

As noted in the Introduction, a sentence with an adverb of quantification and several indefinite descriptions may be ambiguous in that either indefinite description can supply the restriction. (25a) is an example of this kind. On one reading, it is equivalent to (25b); on another, it is equivalent to (25c).

(25). a. (In English text,) a u usually follows a q.
b. Most q's are followed by a u.
c. Most u's follow a q.

The first reading happens to be true: in an English text, when one sees the letter 'q' one usually (indeed, almost always) sees a letter 'u' (immediately) following it. The second reading is false, the letter 'u' being a fairly common

12. Of course, according to standard terminology the pronoun is not a referential one, in the intended reading. But even bound pronouns have reference relative to the assignment functions consulted in a semantic evaluation.

one which occurs in many contexts. These two readings of (25) (there are also other readings, mentioned below) are, at least superficially, prosodically distinguished: the true reading has greatest prominence on "u", while the false reading has greatest prominence on "q". The latter might be consistent with a number of focus markings: the narrowest possible focus—that is, a focus marking on "q," focus marking on the NP $[_{NP}\ a\ q]$, and focus on the verb phrase $[_{VP}\ follows\ a\ q]$. The former might be consistent with a focus on the N "u" or on $[_{NP}\ a\ u]$. Let us examine the semantic consequences of these possibilities in the theory proposed in the previous section.

6.3.1. VP Focus

This option is familiar, since it involves the focus marking I assumed for *A dog is usually intelligent.* Consider an LF where the NPs have essentially their surface scope, that is, the subject is adjoined to S and the object is adjoined to VP.

(26) $[_S \text{ usually } [_S [_{NP} \text{ a u}]_1 [_S\ e_1] [_{VP}[_{NP} \text{ a q}]_2 [_{VP}\text{follows } e_2]]_F]]$

According to the association-with-focus theory, (26) is equivalent to (27a), where the first argument of **usually** has been filled by the focus closure of the second argument, notated with an operator 'FC'. By the reasoning adduced in connection with (13), this is in turn equivalent to (27b), which can be paraphrased in the metalanguage: Most u's follow a q.

(27) a. $\textbf{usually}(\text{FC}([_S [_{NP} \text{ a u}]_1 [_S\ e_1] [_{VP} [_{NP} \text{ a q}]_2 [_{VP}\text{follows } e_2]]_F]),$
$[_S [_{NP} \text{ a u}]_1 [_S\ e_1] [_{VP} [_{NP} \text{ a q}]_2 [_{VP}\text{follows } e_2]]_F])$

b. $\textbf{usually}([_{NP} \text{ a u}]_1, [_{NP} \text{ a q}]_2 \wedge [_S\ e_1 \text{ follows } e_2])$

The argument then has this structure: (i) Consider a version of (25) with greatest prominence on "q." (ii) Such a prominence can realize a focus on $[_{VP}\ follows\ a\ q]$. (iii) (26) is a possible LF for (25) with this focus marking. (iv) Given the focus theory, (26) is equivalent to (27b). (v) Expression (27b) is true if and only if most u's follow a q. (vi) It is not true that most u's follow a q. (vii) Therefore, as desired, (25) with greatest prominence on "q" is false, at least under one reading.

Thus we have an account for the false reading of (25). The proviso "at least under one reading" is required because other LFs, differing in scopes or focus marking, might have other truth conditions.

6.3.2. N Focus

Consider next the narrowest focus possibility, namely, focus on "u" or "q." (28a) and (28b) would correspond to the true and false readings, respectively.

(28) a. $[_S$ usually $[_S [_{NP}$ a $[_N$ u$]_F]_1 [_S$ e$_1 [_{VP} [_{NP}$ a q$]_2 [_{VP}$follows e$_2]]]]]$
b. $[_S$ usually $[_S [_{NP}$ a $[_N$ u$]]_1 [_S$ e$_1 [_{VP} [_{NP}$ a $[_N$ q$]_F]_2 [_{VP}$follows e$_2]]]]]$

As before, the focus closure of the second argument fills the first argument. The effect of focus closure is the same as before: the focused property becomes a trivially true property. Assuming that *thing* expresses a trivial property, we then arrive at (29), where in each expression *thing* replaces the focused phrase.

(29) a. **usually**($[_S [_{NP}$ a $[_N$ thing$]]_1 [_S$ e$_1 [_{VP}[_{NP}$ a q$]_2 [_{VP}$follows e$_2]]]]$,
$[_S [_{NP}$ a $[_N$ u$]_F]_1 [_S$ e$_1 [_{VP}[_{NP}$ a q$]_2 [_{VP}$follows e$_2]]]]$)
b. **usually**($[_S [_{NP}$ a $[_N$ u$]]_1 [_S$ e$_1 [_{VP}[_{NP}$ a $[_N$ thing$]]_2 [_{VP}$follows e$_2]]]]$,
$[_S [_{NP}$ a $[_N$ u$]]_1 [_S$ e$_1 [_{VP}[_{NP}$ a $[_N$ q$]]_2 [_{VP}$follows e$_2]]]]$)

Notice that both indices occur as indices of indefinites in both arguments. But because of the coindexing, the indefinites on the right are in effect anaphoric. This means that the object language paraphrases in (30) are predicted for the narrow focus LFs.[13]

(30) a. When something follows a q, it (the thing doing the following) is usually a u.
b. When a u follows something, it (the thing followed) is usually a q.

This is a good result, since (30a) is true while (30b) is false. In other words, these LFs exhibit the desired correlation between form and meaning.

6.3.3. Non-Equivalence of the Readings

The readings predicted for narrow and broad focus are logically distinguishable. The VP focus reading quantifies u's in general; the reading derived for focus on the N of the object quantifies u's that follow something. The difference is perhaps clearer in (31) below. Here the reading derived for VP focus is: Most nouns are modified by an adjective. This could be false in a model which makes the reading derived for focus on *adjective* come out true. The narrow focus reading is: When something modifies a noun, it is usually an adjective.

13. See the Appendix for a formal derivation of the semantics for (28) which substantiates these claims.

(31) A noun is usually modified by an adjective.

This would be so, for instance, in a model (which we can think of as a specific text) where there are 1,000 nouns, of which 700 are not modified at all, 200 are modified by adjectives, and 100 are modified by prepositional phrases. To my ear, it is easier to get the putative narrow focus reading in a version with bare plural NPs:

(32) Nouns are usually modified by adjectives.

Since the semantic distinction between the readings is fairly clear, it should be possible to look for phonetic correlates of breadth of focus in this construction.

6.3.4. NP Focus

There is another pair of phonologically plausible focus structures, namely those with focus on the NPs. Given the theory as it stands, these produce semantically anomalous readings. Consider an LF where a focused subject is scoped to the S-level:

(33) $[_S$ usually $[_S [_{NP}$ a u$]_{1,F} [_S e_1 [_{VP} [_{NP}$ a q$]_2 [_{VP}$follows $e_2]]]]]$

As we have seen several times, in the focus closure a focused constituent in a conjunctive context drops out. This means that the first argument of **usually** becomes the following:

(34) $[_S e_1 [_{VP} [_{NP}$ a q$]_2 [_{VP}$follows $e_2]]]$

The problem with this is that the trace e_1 has no semantic antecedent. This gives a free reading for the trace, which is perhaps meaningless, or, in a presuppositional theory, a presupposition failure. It is certainly not an observed reading.

We can be content with this result, since we already have LFs for the true and false readings. It is not pernicious for some of the possible LFs of a surface form to be semantically filtered. However, it is probably an artefact of the particular form my analysis has taken that NP focus gives semantic anomaly. I believe that by interpreting indefinites in their surface position (in situ), or by assuming that the semantic part of the scoping operation involves lambda abstraction, one could obtain a sensible NP focus reading, namely, in the case of focus on the object, 'Most u's which follow something follow a q'. This is very close to the result obtained for N focus.

6.3.5. Scope and Focus

The scoping operation played a rather peripheral role in the reasoning above: in most cases, NPs were scoped to a position close to their surface position (S for a subject, VP for an object). Scoping was used just to facilitate semantic interpretation, and one anticipates that interpreting all NPs in situ, using an appropriate semantic rule, would give the same results. As I suggested above, one also anticipates that as in situ interpretation strategy would give meanings for the NP focus examples which are unproblematic as far as variable binding goes, since there would be no trace. Furthermore, there are some potentially problematic interactions of scope and focus. In the VP focus example (26), I marked the focus feature on the maximal VP rather than the minimal one. The alternative LF below has the wrong meaning: since both indefinite NPs are outside the focus, pairs of u's and q's rather than just u's are quantified.

(35) $[_S$ usually $[_S$ $[_{NP}$ a u$]_1$ $[_S$ $e_1]$ $[_{VP}[_{NP}$ a q$]_2$ $[_{VP}$follows $e_2]_F]]]$

An LF where the object NP is scoped to the S-level would give the same undesirable reading.[14]

There is an architectural issue underlying these problematic derivations, reminiscent of conceptual problems in Sag's (1976) theory of ellipsis. Focus is a phenomenon with linked phonological and semantic significance. The phonological significance presumably has to do with phonological properties of surface phrases—say, a phrase focused in some domain being metrically prominent in that domain, and/or some designated part of a focused phrase bearing a pitch accent. But, virtually by definition, where a phrase is scoped we have to perform noncompositional interpretation of surface phrases. What is the semantic significance of the phonological focusing of a phrase with no unitary semantic interpretation? The above example suggests that the interaction of scope and focus must be constrained somehow, minimally so that a prominence on an NP cannot mark a focus on a phrase it scopes out of.[15]

14. That is, a reading that is undesirable for an LF with focus marking on the VP. Note that such a reading where both indefinites contribute to the restriction is in fact the desired reading, and the one the theory generates, for narrow focus on the transitive verb. The reading the theory gives is, 'When a u and a q stand in some relation, the relation is usually the relation of succession.' The intuited reading is more concrete, and logically weaker: 'When a u and a q stand in a relation of (immediate) precedence or a relation of succession, the relation is usually the relation of succession'.

15. This issue is similar to Bresnan's problem of the interaction of *wh*-movement and the stress cycle (Bresnan 1971), though if my speculation about the data is correct, the results are in a sense opposite: she said that the nuclear stress rule could feed *wh*-movement, while (35) suggests

6.4. Bare Plurals

Bare plural noun phrases, I claimed, have the same readings and ambiguities as indefinite descriptions. For instance, (36) may quantify either nouns or adjectives.

(36) Nouns usually follow adjectives.

Gerstner and Krifka (1987) propose that in cases like this, bare plural noun phrases are just plural indefinite descriptions. If so, the analysis I have discussed (presumably along with any other analysis of generic singular indefinite descriptions) extends to bare plurals. The alternative is the hypothesis that bare plural noun phrases in all instances denote *kinds,* a certain variety of individuals (Carlson 1977b, see also chapter 1.3 and 1.4 above). As in effect noted by Schubert and Pelletier (1987), Carlson's hypothesis is consistent with the DRT-style semantics for these examples, which assumes a variety of existential quantification (or whatever we call the Kamp/Heim semantics for indefinites; let us call it *indefinite force*) in the restriction of a two-place adverb.

In his Montague grammar formulation, Carlson makes extensive use of a *realization relation* linking ordinary individuals to kinds.[16] Suppose we are given a predicate of ordinary individuals. Using the realization relation, we define a derived predicate of kinds which is true of a kind if and only if some realization of the kind satisfies the original predicate. For instance, the predicate derived from *live down the road from the Reagan ranch* is true of a kind (say, Movie Stars) if some realization of the kind lives down the road from the Reagan ranch.[17] This is intuitively correct for the existential reading of

---

that the phonological part of the focusing operation cannot feed NP scope assignment. I think the constraint suggested by (35) falls out in a grammar organized according to the rule-by-rule principle using a substitution operation for scoping, or in a strict surface-structure framework such as categorical grammar without quantifier storage. But the construction of concern in this chapter is not really the right empirical domain for an investigation of the issue.

16. I am ignoring here Carlson's distinction between stages and ordinary individuals. See Schubert & Pelletier 1987, pp. 423–425, for criticisms of the use of stages by Carlson and others. The stage concept is strangely peripheral in Carlson's formal theory, in that the empirical predictions of interest would follow just as well if we restricted our attention to models in which the realization relation between stages and ordinary individuals is the identity relation. However, dropping the stage notion would make Carlson's picture as a whole less appealing, in that he uses it to motivate the realization relation and the existential quantification of its stage argument.

17. I am using this example (suggested by Greg Carlson) here, instead of *Dogs are intelligent,* because it has a clear existential reading. The fact that the present theory says that generic readings are existential at a compositional level may be a problem, given that predicates like *be intelligent* give no detectable existential reading for indefinite descriptions and bare plurals in certain contexts, such as tensed main clauses.

(37), given that the realizations of the kind denoted by [$_{NP}$ *movie stars*] are individual movie stars or groups of movie stars.

(37) Movie stars live down the road from the Reagan ranch.

Since a DRT analysis could use indefinite force where Carlson uses existential quantification, Carlson's hypothesis is then at least potentially consistent with a DRT analysis of adverbs of quantification, in particular with the focus theory discussed here.

Let us assume that we want to treat bare plural examples using the association-with-focus theory and some device which introduces indefinite force. This leaves us with a choice: either we follow Gerstner and Krifka and say that the bare plural NPs are indefinite descriptions, or we follow Carlson and say that they denote kinds, the indefinite force being introduced by some kind of operator. In the former case, we have good reason to think that things will work out; in the latter case we have to do some checking.

6.4.1. Carlson's Theory of Kinds

At this point, we are assuming that the bare plural in (36) which supplies the restriction has, at a compositional level not necessarily accessible to intuition, an existential reading.[18] This reading should be arrived at in the way that existential readings for bare plurals in general are arrived at. Thus the choice above is really governed by our opinion about Carlson's thesis: is he right in saying that bare plurals with existential readings denote kinds? The arguments for this position in Carlson 1977b appeared strong, all the more so because the kind theory made a varied range of data fall into place. However, several of the arguments are undermined by counterexamples, alternative analyses, or the fact that the kind theory offers no genuine explanation. The following tabulation is inspired by a similar one in Chierchia 1982b (whose names for the arguments I give in parentheses), though points not relevant to my question are omitted, and one has been added. The way the arguments are stated emphasizes the connection between the data and the kind theory.

Only minimal scope ('opacity,' 'narrow scope'). According to the kind theory, bare plurals denote either individuals or the corresponding generalized quantifiers—objects for which scope is irrelevant. Thus the theory predicts an absence of scope ambiguity, as well as a contrast with real existential or indefinite NPs like [$_{NP}$ *a* ...], [$_{NP}$ *some* ...], and so forth, where there is a scope

18. Given the semantic assumptions we are making, it would be more accurate to call this an indefinite reading. But let us preserve 'existential reading' as a descriptive term.

ambiguity. This is exactly what we observe. For instance, *Mary wants to meet some football players* is ambiguous, but *Mary wants to meet football players* is not.

Reply: There is a detectable ambiguity with respect to negative elements like *fail.* In *The dean failed to act on petitions submitted to his office,* especially if pronounced with an intonation break after *act on,* the accusation can be that there were some petitions the dean did not act on.

Narrower scope than normally possible ('differentiated scope'). In examples like *Max killed rabbits repeatedly/for ten hours,* a bare plural takes narrower scope than a genuine quantifier can take, there being no narrow scope reading for *Max killed a rabbit repeatedly/for ten hours.* This can again be attributed to a type difference between a kind NP and a genuine quantifier, or what amounts to one.

Reply: First, it is not true that no genuine quantifier in object position can take narrow scope with respect to these time adverbs. In the prominent reading of *John ate no cookies for thirty days* the object has narrow scope, as is evident from a comparison with the wide scope paraphrase *No cookies are such that John ate them for thirty days.* Second, it is not clear what the explanation coming from the kind theory for the contrast between [$_{NP}$ *some* ...] and bare plurals is supposed to be. Dowty (1979) analyzes *for*-adverbials as VP- or S-modifiers, meaning that they have a default scope superior to anything in the VP, regardless of its type.[19]

Existential bare plural antecedent, kind pronoun ('differentiated antecedent 1'). A kind-denoting pronoun can have an existential bare plural as antecedent, as in *Condors stole Mary's sweet corn, which is puzzling since they are nearly extinct,* where we assume that *extinct* selects a kind argument. An explanation for this is that the existential bare plural in fact denotes a kind.

Reply: [$_{NP}$ *some* ...] can set up a kind pronoun, as in *Some condors stole her sweet corn, which is puzzling since they are nearly extinct.* Thus the fact that an existential bare plural can set up a kind pronoun is no reason to believe that existential bare plurals have a different semantics from [$_{NP}$ *some* ...].

19. I think the explanation for the aspectual impact of bare plurals given by Dowty (1979) and L. Carlson (1981) does not give force to the differentiated scope argument since it seems to predict an aspectual impact for genuine existentials/indefinites as well. I have not checked whether this is true if one uses algebraic elaborations of the Carlson ontology, such as Hinrichs (1985).

Kind antecedent, existential they ('differentiated antecedent 2'). In *Although condors are nearly extinct, they stole Mary's sweet corn, they* seems to have an existential reading: it is some individual condors who stole Mary's sweet corn. Since there are no individual condors referred to in the prior discourse, either explicitly or implicitly, it must be that *they* refers anaphorically to a kind denoted by *condors*.

Reply: This argument convinces me, at least if we grant the premises that *extinct* selects a kind and that the second clause has an existential reading.[20]

Existential bare plural antecedent, kind reflexive. This version of the antepenultimate argument seeks to take advantage of the fact that the antecedent of a reflexive must stand in a certain command relation to it, namely, m(aximal projection)-command or f(unction)-command. That the antecedent of an ordinary pronoun is not constrained in this way accounts for the fact that *they* in the first condor example above can refer to a kind, though its antecedent, if syntactically present at all, is the noncommanding noun *condors*. Given the command constraint, we predict a difference between a kind-denoting bare plural and a plural indefinite description: the former, but not the latter, should license a kind-denoting reflexive.

Reply: A relevant example is *At the post-WWIII peace meeting, Martians presented themselves as almost extinct,* which most people find okay on a reading where *themselves* denote a kind. *Martians* has what we descriptively call an existential reading, since it was some particular Martian delegates who made the claim. It would not be possible for *themselves* to denote a kind if *Martians* were a plural indefinite description, because the reflexive would have no kind-denoting antecedent bearing the required command relation: the only phrase even possibly codenotative in this case would be the noun *Martians,* the m-command domain of which is the subject NP. We get the same result with f-command given that the argument of the VP on the indefinite description analysis is at the ordinary individual level, not the kind level. Note also that there seems to be a contrast with *At the post-WWIII peace meeting, some Martians presented themselves as almost extinct,* where a kind reading for the

20. Irene Heim (pers. comm.) suggests that one might conceivably take exception to the latter: maybe the argument of the most basic relation denoted by *steal* really is a kind, and the fact that a kind is being blamed for the actions of some of its individual parts is a matter of lexical semantics. An analogous case might be *The ocean destroyed Mary's beach shack.* Given that at a greater level of detail, it was some particular, unusually large storm swells which did the damage, do we say that the semantics for this sentence involves some kind of realization or part relation?

reflexive is, I think, impossible. (Compare the discussion of this sentence in chapter 1.4.6 above.)

My conclusion from this brief survey is that some evidence remains for the hypothesis that existential bare plurals denote kinds. The next question is: Does the focus theory of filling the restriction of adverbs of quantification mesh with some execution of this hypothesis?

6.4.2. The Ordinary-to-Kind Operator

A DRT version of the kind hypothesis can follow Carlson's Montague Grammar theory and introduce kinds as individuals. The main task then is to define the operator introducing indefinite force. Let us start by defining it as a VP operator. In the system of semantic values introduced in the Appendix, the object corresponding to a property is a set of tuples, the last element of which is an individual, the other elements being two assignment functions and a world. The individual corresponds to the argument of the property. Let Φ be a semantic value for a property. The corresponding "property" of kinds should be a set of tuples the last element of which is a kind individual with a realization satisfying the former "property." Letting **R** be the realization relation, a first approximation is the following:

(38) $\{\langle g,j,w,k\rangle \mid \exists x\ [R(x,k) \wedge \langle g,h,w,x\rangle \epsilon \Phi]\}$

What is missing from this formula is the conditions on the assignment function parameters which encode indefiniteness. Note that it is possible to refer anaphorically to the individual realizing the kind, as in (39):

(39) Movie stars live down the road from the Reagan ranch. They are unemployed at the moment.

Here *they* can refer to the particular movie stars who live down the road from the Reagan ranch. The means that a discourse referent or index corresponding to x in (38) should be introduced. Let n be this index; the additional conditions which encode indefinite force are then included as shown in (40).

(40) $$\left\{ \langle g,j,w,k\rangle \mid \exists x \exists h \left[\begin{array}{c} R(x,k) \wedge \\ \mathrm{Dom}(h) = \mathrm{Dom}(g) \cup \{n\} \wedge \\ g \subseteq h \wedge \\ h(n) = x \wedge \\ \langle h,j,w,x\rangle \epsilon \Phi \end{array} \right] \right\}$$

This implementation is fully comprehensible only relative to the Appendix; but for now, in connection with the anaphoric example (39) we can observe that a particular realization of the kind k is recorded as the value of the assignment j (which is an extension of h) on the index n. At the syntactic level, one can introduce a covert operator κ_n with the operator-to-kind semantics indicated above which operates on VPs and phrases of the same type. Then $[\kappa_n[_{VP}\alpha]]$ denotes a property giving an existential reading for a kind argument.

Now we are ready to check our focus theory. The question is whether an LF like (41) has the right meaning, one quantifying realizations of the kind denoted by *movie stars*.

(41) $[_S$ usually $[_S$ $[_{NP}$movie stars$]_2$ $[_{VP}$ κ_3 $[_{VP}$live down the road from the Reagan ranch$]_F]]]$

This follows essentially as before. The minimal S in (41) is equivalent to (42), where D is a domain-regulating operator analogous to '∃'.

(42) $Dx_3[R(x_3,[_{NP}$movie stars$]) \wedge [_S\ e_3\ [_{VP}$live down the road from the Reagan ranch$]]]$

The second conjunct becomes trivial in the focus closure, so that (42) is equivalent to (43a), which in turn is equivalent to the desired (43b).

(43) a. **usually**$(Dx_3R(x_3,[_{NP}$movie stars$]),$

Dx_3 $R(x_3,[_{NP}$movie stars$])\wedge$ $[_S\ e_3\ [_{VP}$live down the road from the Reagan ranch$]]$)

b. **usually**$(Dx_3R(x_3,[_{NP}$movie stars$]),$ $[_S\ e_3\ [_{VP}$live down the road from the Reagan ranch$]])$

6.4.3. Other Positions for the Ordinary-to-Kind-Operator

The operator mapping an ordinary property to a kind property could straightforwardly be defined as a crosscategorical operator, so that the configuration $[_{VP}[\kappa\ \alpha]\ [_{NP}\beta]]$ gives an existential reading for an object NP bare plural $[_{NP}\beta]$. If I am right in saying that there is no systematic narrow scope requirement for bare plurals, we should allow κ to operate on properties derived by lambda abstraction, for instance, the property of being an x such that the dean failed to act on x. Since I formulated κ as an operator on properties, this use requires the assumption that scoping introduces a lambda operator creating a property, contrary to what I said above. Then the LF for the dean example would be this:

(44) $[_S\ [_{NP}$ petitions submitted to his office$]\ [_S\ \kappa_3\lambda x_4[_S$ the dean failed to act on $e_4]]]$

If κ is allowed to combine with properties derived by scoping, there is of course no need to crosscategorialize the ordinary-to-kind operator to deal with bare plurals in object position.

6.4.4. Conclusion on Bare Plurals

The association-with-focus theory is consistent with Carlson's hypothesis that bare plurals always denote kinds: by means of an operator introducing indefinite force, we can assimilate bare plural examples to those involving generic singular indefinites.

It is worth noting again that the theory is also consistent with the hypothesis that when bare plurals have an existential reading (including cases when they have this reading at some embedded compositional level), they are plural indefinite descriptions. The present theory cannot be used as a line of evidence for the hypothesis that bare plurals always denote kinds.

6.5. EVALUATION AND DIRECTIONS FOR INVESTIGATION

A theory of generic indefinites should be evaluated not only on the basis of empirical predictions (to which I return below) but also for generality and explanatoriness. The following argument involving focusing adverbs might serve as an examplar for the claim that the focus theory of adverbs of quantification has an advantage of explanatoriness and generality (cf. Rooth 1985, 62–64). We are interested in an explanation for the fact that (45) presupposes (conventionally implicates) that John introduced someone other than Mary to Sue, and that his introducing this person to Sue was somehow less likely than his introducing Mary to Sue (see, for instance, Karttunen & Peters 1979).

(45) John even introduced Mary_F to Sue.

An explanation using focus semantics starts with a meaning for *even* tailored to examples which either do not involve focus at all or involve the broadest possible focus.

(46) The Mets won the world series. It even rained in Lima.

This discourse suggests that rain in Lima is more improbable than the Mets winning the world series. We can derive this implication if we say that *even* has a covert anaphoric propositional argument in addition to the propositional argument filled by the sentence it combines with. In (46), the covert argument is anaphoric to the proposition denoted by the first sentence. The adverb *even* preserves the assertion of the syntactic argument, and adds a presupposition about the relative likelihood of its two arguments. In addition, the covert argument is presupposed to be true. The latter requirement prevents the covert argument from being anaphoric to some non-asserted proposition, for example, the embedded sentence in *It isn't the case that the Mets won the world series.*

A second premise is that the focus structure of a sentence expresses contrast with, or alternatives to, the proposition denoted by the sentence. In (47) below, John liking Bill (to a certain extent) is contrasted with Mary liking Bill (to a certain extent). These propositions differ in who the person doing the liking is, and it is the NPs denoting the likers that are focused. We model this situation by saying that the function of focus is to constrain the form of a contrasting or alternative proposition: the contrasting proposition must be obtainable from the original one by substituting something for the material corresponding to the focused phrase. This explains what goes wrong in (47b): 'John likes Bill to extent d' is not of the form 'Mary likes y to extent d'.[21]

(47) a. John_F likes Bill more than Mary_F likes Bill.
b. (#) . . . more than Mary likes Bill_F
c. Who likes Bill? Sue_F likes Bill.
d. (#) . . . Sue likes Bill_F

A similar story can be told about (47c) and (47d), using the idea that in the context of the indicated question, propositions of the form 'y likes Bill' are alternatives to the answer 'Sue likes Bill'.

We can now analyze (45). According to the semantic treatment of *even,* it has a covert propositional argument, and another argument supplied by the clause *John introduced Mary to Sue.* Given their proximity as co-arguments, focus in the syntactic argument can presumably express contrast with the covert argument. If it does, the covert argument must be a proposition of the form 'John introduced *y* to Sue'. The presuppositions in this case then are that the covert argument—a proposition of the form 'John introduce *y* to Sue'—is true, and that this proposition is more likely than John introducing Mary to Sue. These presuppositions entail the desired presuppositions described above. For instance, they could not be true unless John introduced someone other than Mary to Sue.

A treatment of the semantic effect of focus in the context of *even* along the above lines achieves the best possible level of parsimony, since it uses nothing specific to the *even*/focus "construction." A corollary is that it provides an

21. The parentheses indicate that focus on *Bill* is okay in certain contexts, such as the context created by the question *What person is such that John likes Bill more than Mary likes that person?* This is not a counterexample, since the focus is motivated by the question in a way modeled by the contrast/alternatives theory.

explanation, in terms of independent properties of *even* and of focus, for the observation that focus has a semantic effect in the context of *even*.

Has a similarly attractive result been achieved for the construction of interest in this chapter? Any theory has to acknowledge that, in examples like (48), the restriction of a quantificational adverb is pragmatically fixed.

(48) It always rains.

Therefore, any theory has to allow for the option of a compositional structure where the syntax specifies only the scope (second argument) of an adverb of quantification. The next question is whether a general theory of focus accounts for the way the restriction (first argument) is filled. Here it is not sufficient that a rule deriving the restriction be statable in terms of focus semantics: rather, this process is supposed to be an instance of the general pragmatic function of focus. The principle stated in section 6.2 was that the restriction of an adverb of quantification is the focus closure of the sentence it combines with. Thus we want to know whether, in general, focus can express ''contrast'' with an existential closure, as well as with a substitution instance as in (47a). Judging by (49), it can.

(49) Sue is living with someone. In fact, she's living with Mary_F.

Can one then claim the advantage for the analysis proposed in this chapter of having the highest possible degree of parsimony? This seems convincing in the examples with narrow focus on an individual-denoting NP such as (6a), repeated as (50) below. Given that *usually* can have an argument which is fixed pragmatically, and that focus can express contrast with an existential closure, the target semantics is derived.

(50) Mary usually took John_F to the movies.

But the theory falls a bit short of the explanatory ideal in the generic indefinite cases which were my central concern. To make their semantics work out, I had to make a very specific choice about the semantics of indefiniteness, a choice which in fact runs counter to what independent evidence there is. Nevertheless, once the semantics for indefinites is set up in this specific way, the generic examples receive a simple and systematic analysis.

6.5.1. A Mixed Theory?

It is possible to adopt my analysis of examples like (50) while giving some other analysis of generic indefinites. The most immediate alternative is one which represents the restrictor directly in compositional structure. (51) is a tripartite structure like the ones Heim used for adverbs of quantification.

(51) $[_S$ usually $[_{NP}$ a dog$]_2$ $[_S$ e_2 is intelligent]]

Moreover, the sisters of *usually* have the appropriate type, the type of S. Finally, (51) has the right meaning. If we wanted to postulate (51) as a logical form, we would have to revise our conception of how LF is derived to allow scoping with daughter adjunction. This does not seem particularly objectionable.

Such an analysis of generic indefinites has no obvious connection to any claims about focus or prosodic structure. (51) has the right meaning, regardless of focus structure. But it does not follow that an LF theory can provide no explanation for a correlation between prosodic form and meaning. After all, pronouncing (47a) as indicated, with a focus on *Mary,* is close to mandatory in the absence of a larger context motivating focus elsewhere, though this has nothing to do with getting to the right asserted proposition in the recursive semantics. In comparative-ellipsis examples like (52) below, focus (on *John* or *Bill*) has a disambiguating effect, though the right theory arguably resolves the ambiguity at LF without reference to focus.

(52) John likes Bill more than Mary.

In this case, I would claim that the choice of focus is dictated by a contrast implicit in the asserted proposition. Though the mechanism is entirely different from that suggested in the "covert-argument-fixing" story, this will give a disambiguating effect for focus at the pragmatic level. Similarly, it might be possible to augment an LF theory of generic indefinites with an account of focus or prosodic patterns. I will not investigate what the specific story might be.

6.5.2. Scope Predictions

Since my focus theory does not represent the restriction structurally at LF, one might think that it is distinguishable from the LF theory outlined above on the basis of constraints on the scope of the indefinite. Unfortunately, the opposite is the case. For the required logical equivalences to work out (see, for instance, the discussion of (14) in section 6.2), the indefinite must be in a conjunctive context at the maximal level of the argument of the adverb of quantification. Both theories thus require essentially maximal scope for the indefinite.[22] This is possibly problematic, since the position of the indefinite seems to be fairly unrestricted. In (3a), repeated here as (53), we have a generic reading for an NP in a relative clause:

(53) At least some people an AIDS victim works with are usually misinformed about the disease.

Example (53) is read as quantifying AIDS victims: note in particular that the existential quantification coming from *at least some* is read as contributing to the scope.[23] If we believe that relative clauses are scope islands (e.g., Rodman 1976), this datum is problematic for either theory.[24] Another problem raised by (53) is that there is no obvious focus or prosodic determinant of the generic reading.

6.6. SUMMARY

We started with some observations, in the form of intuited logical equivalences, about examples where an indefinite description fills the restriction argument of an adverb of quantification. The analysis presented provides a derivation of the equivalences as equivalences of model-theoretic interpretation, in the context of a theory which assigns a central role to parameters of interpretation left undetermined by the standard recursive semantics, and to the contribution of intonational focus to fixing the value of these parameters. While the semantics for adverbs of quantification and indefinites that is by now standard was retained, this semantics is employed in a novel way, in that the restriction argument of an adverb is determined by means of focus semantics, rather than being syntactically represented in a discourse representation or logical form.

22. Thus, while there might or might not be significant differences in the detailed syntax of the LFs demanded by the two theories, both require scoping the indefinite out of the host.

23. There is also a weak reading quantifying just times: at most times, at least some AIDS-victim-coworkers are misinformed about AIDS. It is perhaps easier to get this reading, and harder to get the reading quantifying AIDS victims, if the indefinite description is in the object position of the relative clause: *At least some people who work with an AIDS victim are usually misinformed about the disease.*

24. The work of Fodor and Sag (1982) showing that 'specific' indefinites can violate scope islands may be relevant. This would suggest quite a different theory of generics than the one proposed here. Note, however, that generic indefinites do not have maximal scope, which for Fodor and Sag is criterial for a specific indefinite: at least in the standard conception, the scope of the indefinite is inferior to the scope of the adverb of quantification, and a generic sentence as a whole can certainly be embedded to an arbitrary depth.

APPENDIX: A FORMAL SEMANTICS OF FOCUS, INDEFINITENESS, AND ADVERBS OF QUANTIFICATION

The following is a concrete semantic rule system combining the analysis of focus proposed in Rooth 1985 with the Heim/Kamp semantics for indefiniteness, quantification, and anaphora. Model structures of the kind used here were introduced to me by Barwise (1987). They can be considered a variant, and in some respects a more tractable formulation, of Heim's file change semantics (Heim 1982, 1983b). The rules use possible-worlds semantics: using set theory, semantic values are built from a set of individuals E, a set of possible worlds W, and a set of indices N. Assignments (of individuals to indices) are partial functions from N to E, and G is the set of such assignments. We use g, h, and k as metalanguage assignment variables, and x and y as metalanguage individual variables.

The focus is on semantics, not syntax: though the semantic rules implicitly define a language of logical forms, this is not a subset of the set of realized English logical forms. For instance, no attempt is made to ensure that a scoped NP binds a variable, and no distinction is made between pronouns and traces.

We start with a lexicon L of primitive trees (labeled bracketings) including things like $[_N$ *donkey*$]$, $[_N$ *u*$]$, $[_N$ *q*$]$, $[_{TV}$*follows*$]$, $[_{TV}$*likes*$]$, and $[_{NP}$*Bill*$]$. A primitive lexical denotation function F has values of familiar type: F($[_N$ **donkey**$]$,w) is a subset of E, the extension of $[_N$*donkey*$]$ in the world w. F($[_{TV}$**likes**$]$,w) and F($[_{TV}$**follows**$]$,w) are subsets of $E \times E$, and F($[_{NP}$**Bill**$]$) is an element of E. Our goal is to assign semantic values to certain English logical form phrases and related logical formulas. We do this with recursive semantic rules which interpret local phrase-structural configurations consisting of a mother node and its daughters, and index features on these nodes. In some cases, the rules include conditions on the semantic type of the daughters.

The underlying idea is that a sentence denotes a relation between input and output assignments. The input assignment has the usual role of fixing values for pronouns and other variable-like things. The output assignment records the reference of indefinites. The types of VPs and transitive verbs (TVs) are derived from the type of S: their semantic values have one and two individual arguments respectively, in addition to the assignment arguments. NPs are of two types: one of individual type denotes a function from the set G of assignments to E, written as a relation between assignments and individuals. Indefinite descriptions have the same type as sentences.

The semantic value of an item in the lexicon is defined in terms of F, by adding the assignment arguments; the output assignment matches the input assignment.

B1. If $[_N\ \alpha]$ is an element of L, $[\![[_N\ \alpha]]\!]^\circ = \{\langle g,g,w,x\rangle \mid x \epsilon F([_N\ \alpha], w)\}$.
B2. If $[_{TV}\ \alpha]$ is an element of L, $[\![[_{TV}\ \alpha]]\!]^\circ = \{\langle g,g,w,x,y\rangle \mid \langle x,y\rangle \epsilon F([_{TV}\ \alpha], w)\}$.
B3. If $[_{NP}\ \alpha]$ is an element of L, and n is a natural number, $[\![[_{NP}\ \alpha]_n]\!]^\circ =$ $\{\langle g,x\rangle \mid n \epsilon Dom(g) \wedge x = F([_{NP}\ \alpha]) = g(n)\}$.

Pronouns and traces are treated as variables, picking up their value from the assignment function.

B4. $[\![[_{NP}\ she]_n]\!]^\circ = [\![[_{NP}\ her]_n]\!]^\circ = [\![[_{NP}\ it]_n]\!]^\circ = [\![e_n]\!]^\circ =$ $\{\langle g,x\rangle \mid n \epsilon Dom(g) \wedge g(n) = x\}$.

In the first two recursive rules, **R1** and **R2** below, an NP with individual type fills an argument of a relation. **R3** is the rule for indefinite descriptions. **R4** and **R5** are rules for S and VP scope. **R6** is a semantic rule for a discourse consisting of two sentences. Note that the semantics for this construction is the same as that for an NP with S scope. Finally, **R7** gives the Kamp/Heim semantics for *always,* a two-place ''unselective'' quantifier.

R1. If $[_{NP}\ \alpha]$ has individual type, $[\![[_{VP}\ [_{TV}\ \alpha]\ [_{NP}\ \beta]]]\!]^\circ =$ $\{\langle g,h,w,x\rangle \mid \exists y[\langle g,h,w,x,y\rangle \epsilon [\![[_{TV}\ \alpha]]\!]^\circ \wedge \langle h,y\rangle \epsilon [\![[_{NP}\ \beta]]\!]^\circ]\}$.
R2. If $[_{NP}\ \alpha]$ has individual type, $[\![[_S\ [_{NP}\ \beta]\ [_{VP}\ \alpha]]]\!]^\circ =$ $\{\langle g,h,w\rangle \mid \exists x[\langle g,h,w,x\rangle \epsilon [\![[_{VP}\ \alpha]]\!]^\circ \wedge \langle g,x\rangle \epsilon [\![[_{NP}\ \beta]]\!]^\circ]\}$.
R3. $[\![[_{NP}\ a\ [_N\ \alpha]]_k]\!]^\circ =$

$$\left\{\langle g,h\rangle \mid \exists x \left[\begin{array}{c}\langle g,h,x\rangle \epsilon [\![[_N\ \alpha]]\!]^\circ \wedge \\ Dom(h) = Dom(g) \cup \{k\} \wedge \\ h(k) = x\end{array}\right]\right\}$$

R4. If $[_{NP}\ \alpha]$ has the type of a sentence, then $[\![[_S\ [_{NP}\ \alpha]\ [_S\ \beta]]]\!]^\circ =$ $\{\langle g,k,w\rangle \mid \exists h[\langle g,h,w\rangle \epsilon [\![[_{NP}\ \alpha]]\!]^\circ \wedge \langle h,k,w\rangle \epsilon [\![[_S\ \beta]]\!]^\circ]\}$.
R5. If $[_{NP}\ \alpha]$ has the type of a sentence, then $[\![[_{VP}\ [_{NP}\ \alpha]\ [_{VP}\ \beta]]]\!]^\circ =$ $\{\langle g,k,w,x\rangle \mid \exists h[\langle g,h,w\rangle \epsilon [\![[_{NP}\ \alpha]]\!]^\circ \wedge \langle h,k,w,x\rangle \epsilon [\![[_{VP}\ \beta]]\!]^\circ]\}$.
R6. $[\![[_D\ [_S\ \alpha]\ [_S\ \beta]]]\!]^\circ = \{\langle g,k\rangle \mid \exists h[\langle g,h\rangle \epsilon [\![[_S\ \alpha]]\!]^\circ \wedge \langle h,k\rangle \epsilon [\![[_S\ \beta]]\!]^\circ]\}$.
R7. If α has the type of a sentence, then $[\![$**always** $\alpha\ [_S\ \beta]]\!]^\circ =$ $\{\langle g,g\rangle \mid \forall h[\![\langle g,h\rangle \epsilon [\![[_{NP}\ \alpha]]\!]^\circ \rightarrow \exists k[\langle h,k\rangle \epsilon]\![[_S\ \beta]]\!]^\circ]]]\}$.

The remaining rules of interpretation define the semantics of the logical symbols occasionally used in the text.

L1. If β has individual type, and α has the type of an adjective, noun, or VP (i.e., denotes a relation between two assignments, a world, and an individual), then $[\![\alpha(\beta)]\!]^\circ = \{\langle g,h,w\rangle \mid \exists x[\langle g,h,w,x\rangle \epsilon [\![\alpha]\!]^\circ \wedge \langle g,x\rangle \epsilon [\![\beta]\!]^\circ]\}$.
L2. If β_1 and β_2 have individual type, and α has the type of a TV (i.e., denotes a relation between two assignments, a world, and two individuals), then

$[\![\alpha(\beta_1, \beta_2)]\!]^\circ = \{\langle g,h,w\rangle \mid \exists x_1[\exists x_2[\langle g,h,w,x_1,x_2\rangle \in [\![\alpha]\!]^\circ \wedge \langle g,x_1\rangle \in [\![\beta_1]\!]^\circ \wedge$
$\langle g,x_2\rangle \in [\![\beta_2]\!]^\circ]]\}$

L3. If α and β have the type of a sentence (i.e., denote a relation between two assignments and a world), then $[\![[\alpha \wedge \beta]]\!]^\circ =$
$\{\langle g,k\rangle \mid \exists h[\langle g,h\rangle \in [\![\alpha]\!]^\circ \wedge \langle h,k\rangle \in [\![\beta]\!]^\circ]\}$

Sketch of the Presuppositional Theory

Mirroring the use in file change semantics of partial functions from files (sets of world-assignment pairs) to files (Heim 1983b), the presuppositional theory uses partial relations. This can be formalized by including a truth value argument in the relations serving as semantic values (Barwise 1987). For instance, one might want the semantic value of $[_S\ [_{NP}\ John]_1$ *also likes* $[_{NP}\ Bill]_2]$ to be:

$$\left\{\langle g,g,w,\pi\rangle \;\middle|\; \left[\exists y \left[\begin{array}{c} g(1) = F(\mathbf{John}) \wedge \\ g(2) = F(\mathbf{Bill}) \wedge \\ \left[\begin{array}{c} y \notin F(\mathbf{Bill}) \wedge \\ \langle g(1),g(2)\rangle \in F(w, \mathbf{like}) \wedge \\ \left[\left[\begin{array}{c}\pi = \mathrm{True} \wedge \\ \langle g(1),g(2)\rangle \in F(w, \mathbf{likes})\end{array}\right] \vee \left[\begin{array}{c}\pi = \mathrm{False} \wedge \\ \langle g(1),g(2)\rangle \neq F(w, \mathbf{likes})\end{array}\right]\right]\end{array}\right]\end{array}\right]\right]\right\}$$

The presupposition that John likes someone other than Bill is encoded in the first line. In general, a propositional presupposition is recovered from the semantic value of a sentence (a subset of $G \times G \times W \times \{\mathrm{True}, \mathrm{False}\}$, that is, a set of points in assignment-assignment-world-truth space) by projecting it onto the world axis. Putting the material coming from the proper names into the presupposition is supposed to have the same effect as the rule in DRT that proper names are entered at the top level in a discourse representation. The condition involving **likes** assumes that the primitive lexical semantic value is still total—probably one wants to make it potentially partial as well.

Options for Indefinite Descriptions

Here is the formalization of the three different ideas presented about the semantics of indefiniteness. The novelty condition says that the index of an indefinite description is presupposed to be new. This is reflected in the fact that no input assignment *g* in the relation has 2 in its domain.

$[\![[_{NP}\ \text{a donkey}]_2]\!]^\circ =$
$\{\langle g,h,w,\mathrm{True}\rangle \mid 2 \notin Dom(g) \wedge Dom(h) = Dom(g) \cup \{2\}$
$\wedge\ h(2) \in F(\mathbf{donkey}, w)\} \cup$
$\{\langle g,g,w,\mathrm{False}\rangle \mid 2 \notin Dom(g) \wedge \neg[\exists x\ [x \in F(\mathbf{donkey}, w)]]\}$

A domain regulator approach simply leaves it open whether the index is novel or not:

$$\begin{array}{l}[\![[_{NP} \text{ a donkey}]_2]\!]^\circ = \\ \{\langle g,h,w,\text{True}\rangle \mid \text{Dom}(h) = \text{Dom}(g) \cup \{2\} \wedge h(2)\epsilon F(\textbf{donkey}, w)\} \cup \\ \{\langle g,g,w,\text{False}\rangle \mid \neg[\exists x\ [x\epsilon F(\textbf{donkey}, w)]]\}\end{array}$$

Existential force for indefinite descriptions makes most sense with total assignments. Assuming such assignments, one obtains the following:

$$\begin{array}{l}[\![[_{NP} \text{ a donkey}]_2]\!]^\circ = \\ \{\langle g,h,w,\text{True}\rangle \mid \exists x\ [x\epsilon F(\textbf{donkey}, w)] \wedge \forall n[[n \neq 2 \rightarrow h(n) = g(n)]]\} \\ \cup\{\langle g,g,w,\text{False}\rangle \mid \neg\exists x\ [x\epsilon F(\textbf{donkey}, w)]\}\end{array}$$

Note that in the latter two cases, there is no presupposition.

Disjunctive Split Antecedency

Suppose that disjunction is just union, as in standard Boolean semantics. If we use the existential force semantics for indefiniteness and total assignments, we obtain, for instance, the following semantic values:

$$[\![[_{VP} \text{ sails } [_{NP} \text{ a yacht}]_2]]\!]^\circ =$$

$$\left\{\langle g,h,w,x\rangle \mid \exists y \begin{bmatrix} h(2) = y \wedge \\ \forall n[[n \neq 2 \rightarrow h(2) = g(2)]] \wedge \\ y\epsilon F(\textbf{yacht}, w) \wedge \\ \langle x,y\rangle\epsilon F(\textbf{sails}, w)\end{bmatrix}\right\}$$

$$[\![[_{VP} \text{ flies } [_{NP} \text{ a plane}]_2]]\!]^\circ =$$

$$\left\{\langle g,h,w,x\rangle \mid \exists y \begin{bmatrix} h(2) = y \wedge \\ \forall n[[n \neq 2 \rightarrow h(2) = g(2)]] \wedge \\ y\epsilon F(\textbf{plane}, w) \wedge \\ \langle x,y\rangle\epsilon F(\textbf{flies}, w)\end{bmatrix}\right\}$$

$$\begin{array}{l}[\![[_{VP} [_{VP} \text{ sails } [_{NP} \text{ a yacht}]_2] \text{ or } [_{VP} \text{ flies } [_{NP} \text{ a plane}]_2]]]\!]^\circ = \\ [\![[_{VP} \text{ sails } [_{NP} \text{ a yacht}]_2]]\!]^\circ \cup [\![[_{VP} \text{ flies } [_{NP} \text{ a plane}]_2]]\!]^\circ =\end{array}$$

$$\left\{\langle g,h,w,x\rangle \mid \exists y \begin{bmatrix} h(2) = y \wedge \\ \forall n[[n \neq 2 \rightarrow h(2) = g(2)]] \wedge \\ \left[\begin{bmatrix} y\epsilon F(\textbf{yacht}, w) \wedge \\ \langle x,y\rangle\epsilon F(\textbf{sails}, w)\end{bmatrix} \vee \begin{bmatrix} y\epsilon F(\textbf{plane}, w) \wedge \\ \langle x,y\rangle\epsilon F(\textbf{flies}, w)\end{bmatrix}\right]\end{bmatrix}\right\}$$

The value of the output assignment on 2 encodes a yacht which x sails or a plane which x flies. It will follow that the pronoun *it* in the sentence below can pick up the reference of either antecedent.

When John sails $[_{NP}$ a yacht$]_2$ or flies $[_{NP}$ a plane$]_2$, he always wrecks $[_{NP}$ it$]_2$.

It can be verified that this would also work out if one used either of the other options for the semantics of indefinite descriptions. As we have seen, however, the domain regulator semantics leads to problems elsewhere if one allows indefinite descriptions to be coindexed.

Other examples may motivate using something other than union as the semantics for disjunction in the presuppositional system. Thus we could semantically reconstruct Kamp's DRT analysis of *Either John doesn't have a car or it is in the garage* along the following lines. Say that negation simply inverts the truth value slot, so that if John does have a car in w, a tuple ⟨g,h,w,False⟩ in the semantic value of *John doesn't have a car* records a counterexample (i.e., a car John has) in its output assignment h. Then define disjunction so that if ⟨g,h,w,False⟩ is in the semantic value of Φ and ⟨h,k,w,True⟩ is in the semantic value of Ψ, then ⟨g,k,w,True⟩ is in the semantic value of '$\Phi \vee \Psi$'.

Focus Semantics

The denotation types in the intensional nonpresuppositional theory described here are these:

Individual (e.g., proper name or pronoun): a partial function from G to E.
Proposition (S or indefinite description): a subset of $G \times G \times W$
Property (VP or N): a subset of $G \times G \times W \times E$
Relation (TV): a subset of $G \times G \times W \times E \times E$

Among these we distinguish the sets of semantic values closed from the perspective of both the input and the output assignments:

$Cl_{individual} = \{f\colon G \rightarrow E | f \text{ is a constant function}\}$
$Cl_{proposition} = \{\Phi | \exists p\ [p \subseteq W \wedge \Phi = \{\langle g,g,w,x\rangle | \langle w,x\rangle \epsilon p\}]\}$
$Cl_{property} = \{\Psi | \exists P[P \subseteq W \times E \wedge \Psi = \{\langle g,g,w,x\rangle | \langle w,x\rangle \epsilon P\}]\}$
$Cl_{relation} = \{\Psi | \exists R[R \subseteq W \times E \times E \wedge \Psi = \{\langle g,g,w,x,y\rangle | \langle w,x,y\rangle \epsilon R\}]\}$

Focus gives us a set of alternatives to the ordinary semantic value. We consider this set to be a separate semantic value, $[\![\ ]\!]^f$, consisting of the same things as the ordinary semantic value except that something is possibly substituted into the position of the focused phrase. Formally, this is defined recursively:[25]

F1. The focus semantic value of a focused phrase is the set of closed semantic values matching the ordinary semantic value in type.

F2. The focus semantic value of a nonfocused noncomplex phrase is the unit set of the ordinary semantic value of the phrase.

F3. The focus semantic value of a nonfocused complex phrase is the image of

25. This was the definition given in Rooth 1985, although the semantic values were of course different.

the focus semantic values of the daughter phrases under the semantic combination function for the phrase.

What the focus theory demanded for fixing the restriction of adverbs of quantification was an object with an existentially quantified variable in the position of the focused phrase. We get this as the union of the focus-semantic value. An operator expressing this is FC:

FC1. $[\![FC(\alpha)]\!]^{o} = \cup [\![\alpha]\!]^{o}\}$
FC2. $[\![FC(\alpha)]\!]^{f} = \{[\![\alpha]\!]^{o}\}$

Finally, here is the association-with-focus rule for *always:*

R7. One-place *always*. $[\![[_S \textbf{always} [_S \alpha]]]\!]^{o} =$
$\{\langle g,g\rangle \mid \forall h\, [[\langle g,h\rangle\epsilon \cup [\![\alpha]\!]^{f} \rightarrow \exists k[\langle h,k\rangle\epsilon[\![\alpha]\!]^{o}]]]\}$

VP Focus

Here is a derivation for the VP focus reading of *A u always follows a q,* which corresponds to one of the false readings discussed in the text.

1. $[\![e_2]\!]^{o} =$
$\{\langle h,x\rangle \mid [2\epsilon Dom(h) \wedge h(2) = x]\}$
2. $[\![follows]\!]^{o} =$
$\{\langle h,h,w,x,y\rangle \mid \langle x,y\rangle\epsilon F(\textbf{follows},w)\}$
3. $[\![e_2]\!]^{o}$ = unit set of $[\![e_2]\!]^{o}$
4. $[\![[_{VP}follows\ e_2]]\!]^{o} =$
$\{\langle h,h,w,x\rangle \mid \langle x,h(2)\rangle\epsilon F(\textbf{follows},w)\}$
5. $[\![[_{VP}follows\ e_2]]\!]^{f}$ = unit set of $[\![[_{VP}follows\ e_2]]\!]^{o}$
6. $[\![[_{NP}\ a\ q]_2]\!]^{o} =$
$\{\langle h,k,w\rangle \mid [h \subseteq k \wedge Dom(k) = Dom(h) \cup \{2\} \wedge k(2)\epsilon F(\mathbf{q},w)]\}$
7. $[\![[_{NP}\ a\ q]_2]\!]^{f}$ = unit set of $[\![[_{NP}\ a\ q]_2]\!]^{o}$
8. $[\![[_{VP}[_{NP}\ a\ q]_2\ [_{VP}follows\ e_2]]_F]\!]^{o} =$
$$\left\{\langle h,k,w,x\rangle \;\middle|\; \begin{bmatrix} h \subseteq k \wedge \\ Dom(k) = Dom(h) \cup \{2\} \wedge \\ k(2)\epsilon F(\mathbf{q},w) \wedge \\ \langle x,k(2)\rangle\epsilon F(\textbf{follows},w) \end{bmatrix}\right\}$$
9. $[\![[_{VP}[_{NP}\ a\ q]_2\ [_{VP}follows\ e_2]]_F]\!]^{f} =$
$\{\Phi \mid \exists P[\Phi = \{\langle h,h,w,x\rangle \mid \langle w,x\rangle\epsilon P\}]\}$
10. $[\![[_S\ e_1\ [_{VP}[_{NP}\ a\ q]_2\ [_{VP}follows\ e_2]]_F]]\!]^{o} =$
$$\left\{\langle h,k,w\rangle \;\middle|\; \begin{bmatrix} h \subseteq k \wedge \\ Dom(k) = Dom(k) \cup Dom(h) \cup \{2\} \wedge \\ k(2)\epsilon F(\mathbf{q},w) \wedge \\ \langle h(1),k(2)\rangle\epsilon F(\textbf{follows},w) \end{bmatrix}\right\}$$

11. $[\![[_S\ e_1\ [_{VP}[_{NP}\ \mathrm{a}\ q]_2\ [_{VP}\mathrm{follows}\ e_2]]_F]]\!]^f =$
$\{\Psi \mid \exists P[\Psi = \{\langle h,h,w\rangle \mid [1 \in \mathrm{Dom}(h) \wedge \langle w,h(1)\rangle \in P]\}]\}$
12. $[\![[_{NP}\ \mathrm{a}\ u]_1]\!]^o$
$\{\langle g,h,w\rangle \mid [g \subseteq h \wedge \mathrm{Dom}(h) = \mathrm{Dom}(g) \cup \{1\} \wedge h(1) \in F(\mathbf{u},w)]\}$
13. $[\![[_{NP}\ \mathrm{a}\ u]_1]\!]^f =$ unit set of $[\![[_{NP}\ \mathrm{a}\ u]_1]\!]^o$
14. $[\![[_S\ [_{NP}\ \mathrm{a}\ u]_1\ [_S\ e_1\ [_{VP}[_{NP}\ \mathrm{a}\ q]_2\ [_{VP}\mathrm{follows}\ e_2]]_F]]]\!]^o =$

$$\left\{ \langle g,k,w\rangle \;\middle|\; \begin{bmatrix} g \subseteq k \wedge \\ \mathrm{Dom}(k) = \mathrm{Dom}(g) \cup \{1,2\} \wedge \\ k(1) \in F(\mathbf{u},w) \wedge \\ k(2) \in F(\mathbf{q},w) \wedge \\ \langle k(1),\ k(2)\rangle \in F(\mathbf{follows},w) \end{bmatrix} \right\}$$

15. $[\![[_S\ [_{NP}\ \mathrm{a}\ u]_1\ [_S\ e_1\ [_{VP}[_{NP}\ \mathrm{a}\ q]_2\ [_{VP}\mathrm{follows}\ e_2]]_F]]]\!]^f =$

$$\left\{ \Psi \mid \exists\ P \left[\Psi = \left\{ \langle g,h,w\rangle \;\middle|\; \begin{bmatrix} g \subseteq h \wedge \\ \mathrm{Dom}(h) = \mathrm{Dom}(g) \cup \{1\} \wedge \\ h(1) \in F(\mathbf{u},w) \wedge \\ \langle w,h(1)\rangle \in P \end{bmatrix} \right\} \right] \right\}$$

16. $[\![FC([_S\ [_{NP}\ \mathrm{a}\ u]_1\ [_S\ e_1\ [_{VP}[_{NP}\ \mathrm{a}\ q]_2\ [_{VP}\mathrm{follows}\ e_2]]_F]])]\!]^o =$
$\{\langle g,h,w\rangle \mid [g \subseteq h \wedge \mathrm{Dom}(h) = \mathrm{Dom}(g) \cup \{1\} \wedge h(1) \in F(\mathbf{u},w)]\}$
17. $[\![[_S\ \mathrm{always}\ [_S\ [_{NP}\ \mathrm{a}\ u]_1\ [_S\ e_1\ [_{VP}[_{NP}\ \mathrm{a}\ q]_2\ [_{VP}\mathrm{follows}\ e_2]]_F]]]]\!]^o =$
$\{\langle g,g,w\rangle \mid \forall h[[\langle g,h,w\rangle \in [\![FC([_S\text{—}])]\!]^o \rightarrow \exists k[\langle h,k,w\rangle \in [\![[_S\text{—}]]\!]^o]]]\}$
18. Change variables and do lambda conversion.

$$\left\{ \langle g,g,w\rangle \mid \forall h \begin{bmatrix} \begin{bmatrix} g \subseteq h \wedge \\ \mathrm{Dom}(h) = \mathrm{Dom}(g) \cup \{1\} \wedge \\ h(1) \in F(\mathbf{u},w) \end{bmatrix} \\ \rightarrow \exists k \begin{bmatrix} h \subseteq k \wedge \\ \mathrm{Dom}(k) = \mathrm{Dom}(h) \cup \{1,2\} \wedge \\ k(1) \in F(\mathbf{u},w) \wedge \\ k(2) \in F(\mathbf{q},w) \wedge \\ \langle k(1),k(2)\rangle \in F(\mathbf{follows},w) \end{bmatrix} \end{bmatrix} \right\}$$

19. Use the fact that k extends h and the biconditionals $\exists x[[A \wedge B] \Leftrightarrow A \wedge \exists x[B]]$ (x not free in A) and $[A \wedge B \rightarrow C \wedge B] \Leftrightarrow [A \wedge B \rightarrow C]$.

$$\left\{ \langle g,g,w\rangle \mid \forall h \begin{bmatrix} \begin{bmatrix} g \subseteq h \wedge \\ \mathrm{Dom}(h) = \mathrm{Dom}(g) \cup \{1\} \wedge \\ h(1) \in F(\mathbf{u},w) \end{bmatrix} \\ \rightarrow \exists k \begin{bmatrix} h \subseteq k \wedge \\ \mathrm{Dom}(k) = \mathrm{Dom}(h) \cup \{2\} \wedge \\ k(2) \in F(\mathbf{q},w) \wedge \\ \langle h(1),\ k(2)\rangle \in F(\mathbf{follows},w) \end{bmatrix} \end{bmatrix} \right\}$$

To see what is being quantified, we consider how h can differ from g. According to the antecedent of the conditional, it differs (at most) in its value on the index 1, which is required to be a letter ‘u’ in the model. Thus the above universal quantification of assignments is equivalent to a universal quantification of individuals, with its domain consisting of the set of u’s in the model.

Narrow Focus

Here is a derivation for an example with narrow focus on the noun in the subject.

1. $[\![[_S\ e_1\ [_{VP}[_{NP}\ a\ q]_2\ [_{VP}\text{follows}\ e_2]]]]\!]^\circ =$

$$\left\{ \langle h,k,w\rangle \mid \left[\begin{array}{c} h \subseteq k \wedge \\ Dom(k) = Dom(h) \cup \{2\} \wedge \\ k(2)\epsilon F(\mathbf{q},w) \wedge \\ \langle h(1),\ k(2)\rangle \epsilon F(\mathbf{follows},w) \end{array} \right] \right\}$$

2. $[\![-]\!]^f =$ unit set of $[\![-]\!]^\circ$
3. $[\![[_N\ u]_F]\!]^\circ = \{\langle g,g,w,x\rangle \mid x\epsilon F(\mathbf{u},w)\}$
4. $[\![[_N\ u]_F]\!]^f = \{\Phi \mid \exists P[\Phi = \{\langle g,g,w,x\rangle \mid \langle w,x\rangle \epsilon P\}]\}$
5. $[\![[_{NP}a\ [_N\ u]_F]]\!]^\circ =$
$\{\langle g,h,w\rangle \mid [g \subseteq h \wedge Dom(h) = Dom(g) \cup \{1\} \wedge h(1)\epsilon F(\mathbf{u},w)]\}$
6. $[\![[_{NP}a\ [_N\ u]_F]]\!]^f =$
$\{\Psi \mid \exists P[\Psi = \{\langle g,h,w\rangle \mid [g \subseteq h \wedge Dom(h) = Dom(g) \cup \{1\} \wedge \langle w,h(1)\rangle \epsilon P]\}]\}$
7. $[\![[_S\ [_{NP}\ a\ [_N\ u]_F]_1\ [_S\ e_1\ [_{VP}[_{NP}\ a\ q]_2\ [_{VP}\text{follows}\ e_2]]]]]\!]^\circ =$

$$\left\{ \langle h,k,w\rangle \mid \left[\begin{array}{c} g \subseteq h \wedge \\ Dom(k) = Dom(h) \cup \{1,2\} \wedge \\ k(1)\epsilon F(\mathbf{u},w) \wedge \\ k(2)\epsilon F(\mathbf{q},w) \wedge \\ \langle k(1),\ k(2)\rangle \epsilon F(\mathbf{follows},w) \end{array} \right] \right\}$$

8. $[\![[_S\ [_{NP}\ a\ \{n]_F]1\ [_S\ e_1\ [_{VP}[_{NP}\ a\ q]_2\ [_{VP}\text{follows}\ e_2]]]]]\!]^f =$

$$\left\{ \Psi \mid \exists P \left[\Psi = \left\{ \langle g,h,w\rangle \mid \left[\begin{array}{c} g \subseteq h \wedge \\ Dom(h) = Dom(g) \cup \{1,2\} \wedge \\ \langle w,h(1)\rangle \epsilon P \wedge \\ h(2)\epsilon F(\mathbf{q},w) \wedge \\ \langle h(1),h(2)\rangle \epsilon F(\mathbf{follows},w) \end{array} \right] \right\} \right] \right\}$$

9. $[\![FC([_S\ [_{NP}\ a\ [_N\ u]_F]_1\ [_S\ e_1\ [_{VP}[_{NP}\ a\ q]_2\ [_{VP}\text{follows}\ e_2]]]])]\!]^\circ =$

$$\langle g,h,w\rangle \mid \begin{array}{c} g \subseteq h \wedge \\ Dom(h) = Dom(g) \cup \{1,2\} \wedge \\ h(2)\epsilon F(\mathbf{q},w) \wedge \\ \langle h(1),\ h(2)\rangle \epsilon F(\mathbf{follows},w) \end{array}$$

10. $[\![[_S\ \text{always}\ [_S\ [_{NP}\ a\ [_N\ u]_F]_1\ [_S\ e_1\ [_{VP}[_{NP}\ a\ q]_2\ [_{VP}\text{follows}\ e_2]]]]]]\!]^\circ =$
$\{\langle g,g,w\rangle \mid \forall h[[\langle g,h,w\rangle \epsilon [\![FC([_S—])]\!]^\circ \rightarrow \exists k[\langle h,k,w\rangle \epsilon [\![[_S—]]\!]^\circ]]]\}$

11. That is:

$$\left\{ \langle g,g,w\rangle \mid \forall h \left[\left[\begin{array}{c} g \subseteq h \wedge \\ \mathrm{Dom}(h) = \mathrm{Dom}(g) \cup \{1,2\} \wedge \\ h(2) \in F(\mathbf{q},w) \wedge \\ \langle h(1),\ h(2)\rangle \in F(\mathbf{follows},w) \end{array} \right] \to \exists k \left[\begin{array}{c} h \subseteq k \wedge \\ \mathrm{Dom}(k) = \mathrm{Dom}(h) \cup \{1,2\} \wedge \\ k(1) \in F(\mathbf{u},w) \wedge \\ k(2) \in F(\mathbf{q},w) \wedge \\ \langle k(1),k(2)\rangle \in F(\mathbf{follows}) \end{array} \right] \right] \right\}$$

12. It follows from the domain and subfunction conditions that h = k. Removing redundant conditions in the consequent gives:

$$\left\{ \langle g,g,w\rangle \mid \forall h \left[\begin{array}{c} g \subseteq h \wedge \\ \mathrm{Dom}(h) = \mathrm{Dom}(g) \cup \{1,2\} \wedge \\ h(2) \in F(\mathbf{q},w) \wedge \\ \langle h(1),\ h(2)\rangle \in F(\mathbf{follows},w) \end{array} \to h(1) \in F(\mathbf{u},w) \right] \right\}$$

To see what is being quantified, consider how h can differ from g. According to the antecedent of the conditional, it differs (at most) in its value on the indices 1 and 2. Given the other conditions in the antecedent, the universal quantification of assignments is equivalent to a universal quantification of pairs of individuals: For any x and y such that y is a ‘q’ and x follows y, x is a ‘u’. This corresponds to one of the true readings discussed in the text, the difference being that *usually* has been replaced with *always*. The revised sentence is not really true in the intended model, since sometimes something other than a letter ‘u’ follows a ‘q’, as in *Aqaba*.

7 WHAT SOME GENERIC SENTENCES MEAN

Nicholas Asher and Michael Morreau

7.1. Introduction

Potatoes contain vitamin C, amino acids, protein, and thiamine expresses a true generalization about potatoes. *John smokes a cigar after dinner,* understood in its generic sense as expressing a regularity in John's behavior after dinner, could be true, and it could be false. This realist conviction inspires the theory of genericity which is presented in this chapter. Given that these two sentences can be true at all, their truth should somehow depend on the nutritional value of particular potatoes and on John's behavior on particular occasions after dinner. But this is the puzzling thing about generics: their truth conditions connect them at best only very loosely with particular facts about the world. Potatoes contain vitamin C even though large numbers of them are boiled for so long that it is lost. Potatoes would contain vitamin C even if *all* of them were to be boiled for so long that it is lost. And if John happens to run out of cigars sometimes, or even if he runs out regularly, it does not thereby become untrue that he smokes a cigar after dinner.

This tolerance of exceptions has for a decade or more frustrated efforts in linguistics, philosophy, and artificial intelligence to provide a rigorous account of generic meaning, and of modes of argument to which generic sentences give rise. We offer such an account here, and to this extent our undertaking is an ambitious one. In other ways it is much less ambitious. For one thing, in concentrating on just a few kinds of sentences, we do little justice to the great variety of genericity in natural language which has been documented in this volume and in previous linguistic studies.

There is a useful distinction which will help to mark out the relatively narrow range of generic sentences which concern us here: the distinction between what Manfred Krifka (1987) calls *d-generic* and *i-generic* sentences. The prefixes stand for "definite" and "indefinite" respectively, names chosen in order to reflect the ways in which, according to Krifka, sentences of these types are typically expressed in natural language. The distinction is, in fact, very much a semantic one: d-generic sentences attribute to a kind, a property which could not, without making a category mistake, be attributed to an individual of that kind. *The dinosaur is extinct* is an example of a d-generic sentence, since to say of any particular dinosaur that it is extinct would be to make a category mistake. Kinds of animals can be extinct, but individuals of those kinds can only be dead. To ask how the truth or falsity of this sentence is dependent on that of sentences asserting that particular individual dinosaurs are extinct would be to make the same category mistake, so we will not be concerned with d-generics here. Rather, we will be concerned with i-generics: sentences in which the property attributed to a kind could in principle also be held by individuals of that kind. The first sentence of this chapter is an i-generic sentence, since it is not only true of potatoes as a kind that they contain vitamin C, amino acids, protein, and thiamine. Individual potatoes can contain these things too, and in fact normally they do.

Another limitation of the theory presented here, from the linguist's point of view, is that we have very little to say about how genericity is actually expressed in language, or about translation procedures which associate formal representations with natural language expressions. In the formal language defined below, we assume generic sentences somehow to have been recognized and represented as such. In this language, a generic quantifier can be defined, like the GEN-operator described in chapter 1. Here we leave linguistic issues as much as possible to one side, concentrating instead on providing a theory of what our formal representations of generic sentences mean, and of the reasoning that is appropriate to them.

7.2. TOWARD A THEORY OF GENERIC MEANING: SOME DESIDERATA

Along which dimensions are different candidate semantic theories for generics to be compared? Several answers to this question which we will now discuss should help to motivate the theory of generic meaning presented below.

7.2.1. Generic Sentences Have Truth Values

Generic sentences like the examples mentioned above can be true, and they can be false. Certainly we speak about them as if they can be either, and we take it that an adequate account of generic meaning must have something to say about what it is that makes them true or false. Surprisingly, this is a contentious point. Perhaps in despair of ever finding truth conditions which enable it to be true that *potatoes contain vitamin C* (which most of them in fact do) but at the same time true that *turtles live to be a hundred years or more old* (which most of them do not), it has sometimes been denied that sentences like these have truth conditions at all; or at least, it has been denied that truth conditions are of any interest when it comes to explaining what these sentences mean.

Under the influence of theories of *default reasoning* which have originated in the recent artificial intelligence literature, it is claimed that generic sentences are merely rules of inference, whose significance is not truth conditional, but lies instead in what is called their ''dynamic'' meaning: the contribution they make to how individuals update their beliefs upon obtaining more information. One example of this radical epistemic approach to generic sentences, coming from within linguistic and philosophical circles, is Veltman's recent theory of ''Defaults in Update Semantics'' (Veltman 1995), which denies truth conditions any part whatsoever in the semantics of generic sentences. Veltman puts it this way:

> The heart of the theory . . . [of generics within update semantics] does not consist in a specification of truth conditions but of update conditions. According to this theory the slogan ''You know the meaning of a sentence if you know the conditions under which it is true'' should be replaced by this one: ''You know the meaning of a sentence if you know the change it brings about in the information state of anyone who accepts the news conveyed by it.''

The question of whether generic sentences have truth values, or whether, as Veltman supposes, they merely express rules of default inference, we take to be a very fundamental one. It is unlikely to be settled by amassing intuitive judgments, so it is important to look for other evidence which might bear on the issue. This brings us to a second desideratum.

Theories of generic meaning must be sufficiently general. An adequate theory will provide interpretations not only for simple generic sentences like the ones in the Introduction, but also for composite sentences in which genericity mixes with counterfactuality, belief, knowledge, and even with more genericity, as in the case of ''nested'' generic sentences like *Healthy cats jump at small moving objects,* or *People who work late nights do not wake up early.* Such sentences are nested in that they attribute properties which involve genericity (as expressed here by the ''habitual'' predicates *jumps at small moving objects,* and *wakes up late*) to kinds that are defined by means of generic properties (in this case, *healthy cats,* and *people who work late nights*). Another example of a nested generic sentence, this time one which arguably is logically valid, is *People who don't like to eat out don't like to eat out.* As an example of generics interacting with counterfactuality and propositional attitudes we have the following, even more complex sentence: *John knows that*

Mary loves kissing him, and he would be unhappy if she were to like it less. A theory of what generics mean ought at least to extend to a theory of what they mean in such contexts.

This is where theories like the one presented below part company with theories that treat generic sentences as mere rules of default inference. Where generic sentences are assigned truth values it is immediately clear how to interpret nested generics. And where the truth values are assigned in a possible-worlds framework, as they are below, it is also immediately clear how to embed generic sentences within propositional attitudes, modal contexts, counterfactual and other conditionals, and any other constructions which have been treated within this framework.

Where, on the other hand, generic sentences are interpreted as mere rules of default inference, or functions from information states to information states, it is not even clear how they could be nested even a few levels down without making the formal account phenomenally complicated. This we take to be strong *theoretical* evidence for the importance of truth conditions in a theory of what generic sentences mean, and a strong reminder of the danger of restricting attention to too narrow a range of the phenomena which a theory of generic meaning can be expected to explain.[1]

7.2.2. Reasoning with Generic Sentences

A second dimension along which theories of genericity can be compared is that a theory of generic meaning should explain the ways in which we reason with generic sentences. Logical entailment, the relation which holds between the premises and conclusion of an argument whenever truth is invariably passed from the former to the latter, is one form of reasoning, so the

1. An anonymous reviewer for this volume suggested that nested conditionals can be interpreted even with a dynamic interpretation of conditionals, if the proposition expressed by a sentence is identified with the result of updating an empty information state—call it 0—with that sentence. Whether the interpretation of nested conditionals is straightforward depends, however, on the details of 0 and of updating. Amplifying on his suggestion, let A, B, and C be atomic sentences. The proposition expressed by the nested sentence $(A > B) > C$ can, with a recursive clause for '$>$', be written as follows:

$$\|(A > B) > C\| = \|>\|(\|A > B\|, \|C\|)$$

Now, provided $\|A > B\|$ and $\|C\|$ are the same sort of thing, '$\|>\|$' can be defined once and for all; in this way the fully nested language will have been interpreted. This is what happens on our approach and is standard in modal logic; propositions are just sets of worlds. But in the dynamic approach of Veltman (1995), for example, $\|A > B\|$ and $\|C\|$ are not the same sort of thing; at least not in the versions we have seen. While $[C]0$ is just a set of worlds, $[A > B]0$ is a partially ordered set; and while Veltman says how to define '$\|>\|$' for sets of worlds, he does not say how to do so for partially ordered sets. The challenge is to extend the definition of '$\|>\|$' to the second sort of thing; as far as we know it has not yet been met.

question arises as to which patterns of logical reasoning seem, intuitively speaking, to be valid. There are not many, but the following are at least candidates:

WEAKENING OF THE CONSEQUENT[2]

Lions have manes.
―――――――――――――――
Lions have manes or wings.

We do not claim that whenever it makes sense to assert the premise of this argument it also makes sense to assert the conclusion, but it is plausible that whenever the former is true the latter is true too. Another pattern with a claim to validity is this:

DUDLEY DOORITE

Quakers are politically motivated.
Republicans are politically motivated.
―――――――――――――――
Quakers and Republicans are politically motivated.

Among the intuitively valid generic sentences, those which are entailed by everything, we count *Lions are lions* and the nested sentence *People who don't like to eat out don't like to eat out.*

There are plausible argument patterns besides these, but very few of them. Moreover, the ones we have found relate the truth of generics only to that of other generics, at least when we limit consideration to the fragment formalizable in an extensional, quantificational language augmented by genericity. That generics only associate with other generics in this way ties in, of course, with something which is now very familiar from the writings of Greg Carlson and others: sentences like *Potatoes contain vitamin C* are not to be analyzed extensionally and, except in trivial cases, 'they' do not enter into logical relations with truth-functional compounds of their components.

This makes the intensionality of generics unlike that of the alethic modalities of philosophical logic, or the modalities of indicative conditional analyses like Stalnaker's (1968). Statements involving such modalities may, alone or in combination with modal-free statements, entail other, nontrivial, modal-free statements. Generic statements do not. Genericity in this respect resembles much more closely a deontic or normative modality, since facts about what ought to be the case similarly neither entail, nor are entailed by, facts about what is actually the case. Indeed, in our view the resemblance is not accidental; the intuition underlying the semantics for generics given below is that *Potatoes*

2. The rationale for this name will become clear subsequently.

contain vitamin C is true just in case every individual potato, under normal conditions, contains vitamin C. Understood in this way, generics do not just resemble normative statements. They almost *are* normative statements, since they refer to normal individuals and cases, and that is why their logic is so weak. Essentially, nothing entails a generic except another generic, and nothing is entailed by a generic except another generic.

Be this as it may, not all things which fail to be entailed by a generic statement are equal. For example, among the things not entailed by the generic statement that potatoes contain vitamin C, the particular conclusion that *this* potato contains vitamin C does at least have the distinction of being rendered more plausible. The generic fact makes it somehow reasonable to expect this potato to contain vitamin C, without at the same time making it reasonable to expect any number of other things which are not entailed, like, say, that the moon is made of green cheese. The particular statement, we might say, may *reasonably be inferred* from the generic one in such cases, even if there is no relation of logical entailment between the two.

That genericity gives rise to such reasoning is surely a large part of its cognitive significance, and goes some of the way to explaining why genericity plays such a prominent part in natural language. Genericity enables agents whose information about the world is incomplete to jump to reasonable conclusions, thereby helping them to act intelligently in situations in which they don't have unlimited time available for gathering information. Since lions are normally dangerous, an agent will in general be better off if, when confronted with a lion, he just jumps to the conclusion that the beast is dangerous, without waiting around long enough to find out properly. An agent who is intelligent, and who has been informed that *lions are dangerous,* will do just this. And a theory of genericity, we believe, can be expected to justify his reasoning. It should say which conclusions an agent may jump to on the basis of generic information available to him, and in which sense this information licenses the jumps.

One central formal difference between jumping to reasonable conclusions in this way and a valid argument is that the former is *defeasible*. Merely reasonable conclusions may be withdrawn in the light of new information. For example, the expectation that a particular lion is dangerous is diminished on learning, say, that it has just eaten or that it is drugged and unconscious. The conclusions of valid arguments, on the other hand, are unaffected as premises are added.

Originally challenged by Minsky to formalize simple defeasible reasoning involving generic statements, researchers in the branch of artificial intelligence concerned with nonmonotonic reasoning have discovered a wealth of patterns of defeasible generic inference. While these researchers are generally not explicitly concerned with natural language in itself, they have provided a valuable resource for those interested in the semantics of genericity. Theories of genericity can now be expected to account for patterns of reasonable inference by means of which, in circumstances of incomplete information, generic information contributes to intelligent action; in the virtual absence of valid argument forms, these patterns may serve us as a test bed when developing and comparing theories. Below, roughly in order of increasing complexity, are some defeasible patterns artificial intelligence researchers have come up with. Versions with added premises that defeat the original conclusions have been marked with an asterisk.

DEFEASIBLE MODUS PONENS

Lions are dangerous.	Lions are dangerous.
Lizzy is a lion.	Lizzy is a lion; Lizzy is not dangerous*.
Lizzy is dangerous.	Lizzy is dangerous.

While modus ponens is supposed to be defeasible, it should be insensitive to the addition of premises which are somehow irrelevant to the respective conclusions:

IRRELEVANT INFORMATION

Lions are dangerous.
Lizzy is a lion.
Lizzy is five years old.
―――――
Lizzy is dangerous.

Closely related to the Defeasible Modus Ponens is what we call Defeasible Chaining:

DEFEASIBLE CHAINING

Birds fly.
Sparrows are birds.
Tweety is a sparrow.
―――――
Tweety flies.

The conclusion that Tweety flies should be defeated on the addition of the premise *Tweety does not fly,* as in the case of the Defeasible Modus Ponens. According to the last pattern we shall consider for the moment, a match between two instances of modus ponens whose conclusions are mutually exclusive should end in a draw: both of the conclusions should be defeated:

Nixon Diamond

Republicans are nonpacifists.
Dick is a Republican.
Quakers are pacifists.
Dick is a quaker.*

Dick is a nonpacifist.
Dick is a pacifist.

Most people who have worked on nonmonotonic reasoning find the above patterns of reasonable inference compelling. In our opinion, an acceptable theory of genericity must respect the distinction between logical entailment and reasonable inference, and it must realistically model the reasoning belonging to each area. In particular, the semantics must reflect the fact that these defeasible patterns of inference introduce a dependence on epistemic contexts which is not at all present in the case of the valid patterns; their conclusions are defeated as one obtains information that brings them into question. Realistically modeling such defeasible reasoning will lead us to model information states explicitly in the semantics of generic sentences.

7.2.3. An Outline of This Theory of Generic Meaning

Chapter 1 of this volume discusses several different places where one might find inspiration for a theory of generic meaning, including the theory of prototypes, modal and conditional logics, and the theory of nonmonotonic reasoning. The approach we have taken below has roots in several of these areas, in particular in modal and conditional logic and in nonmonotonic logic. More precisely, we have taken the possible-worlds treatment of conditional sentences developed by the philosophers David Lewis, Robert Stalnaker, and Richmond Thomason in the late 1960s, and rebuilt it as a semantics assigning truth values to generic sentences relative to possible worlds. This first, truth-conditional part of our semantics, with its standard notion of entailment, accounts for valid argument forms like those mentioned earlier on. Because it is a conventional possible-worlds theory, we can insert it into general, possible-worlds analyses of counterfactuals, propositional attitudes, and so on. It is then clear how to interpret embedded generic sentences like those discussed above.

On the basis of this truth-conditional account, we then develop an account of the defeasible patterns of reasonable inference discussed above. Our intuitive picture of what goes on when one reasons by Defeasible Modus Ponens, roughly but clearly, is this: First one assumes the premises *Birds fly* and *Tweety is a bird,* and no more than this. Second, one assumes that Tweety is a normal bird if this is consistent with these premises. Finally, one looks to see whether one is assuming that Tweety flies or not, and finds that one is. It is our view that *all* of the patterns of defeasible reasoning outlined in the introduction to this chapter arise in essentially this way, from assuming just their premises, then assuming individuals to be as normal if this is epistemically possible, and finally checking whether one has ended up assuming their conclusions.

Such reasoning about is modeled by means of *information states,* which are just sets of possible worlds taken from the truth-conditional model theory. We define two functions on these: *updating* and *normalization*. The first is eliminative, simply removing from information states all those possible worlds where the sentences with which one is updating are not true. Assuming just the premises of an argument can then be modeled as updating a distinguished, informationally minimal state '☺' with those premises. The second of the two functions, normalization, models the notion of assuming individuals to be normal if this is consistent with the premises. Normalizing the result of updating '☺' with a set of premises Γ yields a set of information states, the fixed points of the normalization process; the conclusions which may reasonably (though not in general validly) be drawn from premises Γ are those sentences then which are true at all the worlds in all of these fixed points. The figure below summarizes this outline of our dynamic theory of reasonable inference. Here '+' represents the function of updating, and the arrows the process of normalization.

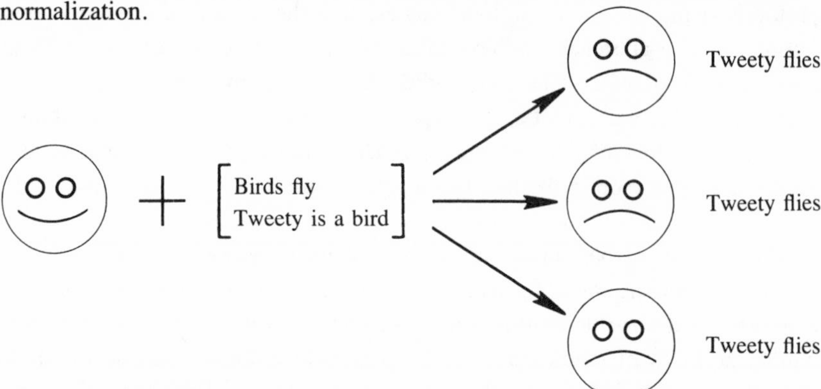

In the rest of this chapter, we will develop a theory of generic meaning and reasoning which fills in this sketch. We begin in the next section by introducing our formal language, illustrating its use in formalizing nested generic sentences, and defending the ideas underlying its semantics against a criticism due to Greg Carlson. Then, in section 7.3.2, we interpret this language in possible-worlds structures. The resulting models determine a monotonic entailment notion which, in section 7.3.3, is given a sound and complete syntactic characterization. This much, though necessary, is all familiar from the literature of conditional logic, but it lays a foundation for the innovation of this chapter—the explanation of defeasible reasoning based on generics.

It is at this point that we get to the intuitive picture given above. Section 7.4.1 is concerned with the left-hand side of the figure. Information states are modeled as sets of possible worlds taken from the models of section 7.3.2, and one of these is set aside as ☺, the informationally minimal state. On these states the update function '+' is defined; between them, ☺ and '+' model the notion of assuming just the premises of an argument. In section 7.4.2 we then intuitively motivate and define the normalization function, which, when iterated, gives rise to the different fixed points mentioned above. Using all of these concepts, in section 7.4.3 the defeasible notion of commonsense entailment is defined.

In section 7.4.4 we return to the patterns of defeasible reasoning with generics that were discussed in section 7.2.2. We prove several facts showing that commonsense entailment goes a long way toward capturing these patterns, and give examples of interesting arguments which, as a consequence of these facts, are defeasibly valid. In section 7.5 we consider different ways of extending the theory presented here to capture other forms of reasoning with generics; in section 7.6 we summarize the theory and compare it with related work in the literature.

7.3. A FORMALIZATION AND TRUTH-CONDITIONAL SEMANTICS FOR GENERICS

At this point it is convenient to introduce the simple formal language in which we formalize generic sentences.

7.3.1. The Language

We consider a first-order language L, augmented with a binary conditional connection '>', by means of which generic sentences are to be represented. The formulas of the resulting language $L_>$ are defined by the usual clauses, together with the following one:

If φ and ψ are formulas, then $\varphi > \psi$ is a formula.

The intended interpretation of $\varphi > \psi$ is that where φ holds, normally ψ holds too. Or, closer to the letter of the model theory to come, if φ were to hold along with all of the things which are normally the case where φ holds, then ψ would hold. This second formulation brings out the counterfactual character of these sentences, and accounts for the choice of the symbol '>' in the formal language. We believe that the generic sentences which interest us should be thought of as universally quantified, normative conditionals of this kind. The sentence *Potatoes contain vitamin C,* for example, we take to mean: Any object would contain vitamin C, if it were a potato and all other things were to hold which would normally hold if it were a potato. This sentence can then be represented in $L_>$ as the following formula:

$$\forall x(\text{potato}(x) > \text{contains-vitamin-C}(x))$$

Note that this definition allows for arbitrarily deep nesting of the conditional '>'. Because of this, nested generics like the intuitively valid sentence mentioned in the Introduction, *People who don't like to eat out normally don't like to eat out,* can be represented as follows. First, the embedded property of not liking to eat out is represented as the monadic predicate $\forall e(\text{eats-out}(x,e) > \text{unhappy}(x,e))$; this predicate is intended to be satisfied by individuals x who, in eating-out events e, are normally unhappy. The entire sentence then comes out as follows:

$$\forall x((\text{person}(x) \,\&\, \forall e(\text{eats-out}(x,e) > \text{unhappy}(x,e))) > \forall(\text{eats-out}(x,e) > \text{unhappy}(x,e))).$$

Carlson once raised what he took to be a problem for any semantics which interprets generic sentences as we are suggesting, quantifying universally over normal or prototypic individuals. He put it like this:

> *Chickens lay eggs* is a true sentence. . . . We also know it to be true that only female chickens lay eggs. It then follows that only female chickens can be included among the normal chickens; if any males were allowed [then *Chickens lay eggs*] would be falsified. So we know that all normal chickens are female. Since all female chickens that lay eggs are hens, the following sentence is predicted to be true: *Chickens are hens.* But [this sentence] is simply not true. (Carlson 1977b, 64–65)

The point which Carlson raises, however, has little to do with the semantics of generics as such. Rather, it points to a much more general difficulty which comes up when determining the logical forms of quantified sentences in natural language. Following work in generalized quantifiers (Lewis 1975), a natural language quantificational structure has three components: the quantificational relation itself, a restrictor, and a nuclear scope. (For a discussion, see Barwise & Cooper 1981.) And in general, determining the restrictor of a natural language quantifier is a nontrivial matter. This is most immediately apparent with universal quantification, since naive translation into logic can produce obvious falsehood; this is what seems to be going on in Carlson's example. It is quite clear that *Chickens lay eggs* cannot mean that *all* normal chickens lay eggs. But it is equally clear that when a faculty chairman surveys the room before a departmental meeting and says, "Everybody is here," he does not intend to assert that all human beings in the universe have flocked to the meeting. Similarly, *John always feeds the cat* does not have the apparent unrestricted universal force that a naive rendering of its logical form would suggest. In no way do the inadequacies of naive translations of these last two sentences call into question the idea that 'always' and 'everybody' involve universal quantification; rather, what they show is that the appropriate restrictors for the quantifiers are not those of the naive translations.

Because the problem he points out is such a general one, Carlson's criticism of the kind of analysis that is offered here seems misdirected. We do not need to change the universal quantificational force that is a feature of our analysis for the quantifiers discussed above. Rather, we need to find a less naive way of determining the restrictors of these universal quantifiers. We need to do this anyway, for other universal quantifiers. An appropriate place to start is with Lewis's (1983) notion of *accommodation*. But this, along with other important issues relating to mapping natural language generics onto their logical representations, is something which we will let lie for the moment.

In the next section, we interpret $L_>$ is possible-worlds structures.

7.3.2. The Truth-Conditional Semantics

The semantic idea underlying our interpretation of '>' is, once again, that for any monadic predicates φ and ψ, the sentence $\forall x(\varphi > \psi)$ should be true at a possible world just in case, at that world, being a normal φ involves being a ψ. The modal frames defined below encode what being a normal φ involves by means of a worlds-accessibility function '*', which assigns to each possible world w and proposition p (or set of possible worlds) a set of possible worlds. Intuitively speaking, *(w,p) is the set of worlds where p holds along with everything which, at w, is normally the case where p holds.

DEFINITION 1: A $L_>$ frame is a triple $F = \langle W,D,* \rangle$ where

(i) W is a nonempty set of worlds,
(ii) D is a nonempty set of individuals, and
(iii) $*: W \times \wp(W) \rightarrow \wp(W)$

For example, let p be the proposition that Big Bird of *Sesame Street* is a bird. Let w be the actual world, where it is true that birds normally can fly and that birds normally have feathers. Then *(w,p) contains only worlds where Big Bird can fly and has feathers. (The actual world w will fall outside of *(w,p), given that the television character is, as birds go, atypical. For one thing, he cannot fly.)

Two things about the above frames should be noticed. First, what is normally the case where p holds is in general a contingent matter, varying from possible world to possible world. This ties in with the fact that generic sentences, too, are in general contingent—at least the ones that are of any interest in language. There should be, for example, possible worlds where Tweety is a perfectly normal bird and yet cannot fly, these quite simply being possible worlds where it is not true that birds can normally fly. Secondly, we do not suppose any absolute normality order on possible worlds. In particular, we explicitly reject the idea that *(w,p) is to be identified with those most normal of all possible worlds where p holds.

Up until now '*' has been left unconstrained, and indeed, in view of the weak logic of generics only a few constraints seem at all reasonable.[3] One which does seem reasonable is this:

FACTICITY: $*(w,p) \subseteq p$

Worlds where p holds together with other propositions which are normally associated with p are in any case worlds where p holds. In other words, p is itself one of the things which normally holds when p holds. This constraint is one we take to be very basic, and all of the frames we consider below will be assumed to satisfy it. Other constraints are less immediately compelling, but could be added to validate others of the argument schemes which were discussed in the section 7.2. For example, the following constraint would validate the Dudley Doorite scheme:[4]

3. One constraint on '*' which is familiar from conditional logic but which we certainly do not want to impose here is the following:

Centering: If $w \in p$, then $w \in *(w,p)$.

That w is a world where p holds is no guarantee that w is a world where everything holds which is normally associated with p. Among the things served to Smith for dinner last week in London was something which was, he was assured, a potato. But many things were not true of this object which normally go with being a potato: it certainly didn't contain vitamin C.

4. One might want to strengthen this to $*(w, p \cup q) = *(w, p) \cup *(w, q)$. But this would trivialize the theory. Suppose that p is a *stronger* proposition than q, by which we mean that $p \subseteq q$. The above equality would then require that $*(w, p) \subseteq *(w, p \cup q) = *(w, q)$. That is, anything which is normally the case when q holds is also normally the case when p holds. This is clearly at odds with the idea that what is normal under certain circumstances may be abnormal under more general circumstances. Not surprisingly, a simple argument shows that the stronger constraint would also trivialize the logic to be given later, by making the fact that birds fly entail that penguins fly.

DUDLEY DOORITE CONSTRAINT: $*(w,p \cup q) \subseteq *(w,p) \cup *(w,q)$

Placing constraints on '*' complicates the construction of models, however, so we leave the latter constraint for further discussion in section 7.5.1. For the meantime, Facticity is the only constraint we will place on our frames.

We now go on to define $L_>$ interpretations in $L_>$ frames in the standard way.

DEFINITION 2: A *base model* M for $L_>$ is a tuple $\langle W,D,*,[\![\,]\!]\rangle$, where
(i) $\langle W,D,*\rangle$ is a $L_>$ frame, and
(ii) $[\![\,]\!]$ is a function from nonlogical constants of L to appropriate intensions (functions from worlds to appropriate extensions).

The satisfaction definition for $L_>$ sentences is largely familiar and uses variable assignments. A variable assignment α is a function from the variables of L into the domain D of a base model. Truth is defined as satisfaction with respect to all assignments.

DEFINITION 3: For any base model M, any possible world w, and any variable assignment α:
(A) $M,w,\alpha \models \varphi$, as usual, for φ an atomic formula of first-order logic.
(B) i) The usual clauses for complex formulas involving $\forall$, $\exists$, v, &, $\rightarrow$, $\neg$.
ii) $M,w,\alpha \models \varphi > \psi$ iff $*(w,\|\varphi\|_{M,\alpha}) \subseteq \|\psi\|_{M,\alpha}$

Here $\|\varphi\|_{M,\alpha}$, *the proposition expressed by φ in* M *relative to α,* is defined to be the following set of possible worlds: $\{w \in W_M: M,w,\alpha \models \varphi\}$. Where φ is a formula lacking free variables, that is, a *sentence,* obviously the subscript α can be dropped. As can the subscript M, where it is clear which model is meant.

Let φ and ψ be any monadic predicates of $L_>$. To get the feel of this definition, note that the sentence $\forall x(\varphi > \psi)$, our representation of the sentence *φ's are normally ψ's,* is true at a possible world w of a model M just in case for each individual δ in the domain of M, $*(w,\|\varphi\underline{\delta}\|_M) \subseteq \|\psi\underline{\delta}\|_M$. In other words, it is true just in case for every individual δ, if we look at the worlds where $\varphi\underline{\delta}$ holds along with everything else which, in w, is normally the case where $\varphi\underline{\delta}$ holds, we find that $\psi\underline{\delta}$ holds. This, then, is our formal rendering of the informal idea mentioned earlier, that $\forall x(\varphi > \psi)$ should be true if "being a normal φ involves being a ψ."

One thing about this account of the truth-conditional meaning of generics is worth noting. The truth of *Birds fly* does not imply the possibility that *all* birds can fly; there need be no worlds where all birds are normal. Indeed, this would be an unnatural assumption. Straightforward adaptations of modal rules like those of Kratzer (1981) to the generic case, as in Heim 1982, do require such absolutely normal worlds, and get into trouble as a result.[5] For example, in order to have the sentence *Turtles live to a grand old age* come out true, they must imagine the most normal worlds to be those where every single turtle lives to a grand old age, instead of dying while very young, as the vast majority do in the actual world. Such worlds would be biologically very strange, and might even violate biological laws; they strike us as most implausible candidates for absolutely normal worlds. In our theory, the truth of this sentence does not bring with it such theoretical liabilities: it just means, roughly speaking, that every individual turtle would live to an old age if it were to develop normally.

Having defined our models, we can now go on to define the notion of *logical consequence* '$\models$' for $L_>$ in the standard way:

DEFINITION 4: Let Γ be a set of formulas, and let φ be a single formula. $\Gamma \models \varphi$ just in case for all $L_>$-models M, for all possible worlds w, and for all variable assignments α: if $M,w,\alpha \models \Gamma$, then $M,w,\alpha \models \varphi$.

A sentence is said to be *logically valid* if it is entailed by the empty set of premises, or, equivalently, by every set of premises. As an example, it is easy to verify that in view of Facticity, the following sentence is logically valid:

$$\forall x((\text{person}(x)\ \&\ \forall e(\text{eats-out}(x,e) > \text{unhappy}(x,e))) > \forall e(\text{eats-out}(x,e) > \text{unhappy}(x,e)))$$

This is the formal representation given earlier of the intuitively valid sentence *People who don't like to eat out don't like to eat out.*

7.3.3. A Derivability Notion

In this section, we provide a syntactic characterization of the entailment notion of the previous section. Such characterizations are of interest in their own right of course. But in this case, the Henkin-style canonical model construction used to prove completeness of the derivability notion is of special importance. We will need the canonical model in the following section, when we come to model the notion of a minimal information state.

First, a notion of derivability without premises is defined by means of the axioms and rules below. As usual, a *derivation* is a finite sequence of formulas,

5. In terms of a Kratzer-like theory that distinguishes a modal relation, a modal base, and an ordering principle to define modalities, our generic quantifier has a quite simple semantics. The modal base is a fixed set of possible worlds, while the antecedent φ of a generic statement $\forall x(\varphi > \psi)$ and the world of evaluation together determine the ordering principle on the spheres relevant to supporting generic reasoning. This will become clear in the next section, when we define the epistemic semantics and information states.

each of which is either an instantiation of one of the above axioms, or follows by means of one of the rules from formulas that appear earlier in the sequence. We say that φ is *derivable,* and write '$\vdash\varphi$', just in case φ is the last formula of some derivation.

A1. Truth-functional $L_>$ tautologies
A2. $\forall x\varphi \rightarrow \varphi[t/x]$ for any term t.
A3. $\forall x\varphi \leftrightarrow \neg\exists x\neg\varphi x$.
A4. $\forall x(\varphi \rightarrow \psi) \rightarrow (\exists x\varphi \rightarrow \psi)$ for x not free in ψ.
A5. $\forall x(\varphi>\psi) \rightarrow (\varphi>\forall x\psi)$, for x not free in φ.
A6. $\varphi>\varphi$.

R1. $\vdash\varphi$ and $\vdash\varphi \rightarrow \psi \Rightarrow \vdash\psi$.
R2. $\vdash(\psi_1 \;\&\; \ldots \;\&\; \psi_n) \rightarrow \psi \Rightarrow \vdash(\varphi>\psi_1 \;\&\; \ldots \;\&\; \varphi>\psi_n) \rightarrow \varphi>\psi$.
R3. $\vdash\varphi \rightarrow \psi[c/x]$, where c is a constant not in φ or $\psi \Rightarrow \vdash\varphi \rightarrow \forall x\psi$.
R4. $\vdash\varphi \Rightarrow \vdash\varphi[t/x]$ where t is a term not in φ.
R5. $\vdash\varphi \leftrightarrow \psi$ and φ a subformula of $\zeta \Rightarrow \vdash\zeta \leftrightarrow \zeta[\psi/\varphi]$.

Here, by way of example, is a (summary of a) derivation of the logically valid sentence

∀x((person(x) & ∀e(eats-out(x,e)>unhappy(x,e))) > ∀e(eats-out(x,e)>unhappy(x,e))).

1. (person(x) & ∀e(eats-out(x,e)>unhappy(x,e))) →
   ∀e(eats-out(x,e)>unhappy(x,e)). **(A1)**
2. (person(x) & ∀e(eats-out(x,e)>unhappy(x,e))) > (person(x) &
   ∀e(eats-out(x,e)>unhappy(x,e))) → (person(x) &
   ∀e(eats-out(x,e)>unhappy(x,e))) > ∀e(eats-out(x,e)>unhappy(x,e)) **(R2, R1)**
3. (person(x) & ∀e(eats-out(x,e)>unhappy(x,e))) > ((person(x) &
   ∀e(eats-out(x,e)>unhappy(x,e))) **(A6)**
4. (person(x) & ∀e(eats-out(x,e)>unhappy(x,e))) >
   ∀e(eats-out(x,e)>unhappy(x,e)) (2, 3, **R1**)
5. ∀x[(person(x) & ∀e(eats-out(x,e)>unhappy(x,e))) >
   ∀e(eats-out(x,e)>unhappy(x,e))] (4, **R3, R4**)

That this sentence should be both valid and derivable without premises is not a coincidence: it is a consequence of the completeness theorem stated below that all valid sentences are derivable without premises, and vice versa. Before stating this completeness theorem, we first generalize the above derivability notion to a notion '$\Gamma \vdash \varphi$' of *derivability from premises Γ*. We say that $\Gamma \vdash \varphi$ just in case for some finite $\Gamma' \subseteq \Gamma$ we have $\vdash \& \Gamma' \rightarrow \varphi$. It is this notion which, according to the completeness theorem, exactly characterizes the notion of entailment defined above.

THEOREM 1 (SOUNDNESS AND COMPLETENESS): For all sets Γ of formulas, and for all individual formulas φ:
$\Gamma \vdash \varphi$ if, and only if, $\Gamma \models \varphi$.

The proof of this theorem is by a straightforward, Henkin-style construction of a canonical model. A standard text such as Chellas 1980 may be consulted for a general introduction to this method. For a proper understanding of the rest of this chapter, only two lemmas need be stated. The first of these is a familiar consequence of the fact that the notion of derivability from premises, as defined above, satisfies compactness and deduction theorems:

LINDENBAUM LEMMA: Let Γ be a $\vdash$consistent set of sentences (that is, for no sentence φ do we have both $\Gamma \vdash \varphi$ and $\Gamma \vdash \neg\varphi$). Then there is a superset Γ' of Γ which is maximal-$\vdash$ consistent (that is, Γ' is $\vdash$ consistent, and has no proper superset which is $\vdash$ consistent).

The second of these lemmas is the greater part of the proof of Theorem 1. Morreau 1992a contains details of the proofs of this and other facts that are stated below without proofs.

HENKIN LEMMA: There is a *canonical* $L_>$ model, $\mathcal{A}_{can}$, such that:

(i) W_{can}, the set of possible worlds of $\mathcal{A}_{can}$, is the set of all maximal-$\vdash$ consistent sets of $L_>$ sentences;

(ii) Let $L_>^+$ be the language obtained from $L_>$ in the Henkin proof, by adding constants as witnesses for existential quantifiers. Then for each $w \in W_{can}$ and each sentence φ of $L_>$:
$*_{can}(w, \|\varphi\|_{can}) = \{v \in W_{can} \mid \text{for all sentences } \psi \text{ of } L_>^+,\ \varphi > \psi \in w \Rightarrow \psi \in v\}$;

(iii) For each $w \in W_{can}$ and sentence φ: $\mathcal{A}_{can}$: $w \models \varphi$ if, and only if, $\varphi \in w$.

For the completeness theorem above, of course, only part (iii) of this lemma matters. In the next section, however, where we deal with patterns of defeasible reasoning to which generic sentences give rise, we will make essential use of this canonical model in modeling the notion of an informationally minimal information state. There (i) and (ii) will be needed to show that the theory captures patterns of nonmonotonic reasoning, including Defeasible Modus Ponens and the Nixon Diamond. It is the following consequence of (i) and (ii) which will be used:

FACT 1: For every sentence φ of $L_>$ and $w \in W_{can}$:
$w \in *_{can}(w, \|\varphi\|_{can})$ if, and only if, for every $L_>$ formula $\psi(\vec{x})$: $\forall\vec{x}((\varphi > \psi) \rightarrow \psi) \in w$.

Another fact should be noted, which will also turn out to be useful in section 7.4. For any formula φ, let $\varphi^{\rightarrow}$ be the result of replacing each occurrence of '>' in φ by an occurrence of '→'. This translation function '→' can be extended in obvious ways to sets Γ of formulas, and to sequences of formulas; in particular, it can be extended to derivations. A straightforward induction on the length of π then shows that $\pi^{\rightarrow}$ is a derivation if π is, and thus provides the proof of the following fact:

FACT 2: If $\Gamma \vdash \varphi$, then $\Gamma^{\rightarrow} \vdash \varphi^{\rightarrow}$.

We conclude this section on the truth-conditional semantics of generic sentences by noting that, as is obvious from the above axioms and rules, both $\models$ and $\vdash$ capture the one pattern of logical entailment discussed above for which a constraint has been placed on *, namely Weakening of the Consequent (see section 7.2.2). The argument form amounts to **A6** and **R2,** since using these two, along with the axioms and rules concerning universal quantification, the following rule is derivable:

$$\vdash \forall x(\psi \rightarrow \gamma) \Rightarrow \ \vdash \forall x(\psi > \psi) \rightarrow \forall x(\varphi > \gamma)$$

Using this rule we obtain, for example, $\vdash \forall x([\varphi > \psi) \rightarrow \forall x(\varphi > \psi \vee \gamma)$, which means that the following formal representation of Weakening of the Consequent has been validated:

$$\frac{\forall x(\varphi > \psi)}{\forall x(\varphi > \psi \vee \gamma)}$$

7.4. AN EPISTEMIC SEMANTICS FOR GENERICS

We have given a truth-conditional semantics for generics which sanctions the patterns of valid inference discussed in section 7.2.2. In this section we show how to capture the patterns of invalid but reasonable inference. It is here that we make formally precise the two important notions mentioned in section 7.2.3: (i) assuming no more than the premises of an argument, and (ii) assuming individuals to be as normal as is consistent with these premises.

7.4.1. Assuming No More than the Premises of an Argument

Earlier we introduced the notion of assuming no more than the premises of an argument, and also the idea of modeling this notion by updating an informationally minimal state with those premises. To make this precise, we now first need to provide a formal model of information states, and to say which information state is informationally minimal; second, we need to define an update function on information states.

Our approach to modeling information states is by now very familiar from philosophy and artificial intelligence. We identify them with sets of possible worlds taken from the base models of Definition 2. One intuition behind this is that to be in an information state s, or to "have" the information in s, is to be informed that the actual world is among the possibilities in s. Alternatively, if information is taken to come in the form of sentences, the information carried by a state is the collection of those sentences that are true at each world of that state.

Updating information states with new information can now be modeled in a particularly simple way. To obtain the information, say, that Sam is a dodo, or that birds fly, is to learn that the actual world is a place where these things are true. Accordingly, in the information models defined below, an information state is updated with a sentence, or more generally, with a set Γ of sentences, by reducing it to those possible worlds where all of the sentences in Γ are true.

DEFINITION 5: The *information model* based on the base model $\langle W,D,*,[\![\,]\!]\rangle$ is the tuple $\langle \wp(W),D,*,[\![\,]\!],+\rangle$, where

$+ : \wp(W) \times \wp(L_{>}) \rightarrow \wp(W)$ is defined such that for all information states $s \in \wp(W)$ and all $\Gamma \in \wp(L_{>})$: $s+\Gamma = s \cap \|\Gamma\|_M$.

Here $\|\Gamma\|_M = \cap\{\|\gamma\|_M \mid \gamma\in\Gamma\}$. As a further convenience, the set $\wp(W)$ of information states of an information model $\mathscr{A} = \langle \wp(W),D,*,[\![\,]\!],+\rangle$ is written 'IS($\mathscr{A}$)'.

According to the next definition, and in line with the discussion above, an information state s *supports* a sentence φ just in case φ is true at each of the possible worlds of s.

DEFINITION 6: Let $\mathscr{A}$ be the information model based on M, let $s \in$ IS($\mathscr{A}$), and let φ be a sentence of $L_{>}$. Then we say that $\mathscr{A}$ and s *support* φ (and we write $\mathscr{A},s \models \varphi$) if, and only if, for all $w\in s$:

$M,w \models \varphi$.

Note that updating is *successful:* for any $\mathscr{A}$, and for any $s \in$ IS($\mathscr{A}$): $\mathscr{A},s+\varphi \models \varphi$.

In order to capture the notion of assuming just the premises of an argument, it remains only to be said which informationally minimal state is to be updated, in the sense defined above, with the premises of that argument. To this end, we isolate a particular information model: $\mathscr{A}_{can}$, the information model based on the canonical model of the Henkin Lemma. (Note that we have already used $\mathscr{A}_{can}$ to refer to this canonical model itself. It is convenient to use the same name for both.) Among the information states of this model is W_{can}, the set of possible worlds of $\mathcal{A}_{can}$, and it is this set which we choose as our informationally minimal state. The following direct consequence of the Lindenbaum and Henkin Lemmas illustrates its suitability for this role in our theory:

FACT 3: For all sentences φ: $\mathcal{A}_{can}$, $W_{can} \models \varphi$ if, and only if, $\vdash \varphi$.

That is to say, the only sentences which are supported by W_{can} are the theorems, or alternatively, the valid sentences of our language. In other words this information state, for which we reserve the rather silly notation '☺' of section 7.2.3, supports no contingent sentences. It might be regarded as the state of information of an ideal agent who, though having perfect logical skills and infinite time on his hands, has no information whatsoever about what the world is actually like.

We can now summarize this section as follows: Assuming just the premises Γ of an argument is modeled as being in the information state ☺ $+\Gamma$ of $\mathcal{A}_{can}$.

7.4.2. Normalization

Having formally modeled the notion of assuming no more than the premises of an argument, we now turn to modeling normalization, the second part of the intuitive picture of reasonable inference given in section 7.2.3. First we will say what it is to assume that a single individual is normal in a single respect; then we will iterate this so as to model the notion of assuming individuals to be normal in a number of respects.

7.4.2.1. *Assuming One Individual to Be as Normal as Possible in One Respect*

Assuming a single individual to be as normal as possible in a single respect is modeled by adding to information models a *normalization function* $\underline{N}$, which takes an information state and a proposition and returns a state which is in general more informative. Intuitively, the idea is that $\underline{N}$(s,p) stands for the result of strengthening s by adding the assumption that where p holds, p holds along with that which, according to the information available in s, is normally the case where p holds. Provided, that is, that this assumption is consistent with s. Otherwise, if making this assumption is precluded by information already available in s, normalization should "fail," and $\underline{N}$(s,p) should just be s itself.

To see how such a function might be of use in formalizing defeasible reasoning with generic sentences, imagine, for example, an information state which contains only the information that birds normally can fly and that Tweety is a bird. The idea is that strengthening this state with the assumption that Tweety is a normal bird should return the information that Tweety can fly. Given an initial state which contains the additional information that Tweety cannot fly, on the other hand, it should not be possible to strengthen the state in this way. In this case it is not consistent with the initial state that Tweety can fly, and the attempt to assume Tweety to be a normal bird should fail. We now go on to define, for any information model $\mathcal{A}$ with its corresponding base model M and worlds-selection function *, a normalization function $\underline{N}$. In the rest of this section the subscript M has been dropped wherever possible, since this same model is intended everywhere.

What is normal and what is not in any given possible world is encoded in the behavior of * at that possible world. The normalization function must, however, utilize the—in general incomplete—information about normality which is carried by information states. So in defining normalization, we need to say how a state's information about what is normally the case where p holds reduces to the behavior of * at the individual possible worlds which make it up. The first step is to generalize * from individual possible worlds to information states:

DEFINITION 7: $*(s,p) := \bigcup_{w \in s} *(w,p)$.

By way of example, let p be the proposition $\|\varphi\delta\|$ expressed by $\varphi\delta$ in M. Then $p \backslash *(w,p)$ stands for the set of possible worlds in which, according to an isolated w, the individual δ is, though a φ, not a normal φ. So $p \backslash *(s,p)$ is the set of worlds where, according to *all* of the worlds in s, δ is an abnormal φ. Now, since the information in s is just everything which holds at each possible world of s, we take this set $p \backslash *(s,p)$ to be the set of worlds where, according to the information in s, δ is an abnormal φ. In order to strengthen s with the assumption that δ is not, according to the information in s, an abnormal φ, these worlds must be removed from s. This is what happens in the following definition:

DEFINITION 8: $\underline{N}(s,p) :=$ $s \backslash (p \backslash *(s,p))$, ... if $s \cap *(s,p) \neq \emptyset$;
s otherwise.

Note that where s already contains the information that p holds (that is, where $s \subseteq p$), this definition simplifies to the following: $\underline{N}(s,p) := s \cap *(s,p)$ provided this set is nonempty; otherwise, $\underline{N}(s,p) := s$.

The restriction in this definition to the case where $s \cap *(s,p) \neq \emptyset$, together with the clause which sets $\underline{N}(s,p)$ equal to s otherwise, has the effect that s is strengthened with the assumption that δ is not an abnormal φ only if this assumption is consistent with s; this is the case where s ∩ *(s,p) ≠ ∅. If this assumption cannot consistently be added to s—that is to say, if s already contains the information that δ is if at all a φ then an abnormal one—then the normalization function does nothing. Assuming δ to be a normal φ is hopeless in this case, so the normalization function "gives up" and simply returns the original state s.

7.4.3.2. *Assuming Individuals to Be Normal in Various Respects*

Consider Defeasible Modus Ponens, with as premises, say, *Birds normally can fly* and *Tweety is a bird*. The information state which assumes just (the formalizations of) these premises is then:

☺ + {∀x(bird(x) > can-fly(x)),bird(t)}

Now, bearing in mind the above discussion of the normalization function, in order to obtain from this an information state which supports the conclusion of the Defeasible Modus Ponens, *Tweety can fly,* we will clearly want to normalize with at least the proposition expressed by *Tweety is a bird,* represented formally here as ||bird(t)||. And it seems right, too, to normalize with this proposition, since *bird* refers to a kind about which the premises have something to say, and *Tweety* refers to an individual about which they have something to say.

Consider as a second example the argument form which we have called the Nixon Diamond, with the premises *Republicans are not pacifists, Quakers are normally pacifists, Dick is a Republican, Dick is a Quaker*. The information state which assumes just these premises is then:

+{∀x(**republican**(x) > ¬**pacifist**(x)), **republican**(**d**), ∀x(**quaker**(x) > **pacifist**(x)), **quaker**(**d**)}

With which propositions do we want to normalize this time around? There are two kinds about which these premises have something to say, Republican and Quaker, and just a single individual d. If we are to fix a normalization strategy on the pattern of the modus ponens, then it seems that we should normalize at least with the two propositions which can be formed from these components: ||republican(d)||, and ||quaker(d)||. That is, the normalization function should be *iterated,* normalizing the above information state first with one of these propositions and then with the other, thus giving rise to a "chain" of increasingly informative information states.

In which order should these propositions show up in the interated normalization? In view of the symmetry of the situation, the only reasonable thing to do is to iterate the normalization both ways, thus obtaining two chains of information states: the one iterated normalization taking first the proposition ||republican(d)|| and then the proposition ||quaker(d)||, the other taking them in the opposite order. Bearing in mind that from these premises we want to draw neither the conclusion pacifist(d) that Dick is a pacifist, nor the conclusion ¬pacifist(d) that Dick is not a pacifist, it is to be hoped that such iterated normalization turns out to be *order sensitive:* a chain in which we normalize first with ||republican(d)|| and then with ||quaker(d)|| should, after each of these normalizations is complete, contain only information states that support the sentence ¬pacifist(d). And a chain which normalizes these propositions in the opposite order should end up supporting pacifist(d). If normalization were to be order sensitive in this way, and if we accept as reasonable conclusions only those sentences which end up being supported whichever way normalization is carried out, then neither the conclusion pacifist(d) nor the conclusion ¬pacifist(d) would be drawn.

Concerning the choice of propositions with which to normalize information states there other possibilities too. For example, instead of choosing propositions for normalization on the basis of the premises of some argument one has in mind—which is the strategy suggested by the above—one might normalize information states using all of the propositions they support. Or even all propositions in the entire model. The definition of the propositions for normalization given below is just one such choice, preferred here because of its relative simplicity in illustrating the usefulness of the notion of normalization, and of our approach in general. Future work to be done on our theory will need to map out the different possibilities that are open here, and how they affect the formal properties of the notion of commonsense entailment.

Let Γ be any set of premises in whose defeasible consequences you are interested. For now, and generalizing from the informal discussion of the above paragraphs, we define the set P_Γ of *propositions for normalization* as follows: first, let Γ^* be the result of rewriting Γ in conjunctive normal form. Then P_Γ is the set of all propositions $\|\varphi(d)\|$, where d is an individual constant appearing in Γ^*, and $\varphi(x)$ is the antecedent of a "positive" occurrence of a universally quantified $>$ conditional in Γ^*.

It is worth writing out a few examples, just to get the feel of this notion. For example, let Γ be the premises of the Defeasible Modus Ponens: $\{\forall x(\varphi>\psi),\varphi(t)\}$. These premises are already in normal form. So P_Γ is the set $\{\|\varphi(t)\|\}$. And letting Γ be the premises of the Nixon Diamond, $\{\forall x(\varphi>\zeta),$ $\forall x(\psi>\neg\zeta),\ \varphi(t),\ \psi(t)\}$, P_Γ is the set $\{\|\varphi(t)\|,\ \|\psi(t)\|\}$.

The following definition now lays down precisely what it is to iteratively normalize an information state s using propositions in some set P.

Definition 9: For any set Γ of sentences, for any countable set P of propositions, and any enumeration ν: $P \rightarrow$ On, the *P-normalization chain* with respect to ν which begins from s is defined to be the following sequence of information states:

$s_\nu^0 = s$

$s_\nu^{\alpha+1} = \underline{N}(s_\nu^\alpha, p)$, where p is that proposition such that (for some limit ordinal λ or with $\lambda = 0$) $\lambda + \nu(p) = \alpha + 1$

$s_\nu^\lambda = \bigcap_{\mu \in \lambda} s_\nu^\mu$

That is, the P-normalization chain with respect to ν which begins from s is the sequence which has s as its first element, and where each state has a successor obtained by normalizing with whatever proposition ν says is next. At limit ordinals, we just take the intersection of all preceding states.

There is one such P-normalization chain for each state and each enumeration ν of P. Since (as is obvious from Definition 8) the normalization process monotonically depletes sets of possible worlds, standard techniques from set theory show that every P-normalization chain reaches a fixed point. That is, for each s and ν there is some ordinal α such that for all larger ordinals β: $s_\nu^\beta = s_\nu^\alpha$. The fixed point of a normalization chain C is denoted 'FIX(C)'.

Iterated normalization turns out to be order sensitive in exactly the way described above in connection with the Nixon Diamond. As we will see when we return to this example in section 7.4.4, different enumerations of the same set of propositions can give rise to different fixed points. Commonsense entailment as defined below cancels out the order sensitivity of normalization by requiring that a conclusion be drawn from a given set of premises only if it is supported by the fixed points of *all* normalization chains to which those premises give rise. According to commonsense entailment, then, it is the order sensitivity of the normalization process which is responsible for skepticism in the case of the Nixon Diamond.

7.4.3. Commonsense Entailment

Equipped with information states, ignorance, updating, and maximal normality, we are now in a position to put together our model of commonsense entailment:

Definition 10 (Commonsense Entailment): $\Gamma | \approx_P \varphi$ if, and only if, for any P-normalization chain C beginning from ☺ $+ \Gamma$:

$\mathcal{A}_{can}$, FIX(C) $\models \varphi$

Where the set P of propositions of normalization chosen is P_Γ (see section 7.4.2.2 above) we can drop the subscript and just write '$\Gamma|\approx \varphi$'. We will see in section 7.4.4 that '$|\approx$' is a defeasible consequence relation which generates the patterns of defeasible reasoning that we set out to capture. Also note that $\Gamma \models \varphi \Rightarrow \Gamma|\approx \varphi$; since '$\models$' is stronger than classical first-order logic, '$|\approx_P$' is too.

7.4.4. Patterns of Reasonable Inference Verified

In this section we return to the patterns of nonmonotonic reasoning introduced in section 7.2.2 and verify that commonsense entailment accounts for them. Before we do so, however, it should be noticed that these patterns are not to be thought of as completely general argument schemes, into which arbitrary generic sentences can be instantiated. The pattern of Defeasible Modus Ponens, for instance, may schematically be represented as follows: from premises $\forall x(\varphi > \psi)$ and $\varphi(t)$ follows $\psi(t)$. But this conclusion is supposed no longer to follow if the premise $\neg\psi(t)$ is added, which intuitively speaking amounts to adding the additional information that t, though a φ, is not a normal φ.

Now, the point is that we cannot expect commonsense entailment to behave like this for arbitrary predicates φ and ψ. For example, if φ and ψ are chosen as one and the same formula A(x), then on adding the premise $\neg A(t)$ we end up with the following premises: $\forall x(A(x) > A(x))$, $A(t)$, $\neg A(t)$. These premises contain A(t), and for this uninteresting reason this sentence will continue to follow (along with everything else, since the premises have become inconsistent). Similar comments apply to the other patterns of defeasible reasoning, and account for the restrictions on the formulas φ, ψ, and γ in the facts reported below.

7.4.4.1. *Defeasible Modus Ponens*

The following fact states conditions under which commonsense entailment captures the patterns of Defeasible Modus Ponens and Irrelevant Information, as discussed in section 7.2.2.

FACT 4:

(i) Let φ and ψ be monadic $L_>$ predicates and let Γ be a set of $L_>$ sentences. Let $(\Gamma \cup \{\forall x(\varphi > \psi), \varphi(t)\})^{\rightarrow}$ be $\vdash$ consistent, and let the set P of propositions of normalization be $\{\|\varphi(t)\|\}$. Then:
$\Gamma, \forall x(\varphi > \psi), \varphi(t) |\approx_P \psi(t)$.

(ii) Let $\Gamma \cup \{\forall x(\varphi > \psi), \varphi(t)\} \vdash \psi(t)$, and let the set P of propositions of normalization be $\{\|\varphi(t)\|\}$. Then:
$\Gamma, \forall x(\varphi > \psi), \varphi(t), \neg\psi(t) \not\approx_P \psi(t)$.

Before proving this fact, we give an example showing that this class of formulas for which Defeasible Modus Ponens holds is large enough to contain some interesting examples.

EXAMPLE: Consider the following informal argument: from *Healthy cats jump at small moving objects,* and *Charlemagne is a healthy cat,* follows, defeasibly, *Charlemagne jumps at small moving objects.* By way of example, this argument is formalized here as an instance of Defeasible Modus Ponens involving nested generic premises. And it is shown that in view of Fact 4(i), the Defeasible Modus Ponens does in fact go through.

First, we need to formalize the premises of the argument. We suppose that our formal language L contains the following distinct predicate and relation symbols, whose arities and intended interpretations are obvious from the discussion below: time, sick, object, event, small, moves-past, pounces-on. Using these symbols new predicates can be defined, by means of which the concepts occurring in this informal argument can be formalized. First, *healthy* is formalized as a monadic predicate satisfied by individuals which are normally not sick:

healthy(x) := ∀t(alive(x,t) > ¬sick(x,t))

The property of jumping at small moving objects is expressed by a predicate satisfied by individuals who, when passed in some event e by a small moving object o, normally pounce on it:

jumps-at-small-moving-objects(x) :=
∀o∀e((object(o) & event(e) & small(o,x) & moves-past(o,x,e))
> pounces-on(x,o,e))

The premises of the argument we are concerned with then come out as the following two nested generic sentences:

∀x(healthy(x) & cat(x) > jumps-at-small-moving-objects(x)),
healthy(Charlemagne) & cat(Charlemagne)

In order to show that the desired conclusion,

jumps-at-small-moving-objects(Charlemagne),

follows from these premises by commonsense entailment, it is sufficient, in view of Fact 4(i), to show that the following two sentences are ⊢ consistent with each other:

(∀x(∀t(alive(x,t) → ¬sick(x,t)) & cat(x))(∀o∀e((object(o) & event(e) & small(o,x) & moves-past(o,x,e)) → pounces-on(x,o,e))))

∀t(alive(Charlemagne,t) → ¬sick(Charlemagne,t)) & cat(Charlemagne)

In virtue of the soundness theorem, Theorem 1, it is sufficient for this purpose to find any base model M and possible world w relative to which both of these sentences are true. Remembering that only constraint on our worlds-selections functions is Facticity, and that alive, sick, and so on are all different predicate symbols, this is now a trivial task. Which completes the demonstration that

{∀x(healthy(x) & cat(x) > jumps-at-small-moving-objects(x)),
healthy(Charlemagne) & cat(Charlemagne)}
|≈ jumps-at-small-moving-objects(Charlemagne).

Having demonstrated the interest of Fact 4, we now prove it. In the proofs of this section the words-selection function of the canonical model and the propositions in it are written without identifying subscripts.

Proof of Fact 4(i)

LEMMA 3: Suppose $(\Gamma\cup\{\forall x(\varphi>\psi), \varphi(t)\})^{\rightarrow}$ is $\vdash$ consistent. Then there is $w \in W_{can}$:
(i) $w \in *(w,\|\varphi(t)\|)$; and
(ii) $\mathcal{A}_{can}, w \models \Gamma \cup \{\forall x(\varphi>\psi), \varphi(t)\}$.

Proof: Sufficient, in view of the Henkin lemma and Fact 1, is:

$\{\forall\vec{x}((\varphi(t)>\gamma)\rightarrow\gamma)$: $\gamma(\vec{x})$ is an $L_>$ formula$\} \cup \Gamma \cup\{\forall x(\varphi>\psi), \varphi(t)\}$ is $\vdash$ consistent.

In view of Fact 2, however, for this it is sufficient that

(a) $\{\forall\vec{x}((\varphi(t)>\gamma)\rightarrow\gamma)$: $\gamma(\vec{x})$ is an $L_>$ formula$\}^{\rightarrow} \cup (\Gamma\cup\{\forall x(\varphi>\psi), \varphi(t)\})^{\rightarrow}$ is $\vdash$ consistent.

Now for any formula γ, $\forall\vec{x}((\varphi(t)>\gamma)^{\rightarrow} = \forall\vec{x}((\varphi(t)^{\rightarrow}\rightarrow\gamma^{\rightarrow})\rightarrow\gamma^{\rightarrow})$. But this latter formula is $\vdash$ equivalent to $\forall\vec{x}(\varphi(t)^{\rightarrow}\vee\gamma^{\rightarrow})$, and is therefore a $\vdash$ consequence of $\varphi(t)^{\rightarrow}$. Since $\varphi(t)^{\rightarrow} \in (\Gamma\cup\{\forall x(\varphi>\psi), \varphi(t)\})^{\rightarrow}$,

$(\Gamma\cup\{\forall x(\varphi>\psi), \varphi(t)\})^{\rightarrow} \vdash \{\forall\vec{x}((\varphi(t)>\gamma)\rightarrow\gamma)$: $\gamma(\vec{x})$ is a formula $\}^{\rightarrow}$.

This reduces (a) to the condition of the lemma.□

The following kind of lemma shows up repeatedly when proving things about commensense entailment:

SURVIVAL LEMMA 4: Let f be the fixed point of the (unique) $\{\|\varphi(t)\|\}$ normalization chain which starts from ☺ $+\Gamma\cup\{\forall x(\varphi>\psi), \varphi(t)\}$.
And let w be the possible world provided by Lemma 3. Then we have $w \in f$.

Proof: The proof is by induction on the normalization chain. The base step, $w \in$ ☺ $+ \Gamma\cup\{\forall x(\varphi>\psi), \varphi(t)\}$, follows from Lemma 3(ii).
For the induction step, the only interesting case is that of successor ordinals. So let

s be any information state of the chain, and suppose as induction hypothesis that $w \in s$. Since there is just the single propositon $\|\varphi(t)\|$ of normalization, the next state in the chain is $\underline{N}(s,\|\varphi(t)\|)$; we need to show that w survives normalization into this set. Now since

$$s \subseteq ☺ + \Gamma \cup \{\forall x(\varphi > \psi), \varphi(t)\} \subseteq \|\varphi(t)\|,$$

by the comment after Definition 8 we have $\underline{N}(s,\|\varphi(t)\|) = s \cap {*}(s,\|\varphi(t)\|)$, provided this set is nonempty. It is indeed nonempty, since by the induction hypothesis and Lemma 3(i), $w \in s \cap {*}(s,\|\varphi(t)\|)$. Thus, as required,

$$w \in \underline{N}(s,\|\varphi(t)\|).$$

This completes the proof that $w \in f$.□

To finish the proof of Fact 4(i), it is now sufficient to prove, using the Survival Lemma 4, that $\mathcal{A}_{can}, f \models \psi(t)$. Once again, let w be the possible world provided by Lemma 3, and let f be the unique fixed point of normalization. Reasoning as in the induction step above, since $f \subseteq \|\varphi(t)\|$ and, by the survival lemma, $w \in f$: $\underline{N}(f,\|\varphi(t)\|) = f \cap {*}(f,\|\varphi(t)\|)$.

Furthermore, since $f \subseteq ☺ + \Gamma \cup \{\forall x(\varphi > \psi), \varphi(t)\} \subseteq \|\forall x(\varphi > \psi)\|$, we have, by the truth conditions for $>$:

$${*}(f, \|\varphi(t)\|) \subseteq \|\psi(t)\|.$$

Combining this with the above, and with the fact that f is a fixed point of normalization:

$$f = \underline{N}(f,\|\varphi(t)\|) \subseteq \|\psi(t)\|$$

In other words, and as required, $\mathcal{A}_{can}, f \models \psi(t)$.

This completes the proof of Fact 4(i).□

It should be noticed that the Survival Lemma 4 also shows that common-sense entailment is consistent, under the condition of Fact 4(i).

Proof of Fact 4(ii). Assuming the condition, choose any $w \in W_{can}$ such that

$$\mathcal{A}_{can}, w \models \Gamma, \forall x(\varphi > \psi), \varphi(t), \neg\psi(t).$$

Let f be the fixed point of the (unique) $\{\varphi(t)\}$ normalization chain which starts from the set X:

$$☺ + \Gamma \cup \{\forall x(\varphi > \psi), \varphi(t), \neg\psi(t)\}.$$

It is sufficient to show that $f = X$; normalization never changes the initial starting point. The proof is by induction on this chain. Of the induction, the only interesting case is that for successor ordinals; so let s be an information state anywhere along this normalization chain, and suppose by way of induction hypothesis that s = X. It is sufficient to show that X = $\underline{N}$(s,‖φ(t)‖). To this end, note first that since s ⊆ ☺+ Γ∪{∀x(φ>ψ), φ(t), ¬ψ(t)}, both

(a) s ⊆ ‖¬ψ(t)‖, and
(b) s ⊆ ‖∀x(φ>ψ)‖,

so by the truth definition for >, *(s,‖φ(t)‖) ⊆ ‖ψ(t)‖. Because of (a) and (b), s∩*(s,‖φ(t)‖) = ∅, so by Definition 8, s = $\underline{N}$(s,‖φ(t)‖) = X.

This completes the inductive proof that f = X, and with it the proof of Fact 4(ii).□

Note that again, the proof also provides the consistency of commonsense entailment, as applied to the premises in question.

7.4.4.2. *Nixon Diamond*

The following fact states a condition under which commonsense entailment is suitably skeptical when applied to premises patterned on the Nixon Diamond.

FACT 5: Let φ, ψ, and γ be monadic, >-free predicates such that neither
φ(t), ψ(t), ∀x(φ>γ), ∀x(ψ>¬γ) ⊢ γ(t), nor
φ(t), ψ(t), ∀x(φ>γ), ∀x(ψ>¬γ) ⊢ ¬γ(t).
And let the set *P* of propositions of normalization be {‖φ(t)‖, ‖ψ(t)‖}.
Then neither
∀x(φ>γ), ∀x(ψ>¬γ), φ(t), ψ(t) $|\approx_P$ γ(t), nor
∀x(φ>γ), ∀x(ψ>¬γ), φ(t), ψ(t) $|\approx_P$ ¬γ(t).

Proof of Fact 5. The proof combines elements of both parts of Fact 4. First, note that the following lemma is easily proved:

LEMMA 5: Assume the conditions of Fact 5. Then there are v,w ∈ W_{can} such that
(i) v ∈ *(v,‖φ(t)‖); w ∈ *(w,‖ψ(t)‖), and
(ii) $\mathcal{A}_{can}$, v ⊢ ∀x(φ>γ), ∀x(ψ>¬γ), φ(t), ψ(t), γ(t);
$\mathcal{A}_{can}$, w ⊨ ∀x(φ>γ), ∀x(ψ>¬γ), φ(t), ψ(t), ¬γ(t).

Proof: We just show the existence of the possible world v, since w can be shown in exactly the same way. Sufficient, in view of Fact 1, is that the following set is ⊢ consistent:

{$\forall\vec{x}$((φ(t)>ζ)→ζ): ζ($\vec{x}$) is an $L_>$ formula} ∪ φ(t), ψ(t), ∀x(φ>γ), ∀x(ψ>¬γ), γ(t)}

In view of the Theorem 1, it is sufficient to find a base model and possible world relative to which this set is true. Define the frame ⟨W,D,*⟩ with W = {v,w}; D = {t}; while for each world x ∈ W: *(x,{v}) = {v}; and *(x,{w}) = *(x,{v,w}) = {w}. Now we turn this frame into a model, M, choosing ⟦⟧ such that t is interpreted as itself and φ, ψ, and γ are interpreted in accordance with this picture. (This can be done since these predicates have been assumed to be >-free.)

v	w
●	●
φ(t)	¬φ(t)
ψ(t)	ψ(t)
γ(t)	¬γ(t)

Now: M,v $\models$ {$\forall\vec{x}((\varphi(t)>\zeta)\rightarrow\zeta)$: $\zeta(\vec{x})$ is an $L_>$ formula} ∪ {φ(t), ψ(t), ∀x(φ>γ), ∀x(ψ>¬γ), γ(t)}.□

We now show that under the conditions of Fact 5, neither

$$\forall x(\varphi>\gamma),\ \forall x(\psi>\neg\gamma),\ \varphi(t),\ \psi(t)\ |{\approx}_P\gamma(t),\ \text{nor}$$
$$\forall x(\varphi>\gamma),\ \forall x(\psi>\neg\gamma),\ \varphi(t),\ \psi(t)\ |{\approx}_P\neg\gamma(t).$$

To this end, it is sufficient, letting v and w be provided by Lemma 5, to find two *P*-normalization chains C and D, both starting from

☺ + {∀x(φ>γ), ∀x(ψ>¬γ), φ(t), ψ(t)},

such that v ∈ FIX (C) and w ∈ FIX (D). Here we just obtain the fixed point C, since D is obtained analogously.

Let C be any *P*-normalization chain starting from

s := $\underline{\text{N}}$(☺ + {∀x(φ>γ), ∀x(ψ>¬γ), φ(t), ψ(t) |φ(t)‖).

We now show by induction that v ∈ FIX (C). The base step, v ∈ s, follows by choice of v, Lemma 5, and Definition 8. The only interesting case of the induction step is that involving successor ordinals; so let t be any information state anywhere along C, and suppose as induction hypothesis that v ∈ t. Since C is a {‖φ(t)‖, ‖ψ(t)‖} normalization chain, the next normalization in the chain must involve a proposition from this set, so it is sufficient if we now can show that v ∈ $\underline{\text{N}}$(t,p), where p ∈ {‖φ(t)‖, ‖ψ(t)‖}.

(a) v ∈ $\underline{\text{N}}$(t,‖φ(t)‖). Since t ⊆ s ⊆ ‖φ(t)‖, by the comment after Definition 8 we have $\underline{\text{N}}$(t,‖φ(t)‖) = t∩*(t,‖φ(t)‖), provided this set is nonempty. It is indeed nonempty, since by the induction hypothesis and Lemma 5(i): v ∈ t∩*(t,‖φ(t)‖). Thus, as required, v ∈ $\underline{\text{N}}$(v,‖φ(t)‖).

(b) $v \in \underline{N}(t,\|\psi(t)\|)$. Again,

(i) $t \subseteq s \subseteq \|\gamma(t)\|$.

Since $t \subseteq s \subseteq \|\forall x(\psi > \neg\gamma)\|$, as above, and with the truth definition of 'v', we also have

(ii) $*(t, \|\psi(t)\|) \subseteq \|\neg\gamma(t)\|$.

(i) and (ii) together give us $t \cap *(t, \|\psi(t)\|) = \emptyset$, so by induction hypothesis and Definition 8, $v \in t = \underline{N}(t,\|\psi(t)\|)$.

This completes the inductive proof that $v \in$ FIX (C), and with it the proof of Fact 5.□

7.5. Extensions of the Basic Theory

We have now presented the main ideas and hope to have made clear that they go a long way toward explaining some interesting facts about the generics in natural language: that generics tolerate exceptions, that they can be nested one within the other, and that in spite of having an almost completely trivial logic they are not void of content, in that they enable us to jump to defeasible conclusions in reasonable ways. Of the valid patterns of argument forms discussed in section 7.2, we have shown the theory to capture Weakening of the Consequent. And we have shown that all of the defeasible patterns that we have mentioned hold, at least within nontrivial fragments of that part of the language within which they can at all be expected to hold.

In this section, we go on to consider some ways in which this basic theory could be elaborated so as to account for additional patterns of reasoning, both valid and defeasible ones. Along the way, we will be pointing out some of the problems on which we will be working in the future. First, we turn to ways in which the logic of generics can be strengthened.

7.5.1. Strengthening the Logic of Generics

One of the things about possible-worlds theories is that they are in a sense modular. Constraints of various kinds can be placed on modal frames independently of one another, thus giving rise to whole families of related entailment notions. Often these constraints are expressed by axioms, similarly independent of each other. In this way, and parallel to the entailment notions, whole families of related axiom systems may originate.

In section 7.2, a pattern of argument was presented—Dudley Doorite—which has been considered valid, but which so far is not validated by our semantics. In this section we validate this argument by introducing an additional modal constraint, along with the axiom scheme that expresses it.

As already mentioned in section 7.3.2, Dudley Doorite is validated if the following constraint is placed on our modal frames:

DUDLEY DOORITE CONSTRAINTS: $*(w,p \cup q) \subseteq *(w,p) \cup *(w,q)$

This constraint is expressed by the following axiom scheme:

$$\varphi > \zeta \ \& \ \psi > \zeta \rightarrow (\varphi \vee \psi) > \zeta$$

If this axiom is added to the system of section 7.3.3, the canonical model construction of Theorem 1 can be modified so as to show that we have a complete characterization of the logic of frames which satisfy Facticity and the above constraint. For details see Morreau 1992a.

The following easily verified lemma shows that such frames exist:

LEMMA 6:

(a) Let W be any nonempty set of possible worlds, and let D be any nonempty set of individuals. Define * to be such that for each $w \in W$ and each $p \subseteq W$, $*(w,p) = p$. then $\langle W,D,*\rangle$ is an $L_>$ frame which satisfies Facticity and the Dudley Doorite Constraint.

(b) Let $\langle W,D,*\rangle$ be a $L_>$ frame which satisifies Facticity and the Dudley Doorite Constraint, and let $V \subseteq W$. Define a new worlds-selection function $*'$ such that for each $w \in W$ and each $p \subseteq W$, $*'(w,p) = *(w,p) \cap V$. Then $\langle W,D,*'\rangle$ is an $L_>$ frame which satisfied Facticity and the Dudley Doorite Constraint.

That this extra constraint and axiom scheme validate the Dudley Doorite argument form of section 7.2 is apparent from the fact that with them, the following scheme is valid and can be derived without premises:

$$\forall x(\varphi > \zeta), \ \& \ \forall x(\psi > \zeta) \rightarrow \forall x((\varphi \vee \psi) > \zeta)$$

With modus ponens, this amounts to the formalization in $L_>$ of Dudley Doorite:

$$\frac{\begin{array}{l}\forall x(\varphi > \zeta)\\ \forall x(\psi > \zeta)\end{array}}{\forall x((\varphi \vee \psi) > \zeta)}$$

This answers the standard questions about how to validate Dudley Doorite in a possible-worlds semantics for generic sentences. But since we are more interested in defeasible reasoning with generics than in their logic, questions still remain to be asked.

The proofs given above of the Defeasible Modus Ponens and the Nixon Diamond involved proving the existence, in the canonical model, of possible worlds with particular structural properties; compare, for example, the essential Lemma 3 in the proof of the Defeasible Modus Ponens, and Lemma 5 in the proof of the Nixon Diamond. After adding a new constraint like the Dudley Doorite Constraint, it must be checked whether these lemmas can still be proved, if we are not to lose all of our defeasible reasoning. In fact, as can easily be checked, the model constructions of the two lemmas both satisfy the new constraint, so that the proofs remain valid.

7.5.2. More Specific Information Takes Precedence: The Penguin Principle

The idea that information about subkinds should take precedence over information about the kinds which subsume them is illustrated in the following argument:

PENGUIN PRINCIPLE

Birds fly.
Penguins do not fly.
Penguins are birds.
Tweety is a penguin.
―――――――――――――
Tweety does not fly.

That penguins do not fly is what might be called a defeasible fact about penguins; there can be exceptions. That penguins are birds, on the other hand, is a taxonomical fact to which there are no exceptions. It is interesting that swapping such a taxonomical fact for a weaker defeasible fact does not much change intuitions about the Penguin Principle:

WEAK PENGUIN PRINCIPLE

Adults are employed.
Students are not employed.
Students are adults.
Sam is a student.
―――――――――――――
Sam is not employed.

The cut-down version of commonsense entailment which we have presented in Section 7.4 does not produce either of these patterns of reasoning. Morreau (1992a) shows that by adding the Dudley Doorite scheme we surprisingly obtain the Penguin Principle. To get the Weak Penguin Principle we must either "prioritize" normalization[6] or, we conjecture, adopt a modal constraint proposed in Asher and Morreau 1991.

SPECIFICITY: If $*(w,p) \subseteq q$, $*(w,p) \cap *(w,q) = \emptyset$, and $*(w,p) \neq \emptyset$, then $*(w,q) \cap p = \emptyset$.

The hope is that after adding the scheme

$$(\varphi > \psi \ \& \ \psi > \zeta \ \& \ \varphi > \neg\zeta) \rightarrow \psi > \neg\varphi$$

to the axioms of section 7.3.3, a canonical model construction like that used earlier can be repeated; if it can, then this constraint should obtain the Weak Penguin Principle. Whether the other results stated above can then still be proved we do not know.

7.5.3. Defeasible Generic Conclusions

Consider the following defeasible argument forms:

DEFEASIBLE TRANSITIVITY

Birds fly.	Slow eaters enjoy their food.
Sparrows are birds.	Those disgusted by their food are slow eaters.
Sparrows fly.	Those disgusted by their food do not enjoy.*
	Those disgusted by their food enjoy it.

DEFEASIBLE STRENGTHENING OF THE ANTECEDENT

Birds fly.	Birds fly.
White birds fly.	Dead birds do not fly.*
	Dead birds fly.

The important feature of these examples is that they involve inferences from generic premises not to particular conclusions, but to generic conclusions. We think that generic conclusions, too, may be among the things rendered more plausible by assuming the normal case. We suggested in Asher & Morreau 1991 that by complicating the normalization function of Definition 8, we might capture such defeasible reasoning toward generic conclusions; the idea was to

6. The idea in prioritized normalization is that in defining iterated normalization chains, we should not be looking at sets of propositions of normalization, but instead at partially ordered sets, $(P, <)$. Intuitively speaking, in the case of premises like the above, we want to be normalizing with the proposition that *Sam is a student* before we normalize with the proposition that *Sam is an adult*. Technically, adding a partial order to the propositions of normalization enables us to exclude those chains where two propositions $p \in P$ and $q \in P$ show up for the first time in the normalization chain in the wrong order. Commonsense entailment may then be redefined as follows, with the subscript '$(P, <)$' instead of just 'P'.

$\Gamma \mid\!\approx_{(P,<)} \varphi$ if, and only if, for any P-normalization chain C which starts from ☺ + Γ and which respects $<$: $\mathcal{A}_{can}$, FIX(C) $\models \varphi$.

add an extra clause which removes possible worlds from information states on the basis of the behavior of '*' at those worlds. So in the case of Defeasible Transitivity, for example, possible worlds would be removed where it does not hold that sparrows fly. This idea, however, led to considerable technical complications, which we did not see our way fully through. Morreau (1993) gives an account of genericity and nonmonotonic reasoning that is based on exactly the same semantics for conditions as we have used here, but in which the technical machinery of defeasible reasoning is much simpler; there, Defeasible Transitivity and Strengthening of the Antecedent can be obtained quite easily. We think it should be possible to have them in an extension of the semantics of section 7.4, too.

7.5.4. Is Normality a Matter of Degree?

Finally, there are intuitively reasonable arguments which would seem to indicate that normality is not an absolute matter but comes in different degrees. Carlson gives the following example:

> Let us look a bit closer at the proposed analysis of "Dogs are mammals." It would say that all normal dogs are mammals. But what if there is something quite abnormal about Fido (e.g., she has two heads, or three legs)? It seems that we would still wish to be able to conclude that Fido is a mammal from the knowledge given above. (Carlson 1977b, 55–56)

We cannot imagine that anyone would propose such an analysis for *Dogs are mammals*. This sentence expresses a strict taxonomic fact, and provided this isn't forgotten when giving the formal analysis of this sentence, the conclusion *Fido is a mammal* will indeed follow in commonsense entailment upon learning that the animal has any combination of heads and legs, since it is a logical consequence of these premises.

A more interesting argument pattern which Carlson seems to be getting at, however, can be illustrated as follows:

GRADED NORMALITY

Dogs are normally hairy.
Dogs normally have four legs.
Fido has three legs.
———————————
Fido is hairy.

And, as Carlson anticipated, this pattern is not captured by the theory we have presented here. We think that the basic ideas could be elaborated in such a way as to capture it, though. We call this pattern Graded Normality since our strategy of assuming individuals to be normal could be expected to give rise to such reasoning if normality were not an absolute matter, as it is assumed to be in this chapter, but were to come in degrees instead. The idea is that on the basis of the premises of the above argument, dogs which are both mammals and four-legged would be more normal than dogs which are mammals but do not have four legs (or those which have four legs but are not mammals), which would in turn be more normal than individuals which lack both of the properties attributed to normal dogs, neither being mammals nor having four legs. The premises of the above argument exclude the possibility that Fido is a completely normal dog. But they do not exclude the possibility that Fido is a halfway normal dog; some mechanism for assuming maximal normality could thus be expected to give rise to the conclusion that Fido is a mammal.

Carlson considers patterns of reasoning such as the above to be foreign to the idea that generic sentences quantify universally over normal individuals; in fact, he brings the whole matter up as a criticism of this approach to the semantics of generics. We have made an effort to explore the idea sketched above of making normality a matter of degree. We have found that it introduces considerable complexities, but we are investigating a semantics to deal with this issue.

7.6. Conclusions and Comparisons with Other Work

In this chapter we have presented a modal theory of nonmonotonic reasoning that represents generic sentences as universally quantified, normative counterfactuals. In our theory, *Birds normally can fly* means, essentially, that every individual would be able to fly if it were to have all of the properties that normally go with being a bird.

After showing how such sentences can be given truth values in possible-worlds structures, and how they can be nested within other contexts that have been analyzed within this framework (such as modal contexts, belief, counterfactuals, and so on), we showed in detail how they give rise to patterns of nonmonotonic reasoning familiar from the artificial intelligence literature. These patterns we take to be an important test for theories of genericity, since a large part of the significance of generic information is the contribution it makes to intelligent guessing, planning, and decision making. The entire development is model theoretic, and for this reason lends considerable intuitive force to the notion of commonsense entailment which is defined here.

Of the various theories of nonmonotonic reasoning present in the artificial intelligence literature, John McCarthy's (1980) theory of *minimal entailment,* and its syntactic counterpart in *circumscription,* provide the most interesting comparison. For while commonsense entailment shares much of the intuitive motivation of minimal entailment, there are some very instructive differences too. Before discussing them, we briefly sketch the outlines of the treatment of generic information within minimal entailment; for a fuller presentation, there is nothing better than McCarthy's original article and Lifschitz's (1986) technical developments.

In minimal entailment, generic sentences of the kind which interest us are also represented as universally quantified conditionals, but entirely within classical logic. *Birds normally can fly,* for example, can be represented as follows:

$$\forall x((\text{bird}(x)\ \&\ \neg\mathbf{Ab}(x)) \rightarrow \text{fly}(x))$$

Here the monadic first-order predicate **Ab** expresses abnormality: an individual falls within its extension just in case it is, intuitively speaking, an abnormal bird. A more sophisticated representation of generic sentences in minimal entailment distinguishes different "respects" in which things can be abnormal. These different respects are treated as abstract objects, allowing the notion of "abnormality in some respect" to be formalized as a relation between these abstract objects and the individuals of whatever kind one is interested in. So **Ab** becomes a binary relation instead of the above monadic predicate, and *Birds normally fly* is represented as follows:

$$\forall x((\text{bird}(x) \wedge \neg\mathbf{Ab}(\text{repect-of-flying},\ x)),\ \rightarrow \text{fly}(x))$$

Obviously minimal entailment draws on informal ideas about what generic sentences mean which are related to ours, but there is also an important difference. The above representations are extensional, and don't enable statements about kinds to be sufficiently independent of what happens to be going on in the world. There are, to take a trivial example, no longer any dinosaurs. For this reason, according to the above representation it is true that *dinosaurs lay eggs,* that *dinosaurs can fly,* that *dinosaurs cannot fly,* and so on. Dinosaurs turn out to have any property you like. This mismatch between the generics of natural language and their representations in Minimal Entailment is not going to worry those in the artificial intelligence field of 'knowledge representation' very much. And it probably shouldn't, either. They are not in the business of theorizing about natural language, and are free to borrow as much genericity from natural language, or as little, as suits them. The mismatch should be noticed by semanticists, though, and it is avoided in the intensional representations of commonsense entailment.

The ways in which nonmonotonicity arises in the two theories are once again intuitively very closely related, but with important differences in technical realization. In minimal entailment, the idea of assuming maximal normality is modeled by restricting attention to a subclass of the models of one's premises, namely those models where **Ab** has a set-theoretically minimal extension. That is, to make a first pass, attention is restricted to models of the premises in which the extension of **Ab** cannot be reduced without losing the truth of the premises. There turn out to be too many of these models, however, so in order to capture patterns of reasoning like the Defeasible Modus Ponens, the class of preferred models is further restricted: one takes into account only those models of the premises in which the extension of **Ab** cannot be reduced without losing the premises, even if the extensions of some designated set of other predicates, the so-called variables, are allowed to vary arbitrarily. Minimal entailment has nothing to say about which predicates must be allowed to vary in order to get which nonmonotonic patterns to come out right. In this sense it is incomplete: one cannot say which conclusions follow from which premises until one has fixed a "minimization strategy," stating which predicates are to be minimized, and in which order, and stating which other predicates are to be allowed to vary, and at which stages in the iterated minimization.

This brings us to a second difference between minimal entailment and commonsense entailment. With a little exaggeration it can be said that commonsense entailment doesn't need to be steered from outside toward the right conclusions in anything like the way that minimal entailment does. If the propositions for normalization are derived from the premises of an argument in the way described in section 7.4.2.2, and if the precedence of more specific information as expressed in our Penguin Principle is accounted for by means of a modal constraint on frames, which is the second alternative described in section 7.5.2, then there are no parameters whatsoever on the turnstile of commonsense entailment. But in minimal entailment priority orders have to be settled, it has to be decided which predicates will be allowed to vary, and so on. Whereas minimal entailment needs a ghost to steer the formalism, with commonsense entailment the right patterns of reasoning seem to fall naturally out of the definitions.

A third important difference between commonsense entailment and minimal entailment is that only the latter comes with anything like a familiar, well-investigated proof theory. McCarthy's (1980) notion of circumscription, which has its origins in the induction scheme of Peano arithmetic, soundly and completely characterizes minimal entailment in a largish and useful fragment of first-order logic, the boundaries of which have been explored by Lifschitz in a series of papers (see, e.g., Lifschitz 1986). Asher (1993) furnishes a sound and complete proof theory for a propositional version of commonsense entailment, but a proof theory for the first-order theory remains very much a topic of current research.

Besides minimal entailment, the other main points of comparison are Reiter's (1980) theory of *default logic* and its close relative, Veltman's (1994) theory of *defaults in update semantics* referred to in section 7.2.1. There are strong reasons to believe that commonsense entailment and minimal entailment on the one hand, and these two theories are on the other, represent two quite essentially different kinds of nonmonotonic reasoning. In section 7.2.1 we mentioned some differences arising from the fact that the representations of generic sentences have a truth-conditional semantics in theories of the first kind, but not in those of the second kind. As a result, the latter are not in position to deal with nested generic sentences. But this difference seems to be a sign of a much deeper difference in conception of what nonmonotonic reasoning is about. In commonsense and minimal entailment, the intuitions are essentially semantic, for example. Generic sentences are taken to be about normal or prototypical individuals, and nonmonotonicity arises where individuals are assumed to be as normal as is compatible with available information. In default logic and in update semantics, on the other hand, the intuitions are essentially syntactic: default rules are mere rules of inference, and nonmonotonicity arises from applying as many of the rules as one can without running into inconsistencies. Morreau (1992b) argues that the differences between these two conceptions of nonmonotonic reasoning run much deeper than meets the eye.

ACKNOWLEDGMENTS

We would like to thank Greg Carlson, Jeff Horty, Dick de Jongh, Hans Kamp, Bob Stalnaker, Rich Thomason, and Frank Veltman for helpful conversations.

8 SEMANTIC CONSTRAINTS ON TYPE-SHIFTING ANAPHORA

Alice ter Meulen

8.1. Introduction

This section introduces some background necessary for the study of type-shifted anaphora, that is, pronouns bound by an antecedent of a different semantic type. The reader familiar with the state of the art in the semantic research on type-shifting in logics with limited types, and the dynamic theories of anaphora, is advised to skip this section and start reading section 8.2, which is concerned with generic information and anaphora.

8.1.1. Three Uses of Definite Descriptions

It is a well-known semantic fact that singular definite descriptions can be used either to refer to an individual or to predicate properties to a given referent. For instance, in (1a) the definite description is referentially used, but in (1b) it is predicatively used.[1]

(1) a. The president is getting old.
b. The president of the club is John.

Partee (1987) argues that there is a third use of definite descriptions, which lacks the existential presupposition characteristic of the referential use and yet seems to share some semantic properties with referential NPs. An example of such a third way of using definite descriptions, which is often called the functional use, is given in (2).

(2) The president is elected every four years.

1. See Doron 1988 for an excellent discussion of the many ways in which definite descriptions may be used to contribute information, and how Situation Semantics accounts for such differences. See also ter Meulen 1987 for some very similar issues, and Janssen 1984, which contains some illuminating discussion of functional NPs as denoting individual concepts (functions from possible worlds to individuals) in a Montague grammar. The well-known problems of logical equivalence in possible-worlds semantics keep me from adopting such an intensional solution. For example, although we can well imagine that the chair of a certain department is by necessity, due to departmental regulations, the chair of its budget committee (and hence both NPs denote identical functions), the former but not the latter may be appointed every four years.

The sentence in (2) expresses that within each period of four years there is one presidential election; it does not presuppose that there is a current president, as (2) is informative even when the institution to be presided over is not yet established. The claim that the functional use is, despite its lack of existential presupposition, referential—even rigidly so—is supported by the facts in (3).

(3) a. John thinks the president is powerful, but Mary thinks the president/he is just a media puppet.
b. His wife provides the president with unpaid advice.
c. Everybody loves the president, no matter what he looks like.

Although each of the sentences in (3) can be interpreted to be about an individual who holds the office of president, they can also be interpreted functionally, as stating relations between properties that are predicated of the function or the role of being president. In the latter interpretation, (3a) shows that two occurrences of the same functionally used NP embedded in an intensional context, or a pronoun and the functionally used NP it follows, refer to the same role; (3b) shows that such functional uses admit backwards anaphora, and (3c) that they are independent of quantificational NPs.

Yet functionally used definite descriptions admit of a form of unselective binding by adverbials as in (4), which is generally assumed to be characteristic of indefinite NPs.

(4) Every time the president reads the State of the Union he reviews the national economy.

In (4) the reading and reviewing must be actions of individuals serving as president, and each occurrence of a president's reading the State of the Union is an antecedent for the occurrence of his reviewing of the economy. Hence the dependency in (4) cannot be interpreted as one between an NP referring to the role and a coreferential pronoun.[2]

These semantic properties seem characteristic of functionally used definite NPs; on the one hand these NPs behave as proper names, referring rigidly to a role or a function; on the other hand they act in some respects as indefinite singulars which can be bound by quantifiers. This chapter attempts to account for this dual character of functionally used NPs within a more general theory of generic information and type-shifting processes between antecedents and

2. A similar claim can be made about the interpretation of the NP *the State of the Union* in (4), but I will ignore the interactions resulting in various distinct possible interpretations here.

anaphora. An interesting connection will be shown to exist between the three uses of definite descriptions and NPs in generic statements.

8.1.2. Typed Denotational Domains

In Partee 1987 the three uses of definite descriptions are related to three denotational domains in Montague grammar, distinguished by their type.[3] Referentially used NPs are interpreted in the domain of individuals, which are of type *e*. Predicatively used ones denote properties, or *propositional functions,* which are of type $\langle e,t \rangle$, encoding the fact that they require satisfaction by an individual to determine a truth value. Functionally used definite descriptions are interpreted as generalized quantifiers of type $\langle\langle e,t \rangle,t \rangle$.

Partee is primarily concerned with the semantic operations between these three domains in Montague Grammar, which change the type of an object in any of the three domains into the type of another domain. Figure 8.1, from Partee 1987 (p. 121), visualizes these type-shifting operations (dotted lines indicate the partial operations).

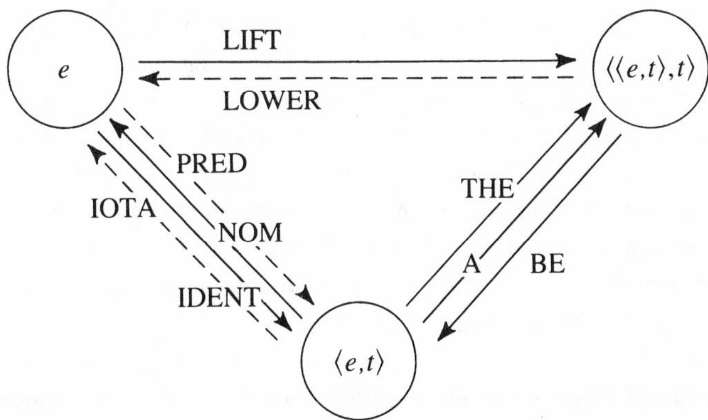

FIGURE 8.1. Three denotational domains (from Partee 1987)

LIFT is the mapping of any entity to the set of all its properties, which is called the *principal ultrafilter* generated by that entity. LOWER is the inverse of LIFT, mapping a principal ultrafilter back to its generator, but this is only

3. Chierchia (1985, 429) points out that this Three Layer Hypothesis, which claims that the intensional logic for natural language semantics need not be based on more than just these three denotational domains Partee recognizes, as well as reference-points, may have a historical precursor in Jespersen 1924, where syntactic categories are grouped into three classes: 'primary'—NP-like entities, 'secondary'—predicates, and 'tertiary'—everything else.

defined for the $\langle\langle e,t\rangle,t\rangle$ objects which are such principal ultrafilters (and there are many that are not, e.g., quantificational or indefinite singular and plural NPs). THE and A, and in fact any determiner, make a property into a generalized quantifier, and BE is Montague's ingenious trick to treat the verb *be* as copula and in identities on a par, by reducing the generalized quantifier type to a predicative property. Note that this operation does not carry any presuppositions and hence is defined for any NP interpreted as generalized quantifier. The two operations from *e* to $\langle e,t\rangle$ are, respectively, the identity function of being identical to the given individual and the extensional version of Chierchia's predication operation, which applies only to entities denoted by nominalized predicates. The two operations from properties to entities are, respectively, NOM, which is an extensional counterpart of Chierchia's nominalization operator mapping any property—except for the viciously self-referential properties that create liar-paradoxes—to its nominalization, and the IOTA-abstraction, which gives for each property the unique entity that has it, if there is just one, but which is undefined for properties that have sets larger than a singleton as extension.[4] Below I will call an entity which is the value of IOTA(P) the *actor* of P; for example, IOTA(president) is the unique individual who is president at the time of evaluation, assuming that context constrains the parameters sufficiently to obtain uniqueness. The reader interested in more details and in the interaction between various type-shifting operators should read Partee's paper and Chierchia's publications, as it is beyond the scope of my current concerns to discuss these issues any further here. These fundamental type-shifting operations on the three denotational domains will come to play an important role in analyzing the constraints on dependencies between antecedents and anaphora in the sections below.

Chierchia (1982a, 1984, 1985) gives these three domains as the only possible denotational types within his intensional logic, which is in addition based on a partially ordered set of times and a set of possible worlds. Properties are not just one-place $\langle e,t\rangle$-type propositional functions, but are generalized to n-place relations, and 0-place properties are propositions. A logic thus restricted does not contain any variable-binding mechanisms for $\langle\langle e,t\rangle,\langle e,t\rangle\rangle$ objects, and hence predicts that determiners, propositions, and adverbials will not be able to function as antecedents for anaphora in natural language. Chierchia calls this predication the *Functor Anaphora Constraint.* We will see that this prediction is supported by the type-shifting anaphora studied here, but that NOM, when used to obtain an anaphoric dependency, needs to be constrained

4. Technically, the interpretation of NOM(P) is the value assigned to P by the mapping *f* from the set of all n-place relations into the domain of individuals.

in its domain of application. Furthermore, I will argue for the existence of a fourth denotational domain—the domain of kinds—and define a number of semantic type-shifting operations between it and the three domains in figure 8.1. Although reference to kinds resembles reference to ordinary individuals in some important respects, some useful explanatory tools are gained when the domains of kinds and individuals are separated.

8.1.3. Dynamic Theories of Anaphora

Although this chapter is not the appropriate place to introduce all the concepts and methods of the recently developed dynamic theories of meaning and interpretation of natural language—some of them were presented in chapter 1—I will outline in this section, briefly and rather informally, what core ideas are common to the various approaches, in as much as they will come to play a role in this study of type-shifting in anaphora. More comprehensive introductions to Discourse Representation Theory (DRT), File Change Semantics, and Situation Semantics (SS) can be found, respectively, in Kamp 1981, Heim 1982, and Barwise & Perry 1983, Barwise 1987. A comparison of DRT and SS is presented in Pinkal 1986 (partly in German), a comparison of DRT and File Change Semantics in Landman 1986b. A theory of dynamic interpretation for generics is given in Schubert & Pelletier 1989.[5]

These distinct theories will have three major related concerns in common:

1. To account for how we interpret expressions in a given context, having only partial information about what is the case
2. To explain the role of pronouns in linking expressions in discourse in a universal and logically satisfactory way
3. To analyze meaning, interpretation, and inference as intrinsically context dependent

These developments have been fostered by the fundamental problems encountered in the established paradigm of possible-worlds semantics in accounting for anaphora, psychological attitudes, perception reports, deixis, and context-dependent expressions.

One major point of difference between DRT and SS is the fact that DRT relies essentially on a configurational level at which informational dependencies are represented, mediating between the natural language syntax and the semantic model theory in which the recursive truth conditions are specified. At the representational level, discourse referents of various kinds serve as arguments for conditions in which properties are attributed to them, and the

5. Recent research by Groenendijk and Stokhof (1991) reformulates the core of dynamic interpretation theories in terms of principles of Montague grammar, preserving compositionality.

set of such referents is structured by hierarchical and subordinating relations. SS does not employ such a representational level, but enriches the model theory with various kinds of primitive objects besides individuals—relations, locations, and truth values, and indeterminates for each of them—and makes heavy use of quantification over partial assignment functions and extensions thereof. Although this point of difference between the two theories leads to deep and far-reaching differences in their accounts of self-referential paradoxes, the issue of type-shifting anaphora this chapter is concerned with can be cast in either of them.[6] Despite my choice to present the proposed analysis with the tools of Situation Semantics, I try to remain rather neutral in my exposition of the problems of type-shifting anaphora, as I believe that pressing the differences actually impedes proper appreciation of the two theories' common goals. Clearly, the configurational representations of DRT appeal strongly to linguistic theory, and they certainly have important heuristic value. On the other hand, structured meanings are more readily represented by structured situation types, which are more clearly semantic objects.[7]

The common insight which spurred these dynamic theories of anaphora was that quantifiers could be interpreted as relations between a set of antecedent conditions consisting the *restrictor* and a set of consequent conditions, that I will call here the *nuclear scope,* following Heim (1982). In the type structure such quantifiers are hence of type $\langle\langle e,t\rangle,\langle\langle e,t\rangle,t\rangle\rangle$, denoting functions from properties to sets of properties. For instance, (5a) is represented as (5b), where the bracketed sequence of variables after the quantifier indicates which variables occur respectively in the restrictor and in the nuclear scope.

(5) a. Every president is happy.
b. **EVERY**[x,x] ([**president**(x)], [**happy**(x)])

The semantics of the universal quantifier requires that every situation that verifies the antecedent conditions can be extended to a situation that, in addition, verifies the conditions in the nuclear scope, assigning identical referents to occurrences of the same variable or 'discourse referent' (the term introduced first by Karttunen in 1969) as arguments of the conditions. Definite referential NPs should be interpreted as referring to an object of type *e* already contained in the representation, independent of any quantificational structure, whereas indefinite NPs introduce new objects of type *e* into the representation, possibly

6. See Barwise & Etchemendy 1987 and Kamp & Asher 1989 for their accounts of truth-functional liar-paradoxes.

7. In this respect I side with the view to which Schubert and Pelletier seem to profess in their 1989 article, where they argue convincingly for the need for structured meanings.

within a quantificational structure. In this dynamic perspective, pronouns are used in discourse when their referent is somehow made available already during the processing of prior discourse. Hence pronouns do not by themselves add any new information, but should rather be identified with a referent already in the representation; further conditions should be attributed to this referent. In requiring identification with an accessible referent in the representation, pronouns are like referential NPs. Referents in the restrictor or nuclear scope are inaccessible to (singular) pronouns in subsequent sentences. Referential NPs provide referents which always remain accessible, indicating that those NPs refer rigidly and bind pronouns in discourse.[8]

It is often been noted that plural pronouns can depend on quantificational antecedents in discourse, contrary to singular pronouns:

(6) a. Every president left the meeting. *He went to the reception.
b. Every president left the meeting. They went to the reception.

Before we turn to the issue of type-shifting anaphora, it is important to register that despite the restrictions on binding by episodic quantificational sentences, generic sentences with quantificational NPs may bind singular or plural pronouns in discourse, as (7) shows:

(7) a. Every president is an elected official. He signs bills into law.
b. All presidents are elected officials. They sign bills into law.

To account for the binding in (7), a general analysis of generic statements is required, which is the topic of the next section.

8.2. PARTICULAR KIND PREDICATION AND CHARACTERISTIC KIND PREDICATION

In earlier work on generics an important distinction has been made among sentences which express generic statements between those, on the one hand, which contain NPs referring rigidly to a kind and a VP attributing a property to it that cannot be distributed to the members of the kind—the *particular kind predication* (PKP)—and those, on the other hand, which express default quantification between a restrictive term and a stative VP denoting a property of (normal) members of the kind in the nuclear scope—the *characteristic kind of predication* (CKP).[9] In this section we will study under which

8. In DRT accessibility conditions are formulated in configurational terms, but in SS in terms of a purely semantic notion of a parametrized set.

9. See especially Carlson 1977b, 1982, Gerstner & Krifka 1987, and also ter Meulen 1986a and chapter 1 of this book.

conditions the LIFT and LOWER operations may be generalized to go back and forth, without loss of information, between PKP-statements and CKP-statements.

One of the characteristics of PKP-statements is that the VP may be progressive, attributing a gradual change in a property to a kind. For instance, in (8) the bare plural NP refers to the kind Elephant and expresses that it is dying out, a property typically predicated of kinds and not of its members.[10]

(8) Elephants are dying out.

Although bare plurals in subject position have commonly been analyzed as referring to kinds, other NPs may have the same semantic function, as was first suggested by Carlson (1977b). Consider (9):

(9) a. The elephant is dying out.
b. This elephant is dying out.
c. Pop art is dying out.

Definite or demonstrative singular NPs as well as bare singular mass terms can be interpreted to refer to kinds in English. Judgments with definite or demonstrative plurals appear to be far less clear; even within the Germanic languages there exists considerable variation (for more detail see section 8.3.2).

Indefinite singular or plural NPs and quantificational NPs are, however, unacceptable in such kind-level predications, unless they can be interpreted taxonomically as referring to or quantifying over a subspecies of elephants, as shown in (10).

(10) a. An elephant is dying out.
b. Every elephant is dying out.
c. Many elephants are dying out.
d. No elephant is dying out.

Similarly, PKP-statements can attribute a modal property to a kind or a past property of a kind in a generic *used-to* construction, as in (11).

(11) a. Elephants may soon be extinct, unless they are protected.
b. Elephants used to dominate the savanna, but now they are dying out.

10. Although the property of dying out is a kind-level predication, if (8) is true it must have some consequences for the truth value of individual-level predications to individual elephants. Lexical constraints will have to be formulated to capture such correlations between kind- and individual-level predications.

In (11a,b) the plural pronoun corefers with the bare plural antecedent to the kind, across opacity-inducing elements, indicating that they both refer rigidly and take wide scope over any quantificational structure.

CKP-statements typically have stative VPs which predicate an essential or default property to the normal, possible members of the kind. Often this is expressed explicitly by an adverbial binding the restrictive term to the variables in the conditions in the nuclear scope, as in (12). The NPs admitted in such CKP-statements include indefinite singulars referring to an arbitrary possible member.

(12) a. An elephant has valuable teeth.
b. The elephant usually has valuable teeth.
c. Elephants ordinarily have valuable teeth.

An important characteristic of CKP-statements is that they can be true even when there are members of the kind which fail to have the property expressed by the VP. An elephant who has lost his teeth does not constitute a counterexample to the claim expressed in (12a). We understand such generic statements to restrict the domain to normal or ordinary cases, where the dimensions that count for 'normality' may depend on the property attributed to the individual. This means that in a CKP-statement like (12a) without overt adverbial, we have to assume a default generic operator DEF of type $\langle\langle e,t\rangle,\langle\langle e,t\rangle,t\rangle\rangle$ relating the restrictive term to the normal cases.[11] In ter Meulen 1986a I proposed a semantic interpretation for such an operator in terms of a conditional correlation which was based on a set of meaningful options, precluding the "deviant" cases from the quantificational structure, and discussed the relationship between such conditionals and atemporal *when* or *whenever*. It is clear from (13) below that conditionals cannot provide additional restrictive conditions in CKP-statements, whereas *when* and *whenever,* which are adjuncts, do, as is predicted by the Kamp/Heim theory and developed in Schubert & Pelletier 1989.

(13) a. Elephants are fearful when they grow older.
b. **DEF** [x,x] ([**elephant**(x), **grow-older**(x)], [**are-fearful**(x)])
c. *Elephants are fearful if they grow older.

PKP-statements can be used in antecedents of generic counterfactuals, but if a CKP-statement is put into the antecedent of a counterfactual, it loses its

11. Schubert and Pelletier (1989) argue that in the absence of overt restrictive clauses a *reference ensemble* is constructed from context and background assumptions.

generic force and is interpreted as unselectively binding indefinites; compare, for instance, (14a,b).

(14) a. If elephants were fearful, Sid would beat them.
b. If an elephant were fearful, Sid would beat it.

In (14a) the PKP-statement in the antecedent makes the entire sentence a conditional generic.[12] It can be paraphrased as: Fearfulness in anything makes Sid beat it; elephants are not fearful, but if they were, Sid would beat them for their fearfulness. There is a way, however, to interpret (14a) as an episodic conditional statement, due to the fact that being fearful is a property of individuals. On that interpretation, (14a) could be paraphrased as: Any situation in which an elephant was being fearful would be one in which Sid beat that elephant, but no such situations arise in the actual world. On that episodic interpretation of (14a), *elephants* would not refer to a kind, but rather be predicatively used and hence rendered as (14c), which is a plain conditional quantifying over (non-actual) cases of fearfulness exhibited in elephants.

(14) c. ⇒ [x,x] ([**elephant**(x), **fearful**(x)], [**beat**(Sid,x)])

Such episodic conditionals seem to lack the explanatory force of generic information and form mere accidental generalizations. In (14c) Sid beats any fearful elephants, but he may also beat other elephants, as well as other animals or beatable things. In contrast, the conditional generic interpretation of (14a) provides much stronger information, because it expresses that fearfulness is the reason for Sid's beatings, so presumably other properties do not give him reason to beat. We see that *when/whenever*-clauses serve to restrict the restrictor in a default quantification, and that only conditionals can set up contexts for the rigidly referring NPs to be interpreted against. The reasons why this interaction between conditionals and PKP- versus CKP-statements is as I illustrated here take us much beyond what is feasible in this chapter.

If we analyze in more detail what the proper interpretation of this default quantification in CKP-statements consists of, the problems of nonmonotonic reasoning that have preoccupied AI-researchers for the past decade appear in all their force. For instance, we interpret (12a) as a CKP-statement, we seem to rely on a host of additional background assumptions when we assume it to hold in our actual world. Antecedents of conditionals do not appear out of

12. In (14a) an individual-level property is 'lifted' to a kind-level property in a PKP-statement. In the text I will discuss how such type-shifting operations between individual-level properties and kind-level properties are obtained by Partee's operations.

the blue; they only make sense against these background conditions. Such background conditions come from a variety of sources: knowledge of the world, of certain physical, biological, or economical laws and regularities, but also of certain inferential relations and semantic properties. In reasoning with conditionals we assume that these background conditions are stable. Most intuitively valid cases of nonmonotonic reasoning seem to change the background—for example, the case of an elephant who has lost his teeth violates the background assumption that elephants have teeth. It is neither practically nor theoretically feasible to spell out exactly what background assumptions play a role in the interpretation of a particular CKP-statement. But at least all PKP-statements about the corresponding kind must be assumed to remain true in the background, which guarantees a minimal modal similarity base for the alternative situations under consideration in the default quantification. A background assumption needs to be made explicit only when it is violated, since in our use of language we may leave unsaid what is assumed to be shared information. Only when conflict arises do we bother to spell out some of what we believe to be warranted assumptions. In the formalization of default quantification given below only some aspects of this stability of background assumptions will be captured.

We can add a domain of kinds to the three domains in figure 8.1 to represent the various mappings between the domains explicitly. The extended model is shown in figure 8.2. Kinds are objects interpreting PKP-NPs only. An entity is a member of a kind when it realizes the kind, and if we think of the set of kinds as a partially ordered taxonomic hierarchy, the realization relation can be turned into a mapping from entities to the "lowest" kind in the taxonomy they realize. This realization relation then has a logical property of monotone increasing functions, namely, 'If x realizes k and $k \leq k'$ then x realizes k'.' For example, an entity that realizes the kind Donkey must realize the kind Animal and the kind Mammal. In addition, there is a DEFAULT-LIFE and -LOWER mapping between the quantificational domain $\langle\langle e,t\rangle,t\rangle$ and the kinds. NPs in CKP-statements are analyzed as quantifiers with DEF as "determiner," hence denote $\langle\langle e,t\rangle,t\rangle$ objects. The mappings between the PKP- and CKP-domains are defined properly below.

DET is any possible determiner of natural language making out of a property a generalized quantifier living on that property, including here also the implicit default operator DEF for CKP-statements. The new mappings APPLY and KIND between kinds and properties of entities are interpreted as follows. APPLY gives for every kind the property its members have, that is, the one

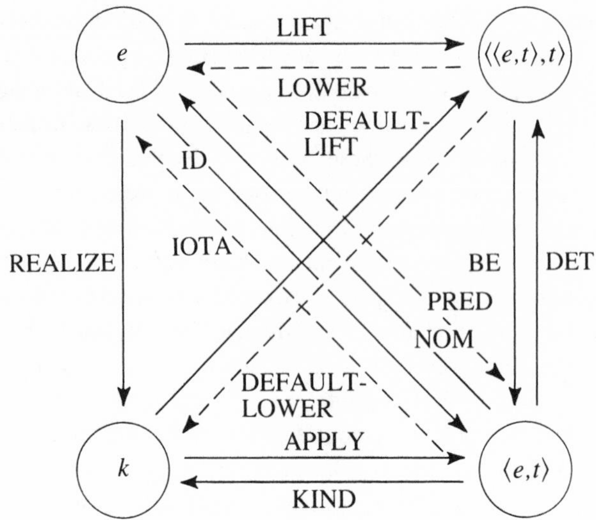

FIGURE 8.2. Four denotational domains

which is true of the set of its possible members. It turns a nominal NP into a predicative NP which has a free argument. KIND is also a total function, mapping a property of individuals to the corresponding kind.[13] If the property is an interpretation of a VP, the corresponding NP will be a gerund, not an infinitive, as in (15).

(15) Walking/*To walk is a healthy activity.

The infinitive could be obtained by NOM, which denotes entities not necessarily ordered in a taxonomic hierarchy (the 'concepts' discussed in chapter 1), as in (16).

(16) To walk is to do something healthy.

DEFAULT-LIFT is a total function from interpretations of PKP-NPs referring rigidly to the kind to a generalized quantifier living on the corresponding property. It is clear that DEFAULT-LIFT(k) is definable as λP.DEF(APPLY(k),P). But if it is assumed to be a primitive mapping, as is common in inheritance logics, the other mappings could be defined in terms of it.[14] One linguistic consequence of this abstract modeling is that any PKP-NP

13. It was pointed out by a referee that for KIND to be total we need to assume "non-natural" and perhaps even fictional kinds. That assumption seems harmless in natural language semantics.

14. Here DEF stands for the default determiner for CKP-statements, subsumed under DET as mentioned above.

may be used in a CKP-statement where the VP denotes a property of individuals, as in (17). Lacking any further disambiguating context, (17) can be interpreted as referring either to an individual given elephant or to the kind.

(17) The elephant has valuable teeth.

The inverse, DEFAULT-LOWER, is a partial relation, taking only definite NPs interpreted as generalized quantifiers, which contain all default properties to the corresponding kind. The characteristic indefinite NPs in CKP-statements are hence blocked from lowering into the kind. This is borne out by the facts in (18).

(18) a. An elephant has valuable teeth/was shot. *It is dying out.
b. Many elephants lost their teeth to poachers. ?They are dying out.
c. Elephants have valuable teeth. They are dying out.
d. The African elephant has valuable teeth. It is dying out.

As (18a) shows, the kind-level property of dying out cannot be predicated of the referential singular pronoun depending on an indefinite NP in a CKP-statement or an episodic statement. In (18c,d), with a bare plural or definite NP as antecedent, this kind of dependency is perfectly possible, since DEFAULT-LOWER applies to the restrictive term and constructs the appropriate kind for a PKP-statement without requiring any additional information. For (18b) a new semantic operation can be defined which allows plural pronouns to occur in PKP-statements, even when they depend on indefinite plural antecedents. This operation is called *copying* and is properly introduced below.

The new operations are accordingly definable as follows (where k is a variable of type *k*, x of type *e*, P of type $\langle e,t\rangle$, and δ of type $\langle\langle e,t\rangle,t\rangle\rangle$[15]

APPLY(k) $=_{def.}$ λx.x REALIZE k
KIND(P) $=_{def.}$ ιk.k is the lowest kind k′ such that P = {x:x REALIZE k′}
Let DEF be the default determiner; then
DEFAULT-LIFT(k) $=_{def.}$ λP.DEF(APPLY(k), P)
DEFAULT-LOWER ($\mathcal{P}$,k) $=_{def.}$ DEFAULT-LIFT(k) = $\mathcal{P}$

Accordingly, DEFAULT-LOWER is the partial inverse of the total DEFAULT-LIFT function. But DEFAULT-LOWER may well be a relation—for example, the beech and the elm remain two kinds, despite the fact they may be attributed the same default properties. Furthermore, DEFAULT-LOWER

15. These definitions were added at the suggestion of a referee, which I gratefully accepted. It may prove to be advantageous for semantic theory to assume DEFAULT-LIFT and APPLY as primitive mappings, from which all others are defined, as is common in computational inheritance logics. I cannot pursue these issues further here.

remains undefined in cases where there is no unique set of properties that apply by default to the set of entities realizing the kind. It is quite obvious now that DEFAULT-LIFE is a stronger operation than DEFAULT-LOWER, and this provides the model-theoretic basis for our explanation of the linguistic data.

This analysis predicts that universal NPs with restrictive clauses should not allow DEFAULT-LOWER to apply to the kind, since they would construct a kind with the same restriction, contrary to the requirement that PKP-statements are only acceptable for well-established kinds. For instance, it is at least harder for most English speakers to admit the PKP-interpretation of the pronoun in (19a) than its normal episodic interpretation as referring to the set in (19b) or the CKP-statement in (19c).[16]

(19) a. Sid sold every elephant he owned. ?/*They are dying out.
b. Sid sold every elephant he owned. They were getting too old.
c. Sid sold every elephant he owned. They are good pack animals.

For (19a) 'DEFAULT-LOWER(every-elephant-Sid-owned)' is not defined, nor indirectly definable as 'KIND(DEF^{-1}(every-elephant-Sid-owned))', for the latter constructs the kind of elephant owned by Sid, using the properties applying to them by default. In (19b) the pronoun refers to the unique set containing all the elephants sold by Sid. Its interpretation is of type *e*, a plural individual or collective, which is constructed by 'IOTA(BE(every-elephant-Sid-owned))'. In (19c) the pronoun occurs in a CKP-statement, attributing to every possible elephant—given our modal base—the default property of being a good pack animal. Although this pronoun is referential, it does not refer rigidly to the kind as a PKP-pronoun would. Rather, its interpretation is based on a quantificational NP which is its antecedent. In detail, (19c) is rendered as

(19) c′. **EVERY** [x,x] ([**elephant**(x), **owns**(Sid,x)], [**sold**(Sid,x)])
DEF [x,x] ([**elephant**(x)], [**good-pack-animal**(x)])

In (19c′) the restrictive term of the default operator DEF is obtained by copying conditions from the restrictive term in the antecedent NP. It may not be necessary to include every condition in the restrictive term in this copying, although that is always possible, and perhaps even preferred for (19c). A compositional theory of meaning will need to spell out exactly which conditions must be copied under what linguistic conditions, but this is undoubtedly also constrained by pragmatic and real-world considerations.

16. Note that the same facts can be illustrated with definite descriptions:
(i) a. Every president left the meeting early. ?/*They are elected annually.
b. Every president left the meeting early. They went to the cocktail party.
c. Every president left the meeting early. They can vote in absentia.

The last point needing clarification is the semantics of the default operator DEF subsumed under DET. It will be necessary to introduce some additional model-theoretic concepts from Situation Semantics for this purpose.[17] A situation *s* is an *n*-tuple consisting of a relation with individuals and a positive or negative polarity. A situation type S is a situation where at least one constituent is unsaturated; this is called an *indeterminate* (*constituent*). A situation s is of type S when for some assignment function *f* from indeterminates to relations and individuals, S[*f*] *is part of* s.[18] A given situation is related by constraints to a set of situations which are its *meaningful options* and to a set of situations which are precluded, or *inaccessible,* to it. These notions are defined as follows: If a constraint C relates the situation types S and S′, and s is of type S and s′ is of type S′, then s′ is a meaningful option for s iff, for every assignment function *f* for all indeterminates in S, if S[*f*] is part of s, then S′[*f*] is part of s′. A situation s′ is inaccessible to s either if they are incompatible due to polarity conflict or contrary properties, or if no assignment function *f* such that S[*f*] is part of s can be extended to *f*′ such that S′[*f*′] is part of s′.

The DEF operator relates every true instance of the restrictive term to a true instance of the nuclear scope, which is an accessible meaningful option to the former. Hence this operator has a modal nature, dependent on a set of constraints and additional contextual parameters. For the DEF operator the additional restrictions expressed in constraints limit the true instances of the conditions in the nuclear scope to those which respect all constraints operative in a given context. To briefly illustrate this analysis of default quantification with one the examples from our prior discussion, the case of an elephant whose teeth are lost is an inaccessible situation for the evaluation of (12a–c), since the background constraint expressed by the generic CKP-statement *An elephant has teeth* is violated.

8.3. TYPE-SHIFTING ANAPHORA

8.3.1. More Facts

In an inspiring and seminal paper on Discourse Representation Theory for plural pronouns, Frey & Kamp 1986, it was proposed that any occurrence of a CN in discourse would simultaneously introduce the kind in the main discourse representation structure, thus giving it wide scope over any quantifi-

17. See also ter Meulen (1986a) for similar concepts. I have simplified the definitions here for sake of expository clarity.

18. This *part-of* notion can be either set-theoretic inclusion or some weaker lattice-theoretic part-of-relation.

cational structure and making it always accessible for anaphora. Support for this hypothesis is presented in (20) and (21).

(20) a. The president is getting old. He is elected every four years.
b. The president is elected every four years. *He is getting old.

(21) a. A president left the meeting. They can vote in absentia.
b. Every president left the meeting. They can vote in absentia.
c. John believes that every president left the meeting. They can vote in absentia.
d. If a president left the meeting, his vote still counts. They can vote in absentia.

This hypothesis appears to be too strong in the light of the discussion above, but it is also too weak, in not being sufficiently general, as we will see below. Consider the facts in (22):

(22) a. The president is getting old. Every American dreams of being *he/*him some day.
b. A president left the meeting. *He is elected annually.
c. A president can vote in absentia. He is elected annually.
d. John is the president. *He is elected annually.

In (22a) the episodic antecedent would, on the Frey/Kamp hypothesis, introduce the role or function of being president, and would allow any subsequent pronoun to pick it up as its referent. However, if the pronoun occurs embedded in a belief context, as in (22a), it seems blocked from such PKP-reference. What every American dreams of is not to be the current president, but rather to fulfill the role of president some day. This can only be circumscribed with *be in his position,* which is still a dependent expression but with rather more informative content than just a mere pronoun. In (22b) we see that, similar to the situation with (18a), an indefinite NP in an episodic statement cannot provide a proper antecedent for a PKP-pronoun with a kind-level VP. Of course, a simple coreference between individuals remains perfectly well possible for (22b), but the VP *be elected annually* is then a property of individuals. In (22c) the indefinite in the CKP-statement can provide a proper antecedent for the pronoun in the PKP-statement, by copying the restrictive term and relating it by DEF to the property of being elected annually, which should be equivalent by DEFAULT-LOWER to the property of being elected annually attributed to the function of president. But as (22d) shows, the predicative uses of CNs cannot provide proper antecedents for PKP-anaphora either. So the context of the antecedent and/or the context of the pronoun seems to determine, at least in some cases, whether a CN provides a proper antecedent for a generically referring PKP-pronoun.

The Frey/Kamp hypothesis concerns CNs only, but properties interpreting other syntactic categories may also introduce kinds. For instance, attributive adjectives allow binding of PKP-pronouns, but other adjectives do not, as seen in (23).

(23) a. Mary mixed blue and red paint. They are primary colors.
b. Mary mixed acrylic and oil paint. They are surface treatments.

Adjectives are attributive (e.g., *red, blue*) that is, of type $\langle e,t\rangle$, if they occur after a copula; otherwise they are not attributive (e.g., *lunar, oil, past, alleged*), that is, of type $\langle\langle e,t\rangle,\langle e,t\rangle\rangle$. Only attributive adjectives provide accessible antecedents for PKP-anaphora. For example, in (23a) the pronoun refers to the colors blue and red, but in (23b) reference is made to the two kinds of paint, not to the properties distinguishing them. For (23a) we obtain the referent of the pronoun by applying the DEF-operator to the $\langle e,t\rangle$-properties **blue**(x) and **red**(y) to obtain the restrictive term of the CKP-statement, which by DEFAULT-LOWER is equivalent to the property attributed to the two colors of being a primary color. The adjectives *acrylic* and *oil* are of the higher type. Only if applied to the property interpreting the CN *paint* do they denote a $\langle e,t\rangle$-type property, which provides the proper antecedent for the plural pronoun referring to the kinds of paint. This is further evidence in support of Chierchia's Functor Anaphora Constraint (cf. section 8.1.2).

We have seen that the restrictor in the interpretation of a CKP-statement is not obtained from a PKP-statement by DEFAULT-LIFT, and does not provide an accessible antecedent for PKP-anaphora. But an antecedent NP in a PKP-statement will always provide an accessible antecedent for CKP-anaphora, singular or plural, and should be configurationally in the main discourse representation structure.

8.3.2. Linguistic Variation in Germanic Languages

As I have remarked several times above, there appears to be some interesting variation in generic reference even in the restricted family of the Germanic languages.

In English, definite plural NPs, as opposed to definite singular NPs, are not generally allowed to be interpreted as PKP- or CKP-reference, in contrast to German; cf. (24).

(24) a. *The elephants are dying out.
b. Die Elephanten sterben aus.
c. *The elephants have valuable teeth.
d. Die Elephanten haben wertvolle Zähne.

Hans Kamp once remarked that in English plurale tantum NPs similarly do not allow PKP- or CKP-reference, as shown in (25) ('*' marks only lack of generic reference; of course episodic reference remains always possible).

(25) a. *The trousers/Trousers were introduced in the Middle Ages.
b. *The glasses/Glasses are a visual aid.
c. *The twins/Twins are born the same day.

Dutch seems to share with German the possibility for definite plurals to refer generically, as in (26), but it does not allow plurale tantum to refer generically.

(26) a. De olifanten/Olifanten sterven uit.
b. De olifanten/Olifanten hebben waardevolle tanden.
c. *De tweelingen/Tweelingen/Een tweeling (indef. sing.) worden/wordt op dezelfde dag geboren.

In English it seems to be acceptable, however, to use a definite plural to refer to a kind which is already introduced in the context, as shown in (27).

(27) There are two kinds of elephants: Indian and African. The African elephants have large ears/are dying out.

Dutch seems more restricted than English in its interpretations of plural pronouns as referring generically, preferring a neuter pronoun or a dependent demonstrative to refer dependently to a kind, but requiring number agreement of the verb with the antecedent, as shown in (28).

(28) a. Piet verkocht al zijn olifanten. Het/Dat zijn zoogdieren/*is een zoogdier.
Peter sold all his elephants. {That are mammals. / *It is a mammal.}
b. Piet verkocht zijn olifant. Dat is een zoogdier.
Peter sold his elephant. That is a mammal.
c. Piet verkocht al zijn olifanten. ?Zij zijn zoogdieren. (episodic only)
Peter sold all his elephants. They are mammals.

The oddity of (28c) lies in the fact that a set of members of a kind is ordinarily not said to have a property belonging to the taxonomic hierarchy.

8.4. CONCLUSION

Let me summarize the constraints we have observed on type-shifted anaphora as follows, citing the corresponding data.

CONSTRAINT 1: A referential NP in an episodic statement does not bind a PKP-anaphor in an attitude context. (See (22a).)

CONSTRAINT 2: An indefinite NP in an episodic statement cannot bind a PKP-anaphor with a kind-level VP. (See (18a), (22b).)

CONSTRAINT 3: A predicatively used CN cannot bind a PKP-anaphor. (See (23).)

In general, it appears that type-shifting from CKP-statements to PKP-statements is significantly more restricted than type-shifting in the other direction. To explain these constraints and the positive data we have discussed in a satisfactory theory of anaphoric dependencies must remain for future research. This chapter has advanced some empirical arguments for separating the domain of kinds from the domain of individuals. The additional type-shifting operations which were defined between the four denotational domains—CKP, PKP, kinds, and individuals—provided basic explanatory insight in the informational equivalences and nonequivalences of generic statements. Perhaps other semantic operations can be defined to turn figure 8.2 into a fully commuting diagram. It would be especially interesting to characterize the exact conditions under which a kind may be considered *as if* it were an individual. This would require spelling out the conceptual process of considering a certain object *as if* it were something else—a task bordering on the analysis of metaphor. Linguistic evidence was presented for constraining the type-shifting, but much more work remains to be done on the issue of type-shifting referential dependencies, both in terms of empirical data collection in natural languages and in terms of the formulations of empirical generalizations, as well as in the formalization of the overall theory of such information content. In the meantime I hope to have shown that assuming a fourth denotational domain serves sound explanatory purposes in a linguistic theory of meaning and interpretation.

9 GENERIC INFORMATION AND DEPENDENT GENERICS

Godehard Link

9.1. Introduction: The Nature of I-Generic Sentences

9.1.1. D-Generics vs. I.-Generics

The distinction between *D-generic* and *I-generic* sentences is due to Gerstner & Krifka 1987 and Krifka 1987. It is a semantic classification of the two basic kinds of generic statements: statements about *kinds* and statements about *instances of a kind.* The distinction obviously presupposes the view that there are such things as kinds in our ontology to begin with. For arguments see chapter 1 of this volume, as well as the classic Carlson 1977b. 'D-generic' stands for "definite generic," 'I-generic' for "indefinite generic"; these syntactic names for a semantic phenomenon serve to hint at the fact that reference to kinds in its purest form is done by employing a definite NP, whereas indefinite generic NPs typically occur in general statements about instances of natural kind terms. Examples of D-generics are given in (1), and some I-generic sentences are listed under (2). In chapter 1, I-generic sentences were called *characteristic sentences.*

(1) a. The mammoth is extinct.
    b. William Shockley invented the transistor.

(2) a. A tiger preys on wild animals.
    b. Babies cry.
    c. The lion has a mane.

D-generic sentences involve *Proper Kind Predication (PKP);* that is, sentences like (1a,b) are used to make *singular statements* about a particular kind (the mammoth, the transistor). I-generic sentences express *Derived Kind Predication (DKP);* that is, sentences like (2a–c) are used to make *general statements* about a certain class of objects (tigers, babies, lions). As can be seen from (2c), the use of a definite generic NP does not entail D-genericity. So the distinction D- vs. I-generic can only serve as a rough orientation.

PKP has been given less attention than DKP, and I, too, would like to concentrate on the latter in this chapter. The main reason is that PKP does not really seem to have an interesting "logic" that would call for a sophisticated analysis. But kinds and PKP are not so spurious as it might look; a realistic generic discourse readily switches from one generic idiom to the other, as can be seen in section 9.3 below, so both constructions are widely used. Also, the discussion there gives rise to what I will call *relational* kind terms, which display an internal structure and therefore should have some logic after all. Finally, there exists regular discourse on the kind level, which may even involve quantification over kinds as the sentences in (3). Such generic sentences are called *taxonomic,* a fitting term due to Krifka (1987). (See also chapter 1.)

(3) a. The tiger is the largest cat in the world.
 b. All deer can run faster than the tiger.

In the present section, however, I'd like to dwell on the other basic generic construction, the DKP. Now there are two ways of expressing general statements: (i) *explicit universal quantification,* correlating with what Croft (1986) calls *closed class quantification* (CCQ); (ii) *I-generic statements,* correlating with *open class quantification* (OCQ). Consider the sentences in (4):

(4) a. All planets of the solar system revolve about the sun on an elliptic orbit. (CCQ)
 b. (All) man-made satellites (will) revolve about the earth on an elliptic orbit. (OCQ)

Without extra information, (4a) is most naturally interpreted as the assertion that each one of the nine planets travels on an elliptic orbit; so the statement is about the *closed* class consisting of the nine planets of the solar system. There is, however, the additional background knowledge, which most of us share, that the elliptic orbit is no accident and will extend to any movement of a satellite in a central force field under appropriate initial conditions. Such a regularity then gives rise to a generic statement about an *open* class of objects, like the one in (4b). While the explicit quantifier may still be used for OCQ, I-generics are definitely inappropriate for expressing a closed class quantification. The reason is that (4a) expresses an *actual universal truth (AUT)*: each member of the actual class described in the domain of the universal quantifier (i.e., the set of planets) is said to travel around the sun on an elliptic orbit. By contrast, the assertion in (4b) extends to any *potential* object that satisfies the restricting condition in the antecedent. (4b) might therefore be called a *schematic truth (ST),* which is best rendered in its standard singular indefinite generic format, in this case (4c):

(4) c. A satellite revolving about the earth travels on an elliptic orbit.

The basic paraphrase for this is: Whatever fits the description of the antecedent, that is, any actual or future satellite circling the earth, will travel on an elliptic orbit. It is this schematic respect in which I-generics crucially differ from regular universal quantification.

9.1.2. Default Quantification and Homogeneous Recognizable Subclasses (HRC)

The second important point of difference between I-generics and classical universal quantification is the well-known fact that in most I-generic contexts *exceptions* are possible. But what else is there to represent those I-generics? A favorite answer is *Default Quantification;* for instance, a paraphrase of (2b) would be: Take an arbitrary baby; it will cry by default. There are lots of ways of explaining the notion of default (which is, by the way, a typical symptom for the pre-paradigmatic phase of the theory); for a test of performance of various approaches, see Morreau 1988. They all try to give something like a ''smart'' rule of behavior, for example to the effect that whenever you are given an object that fits the description of the antecedent of an I-generic you are entitled to assume that it also satisfies the consequent—*unless there is some known information that bars this conclusion.* Now, I think that a distinction is called for here between *the semantic notion of truth condition* on the one hand and *the information to be gained* from a generic statement on the other. A true I-generic sentence expresses a schematic truth which does have universal force, but only with respect to a certain suitably restricted, ''ideal'' or normal condition. Since this condition is formal or schematic, the information to be gained from the generic with regard to a particular instance of its antecedent NP is not complete: we cannot apply universal instantiation, which is truth-conditional; rather, our conclusion has to be based on some *inductive procedure* or other. A rough symbolic representation of the different nature of the conclusion with AUT and ST is the following:

(5) a. AUT: $\forall x(\phi x \rightarrow \psi x),\ \phi a \Rightarrow \psi a$
b. ST: $[\phi x] \supset_G [\psi x]$ (*), $\phi a \Rightarrow c(\psi a \mid \phi a) \geq \alpha$

The generic statement (*) (for the symbol '$\supset_G$' see below) concerns only normal or typical instances, and that is why there is only a certain *inductive* *credibility* c to the proposition that a particular object a, given that it is a ϕ, is also a ψ; this credibility is assumed to exceed a certain level α. By contrast, the transfer of information in (5a), provided by the logical rule of universal instantiation, is complete.

The concept of normality can be informally characterized by the notion of *homogeneity*: in a homogeneous collection of "typical representatives" of a certain kind or concept all idiosyncrasies are ignored. In addition, pragmatic effects restrict the range of applicability of the generic further to some "recognizable subclass." Taken together, these facts mean that a generic statement can only be applied to its relevant *homogeneous recognizable subclass (HRS)*.

What is the appropriate HRS? Again, this is a matter of semantic and pragmatic effects and therefore bound to be somewhat vague. However, the fact is that people do use, and draw information from, generic statements all the time. Therefore, it seems apt to postulate a maxim of the following kind:

MAXIM OF INTERPRETATION: There is always a HRS that can be inferred from grammatical, lexical, contextual, and/or other pragmatic information.

Let me illustrate with a few examples what I have in mind here. (For the informal discussion I represent credibilities by probabilities, which are intuitively well understood; but see below for a different interpretation of c.)

PELLETIER'S SQUISH

(6) a. Snakes are reptiles.
 b. Telephone books are thick books.

(7) a. Birds lay eggs.
 b. The duck lays eggs.
 c. The duck has colored feathers.
 d. Guppies give live birth.

(8) a. Austrians are good skiers.
 b. (The) Chinese eat dogmeat.
 c. Americans are good baseball players.
 d. Germans eat horsemeat. (uttered after WWII)
 e. The tiger even eats grass and soil. (see below)

(9) Unicorns have one horn.

In (6a), *be a reptile* is a taxonomic predicate that admits no exceptions; therefore the HRS is equal to the (open) class of snakes, and any animal that fits the description of being a snake will be a reptile. In (6b) the HRS consists of telephone books of big cities of the present day (and not, say, of those from a hundred years ago). In (7a), laying eggs is a property that entails being female, so the HRS will consist of all normal female birds. Note that HRSs can deal with the apparent puzzle that arises with the simultaneous assertion of (7b) and (7c): the problem is that it is the females that lay eggs, and the males that happen to have colored feathers; the solution is that these sentences are about different HRSs. The only moral to be drawn from this is that we have to be careful when trying to apply a rule of conjunction reduction to a pair of generic sentences with the same subject. (In fact, it would be misleading to express the two facts in question by saying *The duck lays eggs and has colored feathers*. A general strategy to be followed here could be to expand a reduced sentence before it is evaluated.) Finally, in (7d) we have the interference of two effects: first, the relevant HRS are the female guppies; and secondly (if I understand the facts correctly), there seems to be a dispositional component involved such that under appropriate circumstances, guppies might give live birth—this is what brings the probability level α down to less than ½. As a result, applying a default rule of the above sort based on (7d) to a given guppy is not really "smart behavior" when you can't tell the males from the females: you may be wrong in the majority of cases. In (8a–e) we have again a dispositional component superimposed on the regular pattern of a generic assertion, so what enters the HRS here is, respectively the average Austrian, Chinese, American, and German after WWII, and the average tiger in certain circumstances. Thus I don't see the need for postulating still another reading of generic sentences here that Krifka (1987) calls the "distinguishing property" reading of a kind. To conclude, sentence (9) seems to me a perfect schematic truth; there just happen to be no instances of the relevant HRS, the unicorns. So what seems prima facie puzzling about Pelletier's squish, viz. that the number of instances the generic is true of may gradually decrease till it reaches zero, is not after all a serious reason for concern for a theory of I-generics once we introduce a notion like the HRS.

The concept of HRS also explains why the inference in (10) is no good (see Krifka 1987).

(10) a. Tigers have four legs.
b. Three-legged tigers are tigers.
c. Therefore, three-legged tigers have four legs.

In (10a), HRS_1 = tigers, and the taxonomic assertion concerns typical members with no idiosyncratic properties (due to the requirement of homogeneity). In (10b), HRS_2 = three-legged tigers; that the property of three-leggedness is idiosyncratic can be inferred from premise (10a). Hence $HRS_1 \cap HRS_2 = \emptyset$, so the inference is blocked because the premises refer to different collections.

9.2. GENERIC INFORMATION AND BELIEF REVISION

In the preceding section I mentioned the considerable variety of approaches to default reasoning. Although I am convinced that research in linguistic semantics on the nature of generic constructions is rather independent of the issues discussed in those theories I would like to digress somewhat from linguistic matters in this section and suggest one more way of using generic information in language processing.

Ignoring the modal dimension, it seems to be sufficiently appropriate for our purposes to paraphrase an I-generic statement 'F's are G's' by 'All F-typical F's are G's' (where 'F-typical' stands for 'typical with respect to property F'). Typicality is treated by pragmatic considerations, for instance by using the HRS technique or some other procedure. Let us now consider linguistic utterances in the context of information processing. What is the information gained by a hearer X who is given a piece of generic information of the kind 'F's are G's'? Its semantic content is the proposition p that all F-typical F's are G's. X incorporates p into the set of her/his beliefs if (s)he trusts the informant. But this information is of little use unless X is able to apply the predicate 'F-typical' to particular entities in concrete situations. Because the information is only generic, X is not entitled to conclude that an individual a is a G, given that (s)he knows that a is an F, unless the additional information that a is F-typical is available.

Now default logic says: Simply assume that whenever you have an F it is also F-typical. This strategy is stopped by the well-known Nixon Diamond, where Richard Nixon, who is known to be both a Republican and a Quaker, must be assumed to be a pacifist and a nonpacifist at the same time since Quakers typically are pacifists while Republicans typically are not. But when we focus on the transfer of information, a somewhat broadened picture suggests itself. The way generic information is handled by X differs from the way he treats categorical information of the form 'All F's are G's': in the former case there is, so to speak, an additional parameter involved, expressing the firmness with which the assumption of F-typicality is incorporated into X's beliefs. This parameter, call it τ, measures the "epistemic distance" between the proposition that an a is F-typical and its negation. It "corrupts" the ideal infinite epistemic distance between G and its complement G* on F that is based on a genuinely universal propositon of the form 'All F's are G's'. So unlike in that case, the conclusion G for an F-object is subject to potential revision.

A framework in which these ideas are worked out is Wolfgang Spohn's theory of *ordinal conditional functions (OCF);* see Spohn 1988. I shall give a sketch of its basic set-up and try to model the processing of generic information within it. Let W be a set of possible worlds or courses of events; propositions are then subsets of W, as usual. These subsets are assumed to form a complete field of sets Σ over W (i.e., $\Sigma \subseteq 2^W$, $\Sigma \neq \emptyset$, and Σ is closed under arbitrary intersections, unions, and complements; the notation for complements is an attached star '*'). Then κ is called a *Σ-measurable ordinal conditional function (Σ-OCF)* if κ is a function on W with values in the class Ω of ordinals such that

(i) $\kappa^{-1}(0) \neq \emptyset$;

(ii) κ is Σ-measurable, i.e., the restriction of κ to each atom in Σ in a constant function.

Then define $\kappa(A)$:

(iii) $\kappa(A) := \min\{\kappa(w) \mid w \in A\}$ for $A \in \Sigma$, $A \neq \emptyset$.

From this stipulation we have immediately

(iv) $\kappa(A \cup B) = \min\{\kappa(A), \kappa(B)\}$

for all nonempty $A, B \in \Sigma$, and from (iv) in turn, together with condition (i), we infer:

(v) For all *contingent* $A \in \Sigma$ (i.e., those A with A, $A^* \neq \emptyset$): $\kappa(A) = 0$ or $\kappa(A^*) = 0$ or both.

The interpretation of the OCFs is this. Each κ represents a *grading of disbelief* of a person X regarding the possible courses of events: the κ-value of an event w increases with X's distrust in it, and the greater $\kappa(w)$, the greater is w's "surprise value" should the event actually occur. Thus $\kappa(w) = 0$ means that X has no reason to distrust w; in other words, X thinks that w is compatible with the rest of his beliefs, so that X does not believe w not to be the case. Because of (iii) the same is true of whole propositions A if A contains at least one w with $\kappa(w) = 0$. $\kappa(w) = 1$ means that the degree of disbelief in w is 1; $\kappa(w) = 2$, that the degree of disbelief is 2; and so forth. Now if X expresses some nonzero degree of disbelief in each $w' \in A^*$ then it follows that $\kappa^{-1}(0) \subseteq A$ since $0 < \kappa(w')$ for all $w' \in A^*$. By condition (i) the *kernel* $\kappa^{-1}(0)$ is nonzero, and if it is a subset of A, as in the case at hand, we say that X *believes* A to be the case. By contrast, X *disbelieves* or *distrusts* A if $\kappa(A) > 0$. For contingent A it follows from (v) that in the latter case X cannot at the same time distrust A*, for otherwise the kernel would be empty. However, both A and A* can well have the κ-value 0, in which case X is said to be *epistemically indifferent* with respect to A. Moreover, we say that X *believes in* A *with firmness* α if either $\kappa(A^*) > 0$ and $\alpha = \kappa(A^*)$ (i.e., the most plausible course of events in A* has epistemic distance α from A) or else $\kappa(A) > 0$ and $\alpha = -\kappa(A)$ (i.e., X distrusts A with degree $-\alpha$, in which case the belief has negative firmness). Thus, the OCFs do not only give a plausibility ranking of the courses of events in W, but together with the firmness parameter α they provide a measure for the epistemic distance between a proposition A and its complement A*.

Given these concepts we can now proceed to model the dynamics of epistemic states of a person X in terms of the theory of OCFs. An epistemic state is represented by a particular OCF κ. Suppose X receives the information A which suggests itself to X with firmness α. How does the OCF change in the light of the data A? The resulting κ' should assign 0 to A since X believes in A now, and the κ-values on A* should be pushed up at least to level α. The following definition is such that it incorporates this intuition while preserving the respective internal distances on A and A*.

Let $\alpha \in \Omega$, $A, A^* \neq \emptyset$, let κ be an Σ-OCF, and $\kappa(\cdot \mid A)$ the *trace OCF on* $\Sigma \cap A$ with $\kappa(w \mid A) = -\kappa(A) + \kappa(w)$ $(w \in A)$. Then the A,α-*conditionalization* $\kappa_{A,\alpha}$ is that Σ-OCF such that $\kappa_{A,\alpha}(w) = \kappa(w \mid A)$ for $w \in A$, and $\kappa_{A,\alpha}(w) = \alpha + \kappa(w \mid A^*)$ for $w \in A^*$. Now the new epistemic state of X deriving from κ, given the information A (which is incorporated into X's beliefs with firmness α), is then represented by the A,α-conditionalization $\kappa_{A,\alpha}$. The A,α-conditionalization has the following desirable properties (see Spohn 1988, 118f.): (1) it is *reversible;* (2) it is *commutative,* that is, the order of incoming pieces of information does not matter provided these are independent; (3) it works also in the case of new data which is *incompatible* with X's present beliefs: this is exactly the case of nonmonotonic information.

The construction doesn't say anything about the OCF that represents the "initial" epistemic state; but here the situation is no different from the corresponding one in Bayesian statistics, where usually also little is known about the so-called apriori probabilities. However, the mechanism of belief revision in the light of new information is completely determined by the conditionalization procedure. Finally, it might seem somewhat extravagant to admit as values of an OCF the whole range of (possibly transfinite) ordinals. Theoretically, such an objection is not of too much force, since little complication is engendered by not restricting the κ-values to ω, the set of finite ordinals or natural numbers; in fact, the only difference is ordinal addition, which is not commutative beyond the initial segment ω—hence the order of terms in the definition of the trace OCF is important. From a practical point of view, however, we might always think of the OCFs as taking values in ω. In what follows I shall actually restrict the range not to ω but to $\omega + 1 = \omega \cup \{\omega\}$; as briefly mentioned above, one might make use of the value ω in lawlike categorical statements of the form 'All F's are G's' as an indication of the infinite epistemic distance between G and G* on F (here I ignore the fact that in principle every information, even if it is lawlike, might eventually be refuted).

I would now like to apply the framework of OCFs to a standard case of processing generic information, that of Tweety the Penguin (Tweety is to AI what the King of France is to philosophy). In intuitive terms, the situation can be described in the following way. X starts out with a certain set of beliefs, among those: (1) the belief that Tweety is a bird; (2) the belief that birds fly (generic information; symbolically: $B \supset_G F$); (3) the belief that penguins don't fly (categorical information derived from high school biology); and (4) the belief that if Tweety happens to be a penguin it is barely a typical bird. Now X is likely to form the additional belief that Tweety is a typical bird since he has no evidence to the contrary (the possible fact, for instance, that Tweety likes fish need not disturb him, since he knows of lots of typical birds with the same predilection: seagulls, pelicans, cormorans, etc.). But it is clear to X that the typicality assumption is on somewhat shaky ground, so that the epistemic distance to nontypicality (call it τ) is not too great. In the OCF model, then, a κ describing X's epistemic state would assign 0 to Tweety's being a typical bird, and $\tau > 0$ to its complement. Now X learns that Tweety is a penguin after all. He conditionalizes on this proposition with firmness γ, say. Then he believes, of course, that Tweety is a penguin, but at the same time he should not believe anymore in Tweety's typicality. Let us see how this change is properly predicted by the OCF theory.

Let 't' stand for 'Tweety', 'B' for 'bird', 'P' for 'penguin', 'TB' for 'B-typical (bird)', and 'F' for 'flies'. Since we assume from the outset that X believes B(t), we can ignore the worlds which have B*(t). This leaves us with eight worlds out of the sixteen making up the total set W of logically possible worlds that can be built up in our model. The eight worlds are listed in table 9.1.

Since t is the only individual constant involved we henceforth omit it. Thus 'B' is now also short for the whole proposition that Tweety is a bird, and so

Table 9.1

									B	TB	P	F
w_1	B(t)	$\wedge$	TB(t)	$\wedge$	P(t)	$\wedge$	F(t)		+	+	+	+
w_2	B(t)	$\wedge$	TB(t)	$\wedge$	P(t)	$\wedge$	$\neg$F(t)		+	+	+	−
w_3	B(t)	$\wedge$	TB(t)	$\wedge$	$\neg$P(t)	$\wedge$	F(t)		+	+	−	+
w_4	B(t)	$\wedge$	TB(t)	$\wedge$	$\neg$P(t)	$\wedge$	$\neg$F(t)		+	+	−	−
w_5	B(t)	$\wedge$	$\neg$TB(t)	$\wedge$	P(t)	$\wedge$	F(t)		+	−	+	+
w_6	B(t)	$\wedge$	$\neg$TB(t)	$\wedge$	P(t)	$\wedge$	$\neg$F(t)		+	−	+	−
w_7	B(t)	$\wedge$	$\neg$TB(t)	$\wedge$	$\neg$P(t)	$\wedge$	F(t)		+	−	−	+
w_8	B(t)	$\wedge$	$\neg$TB(t)	$\wedge$	$\neg$P(t)	$\wedge$	$\neg$F(t)		+	−	−	−

on. Let Σ be the power set 2^W; then the eight worlds form the subfield of sets $\Sigma \cap B$ which contains the following propositions that are of interest to us:

$$
\begin{aligned}
TB &= \{w_1, w_2, w_3, w_4\} \\
TB^* &= \{w_5, w_6, w_7, w_8\} \\
P &= \{w_1, w_2, w_5, w_6\} \\
P^* &= \{w_3, w_4, w_7, w_8\} \\
F &= \{w_1, w_3, w_5, w_7\} \\
F^* &= \{w_2, w_4, w_6, w_8\}
\end{aligned}
$$

Now, in the initial state S_0 X believes the propositions (i)–(iv) given above. Let κ_0 represent S_0; then we can formulate conditions on the values of κ_0 even if we don't know the exact values. Belief (1) implies the condition that there is a positive firmness α to B, that is, we have $\kappa_0(B^*) = \alpha > 0$. Let us say that whenever a proposition p is believed, the firmness attached to this belief constitutes a (nonzero) malus for the complement p*, that is, every world in p* receives this malus. Thus, α is the malus on B* derived from belief (1). Now, belief (2) is a piece of generic information. Applied to our model, we can say that X concludes from belief (2) that if Tweety is a typical bird it will fly; that is, on TB, the complement F* of F receives the malus τ. For the time being this τ is a parametric value, to be filled with the actual firmness β with which X (if at all) forms the belief TB. Furthermore, since belief (3) is assumed to be categorical or lawlike, we attach the malus ω to $P \cap F$. Finally, from belief (4) we get a malus ρ for $P \cap TB$. Then the middle column of table 9.2 below describes the initial OCF κ_0 (α, τ, and ρ are all assumed to be finite; when w belongs to two propositions with a malus for each, the maluses superimpose).

Table 9.2

B	TB	P	F	S_0 (1)–(4) κ_0	S_1 'TB' κ_1	S_2 'P' κ_2
+	+	+	+	ω	ω	ω
+	+	+	−	$\tau + \rho$	$\beta + \rho$	ρ
+	+	−	+	**0**	**0**	γ
+	+	−	−	τ	β	$\gamma + \beta$
+	−	+	+	ω	ω	ω
+	−	+	−	**0**	β	**0**
+	−	−	+	**0**	β	$\gamma + \beta$
+	−	−	−	**0**	β	$\gamma + \beta$
−				$\geq\alpha$	$\geq\alpha$	$\geq\alpha$

In S_0 we have by the minimum rule:

$$\kappa_0(B) = 0,\ \kappa_0(B^*) = \alpha > 0$$
$$\kappa_0(TB) = 0,\ \kappa_0(TB^*) = 0$$
$$\kappa_0(P) = 0,\ \kappa_0(P^*) = 0$$
$$\kappa_0(F) = 0,\ \kappa_0(F^*) = 0$$

Relative to κ_0 then, X does believe in B but is indifferent toward TB, P, and F.

Now the belief TB is formed, with malus β on TB*. As indicated above we can set $\tau = \beta$. The rule of conditionalization then says that on TB the κ_0-values are shifted "to the left" by $\kappa_0(TB)$, whereas the values for TB* undergo a shift "to the right" by the firmness β. But $\kappa_0(TB) = 0$, so on TB there is no change. Thus $\kappa_1 = (\kappa_0)_{TB,\beta}$ is as shown in table 9.2 (note that ω "swallows" all left summands $<\omega$). For κ_1 we have, again by the minimum rule:

$$\kappa_1(TB) = 0,\ \kappa_1(TB^*) > 0$$
$$\kappa_1(P) = 0,\ \kappa_1(P^*) = 0$$
$$\kappa_1(F) = 0,\ \kappa_1(F^*) > 0$$

That is, X now believes that Tweety is a typical bird and flies, and moreover, that it is not a penguin.

Finally, X learns that P(t), and incorporates this information with firmness γ. Conditionalization on P,γ yields the OCF $\kappa_2 = (\kappa_1)_{P,\gamma}$, representing the third epistemic state S_2. The values on P now shift to the left by $\kappa_1(P) = \min\{\kappa_1(w) \mid w \in P\} = \min\{\beta,\beta + \rho,\omega\} = \beta$, and P* gets the malus γ. The resulting κ_2 is shown again in table 9.2 (ω-values are not affected by the shift, as in ordinal arithmetic, $-\beta + \omega = \omega$ for $\beta < \omega$). The propositions of interest now have the following values:

$$\kappa_2(TB) > 0,\ \kappa_2(TB^*) = 0$$
$$\kappa_2(P) = 0,\ \kappa_2(P^*) > 0$$
$$\kappa_2(F) > 0,\ \kappa_2(F^*) = 0$$

Thus X believes that Tweety is in fact a penguin, that it is not a typical bird, and that it does not fly.

We see that it is possible for X to deal with generic information in a way that takes into account the tentative nature of default conclusions which might have to be given up later on. OCFs show a way of operationalizing such information which cannot be handled by logical semantics alone.

OCF theory also has a more flexible answer to the Nixon Diamond, because of the additional degree of freedom provided by the firmness parameter. Assume that Nixon is both a Republican and a Quaker. With notation carrying over in the obvious way, the generic information that Quakers are pacifists ($Q \supset_G P$) leads to a malus σ on $TQ \cap P^*$, and the generic information that Republicans are nonpacifists ($R \supset_G P^*$) introduces a malus ρ on $TR \cap P$. Now, if X also believes that Nixon is both a typical Republican and a typical Quaker then there are two possibilities: if X thinks Nixon is more of a Republican than a Quaker the firmness ρ is greater than σ, and X ends up believing that Nixon is not a pacifist; whereas in the opposite case, $\sigma > \rho$, he thinks that Nixon is a pacifist in spite of his party allegiance. This is shown in table 9.3, which is to be read in the same way as the Tweety chart.

Table 9.3

R	Q	TR	TQ	$R \supset_G P^*$ P	S_0 $Q \supset_G P$ $\rho > \sigma$ κ_0	S_1 '$TQ \cap TR$' $\sigma > \rho$ κ_1	S_2 '$TQ \cap TR$' κ_2
+	+	+	+	+	ρ	$-\sigma + \rho$	**0**
+	+	+	+	−	σ	**0**	$-\rho + \sigma$
+	+	+	−	+	ρ	$2\rho + \sigma$	$2\rho + \sigma$
+	+	+	−	−	**0**	$\rho + \sigma$	$\rho + \sigma$
+	+	−	+	+	**0**	$\rho + \sigma$	$\rho + \sigma$
+	+	−	+	−	σ	$2\rho + \sigma$	$\rho + 2\sigma$
+	+	−	−	+	**0**	$\rho + \sigma$	$\rho + \sigma$
+	+	−	−	−	**0**	$\rho + \sigma$	$\rho + \sigma$

In the case $\rho > \sigma$ the minimum rule yields $\kappa_1(TR) = 0$, $\kappa_1(TR^*) > 0$; $\kappa_1(TQ) = 0$, $\kappa_1(TQ^*) > 0$; $\kappa_1(P) > 0$, $\kappa_1(P^*) = 0$. Thus X believes that Nixon is both a typical Republican and a typical Quaker, but that he is not a pacifist. The case $\sigma > \rho$ leads to the opposite result. We have $\kappa_2(TR) = 0$, $\kappa_2(TR^*) > 0$; $\kappa_2(TQ) = 0$, $\kappa_2(TQ^*) > 0$; $\kappa_2(P) = 0$, $\kappa_2(P^*) > 0$. So X now thinks Nixon is a pacifist while still entertaining the belief that he is both a typical Republican and a typical Quaker.

9.3. DEPENDENCY

9.3.1. A Logical Format for Representing I-Generics: Event Theory

Let us now return to matters of linguistic semantics. In Link 1987 I presented a semantic framework based on events which seems suited to represent the above distinction between CCQ and OCQ and thereby provide a format for handling I-generics. I will give only a rough indication of the basic idea here and illustrate it with an example; for the technical details of the event formalism the reader is referred to the original paper.

The theory distinguishes between *individual events* and schematic events or *event types*. What used to be called the logical form of a sentence is represented as an event type. The basic format for a *generic conditional* is given in (11):

(11) $[\theta_1 \supset_G \theta_2]$ (where θ_i are event types)

This is the appropriate semantic representation for an I-generic sentence; it says that the event type θ_1 *generically entails* the event type θ_2. For instance, an I-generic sentence like (12a) links two schematic events, that of being a tiger and that of having black stripes (the term 'event' is used here in a rather broad sense; also note that the star in (12b) is the plural operator taken from Link 1983).

(12) a. A tiger has black stripes.
b. [[TIGER(**a**)] $\supset_G$ [*BLACK-STRIPE(**b**) & HAS(**a**,**b**)]]

The representation in (12b) is quantifier-free and is given an interpretation resembling those used in DRT (Kamp 1981). The *open class* character of the quantification involved is provided by a particular feature in the semantics that allows for arbitrary extensions e of the reference event e_o with respect to which every event type is evaluated; the rule then says that whenever there is an object x in e (not just in e_o) that "modulo HRS" fits the description given by the event type θ_1:= [TIGER(**a**)], then it will also fit the description given by the event type θ_2:= [*BLACK-STRIPE(**b**) & HAS(**a**,**b**)] with respect to some suitable anchoring of the parameter **b** (i.e., **b** has to be anchored to an individual sum of black stripes had by x). By contrast, explicit *closed class* quantification is represented by a *sum event type* of the form in (13):

(13) $\Sigma(\theta_1 \mid \theta_2)$

For example:

(14) a. Every student is reading a book.

b. $\Sigma(\text{STUDENT}(\mathbf{a}^1) \mid [\mathbf{e};\rho_1(\mathbf{e}) = \mathbf{a}^1$
$\& \; \rho_2(\mathbf{e}) = \mathbf{b}^1 \; \& \; \text{BOOK}(\mathbf{b})$
$\& \; \tau(\mathbf{e}) = \mathbf{t}^1 \; \& \; \mathbf{t} \geq \mathbf{t}_0$
$\& \; \text{READING}(\mathbf{e})])$.

Sentence (14a) is about a certain class of students who all have to belong to the inventory, or "cast," of the reference event e_o. For the sentence to be true with respect to e_o there has to be a certain sum of reading events in e_o the agents of which are the students and the themes certain books (which also belong to the cast of e_o). It is clear that this quantification is only about a well-defined class of actual objects.

This sketch of the representation of I-generics as generic conditionals will suffice for our present purposes. Note that ter Meulen (1986a) has an analysis of the generic conditional along similar lines, except for the summing device.

9.3.2. Dependent and Independent Generic Noun Phrases

Let us now consider sentence (15a) below; it expresses a simple relation between two kinds, the leopard and the black panther. An indication of the kind level involved here is the fact that in the two NPs naming a kind the indefinite article is bad. Sentence (15b) looks similar to (15a), except that now the indefinite article *is* fine. While the subject NP still seems to be able to refer to a kind (the kind *Leo*), the object NP *a mane* does not denote a kind: there is simply no kind Mane to be had by the kind *Leo* simpliciter. Accordingly, the definite article is bad here. But notice that in (15c) the definite article is acceptable in the same position. It almost appears that the object NP here does refer to a kind, the kind Tail of the Scorpion.

(15) a. The/*A leopard has a close relative, the/*a black panther.

b. The/An (African) lion has a/*the mane.

c. The scorpion has the characteristic bent tail with its poisonous sting.

Even if we want to adopt this language, we still have to make a distinction: there cannot be a kind Mane *independent of* the kind *Leo,* and there cannot be a kind

Tail *independent of* the kind *Scorpio* (or of other species, respectively). That means that we have to analyze the last two sentences in terms of Derived Kind Predication. The predicate *have* really applies to individual animals here, and the sentences express general statements about lions and scorpions, the pattern being roughly, 'For every (typical) instance x of the kind Leo (Scorpio) there is a mane (tail) which x has'. So the sentences are I-generics, in which, as noted above, not only indefinite but also definite NP occur. I call the NP *a mane* in the object position of (15b) a *dependent generic NP*. More examples are given in (16):

(16) a. Indians make baskets.
b. Soldiers wear berets.
c. CIA agents perform covert actions.
d. In this place, young boys pull rickshas for a living.

What is it that makes an NP in a generic sentence dependent? It is not the fact that it stands in direct object position: in (17) we have *double independence:*

(17) a. The poor resent the wealthy.
b. Dogs chase cats.
c. Sheriffs hunt down outlaws.
d. Electrostatic devices attract dust.
e. Gravitating masses influence light rays.

The situation here is that the material of both the subject and the object NP has to be put into the antecedent of the generic conditional; in the semantics, then, the individuals of the corresponding kinds vary independently according to the general pattern, 'For all (typical) x of the subject-kind and all (typical) y of the object-kind the corresponding relation R holds'. That the object position is not even necessary for dependence can be seen from the phenomenon of "inverse dependence"; see below. In settling the question of dependence, number does not seem to play a role either, as (16) above and (18) show.

(18) a. Lions have manes.
b. Unicorns have horns.
c. Cowboys carry guns.

In the sentences in (18), just like those in (16), we have clear dependence, although there is no apparent syntactic difference from the sentences in (17). But notice a possible variation of meaning in sentences (19a–c):

(19) a. A third-grader likes to pick a fight with a classmate.
b. Third-graders like to pick a fight with classmates.
c. Third-graders like to pick a fight with a classmate.

Let us disregard the fact for the moment that these sentences do not seem to be equally acceptable. The two readings we are interested in are clearly there (at least (19b) is ambiguous between them): the sentences can either mean that a (typical) third-grader has some favorite classmate(s) to pick a fight with (e.g., among those further down in the pecking order)—this is the dependent reading—or else that the (typical) third-grader just likes to fight with whoever in his class he can get hold of—the double independent reading. So here we have one single predicate, *picking a fight with,* that gives rise to both readings. The verb *catch* is another one:

(20) a. Frogs catch flies.
b. The Makah Indians catch whales.

While (20a) is clearly double independent, (20b) can also have the dependent reading, in particular when we imagine a custom among the Makah Indians that once in his lifetime, every (male) Makah has to lead a crew catching "his" whale.

The situation laid out so far is highly unsatisfactory, since there seems to be no clue available that decides which reading to choose. The position test failed, and so did the number test. Between, say, *Frogs catch flies* and *Cowboys carry guns* there is not even a detectable difference in stress pattern. The last resort that comes to mind is the idea that the different readings are lexically induced, but this also seems to evaporate in the face of (19) and (20).

Before we explore the lexical hypothesis somewhat further, let us consider the case, hinted at above, where the dependent GNP occurs in subject position, leading to *inverse dependence:*

(21) a. A train passes my house at noon.
b. A computer assists the expert in analyzing her data.
c. In Germany, "guest workers" remove the garbage / do hot jobs in (a/?the) nuclear power plant.

In the intended interpretation, (21a) says that the type of event containing my house at noon has a train passing the house in it; (21b) means roughly that for a given expert there is a computer she can feed with her data. (21c) finally says that for the garbage in Germany there are "guest workers" removing it, or when there is a nuclear power plant and a hot job to be done in it there will be guest workers taking care of it.

The reading described is different from the intonationally unmarked reading which, for example for (21b), says that computers are *designed* to help the expert with analyzing her data. This assertion is about computers, whereas in its intended interpretation, (21b) is about today's experts who enjoy the benefits of a computerized environment. In order to have the hearer interpret the sentence in this intended way, the speaker has to put some extra stress on the dependent subject NP. So here it is intonation that serves as the clue for telling the hearer what the sentence is about. It can thus be seen that the *sentence topic* (see, e.g., Reinhart 1981) influences the logical form of the statement: the topic, or *theme,* of a generic statement is to be placed in the antecedent of the corresponding generic conditional; for some discussion of this observation see Krifka 1987. In the cases at hand that means that since the topic is located in the verb phrase, the subject NP, which is now rhematic, has to get extra stress. Sentence (21a), for instance, can hardly be about trains, which otherwise would have to be made just for passing my house at noon; rather, its topic or theme is the "generic" situation near my house at noon, with an implicit parameter running over days—this material goes into the antecedent. The rheme, then, which is to be placed into the consequent of the generic conditional, expresses the property of there being a train passing my house at the indicated time of day, that is, at noon. For more data on the phenomenon of inverse dependence, in particular in connection with locative phrases, see Carlson 1987.

Returning to the question of dependence vs. double independence, which was left unresolved above, we might now want to entertain the hypothesis that it is the theme–rheme structure of the sentence that settles the issue of dependence. Upon reflection, however, this approach as well seems to be doomed before it can get off the ground. The problem are pairs of sentences like those in (22), which already served as examples above.

(22) a. Frogs catch flies.
b. Cowboys carry guns.

The two sentences have the same unmarked stress contour, so it is natural to assume that in both cases the subject NP is the theme. Still, *guns* is dependent, *flies* is not. Now, it would be bluntly circular, of course, to say that *flies* is part of the theme *because* it is independent: we were just trying to account for (in)dependence in terms of the theme–rheme structure! But let us try a test where the stress pattern (loosely correlated so far with the theme–rheme structure) does influence the dependence relation. Consider (23) (caps indicate main stress).

(23) a. Computers assist EXPERTS.
b. COMPUTERS assist experts.

By reversing the stress in (23b), we have also reversed the basic dependence structure ∀∃ of (23a): while (23a) says about computers that they have the property of assisting (some) experts, (23b) may be the answer to a question of the kind, ''What do you know about today's experts?''; that is, it says about experts that they have the property of being assisted by (some) computers. Now, notice that even though changing stress led to a *reversal* of dependence, this change resulted in a dependent structure only because we started out with one! Compare the double independence case (24a):

(24) a. Cats chase MICE.
b. CATS chase mice.

The reversal of stress does not make *cats* dependent at all; rather, (24b) is the answer to a question like, ''Which animals chase mice?'' That is, while chasing mice is indeed the theme or topic now, this fact by itself does not mean that the NP *mice* inside the theme can subdue the subject NP *cats* and make it dependent. The structure of double independence is preserved.

There is one conclusion, though, which relates the theme–rheme structure and the dependence structure and which does seem to stand up well to the evidence presented so far: while it is wrong to say that rhematicity means dependence, as we saw, we can still maintain that *thematicity means independence*. Let us add that this is not to say that thematic phrases are not subject to further restrictions; in (21c), for instance, the NP *a nuclear power plant* is restricted in its range by the locative phrase *in Germany,* yet it is thematic and thus part of the antecedent.

It is now time to resolve the issue that is still pending, namely, exactly what it is that triggers dependence in examples like (22). I think it is just the logical form of the property expressed by the predicate in question. So *carrying guns* denotes the property of an x such that there are some guns that x carries. Since this property is rhematic in the general statement (22b), the existential quantifier in it comes under the scope of *cowboys.* By contrast, in (22a) there is double independence because the property expressed by the predicate, viz. *catching flies,* does not contain an existential quantifier: it is the property of an x such that (typically) whenever there are flies around x catches them. This property simply doesn't have *existential import.* What I suggest, then, is this:

NPs with existential import in the rhematic part of a generic statement give rise to dependence;

typical examples are those under (16). When the rhematic part itself contains a general property like *catching flies,* the resulting structure in a sentence like

(22a) boils down to double independence, since it is an iterated conditional roughly of the form 'Every (typical) frog x has the property of catching flies', that is, 'Every (typical) frog x is such that (typically) whenever there are flies around x catches them'. This, however, is equivalent to the statement '(Typically) whenever there is a frog x and a fly y around, x catches y'.

Finally, we can see now why the ambiguous sentences in (19) and (20) involving *pick a fight with* and *catch* do not constitute counterexamples to the account just given. To take the third-grader example: *picking a fight with a (some) classmate* and *picking a fight with classmates,* although built up from one and the same verb *pick a fight with,* express different properties. The first one has existential import, the second one does not; the first one gives rise to a dependent structure in a generic statement, the second one leads to double independence in such an environment. In summary, we have shown that while thematicity involves independence, the theme–rheme structure cannot by itself settle the question of dependence of an NP in the rhematic part of a generic statement; the appropriate criterion here is its existential import.

9.4. An Example of a Generic Discourse: *The Tiger*

Any empirical theory has to be measured against its ability to account for the data. In order to convey a feeling for what a realistic generic discourse looks like, excerpts from a nonscientific text on a natural kind, the tiger, are presented in the Appendix below. Such a text has an advantage over a scientific text, say, in a biology book, in that stylistic variation—atypical for a science text—can be expected to display the full range of generic idioms in language. Indeed we find Proper and Derived Kind Predication, generic anaphora, taxonomic quantification, dependent generic NPs, and much more.

One conspicuous feature of the discourse is the ease with which predication levels are switched; for example, one single NP, which occurs in the context of Derived Kind Predication in one sentence, serves as antecedent for a kind-referring pronoun in the next sentence (see, e.g., A(1), (2)). This suggests that there should be a stage in the semantic representation process at which there is a kind-denoting term present even in DKP contexts, so that there is a hook for a kind pronoun in a PKP context later in the discourse. In accordance with Gerstner-Link 1988, I propose to introduce an "up-arrow" operation '$\uparrow$' on nouns producing kind-denoting terms; for instance, if TIGER is a one-place predicate denoting the set of tigers, $\uparrow$ TIGER is a singular term that denotes the kind Tiger. A binary relation **R** of *realization* between object terms and kind terms is then used to relate the kind to its instances over which the generic conditional of a DKP ranges. So we replace (25b) by (25c), which has the explicit kind term in it:

(25) a. The tiger has black stripes.
b. [[TIGER(**a**)] $\supset_G$ [*BLACK-STRIPE(**b**) & HAS(**a**,**b**)]]
c. [**k** = ↑ TIGER] & [[**aRk**] $\supset_G$ [*BLACK-STRIPE(**b**) & HAS(**a**,**b**)]]

Here, **k** is a parameter for kinds. If now the discourse continues with a PKP sentence involving the kind Tiger, the parameter **k** can be taken up, insuring the referential link to this kind. The beginning (A(1),(2)) of the Tiger discourse is to be treated along these lines. The up-arrow operation should not be introduced when the sentence starts with a singular indefinite NP, witness ter Meulen's example given in (26a):

(26) a. An elephant has valuable teeth. *He is dying out.
b. Elephants have valuable teeth. They are dying out.

The bare plural version (26b) is fine again. This suggests that the indefinite singular NP is the only case in DKP in which the kind parameter does not come into play.

In language, relational nouns like *the tail of, the life span of* abound. It is therefore to be expected that Proper Kind Predication does not only apply to basic kind terms like *the tiger,* but also to relational kind terms like *the life span of the tiger*. Is there a need to introduce "dependent" kinds like The Life Span of the Tiger along with the "basic" kinds in our ontology? We already touched this question above when we discussed the lion's mane and the tail of the scorpion. It is obvious that a positive answer would proliferate entities vastly. Still, I think that we could, without too many metaphysical qualms, maintain those dependent or *relational* kinds (let us reserve the notion of dependence for the phenomenon described above), if only for the sake of a higher degree of compositionality in our grammar. Take, for example, the tiger's coat in B(1); it is said there of it that it varies a lot in color. This predicate does not apply to an abitrary instance of a tiger skin (unless it meant variation in color along with the seasons, which is also a possibility). It is a proper kind predicate and can, of course, apply to basic kinds, too, as in *Tigers vary a lot in size*. The relational kind Tiger Skin can also be taken up by a pronoun in the coming discourse, as illustrated by the first *it* in B(2). So it seems hard to draw the line here, and one might indeed well argue that to be relational is by no means an inherent feature of a term. (Is Keyboard relational—viz. Keyboard-of—because a keyboard usually comes with a computer?) Thus I propose to admit relational kind objects along with the ''basic'' kinds. We have to make sure, of course, that those kinds, basic or relational, satisfy certain axioms that give them some structure; tiger claws, for instance, are claws of a wildcat, so the relational kind Claws-of has to respect the ordering relation imposed on the kinds by the taxonomic hierarchy. But I shall not stop now to specify those axioms in detail here.

Rather, I'd like to comment some more, in an informal way, on those features of the Tiger text that are of interest to us here (phrases that deserve attention are underlined). Starting from the top, we have already seen what the basic structure of sentences A(1),(2) should be: along with the generic conditional representing A(1), a discourse marker for the kind Tiger is introduced, which is taken up in the taxonomic assertion A(2). Note further that *walking along a forest path* in A(1) is a generic property with no existential import. A(3)–(5) focus in on male and female tigers, with a change in number. The almost free transition between singular and plural in generic texts is rather characteristic and also crosslinguistically valid (for this phenomenon of *neutralization of number* see Gerstner-Link 1988). We can therefore talk of the subkinds Male Tiger and Female Tiger, which happen to be referred to here by bare plurals. A(3) contains the modal auxiliary *may,* to consider it a verbal modifier and analyze the sentence as a conditional with the diamond on the consequent is somewhat unintuitive semantically, since the sentence does not say that individual tigers vary in size (like Alice in Wonderland happened to after drinking those liquids). A better paraphrase would be: 'It is possible for an instance of the subkind Male Tiger to measure ten feet, etc.' In A(5) males and females are compared by their size, the generic property *being smaller than male tigers* leading to a double independent statement about typical female and male tigers.

In part B, the relational kind Tiger Coat introduced in B(1) is taken up by the pronoun *it* in B(2). Note that the definite NP *the cat* refers to the bearer of the coat in turn, and the following occurrences of *it* refer to the tiger rather than its skin. The modal *can* in B(3), unlike the *may* in A(3), is a VP modifier.

The bare plural *tigers* in C(1) is a kind-referring term in object position. The property of *wandering alone in dense forests* in C(2) has existential import. The status of *most tigers* in C(3) is somewhat unclear: it looks as if the sentence is about the majority of actual tigers, but it does make a generic statement nonetheless; it says that there is this knowledge impressed upon the kind Tiger (viz. that man means danger), and that this knowledge will no doubt be passed on to further generations in the majority of cases. Note also the kind-referring pronoun *him* here. The plural pronoun *they* in C(4) is again kind-referring, whereas *one* at the end of the sentence picks an instance of the kind.

The indefinite NP *a tiger* in D(1) is thematic; it is said here that given a (typical) tiger, watching it is best when *discovering the place where it has killed a large animal* (this property has existential import). In the next sentence, *its meat supply* refers back to the large animal that was killed in the scenario imagined just before. What we have here is something like modal subordination: in an event type where the tiger has killed an animal, there will be meat supply for it, and it will stay near it until it has eaten it.

In E there are a number of relational kind terms, like *habits, tracks, foot, toes, claws*. Part F focuses on the relational kind Tiger Trail.

Part G shows an interesting series of examples of a phenomenon that was already observed by Lawler (1973a). According to him, *John drinks beer* is ambiguous between a universal and an existential reading; it may either mean that John drinks beer at all suitable occasions, or that he might drink beer among other things. Here we have a scale of sentences about the tiger's food, leading from a strictly universal reading (G(2)) to a weak existential reading of a sentence (G(5)) in which the tiger is said to feed on grass and soil on some rare occasions. The existential force that is becoming more and more salient here is accounted for by a *dispositional* element, which is present in many habitual statements.

Relational kind terms occur again in part H, which displays, in addition, another interesting feature. NPs like *the prey* in H(3) and *the victim* in H(4) have what could be called a *modalizing* force: it is only in a certain role (as prey or as victim) that the animals talked about are acted upon in the way the sentence describes. In a semantic representation such modalizers call for a generic conditional in which the antecedent specifies the role indicated by the NP in question.

I(2) is interesting because it seems most natural to assume here that we have a *taxonomic* quantification, that is, an explicit universal quantification over kinds. At the same time it is a Derived Kind Predication since *running faster than* is a relation between animals on the object level rather than between kinds. The following sentence, I(3), is also highly involved. The NP *the tiger* is thematic, and accordingly, the kind Tiger is said to have a certain property P. This P is a generic property with a thematic deer y in it; it is the property of an x such that a necessary condition for x catching y is an undetected creeping of x to within thirty or forty feet of y while y is still unwary. So the 'deer' part of the NP *an unwary deer* goes into the antecedent of the resulting generic conditional, whereas the 'unwary' part is rhematic.

Part J displays instances of modal subordination. J(1) lays out the possibility of a tiger having eaten a certain vast amount of meat; the *then* in J(2) signals that the discourse is carried on assuming just such a situation. Note also the "generic" group of five men further down in J(6), again in a modalized situation—one where a cow weighs five hundred pounds.—Part K has another comparative construction between kinds, the kind Man on the one hand and the kinds Cow or Deer on the other in K(3).

The bare plural *cubs* is thematic in L(1), along with the subject NP *a tigress*. Thus, while being an independent NP in the above sense, *cubs* refers to a relational kind, the kind Tiger Cub.—In M(3) the NP *the tigress* is relational because it refers to the mother of the tiger family introduced in the preceding sentence.—The NPs *the size of a tiger's range* and *the number of prey-animals present* in N(1) are multiply relational, the latter to an even higher degree since it is elliptical; what is meant, of course, are the prey animals present in the tiger's range.

Parts O and P have *generic gerunds* in them: *the repeated calling back and forth* (O(3)), *much roaring* (P(1)), *most of the mating* (P(2)). It seems natural here to give a representation of the sentences involving those phrases in terms of event structures. Note also a case of inverse dependence (*bloody battles*) in O(5).

Part Q starts with a Derived Kind Predication about tigers (Q(1)); the disjunction *male or female* is a syntactic qualification but semantically vacuous and put in only for reasons of salience. Q(1) is about the schematic situation of a tiger placing scent at certain spots along its trail (the property of placing scent has existential import). Beginning with Q(2) this situation is described in more detail. Q(4) is particularly interesting; what is instantiated here is not only the relational kind Tiger Scent but also the generic occasion on which it is sprayed out: *weeks later* refers back to this occasion. Q(6) shows that along with a discourse marker for the relational kind there has to be one for the kind on which it depends (here, Tiger; the sentence is, in fact, more complicated because of the *each-other* construction). The same pattern of introducing the underlying kind after the relational kind belonging to it can be seen in Q(7); note here also the intricate relations across the tiger instances that are established by the NP *another tiger,* as well as the gender distinction *a male tiger* vs. *a tigress.*

APPENDIX: EXCERPTS FROM SCHALLER AND SELSAM (1969), THE TIGER: ITS LIFE IN THE WILD

A (1) The tiger, undisturbed in the wilderness, is a majestic sight as it walks along a forest path or strides through a meadow of grass. (2) It is the largest cat in the world. (3) Male tigers may measure ten feet from the nose to the tip of the tail. (4) They weigh about four hundred pounds. (5) Tigresses are smaller than male tigers—usually eight to nine feet long—and they weigh about three hundred pounds. (6) The life span of a tiger is about twenty years.

B (1) The tiger's coat varies from a rich orange-red to a golden yellow and is striped with black. (2) It blends in so well with its surroundings that the cat becomes almost invisible when it crouches motionless. (3) It can hide behind a small bush or melt into a background of high grass.

C (1) It takes great patience to study tigers. (2) They are shy animals that wander alone in dense forests. (3) Most tigers have learned that man means danger, and they usually avoid him by stealing away or hiding. (4) They hide themselves in the jungle so well that a person rarely sees one.

D (1) The best way of watching a tiger is to discover the place where it has killed a large animal. (2) The tiger remains near its meat supply until it has eaten all of it.

E (1) It is not necessary to actually see tigers to learn about their habits. (2) Much can be gained by studying their tracks. (3) A tiger walks on the ball of its foot and on its toes, not on its whole foot. (4) Its huge claws are withdrawn into a sheath when walking or resting, so they do not leave a mark.

F (1) Each trail of the tiger has its own story to tell. (2) Here the trail may go to a tree; cuts in the bark show where the tiger has sharpened its claws. . . .

G (1) The tiger spends most of its time finding a meal, usually a deer, antelope, or wild pig. (2) But it eats whatever it can catch. (3) Where wild animals are not available, the tiger preys on cattle, goats, and other domestic animals around villages. (4) It also readily eats dead animals. (5) It even eats grass and soil, but nobody knows why.

H (1) The tiger's main source of food are the chital deer. (2) The tiger has formidable weapons with which to catch these deer. (3) Its forelegs are powerful and armed with large, curved claws—ideal for grabbing and pulling the prey to the ground. (4) Its canine or eyeteeth are long and strong, which enable the tiger to kill the victim by biting the neck or throat. (5) Its ears are very sharp as are its eyes. (6) The tiger can see far better than man at night.

I (1) One advantage the tiger does not have is speed. (2) All deer can run faster than the tiger. (3) Because of this, the tiger must creep undetected to within thirty or forty feet of an unwary deer before it has much hope of catching one.

J (1) A tiger can eat a vast amount of meat when it is hungry—as much as fifty pounds in one meal. (2) Then the tiger does not have to eat again for several days. (3) A small animal like a deer or gaur calf may be completely eaten in one night, but a large one like a cow or full-grown gaur sometimes lasts for several days. (4) After killing the animal, the tiger picks it up by the neck and drags it to a shady spot. (5) It is at such times that the tiger shows its full strength. (6) A cow may weigh five hundred pounds; five men would find it difficult to move such a carcass, yet a tiger pulls it easily by itself.

K (1) Although tigers usually prey on deer and other wild animals, occasionally a tiger becomes a man-eater. (2) This often happens when it is old or injured or wounded and thus unable to catch its usual prey. (3) It may then be driven by hunger to prey on man, for man is easier to knock down and kill than a cow or deer.

L (1) When a tigress gives birth to cubs, she hides them in a secluded place. (2) The cubs are blind and helpless at birth and very small. (3) They grow rapidly. (4) By the age of six or seven weeks, they begin to eat meat and follow their mother from the den.

M (1) There is little to interrupt the daily schedule in a tiger's life. (2) Sometimes a villager collecting firewood intrudes accidentally into the resting place of a tiger family. (3) Usually the tigress hears his approach and quietly leads her cubs to safety without being seen.

N (1) The size of a tiger's range varies with the number of prey-animals present. (2) Where deer and other animals are scarcer than at Kanha Park, tiger ranges may be as large as 250 square miles or even larger.

O (1) A male tiger and a tigress come together when courting. (2) A tigress roars when she is looking for a mate. (3) The male answers the roars, and the repeated calling back and forth helps the animals find each other. (4) Sometimes males from nearby ranges are attracted by the calls. (5) Bloody battles may take place between rival tigers.

P (1) In Kanha Park, much roaring can be heard from the last week of October till February, when it reaches a peak. (2) At that time, most of the mating is believed to occur.

Q (1) A tiger, male or female, places scent on bushes and tree trunks. (2) As it walks along, it occasionally stops, raises its tail, and squirts some urine. (3) Mixed with the urine is a very strong scent from two glands located under the tail. (4) This scent is so pungent that a person can smell it at a particular spot weeks later unless the rain washes it away. (5) The scent is, in effect, the tiger's calling card. (6) It enables *tigers* to follow each other in the forest. (7) Scent possibly keeps another tiger from continuing on the same trail, and it may encourage a male tiger to follow on the trail of a tigress.

10 THE SEMANTICS OF THE COMMON NOUN *KIND*

Karina Wilkinson

10.1. Introduction

Bare plural noun phrases can have generic or existential interpretations. In (1) and (2) the subject NPs have generic interpretations, and in (3) the subject has an existential interpretation.

(1) Dinosaurs are extinct.
(2) Kangaroos live in Australia.
(3) Kangaroos ruined my garden.

Wilkinson (1986, 1991), Gerstner and Krifka (1993), Krifka (1987) (partly in collaboration with Gerstner), and Schubert and Pelletier (1987) argue that bare plurals are ambiguous depending on whether they are kind-denoting terms or indefinite NPs. On one of the generic readings, the one in (2), the bare plural is interpreted as an indefinite NP bound by an invisible generic operator.

Following Carlson (1977b), we say that the bare plural in (1) has a kind reading, and the kind-level predicate *extinct* is predicated directly of it. The translation of (1) is as in (4).

(4) **extinct**(**d**) (where **d** abbreviates the dinosaur-kind)

The bare plurals in (2) and (3) are both indefinite. Lewis (1975), Kamp (1981), and Heim (1982) have argued for a treatment of indefinite NPs as variables that receive their quantificational force from unselective quantifiers. On the Kamp/Heim approach an adverb of quantification can bind an indefinite as in (5) and (6) (from Lewis 1975,5).

(5) a. A man who owns a donkey always beats it (now and then).
b. $\mathbf{Always}_{x,y}$ [**man**(x) & **donkey**(y) & **own**(x,y)] [**beat**(x,y)]
(6) a. A quadratic equation usually has two different solutions.
b. $\mathbf{Usually}_{x}$ [**quadratic-equation**(x)] [**has-two-different-solutions**(x)]

Existential closure guarantees that an indefinite NP that is not bound by any other quantifier ends up being quantified by an existential. So, (7) is the representation for (3).

(7) $\exists_x$ [**kangaroo**(x)] [**ruined-my-garden**(x)]

An invisible generic operator can also bind indefinites, as discussed in Farkas & Sugioka 1983 and Wilkinson 1986, 1991. Sentence (2) is represented as in (8).

(8) **Gen**$_x$ [**kangaroo**(x)] [**live-in-Australia**(x)]

The central problem I address in this chapter is how NPs containing the common noun *kind, type,* or *sort* can sometimes have an indefinite reading even with a definite determiner. Two examples of definite *kind*-NPs with existential readings are sentences such as (9), which were first noticed by Carlson (1977b), and *there*-insertion sentences like (12) below.

(9) That kind of book is on the shelf.

Milsark (1974) observed that indefinite NPs are allowed in sentences such as (10).

(10) There are students in Northampton.

Definite NPs only occur in *there*-insertion sentences with a list reading, as in Milsark's (11).

(11) What else is there to worry about?
Well, there's the wolf at the door.

Definite NPs such as *those books* in (13) below behave as expected. Sentence (13) is ungrammatical, but *there*-insertion sentences containing definite NPs with the common noun *kind* as in (12) are acceptable.

(12) There are those kinds of books in the library.
(13) *There are those books in the library.

Similar facts hold for NPs containing common nouns such as *type* and *sort*.

In addition to the existential readings in (9) and (12), definite *kind*-NPs can be bound by adverbs of quantification, so (14) is equivalent in meaning to (15).

(14) That kind of equation usually has two different solutions.
(15) An equation of that kind usually has two different solutions.

Why can these definite NPs behave like indefinites?

To answer this question, I will begin in section 10.2 by discussing Carlson's analysis of the common noun *kind* and his account of sentences like (9). He argues that *kind* is a transitive noun. Since he does not discuss NPs where *kind* is in final position, such as *a book of that kind,* and they do not have an obvious analysis with *kind* as a transitive noun, I will modify his analysis to cover these NPs. In section 10.3, I discuss one modification which makes *kind* ambiguous between a transitive noun meaning and simple one-place predicate. I will show how certain facts about quantification in these NPs are to follow on this view. In section 10.4, I propose that there is a structural ambiguity that accounts for the difference between the generic and the indefinite interpretations of definite *kind*-NPs. Finally, in section 10.5 I present an alternative which does not make the noun *kind* itself ambiguous. Using function composition, I maintain Carlson's analysis of *kind* as a transitive noun and show how the indefinite interpretation is derived compositionally.

10.2. CARLSON'S ACCOUNT OF *KIND*

In this section, I will discuss how Carlson (1977b) accounts for the properties of NPs containing the common noun *kind.* I presuppose some familiarity with his treatment of bare plurals.

Carlson observes:

> The NP 'this kind of animal' behaves very much like the existential use of the bare plural. . . . But the most important fact is that the NP 'this kind of animal' also has 'generic' uses alongside its existential uses, and its existential and generic uses are distributed exactly in the same way as the corresponding uses of the bare plural. (1977b,46)

He argues that the bare plural is unambiguous; it always denotes the name of a kind. The syntactic rule and translation for bare plurals are given in (16) (1977b,398, 411). '$' stands for plural marking.

(16) **S6.** If $\alpha \in P_{CN}$ and α is of the form $\$\beta$,
then $F_5(\alpha) \in P_T$, where $F_5(\alpha) = [\alpha]$
T6. If $\alpha \in P_{CN}$ and α translates as α', then $F_5(\alpha)$ translates as
$\lambda P\ {}^{\vee}P(\iota x^k\ \forall z^o \Box [\mathbf{R}'(z,x) \leftrightarrow \alpha'(z)])$

The translation rule says that a term like *dogs* denotes the unique kind-level individual such that every realization of the kind is a dog and the set of realizations contains every dog. Any existential reading the term receives is the result of quantification over stages introduced by the meaning of a stage-level predicate. Among Carlson's examples of bare plurals or *kind*-NPs that have existential readings are the sentences in (17). The examples in (18) all have generic readings.

(17) a. Bill shot bears / this kind of animal yesterday.
b. Dogs are sitting on my lawn.
c. This kind of animal is sitting on my lawn.
d. I saw bears / this kind of animal in the zoo.

(18) a. Dogs / this kind of animal bark(s).
b. John hates dogs / this kind of animal.
c. Dogs are common.
d. This kind of animal is common. (Carlson 1977b,46–47)

The representation of (17b), for example, is given in (19).

(19) $\exists x^{o}$ [**R**′(x,**d**) & **sitting-on-my-lawn** (x)]

In (19), **d** represents *dogs*. In contrast to the stage-level predicates in (19), the kind-level predicate *common* in (18c) applies directly to the kind *dogs*.

(20) **common(d)**

Carlson represents *dogs* as in (21).

(21) **dogs** $= \lambda P\ {}^{\vee}P(\iota x^{k}\ [\forall y^{o} \Box$ [**R**′(y,x) $\leftrightarrow$ **dog**(y)]])

(21) says that every dog is a realization of the kind *dogs,* and every realization of the dog-kind is a dog.

Carlson notes that *kind* behaves like an adjective semantically, since it takes a CN denotation and yields a CN denotation. He argues that it has the syntactic category CN/CN:

(22) $[[\text{that}]_{\text{Det}}\ [[\text{kind}]_{\text{CN/CN}}\ (\text{of})\ [\text{animal}]]_{\text{CN}}]_{\text{CN}}]_{\text{NP}}$

However, it behaves like a noun in that it takes plural morphology.[1]

Simplifying the meaning of *that$_i$* to $\lambda Q\ \lambda P\ [{}^{\vee}Q(x_i)\ \&\ {}^{\vee}P(x_i)]$ for expository purposes and leaving out Carlson's subkind and disjointness conditions for *kind*, we get the representation in (23) for *that$_i$ kind of animal:*

(23) **that$_i$ kind of animal** =
$\lambda P(\forall y^{o} \Box$ [**R**′(y,x_i^k) $\rightarrow$ **animal**(y)] & ${}^{\vee}P(x_i^k)$)

1. The noun *kind,* in general, agrees in number with the CN in the *of*-phrase. An exception to this (Ileana Comorovski, pers. comm.) is *wh*-phrases, so *what kind of books* is acceptable (cf. **that kind of books*) (see also the discussion of *wh*-phrases in NP modifiers in section 10.4.1). Carlson also points out there are some dialects that, like early modern English, allow *kind* to be singular when the determiner and common noun are plural; e.g., *those kind of men.*

Having the conditional in (23) allows *that$_i$ kind of animal* to be a subkind of the kind *animals,* since not every animal has to be a realization of *that$_i$ kind of animal*.

Again, ignoring for the moment Carlson's conditions that guarantee that the kinds are disjoint and subordinate, *kind* is translated as in (24).

(24) $\mathbf{kind} = \lambda Q\ \lambda x^k\ [\forall z^o\ \Box\ (\mathbf{R}'(z,x) \rightarrow {}^{\vee}Q(z))]$

Applying (24) to the CN *animal* yields the meaning of the common noun *kind of animal* in (25).

(25) $\mathbf{kind\ of\ animal} = \lambda x^k\ [\forall z^o\ \Box\ [\mathbf{R}'(z,x) \rightarrow \mathbf{animal}\ (z)]]$

The denotation of *kind of animal* is a set of kind-level individuals. For a given kind to count as a kind of animal it must have only animals among its realizations, but not every animal needs to realize that kind. This captures the fact that the set of kinds denoted by *kinds of animals* consists of subkinds of the kind denoted by *animals*.

10.3. AMBIGUITY OF *KIND*

Carlson did not discuss NPs such as *an animal of that kind,* but one obvious way of handling NPs with *kind* at the end is to assume that *kind* is ambiguous. In this section I will discuss how making *kind* ambiguous allows for an interpretation of *an animal of that kind* and accounts for the wide scope of *every kind* in *an animal of every kind.* An alternative to making *kind* ambiguous is discussed in section 10.5.

10.3.1. A Simple Predicate: **kind**(x)

Carlson's account generates existential readings of both bare plurals and *kind*-NPs when they are the argument of stage-level predicates. If this were the only translation of *kind,* and the rest of Carlson's fragment were not amended, we would not have an account of *kind* in the following example:

(26) An animal of that kind is sitting on my lawn.

(26) presents a problem for Carlson's treatment, since the sentence doesn't provide the required CN argument for *kind*.

The simplest way I can see to deal with this problem is to let *kind* be ambiguous between a CN/CN meaning and a simple CN meaning, **kind**(x). For *an animal of that$_i$ kind, kind* is translated as **kind,** a predicate over kind-level individuals. To distinguish these two meanings of *kind,* I will call the translation in (24) "$\mathbf{kind}_1$" and the simple predicate "$\mathbf{kind}_2$".

To get from the NP meaning **that kind** to the meaning of the prepositional phrase *of that kind,* I assume that **of** makes a predicate out of *e*-type meanings by simply applying Chierchia's (1984) predication operator π. The expression $\pi(x)(y)$ means 'apply the property corresponding to the individual x to the individual y'. The variable x may be a variable over kinds, while y is a variable over objects. Thus, Carlson's realization operator $\mathbf{R}'$ is just a special case of the predication operator π.

The derivation of *an animal of that kind* is then as follows. As before, **that** contains an indexed variable, but here it also contains the iota operator, so *that$_i$ kind* is a phrase of type e and not a generalized quantifier.

(27) $\mathbf{that}_i = \lambda Q\ [\iota y\ [{}^{\vee}Q(x_i)\ \&\ y = x_i]]$

That applies to **kind$_2$** to give (28).

(28) $\mathbf{that_i\ kind_2} = \iota y\ [\mathbf{kind}(x_i)\ \&\ y = x_i]$

Of makes a predicate out of the NP meaning in (28):

(29) $\mathbf{of\ that_i\ kind_2} =$
$\pi(\iota y[\mathbf{kind}(x_i)\ \&\ y = x_i])$

The predicates *of that$_i$ kind$_2$* and *animal* are conjoined just as in the formation of ordinary relative clauses:

(30) $\mathbf{animal\ of\ that_i\ kind_2} =$
$\lambda z[\mathbf{animal}(z)\ \&\ \pi\ (\iota y\ [\mathbf{kind}(x_i)\ \&\ y = x_i])(z)]$

Taking Montague's 1973 translation of *an,* $\lambda P\ \lambda Q\ \exists x\ [{}^{\vee}P(x)\ \&\ {}^{\vee}Q(x)]$ yields the meaning in (31) for *an animal of that$_i$ kind$_2$*.

(31) $\mathbf{an\ animal\ of\ that\ kind_i\ kind_2} =$
$\lambda P\ \exists z[\mathbf{animal}(z)\ \&\ \pi(\iota y[\mathbf{kind}(x_i)\ \&\ y = x_i])(z)\ \&\ {}^{\vee}P(z)]$

Alternatively, using a Kamp/Heim approach to *an animal of that$_i$ kind,* (30) applies to a discourse referent, say u, as in (32).

(32) $[\mathbf{animal}(u)\ \&\ \pi(\iota y[\mathbf{kind}(x_i)\ \&\ y = x_i])(u)]$

The embedding conditions or satisfaction conditions give the whole NP existential force. Regardless of the choice of the meaning of the indefinite article, the result is an NP meaning that either applies to predicates over objects or is a predicate over objects.

10.3.2. Quantification

Sentences like (33) provide additional support for the simple predicate meaning of *kind*. Here *every kind* has wide scope, which I see no way of accounting for if *kind* has only a CN/CN meaning.

(33) Peter has a coin of every kind.

When *kind* precedes the common noun, as in *every kind of coin,* there is only one quantifier position, but when *kind* follows the noun there are two positions available, e.g.:

(34)

Det		*Det*	
one		every	
every		one	
several	animal(s) of	two (different)	kind(s)
few		any	
each		several	

Notice that not all of the scope possibilities are available here. For example, *an animal of every kind* can only have the wide scope reading for *every*. There is a way of ruling out the narrow scope readings on Carlson's account. Up to now, I have ignored the disjointness condition that Carlson considers part of the meaning of *kind*. He postulates this condition to account for the intuition that (36) follows from (35).

(35) Two kinds of dogs are in the next room.
(36) At least two dogs are in the next room.

He states the condition in (37) as part of the meaning of *kind*.

(37) $\neg \exists x^{o} \exists y^{k} \exists z^{k} [y^{k} \neq z^{k} \,\&\, S_{o}(y) \,\&\, S_{o}(z) \,\&\, \mathbf{R}'(x,y) \,\&\, \mathbf{R}'(x,z)]$

Here S_o is a free variable. Carlson says, "S_o may only contain kinds that are subordinate to the kind corresponding to the CN operated on, and the set of all possible realizations of the members collectively of S_o must be the same set as all possible members of the set of objects operated on" (1977b:348). Roughly, (37) says that there is no object that realizes two different subkinds.

The effect of the disjointness condition is to guarantee that sets of realizations of kinds of animals will be disjoint subsets for any one way of dividing the set of animals into kinds. This is more general than the meaning of the lexical item *kind*. Similar phenomena are observed in other domains where entities in the domain stand in a part–whole relationship (see Kratzer 1989b, Roberts 1987). However such restrictions on quantification fit into the grammar, they should guarantee that the narrow scope reading of *every* in *an animal of every kind* is impossible or at least always false. Similarly, any pairing of quantifiers in (38) that results in one object being of more than one kind will be semantically deviant, indicated by '#' in (38).

(38) *Narrow scope readings for the second quantifier*
#few houses of every kind
#a book of three (different) kinds
#two cats of three (different) kinds

As for the wide scope reading of *every,* consider a reading of (39) where *every kind* is quantified in to the whole sentence.

(39) A cat of every kind disappeared.

Assuming *kind* is ambiguous, only $\mathbf{kind_2}$ can be quantified in. $\mathbf{Kind_1}$ can't occur in NPs that are quantified in, because its argument position is not filled, so the NP would be missing an argument. Using $\mathbf{kind_2}$, (39) is represented as (40):

(40) $\forall x^k\ [\mathbf{kind}(x) \rightarrow \exists y^o\ [\mathbf{cat}(y)\ \&\ \pi(x)(y)\ \&\ \mathbf{disappeared}(y)]]$

Thus, with a one-place predicate meaning for *kind,* we have accounted for NPs such as *an animal of* $that_i$ *kind* and for quantificational NPs.

10.4. EXISTENTIAL READINGS OF *THAT*$_i$ *KIND OF ANIMAL*

Let us turn to the analysis of $that_i$ *kind of animal.* Since *kind* is ambiguous, we have a second way of interpreting $that_i$ *kind of animal,* namely, with the simple predicate **kind**(x). Where the NP has an existential interpretation, I take it that *animal* is the head of the NP, as in (41).

(41) $[[\text{that kind}]_{NP}\ \text{(of) animal}]_{NP}$

If the CN following *kind* is the head, then we have a structure like the one Selkirk (1977) and others argue we have for "pseudo-partitives" such as (42a). In (42a) *people* is the syntactic head of the noun phrase, while in (42b) *number* is the head of the phrase.

(42) a. $[[\text{a number of}]_{QP}\ \text{people}]_{NP}$
b. $[\text{a}[\text{number}\ [\text{of}\ [\text{the people}]_{NP}]_{PP}]_{N'}]_{NP}$

A number of people behaves differently than the true partitive NP *a number of the people.* One piece of evidence Selkirk uses to differentiate the structures in (42) is the fact that extraposition of the prepositional phrase is allowed with the partitive but not the pseudo-partitive.

(43) a. A lot had been eaten of the leftover turkey.
b. *A lot had been eaten of leftover turkey. (Selkirk 1977,305)

Similar data can be constructed with *kind*-NPs, as in (44).

(44) *That kind was sitting on my lawn of animal.

Also, selectional restrictions are determined by the head. Similarly, they are determined by the CN after *kind of*.

I am assuming that the syntax of the phrase is like the pseudo-partitives in that what follows the *of* is a CN and not an NP. I will ignore *kind-of* phrases that are acceptable with an indefinite article preceding the CN, as in *what kind of a guy* and *that kind of an idiot,* since the occurrence of a determiner here is restricted. I cannot find any other determiners that are acceptable. For examples, the following NPs are ungrammatical: **that kind of one book,* **that kind of every book,* and **those kinds of few cars*.

It is difficult to define exactly what class or category of items can occur after the *of*. One might think that the class can be characterized as kind-denoting NPs. *A horse* and *horses* are both NPs that can refer to kinds and are acceptable after the *of*. Assuming that NPs referring to kinds are allowed here leads to the expectation that *the horse* is allowed, but it is not: **that kind of the horse*. Also, the occurrence of bare singular count nouns would be unexplained. A more plausible characterization of the class is as those things that can be predicative (F. Roger Higgins, pers. comm.). Singular and plural common nouns as well as NPs with the indefinite article can be predicative and occur in predicate nominals. The distribution of the bare singular CN is the most limited, although it does occur with role predicates such as *mayor* and in constructions such as *John is poet, philosopher, and friend* (the example is due to F. Roger Higgins). I will leave the NPs with the indefinite article aside and discuss only the phrases where what follows the *of* is a CN, singular or plural.

If *animal* is the head, I assume $\textbf{that}_\mathbf{i}$ combines with $\textbf{kind}_\mathbf{2}$. *That*$_i$ *kind of animal* can be interpreted existentially. It comes out equivalent to *an animal of that*$_i$ *kind* provided that (i) [*that*$_i$ *kind*] becomes a predicate modifier, and (ii) there is some explanation of the existential quantification. I will discuss (i) in the next section and (ii) in section 10.4.2.

10.4.1. Noun Phrase Modifiers

I propose that when *that*$_i$ *kind of animal* gets an existential reading, *animal* is the head and *that*$_i$ *kind* forms a modifier (the *of* is semantically empty). The NP becoming a modifier is reminiscent of expressions like *that size, that color, that length,* and *that weight,* which have been argued by Partee (1987) to have type-shifted interpretations as modifiers. *Color,* on Partee's analysis, is an attributive noun, marked with the feature [+A] which means that it expresses a property of properties. [+A] is a feature that percolates, so the whole NP becomes [+A] and can act like a predicate. Partee treats *every color* in (45) by this mechanism (for details see Partee 1987). *Every color* in (45) is in a context that normally does not allow universally quantified NPs; for example, (46) is disallowed.

(45) This house has been every color.
(46) John has been every student.[2]

Since the [+A] feature percolates, expressions like *that size, that color, that length,* and *that weight* can be used as modifiers:

(47) A dress (of) that size / That size (of) dress — is hard to find.
(48) That length (of) skirt will be in style.
(49) They don't make — that color (of) paint / paint (of) that color — anymore.

Other examples involve nouns such as *age* and *style:*

(50) this age fossil
that style coat

With a *wh*-word the two nouns may disagree in number. That the verbal agreement goes with the second noun further supports the hypothesis that the latter is the head.[3]

(51) a. What size dresses are left?
b. *What size dresses is left?

2. In case John is the only student, (46) would be true, but the speaker would use *the* instead of *every*.

3. One anonymous reviewer suggests that a question such as (i) "suggests a ban on some kind of books," and that (ii) "suggests that many individual books have been banned without there necessarily being any uniform criteria for banning books."
(i) What kind of books has been banned?
(ii) What kind of books have been banned?
I do not share these judgments. For me, (i) is ungrammatical. The reviewer also suggests that the examples in (51)–(53) can be "slightly improved" with *of*. It seems to me that in NPs where the *of* is optional, the variants containing the *of* favor the reading where the first noun is the head, making the singular agreement acceptable.

(52) a. What length skirts are in fashion?
b. *What length skirts is in fashion?

(53) a. What color paints are available?
b. *What color paints is available?

I will follow Partee's analysis that *that* in *that size dress* is a specifier of the NP *that size,* which is predicative, and *dress* is the head of the entire NP. The structure is the same as what I am proposing for *that kind of animal,* except that the *of* is obligatory with *kind.*

(54) $[[[\text{that size}]_{NP}]_{Pred}$ (of) $\text{dress}]_{NP}$

10.4.2. Existential Quantification

For existential readings of *that kind of animal,* there are several ways of accounting for where the existential quantification comes from. The most ad hoc would be to stipulate that there is an implicit indefinite article contained in the NP. Carlson's claim is essentially that the existential quantification is part of the meaning of the verb phrase. Although I am rejecting the idea that it is a quantification over stages introduced by the VP, it would still be possible to have the existential quantification be part of the meaning of the verb phrase. The best solution seems to be along the lines of the Kamp/Heim approach to indefinites. On Kamp's approach, the existential quantification is derived from the embedding conditions for sentences, or on Heim's (1982, chapter 2) approach through existential closure. Given the interpretation for *that$_i$ kind* in (28), we get the open sentence in (55) for the interpretation of *that$_i$ kind of animal.* The free variable z_i gets its reference from the context.

(55) $\textbf{that}_i$ **kind of animal** =
$\pi(\iota y[\textbf{kind}(z_i)\ \&\ y = z_i])(x)\ \&\ \textbf{animal}(x)$

The variable x can be replaced with a discourse referent, and the whole NP gets existential force, or an overt adverb of quantification such as *usually* may bind the variable (cf. (14)). Here, *that$_i$ kind of animal* will take predicates that apply to basic individuals rather than kind-level individuals, and it is equivalent to *an animal of that kind.*

10.4.3. A Problem with the Predicate Meaning for *Kind*

Consider again the translation for *an animal of that$_i$ kind* given in (31):

(31) **an animal of** $\textbf{that}_i\ \textbf{kind}_2$ =
$\lambda P\ \exists z\ [\textbf{animal}(z)\ \&\ \pi(\iota y\ [\textbf{kind}(x_i)\ \&\ y = x_i])(z)\ \&\ {}^{\vee}P(z)]$

The only condition on what is picked out by x_i is that it be a kind. Nothing in the translation requires the kind to be a kind of animal. Something further would have to be said to guarantee that the kind is a kind of animal, which is precisely what is accomplished by having *kind* be a CN/CN. For this reason, I will discuss an alternative to making *kind* ambiguous between a CN/CN and a simple predicate.

However, the quantificational NP *a cat of every kind* in (39), repeated below, is subject to the same objection as was made for *an animal of that kind,* namely, nothing guarantees that the kinds are kinds of cats.

(39) A cat of every kind disappeared.

(40) $\forall^k$ [**kind**(x) $\rightarrow$ $\exists y^o$ [**cat**(y) & π(x)(y) & **disappeared**(y)]]

(40) means, roughly, 'For every kind (cat or non-cat), a cat of it disappeared.' For quantificational NPs, I have not been able to find a solution to this problem even on the alternative approach described in the next section, so the choice between these approaches still remains open.[4]

10.5. AN ALTERNATIVE TO MAKING *KIND* AMBIGUOUS

An alternative to making *kind* ambiguous is to keep Carlson's translation of *kind* in (24), repeated below, for *an animal of that$_i$ kind* and allow **kind** to combine with **that$_i$** even though it is still missing its CN argument.

(24) **kind** = $\lambda Q\ \lambda x^k\ [\forall z^o\ \Box\ (\mathbf{R}'(z,x) \rightarrow\ ^{\vee}Q(z))]$

Supposing that *kind* has the meaning in (24), there is no way of applying the determiner *that* to it directly, since *that* takes CN meanings and *kind* is a CN/CN. However, they can be combined using function composition. Once the meanings are combined, we can derive the existential meaning of *that$_i$ kind of animal* using the method discussed in section 10.4.

First, consider the NP *an animal of that$_i$ kind.* **Kind** takes a CN meaning to give a CN meaning, but in this case, its CN argument, **animal,** precedes it. By composing the meaning of *that$_i$* and *kind* and composing the result with *of,* we end up with an interpretation for *an animal of that kind* that is similar to Carlson's analysis of *such an animal,* given in (56).

4. It would be interesting to pursue an analysis of the quantification, since, as an anonymous reviewer observes, *kind* NPs with a universal quantifier are also allowed in *there*-insertion sentences, in apparent violation of the Definiteness Restriction, as the example in (i) shows.

(i) There are all kinds of animals in the London Zoo.

Hoeksema (1983,72) makes a similar observation. The reviewer also finds *every* in place of *all* in this sentence worse:

(ii) There is every kind of animal in the London Zoo.

(56) **such an animal** =
$\lambda Q\ \exists x^{o}\ [\forall z^{o}\ \Box\ (\mathbf{R}'(z,y^{k}_{i}) \rightarrow \mathbf{animal}(z))\ \&\ \mathbf{R}'(x,y^{k}_{i})\ \&\ {}^{\vee}Q(x)]$

The NP (56) denotes the set of properties that hold of some individual that is the realization of a contextually specified kind, where that kind is a kind of animal.

The derivation proceeds as follows. Taking the meanings given for *that*$_i$ and *kind* in (27) and (24) respectively, we compose them.

(27) $\mathbf{that_i}\ =\ \lambda Q\ [\iota y\ [{}^{\vee}Q(x_i)\ \&\ y\ =\ x_i]]$
(24) $\mathbf{kind}\ =\ \lambda Q\ \lambda x^{k}\ [\forall z^{o}\ \Box\ (\mathbf{R}'(z,x) \rightarrow {}^{\vee}Q(z))]$

The result is (54):

(57) **that$_i$ kind** =
$\lambda P\ [\iota y\ [\forall z^{o}\ \Box\ (\mathbf{R}'(z,x^{k}_{i}) \rightarrow {}^{\vee}P(z))\ \&\ y\ =\ x^{k}_{i}]]$

In order to put this together with **of** to get the right meaning for *of that kind,* **of** has to be able to make a predicate modifier applying to basic individuals out of the NP meaning in (57). The whole *of*-phrase applies to a CN argument, **animal**. Function composition of (57) with *of,* which again is just the predication operation π, gives (58).

(58) **of that kind$_i$** =
$\lambda P\ [\pi(\iota y\ [\forall z^{o}\ \Box\ (\mathbf{R}'(z,x^{k}_{i}) \rightarrow {}^{\vee}P(z))\ \&\ y\ =\ x^{k}_{i}])]$

Example (58) applies to **animal**:

(59) **animal of that$_i$ kind** =
$\pi(\iota y\ [\forall z^{o}\ \Box\ (\mathbf{R}'(z,x^{k}_{i}) \rightarrow \mathbf{animal}(z))\ \&\ y\ =\ x^{k}_{i}])$

Assuming that *an animal of that$_i$ kind* is derived using Montague's translation for the indefinite article, the result of applying **an** to (59) is (60):

(60) **an animal of that$_i$ kind** =
$\lambda Q\ \exists v[\pi(\iota y\ [\forall z^{o}\ \Box\ (\mathbf{R}'(z,x^{k}_{i}) \rightarrow \mathbf{animal}(z))\ \&\ y\ =\ x^{k}_{i}])(v)\ \&\ {}^{\vee}Q(v)]$

An animal of that$_i$ kind is then roughly equivalent to Carlson's translation of *such an animal.*

Turning to *that*$_i$ *kind of animal,* the derivation proceeds in the same way as the previous one, except that what makes *that$_i$ kind* into a predicate modifier is not the *of* now. The *of* is semantically empty. *That$_i$ kind* is made into a predicate modifier by the same process that applies to NPs like *that size* and *that color* discussed above. Also different from the derivation of *an animal of that$_i$ kind* is the absence of the explicit indefinite article. Existential quantification comes in as a result of the embedding conditions.

The indefinite interpretation of *that kind of animal* is (61):

(61) **that kind of animal** =
$\pi(\iota y\ [\forall z^o\ \Box\ (\mathbf{R}'(z,x_i^k) \rightarrow \mathbf{animal}(z))\ \&\ y\ =\ x_i^k])$

This in turn is applied to a discourse referent "bound" by the embedding conditions:

(62) $\pi(\iota y\ [\forall z^o\ \Box\ (\mathbf{R}'(z,x_i^k) \rightarrow \mathbf{animal}(z))\ \&\ y = x_i^k])(u)$.

Again, *that kind of animal* will take predicates that apply to basic individuals rather than individuals from the kind domain, and it is equivalent to *an animal of that kind.*

For (63), the analysis is exactly Carlson's. **Kind** applies directly to **animal** to make a CN as in (25), and the whole NP combines with kind-level predicates.

(63) That kind of animal is common.

Thus, even if *kind* is unambiguously a CN/CN, definite *kind*-NPs can have either a kind-denoting or an indefinite interpretation.

10.6. CONCLUSION

Returning to the *there*-insertion sentences given at the beginning of this chapter, we see why *that kind of animal* is acceptable in *there*-insertion contexts. It can have an existential reading. I have shown that the existential interpretation of NPs such as *that kind of animal* is allowed because of the meaning of *kind* and the structure of the NP. *That kind* in *that kind of animal* can be a predicate modifier, leaving the head, *animal,* without a determiner. Embedding conditions guarantee that the whole NP has existential force if no overt adverb of quantification is present. Adopting Carlson's proposal that *kind* has a transitive meaning, I give a compositional analysis of the generic and indefinite readings of *that kind of animal* that is independent of whether or not *kind* itself is ambiguous.

I have argued that *kind*-NPs are ambiguous. Wilkinson (1991) and others (see chapter 1 of this volume) have argued that bare plurals can be kind-denoting terms; however, with VPs that are non-kind-level predicates they are treated like indefinites in the Kamp/Heim theory. The proposed analysis of *kind*-NPs fits more naturally into a theory that makes bare plurals ambiguous.

ACKNOWLEDGMENTS

I would like to thank Barbara Partee for invaluable help and encouragement. Thanks also to Steve Berman, Greg Carlson, Molly Diesing, F. Roger

Higgins, Angelika Kratzer, Roger Schwarzschild, and Gert Webelhuth for comments on various drafts. This paper is part of my dissertation work on generic NPs. An earlier version appeared in the *Proceedings of WCCFL 8* and was presented at USC in March 1989. I am grateful to Manfred Krifka for allowing an even earlier version to appear in the *Proceedings of the Tübingen Conference on Genericity in Natural Language* (November 1988).

11 COMMON NOUNS: A CONTRASTIVE ANALYSIS OF CHINESE AND ENGLISH

Manfred Krifka

11.1. INTRODUCTION

In chapter 1, especially section 1.3, we implicitly developed a theory of common nouns that covers both their predicational meaning and their meaning as kind-referring expressions. Here I will try to put together some of the results relating to the syntax and semantics of common nouns, and give an outline of a formal theory which encompasses the aspects that are relevant to our subject with respect to two typologically different languages, English and Chinese. The goal of this small contribution is quite modest, mainly for reasons of space and perspicuity.

I will assume an intensional semantic representation language with a set of possible worlds I and a sorted universe A, whose structure will be developed in the course of the chapter. I assume explicit quantification over possible worlds, for which I use the variable i, typically written as a subscript. For entities of the universe, I will use variables x,y,z, etc.

11.2. THE CHINESE CASE

I will start with Chinese, as common noun constructions are more transparent in this classifier language than they are in English. Take as an example the noun *xíong* 'bear'. It can refer to (a) the kind *Ursus* or (b) some specimens of this kind. There is also a measure construction which applies to (c) a specified number of realizations of *Ursus*. And finally, there are two classifier constructions containing *xíong* which apply to a specified number of (d) individual specimens of *Ursus* or (e) subspecies of *Ursus*. (In the glosses, ASP stands for 'aspect' and CL for 'classifier'.)

(1) a. xíong júe zhǒng le
bear vanish kind ASP — 'The bear is extinct.'

b. wǒ kànjiàn xíong le
I see bear ASP — 'I saw (some) bears.'

c. sān qún xíong
three herds bear — 'three herds of bears'

d. sān zhī xíong
three CL bear 'three bears' (objects)

e. sān zhǒng xíong
three CL bear 'three bears' (species)

We assume that the bare noun *xíong* is basically a name of the kind *Ursus,* and that the other uses have to be derived from that (cf. also Dölling 1992, who discusses sort shifts of this type in general). One reason to take the kind-referring use in (1a) as basic is that it seems that every language which allows for bare NPs at all uses them as expressions referring to kinds (see Gerstner-Link 1988). Furthermore, kinds seem to be ontologically prior to specimens; if we want to call some real object a bear, we have to relate this object to the kind *Ursus,* whereas it is not necessary to have some real specimens in mind in order to talk about the kind *Ursus.* Let us represent the syntactic category of kind names by N; as kind names can be used as NPs, we have to assume a syntactic rule NP → N, where the interpretation stays the same—that is, the corresponding semantic rule is $[\![[_{NP}[_{N}\alpha]]]\!] = [\![[_{N}\alpha]]\!]$. Assuming that *Ursus* denotes an element of the universe A of the sort of kinds, we have the following syntactic and semantic derivation:

(2) $[_{N}$ xíong], **Ursus**
|
$[_{NP}$ xíong], **Ursus**

The indefinite, or predicative, use of a bare NP in (1b) can be derived from the definite use by an operator which takes a kind and yields a predicate applying to specimens or subspecies of this kind. In chapter 1, we have introduced the realization relation **R** and the taxonomic relation **T**. In our intensional framework, **R** and **T** will depend on a possible world i. In general, if k is a kind, then $\lambda x.\mathbf{R}_i(x,k)$ applies to specimens or individual sums of specimens of k in world i, and $\lambda x.\mathbf{T}_i(x,k)$ applies to subspecies or individual sums of subspecies of k in world i. (If we think that an individual necessarily belongs to the kind(s) it belongs to, then $\mathbf{R}_i(x,k)$ means that x belongs to k and furthermore exists in i, and similarly for the subspecies relation.) We can conflate these two relations by defining a relation **RT** as follows: $\mathbf{RT}_i(x,y) \leftrightarrow \mathbf{R}_i(x,y) \vee \mathbf{T}_i(x,y)$. To derive the predicative use of a bare noun, I assume the same syntactic rule as above, NP → N, but now with the corresponding semantic rule $[\![[_{NP}[_{N}\alpha]]]\!] = \lambda i\lambda x.\mathbf{RT}_i(x,[\![[_{N}\alpha]]\!])$, which gives us the property of being a specimen or a subspecies, or an individual sum of specimens or subspecies, of the kind $[\![[_{N}\alpha]]\!]$.

(3) $[_N$xíong], **Ursus**
|
$[_{NP}$xíong], $\lambda i\lambda x.\mathbf{RT}_i(x,\mathbf{Ursus})$

The property $\lambda i\lambda x.\mathbf{RT}(x,\mathbf{Ursus})$ applies to single bears or collections consisting of bears, and to single bear species or collections consisting of bear species.

For the measure phrase construction (1c) we can assume two syntactic rules: (i) MP → Num M (where MP stands for 'measure phrase', Num for 'number word', and M for 'measure word'), and (ii) NP → MP N. The corresponding semantic rule is functional application; we have $[\![[_{MP}[_{Num}\alpha][_M\beta]]]\!] = [\![[_M\beta]]\!]([\![[_{Num}\alpha]]\!])$ and $[\![[_{NP}[_{MP}\alpha][_N\beta]]]\!] = [\![[_{MP}\alpha]]\!]([\![[_N\beta]]\!])$. To treat a measure word like *qún* 'herd' we have to assume a function **herd** which for each possible world i, when applied to a (complex) object, yields the number of herds this object consists of; for example, when applied to an object which consists of three herds of animals, it yields the value 3. A natural way to treat measure words like 'herd', 'pound', 'liter', etc., is by additive measure functions (cf. ter Meulen 1980, Krifka 1989). For example, it holds that if $\mathbf{herd}_i(x) = n$ and $\mathbf{herd}_i(y) = m$, and x and y do not overlap—that is, have no common part—then $\mathbf{herd}_i(x \oplus y) = n + m$, where '$\oplus$' is sum formation of individuals and '+' is arithmetic addition. For example, if x are two herds and y are three herds, and x and y do not overlap, then x and y together are five herds. The rules specified so far allow us to derive a phrase like (1c) in the following way:

(4) $[_M$qún], $\lambda n\lambda y\lambda i\lambda x[\mathbf{RT}_i(x,y)\ \&\ \mathbf{herd}_i(x)=n]$
|
| $[_{Num}$sān], **3**
↓
$[_{MP}$sān qún], $\lambda y\lambda i\lambda x[\mathbf{RT}_i(x,y)\ \&\ \mathbf{herd}_i(x)=\mathbf{3}]$
|
| $[_N$xíong], **Ursus**
↓
$[_{NP}$sān qún (de) xíong], $\lambda i\lambda x[\mathbf{RT}_i(x,\mathbf{Ursus})\ \&\ \mathbf{herd}_i(x)=\mathbf{3}]$

If we assume that $\mathbf{herd}_i$ is applicable only to objects and not to kinds, then this predicate applies to objects consisting of three herds of bears. That is, we might replace **RT** by **R** without change of meaning.

The classifier construction (1d) can be treated similarly, with the exception that the measure function now is dependent upon the head noun. So we assume a special operator which, for each possible world, takes a kind and yields a measure function that measures the number of specimens of that kind. Let us call this operator **OU** (for 'object unit'). For example, if x consists of three individual bears, then $\mathbf{OU_i(Ursus)}(x) = \mathbf{3}$; in general, $\mathbf{OU_i}$ (k) will be an additive measure function. Example (1d), then, will be derived as follows:

(5) $[_{M}$zhī], $\lambda n\lambda y\lambda i\lambda x[\mathbf{RT_i}(x,y)\ \&\ \mathbf{OU_i}(y)(x)=n]$

$[_{Num}$sān], **3**

$[_{MP}$sān zhī], $\lambda y\lambda i\lambda x[\mathbf{RT_i}(x,y)\ \&\ \mathbf{OU_i}(y)(x)=\mathbf{3}]$

$[_{N}$xíong], **Ursus**

$[_{NP}$sān zhī xíong], $\lambda i\lambda x[\mathbf{RT_i}(x,\mathbf{Ursus})\ \&\ \mathbf{OU_i(Ursus)}(x)=\mathbf{3}]$

As before, we might replace **RT** by **R,** as $\mathbf{OU_i(Ursus)}$ applies to objects only. It might be considered more appropriate to have the simple realization relation **R** instead of **RT;** I took **RT** for reasons of generality. One could, furthermore, think of getting rid of **RT** altogether by a postulate like $\mathbf{OU_i}(y)(x) = n \rightarrow \mathbf{R_i}(x,y)$. However, I want to distinguish between a qualitative criterion of application and a quantitative criterion of application for predicates. The operator **OU** could reasonably be interpreted in such a way that it yields the same measure function for, say, bears and cats, that is, $\mathbf{OU_i(Ursus)} = \mathbf{OU_i(Felis)}$; in both cases the unit is derived from the notion of a biological organism and may be identified with $\mathbf{OU_i(animal)}$. Then the other component of the operator, the **RT** relation, matters, insofar as it qualitatively distinguishes between bears and cats.

The classifier construction (1e) is similar to the classifier construction (1c), with the exception that the classifier *zhǒng* does not contain a measure function for specimens, but a measure function for subspecies. Let **KU** ('kind unit') be a function which, for each possible world, when applied to a kind, yields a measure function for the number of subspecies of that kind; for example, if x consists of three bear species (say, the polar bear, the grizzly, and the panda), then $\mathbf{KU_i(Ursus)}(x) = \mathbf{3}$. We get the following derivation for (1e):

(6) $[_{M}$zhǒng], $\lambda n\lambda y\lambda i\lambda x[\mathbf{RT_i}(x,y)\ \&\ \mathbf{KU_i}(y)(x)=n]$

$[_{Num}$sān], **3**

$[_{MP}$sān zhǒng], $\lambda y\lambda i\lambda x[\mathbf{RT_i}(x,y)\ \&\ \mathbf{KU_i}(y)(x)=\mathbf{3}]$

$[_{N}$xíong], **Ursus**

$[_{NP}$sān zhǒng xíong], $\lambda i\lambda x[\mathbf{RT_i}(x,\mathbf{Ursus})\ \&\ \mathbf{KU_i(Ursus)}(x)=\mathbf{3}]$

In this case, **RT** may be replaced by **T**.

We have assumed so far that the head noun in classifier constructions refers to a kind. Things are a little bit more complicated when it comes to noun phrases which are modified by adjuncts like adjectives or relative clauses. In Chinese, an adjunct can be either in front of the head noun or in front of the classifier phrase, as the following minimal pair shows (taken from Henne, Rongen, and Hansen 1977, 269; SUB marks a subordinating particle):

(7) a. nèi wèi [chuān lán yīfu de] xiānsheng
that CL wear blue clothing SUB gentleman
'that gentleman, who is wearing blue clothes'

b. [chuān lán yīfu de] nèi wèi xiānsheng
wear blue clothing SUB that CL gentleman
'that gentleman who is wearing blue clothes'

According to Henne et al., the adjunct is 'descriptive' in the first case (which can be rendered as an appositive relative clause in English) and 'restrictive' in the second case. In the second case, the adjunct can be treated as a modifier of a predicative noun. In the first case, however, the adjunct must be treated as a modifier of a kind-referring noun, as it is only the application of the classifier phrase by which an object-referring noun is derived. Thus we have to assume that not only *xiānsheng* 'gentleman', but also *chuān lán yīfu de xiānsheng* 'gentleman wearing blue clothes', refers to a kind.

One possible analysis is to introduce a notion that is more general than that of a kind. So far, kinds were considered to be abstract entities that are well established in the background knowledge of speaker and hearer and can be referred to by definite NPs like *the bear,* which were in the extension of kind predicates like *be extinct* or *be a mammal,* and which were organized in taxonomic hierarchies. Let us now assume a new type of entities, *concepts*. Similar to kinds, concepts are abstract entities related to real objects. However, they need not be well established, but could be construed from scratch. Furthermore, concepts may stand in a subconcept relation (as, e.g., a gentleman wearing blue clothes is a gentleman), but not necessarily in a taxonomic relation (it is not a subspecies of gentleman). Something like this distinction was developed by Pelletier and Schubert (1989, 382), who assumed both 'conventional' kinds (our kinds) and 'formal' kinds (our concepts). To keep our terminology constant, we will use 'kind' as usual in the restricted sense (referring to conventional kinds), but we will assume that kinds form a subset of the more comprehensive sets of concepts. Let **KIND** be the set of kinds and **CONCEPT** the set of concepts; then we have **KIND** $\subseteq$ **CONCEPT**.

We can handle cases like (7a) by assuming that an adnominal modifier, like *lǎo* 'old', can be combined not only with a nominal predicate, but also with the name of a concept, like *xíong,* which yields another concept, like *lǎo xíong* 'old bear', which in turn can be part of a classifier expression, like *sān zhī lǎo xíong* 'three old bears'. In this case, the first concept, but not the second one, is a kind.

How should we integrate the relations **R** and **T** into this enlarged framework? First of all, we need a relation which connects an object with a concept. This relation can be thought of as a generalization of **R**. So let us redefine **R** as a relation between objects and concepts in general: For every possible world i, $\mathbf{R}_i \subseteq \mathbf{OBJECT} \times \mathbf{CONCEPT}$, where **OBJECT** is the set of objects. Second, assume a relation **S,** the *subconcept relation.* It is a two-place relation-in-intension between concepts: for each possible world i, $\mathbf{S}_i \subseteq \mathbf{CONCEPT} \times \mathbf{CONCEPT}$. The relations **R** und **S** are related insofar as every object which belongs to a concept belongs to its superconcepts as well; for example, every old bear is a bear. Therefore we should assume, as a general rule, $\mathbf{R}_i(x,y)$ & $\mathbf{S}_i(y,z) \rightarrow \mathbf{R}_i(x,z)$. Finally, we can think of our taxonomic relation **T** as being the subconcept relation **S** restricted to **KIND,** that is, $\mathbf{T}_i(x,y) \leftrightarrow x \in \mathbf{KIND}$ & $\mathbf{S}_i(x,y)$. For example, the grizzly is a taxonomic subspecies of the bear because it is a subconcept of it and because both the grizzly and the bear are kinds.

We also have to integrate the sum operation $\oplus$ and the operations **OU** and **KU** into this framework. As for the sum operation, we assume that $\oplus$ is a join operation in **OBJECT, KIND,** and **CONCEPT;** that is, $\langle\mathbf{OBJECT},\oplus\rangle$, $\langle\mathbf{KIND},\oplus\rangle$, and $\langle\mathbf{CONCEPT},\oplus\rangle$ each are join semilattices (cf. Link 1983). Now, we can assume that **R** is closed under sum formation for kinds; that is: $y \in \mathbf{KIND}$ & $\mathbf{R}_i(x,y)$ & $\mathbf{R}_1(x',y) \rightarrow \mathbf{R}_i(x \oplus x',y)$. For example, if Yogi and Petz are realizations of **Ursus,** then so is their sum. This is not true for concepts in general; for example, it does not hold for the concept **three bears,** as the sum of two objects which are three bears normally are not three bears. Similarly, we can assume that **T** is closed under sum formation; that is: $\mathbf{T}_i(x,y)$ & $\mathbf{T}_i(x',y) \rightarrow \mathbf{T}_i(x \oplus x',y)$. For example, if the grizzly and the polar bear stand in the subspecies relation to *Ursus,* then the sum of the grizzly and the polar bear stand in the subspecies relation to *Ursus* as well. Furthermore, we can assume that **R** and **S** (and hence, **T**) are even more tightly related to $\oplus$ by claiming: $\mathbf{R}_i(x,y)$ & $\mathbf{R}_i(x',y') \rightarrow \mathbf{R}_i(x \oplus x',y \oplus y')$ and similarly: $\mathbf{S}_i(x,y)$ & $\mathbf{S}_i(x',y') \rightarrow \mathbf{S}_i(x \oplus x', y \oplus y')$. For example, if Simba realizes **Leo** and Yogi realizes **Ursus,** then Simba and Yogi together realize **Leo** and **Ursus** together.

The operator **OU** can also be integrated into the new framework. We have defined **OU** as a function which, relative to a kind, maps an object to a number. However, if we want to stick to our reconstruction of classifier constructions in Chinese and bear in mind that a classifier phrase can be applied to a non-kind concept like **old bear,** we have to assume that **OU** must be specified relative to concepts. Technically, it should be a function from **CONCEPT** to functions from **OBJECT** to numbers. As the object units stay the same with subconcepts (e.g., three old bears are three bears), we should assume that **OU** does not change for subconcepts: $\mathbf{OU_i}(x)(y) = n \;\&\; \mathbf{S_i}(z,x) \rightarrow \mathbf{OU_i}(z)(y) = n$.

To handle adnominal modifications like the modification of the kind-denoting *xíong* by the adjective *lǎo,* we have to introduce an operator which yields, for a given predicate, the concept whose realizations are the entities to which the predicate applies. Let us call this operator σ, following Parsons (1970). It is defined as follows: If P is a property of objects, then σ(P) refers to that concept which has the objects in the extension of P as its realizations. That is, $\sigma(P) = \iota y \forall i \forall x[\mathbf{RT_i}(x,y) \leftrightarrow P_i(x)]$. I assume that concepts are as fine-grained as object properties; that is, for each pair of object properties P,Q, if $P \neq Q$, then $\sigma(P) \neq \sigma(Q)$. To avoid running into Russell's paradox, I simply restrict this condition to properties that apply to objects. There are more general and perhaps adequate solutions to this problem (cf., e.g., Turner 1983).

An adjective like *lǎo,* as a concept modifier, can now be interpreted as $\lambda y.\sigma(\lambda i \lambda x[\mathbf{old.for_i}(x,y) \;\&\; \mathbf{RT_i}(x,y)])$, where $\mathbf{old.for_i}(x,y)$ says that the object x is old for, or with respect to, the concept y in world i (that is, compared to other objects in that concept). Let us write for '$\sigma(\lambda i \lambda x[\mathbf{old.for_i}(x,y) \;\&\; \mathbf{RT_i}(x,y))$' simply '**old**(y)'. Let us assume, as a syntactic rule, N → AP N, where AP is the category of adjective phrases. The corresponding semantic rule is functional application, $[\![[_N[_{AP}\alpha][_N\beta]]]\!] = [\![[_{AP}\alpha]]\!]([\![[_N\beta]]\!])$. As an example derivation, consider the following:

(8) $[_{MP}$ sān zhī], $\lambda y \lambda i \lambda x \mathbf{RT_i}(x,y) \;\&\; \mathbf{OU_i}(y)(x) = \mathbf{3}]$

$[_N$ xíong], **Ursus**

$[_{AP}$ lǎo], **old**

$[_N$ lǎo xíong], **old(Ursus)**

$[_{NP}$ sān zhī lǎo xíong],
$\lambda i \lambda x[\mathbf{RT_i}(x,\mathbf{old(Ursus)}) \;\&\; \mathbf{OU_i}(\mathbf{old(Ursus)})(x) = \mathbf{3}]$

This semantic representation can be clarified a bit. We know that **old(Ursus)** is a subconcept of **Ursus,** which again is a subconcept of **Animal,** and as $\mathbf{OU_i}$

is closed under subconcepts, it follows that $\mathbf{OU_i(old(Ursus))} = \mathbf{OU_i(Animal)}$. This gives us the translation $\lambda i\lambda x[\mathbf{RT_i}(x,\mathbf{old(Ursus)})\ \&\ \mathbf{OU_i(Ursus)}(x)=\mathbf{3}]$. Furthermore, the relation **RT** is distributive and $\mathbf{OU_i(Animal)}$ is additive, that is, $\mathbf{OU_i(Animal)}(x)=\mathbf{3}$ means that x is the sum of three mutually distinct objects x_1, x_2, x_3, for each of which holds $\mathbf{OU_i(Animal)}(xi)=\mathbf{1}$. Hence we can represent (8) as follows:

(9) $\lambda i\lambda x\exists x_1,x_2,x_3[x=x_1\oplus x_2\oplus x_3\ \&\ x_1\neq x_2\ \&\ x_2\neq x_3\ \&\ x_1\neq x_3\ \&$
$\mathbf{RT_i}(x_1,\mathbf{old(Ursus)})\ \&\ \mathbf{OU_i(Animal)}(x_1)=1\ \&$
$\mathbf{RT_i}(x_2,\mathbf{old(Ursus)})\ \&\ \mathbf{OU_i(Animal)}(x_2)=1\ \&$
$\mathbf{RT_i}(x_3,\mathbf{old(Ursus)})\ \&\ \mathbf{OU_i(Animal)}(x_3)=1]$

This is an example for a case with a narrow-scope adnominal modifier. Wide-scope adnominal modifiers, such as in (7b), can be treated as property modifiers. One possible analysis is the following:

(10) $[_{NP}$ sān zhī xíong], $\lambda i\lambda x[\mathbf{RT_i}(x,\mathbf{Ursus})\ \&\ \mathbf{OU_i(Ursus)}(x)=\mathbf{3}]$

$[_{AP}$ lǎo], $\lambda P\lambda i\lambda x[P_i(x)\ \&\ \mathbf{old.for_i}(\sigma(P),x)]$

↓

$[_{NP}$ lǎo sān zhī xíong],
$\lambda i\lambda x[\mathbf{RT_i}(x,\mathbf{Ursus})\ \mathbf{OU_i(Ursus)}(x)=\mathbf{3}\ \&$
$\mathbf{old.for}(\sigma(\lambda i\lambda x[\mathbf{RT_i}(x,\mathbf{Ursus})\ \&\ \mathbf{OU_i(Ursus)}(x)=\mathbf{3}]),x)]$

The resulting property applies to objects that consist of three bears and that are old for the concept **three.bears**. As above, we assume that adjective denotations like **old.for** are distributive. Furthermore, it seems plausible that the change from the concept **Ursus** to the concept **three.bears** in the first argument does not matter: if an object is old as a bear, then it should be old for three bears as well. Thus we would get the same meaning as under (8).

This does not explain the 'descriptive' vs. 'restrictive' distinction observed above. I think that this distinction can only be captured in a semantic model of dynamic interpretation. In the descriptive case, we can assume that the context already provides some concept, and that the nominal modifier just gives additional information about it. In this case, then, the head noun cannot be taken as the name of the kind, but refers to some subconcept. Only in the restrictive case do we construct a new property. I will not work out a formal analysis for this distinction here, but note that the analysis given so far seems promising in one point: It is well known that proper names can only have descriptive relative clauses (e.g., *Xiaoxiao, who is, by the way, only three years old, . . .*). Now, we did analyze the head noun of the classifier construction as the name of a kind, and hence we should expect that an attribute is interpreted as descriptive in case it applies directly to the head noun.

11.3. THE ENGLISH CASE

We have to distinguish between two kinds of common nouns in English: *mass nouns* and *count nouns*. Mass nouns are quite similar to Chinese nouns: they can occur (a) as names of kinds, (b) as indefinite predicates, and (c) in measure constructions. Furthermore, we have (d) taxonomic classifiers, and with a few mass nouns, like *cattle,* we also have (e) object classifiers:

(11) a. Wine contains alcohol.
b. Wine was spilled over the table.
c. Mary bought three bottles of wine.
d. John knows three sorts of wine.
e. The farmer owns thirty heads of cattle.

Mass nouns and mass noun constructions in English can be treated exactly like nouns in Chinese. Count nouns, however, are different. They do not need a classifier, but rather combine directly with a numeral. This difference can be captured in two ways—by assuming that either English numerals or English count nouns have a "built-in" classifier. So, a Chinese NP like *sān zhī xíong* and an English NP like *three bears* actually can mean the same—they rely on different syntactic means to arrive at the same semantic end (see also Sharvy 1978). However, there is at least one difference: whereas *sān zhī xíong* can only apply to collections of three individual bears, *three bears* can also apply to bear species, as in *sān zhǒng xīong*. That is, the measure function in numerals or count nouns is underspecified; it can be either **OU** or **KU,** object unit or kind unit. Let us therefore introduce an operator **OKU** ('object or kind unit'), which is defined as $\mathbf{OKU}_i(x)(y)=n \leftrightarrow \mathbf{OU}_i(x)(y)=n \vee \mathbf{KU}_i(x)(y)=n$. If we assume that the classifier is built into the number word, then we can derive the meaning of *three bears* as follows, using a syntactic rule NP → Num CN with the interpretation $[\![[_{NP}\ [_{Num}\alpha][_{CN}\beta]]]\!] = [\![[_{Num}\alpha]]\!]([\![[_{CN}\beta]]\!])$. We get derivations of the following kind:

(12) $[_{CN}$ bear], **Ursus**

$[_{Num}$ three], $\lambda y \lambda i \lambda x[\mathbf{RT}_i(x,y)\ \&\ \mathbf{OKU}_i(y)(x)=\mathbf{3}]$

$[_{NP}$ three bears], $\lambda i \lambda x[\mathbf{RT}_i(x,\mathbf{Ursus})\ \&\ \mathbf{OKU}_i(\mathbf{Ursus})(x)=\mathbf{3}]$

If, alternatively, we assume that the classifier is built into the noun *bears,* then the kind name *bear* is first transformed to a count noun *bear(s)* by a null operator. This count noun is relational, as it has a number argument; in the case of *bear(s),* we have $\lambda n\lambda i\lambda x[\mathbf{RT}_i(x,\mathbf{Ursus})\ \&\ \mathbf{OKU}(\mathbf{Ursus})(x)=n]$. The number argument is saturated by the number word, here *three,* which has a simple interpretation, in our case **3**. It suffices to assume one syntactic category of nouns, N, for both mass nouns and count nouns, and a rule NP → Num N, with the semantics $[\![[_{NP}\ [_{Num}\alpha][_N\beta]]]\!] = [\![[_N\beta]]\!]([\![[_{Num}\alpha]]\!])$. This rule is prevented from applying to mass nouns, as their interpretation is not relational and cannot be applied to numbers. In this way we can encode in the semantic representation that only a specific class of nouns, the count nouns, can be combined with a numeral.

(13) $[_N$ bear$]$, **Ursus**

ϕ, $\lambda y\lambda n\lambda i\lambda x[\mathbf{RT}_i(x,y)\ \&\ \mathbf{OKU}_i(y)(x)=n]$ (count operator)

$[_N$ bear$]$, $\lambda n\lambda i\lambda x[\mathbf{RT}_i(x,\mathbf{Ursus})\ \&\ \mathbf{OKU}_i(\mathbf{Ursus})(x)=n]$

$[_{Num}$ three$]$, **3**

$[_{NP}$ three bears$]$, $\lambda i\lambda x[\mathbf{RT}_i(x,\mathbf{Ursus})\ \&\ \mathbf{OKU}_i(\mathbf{Ursus})(x)=\mathbf{3}]$

Before I evaluate these two analyses, I want to make two comments which apply to both of them. First, the number of the noun changes in our representations from singular to plural without any change in the semantic representation. I think this is as it should be, as the selection of singular or plural forms seems to be a purely syntactic matter. In English, we have plural forms in cases which lack any semantic plurality (viz. *0 bears* or *1.0 bears*). And in many languages which have a singular/plural distinction, the singular is used with any number, for example in Turkish (viz. *üç elma* lit. 'three apple' = 'three apples' vs. **üç elmalar* 'three apple.PLURAL').

Second, the construction of **OKU** implies that *three bears* can be applied to entities consisting either of three object bears or of three bear species, but not to a complex object containing kinds and objects. This is adequate, as it would be rather strange to call the collection of the grizzly, the polar bear, and the bear Albert in the Edmonton zoo *three bears*.

Now let us discuss our two proposals. The second one, which works with relational count nouns, seems to be preferable at first sight, as we could derive a semantic notion of a count noun and have a simpler syntax (cf. Haider 1988).

However, there are problems with it. One is that many nouns can be used either as count nouns or mass nouns; it might be that this is even true for every noun (see, e.g., Ware 1975, Pelletier & Schubert 1989). So a sharp semantic distinction seems to be less preferable than a syntactic distinction that could be overridden by the syntactic context. Furthermore, if we want to transfer the treatment of adjectives as developed above for the Chinese case to the English case, so that the adjective may modify the kind name directly, we would have to assume for cases like *three old bears* that *old* is first applied to the kind name *bear,* and only then the count operator is applied to *old bear* to change it into a count noun. This would be a strange analysis insofar as the syntactic rule (combination of *old* with *bear*) would have scope over a lexical rule (application of the count operator). Finally, the analysis does not spare us a syntactic distinction between mass nouns and count nouns after all. One of the differences between mass nouns like *wine* and count nouns like *bear* is that the former can be used as names of kinds right away, whereas the latter need a definite article or pluralization to perform this task. The only reason for these operations seems to be syntactic: singular count nouns cannot be used as noun phrases. So we need to distinguish between mass nouns and count nouns anyway. While these are no knockdown arguments, they make the first analysis more plausible, and it is the analysis I will assume in what follows.

Let us now come to the rules for kind-referring NPs in English. A mass noun N can be used as a kind-referring NP directly via the rule NP → N, with $[\![[_{NP}\ [_{N}\alpha]]]\!] = [\![[_{N}\alpha]]\!]$. This is similar to the Chinese case. There is no such rule for count nouns. However, we have a rule NP → Det CN, with $[\![[_{NP}\ [_{Det}\alpha][_{CN}\beta]]]\!] = [\![[_{Det}\alpha]]\!]([\![[_{CN}\beta]]\!])$. We simply have to assume that the definite determiner *the* can be interpreted as the identity function λx.x if applied to a name (something we would need to do anyway for cases like *the Sudan*). Then we get, for the NP *the bear,* the meaning **Ursus:**

(14) $[_{CN}$ bear], **Ursus**

$[_{Det}$ the], λx.x

↓

$[_{NP}$ the bear], **Ursus**

The other way to arrive at a kind-referring noun is to transfer a singular count noun CN to a plural form CNp, as we can assume a syntactic rule NP → CNp which allows for bare plurals. We have seen that the most natural interpretation of a bare plural is the indefinite one—for example, bare plurals in nontopic positions tend to have this interpretation (see chapter 1, section 1.3.2). Therefore we should assume that the semantics of the rule NP → CNp yields a predicate. It can be seen as a special case of the rule NP → Num CN, where the actual number remains unspecified. One option is the interpretation rule $[\![[_{NP}\ [_{CNp}\alpha]]]\!] = \lambda x\exists n[\mathbf{RT}(x,[\![[_{CNp}\alpha]]\!])\ \&\ \mathbf{OKU}([\![[_{CNp}\alpha]]\!])(x)=n]$, where we assume that a plural CNp is interpreted as a kind, just like the corresponding singular CN. One example derivation is given below; we get a predicate which applies to objects which realize the kind **Ursus** and which are any number of object units of **Ursus** (we tacitly assume n > 0).

(15) $[_{CNp}$ bears], **Ursus**
|
$[_{NP}$ bears], $\lambda i\lambda x\exists n[\mathbf{RT}_i(x,\mathbf{Ursus})\ \&\ \mathbf{OKU}_i(\mathbf{Ursus})(x)=n]$

How can we derive the kind-referring interpretation from that? First of all, we note that our category NP is not necessarily maximal, as we have cases like *the bears* or *those three bears,* where the NPs *bears* or *three bears* are combined with additional determiners. There are different ways to treat this—for example, we could follow Abney (1987) and Haider (1988) and introduce a determiner phrase DP which governs an NP. Here, we just assume that rules like NP → DET NP are possible, where the embedded NP is indefinite and the embedding NP is definite. Then it becomes plausible to derive the kind-referring interpretation of an NP like *bears* by a syntactic rule like NP → NP and the corresponding semantic rule $[\![[_{NP}\ [_{NP}\alpha]]]\!] = \sigma([\![[_{NP}\alpha]]\!])$. We get derivations like the following:

(16) $[_{NP}$bears], $\lambda i\lambda x\exists n[\mathbf{RT}_i(x,\mathbf{Ursus})\ \&\ \mathbf{OKU}_i(\mathbf{Ursus})(x)=n]$
|
$[_{NP}$bears], $\sigma(\lambda i\lambda x\exists n[\mathbf{RT}_i(x,\mathbf{Ursus})\ \&\ \mathbf{OKU}_i(\mathbf{Ursus})(x)=n])$
$= \iota y\forall i\forall x[\exists n[\mathbf{RT}_i(x,\mathbf{Ursus})\ \&\ \mathbf{OKU}_i(\mathbf{Ursus})(x)=n] \leftrightarrow \mathbf{RT}_i(x,y)]$

This concept should be identical to the kind **Ursus,** as any realization of **Ursus** will be in the extension of the predicate, and vice versa. Therefore the noun phrase *bears* may also refer to the kind **Ursus**. Note that the σ-operator may be applied to other predicates as well, for example to *three bears,* which I have rendered as $\lambda x[\mathbf{Rx}_i(x,\mathbf{Ursus})\ \&\ \mathbf{OKU}_i(\mathbf{Ursus})(x)=\mathbf{3}]$. In this case, however, $\sigma(\lambda i\lambda x[\mathbf{RT}_i(x,\mathbf{Ursus})\ \&\ \mathbf{OKU}_i(\mathbf{Ursus})(x)=\mathbf{3}]$ yields a concept which is not a kind. In the case at hand, this can be proved, as **R** is not closed under sum formation for this concept: If x and y are three bears, then their sum isn't three bears anymore. Thus, only those predicates which really correspond to a kind can be mapped to a kind by σ.

For adjectives, finally, we can assume that they can be combined either with N or with CN and CNp, that is, we have the rules N → AP N, CN → AP CN, and CNp → AP CNp. The interpretation is similar to the Chinese case.

11.4. KUNG-SUN LUNG'S PARADOX

Let us end this short comparison of common nouns in Chinese and in English with a remark on the famous paradox of the ancient Chinese logician Kung-sun Lung, who stated that the (Classical Chinese) sentence in (17) can be asserted—that is, it has a noncontradictory and even true reading, to the puzzlement of many interpreters (cf. Hansen 1983 for a discussion).

(17) pai ma fei ma
white horse not horse
'white horse is-not horse'

The theory of common nouns developed in this chapter, together with the genericity theory sketched in chapter 1, predicts that this sentence indeed has a noncontradictory and true reading, in addition to a contradictory one. We get the noncontradictory reading by the assumption that *pai ma* and *ma* can be taken as referring to concepts, and by taking *fei* as a negation of the relation **IS** (cf. section 1.3.5), which is reduced to simple identity if both arguments are kinds (cf. (17′a) below). This reading can be rendered as 'The (kind of the) white horse is not the (the kind of the) horse', which is of course true, for not every horse is necessarily white. By contrast, under the assumption that *pai ma* and *ma* are indefinite NPs and the sentence is a negated generic sentence, we get the contradictory reading, as every object which is a white horse will be an object that is a horse, given that *pai* is an intersective adjective (cf. (17′b)). This reading can be rendered as 'A white horse is not a horse'. I give the analysis with a narrow-scope negation; the wide-scope negation would yield an equally contradictory result. The **GEN**-operator is interpreted as a modal quantifier in this setting that binds the possible world variable i.

(17′) a. $\neg\ [\mathbf{IS}_i(\mathbf{white(Caballus)},\mathbf{Caballus})]$
$= \sigma(\lambda i\lambda x[\mathbf{white}_i(x)\ \&\ \mathbf{RT}_i(x,\mathbf{Caballus})]) \neq \mathbf{Caballus}$

b. $\mathbf{GEN}[i,x;](\mathbf{IS}_i(x,\mathbf{white(Caballus)}); \neg\mathbf{IS}_i(x,\mathbf{Caballus}))$
$= \mathbf{GEN}[i,x;](\mathbf{RT}_i(x,\mathbf{white(Caballus)}); \neg\ \mathbf{RT}_i(x,\mathbf{Caballus}))$
$= \mathbf{GEN}[i,x;](\mathbf{white}_i(x)\ \&\ \mathbf{RT}_i(x,\mathbf{Caballus}); \neg\mathbf{RT}_i(x,\mathbf{Caballus}))$

Thus it is essentially the lack of a clear distinction between kind-referring uses and predicative uses in Chinese that creates this paradox.

I have argued that in English, mass nouns show a similar nondistinctiveness between the kind-referring and the predicative reading as in Chinese. Consequently, we can capture Kung-sun Lung's paradox in English using mass nouns in examples like *White wine is not wine,* which arguably has both a contradictory and a noncontradictory reading.

This concludes our short discussion of two grammars—Chinese and English—which handle the basic noun phrase structure quite differently.

12 THE MARKING OF THE EPISODIC/ GENERIC DISTINCTION IN TENSE-ASPECT SYSTEMS

Östen Dahl

12.1. Introduction

The question that I shall try to answer in this chapter is the following: given that the distinction between 'episodic' and 'generic' sentences has turned out to be an important one in the semantics of natural language,[1] to what extent is that distinction reflected in the grammars of individual languages, in particular, in their tense-aspect systems?

I think it may be appropriate to start by quoting two earlier partial answers to this question. This first is my own, from Dahl 1975:

> A possible objection to my approach would be that . . . I have not demonstrated that 'generic tense' . . . is a category which has any interesting grammatical properties. One way of giving an answer to this is to show that there are languages where 'generic tense' is marked morphologically. At first glance, English might seem to be such a language. . . . However, the generic-nongeneric distinction is clearly not the main distinction underlying the opposition between simple and progressive tenses. . . . We have to look for other languages. Turkish seems to be a suitable candidate. Lewis . . . describes the difference . . . in the following way: ''Fundamentally *yaparım* means 'I am a doer' . . . *yapıyorum* means 'I have undertaken, and am now engaged in, the job of doing'.'' . . . In this language, there is an opposition between so-called 'aorist' and 'nonaorist' tenses. . . . Hopi is another language we could mention. The 'nomic' category in Hopi according to Whorf . . . ''does not declare any particular situation, but offers the statement as general truth. . . .'' (Pp. 107–108)

1. Exactly what is understood by 'generic' varies from author to author, and sometimes between different works by the same author (cf., e.g., Dahl 1975 and Dahl 1985). Since this chapter relates to the distinction 'generic'/'episodic' as made, for instance, in Carlson 1988, I will use the term in the widest possible sense, including also cases that would often rather be termed 'habitual', such as *John walks to school.* This is in agreement then with the use in both the papers quoted in this section.

The second quotation is more recent, from Carlson 1988:

> Generic sentences would appear to be formally based on episodics—a generic like "The sun rises in the East" has a corresponding episodic "The sun rose in the East," matters of tense (and aspect) aside. As a wider array of languages are examined, this basic observation receives consistent support. No language I am aware of takes generic forms as basic and derives episodics from them, yet there are a lot that seem to work the other way around (then there is a very large class, including German, French, and English, in which they are treated roughly the same). (Pp. 36–37)

It is not crystal clear what the authors of these quotations want to claim, but at least the reader gets the impression that both make the following points:

(i) There are at least some or even "a lot" of languages in which genericity—or the generic/episodic distinction—is relevant in the grammar.

(ii) In those languages, the generic interpretation is the "marked" or "derived" case relative to the episodic one.

The first problem we stumble on when trying to evaluate these claims is the relation between genericity and the notions of tense and aspect. Dahl uses the term 'generic tense' without really motivating it. Carlson, on the other hand, brushes the problem aside in a somewhat baffling way, saying that "generic sentences would appear to be formally based on episodics . . . matters of tense (and aspect) aside." At the same time, what is probably the most common view is expressed in Comrie 1976, where genericity is treated as an aspectual notion, under the label of 'habituality' or 'habitual aspect'.[2] Both Dahl's use of 'tense' and Comrie's use of 'aspect' are of course motivated by the observation that such differences as are found between generic and episodic sentences tend to be naturally subsumed under the categories of tense and aspect. In any case, it is not clear how one can treat the marking of genericity separately from a discussion of those categories.

My main concern in this chapter, then, will be to scrutinize the claims

2. Comrie's definition of habituality goes as follows: "The feature that is common to all habituals . . . is that they describe a situation which is characteristic of an extended period of time, so extended in fact that the situation referred to is viewed not as an incidental property of the moment but, precisely, as a characteristic feature of a whole period" (1976, 27). Most of Comrie's discussion concerns past habituals, which may partly explain his emphasis on 'extended periods', a notion which is less prominent in, for example, the papers of Carlson and Dahl; still, his use of 'incidental' and 'characteristic' makes it clear that he is having basically the same distinction in mind. In Comrie 1985, the possibility of habituality being part of the modal system of a language is also mentioned (see footnote 4 below).

under (i)–(ii) in the light of available data on tense-aspect systems in natural languages. First, however, a few words on the character of those data.

12.2. THE DATABASE

The database I shall be using here is essentially the same as the one that underlies the investigation reported in Dahl 1985, viz. the translations into 65 languages of a questionnaire containing around 200 sentences. (Some ten languages have been added later).[3] In Dahl 1985, the focus was on identifying crosslinguistically valid types of grammatical constructions and/or morphemes—henceforth called *grams*—in tense-aspect systems and making generalizations about the relation between the semantics of grams and their mode of expression (periphrastic or inflectional). In later work, the interest shifted toward the study of the processes by which tense-aspect grams arise and develop (see Bybee & Dahl 1989; cf. also Bybee 1985). Inflectionally expressed grams were then seen as the endpoint of a gradual process of grammaticalization by which constructions acquire more and more of the typical properties of inflectional categories.

The questionnaire contained a number of more or less clear examples of generic sentences. A natural way of approaching the question addressed in the Introduction above is then to look at the ways in which these sentences are marked grammatically in the different languages, and what the distribution of each of the relevant grammatical markings is—in particular, whether it coin-

3. The following are the languages in the present sample: Afrikaans (Indo-European), Akan (Niger-Congo), Alawa (Australian), Amharic (Afro-Asiatic), Arabic (Classical) (Afro-Asiatic) (Tunisian), Avokaya (Nilo-Saharan), Azerbaijani (Altaic), Bandjalang (Australian), Beja (Afro-Asiatic), Bengali (Indo-European), Bugis Makassar (Austronesian), Bulgarian (Indo-European), Catalan (Indo-European), Cebuano (Austronesian), Chinese (Mandarin) (Sino-Tibetan), Czech (Indo-European), Didinga (Nilo-Saharan), Dutch (Indo-European), English (Indo-European), Estonian (Uralic), Finnish (Uralic), Fitzroy Crossing Kriol (Indo-European), French (Indo-European), Georgian (Caucasian), German (Indo-European), Greek (Modern) (Indo-European), Greenlandic Eskimo (Eskimo-Aleut), Guarani (Andean-Equatorial), Hawaiian (Austronesian), Hebrew (Afro-Asiatic), Hindi/Urdu (Indo-European), Hungarian (Uralic), Indonesian (Austronesian), Inuktitut (Eskimo-Aleut), Isekiri (Niger-Congo), Italian (Indo-European), Japanese (Altaic), Javanese (Austronesian), Kammu (Mon-Khmer), Karaboro (Niger-Congo), Kikuyu (Niger-Congo), Kurdish (Indo-European), Latin (Indo-European), Latvian (Indo-European), Limouzi (Indo-European), Luganda (Niger-Congo), Maltese (Afro-Asiatic), Maori (Austronesian), Montagnais (Algonquian), Oneida (Iroquois), Oromo (Galla) (Afro-Asiatic), Persian (Indo-European), Polish (Indo-European), Portuguese (Indo-European), Punjabi (Indo-European), Quechua (Andean-Equatorial), Rendille (Afro-Asiatic), Rumanian (Indo-European), Russian (Indo-European), Seneca (Iroquois), Somali (Afro-Asiatic), Sotho (Niger-Congo), Spanish (Indo-European), Sundanese (Austronesian), Swedish (Indo-European), Swedish Sign Language, Tamil (Dravidian), Thai (Kam-Tai), Tigrinya (Afro-Asiatic), Turkish (Altaic), Wolof (Niger-Congo), Yoruba (Niger-Congo), Yucatec Maya (Penutian), Zulu (Niger-Congo).

cides with the generic/episodic distinction as we would like to define it, or whether other notions are involved. An obvious and unavoidable limitation of this approach is that there may be crucial cases which are not reflected in the questionnaire.

12.3. THE MINIMAL MARKING TENDENCY

Consider the following English sentences, where (1) and (2) exemplify generics and (3) and (4) episodics:

(1) Cats meow.
(2) I smoke a pipe.
(3) I am smoking a pipe right now.
(4) I smoked a pipe yesterday after dinner.

It can be seen immediately that (1) and (2) differ from both (3) and (4) in their tense-aspect marking, although on different dimensions. According to the standard account, they differ from (3) in being a non-Progressive rather than in a Progressive form and from (4) in being in the Present rather than in the Past tense. From this account, there does not seem to be any simple feature that distinguishes (1,2) and (3,4) as groups. However, there is one property that singles out the generic sentences (1,2): they do not contain any overt tense-aspect marking—the forms *meow* and *smoke,* although analyzed as 1st person singular and 3rd person plural of the Simple Present, respectively, are identical to the stem of the verbs. If we look at English only, this may appear to be at least partly an accident, but it turns out that the most general statement that can be made about generics is indeed that they are not overtly marked for tense and aspect, or alternatively, that they employ the least marked tense-aspect choice in the language. This tendency—which we shall refer to as the *minimal marking tendency*—is strongest for the type of generic sentence exemplified by (1); we shall return to the differences between different generics below.

The tendency for generics to be minimally marked for tense-aspect is relatively independent of what the tense-aspect system looks like in other respects (with important exceptions to be discussed later). In the English examples above, sentences (3) and (4) contain Progressive and Past markings, respectively. Other languages may have counterparts to only one of these. Thus in Thai, the counterpart of (3) would contain a Progressive marker, whereas (4) would be wholly unmarked. In Afrikaans, on the other hand, (3) would be unmarked, whereas (4) would contain a Past (historically a perfect) marking. It then looks as if Thai lumped generics together with events in the past and Afrikaans put them in one bag with ongoing processes in the present. Such an interpretation is misleading, however: the generic contexts will tend to share the unmarked expression with whatever other types of sentences happen to be unmarked in the system. Indeed, there are certain other cases where there is a strong tendency for zero tense-aspect marking, notably verbs which denote successive events in a narrative. Thus, even languages like Afrikaans which otherwise mark past time reference tend not to do so in narratives. This means that generics and narratives are unmarked in both Thai and Afrikaans, although the tense-aspect systems of these languages are not particularly similar in other respects. (English could also be included here if we consider the use of the 'historical present' as a case of lack of tense-aspect marking in narratives.) Again, this should not be taken primarily as a sign of a close semantic relation between generics and narratives—rather, the lack of marking should be explained separately for each case.

In the case of generics, our main concern here, there are slightly different ways of explaining the tendency toward minimal tense-aspect marking. At least with respect to tense, it would appear natural to connect the lack of marking with the lack of specific time reference in generic sentences. If one tries to flesh out this idea, there is a possible conflict with Carlson's thesis about the basicness of episodic sentences, since episodic sentences would appear to contain something that generics lack, viz. specific time reference.

Another possibility is to try to explain the lack of tense-aspect marking in generic sentences as a consequence of the ways tense-aspect grams are grammaticalized. As argued in Bybee & Dahl 1989, there is a limited set of crosslinguistic gram types, and a limited set of points in semantic space from which tense-aspect markings can arise and spread. One way of formulating the minimal marking generalization is to say that it so happens that generics occupy a region of semantic space that is not close to any of the points of origin of tense-aspect grams. It is of course questionable whether this takes us anywhere as long as we have not explained why the points of origin occur where they do. Still, a closer look at the individual paths of grammaticalization may be worthwhile, in particular to explain the exceptions to the minimal marking tendency.

12.4 Generics and Imperfectives

The following are the most frequent paths of grammaticalization among tense-aspect grams (Bybee & Dahl 1989):

(i) Perfects develop into pasts or perfectives
(ii) Futures develop out of so-called prospectives or constructions expressing intention, volition, or obligation
(iii) (Present) progressives develop into presents or imperfectives

Of these, generics are involved only in (iii), the source of which is quite common among languages: progressive constructions appear in about 30 languages in the sample, although they vary considerably as to degree of grammaticalization. As we have already seen, a grammatical opposition between progressive and nonprogressive may serve to distinguish a certain type of episodic sentences from their generic counterparts ((3) vs. (2) above).

As we have also seen, however, generics may in such a system be nondistinct in their expression from various other kinds of sentences. In particular, the following kinds of contexts do not normally take progressive markings and will therefore tend to have the same form as generics: (i) statives (e.g., verbs like 'know', 'love', etc.) (ii) performatives (e.g., *I promise to go*), (iii) narratives and especially discourses in what is sometimes called 'reportive present', that is, accounts of an ongoing sequence of events, such as sportscasts.

When a progressive construction is subject to further grammaticalization, this typically means that its domain of use comes to include both the contexts listed in the preceding paragraph and generics. Accordingly, we find quite a few examples of generics being expressed by forms which at an earlier stage had progressive meaning only. Consider, for example, the Hindi form called the 'Present' in grammars, as in *bolta hai* '(he) speaks'. This form consists of an original present participle followed by a form of the copula—a relatively typical makeup for a progressive construction—and apparently was earlier restricted to progressive interpretations. When it expanded, the old 'Simple Present' (for the verb *bole* 'speak') became restricted to subordinate clauses and is nowadays labeled 'Subjunctive'. In this case, then, the form used in generics is not the minimally marked one, in terms of how many overt tense-(mood-)aspect marking morphemes it contains. This type of case, where an overtly marked imperfective (or sometimes an overtly marked present or present indicative) develops out of a progressive, constitutes one of the main kinds of exceptions to the minimal marking generalization. It is somewhat hard, however, to state exactly what languages belong to this group, for at least two reasons. One is that in such systems, it is often hard to identify any member as the 'minimally marked' one. The second is that later developments, in particular the rise of new progressive constructions, tend to obscure the situation. For instance, in Hindi, the form *boltā hai* is nowadays not used in prototypical progressive contexts: a new construction *bol rahā hai* appears instead. A rather curious situation thus arises, where what was originally a progressive construction has now only nonprogressive uses.

The use of overtly marked imperfectives in generic contexts is of course of rather marginal interest for the understanding of generics. What is more relevant is that in the course of the transition from progressive to imperfective, various intermediate situations may arise, in which a certain form may come to be more or less exclusively used for generic contexts. A case in point is Turkish, which happens to be one of the two languages mentioned in the quotation above from Dahl 1975. (The most complete account of the Turkish tense-aspect system is found in Johanson 1971.) The following examples from the questionnaire material illustrate the use of the two suffixes *-yor* and *-Ir* mentioned in the quotation:

(5) mektup yazıyor 'he is writing letters'
(6) mektup yazar 'he writes letters'
(7) miyavlar 'they (cats) meow'

Relatively recently, the *-yor* forms seem to have had progressive meaning only. In the modern language, however, they have a wider distribution than progressives normally do: for instance, they occur systematically in stative contexts (e.g., with verbs like 'know') and with performative verbs ('I promise that . . .') and in the 'reportive present'. In generics, the *-Ir* forms—usually referred to as the 'Aorist'—seem to predominate, but the *-yor* forms seem to be expanding into this area too, especially in the spoken language. The Aorist is also used to express future time reference and may occur, e.g., in narratives, as a kind of 'historical present'. This combination of uses is natural if we interpret the Aorist as a receding nonprogressive category. Two things are worth emphasizing here: first, the generic reading is only one of several uses that this form has; second, the situation appears unstable—the *-yor* form is still expanding. In the closely related Azerbaijani, the expanion has gone further in that the Aorist is now used more or less exclusively with future time reference.

A rather analogous situation is found in Tamil, where the form referred to in the grammars as 'Future' is also used fairly regularly in generic contexts. Historically, this form was probably a general nonpast, which has now been superseded in contexts with present time reference by a formerly progressive construction (referred to in grammars as the 'Present').

A further language which seems to behave in a rather similar way as to the marking of generics is Cebuano (Wolff 1966), although we do not have sufficient information about the history of the language to be able to make a judgment about the ways in which it has developed. In Cebuano, progressive contexts are distinguished from generic ones in that the former have the verb in the 'real durative' form, while the latter tend to use an 'unreal' form, commonly the 'unreal volitional'; compare, e.g., *ga-suwat* 'he is writing' vs.

mu-suwat 'he (usually) writes'. As can be seen from the examples, tense-aspect distinctions are marked primarily by prefixes in Cebuano, and no form is clearly unmarked in the system. The 'unreal volitional' might then seem to be a candidate for a habitual-generic gram. However, it is also used in a number of other contexts: (i) for future time reference—the form *mu-suwat* also occurs in the questionnaire with the interpretation 'is going to write'; (ii) with the adverbs 'twice', 'seven times', 'many times'; and (iii) instead of the 'real' forms under the scope of negation. This kind of pattern of use suggests that here too we may be dealing with a form which had a wider distribution earlier and which has undergone a development similar to the one found in the Turkic and Dravidian languages.[4]

In the languages described above, what looks like a grammatical opposition between episodic and generic sentences is thus rather a situation where the generic reading comes to be one of the more salient remaining interpretations of a gram which is in the process of yielding its territory to an expanding one. The relatively low frequency of this type of system, together with the observable synchronic variation in a language like Turkish, suggest that this is a transitional stage between two more stable states in tense-aspect systems. It is thus relatively implausible that a gram like the Turkish Aorist could develop into a proper marker of genericity.

The tendency for generics to go with imperfective aspect is fairly strong, but it is not without its exceptions. It is argued in Dahl 1985 and Bybee & Dahl 1989 that the aspect systems of Slavic languages are somewhat deviant in various respects. In the Slavic languages, in particular in Czech, Slovak, Serbian, Serbo-Croatian, and Slovene, but to a lesser extent also, e.g., in

4. The 'real'/'unreal' distinction is often found in descriptions of the verb systems of languages in Australia and other parts of Oceania. The 'unreal' verb forms typically are used as future tenses, but also have a number of other, usually modal uses. I do not have enough data to be able to say how often it happens that unreal forms have generic uses. One such case is mentioned by Comrie 1985, viz. Dyirbal (Australian) as described by Dixon 1972. Comrie explains the use of a modal category for habituality by saying that "it involves induction from limited observations about the actual world to a generalization about possible worlds." Indeed, it is sometimes possible to use a construction with predictive meaning, such as the English *will,* to express generics (of the 'hidden conditional' variety), the standard example being *Oil will float on water.* This suggests that future and other similar modal categories might be historical sources for forms expressing genericity. I do not know of any clear such cases; notice that they would be different from situations where a form has 'residual' future and habitual uses. In the case of Dyirbal, the facts are rather unclear: the unreal form with suffix *-ny* is opposed to a general 'present-past' form in *-nyu*/*-n* (*-nyu* was originally a past marker, to judge from the facts presented in Dixon 1980), so one could equally well assume that the 'unreal' is a residual category as that it has developed out of a marked future construction.

Russian, it is possible to use the perfective aspect for generics when a 'bounded' event is referred to, as in the following Serbo-Croatian sentence, quoted from Mønnesland (1984,62):

(8) Svako jutro popijem čašu rakije 'every morning I drink a glass of brandy'

Since the perfective aspect is overtly marked in this sentence (*popijem* vs. imperfective *pijem*), it looks like another exception to the minimal marking tendency. It should be noted, though, that since the imperfective is still possible in generics in Slavic, it is rather a question of an aspectual distinction which also occurs elsewhere being upheld in generics. However, this in itself can be regarded as a case of deviant behavior, since aspectual distinction—in particular that between imperfective and perfective aspect—tend to be neutralized in generics.

12.5. Generics from Habituals

We shall now consider another pattern of tense-aspect marking in generic sentences. Consider the following sentences from my questionnaire:[5]

(9) [Q: What your brother DO right now? (= What activity is he engaged in?) Answer by someone who can see him:] He WRITE letters.

(10) [Q: What your brother usually DO after breakfast? A:] He WRITE letters.

(11) [A: My brother works at an office. B: What kind of work he DO? A:] He WRITE letters.

(9) is a prototypical example of a progressive context. (10) and (11) would both be 'generics' in the wide sense.

The contexts of (10) and (11) would not seem to differ radically. Yet, as to tense-aspect marking, (10) and (11) behave differently in a sizable proportion of the languages in the questionnaire material. In 24 languages out of 76 (weighted percentage: 39),[6] we find relatively clear cases of markings in the translations of (10) not found in the translations of the progressive in (9). In only 7 of these languages (weighted percentage: 9) do we find the same marking in (11).[7] The inverse case—an overt marking in (11) but not in (9–10)—is not found at all. In

5. In the questionnaire, all verbs were given in the infinitive.

6. The 'weighted percentage' is calculated on the basis that languages belonging to the same language family are counted as if they were one language (this is done recursively, on every level of the genetic classification). This aim is to avoid areal and genetic biases.

7. These languages are Georgian, Işẹkiri, Maori, West Greenlandic Eskimo, Salliut Inuktitut, Wolof, and Yoruba.

17 languages (weighted percentage: 22),[8] then, there is a tense-aspect marking which occurs in (10) only. In most cases, this is either an auxiliary or a nonbound particle (or adverb); in a few cases, the marking is an affix. Swedish and Czech illustrate the periphrastic and bound alternatives, respectively:

SWEDISH (auxiliary *bruka*)

(12) Han brukar skriva brev. (= (10))

(13) Han skriver brev. (= (11))

CZECH ('iterative' suffix *-vá-*)

(14) Psává dopisy. (= (10))

(15) Piše dopisy. (= (11))

A closer inspection of the questionnaires reveals that the difference between (10) and (11) is probably seldom categorical. When there are responses from more than one informant for one language, or the same informant has given alternative translations, it turns out that the use of the marker tends to be optional in at least one of the sentences. However, the tendency is still very clear: either it is obligatory (to judge from the data) in (10) and optional in (11), or it is optional in (10) and does not occur at all in (11).

What kind of semantics can be assigned to those markers that would explain this difference in behavior? The crucial factor seems to be the presence in the context of (10) of the adverb *usually*. Compare the following English sentences:

(16) John walks to school.

(17) John usually walks to school.

The addition of *usually* in (17) fairly clearly carries the implicature that John at least sometimes does not walk to school. The same goes for the verb *bruka* in Swedish and the Czech iterative suffix (to judge from the glosses given in Kučera 1981). Supposing that this is true of the corresponding markers in other languages too, it appears that their function is not to mark genericity per se but to serve as a kind of quantifier over situations with, roughly, the semantics of 'most'. Following the terminology of Dahl 1985, let us refer to this kind of tense-aspect markers as 'habituals'. A relatively safe generalization is that habituals in general exhibit a low degree of grammaticalization. They are of potential interest to our topic mainly as possible sources of a grammaticalization path yielding what would be the primary candidates for a gram that systematically marks genericity. We shall now proceed to look at the languages in

8. These languages are Arabic (Classical), Akan, Catalan, Czech, Didinga, German, Guarani, Hungarian, Kammu, Limouzi, Montagnais, Sotho, Spanish, Swedish, Swedish Sign Language, Yucatec Maya, Zulu.

which such markers are found. In contradistinction to the ones we have talked about so far, these markers appear not only in (10) and (11) but also—to judge from the data, obligatorily—in a prototypical generic sentence such as (18), taken from the questionnaire.

(18) [Q: What kind of sound do cats make?] They MEOW.

In the questionnaire material, there are four fairly clear examples of such markings: Iṣẹkiri (Niger-Kordofanian), Wolof (Niger-Kordofanian), Maori (Austronesian), and West Greenlandic Eskimo (Eskimo-Aleut). The weighted percentage for these four languages in the sample is 8. A less clear case is Seneca (Iroquoian), which, if we include it, makes the total weighted percentage 9. We shall now look at these five languages in turn.

In Iṣẹkiri (Niger-Kordofanian), the preverbal particle *ká* marks generic contexts:

(19) o ká ya iwɛ́ 'he (usually) writes letters' (cf. o wínɔ́rɔ́ ya iwɛɛ́ 'he is writing letters')

(20) dí aghan aŋã ká ké 'cats meow'

It is also used in conditional constructions like the following:

(21) a má gbà ipósí dá ìtɛ̀, dí o ká ké 'if you tease a cat, it cries'

In Wolof (Niger-Kordofanian), two different periphrastic constructions are used in progressive and generic contexts, respectively:

(22) munge binda letar 'he is writing letters'

(23) dafa de binda letar 'he (usually) writes letters'

(24) dany de ngew 'they meow'

The latter construction is also used together with the adverb 'often'.

In the questionnaire data on Maori (Austronesian), the postverbal particle *ai* is used eight times in generic contexts:

(25) tuhituhi reta ai ia 'he writes letters' (cf. e tuhituhi reta ana ia 'he is writing letters' with Progressive marker *e . . . ana*)

(26) miao ai 'they meow'

In some types of generics, an alternative nominalization construction can be used; for example:

(27) he tuhituhi reta ia 'he writes letters' (lit. 'this is letter-writing')

In West Greenlandic Eskimo (Eskimo-Aleut), an 'iterative' is opposed to the very general 'indicative' by the suffix *-sar-/-tar-*, as in the following:

(28) allakkanik allapoq 'he is writing/was writing/wrote letters'
(29) allakkanik allattarpoq 'he (usually) writes letters'

The 'iterative' occurs 30 times in the questionnaire. It is used consistently in all habitual and generic contexts; for example:

(30) arfinermut makittarpunga 'I get up at six o'clock'
(31) miaartortarput 'they (i.e., cats) meow'

It is also used in the main clause of a conditional sentence such as the following:

(32) qitsuk qinngasaarnoqaraangami miaartortarpoq 'if you tease a cat, it meows'

The verb for 'cough' appears in the iterative together with the adverbs 'seven times', 'many times', 'for a while', and 'often'. The iterative is given as an alternative to the indicative with the adverbs 'twice' and 'for an hour'. In passing, it can be mentioned that the other Eskimo language in the sample—Salliut Inuktitut—lacks a counterpart to *-sar/tar-* but has a habitual suffix *-suu-/-juu-*.

So much for the clear cases of generic marking. As for the more questionable case, Seneca (Iroquoian), there is a distinction between what Chafe (1967) calls 'descriptive' and 'iterative' aspect, for example in the following sentences:

(32) kosyɔnyowa:eh 'she is washing a piece of clothing'
(33) yɔsyɔnyowa:eh 'she washes a piece of clothing (regularly)'

It does not seem possible to isolate a clear marking relation between the two aspects. Compare the following pairs of 3rd person sg. forms:

Descriptive	*Iterative*	
howɛtaɔh	hawɛ:tas	'die'
hoiote	hatyo:ta:s	'work'
hotaɔh	hotawas	'sleep'
hoteyɛstɔh	hateyɛstha	'read'

The descriptive has a rather wide range of uses, making it look rather like a general Imperfective. (For example, it is the default form used in stative contexts.)

The frequency of the iterative in the questionnaire is 22. It is generally used in generics, as in (34):

(34) wɛnɔ́staha 'they (i.e., cats) meow'

It competes with the nonbound habitual particle *kɛs,* which combines with the 'punctual' (perfective) aspect, as in (35):

(35) ɛyɔsyɔnyowae hɔ: kɛs 'she used to wash clothes'

In addition, the verb for 'cough' was translated with the iterative aspect when combined with the adverbs 'many times' and 'for an hour' (but not with 'twice' and 'seven times', where the punctual aspect was used).

Hopi, as described by Whorf in the quotation at the beginning of this chapter, may in fact also be an example of a language with an overt marker of genericity. According to Whorf (1956, 113), the 'nomic' (suffix *-ŋʷi*) in Hopi is one of three 'assertions', the other two being the 'reportive' (zero form) and the 'expective' (suffix *-ni*). Except for the English examples given above, Whorf does not exemplify the use of the nomic, however. This makes it somewhat difficult to draw any firm conclusions.

The markings of generic sentences that we have now looked at seem to exhibit a higher degree of grammaticalization than habituals in general. They are usually given without alternatives in the questionnaires. If we include Seneca, the marking is morphological in two out of five cases. In one clear case, West Greenlandic Eskimo, the marking is morphological. Regrettably, I have not been able to establish the historical origin of these markings, but as I have already suggested, one relatively plausible hypothesis is that they have arisen by grammaticalization of habituals as defined above.

As for the semantics, the distribution of the grams in at least Wolof, Iṣẹkiri, and Maori seems to fit the hypothesis that they are indeed markers of genericity. West Greenlandic Eskimo and Seneca are more of a problem, since the grams called 'iterative' in those languages occur also in contexts which could hardly be labeled 'generic', for example with adverbs such as 'twice' (Greenlandic) or 'for an hour' (Seneca). It may be that in those languages, 'iterativity' (however that notion should be defined) is more relevant than genericity, as the traditional labels also suggest.

Prototypical generics concern regularities, norms, or habits that either hold independent of time or during a period of time including the time of speech. At least if we use the term 'generic' in the wide sense, however, generics restricted to the past or the future do occur in languages, and this raises the issue of tense-marking in generics. In addition to combinations of regular past or future tense markings and the different types of markers discussed above there are also a few cases of specific 'habitual past' grams, that is, forms or constructions which like the English *used-to* construction are not just the past of a general habitual but have to be treated by themselves in the description of the language. In this group, the degree of grammaticalization varies considerably. (See Dahl 1985, chapter 3 for details.)

12.6. Conclusion

The picture that emerges from the above survey of the available facts is the following. Indeed, no language seems to have a general overt marking of all and only episodic sentences; however, it is probably true for the majority of all human languages that prototypical generic sentences are minimally marked with respect to tense and aspect—that is, that they either lack overt tense-aspect marking or that they use the least marked form in the system. Furthermore, whatever form is used for generics is also used in other, nongeneric contexts, although what these contexts are in a specific language depends on the rest of the tense-aspect system. The exceptions to these generalizations can be classified into the following types: (i) generics expressed by a marked imperfective (or possibly present tense) form, (ii) generics expressed by a receding nonprogressive, (iii) cases where there is an overt marker of genericity. How many languages there are in group (i) is somewhat difficult to determine; the total weighted percentage in the questionnaire material of the languages in groups (ii) and (iii) is about 15 each, suggesting that the tendency for systematic overt marking of generics is not too strong. In addition, as we have seen, even in these groups, generics sometimes share their expression with other types of sentences.

What is the moral to be drawn from the above? We have seen that it is not entirely easy to find clear examples of grammatical distinctions that coincide with the episodic/generic distinction in semantics. But looking around, we see that this is no unique situation: it is indeed rather rare for a grammatical marker to have a domain which is neatly delineated by a single semantic distinction. At best, the distinctions that interest semanticists are relevant in the straightforward cases of a grammatical opposition, but even then secondary readings may spoil what appeared to be nice generalizations. However, there are a couple of peculiarities regarding the marking of generics that the student of this sentence type should keep in mind, in my opinion. The first is the strong tendency for generic sentences to be completely devoid of any tense-aspect marking. This, I think, is something that an adequate semantic theory should account for. The second peculiarity is the parallel between the scarcity of grams that specifically mark verbs in generic sentences and the way in which generic NPs are marked. To my knowledge, there is no language that has a 'generic' article, that is, an article which is used exclusively with generic NPs. Thus, however sad this may be for those of us to whom the episodic/generic distinction is dear, this distinction more often than not is only indirectly reflected in speakers' choices between grammatical markers.

BIBLIOGRAPHY OF RECENT WORK ON GENERICITY

Manfred Krifka and Francis Jeffry Pelletier

This bibliography is an up-to-date (1993) account of work on genericity in the linguistic literature (with some input from the philosophical and artificial intelligence literature), especially work done after 1985. For a bibliography up to 1985, see M. Galmiche and G. Kleiber, *Langages* 79:118–126 (1985). The present bibliography is also a comprehensive reference list for all the chapters in this anthology.

Abbott, Barbara. 1989. "Nondescriptionality and Natural Kind Terms." *Linguistics and Philosophy* 12:269–291.

Abney, Steve. 1987. *The English Noun Phrase in Its Sentential Aspect.* Ph.D. dissertation, MIT.

Alho, Irja H. 1990. "Distinguishing Kind and Set in Finnish." Ms., University of Illinois at Urbana.

Allerton, D. J., and Alan Cruttenden. 1979. "Three Reasons for Accenting a Definite Subject." *Journal of Linguistics* 15:49–53.

Anderson, John M. 1973a. "The Ghost of Times Past." *Foundations of Language* 9:481–491.

Anderson, John M. 1973b. "Universal Quantifiers." *Lingua* 31:125–176.

Arnauld, Antoine. 1662. "La Logique ou L'Art de Penser." In J. Dickoff and P. James, translators and eds., *The Art of Thinking: Port-Royal Logic.* Indianapolis: Bobbs-Merrill Co.

Asher, Nicholas. 1993. "Extensions for Commonsense Entailment." Paper presented at the IJCAI-93 Workshop on Conditionals, Chambery, France.

Asher, Nicholas, and Michael Morreau. 1991. "Commonsense Entailment: A Modal Theory of Nonmonotonic Reasoning." *Proceedings of the 12th IJCAI,* 387–392. San Mateo, Cal.: Morgan Kaufmann.

Auger, J. 1993. "Syntax, Semantics and 'Ca': On Genericity in Colloquial French." *The Penn Review of Linguistics* 17:1–12.

Authier, Jean-Marc P. 1989. "Arbitrary Null Objects and Unselective Binding." In O. Jaeggli and K. Safir, eds., *The Null Subject Parameter,* 45–67. Dordrecht: Kluwer.

Åqvist, Lennart, Jaap Hoepelman, and Christian Rohrer. 1980. "Adverbs of Frequency." In C. Rohrer, ed., *Time, Tense, and Quantifiers,* 1–17. Tübingen: Niemeyer.

Babby, Leonard. 1980. *Existential Sentences and Negation in Russian.* Ann Arbor: Karoma.

Bach, Emmon. 1981. "On Time, Tense, and Aspect: An Essay in English Metaphysics.'' In P. Cole, ed., *Radical Pragmatics,* 63–81. New York: Academic Press.

Bach, Emmon. 1986. ''The Algebra of Events.'' *Linguistics and Philosophy* 9:5–16.

Bach, Emmon, and Robin Cooper. 1978. ''The NP-S Analysis of Relative Clauses and Compositional Semantics.'' *Linguistics and Philosophy* 2:145–150.

Bach, Emmon, and Barbara Partee. 1980. ''Anaphora and Semantic Structure.'' In K. J. Kreiman and A. E. Ojeda, eds., *Papers from the Parassession on Pronouns and Anaphora,* 1–28. Chicago: Chicago Linguistic Society.

Bacon, John. 1973a. ''The Semantics of Generic 'The'.'' *Journal of Philosophical Logic* 2:323–339.

Bacon, John. 1973b. ''Do Generic Descriptions Denote?'' *Mind* 82:331–347.

Bacon, John. 1974. ''The Untenability of Genera.'' *Logique et Analyse* 17:199–208.

Baker, Carl Lee. 1973. ''Definiteness and Indefiniteness in English.'' Distributed by Indiana University Linguistics Club.

Baker, Mark. 1988. *Incorporation: A Theory of Grammatical Function Changing.* Chicago: University of Chicago Press.

Barwise, Jon. 1986. ''Conditionals and Conditional Information.'' In E. Traugott, A. ter Meulen, J. Snitzer-Reilly, and C. Ferguson, eds., *On Conditionals,* 21–54. Cambridge: Cambridge University Press.

Barwise, Jon. 1987. ''Noun-phrases, Generalized Quantifiers and Anaphora.'' In P. Gärdenfors, ed., *Generalized Quantifiers,* 1–29. Dordrecht: Kluwer.

Barwise, Jon, and Robin Cooper. 1981. ''Generalized Quantifiers and Natural Language.'' *Linguistics and Philosophy* 4:159–219.

Barwise, Jon, and John Etchemendy. 1987. *The Liar: An Essay in Truth and Circularity.* New York: Oxford University Press.

Barwise, Jon, and John Perry. 1983. *Situations and Attitudes.* Cambridge, Mass.: MIT Press.

Bäuerle, Rainer. 1988. ''Ereignisse und Repräsentationen.'' Lilog-Report 43, IBM-Deutschland GmbH, Stuttgart.

Bäuerle, Rainer, and U. Egli. 1985. ''Anapher, Nominalphrase und Eselsätze.'' Arbeitspapier 105 des SFB 99, University of Konstanz.

Bäuerle, Rainer, Christoph Schwarze, and Arnim von Stechow, eds. 1983. *Meaning, Use, and Interpretation of Language.* Berlin: de Gruyter.

Bealer, George. 1975. ''Predication and Matter.'' *Synthèse* 31:493–508. Reprinted in F. J. Pelletier, ed., 1979, *Mass Terms: Some Philosophical Problems,* 279–294. Reidel: Dordrecht.

Bealer, George, and Uwe Mönnich. 1989. ''Property Theories.'' In D. Gabbay and F. Guenthner, eds., *Handbook of Philosophical Logic,* vol. 4, 133–251. Dordrecht: Reidel.

Bech, G. 1955/1957. ''Studien über das deutsche Verbum infinitum.'' *Historisk-filologiske Meddelelser* 35, no. 2, 1955; 36, no. 6, 1957. Copenhagen: Det Kangelige Danske Videnskabernes Selskabs.

Beck-Busse, Gabriele. 1990. ''La généricité 'aspectuelle': les states.'' *Revue de l'institute supérieur de traducteurs et interprètes des Bruxelles* 17/18:19–30.

Berlin, Brent, Dennis E. Breedlove, and Peter H. Raven. 1973. ''General Principles of Classification and Nomenclature in Folk Biology.'' *American Anthropologist* 75:214–242.

Berman, Steve. 1987. ''Situation-Based Semantics for Adverbs of Quantification.'' *Proceedings of WCCFL 6,* 17–31. Stanford, Cal.: Stanford Linguistics Association, Stanford University.

Berman, Steve. 1990. ''Towards the Semantics of Open Sentences: WH-phrase and Indefinites.'' In M. Stokhof and L. Torenvliet, eds., *Proceedings of the 7th Amsterdam Colloquium,* 53–78. Amsterdam: ITLI, University of Amsterdam.

Bierwisch, Manfred. 1987. ''Semantik der Graduierung.'' In M. Bierwisch and E. Lang, eds., *Grammatische und konzeptuelle Aspekte von Dimensionsadjektiven,* 91–286. Berlin: Akademie Verlag.

Biggs, Colin. 1978. ''Generic Generalizations.'' *Akten des XII Kongresses für Linguistik,* Vienna, 169–172. Innsbruck: Innsbrucker Berträge zur Sprachwissenschaft.

Blutner, Reinhard. 1985. ''Prototyp-Theorien und strukturelle Prinzipien der mentalen Kategorisierung.'' *Linguistische Studien* 125:86–135.

Blutner, Reinhard. 1988. ''Defaults and the Meaning of Generic Sentences.'' In M. Krifka, ed., *Genericity in Natural Language,* 3–30. SNS-Bericht 88-42, University of Tübingen.

Bolinger, Dwight. 1980. ''Syntactic Diffusion and the Indefinite Article.'' Distributed by Indiana University Linguistics Club.

Bowers, John. 1993a. ''The Syntax of Predication.'' *Linguistic Inquiry* 24:591–656.

Bowers, John. 1993b. ''The Syntax and Semantics of Individual and Stage Level Predicates.'' Paper presented at SALT 3, UC Irvine.

Bresnan, Joan. 1971. ''Sentence Stress and Syntactic Transformations.'' *Language* 47:257–280.

Brockett, Chris. 1990. ''The Syntax of Generics: Japanese Evidence for the Quantificational Model.'' *Proceedings of WCCFL9,* 59–74. Stanford, Cal.: Stanford Linguistics Association, Stanford University.

Bunt, Harry. 1985. *Mass Terms and Model-Theoretic Semantics.* Cambridge: Cambridge University Press.

Burton-Roberts, Noel. 1976. ''On the Generic Indefinite Article.'' *Language* 52: 427–448.

Burton-Roberts, Noel. 1977. ''Generic Sentences and Analyticity.'' *Studies in Language* 1:155–196.

Burton-Roberts, Noel. 1981. ''Review of Hawkins (1978).'' *Language* 57:191–196.

Bybee, Joan. 1985. *Morphology: A Study of the Relation between Meaning and Form.* Amsterdam: John Benjamins.

Bybee, Joan, and Östen Dahl. 1989. ''The Creation of Tense and Aspect Systems in the Languages of the World.'' *Studies in Language* 13:51–103.

Campbell, Richard. 1989. *The Grammatical Structure of Verbal Predicates.* Ph.D. dissertation, UCLA.

Carlson, Gregory N. 1977a. ''A Unified Analysis of the English Bare Plural.'' *Linguistics and Philosophy* 1:413–456.

Carlson, Gregory N. 1977b. *Reference to Kinds in English.* Ph.D. dissertation, University of Massachusetts, Amherst. Published 1980 by Garland Press, New York.

Carlson, Gregory N. 1979. "Generics and Atemporal 'When'." *Linguistics and Philosophy* 3:49–98.

Carlson, Gregory N. 1982. "Generic Terms and Generic Sentences." *Journal of Philosophical Logic* 11:145–181.

Carlson, Gregory N. 1987. "Exceptions to Generic Generalizations." In A. Manaster-Ramer, ed., *Mathematics of Language,* 19–32. Philadelphia: John Benjamins.

Carlson, Gregory N. 1988. "Truth-Conditions of Generic Sentences: Two Contrasting Views." In M. Krifka, ed., *Genericity in Natural Language,* 31–51. SNS-Bericht 88-42, University of Tübingen.

Carlson, Gregory N. 1989. "The Semantic Composition of English Generic Sentences." In G. Chierchia, B. Partee, and R. Turner, eds., *Properties, Types, and Meaning,* vol. 2: *Semantic Issues,* 167–191. Dordrecht: Kluwer.

Carlson, Lauri. 1981. "Aspect and Quantification." In P. Tedeschi and A. Zaenen, eds., *Syntax and Semantics 14: Tense and Aspect,* 31–64. New York: Academic Press.

Carlstrom, I. F. 1975. "Truth and Entailment for a Vague Quantifier." *Synthèse* 30: 461–495.

Cartwright, Nancy. 1989. *Nature's Capacities and Their Management,* esp. 198–202. Oxford: Clarendon Press.

Casadio, Claudia. 1990. "Interpretazione generica e metafora." Ms., Lecce, Milella.

Casadio, Claudia, and A. Orlandini. 1991. "On the Interpretation of Generic Statements in Latin." In R. Coleman, ed., *New Studies in Latin Linguistics: Selected Papers from the 4th International Colloquium on Latin Linguistics, Cambridge 1987.* Amsterdam: John Benjamins.

Chafe, Wallace. 1967. *Seneca Morphology and Dictionary.* Washington, D.C.: The Smithsonian Press.

Chafe, Wallace. 1970. *Meaning and the Structure of Language.* Chicago: University of Chicago Press.

Chellas, Brian. 1980. *Model Logic: An Introduction.* Cambridge: Cambridge University Press.

Chierchia, Gennaro. 1982a. "Nominalization and Montague Grammar: A Semantics without Types for Natural Languages." *Linguistics and Philosophy* 5:303–354.

Chierchia, Gennaro. 1982b. "Bare Plurals, Mass Nouns, and Nominalization." *Proceedings of WCCFL 1,* 243–255. Stanford, Cal.: Stanford Linguistics Association, Stanford University.

Chierchia, Gennaro. 1984. *Topics in the Syntax and Semantics of Infinitives and Gerunds.* Ph.D. dissertation, University of Massachusetts, Amherst.

Chierchia, Gennaro. 1985. "Formal Semantics and the Grammar of Predication." *Linguistic Inquiry* 16:417–443.

Chierchia, Gennaro. 1988. "Dynamic Generalized Quantifiers and Donkey Anaphora." In M. Krifka, ed., *Genericity in Natural Language,* 53–83. SNS-Bericht 88-42, University of Tübingen.

Chierchia, Gennaro. 1990. "The Variability of Impersonal Subjects." Amsterdam: ITLI Prepublication Series, University of Amsterdam.

Chierchia, Gennaro. 1992. ''Anaphora and Dynamic Binding.'' *Linguistics and Philosophy* 15:111–183.

Chierchia, Gennaro. 1994. ''A Note on the Individual-Level vs. Stage-Level Contrast in German.'' Forthcoming in *Proceedings of the Cortona Meeting on Tense and Aspect.* Turin: Rosenberg & Sellier Publishers.

Chierchia, Gennaro, and Raymond Turner. 1988. ''Semantic and Property Theory.'' *Linguistics and Philosophy* 11:261–302.

Chierchia, Gennaro, Barbara Partee, and Ray Turner, eds. 1989. *Properties, Types, and Meaning* (2 vols.). Dordrecht: Kluwer.

Chomsky, Noam. 1975. ''Questions of Form and Interpretation.'' *Linguistic Analysis* 1:75–109.

Chomsky, Noam. 1982. *Some Concepts and Consequences of the Theory of Government and Binding.* Cambridge, Mass.: MIT Press.

Chomsky, Noam. 1993. ''A Minimalist Program for Linguistic Theory.'' In K. Hale and S. J. Keyser, eds., *The View from Building 20: Essays in Linguistics in Honor of Sylvain Bromberger,* 1–52. Cambridge, Mass.: MIT Press.

Chomsky, Noam, and Howard Lasnik. 1977. ''Filters and Control.'' *Linguistic Inquiry* 8:425–504.

Christophersen, P. 1939. *The Articles: A History of Their Theory and Use in English.* Copenhagen: Mungaard.

Churchland, Patricia. 1984. *Matter and Consciousness.* Cambridge, Mass.: MIT Press.

Cinque, Giulio. 1988. ''On Si Constructions and the Theory of Arb.'' *Linguistic Inquiry* 19:521–581.

Clark, Romaine. 1973. ''Prima facie Generalizations.'' In G. Pearce and P. Maynard, eds., *Conceptual Change,* 42–54. Dordrecht: Reidel.

Code, Alan. 1985. ''On the Origins of Some Aristotelean Theses about Predication.'' In J. Bogen and J. McGuire, eds., *How Things Are,* 101–131. Dordrecht: Reidel.

Code, Alan. 1986. ''Aristotle: Essence and Accident.'' In R. Grandy and R. Warner, eds., *Philosophical Grounds of Rationality: Intentions, Categories, Ends,* 411–439. New York: Oxford University Press.

Combettes, Bernard. 1988. ''Marqueurs de généricité et ordre des mots: article défini et déterminant zéero en moyen-francais.'' In G. Kleiber, ed., *Rencontre(s) avec la Généricité,* 9–32. Récherches linguistiques 12, Université de Metz.

Comrie, Bernard. 1976. *Aspect: An Introduction to the Study of Verbal Aspect and Related Problems.* Cambridge: Cambridge University Press.

Comrie, Bernard. 1985. *Tense.* Cambridge: Cambridge University Press.

Condoravdi, Cleo. 1989a. ''Indefinite and Generic Pronouns.'' *Proceedings of WCCFL 8,* 71–84. Stanford, Calif.: Stanford Linguistics Association, Stanford University.

Condoravdi, Cleo. 1989b. ''The Middle: Where Semantics and Morphology Meet.'' MIT Working Papers in Linguistics 11, Department of Linguistics and Philosophy, MIT.

Condoravdi, Cleo. 1992. ''Strong and Weak Novelty and Familiarity.'' *Proceedings of SALT 2,* 17–37. Ohio State University Working Papers in Linguistics 10, Department of Linguistics, Ohio State University.

Conrad, Bent. 1982. "Referring and Non-referring Phrases: A Study in the Use of the Gerund and the Infinitive." Publications in the Department of English, University of Copenhagen.

Cooper, Robin. 1979. "The Interpretation of Pronouns." In F. Heny and H. Schnelle, eds., *Syntax and Semantics 10,* 61–92. New York: Academic Press.

Corblin, F. 1987. *Indéfini, défini et démonstratif.* Genève-Paris: Droz.

Croft, Bill. 1986. "Universal Quantifiers and Generic Expressions." Ms., Stanford University.

Cruse, D. A. 1986. *Lexical Semantics.* Cambridge: Cambridge University Press.

Dahl, Östen. 1970. "Some Notes on Indefinites." *Language* 46:33–41.

Dahl, Östen. 1975. "On Generics." In E. Keenan, ed., *Formal Semantics of Natural Language,* 99–111. Cambridge: Cambridge University Press.

Dahl, Östen. 1985. *Tense and Aspect Systems.* Oxford: Blackwell.

Dahl, Östen. 1988a. "Inherited Genericity." in M. Krifka, ed., *Genericity in Natural Language,* 85–94. SNS-Bericht 88-42, University of Tübingen.

Dahl, Östen. 1988b. "The Expression of the Episodic/Generic Distinction in Tense-Aspect Systems." In M. Krifka, ed., *Genericity in Natural Language,* 95–105. SNS-Bericht 88-42, University of Tübingen.

Danon-Boileau, L. 1989. "La détermination du sujet." *Langages* 94:39–72.

Davidson, Donald. 1967. "The Logical Form of Action Sentences." In N. Rescher, ed., *The Logic of Decision and Action,* 81–95. Pittsburgh: University of Pittsburgh Press.

Declerck, Renaat. 1986. "The Manifold Interpretations of Generic Sentences." *Lingua* 68:149–188.

Declerck, Renaat. 1987a. "A Puzzle About Generics." *Folia Linguistica* 21:143–153.

Declerck, Renaat. 1987b. "Definiteness and Inclusive Reference." *Journal of Literary Semantics* 16:12–29.

Declerck, Renaat. 1988. "Restrictive When-clauses." *Linguistics and Philosophy* 11: 131–168.

Declerck, Renaat. 1991. "The Origins of Genericity." *Linguistics* 29:79–102.

de Groot, C., and H. Tommola, eds. 1984. *Aspect Bound. A Voyage into the Realm of Germanic, Slavonic and Finno-Ugrian Aspectology.* Dordrecht: Foris.

De Hoop, Helen. 1992. *Case Configuration and Noun Phrase Interpretation.* Ph.D. dissertation, Rijksuniversiteit Gröningen.

De Hoop, Helen, and Henriette De Swart. 1989. "Over Indefiniete Objecten en te Relatie tussen Syntaxis en Semantiek." *Glot* 12:19–35.

Dekker, P. 1990. "Existential Disclosure." Paper presented at the Third Symposium on Logic and Language, Refvulop, Hungary.

Delgrande, J. 1987. "A Semantics for Defaults Using Conditional Logic." *Artificial Intelligence* 33:105–130.

Delgrande, J. 1988. "An Approach to Default Reasoning Based on First-Order Conditional Logic. Revised Report." *Artificial Intelligence* 36:63–90.

de Mey, Sjaak. 1980. "Stages and Extensionality: The Carlson Problem." In S. Daalder and M. Gerritsen, eds., *Linguistics in the Netherlands,* 191–202. Amsterdam: North-Holland.

de Mey, Sjaak. 1982. "Aspects of the Interpretation of Bare Plurals." In S. Daalder and M. Gerritsen, eds., *Linguistics in the Netherlands,* 115–126. Amsterdam: North-Holland.

Desclés, J. P. 1987. "Implication entre concepts: la notion de typicalité." In M. Riegel and I. Tamba, eds., *L'implication dans les langues naturelles et dans les langues artificiels,* 179–202. Paris: Kliencksieck.

de Swart, Henriëtte. 1988. "Phrases habituelles et sémantique de situations." In G. Kleiber, ed., *Rencontre(s) avec la Généricité,* 261–279. Récherches linguistiques 12, Université de Metz.

de Swart, Henriëtte. 1991. *Adverbs of Quantification: A Generalized Quantifiers Approach.* Ph.D. dissertation, Rijksuniversiteit Gröningen.

Diesing, Molly. 1988. "Bare Plural Subjects and the Stage/Individual Contrast." In M. Krifka, ed., *Genericity in Natural Language,* 107–154. SNS-Bericht 88-42, University of Tübingen.

Diesing, Molly. 1990. "Verb Movement and the Subject Position in Yiddish." *Natural Language and Linguistic Theory* 8:41–81.

Diesing, Molly. 1992. *Indefinites.* Cambridge, Mass.: MIT Press.

Dixon, R. M. W. 1972. *The Dyirbal Language of North Queensland.* Cambridge: Cambridge University Press.

Dixon, R. M. W. 1980. *The Languages of Australia.* Cambridge: Cambridge University Press.

Dölling, J. 1992. "Flexible Interpretation durch Sortenverschiebung." In I. Zimmermann and A. Strigin, eds., *Fügungspotenzen,* 23–62. Berlin: Akademie Verlag.

Donnellan, Keith S. 1966. "Reference and Definite Descriptions." *The Philosophical Review* 75:281–304.

Donnellan, Keith S. 1972. "Proper Names and Identifying Descriptions." In D. Davidson and G. Harman, eds., *Semantics of Natural Language,* 356–379. Dordrecht: Reidel.

Doron, E. 1988. "The Semantics of Predicate Nominals." *Linguistics* 26:281–301.

Dowty, David. 1979. *World Meaning and Montague Grammar.* Dordrecht: Kluwer.

Ducrot, O. 1970. "Les indéfinis et l'énonciation." *Langages* 17:91–111.

Ebert, Karen. 1971a. "Referenz, Sprechsituation und die bestimmten Artikel in einem nordfriesischen Dialekt (Fering)." *Studien und Materialien* 4, Nordfrilisk Instituut, Bräist/Bredstedt.

Ebert, Karen. 1971b. "Zwei Formen des bestimmten Artikels." In D. Wunderlich, ed., *Probleme und Fortschritte der Transformationsgrammatik,* 159–174. München: Hueber.

Enç, Mürvet. 1981. *Tense without Scope.* Ph.D. dissertation, University of Wisconsin, Madison.

Enç, Mürvet. 1991. "The Semantics of Specificity." *Linguistic Inquiry* 22:1–26.

Evans, Gareth. 1977. "Pronouns, Quantifiers, and Relative Clauses. Parts 1 and 2." *Canadian Journal of Philosophy* 7:467–536, 777–797.

Evans, Gareth. 1980. "Pronouns." *Linguistic Inquiry* 2:337–362.

Farkas, Donka, and Yoko Sugioka. 1983. "Restrictive If/When Clauses." *Linguistics and Philosophy* 6:225–258.

Féry, Catherine. 1991. "Prosodic and Tonal Structure of Standard German." Arbeitspapier 9 der Fachgruppe Sprachwissenschaft, University of Konstanz.

Findler, Nicholas. 1979. *Associative Networks*. New York: Academic Press.

Fine, Kit. 1985. *Reasoning with Arbitrary Objects*. Oxford: Blackwell.

Fodor, Janet D., and Ivan A. Sag. 1982. "Referential and Quantificational Indefinites." *Linguistics and Philosophy* 5:355–398.

Fodor, Jerry A. 1987. *Psychosemantics*. Cambridge, Mass.: MIT Press.

Frege, Gottlob. 1892. "Über Begriff und Gegenstand." *Vierteljahrsschrift für wissenschaftliche Philosophie* 16:192–205. Translated as "On Concept and Object." In P. Geach and M. Black, eds., 1966, *Translations from the Philosophical Writings of Gottlob Frege*, 42–55. Oxford: Blackwell.

Frey, Werner, and Hans Kamp. 1986. "Plural Anaphora and Plural Determiners." Ms., Institut für maschinelle Sprachverarbeitung, Stuttgart University.

Fuchs, Anna. 1980. "Accented Subjects in 'All-New' Utterances." In G. Brettschneider and C. Lehmann, eds., *Wege zur Universalienforschung; Sprachwissenschaftliche Beiträge zum 60. Geburtstag von Hansjakob Seiler*, 449–461. Tübingen: Narr.

Furukawa, N. 1986. *L'article et le probléme de la référence en francais*. Tokyo: Editions France Tosho.

Galmiche, Michel. 1983. "L'utilisation des articles génériques comme mode de denotation de la vérite." *LINX* 9:29–87.

Galmiche, Michel. 1985. "Phrases, syntagmes et articles génériques." *Langages* 79:1–39.

Gazdar, Gerald. 1979. *Pragmatics*. New York: Academic Press.

Gerstner, Claudia. 1979. *Über Generizität*. M.A. thesis, University of Munich.

Gerstner-Link, Claudia. 1988. *Über Generizität. Generische Nominalphrasen in singulären Aussagen und generischen Aussagen*. Ph.D. dissertation, University of Munich.

Gerstner, Claudia, and Manfred Krifka. 1993. "Genericity." In J. Jacobs, A. von Stechow, W. Sternefeld, and Th. Vennemann, eds., *Handbuch der Syntax*, 966–978. Berlin: de Gruyter.

Geurts, Bart. 1985. "Generics." *Journal of Semantics* 4:247–255.

Geurts, Bart. 1988. "The Representation of Generic Knowledge." In M. Krifka, ed., *Genericity in Natural Language*, 155–174. SNS-Bericht 88-42, University of Tübingen.

Goodman, Nelson. 1955. *Fact, Fiction and Forecast*. Cambridge, Mass.: Harvard University Press.

Grice, H. Paul, and Alan Code. 1979. "The Realm between Form, Matter, and Composite in Aristotle's *Metaphysics Z*. Paper presented at the Conference on Ancient Philosophy, University of Victoria.

Grimshaw, Jane. 1987. "Psych Verbs and the Structure of Argument Structure." Ms., Brandeis University.

Grimshaw, Jane. 1990. *Argument Structure*. Cambridge, Mass.: MIT Press.

Groenendijk, Jereon, and Martin Stokhof. 1987. "Dynamic Predicate Logic." Paper presented at the ASL/LSA Logic and Linguistics meeting, Stanford, Cal.

Groenendijk, Jereon, and Martin Stokhof. 1989. "Dynamic Predicate Logic." ITLI

LP-89-02. Institute for Language, Logic, and Information, University of Amsterdam.

Groenendijk, Jereon, and Martin Stokhof. 1990. "Dynamic Montague Grammar." In L. Kálmán and L. Pólos, eds., *Proceedings of the Second Symposium on Logic and Language,* 3–48. Budapest: Akadémiai Kiadó.

Groenendijk, Jereon, and Martin Stokhof. 1991. "Dynamic Predicate Logic." *Linguistics and Philosophy* 14:39–100.

Guericolas, Claude. 1988. "Les phrases dispositionelles: une approche informelle." In G. Kleiber ed., *Rencontre(s) avec la Généricité,* 33–57. Récherches linguistiques 12; Université de Metz.

Gussenhoven, Carlos. 1983. "Focus, Mode, and the Nucleus." *Journal of Linguistics* 19:377–417.

Haider, Hubert. 1988. "Die Struktur der deutschen Nominalphrase." *Zeitschrift für Sprachwissenschaft* 7:32–59.

Halliday, M. A. K. 1970. *A Course in Spoken English: Intonation.* Oxford: Oxford University Press.

Hamblin, C. L. 1973. "Questions in Montague English." *Foundations of Language* 10:41–53. Reprinted in B. Partee, ed., 1976, *Montague Grammar,* 247–259. New York: Academic Press.

Hansen, Chad. 1983. *Language and Logic in Ancient China.* Ann Arbor: The University of Michigan Press.

Harweg, R. 1969. "Unbestimmter und bestimmter Artikel in generalisierender Funktion." *Orbis* 18:297–331.

Hawkins, John A. 1978. *Definiteness and Indefiniteness: A Study in Reference and Grammaticality Prediction.* New York: Humanities Press.

Heim, Irene. 1982. *The Semantics of Definite and Indefinite Noun Phrases.* Ph.D. dissertation, University of Massachusetts, Amherst, and SFB-Papier 73, University of Konstanz.

Heim, Irene. 1983a. "On the Projection Problem for Presuppositions." *Proceedings of WCCFL 2,* 114–125. Stanford, Cal.: Stanford Linguistics Association, Stanford University.

Heim, Irene. 1983b. "File Change Semantics and the Familiarity Theory of Definiteness." In R. Bäuerle, C. Schwarze, and A. von Stechow, eds., *Meaning, Use and the Interpretation of Language,* 164–189. Berlin: de Gruyter.

Heim, Irene. 1984. "A Note on Negative Polarity and Downward Entailingness." *Preceedings of NELS 14,* 98–107. Amherst, Mass.: GLSA, University of Massachusetts.

Heim, Irene. 1987a. "E-type Pronouns in 1987." Talk given at Stuttgart University, 11 December.

Heim, Irene. 1987b. "Where Does the Definiteness Restriction Apply? Evidence from the Definiteness of Variables." In E. Reuland and A. ter Meulen, eds., *The Representation of (In)Definiteness,* 21–42. Cambridge, Mass.: MIT Press.

Hempel, Carl, and Robert Oppenheim. 1936. *Der Typusbegriff im Lichte der neueren Logik.* Leiden: Sijhoff.

Henne, M., O. B. Rongen, and L. J. Hansen. 1977. *A Handbook on Chinese Language Structure.* Oslo: Universitaetsforlaget.

Herschensohn, J. 1980. "Genericness and Intensionality." *Cornell Working Papers in Linguistics,* 1:93–102. Ithaca, N.Y.: Cornell University Press.

Heyer, Gerhard. 1985. "Generic Descriptions, Default Reasoning, and Typicality." *Theoretical Linguistics* 11:33–72.

Heyer, Gerhard. 1987. *Generische Kennzeichnungen. Zur Logik und Ontologie generischer Bedeutungen.* Munich: Philosophia.

Heyer, Gerhard. 1988. "A Frame-Based Approach to Generic Descriptions." In M. Krifka, ed., *Genericity in Natural Language,* 175–197. SNS-Bericht 88-42, University of Tübingen.

Heyer, Gerhard. 1990. "Semantics and Knowledge Representation in the Analysis of Generic Descriptions." *Journal of Semantics* 7:93–110.

Higginbotham, James. 1983. "The Logic of Perceptual Reports: An Extensional Alternative to Situation Semantics." *Journal of Philosophy* 80:100–127.

Higginbotham, James. 1985. "On Semantics." *Linguistic Inquiry* 16:547–593.

Higginbotham, James. 1988. "Elucidations of Meaning." Lexicon Project Working Papers 19, MIT Center for Cognitive Science.

Higgins, Roger. 1973. *The Pseudocleft Construction in English.* Ph.D. dissertation, MIT. Published 1979 by Garland Press, New York.

Hill, Archibald A. 1966. "A Re-Examination of the English Articles." Monograph Series on Languages and Linguistics 19. Washington, D.C.: Georgetown University Press.

Hinrichs, Erhard. 1981. *Temporale Anaphora im Englischen.* Zulassungsarbeit (ms.), University of Tübingen.

Hinrichs, Erhard. 1985. *A Compositional Semantics for Aktionsarten and NP Reference in English.* Ph.D. dissertation, Ohio State University.

Hintikka, Jaakko. 1980. "On the *Any*-Thesis and the Methodology of Linguistics." *Linguistics and Philosophy* 4:101–122.

Hintikka, Jaakko, and Lauri Carlson. 1979. "Conditionals, Generics, Quantifiers, and Other Applications of Subgames." In F. Guenthner and F. Schmidt, eds., *Formal Semantics and Pragmatics for Natural Languages,* 1–36. Dordrecht: Reidel.

Hirschbühler, Paul. 1982. "VP Deletion and Across the Board Quantifier Scope." In J. Pustejovsky and P. Sells, eds., *Proceedings of NELS 12,* 132–139. Amherst, Mass.: GLSA, University of Massachusetts.

Hoeksema, J. 1983. "Plurality and Conjunction." in A. ter Meulen, ed., *Studies in Modeltheoretic Semantics,* 63–83. Dordrecht: Foris.

Horn, Larry. 1969. "A Presuppositional Analysis of *Only* and *Even.*" *CLS* 5, 98–107. Chicago: Chicago Linguistic Society.

Horty, Jeffry, Richmond Thomason, and David Touretsky. 1990. "A Skeptical Theory of Inheritance in Non-Monotonic Semantic Nets." *Artificial Intelligence* 42: 311–348.

Huang, C.-T. J. 1982. *Logical Relations in Chinese and the Theory of Grammar.* Ph.D. dissertation, MIT.

Jackendoff, Ray. 1972. *Semantic Interpretation in Generative Grammar.* Cambridge, Mass.: MIT Press.

Jackendoff, Ray. 1977. *X' Syntax: A Study of Phrase Structure.* Cambridge, Mass.: MIT Press.

Jacobs, Joachim. 1983. *Fokus und Skalen: Zur Syntax und Semantik von Gradpartikeln im Deutschen.* Tübingen: Niemeyer.

Jacobs, Joachim. 1984. "Funktionale Satzperspektive und Illokutionssemantik." *Linguistische Berichte* 91:25–58.

Jacobs, Joachim. 1991. "Focus Ambiguities." *Journal of Semantics* 8:1–36.

Jacobson, Polly. 1990. "Raising as Function Composition." *Linguistics and Philosophy* 13:423–475.

Jacobson, Polly. 1991. "On the Quantification Force of English Free Relatives." To appear in E. Bach et al., eds., *Crosslinguistic Quantification,* Dordrecht: Kluwer.

Jaeggli, Osvaldo. 1986. "Arbitrary Plural Pronominals." *Natural Language and Linguistic Theory* 4:43–76.

Jakubczak, I. 1973. "Some Remarks on Generic Relative Constructions in English and Polish." *Papers and Studies in Contrastive Linguistics* 2:227–232.

Janssen, Th. 1984. "Individual Concepts Are Useful." In F. Landman and F. Veltman, eds., *Varieties of Formal Semantics,* 171–192. GRASS 3. Dordrecht: Foris.

Jespersen, Otto. 1924. *The Philosophy of Grammar.* Republished 1965 by Norton, New York.

Johanson, L. 1971. *Aspekt im Türkischen: Vorstudien zu einer Beschreibung des türkeitürkischen Aspektsystems.* Acta Universitatis Upsaliensis, Studia Turcica Upsaliensia 1. Stockholm: Almqvist & Wiksell.

Joly, A. 1986. "La determination nominale et al querelle des universels." In J. David and G. Kleiber, eds., *Déterminants: Syntaxe et sémantique,* 113–133. Paris: Klincksieck.

Jonasson, K. 1986a. "L'article indéfini générique et la structure de l'énoncé." *Travaux de linguistique et de littérature* 24:309–345.

Jonasson, K. 1986b. "L'article indéfini générique et l'interpretation des modaux." In J. David and G. Kleiber, eds., *Déterminants: syntaxe et sémantique,* 217–226. Paris: Kliencksieck.

Kadmon, Nirit. 1987. *On Unique and Non-Unique Reference and Asymmetric Quantification.* Ph.D. dissertation, University of Massachusetts, Amherst.

Kadmon, Nirit. 1990. "Uniqueness." *Linguistics and Philosophy* 13:273–324.

Kadmon, Nirit, and Fred Landman. 1993. "Any." *Linguistics and Philosophy* 16: 353–442.

Kálmán, Lászl6. 1987. "Generics, Common-Sense Reasoning, and Monotonicity in Discourse Representation Theory." In J. Ruzsa and A. Szabolcsi, eds., *Logic and Language: Proceedings of the '87 Debrecen Conference,* 95–110. Budapest: Académiai Kiad6.

Kamareddine, Fairouz. 1988. "Internal Definability and Collections." In M. Krifka, ed., *Genericity in Natural Language,* 199–219. SNS-Bericht 88-42, University of Tübingen.

Kamp, Hans. "Two Theories about Adjectives." In E. Keenan, ed., *Formal Semantics of Natural Language,* 123–155. Cambridge: Cambridge University Press.

Kamp, Hans. 1981. "A Theory of Truth and Semantic Representation." In J. Groenendijk, T. Janssen, and M. Stokhof, eds., *Formal Methods in the Study of Language,* 277–322. Mathematical Centre Tracts 135, Mathematisch Centrum, Amsterdam. Reprinted in J. Groenendijk, T. Janssen, and M. Stokhof, eds., 1984, *Truth, Interpretation and Information,* 1–41. Dordrecht: Foris.

Kamp, Hans. 1983. "Events, Instants and Temporal Reference." In R. Bäuerle, U. Egli, and A. von Stechow, eds., *Semantics from Different Points of View,* 376–417. Berlin: Springer-Verlag.

Kamp, Hans, and Nicholas Asher. 1989. "Self-Reference, Attitudes and Paradox." In G. Chierchia, B. H. Partee, and R. Turner, eds., *Properties, Types, and Meaning,* vol. 2: *Semantic Issues,* 85–158. Dordrecht: Kluwer.

Kanouse, David. 1972. "Verbs as Implicit Quantifiers." *Journal of Verbal Learning and Verbal Behavior* 11:141–147.

Kanski, Z. 1992. "Impersonal Constructions as a Strategy for Second-Order Predication." In M. Kefer and J. van der Auwera, eds., *Meaning and Grammar: Cross-Linguistic Perspectives,* 95–121. Berlin: Mouton de Gruyter.

Karimi, Ezat. 1989. "Null Pronominals with Arbitrary Interpretation." Ms., University of Texas at Austin.

Karttunen, Lauri. 1969. "Discourse Referents." Published in J. McCawley, ed., 1976, *Syntax and Semantics 7: Notes from the Linguistic Underground* 363–385. New York: Academic Press.

Karttunen, Lauri, and Stanley Peters. 1979. "Conventional Implicature." In C.-K. Oh and D. Dinneen, eds., *Syntax and Semantics 11: Presupposition,* 1–56. New York: Academic Press.

Kay, Paul. 1971. "Taxonomy and Semantic Contrast." *Language* 47:866–887.

Keenan, Edward L., ed. 1975. *Formal Semantics of Natural Language.* Cambridge: Cambridge University Press.

Keenan, Edward L. 1987. "A Semantic Definition of 'Indefinite NP'." In E. Reuland and A. ter Meulen, eds., *The Representation of (In)definiteness,* 286–317. Cambridge, Mass.: MIT Press.

Kenny, Anthony. 1963. *Action, Emotion and Will.* London: Routledge & Kegan Paul.

Kim, Boomee. 1991. "A Uniform Analysis of Arbitrary Null Subjects and Objects." *Proceedings of WCCFL 10,* 283–296. Stanford, Cal.: Stanford Linguistics Association, Stanford University.

Kiparsky, Paul. 1973. "'Elsewhere' in Phonology." In S. Anderson and P. Kiparsky, eds., *A Festschrift for Morris Halle,* 93–106. New York: Holt, Rinehart and Winston.

Kitagawa, Y. 1986. *Subjects in Japanese and in English.* Ph.D. dissertation, University of Massachusetts, Amherst.

Kitagawa, Y. 1989. "Deriving and Copying Predication." *Proceedings of NELS 19,* 279–300. Amherst, Mass.: GLSA, University of Massachusetts.

Kleiber, Georges. 1981. *Problèmes de référence: descriptions définies et noms propres.* Paris: Klienccksieck.

Kleiber, Georges. 1985. "Du côté de la genericité verbale: les approches quantificationelles." *Langages* 79:61–88.

Kleiber, Georges. 1988a. "Comment analyser les phrases habituelles du français?" In

M. Krifka, ed., *Genericity in Natural Language,* 221–245. SNS-Bericht 88-42, University of Tübingen.

Kleiber, Georges. 1988b. "Phrases génériques et raisonnement par défault." *Le francais moderne* 56:1–14.

Kleiber, Georges. 1989a. "LE générique: un massif?" *Langages* 94:73–113.

Kleiber, Georges. 1989b. "Comment traiter LE générique?" In *Traveaux de linguistique, Actes du Colloque de Bruxelles de décembre 1988 sur généricité, spécificité, aspect.*

Kleiber, Georges. 1989c. "LE générique: un article intensionel?" In E. Faucher, F. Hartweg, and J. Janitza, eds., *Sens et Etre. Mélanges en l'honneur de Jean-Marie Zemb,* 117–128. Nancy: Presses Universitaires de Nancy.

Kleiber, Georges. 1990. *L'article LE générique: La généricité sur la mode massif.* Geneva: Librarie Droz.

Kleiber, Georges, and Helene Lazzaro. 1988. "Qu'est-ce qu'un syntagme nominale générique? Ou les carottes qui poussent ici sont plus grosses que les autres." In G. Kleiber, ed., *Rencontre(s) avec la Généricité,* 73–112. Récherches linguistiques 12, Université de Metz.

Klein, Wolfgang, and Arnim von Stechow. 1982. "Intonation und Bedeutung von Fokus." *Arbeitspapier 77 des SFB 99,* University of Konstanz.

Koene, Netta. 1989. "Ambiguity: Syntactic and Prosodic Form in Empirical Semantics." In R. Bartsch, J. van Benthem, and P. van Emde Boas, eds., *Semantics and Contextual Expressions,* 57–73. Dordrecht: Foris.

Koopman, Hilda, and Dominique Sportiche. 1985. "Θ-Theory and Extraction." Paper presented at Colloquium on Parametric Typology, Brussels.

Koopman, Hilda, and Dominique Sportiche. 1988. "Subjects." Ms., UCLA.

Kratzer, Angelika. 1978. *Semantik der Rede, Kontexttheorie-Modalwörter, Konditionalsätze.* Königstein: Scriptor.

Kratzer, Angelika. 1980. "Die Analyse des bloßen Plural bei Gregory Carlson." *Linguistische Berichte* 70:47–50.

Kratzer, Angelika. 1981. "The Notional Category of Modality." In H.-J. Eikmeyer and H. Rieser, eds., *Words, Worlds, and Contexts: New Approaches to Word Semantics,* 38–74. Berlin: de Gruyter.

Kratzer, Angelika. 1986. "Conditionals." In A. M. Farley, P. Farley, and K. E. McCullough, eds., *Papers from the Parasession on Pragmatics and Grammatical Theory,* 1–15. Chicago: Chicago Linguistic Society.

Kratzer, Angelika. 1988. "Stage-Level and Individual-Level Predicates." In M. Krifka, ed., *Genericity in Natural Language,* 247–284. SNS-Bericht 88-42, University of Tübingen.

Kratzer, Angelika. 1989. "An Investigation of the Lumps of Thought." *Linguistics and Philosophy* 12:607–653.

Kratzer, Angelika. 1991. "The Representation of Focus." In A. von Stechow and D. Wunderlich, eds., *Semantik/Semantics: Ein internationales Handbuch der zeitgenössischen Forschung/An International Handbook of Contemporary Research,* 825–834. Berlin: de Gruyter.

Krifka, Manfred. 1987. *An Outline of Genericity,* partly in collaboration with Claudia Gerstner. SNS-Bericht 87-23, University of Tübingen.

Krifka, Manfred. 1988a. "The Relational Theory of Genericity." In M. Krifka, ed., *Genericity in Natural Language,* 285–312. SNS-Bericht 88-42, University of Tübingen.

Krifka, Manfred. 1988b. "Review of G. Heyer, *Generische Kennzeichnungen: Zur Logik und Ontologie generischer Bedeutungen.*" *Journal of Semantics* 6: 161–168.

Krifka, Manfred. 1989. "Nominal Reference, Temporal Constitution and Quantification in Event Semantics." In J. van Benthem, R. Bartsch, and P. van Emde Boas, eds., *Semantics and Contextual Expression,* 75–115. Dordrecht: Foris.

Krifka, Manfred. 1991a. "A Compositional Semantics for Multiple Focus Constructions." *Linguistische Berichte* (Sonderheft) 4:17–54.

Krifka, Manfred. 1991b. "A Compositional Semantics for Multiple Foci." *Proceedings of SALT 1,* 127–158. Cornell Working Papers in Linguistics 10. Ithaca, N.Y.: Cornell University Press.

Krifka, Manfred. 1992a. "Definite NPs Aren't Quantifiers." *Linguistic Inquiry* 23: 156–163.

Krifka, Manfred. 1992b. "A Framework for Focus-Sensitive Quantification." *Proceedings of SALT 2,* 215–236. Ohio State University Working Papers in Linguistics 40, Department of Linguistics, Ohio State University.

Krifka, Manfred. 1992c. "Focus, Quantification, and Dynamic Interpretation." Presented at the Eighth Amsterdam Colloquium.

Krifka, Manfred. 1993. "Some Remarks on Polarity Items." In D. Zaefferer, ed., *Semantic Universals and Universal Semantics,* 150–189. Berlin: Foris.

Kripke, Saul A. 1972. "Naming and Necessity." In D. Davidson and G. Harman, eds., *Semantics of Natural Language,* 253–355. Dordrecht: Reidel.

Kučera, H. 1981. "Aspect, Markedness and t_0." In P. Tedeschi and A. Zaenen, eds., *Syntax and Semantics 14: Tense and Aspect,* 177–190. New York: Academic Press.

Kuroda, S.-Y. 1972. "The Categorical and the Thetic Judgment: Evidence from Japanese Syntax." *Foundations of Language* 9:153–185.

Kuroda, S.-Y. 1988. "Whether We Agree or Not: A Comparative Syntax of English and Japanese." *Linguisticae Investigationes* 12:1–47.

Kyburg, Henry. 1990. "Probabilistic Inference and Nonmonotonic Inference." In R. Shachter, T. Levitt, L. Kanal, and J. Lemmer, eds., *Uncertainty in Artificial Intelligence 4,* 319–326. Amsterdam: North-Holland.

Laca, Brenda. 1990. "Generic Objects: Some More Pieces of the Puzzle." *Lingua* 81:25–46.

Ladusaw, William. 1979. *Polarity Sensitivity as Inherent Scope Relations.* Ph.D. dissertation, University of Texas at Austin.

Landman, Fred. 1986a. "Pegs and Alecs." In J. Halpern, ed., *Theoretical Aspects of Reasoning about Knowledge,* 45–61. Los Altos: Morgan Kaufmann.

Landman, Fred. 1986b. "Towards a Theory of Information: The Status of Partial Objects in Semantics." GRASS 6. Dordrecht: Foris.

Landman, Fred. 1989. "Groups I," "Groups II." *Linguistics and Philosophy* 12:559–605, 723–744.

Landman, Fred. 1992. "The Progressive." *Natural Language Semantics* 1:1–32.

Langford, C. H. 1949. "The Institutional Use of 'The'." *Philosophy and Phenomenological Research* 10:115–120.

Laparra, Marceline. 1988. "Degrés de l'explicitation de la lecture générique de certains syntagmes nominaux dans un corpus de langue orale." In G. Kleiber, ed., *Rencontre(s) avec la Généricité,* 113–131. Récherches linguistiques 12, Université de Metz.

Lawler, John. 1972. "Generic to a Fault." *CLS* 8, 247–258. Chicago: Chicago Linguistic Society.

Lawler, John. 1973a. *Studies in English Generics.* University of Michigan Papers in Linguistics 1:1. Ann Arbor: University of Michigan Press.

Lawler, John. 1973b. "Tracking the Generic Toad." *CLS* 9, 320–331. Chicago: Chicago Linguistic Society.

Léard, Jean-Marcel. 1984. "Morphogénèse et lexigénèse." *Revue Québécoise de Linguistique* 13:325–379.

Léard, Jean-Marcel. 1988. "Quelques aspects morpho-syntaxiques des syntagmes et des phrases génériques." In G. Kleiber, ed., *Rencontre(s) avec la Généricité,* 133–155. Récherches linguistiques 12, Université de Metz.

Lemmon, E. J. 1967. "Comments on D. Davidson's 'The Logical Form of Action Sentences'." In N. Rescher, ed., *The Logic of Decision and Action,* 96–103. Pittsburgh: University of Pittsburgh Press.

Lerner, J. Y., and Wolfgang Sternefeld. 1984. "Zum Skopus der Negation im komplexen Satz des Deutschen." *Zeitschrift für Sprachwissenschaft* 3:159–202.

Lewis, David. 1973. *Counterfactuals.* Cambridge, Mass.: Harvard University Press.

Lewis, David. 1975. "Adverbs of Quantification." In E. Keenan, ed., *Formal Semantics of Natural Languages,* 3–15. Cambridge: Cambridge University Press.

Lewis, David. 1983. "Scorekeeping in a Language Game." In R. Bäuerle, U. Egli, and A. von Stechow, eds., *Semantics from Different Points of View,* 172–187. Berlin: Springer-Verlag.

Lewis, G. L. 1967. *Turkish Grammar.* Oxford: Clarendon Press.

Lifschitz, V. 1986. "On the Satisfiability of Circumscription." *Artificial Intelligence* 28:17–27.

Link, Godehard. 1983. "The Logical Analysis of Plurals and Mass Terms: A Lattice-Theoretical Approach." In R. Bäuerle, C. Schwarze, and A. von Stechow, eds., *Meaning, Use and Interpretation of Language,* 303–323. Berlin: de Gruyter.

Link, Godehard. 1987. "Algebraic Semantics of Event Structures." In J. Groenendijk, M. Stokhof, and F. Veltman, eds., *Proceedings of the Sixth Amsterdam Colloquium,* 243–262. Amsterdam: ITLI, University of Amsterdam.

Link, Godehard. 1988. "Dependency in the Theory of Generics." In M. Krifka, ed., *Genericity in Natural Language,* 313–335. SNS-Bericht 88-42, University of Tübingen.

Löbner, Sebastian. 1987. "Natural Language and Generalized Quantifier Theory." In P. Gärdenfors, ed., *Generalized Quantifiers: Linguistic and Logic Approaches,* 181–201. Dordrecht: Reidel.

Lyons, John. 1977. *Semantics.* (2 vols.). Cambridge: Cambridge University Press.

Maillard, Michel. 1988. "'Un zizi, ca sert à faire pipi debout!' Les références génériques de ca en grammaire francaise." In G. Kleiber, ed., *Rencontre(s) avec la Généricité,* 157–205. Récherches linguistiques 12, Université de Metz.

Martin, R. 1986. "Les usages génériques de l'article LA et la pluralité." In J. David and D. Kleiber, eds., *Déterminants: syntaxe et semantique,* 187–202. Paris: Kliencksieck.

Martin, R. 1987. *Langage et croyance: les "univers de croyence" dans la théorie sémantique.* Brussels: P. Mardaga.

May, Robert. 1977. *The Grammar of Quantification.* Ph.D. dissertation, MIT.

May, Robert. 1985. *Logical Form: Its Structure and Derivation.* Cambridge, Mass.: MIT Press.

Mayer, Rolf. 1980. *Ontologische Aspekte der Nominalsemantik.* Tübingen: Niemeyer.

McCarthy, John. 1980. "Circumscription: A Form of Non-Monotonic Reasoning." *Artificial Intelligence* 13:27–39.

McCarthy, John. 1986. "Applications of Circumscription to Formalizing Common Sense Knowledge." *Artificial Intelligence* 28:89–116.

McDermott, Drew, and Jon Doyle. 1980. "Non-Monotonic Logic I." *Artificial Intelligence* 13:41–72.

Mehlig, H. R. 1982a. "Generic States and Specific States." In K. Detering, *Sprache, Erkennen und Verstehen,* 28–37. Tübingen: Niemeyer.

Mehlig, H. R. 1982b. "Nominale Referenz, Zeitreferenz und Prädikatssemantik." In H. R. Mehlig, ed., *Slavistische Linguistik,* 48–75. Munich: Sagner.

Milner, J. C. 1978. *De la syntaxe à l'interpretation: quantites, insultes, exclamations.* Paris: Le Seuil.

Milsark, Gary. 1974. *Existential Sentences in English.* Ph.D. dissertation, MIT. Distributed by Indiana University Linguistics Club.

Milsark, Gary. 1977. "Toward an Explanation of Certain Peculiarities of the Existential Construction in English." *Linguistic Analysis* 3:1–30.

Mithun, Marianne. 1984. "The Evolution of Noun Incorporation." *Language* 60: 847–894.

Moens, M., and M. Steedman. 1988. "Temporal Ontology and Temporal Reference." *Computational Linguistics* 14:15–28.

Moltmann, Friederike. 1995. *Parts and Wholes in Semantics.* Oxford: Oxford University Press.

Mønnesland, S. 1984. "The Slavonic Frequentative Habitual." In C. de Groot and H. Tommola, eds., *Aspect Bound,* 53–76. Dordrecht: Foris.

Montague, Richard. 1973. "The Proper Treatment of Quantification in Ordinary English." In J. Hintikka, J. Moravcsik, and P. Suppes, eds., *Approaches to Natural Language,* 221–242. Dordrecht: Reidel. Also in R. Thomason, ed., 1974, *Formal Philosophy: Selected Papers of Richard Montague.* New Haven, Conn.: Yale University Press.

Moore, Robert. 1984. "Possible-World Semantics for Autoepistemic Logic." In *Proceedings of the 1984 AAAI Workshop on Nonmonotonic Reasoning,* 334–354. Menlo Park, Cal.: American Association for Artificial Intelligence.

Morreau, Michael. 1988. "Default Formalisms for Generics: A Consumer Report."

In M. Krifka, ed., *Genericity in Natural Language,* 337–356. SNS-Bericht 88-42, University of Tübingen.

Morreau, Michael. 1992a. *Conditionals in Philosophy and Artificial Intelligence.* Ph.D. dissertation, University of Amsterdam.

Morreau, Michael. 1992b. "Norms or Inference Tickets? A Frontal Collision between Intuitions." In T. Briscoe, V. De Paiva, and A. Copestake, eds., *Inheritance, Defaults, and the Lexicon,* 58–73. Cambridge: Cambridge University Press.

Morreau, Michael. 1993. "The Conditional Logic of Generalizations." Paper presented at the IJCAI-93 Workshop on Conditionals, Chambery, France.

Mourelatos, Alexander P. D. 1978. "Events, Processes and States." *Linguistics and Philosophy* 2:415–434.

Mufwene, Salikoko. 1986. "Number Delimitation in Gullah." *American Speech* 61: 33–60.

Muller, Claude. 1988. "A propos de l'indéfini générique." In G. Kleiber, ed., *Rencontre(s) avec la Généricité,* 207–233. Récherches linguistiques 12, Université de Metz.

Newton, Brian. 1979. "Scenarios, Modality and Verbal Aspect in Modern Greek." *Language* 55:139–167.

Nunberg, Geoff. 1993. "Indexicality and Deixis." *Linguistics and Philosophy* 16:1–44.

Nunberg, Geoff, and C. Pan. 1975. "Inferring Quantification in Generic Sentences." *CLS* 11, 412–422. Chicago: Chicago Linguistic Society.

Ojeda, Almerindo E. 1991. "Definite Descriptions and Definite Generics." *Linguistics and Philosophy* 14:367–397.

Oomen, I. 1977. *Determination bei generischen, definiten und indefiniten Beschreibungen.* Tübingen: Niemeyer.

Parsons, Terence. 1970. "An Analysis of Mass Terms and Amount Terms." *Foundations of Language* 6:362–388. Reprinted in F. J. Pelletier, ed., 1979, *Mass Terms: Some Philosophical Problems,* 137–166. Dordrecht: Reidel.

Parsons, Terence. 1980. "Modifiers and Quantifiers in Natural Language." In F. J. Pelletier and C. Normore, eds., *New Essays in Philosophy of Language. Canadian Journal of Philosophy,* suppl. vol. 6:29–60.

Parsons, Terence. 1985. "Underlying Events in the Logical Analysis of English." In E. LePore and B. P. McLaughlin, eds., *Actions and Events: Perspectives on the Philosophy of Donald Davidson,* 235–267. Oxford: Blackwell.

Parsons, Terence. 1990. *Events in the Semantics of English.* Cambridge, Mass.: MIT Press.

Partee, Barbara. 1973. "Some Structural Analogies between Tenses and Pronouns in English." *The Journal of Philosophy* 70:601–609.

Partee, Barbara. 1977. "John is Easy to Please." In A. Zampolli, ed., *Linguistic Structures Processing,* 281–312. Amsterdam: North-Holland.

Partee, Barbara. 1978. "Bound Variables and Other Anaphora." In D. Waltz, ed., *Proceedings of TINLAP-2,* 79–85. New York: Association for Computing Machinery.

Partee, Barbara. 1984. "Nominal and Temporal Anaphora." *Linguistics and Philosophy* 7:243–286.

Partee, Barbara. 1987. "Noun-Phrase Interpretation and Type-Shifting Principles." In J. Groenendijk and M. Stockhof, eds., *Studies in Discourse Representation Theory and the Theory of Generalized Quantifiers,* 115–143. GRASS 8. Dordrecht: Foris.

Partee, Barbara. 1991. "Topic, Focus, and Quantification." In *Proceedings of SALT 1,* 257–280. Cornell Working Papers in Linguistics 40. Ithaca, N.Y.: Cornell University Press.

Partee, Barbara, and Mats Rooth. 1983. "Generalized Conjunction and Type Ambiguity." In R. Bäuerle, C. Schwarze, and A. von Stechow, eds., *Meaning, Use and Interpretation of Language,* 361–383. Berlin: de Gruyter.

Pease-Gorrissen, Margarita. 1980. "The Use of the Article in Spanish Habitual and Generic Sentences." *Lingua* 51:311–336.

Pease-Gorrissen, Margarita. 1982. *Generic Sentences with Special Reference to Spanish.* Dissertation Abstracts International, 42/10, 4437-A.

Pelletier, Francis Jeffry. 1974. "On Some Proposals for the Semantics of Mass Terms." *Journal of Philosophical Logic* 3:87–108.

Pelletier, Francis Jeffry. 1979. "Aristotle on Sameness and Referential Opacity." *Noûs* 13:283–311.

Pelletier, Francis Jeffry. 1991. "Mass Terms." In B. Smith, ed., *Handbook of Metaphysics and Ontology,* 495–499. Munich: Philosophia.

Pelletier, Francis Jeffry, and Lenhart K. Schubert. 1989. "Mass Expressions." In D. Gabbay and F. Guenthner, eds., *Handbook of Philosophical Logic,* vol. 4, 327–407. Dordrecht: Kluwer.

Perlmutter, David. 1970. "On the Article in English." In M. Bierwisch and K. Heidolph, eds., *Progress in Linguistics,* 233–248. The Hague: Mouton.

Perlmutter, David. 1978. "Impersonal Passives and the Unaccusative Hypothesis." *Berkeley Linguistics Society* 4, 157–189.

Pesetsky, David. 1982. *Paths and Categories.* Ph.D. dissertation, MIT.

Picabia, Lelia. 1988. "Quand y a-t-il générique?" In G. Kleiber, ed., *Rencontre(s) avec la Généricité,* 235–259. Récherches linguistiques 12, Université de Metz.

Pierrehumbert, Janet. 1980. *The Phonology and Phonetics of English Intonation.* Ph.D. dissertation, MIT.

Pinkal, M., ed. 1986. "Tutorial: Situationssemantik und Diskursrepräsentationstheorie." In H. Stoynan, ed., *GWAI-85,* 395–471. Informatik Fachberichte 188. Berlin: Springer-Verlag.

Platteau, F. 1980. "Definite and Indefinite Generics." In J. van der Auwera, ed., *The Semantics of Determiners,* 112–123. London: Croom Helm.

Porterfield, Leslie, and Veneeta Srivastav. 1988. "(In)definiteness in the Absence of Articles: Evidence from Hindi and Indonesian." *Proceedings of WCCFL 7,* 265–276. Stanford, Cal.: Stanford Linguistics Association, Stanford University.

Portner, Paul. 1992. *Situation Theory and the Semantics of Propositional Expressions.* Ph.D. dissertation, University of Massachusetts, Amherst.

Postal, Paul. 1970. "On Coreferential Subject Deletion." *Linguistic Inquiry* 1: 439–500.

Putnam, Hilary. 1970. "Is Semantics Possible?" In H. E. Kiefer and M. K. Munitz, eds., *Language, Belief and Metaphysics,* 50–63. Albany, N.Y.: State University of New York Press. Also in H. Putnam, 1975, *Mind, Language and Reality* (*Philosophical Papers,* vol. 2), 139–152. Cambridge: Cambridge University Press.

Putnam, Hilary. 1975. "The Meaning of 'Meaning'." In K. Gunderson, ed., *Language, Mind and Knowledge,* 131–193. Minneapolis: University of Minnesota Press. Also in H. Putnam (1975), *Mind, Language and Reality* (*Philosophical Papers,* vol 2), 215–271. Cambridge: Cambridge University Press.

Quine, Willard Van Orman. 1960. *Word and Object.* Cambridge, Mass.: MIT Press.

Quirk, Randolph, Sidney Greenbaum, Geoffrey Leech, and Jan Svartvik. 1985. *A Comprehensive Grammar of the English Language.* London: Longman.

Reinhart, Tanya. 1981. "Pragmatics and Linguistics: An Analysis of Sentence Topics." *Philosophica* 27:53–93.

Reiter, Ray. 1980. "A Logic for Default Reasoning." *Artificial Intelligence* 13: 81–132.

Reiter, Ray. 1987. "Nonmonotonic Reasoning." *Annual Reviews of Computer Science* 2:147–187.

Rizzi, Luigi. 1986. "Null Objects in Italian and the Theory of *Pro.*" *Linguistic Inquiry* 17:501–557.

Rizzi, Luigi. 1990. *Relativized Minimality.* Cambridge, Mass.: MIT Press.

Roberts, Craige. 1987. *Modal Subordination, Anaphora, and Distributivity.* Ph.D. dissertation, University of Massachusetts, Amherst.

Roberts, Craige. 1989. "Modal Subordination and Pronominal Anaphora in Discourse." *Linguistics and Philosophy* 12:683–721.

Rochemont, Michael. 1986. *Focus in Generative Grammar.* Amsterdam: John Benjamins.

Rodman, R. 1976. "Scope Phenomena, 'Movement Transformations', and Montague Grammar." In B. H. Partee, ed., *Montague Grammar,* 165–176. New York: Academic Press.

Root, Rebecca. 1986. *The Semantics of Anaphora in Discourse.* Ph.D. dissertation, University of Texas at Austin.

Rooth, Mats. 1985. *Association with Focus.* Ph.D. dissertation, University of Massachusetts, Amherst.

Rooth, Mats. 1987. "Noun Phrase Interpretation in Montague Grammar, File Change Semantics, and Situation Semantics." In P. Gärdenfors, ed., *Generalized Quantifiers: Linguistic and Logical Approaches,* 237–268. Dordrecht: Kluwer.

Rosch, Eleanor. 1978. "Principles of Categorization." In E. Rosch and B. B. Lloyd, eds., *Cognition and Categorization,* 27–48. Hillsdale, N.J.: Lawrence Erlbaum.

Ryle, Gilbert. 1949. *The Concept of Mind.* London: Hutchinson.

Sag, Ivan. 1976. *Deletion and Logical Form.* Ph.D. dissertation, MIT. Published 1980 by Garland Press, New York.

Saito, M. 1985. *Some Asymmetries in Japanese and Their Theoretical Consequences.* Ph.D. dissertation, MIT.

Salmon, Nathan. 1989. "Reference and Information Content: Names and Descriptions." In D. Gabbay and F. Guenthner, eds., *Handbook of Philosophical Logic,* vol. 4, 409–461. Dordrecht: Kluwer.

Sasse, Hans-Jürgen. 1987. "The Thetic/Categorical Distinction Revisited." *Linguistics* 25:511–580.

Scha, Remko. 1981. "Distributive, Collective and Cumulative Quantification." In J. Groenendijk, T. Janssen, and M. Stokhof, eds. *Formal Methods in the Study of Language,* 483–512. Mathematical Centre Tracts 135, Mathematisch Centrum, Amsterdam.

Schaller, George B., and Millicent E. Selsam. 1969. *The Tiger: Its Life in the Wild.* New York: Harper and Row. (A book dealing with the natural history of tigers, from which example sentences have been taken).

Scheutz, Hannes. 1988. "Determinantien und Definitheitsarten im Bairischen und Standarddeutschen." In P. Stein, A. Weiss, and G. Hayer, eds., *Festschrift für Ingo Reiffenstein zum 60. Geburtstag,* 231–258. Göppingen: Kümmerle.

Schubert, Lenhart K., and Francis Jeffry Pelletier. 1987. "Problems in the Representation of the Logical Form of Generics, Plurals, and Mass Nouns." In E. LePore, ed., *New Directions in Semantics,* 385–451. London: Academic Press.

Schubert, Lenhart K., and Francis Jeffry Pelletier. 1988. "An Outlook on Generic Statements." In M. Krifka, ed., *Genericity in Natural Language,* 357–372. SNS-Bericht 88-42, University of Tübingen.

Schubert, Lenhart K., and Francis Jeffry Pelletier. 1989. "Generically Speaking; Or, Using Discourse Representation Theory to Interpret Generics." In G. Chierchia, B. Partee, and R. Turner, eds., *Properties, Types and Meaning,* vol. 2: *Semantic Issues,* 193–268. Dordrecht: Kluwer.

Schwartz, Stephen P. 1977. *Naming, Necessity and Natural Kinds.* Ithaca, N.Y.: Cornell University Press.

Searle, John. 1969. *Speech Acts.* Cambridge: Cambridge University Press.

Selkirk, Elizabeth. 1977. "Some Remarks on Noun Phrase Structure." In P. Culicover, T. Wasow, and A. Akmajian, eds., *Formal Syntax,* 285–316. New York: Academic Press.

Selkirk, Elizabeth. 1984. *Phonology and Syntax: The Relation Between Sound and Structure.* Cambridge, Mass.: MIT Press.

Sellars, Wilfred. 1963. "Abstract Entities." *Review of Metaphysics* 16:627–671. Reprinted in Wilfred Sellars, 1967, *Philosophical Perspectives,* 229–269. Springfield, Ill.: Charles Thomas Publ.

Sharvy, Richard. 1978. "Maybe English Has No Count Nouns: Notes on Chinese Semantics. An Essay in Metaphysics and Linguistics." *Studies in Language* 2:345–365.

Sharvey, Richard. 1980. "A More General Theory of Definite Descriptions." *The Philosophical Review* 89:607–624.

Smith, Carlota. 1964. "Determiners and Relative Clauses in Generative Grammar of English." *Language* 40:37–52.

Smith, Neil. 1975. "On Generics." *Transactions of the Philological Society,* 27–48.

Spears, A. K. 1974. "On the Notion Occasion and the Analysis of Aspect." *CLS* 10, 672–683. Chicago: Chicago Linguistic Society.

Spohn, Wolfgang. 1988. "Ordinal Conditional Functions: A Dynamic Theory of Epistemic States.'' In W. L. Harper and B. Skyrms, eds., *Causation in Decision, Belief Change, and Statistics,* vol. 2, 105–134. Dordrecht: Kluwer.

Srivastav, Veneeta. 1991. *WH-Dependencies in Hindi and the Theory of Grammar.* Ph.D. dissertation, Cornell University.

Stalnaker, Robert. 1968. ''A Theory of Conditionals.'' In N. Rescher, ed., *Studies in Logical Theory,* 98–112. Oxford: Blackwell.

Stalnaker, Robert. 1978. ''Assertion.'' In P. Cole, ed., *Syntax and Semantics 9: Pragmatics,* 315–332. New York: Academic Press.

Stalnaker, Robert. 1987. *Inquiry*. Cambridge, Mass.: MIT Press.

Stowell, Tim. 1978. ''What Was There Before There Was There.'' In D. Farkas, W. Jacobson, and K. Todrys, eds., *CLS* 14, 458–471. Chicago: Chicago Linguistic Society.

Strigin, Anatoli. 1985. ''Eine Semantik für generische Sätze.'' *Linguistische Studien* 125:1–85.

Stump, Gregory. 1981. *Formal Semantics and Pragmatics of Free Adjuncts and Absolutes.* Ph.D. dissertation, Ohio State University.

Stump, Gregory. 1985. *The Semantic Variability of Absolute Constructions.* Dordrecht: Reidel.

Tamba, Irene. 1988. ''Quelques aspects des expressions génériques en japonais.'' In G. Kleiber, ed., *Rencontre(s) avec la Généricité,* 281–300. Récherches linguistiques 12, Université de Metz.

Tateishi, K. 1988. ''On the Universality of X-bar Theory: The Case of Japanese.'' *Proceedings of WCCFL 7,* 331–345. Stanford, Cal.: Stanford Linguistics Association, Stanford University.

ter Meulen, Alice. 1980. *Substances, Quantities and Individuals.* Ph.D. dissertation, Stanford University. Distributed by Indiana University Linguistics Club.

ter Meulen, Alice. 1981. ''An Intensional Logic for Mass Terms.'' *Philosophical Studies* 40:105–126.

ter Meulen, Alice. 1986a. ''Generic Information, Conditional Contexts and Constraints.'' In E. Traugott, A. ter Meulen, J. Snitzer-Reilly, and C. Ferguson, eds., *On Conditionals,* 123–145. Cambridge: Cambridge University Press.

ter Meulen, Alice. 1986b. ''Plural Pronouns with Nominal and Predicative Antecedents.'' *Proceedings of WCCFL 5,* 165–177. Stanford, Cal.: Stanford Linguistics Association, Stanford University.

ter Meulen, Alice. 1987. ''The Dynamic Interpretation of Discourse.'' In T. Ballmer and W. Wilden, eds., *Process Linguistics,* 283–308. Tübingen: Niemeyer.

ter Meulen, Alice. 1988. ''Semantic Constraints on Type-Shifting Anaphora.'' In M. Krifka, ed., *Genericity in Natural Language,* 373–393. SNS-Bericht 88-42, University of Tübingen.

Thomason, Richmond. 1988. ''Theories of Nonmonotonicity and Natural Language Generics.'' In M. Krifka, ed., *Genericity in Natural Language,* 395–406. SNS-Bericht 88-42, University of Tübingen.

Thrane, T. 1980. *Referential-Semantic Analysis: Aspects of a Theory of Linguistics.* Cambridge: Cambridge University Press.

Tichy, Pavel. 1980. ''The Semantics of Episodic Verbs.'' *Theoretical Linguistics* 7: 263–296.

Traugott, E., A. ter Meulen, J. Snitzer-Reilly, and C. Ferguson, eds. 1986. *On Conditionals*. Cambridge: Cambridge University Press.

Turner, Raymond. 1983. "Montague Grammar, Nominalizations and Scott's Domains." *Linguistics and Philosophy* 6:259–288.

Uhmann, Susanne. 1991. *Fokusphonologie. Eine Analyse deutscher Intonationskonturen im Rahmen der nicht-linearen Phonologie*. Tübingen: Niemeyer.

van Benthem, Johan. 1984. "Foundations of Conditional Logic." *Journal of Philosophical Logic* 13:303–349.

van Benthem, Johan, and Alice ter Meulen, eds. 1985. *Generalized Quantifiers in Natural Language*. GRASS 5. Dordrecht: Foris.

van Langendonck, Willy. 1980a. "Indefinites, Exemplars, and Kinds." In J. van der Auwera, ed., *The Semantics of Determiners*, 211–231. London: Croom Helm.

van Langendonck, Willy. 1980b. "On a Narrow Conception of Genericness." *Linguistics* 18:1085–1094.

van Riemsdijk, Henk. 1987. "Movement and Regeneration: A First Short Outline." Ms., Tilburg University.

Vater, Hans. 1979. *Das System der Artikelformen im gegenwärtigen Deutsch*. 2d ed. Tübingen: Niemeyer.

Veltman, Frank. 1995. "Defaults in Update Semantics." Forthcoming in *The Journal of Philosophical Logic*.

Vendler, Zeno. 1967. *Linguistics in Philosophy*. Ithaca, N.Y.: Cornell University Press.

von Stechow, Arnim. 1982. "Structured Propositions." Forschungsbericht 59 des SFB 99, University of Konstanz.

von Stechow, Arnim. 1986. "Alternative Semantics for Questions." Ms., University of Konstanz.

von Stechow, Arnim. 1989. "Focusing and Backgrounding Operators." Arbeitspapier 6 der Fachgruppe Sprachwissenschaft, University of Konstanz.

von Stechow, Arnim, and Wolfgang Sternefeld. 1988. *Bausteine syntaktischen Wissens: Ein Lehrbuch der generativen Grammatik*. Opladen: Westdeutscher Verlag.

von Stechow, Arnim, and Susanne Uhmann. 1986. "Some Remarks on Focus Projection." In W. Abraham and S. de Mey, eds., *Topic, Focus and Configurationality*, 295–320. Amsterdam: John Benjamins.

Ware, Robert X. 1975. "Some Bits and Pieces." *Synthèse* 31:379–393. Reprinted in F. J. Pelletier, ed., 1979, *Mass Terms: Some Philosophical Problems*, 15–29. Dordrecht: Reidel.

Wasow, Tom. 1972. *Anaphoric Relations in English*. Ph.D. dissertation, MIT.

Wasow, Tom. 1979. *Anaphora in Generative Grammar*. Gent: Story-Scientia.

Webber, Bonnie Lynn. 1978. *A Formal Approach to Discourse Anaphora*. Ph.D. dissertation, Harvard University.

Webelhuth, Gerd. 1985. "German is Configurational." *Linguistic Review* 4:203–246.

Webelhuth, Gerd. 1989. *Syntactic Saturation Phenomena and the Modern Germanic Languages*. Ph.D. dissertation, University of Massachusetts, Amherst.

Weir, Carl Edward. 1986. *English Gerundive Constructions*. Ph.D. dissertation, University of Texas at Austin.

Westerståhl, Dag. 1985. "Logical Constants in Quantifier Languages." *Linguistics and Philosophy* 8:387–413.

Westerståhl, Dag. 1989. "Quantifiers in Formal and Natural Languages." In D. Gabbay and F. Guenthner, eds., *Handbook of Philosophical Logic,* vol. 4, 1–131. Dordrecht: Reidel.

Whorf, Benjamin L. 1956. *Language, Thought, and Reality: Selected Writings of B. L. Whorf.* Ed. J. B. Carroll. London: Chapman & Hall; Cambridge, Mass.: MIT Press.

Wilkinson, Karina. 1986. "Genericity and Indefinite NPs." Ms., University of Massachusetts, Amherst.

Wilkinson, Karina. 1988. "The Semantics of the Common Noun 'Kind'." In M. Krifka, ed., *Genericity in Natural Language,* 407–429. SNS-Bericht 88-42, University of Tübingen. A revised version titled "(In)definites and *kind* NPs" appeared in E. J. Fee and K. Hunt, eds., *Proceedings of the WCCFL-8* (1989), 414–428, Stanford Linguistics Association, Stanford, Cal.

Wilkinson, Karina. 1991. *Studies in the Semantics of Generic Noun Phrases.* Ph.D. dissertation, University of Massachuseetts, Amherst.

Williams, Edwin. 1977. "Discourse and Logical Form." *Linguistic Inquiry* 18: 101–139.

Williams, Edwin. 1981. "Argument Structure and Morphology." *The Linguistic Review* 1:81–114.

Williams, Edwin. 1987. "NP-trace in Θ-Theory." *Linguistics and Philosophy* 10: 433–447.

Wilmet, Marc. 1985. "*A Kiwi Abounds in this Area: Note sur l'article «indéfini générique»." In G. Debusscher and J.-P. van Noppen, eds., *Communiquer et traduire,* 219–226. Brussels: Éditions de l'Université.

Wilmet, Marc. 1988. "Contre la généricité." *Lingua* 75:231–250.

Wittgenstein, Ludwig. 1953. *Philosophical Investigations.* Oxford: Blackwell.

Wolff, J. U. 1966. *Beginning Cebuano.* Part 1 and 2. New Haven, Conn.: Yale University Press.

Woolford, Ellen. 1988. "VP Internal Subjects in VSO and Non-Configurational Languages." Ms., Pennsylvania State University.

Ziff, Paul. 1972. *Understanding Understanding.* Ithaca, N.Y.: Cornell University Press.

Zuber, Ryszard. 1978. "Analyticity and Genericness." *Grazer Philosophische Studien* 6:63–73.

Zuber, Ryszard. 1989. "Phrases génériques et oppositions privatives." *Traveaux de Linguistique* 18:95–111.

Zucchi, Alessandro. 1990. *The Language of Propositions and Events.* Ph.D. dissertation, University of Massachusetts, Amherst.

Zwarts, Joost. 1988. "An Analysis of Genericity and Its Translation in Rosetta." Report of Philips Research Laboratories, Eindhooven, and Instituut A. W. de Groot voor Algemene Taalwetenschap, Utrecht.

Zwarts, Joost. 1990. "Kinds and Generic Terms." In M. Stokhof and L. Torenvliet, eds., *Proceedings of the Seventh Amsterdam Colloquium,* 685–705. Amsterdam: ITLI, University of Amsterdam.

NAME INDEX

Abbot, B., 112
Abney, S., 409
Alho, I., 106
Anderson, J., 79n
Aristotle, 86n
Arnauld, A., 42, 44, 81, 82
Asher, N., 5, 50, 59, 60, 101, 233, 333, 337, 344n
Authier, J., 124

Babby, L., 147
Bach, E., 126, 175, 203n, 211n
Bacon, J., 64
Baker, C., 15
Baker, M., 88
Barwise, J., 57, 96, 97n, 190n, 210–12, 291, 293, 310, 343, 344n
Bäuerle, R., 157, 163, 167, 170
Bealer, G., 66, 124
Bech, G., 144, 145
Berlin, B., 76
Berman, S., 157, 167, 169, 171, 175, 190n, 396
Bierwisch, M., 76
Bonomi, A., 223
Bowers, J., 176n, 185n, 223
Breedlove, E., 76
Bunt, H., 66, 67
Burton-Roberts, N., 11, 13, 49, 54, 74, 98, 101
Bybee, J., 414, 416, 419

Campbell, R., 38
Carlson, G., 4, 5, 10, 11, 17, 20n, 21–24, 31, 36, 44, 48n, 59, 64–67, 70, 83, 84, 95, 102, 105, 114–17, 119–21, 121n, 122, 123, 125, 126, 138, 141, 146, 176, 178, 188n, 192, 201, 225, 228, 230, 238, 265, 280, 280nn, 281, 282n, 284, 286, 304, 308, 310, 311, 334, 335, 338, 345n, 346, 358, 374, 383–89, 393, 394, 396, 412n, 413, 413n, 396
Carlson, L., 282n
Casalegno, P., 223
Chellas, B., 316
Chierchia, G., 16–18, 39, 102, 114n, 124, 171, 172, 190n, 215, 220n, 269n, 270, 281, 341n, 342, 386
Chomsky, N., 27, 29, 131, 193n
Churchland, P. A., 236
Cinque, G., 124
Code, A., 86n
Comorovski, I., 94, 386
Comrie, B., 413, 413n, 419
Condoravi, C., 80, 124
Conrad, B., 30n, 31, 102, 103
Cooper, R., 96, 97n, 142, 159–61, 190n, 203n, 210–12, 211n, 310
Corblin, F., 93
Croft, B., 45, 359
Cruse, D., 76

Dahl, Ö., 8, 10, 11, 13, 16, 20, 41, 43, 45, 49, 228, 230n, 233, 412–14, 412n, 413n, 416, 418, 419, 421, 424
Davidson, D., 126, 128, 129, 131, 135, 137, 138, 154, 155, 169, 171, 176, 181, 204, 206, 219, 221, 248
Declerck, R., 4, 25, 35, 36, 39, 45, 48, 71n, 74, 190, 190n
De Hoop, H., 215
Delgrande, J., 49
de Mey, S., 26, 27, 116
de Swart, H., 33, 215
Diesing, M., 26, 27, 122, 132, 133, 135–37, 140–43, 147–49, 175, 176, 176n, 186n, 187, 193, 214, 218–20, 219n, 220n, 223, 238, 396
Dixon, R., 419

Dölling, J., 399
Donnellan, K., 107
Doron, E., 339n
Dowty, D., 177, 196n, 232, 268n, 282, 282n
Doyle, J., 59

Ebert, K., 69
Egli, U., 157, 163, 167, 170
Enç, M., 15, 102, 206
Etchemendy, J., 344n
Evans, G., 142, 159, 160, 161

Farkas, D., 25, 25n, 140, 384
Ferguson, C., 50
Féry, C., 241
Findler, N., 77
Fine, K., 47
Fodor, J. D., 15, 290n
Frege, G., 64, 108, 191n
Frey, W., 105, 353–55
Frisé, A., 109
Fuhrmann, A., 113

Galmiche, M., 74, 83n
Gerstner, C., 4, 83, 89, 116, 138, 140, 141, 188n, 191, 280, 281, 345n, 358, 383
Gerstner-Link, C., 57, 67, 73, 113, 376, 378, 399
Geurts, B., 48, 82
Goodman, N., 13, 233
Greenbaum, S., 10
Grice, H. P., 86n
Grimshaw, J., 136
Groenendijk, J., 171, 190n, 246, 250, 269n, 343n

Haider, H., 407, 409
Halliday, M., 24n
Hansen, C., 402, 410
Heim, I., 23, 25, 26, 29, 49, 50, 52, 53, 55, 101, 107, 129–31, 139–42, 144n, 148, 150, 157–61, 157n, 161n, 163, 171–75, 211n, 246, 266, 268–71, 269n, 273, 280, 283, 289, 291–93, 314, 343, 344, 347, 383, 393, 396
Hempel, C., 46
Henkin, L., 314, 318, 319
Henne, M., 402
Heyer, G., 13, 46, 46n, 55, 64, 65, 78, 81, 83
Higginbotham, J., 126, 209
Higgins, R., 206n, 391, 396, 397
Hinrichs, E., 22, 36, 90, 248, 268, 282n
Hintikka, J., 99
Hirschbühler, P., 187
Hoeksema, J., 294n
Horn, L., 241
Horty, J., 338
Huang, C., 133

Jackendoff, R., 239, 240
Jacobs, J., 239–42
Jacobson, P., 183n, 190n, 211n, 223
Jaeggli, O., 124
Janssen, T., 339n
Jespersen, O., 342n
Johanson, L., 418

Kadmon, N., 101, 102, 142, 157, 160, 162, 163, 171, 175, 189n
Kafka, F., 108
Kamp, H., 23, 25, 29, 105, 129, 130, 139–42, 157–59, 171–74, 196n, 246, 266, 268–73, 268n, 280, 291, 292, 295, 338, 343, 344n, 347, 353–56, 370, 383, 396
Kanouse, D., 71n
Kanski, Z., 124
Karimi, E., 124
Karttunen, L., 286, 344
Kay, P., 76
Keenan, E., 211n
Kim, B., 124
Kiparsky, P., 236
Kitagawa, Y., 132, 185
Kleiber, G., 30n, 31, 55, 59, 64, 80, 84, 90, 91, 93, 94
Koopman, H., 132, 185n
Kratzer, A., 11, 17, 22, 25, 31, 33, 49–51, 55, 119, 129, 130, 176, 187, 190, 196nn, 208, 208n, 215–20, 220n, 233, 255, 314, 389, 397
Krifka, M., 4, 27, 28, 30n, 31, 42, 67, 83, 93, 101, 116, 138, 140, 141, 188n, 189n, 191, 230n, 242, 244, 255, 280, 281, 300, 345n, 358, 359, 362, 374, 383, 397, 400
Kripke, S., 107–9, 111

Kucera, H., 421
Kuroda, S.-Y., 73, 132, 185n, 196n
Kyburg, H., 61

Laca, B., 13, 40, 42, 43, 54, 71n, 72, 94, 118
Ladusaw, W., 99, 100
Landman, F., 48, 101, 102, 196n, 343
Lang, E., 54
Langford, C., 65
Lawler, J., 13, 20, 30, 30n, 41, 43, 49, 55, 71n, 230, 239, 379
Léard, J., 43
Leech, G., 10
Lemmon, E. J., 128, 155
Lerner, J., 144
Lewis, D., 25, 49, 50, 56, 129, 130, 139–42, 150, 157, 159, 171–74, 195, 196nn, 233, 245, 255, 266, 307, 310, 311, 383
Lifschitz, V., 336, 337
Link, G., 27–29, 370
Lung, K., 410, 411
Lyons, J., 6, 10, 44

Martin, R., 62
May, R., 141, 184, 193n
Mayer, R., 64
McCarthy, J., 60, 334, 336, 337
McDermott, D., 59
Milsark, G., 23, 23n, 119, 125, 139, 204, 210, 212, 384
Minsky, M., 305
Mithun, M., 87
Moens, M., 34n
Moltmann, F., 94
Monnesland, S., 420
Mönnich, U., 124
Montague, R., 181, 183, 190, 195n, 268, 269n, 284, 339n, 341, 343n, 388, 395
Moore, R., 59
Morreau, M., 5, 50, 59, 60, 101, 233, 316, 331–34, 338, 360
Mourelatos, A., 16
Mufwene, S., 67
Musil, R., 108, 109

Newton, B., 30n, 31, 36n, 42, 43
Nunberg, G., 11, 13, 46, 49, 85n, 98, 101

Ojeda, A., 64, 80
Oppenheim, R., 46

Pan, C., 11, 13, 46, 49, 98, 101
Parsons, T., 66, 126, 176, 181, 209, 221, 404
Partee, B., 23n, 25, 30n, 38, 98, 124, 142, 155, 157, 175, 183, 203n, 248, 268, 269n, 339, 341, 342, 348n, 392, 393, 396
Pelletier, F. J., 6n, 23n, 25, 25n, 26, 30, 30n, 31, 33, 33n, 34, 34n, 35n, 42, 44, 66, 67n, 75, 76, 79, 80n, 81, 84, 86n, 107, 113, 116, 119, 140, 150, 161, 171, 172, 174, 201, 239, 264, 280, 280n, 343, 344n, 347, 347n, 361, 362, 383, 402, 408
Perlmutter, D., 98, 135
Perry, J., 57, 343
Pesetsky, D., 147, 175
Peters, S., 286
Pinkal, M., 343
Platteau, F., 46, 83n
Porterfield, L., 69, 74
Portner, P., 102
Postal, P., 107
Putnam, H., 43, 48, 49, 107, 109–12, 111n

Quine, W. V., 32n, 66
Quirk, R., 10

Raven, H., 76
Reinhart, T., 374
Reiter, R., 59, 60, 338
Roberts, C., 34, 107, 161n, 389
Rodman, R., 290
Rongen, O., 402
Root, R., 105
Rooth, M., 25, 27, 42, 101, 115, 173, 183, 189n, 239, 244, 246, 266–68, 269nn, 272, 286, 291, 295
Rosch, E., 46, 48
Ross, J., 235, 236
Russell, B., 159, 191n, 404
Ryle, G., 37

Sag, I., 15, 187, 279, 290n
Saito, M., 132, 151
Salmon, N., 108
Sasse, H.-J., 73

Schaller, G., 380
Scheutz, H., 69
Schubert, L., 6n, 23n, 25, 25n, 26, 30, 30n, 31, 33n, 34, 35n, 42, 44, 66, 67n, 75, 76, 79, 80n, 81, 84, 107, 116, 119, 140, 150, 161, 171, 172, 174, 201, 239, 264, 280, 280n, 343, 344n, 347, 347n, 383, 402, 408
Schwartz, S., 108
Schwarzschild, R., 397
Searle, J., 195n
Selkirk, E., 175, 241, 390, 391
Selsam, E., 380
Sharvy, R., 80, 406
Smith, N., 70, 78, 98, 100
Snitzer-Reilly, J., 50
Spears, A., 30n, 31
Spohn, W., 363–65
Sportiche, D., 132, 185n
Srivastav, V., 69, 74, 211n
Stalnaker, R., 50, 195, 196n, 233, 246, 304, 307, 338
Steedman, M., 34n
Sternefeld, W., 144, 151
Stokhof, M., 171, 190n, 246, 250, 269n, 243n
Stowell, T., 203, 211
Strigin, A., 59
Stump, G., 23, 30n, 125, 267
Sugioka, Y., 25, 25n, 140, 384
Svartvik, J., 10

Tarski, A., 273n
Tateishi, K., 132
ter Meulen, A., 25, 50, 57, 66, 70, 105, 105n, 115, 339n, 345n, 347, 353n, 371, 400
Thomason, R., 307, 338
Thrane, T., 49
Tichy, P., 16
Traugott, E., 49
Turner, R., 124, 404

Uhmann, S., 241

van Benthem, J., 49
van Langendonck, W., 11, 106n, 116
van Riemsdijk, H., 134
Veltman, F., 59, 302, 303, 338
Vendler, Z., 11, 16, 98
von Stechow, A., 151, 175, 239, 241

Ware, R., 408
Wasow, T., 107
Webber, B., 105, 106n
Webelhuth, G., 132, 145, 151, 397
Weir, C., 23, 102, 104, 116, 117
Westerståhl, D., 96
Wilkinson, K., 4, 75, 78, 116, 138, 140, 141, 175, 296, 383, 384
Williams, E., 135, 136, 183n, 187
Wilmet, M., 4, 74, 83
Wittgenstein, L., 231
Wolff, J., 418
Woolford, E., 132

Ziff, P., 43
Zucchi, A., 105

LANGUAGE INDEX

Afrikaans, 415–16
Akan, 421n
Arabic, Classical, 421n
Azerbaijani, 418

Catalan, 421n
Cebuano, 418–19
Chinese, 67–68, 75, 398
Creoles, 67
Czech, 419, 421

Didinga, 421n
Dravidian languages, 419
Dutch, 26–27, 106n, 356
Dyirbal, 419n

English, 6, 7, 19, 38, 64–65, 67, 73, 83, 90–91, 113, 118, 119, 228, 355–56, 398, 412, 413, 416
English-based creoles, 67
Eskimo, 420n, 422–24

Finnish, 106, 117–18
French, 43, 68, 90–91, 94, 106n, 118, 124, 228, 413
Frisian, 69

Georgian, 420n
German, 19, 26, 27, 65, 68, 73–75, 77, 83, 87–88, 91, 106, 113, 119, 124, 228, 355–56, 413, 421n; dialects, esp. Bavarian, 69
Greek, Modern, 36n, 43, 124
Guarani, 421n

Hindi, 69, 74, 417
Hopi, 412, 424
Hungarian, 421n

Indonesian, 69, 74
Isekiri, 420n, 422, 424
Italian, 124

Japanese, 27, 118

Kammu, 421n
Korean, 124

Limouzi, 421n

Maori, 420n
Mayan, 421n
Modern Greek, 36n, 43, 124
Montagnais, 421n

Persian, 124
Polish, 124

Romanian, 94
Russian, 420

Salliut Inuktitut, 420n, 423
Seneca, 422–24
Serbo-Croatian, 412–20
Slavic languages, 419–20
Slovak, 419
Slovene, 419
Sotho, 421n
Spanish, 17, 43, 72, 94, 421n

Swahili, 8, 19
Swedish, 421
Swedish Sign Language, 421n

Tamil, 418
Thai, 415–16
Turkish, 412, 418–19

West Greenlandic Eskimo, 420n, 422–24
Wolof, 420n, 422, 424

Yoruba, 420n
Yucatec Maya, 421n

Zulu, 421n

SUBJECT INDEX

Abnormalcy, 60
"Aboutness," 3ff., 121, 122
Absolute constructions, 23
Absolutive construction, 125
Accent, 73, 82, 239
Accidental vs. lawlike generalizations, 44, 45. *See also* Regularity
Accidental properties, 13, 13n, 95
Accommodation, 56, 58, 70, 113, 191
Active 'be,' 38
Adjectives, 7, 112n, 179, 404
Adverbial quantification, 7, 25, 30ff., 96, 180–81, 188–95, 198, 204, 215–16, 219, 244, 252, 265, 266
Adverbs, 129, 150, 221
Adverbs of quantification. *See* Adverbial quantification
Agent/theme, 135
Aktionsarten, 169
Alternatives, construction of, 101, 241, 245, 250–52, 263–64
Alternative semantics, 244
Ambiguity, 5, 114. *See also* Kind reference; Scope
Analytic philosophy, 63, 107ff.
Anaphora, 69, 85, 87, 88, 105–7, 115–16, 119f., 123, 248
Anchoring of parameters, 57f.; and imperfectives, 416–20
'Any' as quantifier, 99
'Any'-NPs, 98–102
Aorist, 412, 418, 419
Appositive vs. restrictive, 405
Arbitrary control, 103
Arbitrary interpretations, 123, 124
Arbitrary objects, 47
ARE-relation. *See* IS-relation
Argument linking, 135
Aristotle, 86n
Artifacts, 21n, 111, 111n
Artificial intelligence, 5, 50, 58, 63, 77, 305–6, 335
Aspect, 6, 36n, 68, 104, 178, 197, 204, 207, 232, 413
Assignment function, 246
Association-with-Focus theory, 266–68
Asymmetric readings. *See* Proportion problem
Asymmetry, of subtype relation, 77n
Atelic/telic distinction, 104
Atomic individuals, 28, 90
Autoepistemic reasoning, 59–60
Avant-Garde interpretation, 78, 83–84, 87, 117
Average Property interpretation; 78, 80–81; ambiguity with, 81
Average property adjectives, 80

Background knowledge, 69, 240–42
Baptism, 109
Bare NPs, 11, 68, 74, 103, 114–22, 179–80, 190–91, 200, 212–15, 383–85
Bare plurals, 5, 10, 26, 70–74, 105, 114–16, 117, 123, 125ff., 179–80, 191–92, 200, 212, 266, 278, 280, 346; definite interpretation of, 72–73
Basic generics, 232
"Basic-level" words, 76, 84
Belief, 235, 363–67
Bishop sentences, 173

C-command, 142
Case, 138

The letter *n* identifies pages with footnotes; *f.* and *ff.* mean "and following."

"Cases," 30ff., 42
Categorical sentence, 72f.
Causal theory of reference, 109–112
Characterizing vs. particular predications, 3, 5, 12, 13, 14–15
Characterizing property interpretation, 78, 81
Characterizing sentences, 6–8; as indeterminate, figurative, or metaphorical, 3; containing kind reference, 3; distinguished from non-characterizing, 9–10, 19–63; and predication, 2, 122, 259, 388
Circumscription, 60, 335
Classifier phrase, 68, 75, 398, 400, 401
Clause splitting, 190–95, 213, 222–23
Closure, 179, 190
Coercion, 18, 33, 33n, 34, 34n, 37n, 38, 73
Cognitive psychology, 63
Cognitive science, 5
Collective Property interpretation, 78, 79–80; ambiguity with, 81
Collectives. *See* Sum individuals; Groups; Objects, plural
Common nouns, 66ff., 196, 204–7
Commonsense entailment, 323, 335, 337
Commutativity, of identity, 86
Comparison class, 77
Completeness proof of logic-incorporating generics, 337
Compositionality, 35n, 69, 70, 113
Concepts, 93–94, 123, 402
Conceptual description, 109
Conditionals, 25, 31, 49f., 51f., 100, 216–18, 422
Conjunction, 116, 220–21, 249
Connectionism, 236
Constraints, 57–58
Context, 192, 195–6, 208, 211n
Context-change semantics, 107, 190
Contextual restriction of quantifiers, 45
Control, 103
Conversational background, 50
Conversational implicature, 160
Counterfactuals, 49f., 216–18, 220, 233
Count nouns, 5, 67, 68, 71, 74, 75, 92, 105
Covert operators, 52–53. *See also* Hidden GEN-operator
Cultural norm, 49. *See also* Stereotypes
Cumulative/distributive readings, 28f., 35, 90f.

D-generic, 4n, 300, 301
Davidsonian argument, 176, 181, 204, 206, 221, 248
Default, 59, 61, 302–3, 338, 362, 363
Defeasible reasoning, 305–7, 332, 333
Deferred reference, 85n
Definite NPs, 5, 65, 74, 90–91, 190–91, 194–95; singular, 5, 106
Definiteness effect, 210–12
Deising's conjecture, 133
Deising's proposal, 140
Deising's slogan, 143, 149, 154
Demonstrative NPs, 74
Denotational domains, 341, 342, 350
Deontic modality. *See* Modality
Dependent generics, 371f.
Dependent NPs, 94
Dependent plurals, 27f., 29
Derived kind, 376, 380, 388
Derived kind predicates, 79, 372
Descriptive (Seneca), 423
Descriptive content, 161
Determiner Phrase hypothesis, 409
Determiners, zero, 145
Direct reference, 108f.
Discourse referent, 73, 246
Discourse Representation Theory, 129, 189, 191, 246, 268, 272, 343
Disposition, 41, 362
Dispositional predicate, 37, 38, 39, 50
Dispositional sentences, 3
Distinguishing Property interpretation, 49, 78, 81–83
Distributive/cumulative readings, 28f., 35, 90f.
Domain of quantification. *See* Quantification
Domain restriction, 129
Donkey sentences, 269–79. *See also* Proportion problem
Downward-entailing operator, 99, 100, 101
DST-operator, 28, 90
Dudley Doorite constraint, 313, 331
Durative, 418
Dyadic operator, 238
Dynamic, 12, 16f., 18, 190, 246, 250, 302, 405

E-type pronouns, 142, 150, 159, 172
Entailment, 234–36
Ep-operator, 21

Episodic predicate, 37, 92, 94, 114–22
Episodic sentences, 2, 16f., 21, 102, 176–77, 247
Episodic/stative distinction, 38
Episodic statives, 36
Epistemic, 302, 365
Epistemic modality. *See* Modality
Equivalence relation, assumed by causal theory, 109, 111
Essential properties, 13, 13n, 19
Established kinds. *See* Well-established kinds
Event, 12, 16, 17, 75, 104, 125, 232, 370
Event-argument, 125, 125–75, 176, 188, 204, 206, 219, 221; Davidsonian, 126, 154; part/whole relations of, 168
Exceptions, 4, 44ff., 195
Exhaustivity, 244
Existential, 179, 190; analysis of bare plurals, 26f., 114f., 117; closure, 29f., 34, 36, 140, 142, 147ff., 190, 383, 393; interpretation of 'gen,' 41, 117
Expective, 424
Explicitness, 32n
Extension/intension distinction, 47, 64, 72, 108
External arguments, 135, 156
Extraction domains, conditions on, 133

Fact, 104
File Change Semantics, 246, 343
Focus, 42, 189n, 266
Focus-background structures, 42, 240
Focus operator, 239, 240
Focus-sensitive quantifiers, 240, 241, 252
Free-choice 'any,' 102
Free focus, 241
Frequency, 97
Functor anaphora constraint, 342, 355

G-operator, 140
General sentences, 3
Generalization, 26, 33, 91, 225; descriptive vs. normative, 13; over events, 2; over situations, 38
Generalized quantifiers, 96ff., 190, 193n, 211, 341
"Generic class," 105
"Generic fact," 33
Generic interpretations, 132, 154
Generic nouns, marking of, 67
Generic phenomena, classified, 14–18
Generic polarity, 202, 222
Generic quantifier, 256
Generic tense, 157
Generic vs. episodic, 224, 415
Generic vs. particular sentences, 3
Genericity, 176, 188; diagnostic tests for, 8–14; as not a uniform concept, 2–5, 122; varieties of, 2–8
Generics, marking of, 416, 419, 422, 424; overt markers, 420, 424, 425
Genitive of negation, 147. *See also* Negation
Genus, 2
GEN-operator, 188, 195–98, 200, 202–15, 219–22, 238, 255, 383, 384, 410; dyadic analysis, 23–30, 30ff., 122, 188; hidden GEN operations, 41, 123, 198–201; interpretation of GEN, 195–96; monadic analysis, 20–23; 'most' as analysis of GEN, 44; nested, 92
Gerundives, 102–5, 123
Gn-operator, 22
Gnomic, 3
Grammaticalization, 414, 416, 417, 421, 424
Groups, 6n, 89, 90, 106

Habit, 2, 17f., 19, 32f., 36–43, 79, 104, 105, 122, 196, 420–24
Habitual morpheme, 196–99, 202
Habitual predicate, 32, 36–43, 79
HAS-relation, 85n
Henkin lemma, 318–19
Hidden GEN operators, 41, 123, 198–201
Homogeneity, 361

I-generic, 4n, 300, 301; vs. d-generic, 359
Identical Projection Function model, 145
Identity, 85ff., 85n
Idioms, 69
Imperfective, 416–20, 423, 425
Implicit arguments. *See* Event-argument, Davidsonian
Implicit restrictions, 195, 263
Indefinite lazy reading, 161
Indefinite NPs, 10, 29, 72, 74, 92, 99, 107, 124, 180, 189–92, 194–96, 200, 210, 212, 220, 247, 399; pronouns, 106; "indefinite generic article," 98; indefinite objects, 151, 153

Index, 193
Indicative, 422, 423
Individual-level predicate, 21, 176–7, 198–222; vs. stage-level predicates, 21, 22, 122, 177–81, 198, 217–18, 220
Individuals, 20, 65; atomic, 28
Induction, 224–30
Infinitival nouns, 102–5, 123
INFL, 185, 197, 247, 248
Information model, 317–18
Information states, 302, 308
Inherent generics, 198–206, 219, 222. *See also* Basic generics
Input assignment, 246
Instrumental modality, 50
Intension/extension distinction, 47, 64, 72, 108, 181–82, 304
Intensions, 64, 72, 77
Internal Comparison interpretation, 78, 84
Intonation, 143, 163
Irreflexivity, of realization relation, 66
ISA-relation, 77
IS-relation, 85, 86, 85n, 88, 89, 91, 92
Iterative, 421–24

Kind(s), 2, 64, 280, 281, 346, 358, 376–77; ambiguous between quantifying and non-quantifying, 64; analysis of, 64, 65–74; as proper names, 6, 64, 65, 66ff., 109, 123; as quantificational, 64; characteristic, 345; establishment of, 107–13, 123 (*see also* well-establisher kind); Natural, 21n, 107–13, 123, 402; Nominal, 107–13; Proper, 358, 376; relation of to instances, 78ff.; Syntactic positions for, 2n, 10, 36–43, 63, 70, 71, 73, 111
Kind denoting, 71, 117, 190–92, 195
Kind predicate interpretation, 78–79, 121
Kind predicates, 10, 64, 95ff., 123, 346, 383–85, 396
Kind reference, 2, 4n, 6, 6n, 14, 63–94, 98, 102ff., 106, 114ff., 138–43, 216, 372, 383–96; vs. object reference, 2, 10–15, 22, 63–94; vs. predicative Ns, 6, 66f., 71, 72, 74, 89; kind-referring interpretation, 67
Kohäsion, 145
Kung-sun Lung's paradox, 410

Lattice, 76
Lawlikeness, 7. *See also* Regularity
Lexical: characterizing predicates, 17, 18, 19, 36–43; decomposition, 37, 199–201, 203–4; dispositional predicate, 39, 79; items that indicate kind-reference, 6; items that enforce characterizing sentences, 7–8; statives, 36, 38
Lexical kind predicates, 79. *See also* Basic generics
Local licensing, 202–4, 212–14
Locations. *See* Minimal location
Locatives, 126, 155, 176, 178, 199, 207–10; locative adverbials, 177, 207–9
Logic, 5, 58
Logical inference rules, 303
Lottery paradox, 61
Lumping, 217–18

Mapping Hypothesis, 219; marked or derived, 413
Mass nouns, 5, 66, 67n, 68, 71, 80n, 91, 105, 406; mass/count nouns, 5, 67, 75, 406, 408; nominal vs. predicative, 66
Measure phrase, 400
Mereology, 64, 80, 80n; part/whole relations of events, 168
Metrical quantifiers, 97
Middle voice, 7
Minimal entailment, 60, 335–37
Minimal locations, 169
Minimal marking tendency, 415–17, 420
Modal: background, 50, 82, 255; base, 50, 55, 62–63, 313–14; interpretation of GEN, 49–57; operators, 50, 61; relation, 50; subordination, 107, 380
Modality, 144, 188, 195, 204, 210; deontic, 50, 51; epistemic, 129, 174; Scope, 144
Modals, 378
Modification, 207–9, 391–92, 402, 404
Modus Ponens, 321, 324–25
Montague grammar, 195n, 268, 280, 341
Moral vs. metaphysical universal, 44
Multiple Foci, 242

Names: proper *(see main entry)*; poetic, 65; of kinds, 65–66, 68–69 (*see also* Kind reference)
Narrative, 416, 417
Necessity: mathematical, 53; linguistic, 54

Negation, 123, 214, 419; genitive of, 147; negation merging, 146; negative polarity, 99, 100, 101, 102, 202, 213–14; negative-polarity 'any,' 102, 214
Nixon Diamond, 307, 322–23, 328–30
Nomic, 3, 412, 424
Nominal kinds. *See* Kind(s)
Nominalizations, 102–5, 123, 124, 135, 422
Non-accidental, 233, 359. *See also* Lawlikeness; Regularity; Essential properties
Noncomposite words, 76
Non-configurational languages. *See* Scrambling
Nonconservative quantifiers, 97n
Nondispositional stative predicate, 38
Non-equivalence relation, of IS-relation, 86
Non-monotonic reasoning, 58–63, 101, 233, 306, 363–70
Non-overt operators, 130, 138, 142
Non-progressive, 417, 418, 425
Nonspecific vs. specific: NPs, 115 (*see also* Indefinite NPs); readings, 29
Nonspecificity, 15, 15n, 16, 32
Non-symmetry, of IS-relation, 86
Norm, cultural, 49. *See also* Stereotypes
Normalcy conditions, 31, 56, 62
Normality, 255, 319–23, 334–36; notions, 93–94, 123
Normalization, 308, 333
"Normal" situations, 31
Normative, 309–10
Noun incorporation, 87f.
Novelty condition, 148
NPs: as ambiguous between kind-referring and not, 6, 8; quantified, 74, 96; kind-referring, 6; in characterizing sentences, 8. *See also* Indefinite NPs; Proper nouns; Names
Nuclear scope, 344. *See also* Tripartite quantifier structures
Numerals, 35, 40, 74, 406, 407

Object asymmetric readings. *See* Proportion problem
Object predications, 2
Object-referring NPs, 2
Objects: arbitrary, 47; generalizations over, 20–36; ordinary, 20; partial, 48; plural, 40, 90 (*see also* Sum individuals); social (*see* Stereotypes); underspecified, 48. *See also* Individuals; Kind(s)
Occasions, 189, 191
Of, 391, 395
Open class, 61
Operators, non-overt, 130, 138, 142
Ordering source, for modality, 51
Ordinal conditional functions, 364
Output assignment, 246

Paradigms, 109, 110. *See also* Prototypes
Parameters of situations, 57f.
Partial orderings, on hierarchies, 76
Particular kind, 345
Particular vs. characterizing predications, 3, 5, 12, 13, 14–15
Particular vs. generic sentences, 3
Part/whole relations. *See* Mereology
Passive voice, 71, 72
Past tense, 79, 99n
Perception reports, 178–79, 209–10
Perfective, 6, 416, 420, 423, 424
Performative, 195n, 417, 418
"Personal generic," 87
Plato, 66n, 98
Plurality, 20n, 23–30, 27f., 35, 40, 67, 68, 90–91, 106; plural pronouns, 105, 106
Plural object, 40. *See also* Sum individuals
Port-Royal puzzle, 42, 81–83
Positive adjective, 76–77
Possible worlds, 195–96, 216, 246, 307, 398
Pragmatics, 31, 101; vs. semantics, 87
Predicate NPs, 204–6
Predication, 185–87, 341, 388
Preemption, 226
Presupposition, 30ff., 105, 150, 160, 216, 286, 339, 340
Presupposition accommodation. *See* Accommodation
Progressive, 6, 12, 17n, 36, 415–18, 420, 422
Proper name, 65, 107; descriptional theories of, 108; as syntactically complex, 70; with definite article, 67, 68
Properties, 231
Property, general, 2
Proportion problem, 157, 162; Bishop sentences, 174
Proposition, 104

Prospective, 416
Prototypes, 46–48, 110
Pseudo-kinds, 93–94
Pseudo-partitives, 390, 391
Punctual (Seneca), 423, 424

Quantification, 191, 200n, 202, 204, 216, 232, 359, 389; domain of, 169; and negative quantifiers, 144; over cases, 42, 245, 421; vacuous, prohibition against, 131, 148, 162
Quantificational adverbials. *See* Adverbial quantification
Quantificational predicates, 95–98, 123
Quantificational view of generics, 227
Quantified NPs, 74, 96, 183
Quantifier raising, 183–84
Quantifiers, 3n, 29f., 103, 181, 183, 206, 210, 250
Quantifier scope, 142, 144
Quantifier split, 133

Raising, 186
Readings, 390f.
Real, 419
Realization relation, 20–21, 66, 77, 85, 90, 106, 139, 280, 284, 376, 377, 385, 386, 399, 403
Reciprocals and reflexives, 91, 115, 120, 124, 204
Reconstruction, 184–87, 193
Reduction of kind properties to instances, 79ff.
Reflexives. *See* Reciprocals and reflexives
Reflexivity, of IS-relation, 86
Registers of language, 83
Regularity, 2, 12. *See also* Lawlikeness
Relative clauses, 290, 402; extraction of, 134
"Relevant quantification," 45–46
Reportive (Hopi), 424
Reportive present, 417, 418
Representative Object interpretation, 78, 83, 85, 87, 117; restrictions on, 310–11
Restrictive clauses. *See* Tripartite quantifier structures
Restrictor, 31, 40, 43, 188–95, 199, 206, 208, 210, 212, 265, 344
Restrictor/matrix, 23–30, 30ff., 82, 238, 239
Rigid designator, 109ff.
Rule, 224ff.
Russell-contradiction, 66n, 404

Sage Plant sentences, 158
Scalar implicature, 161
Scope, 114–15, 119, 122, 123, 185, 188–95, 208, 213, 219, 265; quantifier, 142, 144
Scrambling, 134, 125–75, 148, 151
Second-order predicates, 96, 98
Selectional restrictions, 2n, 10, 36–43, 63f., 70, 71, 73, 95
Semantic net, 77
Semantic partition, 188–89, 190–95, 213, 222–23, 238
Sense/denotation distinction, 108
Sentence accent, 27, 27n, 82
Sentence intonation, 27
Similarity, 233–34
Singular vs. plural, 407
Situation argument, 30ff., 33, 36, 189, 193–95, 208–9, 216–17, 221
Situations, 30–36, 57, 62, 89, 122, 181, 191, 196, 206–7, 244, 247, 258
Situation semantics, 57–58, 169, 208n, 343, 353
Situation types, 35, 57
Spatiotemporal location argument, 126. *See also* Event-argument
Specificity, 15, 15n, 16, 23–30, 36; NPs, 115 (*see also* Indefinite NPs); readings, 29
Specimen of kind, 399
Stability, 176, 177, 196, 199, 207
'So-called' construction, 65
Stage, 20, 66, 385, 386
Stage/individual-level predicates, 125–75
Stage-level predicate, 17, 21, 22, 23, 36, 121, 122, 176–78, 198, 200, 217–18
Stative/episodic distinction, 38, 104
Stative sentences, 12, 16f., 73, 232
Stativity, 16, 17n, 21, 33, 37f., 63, 177–79, 195, 207, 249, 417, 418
Stereotypes, 48–49, 55, 82, 196n
Stress, 238–39, 322–25
Stress placement, 27, 42, 82, 238
Strong NPs, 210
Structured meanings, 239–41, 250
Subconcept, 77f.

Subject-object asymmetry, 73–74
Subjunctive, 417
Subkinds, 378, 387, 389
Sum events, 321
Sum individuals, 27f., 35, 64, 89, 90, 399, 400
Sum situations, 40
Symmetric readings. *See* Proportion problem

T-relation, 77
Taxonomic hierarchy, 5, 76, 84, 359, 361
Taxonomic interpretation, 10, 14, 71, 71n, 74–77, 92, 96, 123
Taxonomic relation, 399
Telic/atelic, 104
Temporal, 177, 189, 204, 206, 248
Temporal stability, 177–78
Tense, 155; generic, 157; past, 6, 79n, 99n; reportive present, 6
Theme/agent, 135
Theme marker, 43, 94
Theme/rheme, 374–76
Theories of anaphora, 343
"There"-construction, 23, 27, 97n, 118, 119, 125, 179, 210–12, 384
Thetic/topic, 72f.
Third Man argument, 66n
Tigers, 362, 370, 376–82
"Timeless," 6
Topology, 97
Transitivity: of identity, 86; of subtype relation, 77n
Tripartite analysis, 25, 27, 188
Tripartite quantifier structures, 130ff., 149
Truth conditions: for generics, 195, 224–29, 301–3; of characterizing sentences, 3; truth of, 224–25, 359–60
Types, 182
Type-shifting, 182–83, 190–92, 341, 342
Type-shifting anaphora, 353
Type theory, 124
Typicality, 80, 111ff., 363f.

Unaccusatives, 180, 185–88, 215
Unaccusative/unergative, 132, 125–75, 142, 165
Unboundedness, 35, 36, 40
Universal: moral, 44; metaphysical, 44
Universal interpretation: of GEN, 4, 41–45, 195; of bare plurals, 26f. *See also* Generic interpretations
Unreal, 418
Upward-entailing, 13, 101
"Used-to" construction, 7, 346

Verb-second, 133
Volitional, 418, 419
VP-ellipsis, 187–88, 204, 221
VP-internal hypothesis, 132–33, 125–75
VP-internal subjects, 185–87, 220; vs. episodic, 224, 227, 228, 412, 415, 425; vs. habituals, 420–24; vs. stage-level predicates, 176–81, 198, 202–3, 207; vs. unreal, 419f.

Weak and strong quantifiers, 210
Well-established kinds, 11, 11n, 12, 13n, 63, 69, 70, 93, 95, 103, 104, 112, 113
"When"-clause, 25, 34, 104, 129–32, 148, 180, 265, 273
Word order, 27